Random House
French
Dictionary

D0963357

Random House
French
Dictionary

Second Edition

FRENCH • ENGLISH
ENGLISH • FRENCH
FRANÇAIS • ANGLAIS
ANGLAIS • FRANÇAIS

Edited by
Francesca L. V. Langbaum
UNIVERSITY OF VIRGINIA

Revised by
Susan Husserl-Kapit, Ph.D.

RANDOM HOUSE
NEW YORK

ISBN: 0-679-76430-5

Typeset and printed in the United States of America
Second Edition
9 8 7 6 5 4 3 2 1

New York   Toronto   London   Sydney   Auckland

Concise Pronunciation Guide

The following concise guide describes the approximate pronunciation of the letters and frequent combinations of letters occurring in the French language. A study of it will enable the reader to pronounce French adequately most of the time. While the guide cannot list all the exceptions to the established pronunciations, or cover the manner in which adjacent words affect each other in speech, such exceptions and variations will readily be learned as one develops facility in the language.

French Letter	Description of Pronunciation
a, à	Between *a* in *calm* and *a* in *hat*.
â	Like *a* in *calm*.
ai	Like *e* in *bed*.
au	Like *oa* in *coat*.
b	As in English. At end of words, usually silent.
c	Before *e*, *i*, *y*, like *s*. Elsewhere, like *k*. When *c* occurs at the end of a word and is preceded by a consonant, it is usually silent.
ç	Like *s*.
cc	Before *e*, *i*, like *x*. Elsewhere, like *k*.
ch	Usually like *sh* in *short*. *ch* is pronounced like *k* in words of Greek origin before *a*, *o*, and *u* and before consonants.
d	At beginning and in middle of words, as in English. At end of words, usually silent.
e	At end of words, normally silent; indicates that preceding consonant letter is pronounced. Between two single consonant sounds, usually silent. Elsewhere, like English *a* in *sofa*.
é	Approximately like *a* in *hate*.
è, ê, ei	Like *e* in *bed*.
eau	Like *au*.
ent	Silent when it is the third person plural ending.
er (end of words)	At end of words of more than one syllable, usually like *a* in *hate*, the *r* being silent; otherwise like *air* in *chair*.
es	Silent at end of words.
eu	A vowel sound not found in English; like French *e*, but pronounced with the lips rounded as for *o*.

French Letter	Description of Pronunciation
ez	At end of words, almost always like English *a* in *hate,* the *z* being silent.
f	As in English; silent at the end of a few words.
g	Before *e, i, y,* like *z* in *azure.* Elsewhere, like *g* in *get.* At end of words, usually silent.
gn	Like *ni* in *onion.*
gu	Before *e, i, y,* like *g* in *get.* Elsewhere, like *g* in *get* plus French *u* (see below).
h	In some words, represents a slight tightening of the throat muscles (in French, called "aspiration"). In most words, silent.
i, î	Like *i* in *machine.*
ill	(-il at end of words) like *y* in *yes,* in many but not all words.
j	Like *z* in *azure.*
k	As in English.
l	As in English, but always pronounced "bright," with tongue in front of mouth.
m, n	When double, and when single between two vowel letters or at beginning of word, like English *m* and *n* respectively. When single at end of syllable (at end of word or before another consonant), indicates nasalization of preceding vowel.
o	Usually like *u* in English *mud,* but rounder. When final sound in word, and often before *s* and *z,* like *ô.*
ô	Approximately like *oa* in *coat.*
oe, oeu	Like *eu.*
oi	Approximately like a combination of the consonant *w* and the *a* of *calm.*
ou, oû, où	Like *ou* in *tour.*
p	At end of words, usually silent. Between *m* and *t, m* and *s, r* and *s,* usually silent. Elsewhere, as in English.
pn, ps	Unlike English, when *pn* and *ps* occur at the beginning of words the *p* is usually sounded.
ph	Like *f.*
qu	Usually like *k.*

French Letter	Description of Pronunciation
r	A vibration either of the uvula, or of the tip of the tongue against the upper front teeth. See above under *er*.
s	Generally, like *s* in *sea*. Single *s* between vowels, like *z* in *zone*. At end of words, normally silent.
sc	Before *e* or *i*, like *s*. Elsewhere, like *sk*.
t	Approximately like English *t*, but pronounced with tongue tip against teeth. At end of words, normally silent. When followed by *ie, ion, ium, ius*, and other diphthongs beginning with a vowel, *t* generally is like English *s* in *sea* (unless the *t* itself is preceded by an *s* or an *x*).
th	Like *t*.
u, û	A vowel sound not found in English; like the *i* in *machine* but with lips rounded as for *ou*.
ue	After *e* or *g* and before *il*, like *eu*.
v	As in English.
w	Usually like *v;* in some people's pronunciation, like English *w*.
x	Generally sounds like *ks;* but when the syllable *ex* begins a word and is followed by a vowel, *x* sounds like *gz*. At end of words, usually silent.
y	Generally like *i* in *machine;* but when between two vowels, like *y* in *yes*.
z	Like *z* in *zone*. At end of words, often silent (see above under *ez*).

Note on Pronunciation

A few minutes' study of the *Concise Pronunciation Guide* on pages v–vii will enable you to pronounce most French words without having to look each word up in the dictionary. For the relatively few cases in which the pronunciation does not follow the usual pattern, this dictionary provides a transcription in simple and familiar symbols.

ă	bat	ô	order
ā	cape	œ	[a vowel made with the lips rounded in position for *o* as in *over*, while trying to say *a* as in *able*]
â	dare		
ä	calm		
à	[a vowel intermediate in quality between the *a* of *cat* and the *a* of *calm*, but closer to the former]	oi	oil
		o͝o	book
		o͞o	ooze
		ou	loud
ĕ	set	ŭ	up
ē	bee	ū	cute
ĭ	big	û	burn
ī	bite	y	[a vowel made with the lips rounded in position for *oo* as in *ooze*, while trying to say *e* as in *easy*]
N	[a symbol used to indicate nasalized vowels. There are four such vowels in French, found in *un bon vin blanc* (œN bôN văN blä̆N)]		
		ə	[indicates the sound of *a* in *alone*, *e* in *system*, *i* in *easily*, *o* in *gallop*, *u* in *circus*]
ŏ	hot		
ō	no		

Irregular Verbs

Infinitive	Pres. Part.	Past Part.	Pres. Indic.	Future
aller	allant	allé	vais	irai
asseoir	asseyant	assis	assieds	assiérai
atteindre	atteignant	atteint	atteins	atteindrai
avoir	ayant	eu	ai	aurai
battre	battant	battu	bats	battrai
boire	buvant	bu	bois	boirai
conduire	conduisant	conduit	conduis	conduirai
connaître	connaissant	connu	connais	connaîtrai
courir	courant	couru	cours	courrai
craindre	craignant	craint	crains	craindrai
croire	croyant	cru	crois	croirai
devoir	devant	dû	dois	devrai
dire	disant	dit	dis	dirai
dormir	dormant	dormi	dors	dormirai
écrire	écrivant	écrit	écris	écrirai
envoyer	envoyant	envoyé	envoie	enverrai
être	étant	été	suis	serai
faire	faisant	fait	fais	ferai
falloir	———	fallu	(il) faut	(il) faudra
joindre	joignant	joint	joins	joindrai
lire	lisant	lu	lis	lirai
mettre	mettant	mis	mets	mettrai
mourir	mourant	mort	meurs	mourrai
naître	naissant	né	nais	naîtrai
ouvrir	ouvrant	ouvert	ouvre	ouvrirai
plaire	plaisant	plu	plais	plairai
pleuvoir	pleuvant	plu	(il) pleut	(il) pleuvra
pouvoir	pouvant	pu	peux	pourrai
prendre	prenant	pris	prends	prendrai
recevoir	recevant	reçu	reçois	recevrai
rire	riant	ri	ris	rirai
savoir	sachant	su	sais	saurai
suffire	suffisant	suffi	suffis	suffirai
suivre	suivant	suivi	suis	suivrai
tenir	tenant	tenu	tiens	tiendrai
valoir	valant	valu	vaux	vaudrai
venir	venant	venu	viens	viendrai
vivre	vivant	vécu	vis	vivrai
voir	voyant	vu	vois	verrai
vouloir	voulant	voulu	veux	voudrai

Abbreviations

abbr.	abbreviation	*lit.*	literal, literally
adj.	adjective	*m.*	masculine
adv.	adverb	*med.*	medical
arch.	architecture	*mil.*	military
arith.	arithmetic	*n.*	noun
art.	article	*naut.*	nautical
comm.	commercial	*pl.*	plural
conj.	conjunction	*pred.*	predicate
eccles.	ecclesiastical	*prep.*	preposition
f.	feminine	*pron.*	pronoun
fig.	figurative	*sg.*	singular
geog.	geography	*tr.*	transitive (used only
geom.	geometry		with verbs which also
gramm.	grammar,		have reflexive use to
	grammatical		indicate intransitive
interj.	interjection		meaning)
interr.	interrogative	*vb.*	verb
intr.	intransitive		

A

à, *prep.* at, in, to.

abaisser, *vb.* depress, lower.

abandon, *n.m.* desertion, abandonment.

abandonné, *adj.* forlorn.

abandonner, *vb.* forsake, leave (desert). **s'a.**, give up, resign oneself.

abasourdir, *vb.* astound.

abat-jour, *n.m.* lampshade.

abattage, *n.m.* slaughter.

abattement, *n.m.* depression, dejection.

abattoir, *n.m.* slaughterhouse.

abattre, *vb.* depress, reduce; slaughter. **s'a.**, alight.

abbaye, *n.f.* abbey.

abbé, *n.m.* abbot.

abbesse, *n.f.* abbess.

abcès, *n.m.* abscess.

abdiquer, *vb.* abdicate.

abdomen, *n.m.* abdomen.

abeille, *n.f.* bee.

aberrant, *adj.* absurd.

aberration, *n.f.* aberration.

abîme, *n.m.* abyss.

abîmer, *vb.* injure, spoil.

abject, *adj.* abject, low.

aboiement, *n.m.* barking.

abolir, *vb.* abolish.

abolition, *n.f.* abolition.

abominable, *adj.* vile, objectionable.

abondamment, *adv.* fully.

abondance, *n.f.* plenty.

abondant, *adj.* plentiful. **peu a.**, scanty.

abonder de, *vb.* abound in.

abonné, *n.m.* subscriber.

abonnement, *n.m.* subscription.

abonner, *vb.* **s'a.**, subscribe.

abord, 1. *n.m.* approach. 2. *adv.* **d'a.**, at first.

abordable, *adj.* approachable, affordable.

aborder, *vb.* accost.

aboutir, *vb.* end (in).

aboyer, *vb.* bark.

abrégé, *n.m.* summary.

abréger, *vb.* abridge, shorten, abbreviate.

abreuver, *vb.* water (animals).

abréviation, *n.f.* abbreviation.

abri, *n.m.* shelter. **à l'a. de**, safe from.

abricot, *n.m.* apricot.

abriter, *vb.* shelter.

abroger, *vb.* repeal.

abrupt (-pt), *adj.* steep.

abrutir, *vb.* exhaust. **s'a.**, become dazed.

absence, *n.f.* absence.

absent, *adj.* absent. **rester a.**, stay away.

absenter, *vb.* **s'a.**, go away.

abside, *n.f.* apse.

absinthe, *n.f.* absinthe.

absolu, *adj.* utter, absolute.

absolument, *adv.* absolutely.

absolution, *n.f.* absolution.

absorbant, *adj. and n.m.* absorbent.

absorbé dans, *adj.* intent on.

absorber, *vb.* engross, absorb. **s'a. dans**, pore over.

absorption, *n.f.* absorption.

absoudre, *vb.* absolve.

abstenir, *vb.* forbear. **s'a. de**, abstain from.

abstinence, *n.f.* abstinence.

abstraction, *n.f.* abstraction.

abstrait, *adj.* abstract.

absurde, *adj.* absurd, preposterous.

absurdité, *n.f.* nonsense, absurdity.

abus, *n.m.* abuse.

abuser de, *vb.* abuse.

académie, *n.f.* academy.

académique, *adj.* academic.

acajou, *n.m.* mahogany.

accablant, *adj.* oppressive.

accabler, *vb.* overwhelm, burden.

accalmie, *n.f.* lull.

accaparer, *vb.* get a corner on.

accéder, *vb.* reach.

accélérateur, *n.m.* accelerator.

accélération, *n.f.* acceleration.

accélérer, *vb.* quicken, hurry.

accent, *n.m.* stress, emphasis, accent.

accentuer, *vb.* accentuate, accent, emphasize.

acceptable, *adj.* acceptable.

acceptation, *n.f.* acceptance.

accepter, *vb.* accept, admit.

accepteur, *n.m.* accepter.

accès, *n.m.* access, approach; fit (of anger); bout (of fever).

accessible, *adj.* accessible.

accessoire, *n.m. and adj.* accessory, adjunct.

accident, *n.m.* crash, accident.

accidenté, *adj.* damaged; (terrain) hilly.

accidentel, *adj.* accidental.

acclamation, *n.f.* acclamation.

acclamer, *vb.* acclaim, cheer.

accommodant, *adj.* accommodating.

accommoder, *vb.* accommodate.

accompagnateur, *n.m.* accompanist, (travel) guide.

accompagnement, *n.m.* accompaniment.

accompagner, *vb.* accompany, go with.

accompli, *adj.* accomplished, complete, perfect.

accomplir, *vb.* accomplish, achieve, fulfill, carry out, perform.

accomplissement, *n.m.* performance, accomplishment, fulfillment, achievement.

accord, *n.m.* agreement, harmony; settlement; chord, tune. **être d'a.,** agree, concur.

accorder, *vb.* grant, bestow; allow; tune. **s'a.,** agree.

accouchement, *n.m.* delivery (baby).

accoucher, *vb.* deliver (baby).

accoucheur, *n.m.* **médecin-a.,** obstetrician.

accouder, *vb.* **s'a.,** lean.

accourir, *vb.* flock, run up.

accoutumer, *vb.* accustom, habituate.

accréditer, *vb.* accredit.

accro, *n.m.* (drug) addict.

accroc, *n.m.* tear, snag; hitch (fig.).

accrocher, *vb.* hook, hitch, hang (up).

accroissement, *n.m.* growth, addition.

accroître, *vb.* increase.

accroupir, *vb.* **s'a.,** squat, crouch.

accru, *adj.* greater, increased.

accueil, *n.m.* reception, greeting.

accueillir, *vb.* receive, greet.

acculer, *vb.* corner.

accumuler, *vb.* heap up.

accusateur, *n.m.* accuser.

accusatif, *n.m.* accusative.

accusation, *n.f.* accusation.

accusatrice, *n.f.* accuser.

accusé, *n.m.* defendant.

accuser, *vb.* arraign, accuse.

acerbe, *adj.* bitter.

acharné, *adj.* eager, relentless.

acharner, *vb.* **s'a.,** go at intensely.

achat, *n.m.* purchase.

acheminer, *vb.* start (toward).

acheter, *vb.* buy.

acheteur, *n.m.* buyer.

achèvement, *n.m.* completion.

achever, *vb.* complete, finish, achieve.

acide, *adj. and n.m.* acid.

acidité, *n.f.* acidity.

acier, *n.m.* steel.

acné, *n.f.* acne.

acolyte, *n.m.* associate.

acompte, *n.m.* deposit, installment.

à-côté, *n.m.* side-issue.

à-c.s., extras.

à-coup, *n.m.* jolt. **par à-c.s.,** by fits and starts.

acoustique, *n.f.* acoustics.

acquérir, *vb.* acquire, get, obtain.

acquiescement, *n.m.* acquiescence, compliance.

acquiescer à, *vb.* acquiesce, consent.

acquisition, *n.f.* acquisition, purchase.

acquittement, *n.m.* acquittal.

acquitter, *vb.* acquit.

âcre, *adj.* sharp.

acrobate, *n.m.f.* acrobat.

acrobatie, *n.f.* acrobatics.

acte, *n.m.* act. **a. notarié,** deed. **a. de naissance,** birth certificate.

acteur, *n.m.* actor.

actif, 1. *n.m.* assets (*comm.*). **2.** *adj.* active.

action, *n.f.* action, deed, act; (*comm.*) share.

action de contrôle en retour, *n.f.* feedback.

actionnaire, *n.m.* shareholder.

actionner, *vb.* operate.

activement, *adv.* busily.
activer, *vb.* activate, fan, hurry.
activité, *n.f.* activity.
actrice, *n.f.* actress.
actualiser, *vb.* update.
actualité, *n.f.* topicality.
actualités, *n.f.pl.* current events, TV news.
actuel, *adj.* present.
actuellement, *adv.* now, at present.
acuité, *n.f.* acuteness.
acupuncture, *n.f.* acupuncture.
adaptateur, *n.m.* adapter.
adaptation, *n.f.* adaptation.
adapter, *vb.* adapt, fit, adjust, suit.
additif, *n.m.* additive.
addition, *n.f.* addition, bill.
additionnel, *adj.* additional.
additionner, *vb.* add.
adepte, *n.m.f.* follower.
adéquat, *adj.* appropriate.
adhérent, *n.m.* member.
adhérer, *vb.* adhere, join.
adhésif, *adj.* adhesive.
adieu, *n.m. and interj.* good-bye, farewell. **faire ses adieux,** take one's leave.
adjacent, *adj.* adjacent.
adjectif, *n.m.* adjective.
adjoindre, *vb.* add, attach.
adjoint, *n.m.* fellow-worker, associate.
adjuger, *vb.* grant, award.
admettre, *vb.* allow, admit, grant.
administrateur, *n.m.* administrator, director, manager.
administratif, *adj.* administrative.
administration, *n.f.* administration, direction.
administrer, *vb.* administer, manage.
admirable, *adj.* admirable.
admirateur, *n.m.* admirer.
admiration, *n.f.* admiration.
admirer, *vb.* admire.
admissible, *adj.* eligible.
admission, *n.f.* confession, admission.
adolescence, *n.f.* adolescence.
adolescent, *adj. and n.m.* adolescent.
adonner, *vb.* s'a. à, indulge in, become addicted to.
adopter, *vb.* adopt.

adoptif, *adj.* adoptive.
adoption, *n.f.* adoption.
adoration, *n.f.* adoration.
adorer, *vb.* worship, adore.
adosser, *vb.* s'a. à, lean on.
adoucir, *vb.* soothe, soften, sweeten.
adresse, *n.f.* address; skill, ability.
adresser, *vb.* address (a letter); direct. s'a. à, apply to.
adroit, *adj.* skillful, clever, handy.
aduler, *vb.* adulate.
adulte, *adj. and n.m.f.* adult.
adultère, *n.m.* adultery.
adultérer, *vb.* adulterate.
advenir, *vb.* happen, occur.
adverbe, *n.m.* adverb.
adversaire, *n.m.f.* opponent.
adverse, *adj.* adverse.
adversité, *n.f.* adversity.
aéré, *adj.* airy.
aérer, *vb.* air (a room).
aérien, *adj.* aerial, overhead.
aérobic, *n.m.* aerobics.
aérodynamique, *adj.* streamlined, aerodynamic.
aérogare, *n.f.* airline (city) terminal.
aéroglisseur, *n.m.* hovercraft.
aérogramme, *n.m.* airmail letter, aerogram.
aéronautique, 1. *n.m.* aeronautics. **2.** *adj.* aeronautical.
aéroport, *n.m.* airport.
aérospatial, *adj.* aerospace.
affable, *adj.* affable.
affaiblir, *vb.* weaken.
affaire, *n.f.* affair, matter; deal; *(pl.)* business. se tirer d'a., manage (somehow). **homme d'a.s,** businessman.
affairé, *adj.* busy.
affairer, *vb.* s'a., be busy.
affaissement, *n.m.* collapse.
affaisser, *vb.* s'a., collapse.
affaler, *vb.* s'a., collapse.
affamé, *adj.* hungry, famished.
affamer, *vb.* starve.
affectation, *n.f.* affectation.
affecter, *vb.* affect; assign.
affectif, *adj.* emotional.
affection, *n.f.* affection.
affectueux, *adj.* affectionate.
affermir, *vb.* strengthen.
affiche, *n.f.* poster.

afficher, *vb.* post, announce.
affilée (d'), *adv.* in a row.
affilier, *vb.* affiliate.
affiner, *vb.* refine.
affinité, *n.f.* affinity.
affirmatif, *adj.* affirmative.
affirmation, *n.f.* statement.
affirmer, *vb.* assert, state, maintain, testify, affirm.
affliction, *n.f.* affliction.
affligé, *adj.* sorrowful.
affliger, *vb.* distress, afflict, grieve.
affluence, *n.f.* crowd. **heures d'a.,** rush hour.
affluent, *n.m.* tributary.
affluer, *vb.* flow into.
affolement, *n.* panic.
affoler, *vb.* drive mad.
affranchir, *vb.* free.
affranchissement, *n.m.* postage.
affréter, *vb.* charter (boat).
affreusement, *adv.* terribly.
affreux, *adj.* dreadful, terrible, horrid, dire.
affront, *n.m.* affront, insult.
affronter, *vb.* confront, face.
afin, 1. **a. de,** *prep.* in order to. 2. *conj.* **a. que,** so that.
Africain, *n.m.* African.
africain, *adj.* African.
Afrique, *n.f.* Africa.
agacer, *vb.* vex, irritate.
âge, *n.m.* age. **d'un certain â.,** elderly. **le moyen â.,** the Middle Ages.
âgé, *adj.* aged.
agence, *n.f. (comm.)* agency.
agencer, *vb.* organize, arrange.
agenda, *n.m.* datebook.
agenouiller, *vb.* s'a., kneel.
agent, *n.m.* agent. **a. de police,** policeman. **a. de change,** stockbroker.
agglomération, *n.f.* built-up area, town.
aggloméré, *n.m.* chipboard.
agglomérer, *vb.* s'a., pile up.
agglutiner, *vb.* s'a. stick together.
aggraver, *vb.* aggravate.
agile, *adj.* nimble.
agir, *vb.* act. s'a. de, be a question of.
agitateur, *n.m.* agitator.
agitation, *n.f.* excitement, disturbance, commotion, flutter.

agité, *adj.* upset, excited.
agiter, *vb.* agitate, wave, wag, shake, stir. s'a., toss; flutter.
agneau, *n.m.* lamb.
agonie, *n.f.* agony.
agoniser, *vb.* be dying.
agrafe, *n.f.* clasp, staple.
agrafer, *vb.* clasp, staple.
agrafeuse, *n.f.* stapler.
agrandir, *vb.* enlarge.
agréable, *adj.* likable, pleasant, enjoyable, agreeable.
agréer, *vb.* accept, consent.
agrégation, *n.f.* aggregation; fellowship.
agrément, *n.m.* pleasure, approval.
agresser, *vb.* attack.
agresseur, *n.m.* aggressor, attacker.
agressif, *adj.* aggressive, hostile.
agression, *n.f.* aggression.
agricole, *adj.* agricultural.
agriculture, *n.f.* agriculture.
agripper, *vb.* s'a. à, grab.
agroalimentaire, *n.m.* food industry.
agrumes, *n.m.pl.* citrus fruit(s).
aguerrir, *vb.* harden.
aguets, *n.m.pl.* être aux a., be on the look-out.
aguicher, *vb.* entice.
ahurir, *vb.* bewilder, fluster.
aide, *n.f.* help, aid.
aider, *vb.* help, aid.
aïe, *interj.* ouch!
aïeul (ä yœl), *n.m.* grandfather.
aïeule (ä yœl), *n.f.* grandmother.
aïeux, *n.m.pl.* ancestors.
aigle, *n.m.f.* eagle.
aiglefin, *n.m.* haddock.
aigre, *adj.* sour.
aigu, *m.* **aiguë** *f.* *adj.* shrill, sharp, pointed.
aiguille, *n.f.* needle.
aiguisé, *adj.* keen.
aiguiser, *vb.* sharpen.
ail (ä ē) *n.m.* garlic.
aile, *n.f.* wing.
aileron, *n.m.* fin.
ailleurs, *adv.* elsewhere. **d'a.,** in addition, anyhow.
aimable, *adj.* kind, pleasant, amiable.
aimant, *n.m.* magnet.

aimer, vb. love, like.

aine, n.f. groin.

aîné (ě' nā), **1.** adj. and n.m. elder. **2.** adj. eldest, senior.

ainsi, adv. thus, so, like this.

air, n.m. air, looks. **en plein a.**, in the open air.

aire, n.f. area.

aisance, n.f. ease, affluence.

aise, n.f. ease, comfort. **à l'a.**, comfortable.

aisé, adj. substantial, well-to-do; easy.

aisselle, n.f. armpit.

ajourner, vb. put off. **s'a.**, adjourn.

ajouter, vb. add.

ajustage, n.m. fitting.

ajuster, vb. fit, fix, adjust.

alarme, n.f. alarm.

alarmer, vb. alarm.

albâtre, n.m. alabaster.

albatros, n.m. albatross.

album, n.m. album.

albumine, n.f. albumin.

alcool (-kôl), n.m. alcohol.

alcoolique (-kôl-), adj. and n.m.f. alcoholic.

alcoolisé, adj. alcoholic (drink).

alcootest, n.m. Breathalyzer test.

alcôve, n.f. alcove.

aléas, n.m.pl. hazards.

aléatoire, adj. uncertain, random.

alentour, adv. around.

alentours, n.m.pl. neighborhood, surroundings.

alerte, adj. spry, active, alert.

algarade, n.f. altercation.

algèbre, n.f. algebra.

Alger, n.f. Algiers.

Algérie, n.f. Algeria.

Algérien, n.m. Algerian.

algérian, adj. Algerian.

algue, n.f. seaweed.

alias, adv. alias.

alibi, n.m. alibi.

aliéné, n.m. lunatic.

aliéner, vb. alienate.

aligner, vb. line up.

aliment, n.m. food.

alimentation, n.f. feeding.

alimenter, vb. feed.

alinéa, n.m. paragraph.

aliter, vb. **s'a.**, take to one's bed.

allaiter, vb. nurse, feed.

allécher, vb. tempt.

allée, n.f. path, avenue, aisle.

allégation, n.f. allegation.

alléger, vb. lighten, soothe.

allégresse, n.f. glee, delight, mirth.

alléguer, vb. plead, allege.

Allemagne, n.f. Germany.

Allemand, n.m. German (person).

allemand, **1.** n.m. German (language). **2.** adj. German.

aller, vb. go. **s'en a.**, go away. **a. à**, fit. **se laisser a.**, drift. **a. bien**, be well. **a. mal**, be not well. **a. et retour**, round trip.

allergique, adj. allergic.

alliage, n.m. alloy.

alliance, n.f. alliance, union.

allié, **1.** n.m. ally, relation. **2.** adj. allied.

allier, vb. ally. **s'a. à**, join with.

allô, interj. hello.

allocation, n.f. allowance. **a.s familiales**, family allowance.

allocution, n.f. short speech.

allonger, vb. lengthen, prolong.

allons, interj. well, come now.

allouer, vb. grant.

allume-cigare, n.m. cigar lighter.

allumer, vb. light.

allumette, n.f. match.

allure, n.f. pace, gait.

allusion, n.f. hint, allusion. **faire a. à**, allude to.

almanach (-nä), n.m. almanac.

aloi, n.m. **de bon a.**, of genuine quality.

alors, **1.** adv. then. **2.** conj. **a. que**, when.

alouette, n.f. lark.

aloudir, vb. weigh down.

Alpes, n.f.pl. Alps.

alphabet, n.m. alphabet.

alphabétiser, vb. teach to read and write.

alpinisme, n.m. mountaineering.

Alsace, n.f. Alsace.

altérer, vb. change.

alternatif, adj. alternate.

alternative, n.f. alternative.

alterner, vb. alternate.

Altesse, n.f. Highness (title).

altitude, n.f. altitude.

alto, n.m. viola.

altruisme, n.m. altruism.

aluminium, n.m. aluminum.

amabilité, n.f. kindness.

amadouer, vb. soothe, coax.

amaigrir, vb. to make thin(ner).

amalgame, n.m. combination.

amalgamer, vb. amalgamate.

amande, n.f. kernel; almond.

amant, n.m. lover.

amarrer, vb. moor.

amas, n.m. hoard, mass.

amasser, vb. hoard, gather, amass.

amateur, n.m. amateur. **a. de**, lover of.

ambassade, n.f. embassy.

ambassadeur, n.m. ambassador.

ambassadrice, n.f. ambassadress.

ambiance, n.f. atmosphere.

ambiant, adj. surrounding.

ambigu m., **ambiguë** f. adj. ambiguous.

ambiguïté, n.f. ambiguity.

ambitieux, adj. ambitious.

ambition, n.f. ambition.

ambre, n.m. amber.

ambulance, n.f. ambulance.

ambulant, adj. traveling.

âme, n.f. soul.

amélioration, n.f. improvement.

améliorer, vb. improve.

aménagement, n.m. development.

aménager, vb. fit up.

amende, n.f. fine. **mettre à l'a.**, fine.

amendement, n.m. amendment.

amender, vb. amend.

amener, vb. bring, lead.

amenuiser, vb. **s'a.**, dwindle, lessen.

amer (-r), adj. bitter.

Américain, n.m. American.

américain, adj. American.

Amérique, n.f. America.

A. du Nord, North America.

A. du Sud, South America.

amertume, n.f. bitterness.

ameublement, n.m. furniture.

ami m., **amie** f. n. friend.

amiable, adj. conciliatory. **à l'a.**, out of court.

amiante, n.m. asbestos.

amical, adj. friendly, amicable.

amidon, n.m. starch.

amiral, n.m. admiral.

amitié, n.f. friendship.

ammoniaque, n.f. ammonia.

amniocentèse, n.f. amniocentesis.

amoindrir, vb. lessen, reduce.

amollir, vb. soften.

amonceler, vb. pile up. **s'a.**, pile up, (fig.) accumulate.

amont, adv. **en a.**, upstream, uphill.

amorce, n.f. bait, beginning.

amorcer, vb. bait, begin.

amorphe, adj. listless.

amortir, vb. deaden, soften.

amortisseur, n.m. shock absorber.

amour, n.m. love.

amoureux, 1. n.m. lover. 2. adj. in love, amorous.

amour-propre, n.m. vanity, pride, conceit.

ampère, n.m. amp(ere).

ample, adj. ample, spacious.

ampleur, n.f. plenty; compass.

amplificateur, n.m. amplifier.

amplifier, vb. increase, enlarge, develop.

ampoule, n.f. blister; (electric) bulb.

amputer, vb. amputate.

amusant, adj. funny, enjoyable.

amusement, n.m. fun, pastime, entertainment.

amuser, vb. entertain. **s'a.**, have a good time.

amygdale, n.f. tonsil.

an, n.m. year.

analogie, n.f. analogy.

analogique, adj. analogue.

analogue, adj. similar, analogous.

analphabète, n.m.f. illiterate.

analyse, n.f. analysis.

analyser, vb. analyze.

ananas, n.m. pineapple.

anarchie, n.f. anarchy.

anathème, n.m. anathema.

anatomie, n.f. anatomy.

ancêtre, n.m. forefather, ancestor.

anche, n.f. reed.

anchois, n.m. anchovy.

ancien m., **ancienne** f. adj. ancient, old; former.

ancre, n.f. anchor.

ancrer, vb. anchor.

Andorre, n.f. Andorra.

andouille, n.f. sausage made of chitterlings; (colloqiuial) idiot.

âne m., **ânesse** f. n. ass, donkey.

anéantir, vb. annihilate, destroy.

anecdote, n.f. anecdote.

anémie, n.f. anemia.

ânerie, n.f. stupidity.

anesthésie, *n.f.* anesthesia.

anesthésique, *adj. and n.m.* anesthetic.

ange, *n.m.* angel.

angine, *n.f.* throat infection.

Anglais, *n.m.* Englishman.

anglais, *adj. and n.m.* English.

Anglaise, *n.f.* Englishwoman.

angle, *n.m.* angle, corner.

Angleterre, *n.f.* England.

angoissant, *adj.* in anguish.

angoisse, *n.f.* agony, pang, anguish.

anguille, *n.f.* eel.

anguleux, *adj.* angular.

anicroche, *n.f.* hitch.

animal, *adj. and n.m.* animal.

animateur, *n.m.* leader, organizer.

animation, *n.f.* animation.

animer, *vb.* enliven, animate.

anis, *n.m.* aniseed.

ankyloser, *vb.* s'a., become stiff.

animosité, *n.f.* animosity.

anneau, *n.m.* ring, circle.

année, *n.f.* year; vintage.

annexe, *n.f.* annex.

annexer, *vb.* annex.

annexion, *n.f.* annexation.

anniversaire, *n.m.* anniversary; birthday.

annonce, *n.f.* advertisement; announcement.

annoncer, *vb.* advertise; announce.

annotation, *n.f.* annotation.

annoter, *vb.* annotate.

annuaire, *n.m.* directory.

annuel, *adj.* yearly, annual.

annuité, *n.f.* annual payment.

annulaire, *n.m.* ring finger.

annulation, *n.f.* cancellation.

annuler, *vb.* cancel, void, annul.

anodin, *adj.* harmless, minor.

ânonner, *vb.* stammer.

anonyme, *adj.* anonymous.

anorak, *n.m.* anorak.

anorexie, *n.f.* anorexia.

anormal, *adj.* irregular, abnormal.

anse, *n.f.* handle; bay (water).

antagonisme, *n.m.* antagonism.

antarctique, *adj.* antarctic.

antécédent, *adj. and n.m.* antecedent.

antécédents, *n.m.pl.* record.

antenne, *n.f.* antenna.

antérieur, *adj.* previous; fore, front.

anthracite, *n.m.* anthracite.

antichambre, *n.f.* entrance hall.

anticipation, *n.f.* anticipation.

anticiper, *vb.* anticipate.

anticorps, *n.m.* antibody.

antidote, *n.m.* antidote.

antihistaminique, *n.m.* antihistamine.

Antilles, *n.f.pl.* West Indies.

antilope, *n.f.* antelope.

antinucléaire, *adj.* antinuclear.

antipathie, *n.f.* antipathy.

antiquaire, *n.m.* antique dealer.

antique, *adj.* ancient, antiquated, antique.

antiquité, *n.f.* antiquity.

antisémite, 1. *n.m.* anti-Semite. **2.** *adj.* anti-Semitic.

antiseptique, *adj. and n.m.* antiseptic.

antre, *n.m.* den.

anxiété, *n.f.* anxiety, worry.

anxieux, *adj.* anxious.

août (ōō), *n.m.* August.

apaiser, *vb.* allay, quiet, appease.

apanage, *n.m.* l'a. de, privilege of.

aparté, *n.m.* aside.

apathie, *n.f.* apathy.

apatride, *n.m.* stateless person.

apercevoir, *vb.* perceive. s'a. de, realize.

aperçu, *n.m.* outline.

apéritif, *n.m.* appetizer.

à-peu-près, *n.m.* approximation.

apeuré, *adj.* scared.

aphone, *adj.* voiceless.

apitoyer, *vb.* move (emotionally).

aplanir, *vb.* even off.

aplatir, *vb.* flatten.

aplomb, *n.m.* poise, boldness.

apogée, *n.m.* peak.

apologie, *n.f.* vindication.

apoplexie, *n.f.* apoplexy.

apostolique, *adj.* apostolic.

apostrophe, *n.f.* apostrophe.

apothéose, *n.f.* crowning glory.

apôtre, *n.m.* apostle.

apparaître, *vb.* appear.

appareil, *n.m.* gear, appliance, device. **a. photographique,** camera.

apparence, *n.f.* appearance, looks.

apparent, *adj.* noticeable, apparent.

apparenté, *adj.* related.
apparition, *n.f.* appearance, ghost.
appartement, *n.m.* apartment.
appartenir, *vb.* belong; pertain.
appât, *n.m.* bait.
appauvrir, *vb.* impoverish.
appel, *n.m.* call, appeal.
appeler, *vb.* call, summon, appeal. **s'a.**, be named.
appendice, *n.m.* appendix.
appesantir, *vb.* **s'a.**, grow heavier.
appétissant, *adj.* appetizing.
appétit, *n.m.* appetite.
applaudir, *vb.* applaud.
applaudissements, *n.m.pl.* applause.
applicable, *adj.* applicable.
application, *n.f.* application, industry.
appliqué, *adj.* industrious.
appliquer, *vb.* apply (put on), stick. **s'a.**, work hard.
appoint, *n.m.* contribution.
appointements, *n.m.pl.* salary.
apport, *n.m.* contribution.
apporter, *vb.* bring, fetch.
apposer, *vb.* affix.
appréciable, *adj.* appreciable.
appréciation, *n.f.* appreciation.
apprécier, *vb.* appreciate, value.
appréhension, *n.f.* apprehension.
apprendre, *vb.* learn. **a. à**, teach (to). **a. par cœur**, memorize.
apprenti, *n.m.* apprentice.
apprentissage, *n.m.* apprenticeship.
apprêt, *n.m.* preparation.
apprêter, *vb.* **s'a.**, prepare, get ready.
apprivoiser, *vb.* tame.
approbation, *n.f.* endorsement, approval, approbation.
approche, *n.f.* approach.
approcher, *vb.* **s'a. de**, approach, go toward.
approfondir, *vb.* deepen.
appropriation, *n.f.* appropriation.
approprier, *vb.* **s'a.**, take over, appropriate.
approuver, *vb.* approve.
approvisionnement, *n.m.* supply.
approvisioner, *vb.* supply.
approximatif, *adj.* approximate.
appui (-pwē), *n.m.* support.
appuyer (-pwē-), *vb.* support, endorse, advocate. **a. sur**, emphasize.
âpre, *adj.* bitter.
après, **1.** *adv.* after. **2.** *conj.* **a. que**, after. **d'a.**, according to.
après-demain, *n.m.* day after tomorrow.
après-midi, *n.m.f.* afternoon.
âpreté, *n.f.* harshness, bitterness.
à-propos, *n.m.* fitness.
apte à, *adj.* apt, suitable for.
aptitude, *n.f.* fitness, ability, aptitude.
aqualit, *n.m.* waterbed.
aquarelle (-kwä-), *n.f.* watercolor.
aquarium (-kwä-), *n.m.* aquarium.
aquatique (-kwä-), *adj.* aquatic.
aqueux, *adj.* watery.
Arabe, *n.m.f.* Arab, Arabian.
arabe, **1.** *n.m.f.* Arab, Arabian, Arabic. **2.** *adj.* Arab, Arabian, Arabic.
arachide, *n.f.* peanut.
araignée, *n.f.* spider. **toile d'a.**, cobweb.
arbitrage, *n.m.* arbitration.
arbitraire, *adj.* arbitrary.
arbitre, *n.m.f.* umpire, arbitrator.
arbitrer, *vb.* arbitrate.
arbre, *n.m.* tree.
arbrisseau, *n.m.* shrub.
arc (-k), *n.m.* arc, arch, bow.
arcade, *n.f.* arcade.
arc-boutant, *n.m.* flying buttress.
arc-en-ciel, *n.m.* rainbow.
archaïque (ärk-), *adj.* archaic.
arche, *n.f.* arch (of bridge); ark. **a. de Noé**, Noah's Ark.
archéologie, *n.f.* archeology.
archet, *n.m.* bow.
archevêque, *n.m.* archbishop.
archi-, *prefix.* very.
archipel, *n.m.* archipelago.
architecte, *n.m.* architect.
architectural, *adj.* architectural.
architecture, *n.f.* architecture.
archives, *n.f.pl.* files, archives.
arctique, *adj.* arctic.
ardemment, *adv.* eagerly.
ardent, *adj.* eager, fiery, ardent.
ardeur, *n.f.* ardor.
ardoise, *n.f.* slate.
arène, *n.f.* arena, ring.
arête, *n.f.* fish bone.
argent, *n.m.* silver, money.
argenté, *adj.* silver(y).

argenterie, *n.f.* silverware.
Argentin, *n.m.* Argentine.
argentin, *adj.* Argentine.
argile, *n.f.* clay.
argot, *n.m.* slang.
argument, *n.m.* argument (reasoning).
argumenter, *vb.* argue (reason).
aride, *adj.* arid.
aristocrate, *n.m.f.* aristocrat.
aristocratie, *n.f.* aristocracy.
aristocratique, *adj.* aristocratic.
arithmétique, *n.f.* arithmetic.
arme, *n.f.* weapon; arm.
armée, *n.f.* army.
armement, *n.m.* armament.
arme nucléaire, *n.f.* nuclear weapon.
armer, *vb.* arm.
armistice, *n.m.* armistice.
armoire, *n.f.* cupboard, closet, wardrobe.
armure, *n.f.* armor.
arnaque, *n.f.* swindle.
aromatique, *adj.* aromatic.
arome, *n.m.* flavor, aroma.
arpenter, *vb.* pace.
arrache-pied, *adv.* **d'a.,** relentlessly.
arracher, *vb.* snatch.
arrangement, *n.m.* arrangement, settlement.
arranger, *vb.* settle, trim, fix, arrange.
arrestation, *n.f.* arrest, apprehension. **en état d'a.,** under arrest.
arrêt, *n.m.* stop.
arrêté, *n.m.* decree.
arrêter, *vb.* stop, check, halt, arrest.
arrhes, *n.f.pl.* deposit.
arrière, *adv.* behind, back. **en a.,** backward. **marche a.,** reverse (gear).
arriéré, 1. *n.m.* arrear. **2.** *adj.* backward.
arrière-garde, *n.f.* rear guard.
arrivée, *n.f.* arrival.
arriver, *vb.* happen, reach, arrive.
arrogance, *n.f.* arrogance.
arrogant, *adj.* arrogant.
arroger, *vb.* arrogate, assume.
arrondir, *vb.* round off.
arrondissement, *n.m.* district.

arroser, *vb.* water, sprinkle; baste (meat).
arsenal, *n.m.* arsenal.
arsenic, *n.m.* arsenic.
art, *n.m.* art. **beaux-a.s,** fine arts.
artère, *n.f.* artery.
artériel, *adj.* arterial.
arthrite, *n.f.* arthritis.
arthrose, *n.f.* osteoarthritis.
artichaut, *n.m.* artichoke.
article, *n.m.* article, item; entry. **a. de fond,** editorial.
articulation, *n.f.* joint, articulation.
articuler, *vb.* articulate.
artifice, *n.m.* artifice.
artificiel, *adj.* artificial.
artificieux, *adj.* artful.
artillerie, *n.f.* artillery.
artisan, *n.m.* craftsman, artisan.
artiste, *n.m.f.* artist.
artistique, *adj.* artistic.
as (äs), *n.m.* ace.
ascenseur, *n.m.* elevator.
ascension, *n.f.* ascent (of a mountain).
ascète, *n.m.f.* ascetic.
aseptique, *adj.* aseptic.
aseptiser, *vb.* disinfect.
Asiatique, *n.m.f.* Asian.
asiatique, *adj.* Asian.
Asie, *n.f.* Asia.
asile, *n.m.* haven, refuge, asylum.
aspect (-pě), *n.m.* looks, appearance, aspect.
asperger, *vb.* sprinkle.
asperges, *n.f.pl.* asparagus.
aspérité, *n.f.* bump.
asphalte, *n.m.*, asphalt.
asphyxier, *vb.* suffocate.
aspirateur, *n.m.* vacuum cleaner.
aspiration, *n.f.* aspiration, longing.
aspirer, *vb.* aspire, breathe.
aspirine, *n.f.* aspirin.
assaillant, *n.m.* assailant.
assaillir, *vb.* assail, attack.
assaisonner, *vb.* season.
assassin, *n.m.* assassin, murderer.
assassinat, *n.m.* assassination, murder.
assassiner, *vb.* assassinate, murder.
assaut, *n.m.* assault, attack.
assemblage, *n.m.* collection.

assemblée, *n.f.* congregation, assembly.

assembler, *vb.* convene, gather. **s'a.,** assemble.

assener, *vb.* deal (a blow).

assentiment, *n.m.* assent.

asseoir, *vb.* seat. **s'a.,** sit down.

assermenté, *adj.* sworn.

assertion, *n.f.* assertion.

asservir, *vb.* enslave.

assez (de), *adv.* enough (of); pretty much.

assidu, *adj.* assiduous, industrious.

assiduité, *n.f.* industry.

assiéger, *vb.* besiege.

assiette, *n.f.* plate.

assigner, *vb.* assign.

assimiler, *vb.* assimilate.

assis, *adj.* seated.

assistance, *n.f.* those present.

assister à, *vb.* attend, be present at.

association, *n.f.* soccer; association, company; connection.

associé, 1. *n.m.* partner, associate. **2.** *adj.* associated.

associer, *vb.* associate.

assoiffé, *adj.* thirsty.

assombrir, *vb.* **s'a.,** grow dark.

assommer, *vb.* murder, slaughter.

Assomption, *n.f.* (*eccles.*) Assumption.

assorti, *adj.* matching.

assortiment, *n.m.* assortment.

assortir, *vb.* match; tune.

assoupir, *vb.* **s'a.,** get drowsy.

assouplir, *vb.* make supple.

assourdir, *vb.* deafen.

assouvir, *vb.* satisfy, appease.

assujetti, *adj.* subject.

assujettir, *vb.* subject.

assumer, *vb.* assume.

assurance, *n.f.* assurance, insurance.

assuré, *adj.* sure.

assurer, *vb.* insure; assure. **assure. s'a. de,** make certain.

assureur, *n.m.* insurer.

astérisque, *n.m.* asterisk.

asthme, *n.m.* asthma.

astiquer, *vb.* polish.

astre, *n.m.* star.

astronaute, *n.m.* astronaut.

astronome, *n.m.* astronomer.

astronomie, *n.f.* astronomy.

astuce, *n.f.* shrewdness; trick.

astucieux, *adj.* tricky.

atelier, *n.m.* studio, (work)shop.

athée, *n.m.f.* atheist.

Athènes, *n.f.* Athens.

athlète, *n.m.f.* athlete.

athlétique, *adj.* athletic.

atlantique, *adj.* Atlantic.

atlas (-s), *n.m.* atlas.

atmosphère, *n.f.* atmosphere.

atmosphérique, *adj.* atmospheric.

atome, *n.m.* atom.

atomique, *adj.* atomic.

atout, *n.m.* trump.

atroce, *adj.* atrocious, outrageous.

atrocité, *n.f.* atrocity.

attachement, *n.m.* attachment, affection.

attacher, *vb.* tie, fasten, join, attach.

attaque, *n.f.* attack.

attaquer, *vb.* attack.

attardé, *adj.* belated.

attarder, *vb.* **s'a.,** linger; delay.

atteindre, *vb.* reach, attain; strike.

atteint, *adj.* stricken.

atteinte, *n.f.* reach. **hors d'a.,** out of reach.

attelage, *n.m.* team.

atteler, *vb.* hitch up, harness.

attenant, *adj.* adjoining.

attendre, *vb.* wait (for), await. **s'a. à,** expect.

attendrir, *vb.* soften, move. **se laisser a.,** relent.

attendrissement, *n.m.* feeling, emotion.

attentat, *n.m.* criminal attack, outrage.

attente, *n.f.* expectation, wait.

attenter à, *vb.* make an attempt on.

attentif, *adj.* thoughtful, attentive.

attention, *n.f.* notice, heed, attention. **faire a.,** heed, pay attention.

atténuer, *vb.* extenuate.

atterrir, *vb.* land.

attester, *vb.* attest.

attirant, *adj.* attractive.

attirer, *vb.* attract, entice, lure.

attitude, *n.f.* attitude.

attouchement, *n.m.* touch.

attraction, *n.f.* attraction.

attrait, *n.m.* charm.

attraper, *vb.* catch.

attrayant, *adj.* attractive.
attribuer, *vb.* ascribe, attribute.
attribut, *n.m.* attribute, characteristic.
attrister, *vb.* grieve.
au, *m.,* **à la,** *f.,* **aux,** *pl.* *prep.* to the, in the.
aubaine, *n.f.* godsend.
aube, *n.f.* dawn.
auberge, *n.f.* inn.
aubergine, *n.f.* eggplant.
aubergiste, *n.m.* innkeeper.
aucun, *pron.* none.
aucunement, *adv.* not at all.
audace, *n.f.* audacity.
audacieux, *adj.* daring, bold.
au-delà, *adv.* beyond.
au-dessous, 1. *adv.* below. **2.** *prep.* **au-d. de,** beneath, under.
au-dessus, 1. *adv.* above. **2.** *prep.* **au-d. de,** over, above.
audience, *n.f.* audience.
Audimat, *n.m.* (trademark) TV ratings.
audiovisuel, *adj.* audiovisual.
auditeur, *n.m.* listener.
auditoire, *n.m.* audience, assembly.
auge, *n.f.* trough.
augmentation, *n.f.* increase, raise, rise.
augmenter, *vb.* increase.
augure, *n.m.* omen, augury. **de bon a.,** auspicious. **de mauvais a.,** ominous.
augurer, *vb.* augur.
aujourd'hui, *adv.* today.
aumône, *n.f.* alms.
aumônier, *n.m.* chaplain.
auparavant, *adv.* before (time).
auprès de, *prep.* next, near, beside.
auréole, *n.f.* halo.
aurore, *n.f.* dawn.
ausculter, *vb.* examine with a stethoscope.
auspice, *n.m.* auspice.
aussi, *adv.* too, also; so, as; therefore.
aussitôt, *adv.* immediately.
austère, *adj.* austere, severe.
austérité, *n.f.* austerity.
Australie, *n.f.* Australia.
Australien, *n.m.* Australian.
australien, *adj.* Australian.
autant, *adv.* so much, as much. **a.**

que, as (so) much as. **d'a. que,** since. **a. plus,** so much the more.
autel, *n.m.* altar.
auteur, *n.m.* author, originator.
authentique, *adj.* true, genuine, authentic.
auto, *n.f.* auto.
auto-, *prefix.* self-, auto-.
autobus (-s), *n.m.* bus.
automatique, *adj.* automatic.
automne (-tôn), *n.m.* fall.
automobile, *n.f.* automobile.
autonomie, *n.f.* autonomy.
autopsie, *n.f.* autopsy.
autorail, *n.m.* train car.
autorisation, *n.f.* license, authorization.
autoriser, *vb.* authorize.
autoritaire, *adj.* authoritative.
autorité, *n.f.* authority.
autoroute, *n.f.* highway.
auto-stop, *n.m.* hitchhiking.
autour, 1. *adv.* around. **2.** *prep.* **a. de,** around.
autre, 1. *adj.* other. **2.** *pron.* other, else. **l'un l'a.,** one another. **quelqu'un d'a.,** someone else.
autrefois, *adv.* formerly.
autrement, *adv.* otherwise.
Autriche, *n.f.* Austria.
Autrichien, *n.m.* Austrian.
autrichien, *adj.* Austrian.
autruche, *n.f.* ostrich.
autrui, *pron.* someone else, others.
auxiliaire, *adj.* auxiliary.
avalanche, *n.f.* avalanche.
avaler, *vb.* swallow.
avance, *n.f.* advance. **d'a.,** beforehand. **en a.,** fast (clock).
avancé, *adj.* forward, advanced.
avancement, *n.m.* advance; advancement; promotion.
avancer, *vb.* proceed; come *or* go forward *or* onward.
avances, *n.f.pl.* advance. **faire des a. à,** make approaches to.
avant, 1. *n.m.* fore, bow. **2.** *adv.,* *prep.* before. **3.** *conj.* **a. que,** before. **en a.,** forward, onward. **en a. de,** ahead of.
avantage, *n.m.* advantage.
avantageux, *adj.* advantageous; favorable; profitable.
avant-bras, *n.m.* forearm.
avant-garde, *n.f.* vanguard.

avant-hier (-yâr), *n.m.* day before yesterday.

avant-toit, *n.m.* eaves.

avare, 1. *n.m.f.* miser. **2.** *adj.* miserly, stingy.

avarice, *n.f.* avarice.

avec, *prep.* with.

avenant, *adj.* comely. **à l'a.,** accordingly.

avenir, *n.m.* future.

Avent, *n.m.* *(eccles.)* Advent.

aventure, *n.f.* adventure.

aventurer, *vb.* s'a., take a chance.

aventureux, *adj.* adventurous.

aventurier, *n.m.* adventurer.

avenue, *n.f.* avenue.

avérer, *vb.* s'a., prove (to be).

averse, *n.f.* shower (rain).

aversion, *n.f.* aversion, dislike.

avertir, *vb.* notify, warn.

avertissement, *n.m.* warning.

avertisseur d'incendie, *n.m.* fire alarm.

aveu, *n.m.* admission, confession.

aveugle, *adj.* blind.

aveuglement, *n.m.* blindness.

aveuglément, *adv.* blindly.

aveugler, *vb.* blind.

aviateur, *n.m.* flier, aviator.

aviation, *n.f.* air force, aviation.

avide, *adj.* eager, greedy, avid.

avidité, *n.f.* greediness.

avilir, *vb.* debase, disgrace.

avion, *n.m.* airplane. **a. de bombardement,** bomber. **par a.,** via air mail.

avis, *n.m.* notice, opinion, advice (*comm.*).

aviser, *vb.* inform, notify. **s'a. (de),** decide.

avocat, *n.m.* lawyer; advocate.

avoine, *n.f.* oat.

avoir, *vb.* have. **il y a,** ago.

avortement, *n.m.* abortion.

avoué, *n.m.* attorney, lawyer.

avouer, *vb.* confess, admit, avow.

avril (-l), *n.m.* April.

axe, *n.m.* axis.

axer, *vb.* center.

axiome, *n.m.* axiom.

ayatollah, *n.m.* ayatollah.

azote, *n.m.* nitrogen.

azur, *n.m.* azure, blue.

azuré, *adj.* azure.

B

babeurre, *n.m.* buttermilk.

babil, *n.m.* babble.

babiller, *vb.* babble.

bâbord, *n.m.* *(naut.)* port.

babouin, *n.m.* baboon.

baby-foot, *n.m.* table football.

bac, *n.m.* ferryboat. **passage en b.,** ferry, high school diploma.

baccalauréat, *n.m.* high school diploma.

bachelier, *n.m.* graduate.

bachot, *n.m.* (colloquial) high school diploma.

bacille (-l), *n.m.* bacillus.

bactérie, *n.f.* bacterium.

bactériologie, *n. f.* bacteriology.

badaud, *adj.* silly.

baffe, *n.f.* (colloquial) slap.

bagages, *n.m.pl.* luggage.

bagatelle, *n.f.* trifle.

bagnole, *n.f.* (colloquial) car.

bague, *n.f.* ring.

baguette, *n.f.* wand, stick; long, thin loaf of bread.

baie, *n.f.* bay; creek; berry.

baigner, *vb.* bathe.

baigneur, *n.m.* bather.

baignoire (bĕn wär), *n.f.* bathtub.

bail, *n.m.* lease.

bâillement, *n.m.* yawn.

bâiller, *vb.* yawn.

bâillon, *n.m.* gag.

bain, *n.m.* bath.

baïonnette, *n.f.* bayonet.

baiser, *n.m. and vb.* kiss (hand, forehead, etc.).

baissé, *adj.* downcast.

baisser, *vb.* lower, sink.

bal, *n.m.* ball (dance).

balade, *n.f.* stroll.

baladeur, *n.m.* portable cassette player or radio; (trademark) Walkman.

balai, *n.m.* broom. **b. à laver,** mop.

balance, *n.f.* scales, balance.

balancement, *n.m.* rocking, swinging.

balancer, vb. rock, swing, sway. **se b.,** roll, hover.

balayer, vb. sweep.

balbutier, vb. stammer.

balcon, n.m. balcony.

baldaquin, n.m. canopy.

baleine, n.f. whale.

ballade, n.f. ballad.

balle, n.f. bullet; ball; bale.

ballet, n.m. ballet.

ballon, n.m. balloon.

ballot, n.m. bundle.

ballotter, vb. shake.

balnéaire, adj. seaside.

balsamique, adj. balmy.

bambin, n.m. small child.

bambou, n.m. bamboo.

ban, n.m. ban. **mettre au b.,** ban.

banal, adj. trite.

banane, n.f. banana.

banc, n.m. bench.

bancaire, adj. banking.

bandage, n.m. bandage.

bande, n.f. strip, stripe; pack, gang, band.

bande magnétique, n.f. tape.

bande vidéo, n.f. videotape.

bandit, n.m. bandit, robber, knave.

banlieue, n.f. suburbs.

bannière, n.f. banner.

bannir, vb. banish.

bannissement, n.m. banishment.

banque, n.f. bank. **billet de b.,** banknote.

banqueroute, n.f. bankruptcy.

banquet, n.m. banquet, feast.

banquier, n.m. banker.

baptême, (bä těm), n.m. christening, baptism.

baptiser (bä tē-), vb. christen, baptize.

Baptiste (bä těst), n.m. Baptist.

baptistère (bä těs-), n.m. baptistery.

bar, n.m. bar; bass (fish).

baraque, n.f. booth, stall; (colloquial) house.

baratin, n.m. smooth talk.

barbare, 1. n.m.f. barbarian. **2.** adj. barbarian, barbarous, wild.

barbarie, n.f. cruelty.

barbe, n.f. beard.

barbouiller, vb. daub, blur.

barbu, adj. bearded.

baril, n.m. barrel, keg.

baromètre, n.m. barometer.

baron, n.m. baron.

baroque, adj. baroque, weird.

barque, n.f. boat.

barrage, n.m. dam.

barre, n.f. bar, rail(ing). **b. du gouvernail,** helm.

barreau, n.m. bar.

barrer, vb. shut out.

barricade, n.f. barricade.

barrière, n.f. gate; bar, barrier; fence.

barrique, n.f. barrel, cask.

bas, n.m. stocking.

bas m., **basse** f. adj. base, low, soft. **en b.,** down(ward), downstairs. **b. côté,** aisle.

bascule, n.f. seesaw. **chaise à b.,** rocking-chair.

basculer, vb. fall over.

base, n.f. base, basis.

basilic, n.m. basil.

basket, n.m. basketball; sneaker.

Basque, n.m. Basque (person).

basque, 1. n.m. Basque (language). **2.** adj. Basque.

basse, n.f. bass (voice).

basse-cour, n.f. barnyard.

bassesse, n.f. baseness.

bassin, n.m. basin, dock.

bataille, n.f. battle.

bataillon, n.m. battalion.

bâtard, adj. and n.m. bastard.

bateau, n.m. boat.

bâtiment, n.m. building.

bâtir, vb. build.

bâton, n.m. stick, staff.

battant, n.m. flap, door.

batte, n.f. bat.

battement, n.m. beat.

batterie, n.f. battery; drums.

battre, vb. beat, strike; flap, pulsate. **se b.,** fight.

baume, n.m. balm.

bavard, adj. talkative, gossipy.

bavardage, n.m. gossip, chatter.

bavarder, vb. gossip, chat(ter).

bavette, n.f. bib.

bavure, n.f. smudge, mistake.

bazar, n.m. bazaar.

BCBG, adj. preppy. (bon chic bon genre).

BD, n.f. comic strip. (bande dessinée).

béatitude, n.f. bliss.

beau, bel *m.,* **belle** *f. adj.* beautiful, handsome, fair, lovely, fine. **avoir b.,** (to do something) in vain. **faire b.,** be fine (weather).

beaucoup (de), *adj.* a lot, a great deal; much, many. **de b., by** by far.

beau-frère, *n.m.* brother-in-law.

beau-père, *n.m.* father-in-law; stepfather.

beauté, *n.f.* beauty. **grain de b.,** mole.

bébé, *n.m.* baby.

bec, *n.m.* beak, bill; spot; burner; **b. sucré,** sweet tooth.

bécane, *n.f.* (colloquial) bike.

bêche, *n.f.* spade.

bêcher, *vb.* dig.

becqueter, *vb.* peck.

bée, *adj.* **rester bouche b.,** stand gaping.

bégayer, *vb.* stammer.

beignet, *n.m.* fritter.

bêler, *vb.* bleat.

Belge, *n.m.f.* Belgian.

belge, *adj.* Belgian.

Belgique, *n.f.* Belgium.

bélier, *n.m.* ram.

belle-fille, *n.f.* daughter-in-law.

belle-mère, *n.f.* mother-in-law; stepmother.

belligérant, *adj. and n.m.* belligerent.

bémol, *n.m.* flat (music).

bénédiction, *n.f.* blessing, benediction.

bénéfice, *n.m.* benefit, advantage, profit.

bénéficier, *vb.* benefit, profit.

bénin, bénigne *f. adj.* benign.

bénir, *vb.* bless.

béquille, *n.f.* crutch.

berceau, *n.m.* cradle, bower.

bercer, *vb.* rock.

berge, *n.f.* bank (river, etc.).

berger, *n.m.* shepherd.

besogne, *n.f.* (piece) of work.

besoin, *n.m.* need, want. **avoir b.,** need.

bestiaux, *n.m.pl.* cattle.

bétail, *n.m.* cattle, animals.

bête, 1. *n.f.* beast, animal. 2. *adj.* stupid, dumb.

bêtise, *n.f.* nonsense.

béton, *n.m.* concrete.

betterave, *n.f.* beet.

Beur, *n.m.f.* North African in France of immigrant parents.

beurre, *n.m.* butter.

bévue, *n.f.* blunder, boner.

biais, *n.m.* slant; bias. **en b.,** at an angle.

bibelot, *n.m.* trinket.

biberon, *n.m.* baby's bottle.

Bible, *n.f.* Bible.

bibliothèque, *n.f.* library; bookcase.

biblique, *adj.* biblical.

bicyclette, *n.f.* bicycle. **faire de la b.,** cycle.

bidet, *n.m.* bidet.

bidon, *n.m.* can.

bidonville, *n.m.* shanty town.

bien, *n.m.* good; *(pl.)* goods, property, estate. **faire du b. à,** benefit.

bien, *adv.* well. **b. entendu,** of course. **aller b.,** be well. **vouloir b.,** be willing. **b. que,** although.

bien-aimé, *n.m. and adj.* darling.

bien-être, *n.m.* welfare.

bienfaisant, *adj.* beneficent, kind, humane.

bienfait, *n.m.* benefit.

bienfaiteur, *n.m.* benefactor.

bienheureux, *adj.* blessed.

bienséant, *adj.* proper.

bientôt, *adv.* soon.

bienveillance, *n.f.* benevolence, kindness.

bienveillant, *adj.* benevolent, kindly.

bienvenu, *adj.* welcome.

bière, *n.f.* beer, ale.

biffer, *vb.* cancel, erase.

bifteck, *n.m.* beefsteak.

bifurquer, *vb.* branch off, fork.

bigamie, *n.f.* bigamy.

bigot, *n.m.* bigot.

bigoterie, *n.f.* bigotry.

bijou, *n.m.* jewel.

bijouterie, *n.f.* jewelry.

bilan, *n.m.* balance sheet; outcome.

bile, *n.f.* bile. **se faire de la b.,** worry.

bilingue, *adj.* bilingual.

billard, *n.m.* billiards.

bille, *n.f.* marble (toy).

billet, *n.m.* ticket, note. **b. de banque,** banknote.

billetterie, *n.f.* ticket dispenser.

billion (-l-), *n.m.* billion.

biochimie, *n.f.* biochemistry.

biographie, *n.f.* biography.

biologie, *n.f.* biology.

bis, 1. *n.m.* encore. **2.** *adv.* A or a (in addresses).

biscuit, *n.m.* biscuit.

bise, *n.f.* (colloquial) kiss.

bisou, *n.m.* (colloquial) kiss.

bit, *n.m.* bit.

bizarre, *adj.* queer, odd, strange.

blâme, *n.m.* blame.

blâmer, *vb.* blame.

blanc *m.,* **blanche** *f. adj.* white, blank. **en b.,** blank.

blancheur, *n.f.* whiteness.

blanchir, *vb.* whiten.

blanchisserie, *n.f.* laundry.

blasé, *adj.* sophisticated.

blasphème, *n.m.* blasphemy.

blasphémer, *vb.* curse, blaspheme.

blatte, *n.f.* cockroach.

blé, *n.m.* wheat.

bled, *n.m.* inland country.

blême, *adj.* pale.

blesser, *vb.* wound, hurt, injure.

blessure, *n.f.* wound, hurt, injury.

bleu, *adj.* blue; extremely rare (meat).

bloc, *n.m.* pad, block.

blocus (-s), *n.m.* blockade.

blond, *adj.* fair, blond(e).

bloquer, *vb.* block.

blottir, *vb.* **se b.,** cower.

blouse, *n.f.* blouse.

blouson, *n.m.* windbreaker.

blue jeans, *n.m.pl.* blue jeans.

bluff, *n.m.* bluff.

bluffeur, *n.m.* bluffer.

bobine, *n.f.* spool, reel.

bœuf (bœf), *n.m.* ox, beef. **jeune b.,** steer.

bogue, *n.m.* bug (computers).

Bohème, *n.f.* Bohemia.

bohème, 1. *n.m.f.* bohemian, happy-go-lucky person. **2.** *n.f.* artistic underworld. **3.** *adj.* bohemian.

Bohémien, *n.m.* Bohemian; gypsy.

bohémien, *adj.* Bohemian.

boire, *vb.* drink. **b. à petits coups,** sip.

bois, *n.m.* wood, forest, lumber.

boiserie, *n.f.* woodwork.

boisseau, *n.m.* bushel.

boisson, *n.f.* beverage, drink.

boîte, *n.f.* box; can (food). **b. aux lettres,** mail-box.

boiter, *vb.* limp.

boiteux, *adj.* lame.

bol, *n.m.* bowl.

bombardement, *n.m.* bombardment.

bombarder, *vb.* bomb, bombard.

bombe, *n.f.* bomb, shell.

bombe à neutrons, *n.f.* neutron bomb.

bon *m.,* **bonne** *f. adj.* good, kind. **de b. heure,** early. **b. marché,** cheap.

bon, *n.m.* bond.

bonbon, *n.m.* candy, bonbon.

bond, *n.m.* bound, leap.

bonder, *vb.* overcrowd, jam.

bondir, *vb.* bound, leap, spring.

bonheur, *n.m.* happiness.

bonhomme, *n.m.* fellow.

bonjour, *interj. and n.m.* good morning.

bonne, *n.f.* maid.

bonnement, *adv.* simply.

bonnet, *n.m.* cap, hood.

bonsoir, *interj. and n.m.* good evening.

bonté, *n.f.* kindness, goodness.

bord, *n.m.* edge, rim, brim. **b. du toit,** eaves.

bordeaux, *n.m.* Bordeaux (wine).

border, *vb.* bound, edge, border, hem.

borne, *n.f.* bound, limit.

borner, *vb.* bound, limit.

Bosnie-Herzégovine, *n.f.* Bosnia (and) Herzegovina.

bosquet, *n.m.* clump (trees).

bosse, *n.f.* bump.

bosselure, *n.f.* dent.

bosser, *vb.* (colloquial) work.

bossu, *adj.* hunchbacked.

botanique, *n.f.* botany.

botte, *n.f.* boot; bunch.

Bottin, *n.m.* (trademark) phone book.

bottine, *n.f.* ankle boot.

bouche, *n.f.* mouth.

boucher, *vb.* stop up.

boucher, *n.m.* butcher.

boucherie, *n.f.* butcher shop.

bouchon, *n.m.* cork.

boucle, *n.f.* curl, loop, buckle. **b. d'oreille,** earring.

boucler, *vb.* curl.

bouclier, *n.m.* shield.
bouder, *vb.* sulk.
boudin, *n.m.* black pudding.
boue, *n.f.* mud.
bouée, *n.f.* buoy.
boueur, *n.m.* scavenger.
boueux, *adj.* muddy.
bouffe, *n.f.* (colloquial) food, grub.
bouffée, *n.f.* puff.
bouffon, *n.m.* clown, fool.
bouffonerie, *n.f.* antic(s).
bouger, *vb.* stir, move, budge.
bougie, *n.f.* candle; spark plug.
bouillabaisse, *n.f.* bouillabaisse.
bouillir, *vb.* boil.
bouilloire, *n.f.* kettle.
bouillon, *n.m.* broth.
bouillonner, *vb.* bubble.
bouillotte, *n.f.* kettle.
boulanger, *n.m.* baker.
boulangerie, *n.f.* bakery.
boule, *n.f.* ball.
bouleau, *n.m.* birch.
bouledogue, *n.m.* bulldog.
boulevard, *n.m.* boulevard.
bouleversement, *n.m.* upset.
bouleverser, *vb.* upset, overturn.
boulot, *n.m.* (colloquial) work.
boum, 1. *n.m.* bang. **2.** *n.f.* party.
bouquet, *n.m.* cluster, bunch, bouquet.
bouquiniste, *n.m.* (secondhand) bookseller.
bourbeux, *adj.* sloppy.
bourdon, *n.m.* bumblebee.
bourdonnement, *n.m.* buzz.
bourdonner, *vb.* hum, buzz.
bourg, *n.m.* borough, village.
bourgeois, *adj.* middle-class, bourgeois.
bourgeoisie, *n.f.* middle class.
bourgeon, *n.m.* bud.
bourgeonner, *vb.* bud.
bourgogne, 1. *n.m.* Burgundy (wine). **2.** *n.f.* **la B.,** Burgundy.
bourre, *n.f.* stuffing.
bourreau, *n.m.* executioner, hangman; brute.
bourrelet, *n.m.* pad.
bourrer, *vb.* stuff, pad.
bourru, *adj.* gruff.
bourse, *n.f.* purse, bag; stock exchange; scholarship, fellowship.
boursoufler, *vb.* bloat.

bousculer, *vb.* jostle.
bousiller, *vb.* bungle.
boussole, *n.f.* compass.
bout, *n.m.* end, tip, butt, stub.
bouteille, *n.f.* bottle.
boutique, *n.f.* shop.
bouton, *n.m.* button, bud; pimple.
boutonnière, *n.f.* buttonhole.
boxe, *n.f.* boxing.
boxeur, *n.m.* boxer.
boycotter, *vb.* boycott.
bracelet, *n.m.* bracelet.
braconnier, *n.m.* poacher.
brailler, *vb.* bawl.
braise, *n.f.* coals, embers.
brancard, *n.m.* stretcher.
branche, *n.f.* branch, bough, limb.
branché, *adj.* trendy.
brandir, *vb.* brandish.
branler, *vb.* waver.
braquer, *vb.* aim, point.
bras, *n.m.* arm.
brasse, *n.f.* fathom; breaststroke.
brasser, *vb.* brew.
brasserie, *n.f.* brewery; beer-joint.
bravade, *n.f.* bravado.
brave, *adj.* fine, good, brave.
braver, *vb.* brave, face, defy.
bravoure, *n.f.* courage.
break, *n.m.* station wagon.
brebis, *n.f.* lamb.
brèche, *n.f.* breach, gap.
bref, 1. *adj. m.,* **brève** *f.* brief, short. **2.** *adv.* in short.
Brésil, *n.m.* Brazil.
Bretagne, *n.f.* Brittany.
brevet, *n.m.* commission. **b. d'invention,** patent.
bribe, *n.f.* scrap, bit.
bricoler, *vb.* do odd jobs.
bride, *n.f.* bridle.
brider, *vb.* curb.
bridge, *n.m.* bridge (game).
brièveté, *n.f.* brevity.
brigade, *n.f.* brigade.
brigadier, *n.m.* corporal.
brigant, *n.m.* robber, knave.
brillant, *adj.* brilliant, bright, glowing.
briller, *vb.* shine, glisten, glare.
brin, *n.m.* blade (grass).
brindille, *n.f.* twig.
brioche, *n.f.* bun.
brique, *n.f.* brick.

briquet, *n.m.* lighter. **pierre à b.,** flint.
brise, *n.f.* breeze.
briser, *vb.* break, shatter, smash.
britannique, *adj.* British.
brocart, *n.m.* brocade.
broche, *n.f.* spit, spindle; brooch.
brochette, *n.f.* skewer.
brochure, *n.f.* pamphlet.
broder, *vb.* embroider.
broderie, *n.f.* embroidery.
bronchite, *n.f.* bronchitis.
bronze, *n.m.* bronze.
broquette, *n.f.* tack.
brosse, *n.f.* brush.
brouhaha, *n.m.* uproar.
brouillard, *n.m.* fog, mist.
brouiller, *vb.* jumble, embroil; scramble (eggs). **se b.,** quarrel.
brouillon, *n.m.* (rough) draft.
broussailles, *n.f.pl.* brushwood.
brousse, *n.f.* **la b.,** the bush.
brouter, *vb.* browse.
broyer, *vb.* crush.
bruine, *n.f.* drizzle.
bruiner, *vb.* drizzle.
bruissement, *n.m.* rustle.
bruit, *n.m.* noise, clatter; report, rumor.
brûler, *vb.* burn.
brume, *n.f.* mist. **b. légère,** haze.
brumeux, *adj.* foggy, misty.
brun, *adj.* brown.
brune, *adj. and n.f.* brunette.
brusque, *adj.* abrupt, curt, blunt, gruff, brusque.
brut, *adj.* crude, gross.
Bruxelles, *n.f.* Brussels.
brutal, *adj.* brutal, savage.
brutalité, *n.f.* brutality.
brute, *n.f.* brute.
bruyant, *adj.* noisy, loud.
bruyère, *n.f.* heath, heather.
bûche, *n.f.* log.
bûcheron, *n.m.* wood-cutter.
budget, *n.m.* budget.
buffet, *n.m.* buffet.
buffle, *n.m.* buffalo.
buis, *n.m.* box (tree).
buisson, *n.m.* bush, shrub, thicket.
buissonneux, *adj.* bushy.
bulbe, *n.m.* bulb.
Bulgarie, *n.f.* Bulgaria.
bulle, *n.f.* bubble; (papal) bull.
bulletin, *n.m.* bulletin, ticket.
bureau, *n.m.* office, bureau; desk. **b. de location,** box office.
burin, *n.m.* chisel.
burlesque, *adj.* ludicrous.
bus, *n.m.* bus.
buste, *n.m.* bust.
but, *n.m.* aim, goal, purpose.
butin, *n.m.* spoils, booty.
butte, *n.f.* hill, knoll.
buvard, *n.m.* blotter.
buvette, *n.f.* bar.

C

ça, *pron.* that.
cabane, *n.f.* cabin, hut.
cabaret, *n.m.* cabaret; tavern.
cabine, *n.f.* cabin, booth.
cabinet, *n.m.* closet; office. **c. de toilette,** lavatory. **c. de travail,** study.
câble, *n.m.* cable, rope.
câbler, *vb.* cable.
câblogramme, *n.m.* cablegram.
cacahuète, *n.f.* peanut.
cacao, *n.m.* cocoa.
cacher, *vb.* hide, conceal. **se c.,** lurk.
cacher, *m.,* **cachère** *f. adj.* kosher.
cachet, *n.m.* seal.
cadavre, *n.m.* corpse.
cadeau, *n.m.* gift, present.
cadence, *n.f.* cadence.
cadet, 1. *n.m.* cadet 2. *adj.* junior.
cadran, *n.m.* dial.
cadre, *n.m.* frame.
café, *n.m.* coffee; café.
cage, *n.f.* cage.
cahier, *n.m.* notebook.
caille, *n.f.* quail.
caillot, *n.m.* clot.
caillou, *n.m.* pebble.
caisse, *n.f.* crate, case, box.
caissier, *n.m.* cashier, teller.
cajoler, *vb.* coax.
calamité, *n.f.* calamity.
calcium, *n.m.* calcium.
calcul, *n.m.* calculation.
calculateur, *n.m.* calculator.
calculatrice, *n.f.* calculator.

calculer, *vb.* figure, reckon, calculate.

cale, *n.f.* hold (ship).

calembour, *n.m.* pun.

calendrier, *n.m.* calendar.

calibre, *n.m.* caliber.

calicot, *n.m.* calico.

callosité, *n.f.* callus.

calmant, *n.m.* sedative.

calme, *adj. and n.m.* quiet, calm.

calmer, *vb.* soothe, quiet, calm.

calomnie, *n.f.* slander.

calomnier, *vb.* slander.

calorie, *n.f.* calorie.

calotte, *n.f.* crown (of hat).

Calvaire, *n.m.* Calvary.

camarade, *n.m.f.* comrade; companion, mate.

camaraderie, *n.f.* companionship, fellowship.

cambrioleur, *n.m.* burglar.

camembert, *n.m.* Camembert cheese.

camera, *n.f.* camera.

caméscope, *n.m.* camcorder.

camion, *n.m.* truck.

camoufler, *vb.* camouflage.

camp, *n.m.* camp.

campagnard, 1. *n.m.* countryman, peasant. **2.** *adj.* peasant.

campagne, *n.f.* country; campaign.

camper, *vb.* camp.

camphre, *n.m.* camphor.

Canada, *n.m.* Canada.

Canadien, *n.m.* Canadian.

canadien, *adj.* Canadian.

canaille, *n.f.* rabble; scoundrel.

canal, *n.m.* channel, canal.

canapé, *n.m.* sofa, couch; canapé.

canard, *n.m.* duck.

canari, *n.m.* canary.

cancer (-r), *n.m.* cancer.

cancérogène, *adj.* carcinogenic.

candeur, *n.f.* purity; candor.

candidat, *n.m.* candidate, applicant.

candidature, *n.f.* candidacy.

candide, *adj.* frank, open, candid.

canevas, *n.m.* canvas. **gros c.,** burlap.

canicule, *n.f.* heat wave.

canin, *adj.* canine.

canne, *n.f.* cane, stick.

canneberge, *n.f.* cranberry.

cannelle, *n.f.* cinnamon.

cannibale, *adj. and n.m.f.* cannibal.

canoë (-ŏ ă), *n.m.* canoe.

canon, *n.m.* cannon.

canot, *n.m.* boat, canoe. **c. automobile,** motorboat.

cantaloup, *n.m.* cantaloupe.

cantine, *n.f.* canteen, dining hall.

cantique, *n.m.* hymn.

canton, *n.m.* district, canton.

caoutchouc (-chōō), *n.m.* rubber.

cap (-p), *n.m.* cape (headland).

capable, *adj.* efficient, fit, capable, competent.

capacité, *n.f.* capability; capacity.

cape, *n.f.* cape (clothing).

capitaine, *n.m.* captain.

capital, *adj. and n.m.* capital.

capitale, *n.f.* capital (city).

capitaliser, *vb.* capitalize.

capitalisme, *n.m.* capitalism.

capitaliste, *n.m.f.* capitalist.

caporal, *n.m.* corporal.

capot, *n.m.* hood.

capote, *n.f.* hood.

câpre, *n.f.* caper.

caprice, *n.m.* whim, fancy.

capricieux, *adj.* fickle, capricious.

capsule, *n.f.* capsule.

captif, *adj. and n.m.* captive.

captiver, *vb.* captivate, charm.

captivité, *n.f.* captivity.

capture, *n.f.* capture.

capturer, *vb.* capture.

capuchon, *n.m.* hood.

car, *conj.* for.

caractère, *n.m.* character, nature, disposition; type.

caractériser, *vb.* characterize; distinguish; mark.

caractéristique, *adj.* characteristic.

carafe, *n.f.* decanter, water-bottle.

caraïbe, *adj.* Caribbean.

Caraïbes, *n.f.pl.* **les C.,** the Caribbean.

caramel, *n.m.* caramel.

carat, *n.m.* carat.

caravane, *n.f.* caravan.

carbone, *n.m.* carbon.

carboniser, *vb.* char.

carburant, *n.m.* fuel.

carburateur, *n.m.* carburetor.

carcasse, *n.f.* shell; carcass.

cardinal, *n.m.* cardinal.

Carême, *n.m.* Lent.
caresse, *n.f.* caress.
caresser, *vb.* fondle, stroke, caress.
cargaison, *n.f.* cargo.
caricature, *n.f.* caricature.
carie, *n.f.* decay.
carillon, *n.m.* chime.
carilloner, *vb.* chime.
carnaval, *n.m.* carnival.
carnet, *n.m.* notebook.
carnivore, *adj.* carnivorous.
carotte, *n.f.* carrot.
carré, *n.m. and adj.* square.
carreau, *n.m.* diamond (cards); pane; tile.
carrefour, *n.m.* crossroads.
carrément, *adv.* bluntly, altogether.
carrière, *n.f.* career; scope; quarry.
carriole, *n.f.* (light) cart.
carrosse, *n.m.* coach.
cartable, *n.m.* school bag.
carte, *n.f.* chart, map, card. **c. de crédit,** credit card. **c. du jour,** bill of fare.
carton, *n.m.* cardboard; box, carton.
cartouche, *n.f.* cartridge.
cas, *n.m.* case; event.
cascade, *n.f.* waterfall.
cascadeur, *n.m.* stuntman.
case, *n.f.* pigeonhole; hut, shed.
caserne, *n.f.* barracks.
casier, *n.m.* filing cabinet, compartment.
casque, *n.m.* helmet.
casque a écouteurs, *n.m.pl.* headphones.
casquette, *n.f.* cap.
cassable, *adj.* breakable.
casse-croûte, *n.m.* snack.
casser, *vb.* break, crack.
casserole, *n.f.* pan.
cassette, *n.f.* **1.** casket. **2.** cassette.
cassis, *n.m.* black currant.
cassure, *n.f.* break.
caste, *n.f.* caste.
castor, *n.m.* beaver.
casuel, *adj.* casual.
catalogue, *n.m.* catalogue.
cataracte, *n.f.* cataract.
catarrhe, *n.m.* catarrh.
catastrophe, *n.f.* disaster, catastrophe.
catéchisme, *n.m.* catechism.

catégorie, *n.f.* category.
cathédrale, *n.f.* cathedral.
catholicisme, *n.m.* Catholicism.
catholique, *adj.* Catholic.
cauchemar, *n.m.* nightmare.
cause, *n.f.* case; cause.
causer, *vb.* chat; cause.
causerie, *n.f.* chat, talk.
causette, *n.f.* chat.
caution, *n.f.* bail, security.
cavalerie, *n.f.* cavalry.
cavalier, *n.m.* rider, horseman; escort.
cave, *n.f.* cellar, cavern.
cavité, *n.f.* cavity.
CD, *n.m.* compact disc.
ce (sa), cet (sĕt) *m.,* **cette** (sĕt) *f.,* **ces** (sā) *pl. adj.* that, this.
ceci, *pron.* this.
cécité, *n.f.* blindness.
céder, *vb.* yield, give in, cede.
cédille, *n.f.* cedilla.
cèdre, *n.m.* cedar.
ceindre, *vb.* gird.
ceinture, *n.f.* belt, sash.
cela, *pron.* that.
célébration, *n.f.* celebration.
célèbre, *adj.* famous, noted.
célébrer, *vb.* celebrate.
célébrité, *n.f.* celebrity.
céleri, *n.m.* celery.
céleste, *adj.* heavenly, celestial.
célibataire, 1. *n.m.* bachelor. **2.** *adj.* single.
celle, *pron. f.* See **celui.**
cellule, *n.f.* cell.
celluloïd (-lô ĕd), *n.m.* celluloid.
celtique, *adj.* Celtic.
celui *m.,* **celle** *f.,* **ceux** *m.pl.,* **celles** *f.pl.* *pron.* the one. **celui-ci,** this one; the latter. **celui-là,** that one; the former.
cendre, *n.f.* ashes, cinders.
cendrier, *n.m.* ashtray.
censé, *adj.* **être c. faire,** be supposed to do.
censeur, *n.m.* censor, vice-principal.
censure, *n.f.* censure.
censurer, *vb.* censor.
cent, *adj. and n.m.* hundred. **pour c.,** percent.
centaine, *n.f.* about a hundred.
centenaire, *adj. and n.m.* centenary, centennial.

centième, *adj.* hundredth.
centigrade, *adj.* centigrade.
centimètre, *n.m.* centimeter.
central, *adj.* central.
centraliser, *vb.* centralize.
centre, *n.m.* center.
cep, *n.m.* vine stock.
cependant, *adv.* however, still, yet.
cercle, *n.m.* circle, ring, hoop; club.
cercueil, *n.m.* coffin.
céréale, *adj. and n.f.* cereal.
cérémonial, *adj. and n.m.* ceremonial.
cérémonie, *n.f.* ceremony. **sans c.,** informal.
cérémonieux *adj.* formal, ceremonious.
cerf (sèr), *n.m.* deer.
cerf-volant, *n.m.* kite.
cerise, *n.f.* cherry.
certain, *adj.* certain, sure; *(pl.)* some.
certes, *adv.* indeed.
certificat, *n.m.* credentials; certificate.
certifier, *vb.* certify.
certitude, *n.f.* certainty, assurance.
cerveau, *n.m.* brain.
cervelle, *n.f.* brains.
cessation, *n.f.* stopping, cessation.
cesser, *vb.* stop, desist, cease.
cession, *n.f.* assignment (law).
cet, cette, *pron.* See ce.
chacun, *pron.* everybody, everyone; each.
chagrin, 1. *n.m.* grief, vexation. **2.** *adj.* fretful.
chagriner, *vb.* grieve.
chaîne, *n.f.* chain; range.
chaîne stéréo, *n.f.* stereo system.
chaînon, *n.m.* link.
chair, *n.f.* flesh.
chaire, *n.f.* pulpit, rostrum.
chaise, *n.f.* chair.
chaland, *n.m.* barge.
châle, *n.m.* shawl.
chaleur, *n.f.* warmth, heat, glow.
chaloupe, *n.f.* launch.
chambre, *n.f.* room, chamber; House (parliament). **c. à coucher,** bedroom.
chameau, *n.m.* camel.
chamois, *n.m.* chamois.

champ, *n.m.* field.
champagne, *n.m.* champagne.
champêtre, *adj.* rural.
champignon, *n.m.* mushroom.
champion, *n.m.* champion.
championnat, *n.m.* championship.
chance, *n.f.* luck; risk, chance.
chanceler, *vb.* stagger, reel.
chancelier, *n.m.* chancellor.
chandail, *n.m.* sweater.
chandelier, *n.m.* candlestick.
chandelle, *n.f.* candle.
change, *n.m.* exchange.
changeant, *adj.* changeable.
changement, *n.m.* change, shift.
changer, *vb.* alter, shift, change.
chanson, *n.f.* song.
chant, *n.m.* song, chant. **c. du coq,** cock-crow.
chantage, *n.m.* blackmail.
chanter, *vb.* sing, chant.
chanteur, *n.m.* singer.
chantier, *n.m.* (work)yard.
chaos (k-), *n.m.* chaos.
chaotique (k-), *adj.* chaotic.
chapeau, *n.m.* hat, bonnet.
chapelle, *n.f.* chapel.
chaperon, *n.m.* chaperon.
chapiteau, *n.m.* capital.
chapitre, *n.m.* chapter.
chapon, *n.m.* capon.
chaque, *adj.* every, each.
char, *n.m.* chariot. **c. d'assaut,** (military) tank.
charbon, *n.m.* coal. **c. de bois,** charcoal.
charcuterie, *n.f.* delicatessen.
charge, *n.f.* load, charge.
charger, *vb.* load, burden, charge.
chariot, *n.m.* wagon; baggage cart.
charisme, *n.m.* charisma.
charitable, *adj.* charitable.
charité, *n.f.* charity.
charlatan, *n.m.* charlatan.
charmant, *adj.* delightful, lovely, charming.
charme, *n.m.* spell, charm.
charmer, *vb.* charm.
charnel, *adj.* carnal.
charnu, *adj.* fleshy.
charpente, *n.f.* framework.
charpentier, *n.m.* carpenter.
charretier, *n.m.* carter.
charrette, *n.f.* cart.
charrue, *n.f.* plow.

charte, *n.f.* charter.
chasse, *n.f.* hunt(ing), chase.
châsse, *n.f.* shrine.
chasse-neige, *n.m.* snowplow.
chasser, *vb.* hunt, chase; drive away.
chasseur, *n.m.* hunter; bellboy.
châssis, *n.m.* (window) sash; chassis.
chaste, *adj.* chaste.
chasteté, *n.f.* chastity.
chat *m.*, **chatte** *f. n.f.* cat.
châtaigne, *n.f.* chestnut.
château, *n.m.* mansion, castle.
châtier, *vb.* punish, chastise.
chaton, *n.m.* kitten.
chatouiller, *vb.* tickle.
chatouilleux, *adj.* ticklish.
chaud, *adj.* hot, warm.
chaudière, *n.f.* boiler.
chauffage, *n.m.* heating.
chauffer, *vb.* heat, warm.
chauffeur, *n.m.* driver, chauffeur.
chaumière, *n.f.* cottage.
chaussée, *n.f.* road.
chausser, *vb.* wear shoes. **se c.**, put on shoes.
chaussette, *n.f.* sock.
chaussure, *n.f.* footgear.
chauve, *adj.* bald.
chauve-souris, *n.f.* bat.
chaux, *n.f.* lime.
chavirer, *vb.* capsize.
chef, *n.m.* leader, chief.
chef-d'œuvre (shĕ-), *n.m.* masterpiece.
chemin, *n.m.* road. **c. de fer**, railway. **à mi-c.**, halfway. **c. de table**, table runner.
chemineau, *n.m.* tramp.
cheminée, *n.f.* fireplace, chimney; funnel.
chemise, *n.f.* shirt. **c. de nuit**, nightgown.
chemisier, *n.m.* blouse.
chêne, *n.m.* oak.
chenille, *n.f.* caterpillar.
chèque, *n.m.* check.
chèque de voyage, *n.m.* traveler's check.
cher (-r), *adj.* dear, expensive.
chercher, *vb.* seek, look for, search. **aller c.**, fetch.
chère, *n.f.* fare, food. **aimer la bonne c.**, be fond of good living. **faire bonne c.**, have a good meal.
chéri, *adj. and n.m.* beloved, darling.
chérir, *vb.* cherish.
chétif, *adj.* puny.
cheval, *n.m.* horse. **à c.**, on horseback. **monter à c.**, ride (horseback). **fer à c.**, horseshoe.
chevaleresque, *adj.* chivalrous.
chevalerie, *n.f.* chivalry.
chevalet, *n.m.* easel; knight.
chevalier, *n.m.* knight.
cheveu, *n.m., pl.* **cheveux**, hair.
cheville, *n.f.* ankle; peg.
chèvre, *n.f.* goat.
chevreau, *n.m.* kid.
chevreuil, *n.m.* roe.
chevron, *n.m.* rafter.
chevroter, *vb.* quaver.
chevrotine, *n.f.* buckshot.
chez, *prep.* at . . .'s (house, office, shop, etc.).
chic, *adj.* stylish.
chien, *n.m.* dog.
chienne, *n.f.* bitch.
chiffon, *n.m.* rag.
chiffonner, *vb.* crumple.
chiffre, *n.m.* figure.
chiffrer, *vb.* figure.
Chili, *n.m.* Chile.
Chilien, *n.m.* Chilean.
chilien, *adj.* Chilean.
chimie, *n.f.* chemistry.
chimiothérapie, *n.f.* chemotherapy.
chimique, *adj.* chemical.
chimiste, *n.m.f.* chemist.
Chine, *n.f.* China.
Chinois, *n.m.* Chinese (person).
chinois, **1.** *n.m.* Chinese (language). **2.** *adj.* Chinese.
chiper, *vb.* (colloquial) swipe.
chiquenaude, *n.f.* flip.
chirurgie, *n.f.* surgery.
chirurgien, *n.m.* surgeon.
chlore (k-), *n.m.* chlorine.
chloroforme (k-), *n.m.* chloroform.
choc, *n.m.* shock, clash, brunt.
chocolat, *n.m.* chocolate.
chœur (k-), *n.m.* choir, chorus.
choisir, *vb.* choose, select, pick.
choix, *n.m.* choice.

chômage, *n.m.* stoppage (of work).

chômer, *vb.* be unemployed.

choquer, *vb.* shock, clash.

choral (k-), *adj.* choral.

chose, *n.f.* thing, matter. **quelque c.,** anything.

chou, *n.m.* cabbage.

choucroute, *n.f.* sauerkraut.

chouette, 1. *n.f.* owl. **2.** *adj.* great, neat.

chou-fleur, *n.m.* cauliflower.

choyer, *vb.* pamper.

chrétien (k-), *adj. and n.m.* Christian.

chrétienté (k-), *n.f.* Christendom.

christianisme (k-), *n.m.* Christianity.

chronique (k-), **1.** *n.f.* chronicle. **2.** *adj.* chronic.

chronologique (k-), *adj.* chronological.

chronomètre (k-), stopwatch.

chronométrer (k-), *vb.* time.

chrysanthème (k-), *n.m.* chrysanthemum.

chuchoter, *vb.* whisper.

chut (shYt), *interj.* sh!

chute, *n.f.* fall, drop, downfall.

Chypre, *n.f.* Cyprus.

cible, *n.f.* target.

cicatrice, *n.f.* scar.

cidre, *n.m.* cider.

ciel, *n.m.*, sky. *(pl.)* **cieux,** heaven.

cierge, *n.m.* (church) candle.

cigale, *n.m.* locust.

cigare, *n.m.* cigar.

cigarette, *n.f.* cigarette.

ci-gît, *adv. and vb.* here lies.

cigogne, *n.f.* stork.

ci-joint, *adj.* enclosed.

cil (-l), *n.m.* eyelash.

cime, *n.f.* top, summit.

ciment, *n.m.* cement.

cimenter, *vb.* cement.

cimetière, *n.m.* churchyard, cemetery.

cinéaste, *n.m.f.* film-maker.

cinéma, *n.m.* cinema.

cinémathèque, *n.f.* film library.

cinglant, *adj.* scathing.

cinq (-k), *adj. and n.m.* five.

cinquante (-k), *adj. and n.m.* fifty.

cinquième, *adj. and n.m.f.* fifth.

cintre, *n.m.* semicircle; arch.

circonférence, *n.f.* circumference.

circonflexe, *adj.* circumflex.

circonscription, *n.f.* **c. électorale,** borough.

circonscrire, *vb.* circumscribe.

circonstance, *n.f.* event, circumstance. **c. critique,** emergency.

circonvenir, *vb.* circumvent.

circuit, *n.m.* circuit. **hors c.,** disconnected.

circulaire, *adj.* circular.

circulation, *n.f.* traffic; circulation.

circuler, *vb.* circulate, turn, revolve.

cire, *n.f.* wax.

cirer, *vb.* polish, shine.

cireur, *n.m.* bootblack.

cirque, *n.m.* circus.

cirrhose, *n.f.* cirrhosis.

cisailles, *n.f.pl.* shears.

ciseau, *n.m.* chisel; *(pl.)* scissors.

ciseler, *vb.* chisel.

citadelle, *n.f.* citadel.

citation, *n.f.* quotation, citation.

cité, *n.f.* city. **droit de c.,** citizenship.

citer, *vb.* quote, cite.

citoyen, *n.m.* citizen.

citron, *n.m.* lemon. **c. pressé,** lemonade.

citrouille, *n.f.* pumpkin.

civil, 1. *n.m.* civilian. **2.** *adj.* civil.

civilisation, *n.f.* civilization.

civilisé, *adj.* civilized.

civiliser, *vb.* civilize.

civique, *adj.* civic.

clair, *adj.* clear, bright. **c. de lune,** moonlight.

clairière, *n.f.* glade, clearing.

clairon, *n.m.* bugle.

clameur, *n.f.* clamor, outcry.

clandestin, *adj.* clandestine.

clapoteux, *adj.* choppy (sea).

claque, *n.f.* slap.

claquer, *vb.* slap, smack; chatter (teeth); bang.

clarifier, *vb.* clarify.

clarinette, *n.f.* clarinet.

clarté, *n.f.* clarity; light.

classe, *n.f.* class.

classement, *n.m.* classification.

classer, *vb.* classify, order, file, grade.

classeur, n.m. file, filing cabinet.
classification, n.f. classification.
classifier, vb. classify.
classique, adj. classic, classical.
clause, n.f. clause.
clavecin, n.m. harpsichord.
clavicule, n.f. collarbone.
clavier, n.m. keyboard.
clef (klā), **clé,** n.f. key.
clémence, n.f. clemency.
clément, adj. merciful.
clerc, n.m. clerk.
clergé, n.m. clergy.
clérical, adj. clerical.
cliché, n.m. cliché; snapshot; negative.
client, n.m. customer, patron, client.
clientèle, n.f. customers; practice.
cligner (de l'œil), vb. wink.
clignoter, vb. blink, wink.
clignotant, n.m. turn signal.
climat, n.m. climate.
climatisation, n.f. air conditioning.
climatiser, vb. air-condition.
clin, n.m. **c. d'œil,** wink.
clinique, 1. n.f. clinic. **2.** adj. clinical.
cloche, n.f. bell.
clocher, n.m. belfry. **de c.,** parochial.
cloison, n.f. partition.
cloître, n.m. cloister, convent.
clôture, n.f. fence.
clou, n.m. nail.
clouer, vb. nail, tack.
club (-b), n.m. club.
coaguler, vb. coagulate.
coalition, n.f. coalition.
coasser, vb. croak (frogs).
cobaye, n.m. guinea pig.
coca, n.m. Coke (trademarked name of soft drink).
cocaïne, n.f. cocaine.
cochon, n.m. pig.
coco, n.m. **noix de c.,** coconut.
cocon, n.m. cocoon.
cocotte, n.f. casserole.
cocu, n.m. cuckold.
code, n.m. code; laws.
code postal, n.m. zip code.
cœur, n.m. heart.
coffre, n.m. bin; coffer.
cognac, n.m. brandy, cognac.

cogner, vb. bump, strike, run into, knock (down).
cohérent, adj. coherent.
cohésion, n.f. cohesion.
coiffer, vb. dress (hair).
coiffeur, n.m. hairdresser, barber.
coiffure, n.f. hairdo.
coin, n.m. corner, wedge.
coincé, adj. stuck; inhibited.
coincer, vb. get stuck, jam.
coïncidence (kō ăN-), n.f. coincidence.
coïncider (kō ăN-), vb. coincide.
col, n.m. collar; pass.
colère, n.f. anger, temper. **en c.,** angry.
colimaçon, n.m. snail.
colique, n.f. diarrhea.
colis, n.m. parcel.
collaborateur, n.m. fellow-worker.
collaboration, n.f. assistance, collaboration.
collaborer, vb. work together, collaborate.
collant, n.m. pantyhose.
collatéral, adj. and n.m. collateral.
colle, n.f. glue, paste.
collecte, n.f. collection.
collectif, adj. collective.
collection, n.f. collection.
collectionneur, n.m. collector.
collège, n.m. secondary school.
collègue, n.m.f. colleague.
coller, vb. glue, paste; stick.
collier, n.m. necklace; collar (dog).
colline, n.f. hill.
collision, n.f. collision.
colombe, n.f. dove.
Colombie, n.f. Colombia.
colon, n.m. settler, colonist.
colonel, n.m. colonel.
colonial, adj. colonial.
colonie, n.f. settlement, colony.
coloniser, vb. colonize.
colonne, n.f. column.
coloré, adj. colorful.
colorer, vb. color.
colossal, adj. huge, colossal.
colosse, n.m. giant, colossus.
colporter, vb. peddle.
colporteur, n.m. peddler.
combat, n.m. fight, battle. **hors de c.,** disabled.
combattant, adj. and n.m. combatant.

combattre, *vb.* fight.

combien (de), *adv.* how much, how many.

combinaison, *n.f.* combination; slip, B.V.D.'s.

combine, *n.f.* trick, scheme.

combiner, *vb.* devise, combine.

combiné, *n.m.* (phone) receiver.

comble, *n.m.* climax, top.

combler, *vb.* heap up, fill.

combustible, 1. *n.m.* fuel. **2.** *adj.* combustible.

combustion, *n.f.* combustion.

comédie, *n.f.* comedy.

comédien, *n.m.* actor, comedian.

comestible, *adj.* edible.

comète, *n.f.* comet.

comique, *adj.* funny, comic(al).

comité, *n.m.* committee.

commandant, *n.m.* major, commander.

commande, *n.f.* order; commission.

commandement, *n.m.* command, commandment.

commander, *vb.* order, command.

commanditer, *vb.* finance.

comme, 1. *adv.* as, how. **2.** *prep.* as, like. **c. il faut,** proper, decent.

commémoratif, *adj.* memorial.

commémorer, *vb.* commemorate.

commencement, *n.m.* beginning, start.

commencer, *vb.* begin, start.

comment, *adv.* how.

commentaire, *n.m.* comment, commentary.

commentateur, *n.m.* commentator.

commenter, *vb.* comment on.

commerçant, *n.m.* trader.

commerce, *n.m.* trade, commerce.

commercer, *vb.* trade.

commercial, *adj.* commercial.

commettre, *vb.* commit.

commis, *n.m.* clerk.

commissaire, *n.m.* commissary, commissioner.

commissariat, *n.m.* police station.

commission, *n.f.* errand; commission.

commode, 1. *n.f.* dresser, bureau. **2.** *adj.* handy, convenient; comfortable.

commodité, *n.f.* convenience.

commun, *adj.* joint, common.

communauté, *n.f.* community.

commune, *n.f.* commune, town(ship).

communicatif, *adj.* communicative.

communication, *n.f.* communication.

communion, *n.f.* communion.

communiquer, *vb.* communicate.

communisme, *n.m.* communism.

communiste, *adj. and n.m.f.* communist.

commutateur, *n.m.* switch.

compacité, *n.f.* compactness.

compact (-kt), *adj.* compact.

compact disc, *n.m.* compact disc.

compagne, *n.f.* mate, companion.

compagnie, *n.f.* company.

compagnon, *n.m.* mate, fellow, companion.

comparable, *adj.* comparable.

comparaison, *n.f.* comparison.

comparaître, *vb.* appear.

comparatif, *adj. and n.m.* comparative.

comparer, *vb.* compare.

compartiment, *n.m.* compartment.

compas, *n.m.* compass.

compassion, *n.f.* sympathy, compassion.

compatible, *adj.* compatible.

compatissant, *adj.* sympathetic, compassionate.

compatriote, *n.m.f.* compatriot.

compensation, *n.f.* amends; compensation.

compenser, *vb.* compensate.

compétence, *n.f.* qualification, efficiency, competence.

compétition, *n.f.* competition.

compiler, *vb.* compile.

complaire, *vb.* please.

complaisance, *n.f.* kindness, compliance.

complaisant, *adj.* obliging, kind.

complément, *n.m.* object; complement.

complet, 1. *n.m.* suit. **2.** *adj.* full, thorough, complete.

compléter, *vb.* complete.

complexe, *adj. and n.m.* complex.

complexité, *n.f.* complexity.

complication, n.f. complication.

complice, n.m.f. party to, accomplice.

compliment, n.m. compliment.

compliqué, adj. intricate, involved, complicated.

compliquer, vb. complicate.

complot, n.m. plot.

comporter, vb. se c., act, behave.

composant, adj. and n.m. component.

composé, adj. and n.m. compound.

composer, vb. compound, compose.

compositeur, n.m. composer.

composition, n.f. essay, theme, composition.

composter, vb. date-stamp, punch.

compote, n.f. stewed fruit.

compréhensible, adj. understandable.

compréhensif, adj. comprehensive.

compréhension, n.f. comprehension.

comprendre, vb. understand, realize; comprise, include. **c. mal,** misunderstand.

compresse, n.f. compress.

compression, n.f. compression.

comprimé, n.m. tablet (med.).

comprimer, vb. compress.

compromettre, vb. compromise.

compromis, n.m. compromise.

comptabilité, n.f. accounting, bookkeeping.

comptable, n.m. accountant.

comptant, adv. payer c., pay cash.

compte, n.m. account, count. **rendre c. de,** account for. **tenir c. de,** allow for.

compte-gouttes, n.m. dropper.

compter, vb. count, reckon. **c. sur,** rely on.

compteur, n.m. meter.

comptoir, n.m. counter.

comte, n.m. count.

comté, n.m. county.

comtesse, n.f. countess.

concave, adj. concave.

concéder, vb. grant, concede.

concentration, n.f. concentration.

concentrer, vb. condense; concentrate.

concept (-pt), n.m. concept.

conception, n.f. conception.

concernant, prep. concerning.

concerner, vb. concern.

concert, n.m. concert.

concerter, vb. organize, prepare.

concession, n.f. grant, license, admission, concession.

concessionnaire, n.m. dealer.

concevable, adj. conceivable.

concevoir, vb. conceive, imagine.

concierge, n.m.f. janitor, doorkeeper, porter.

concile, n.m. council.

conciliation, n.f. conciliation.

concilier, vb. reconcile, conciliate.

concis, adj. concise.

concision, n.f. conciseness.

concitoyen, n.m. fellow citizen.

concluant, adj. conclusive.

conclure, vb. complete, conclude, infer.

conclusion, n.f. conclusion.

concombre, n.m. cucumber.

concourir, vb. concur, contribute, compete.

concours, n.m. contest.

concret, adj. concrete.

concrétiser, vb. put in concrete form.

concurrence, n.f. competition.

concurrent, n.m. rival, competitor.

condamnation (-dä nä-), n.f. conviction, condemnation, sentence.

condamner (-dä nä), vb. convict, doom, condemn, sentence.

condensation, n.f. condensation.

condenser, vb. condense.

condescendance, n.f. condescension.

condescendre, vb. condescend.

condiment, n.m. condiment.

condisciple, n.m. classmates.

condition, n.f. condition.

conditionnel, adj. and n.m. conditional.

conditionnement, n.m. conditioning.

conditionner, vb. condition.

condoléance, n.f. condolence. **faire ses c.s à,** condole with.

condominium, *n.m.* condominium.

conducteur, *n.m.* conductor.

conduire, *vb.* lead, take, drive, conduct. se c., behave, act.

conduite, *n.f.* behavior, conduct.

cône, *n.m.* cone.

cône de charge, *n.m.* warhead.

confection, *n.f.* making (e.g. clothes); ready-made garment.

confédération, *n.f.* confederacy, confederation.

confédéré, *adj. and n.m.* confederate.

conférence, *n.f.* lecture, talk, conference.

conférer, *vb.* confer, grant.

confesser, *vb.* confess, admit.

confesseur, *n.m.* confessor.

confession, *n.f.* denomination; confession.

confiance, *n.f.* trust, belief, confidence. digne de c., dependable.

confiant, *adj.* confident.

confidence, *n.f.* confidence.

confident, *n.m.* confidant.

confidentiel, *adj.* confidential.

confier, *vb.* confide, entrust. se c. à, trust.

configuration, *n.f.* configuration.

confiner, *vb.* confine, limit.

confirmation, *n.f.* confirmation.

confirmer, *vb.* confirm.

confiserie, *n.f.* confectionery.

confisquer, *vb.* confiscate.

confit, *adj.* candied.

confiture, *n.f.* jam, jelly.

conflit, *n.m.* conflict.

confondre, *vb.* confuse, confound.

confondu, *adj.* overwhelmed.

conforme à, *adv.* in accordance with.

conformément, *adv.* in accordance.

conformer, *vb.* conform. se c. à, comply with.

conformité, *n.f.* accordance.

confort, *n.m.* comfort.

confortable, *adj.* cozy, snug, comfortable.

confrère, *n.m.* colleague.

confronter, *vb.* confront.

confus, *adj.* confused.

confusion, *n.f.* confusion.

congé, *n.m.* discharge; leave of absence.

congédier, *vb.* discharge, dismiss.

congélateur, *n.m.* freezer.

congeler, *vb.* congeal.

congénère, *n.m.f.* fellow human.

congénital, *adj.* congenital.

congestion, *n.f.* congestion.

conglomération, *n.f.* conglomeration.

congrès, *n.m.* congress, assembly, conference.

conjecture, *n.f.* guess, conjecture.

conjoint, 1. *n.m.* spouse. **2.** *adj.* joint.

conjonction, *n.f.* conjunction.

conjugaison, *n.f.* conjugation.

conjugal, *adj.* conjugal.

conjuguer, *vb.* conjugate.

conjuration, *n.f.* conspiracy.

conjurer, *vb.* conspire, plot.

connaissance, *n.f.* knowledge, acquaintance. sans c., unconscious. faire la c. de, meet.

connaisseur, *n.m.* connoisseur.

connaître, *vb.* be acquainted with, know.

connecté, *adj.* on line.

connecter, *vb.* connect.

connexion, *n.f.* connection.

conquérir, *vb.* conquer.

conquête, *n.f.* conquest.

consacrer, *vb.* consecrate, devote, dedicate, hallow.

conscience, *n.f.* conscience, consciousness.

consciencieux, *adj.* conscientious.

conscient, *adj.* conscious.

conscription, *n.f.* draft.

conscrit, *adj. and n.m.* conscript.

consécration, *n.f.* consecration.

consécutif, *adj.* consecutive.

conseil, *n.m.* advice, counsel; council, board; staff.

conseiller, 1. *vb.* advise, counsel. **2.** *n.m.* advisor.

consentement, *n.m.* consent.

consentir, *vb.* consent, assent, accede.

conséquence, *n.f.* outgrowth, result, consequence.

conséquent, *adj.* consequent; consistent. par c., consequently.

conservateur, *adj. and n.m.* conservative.

conservation, *n.f.* conservation.
conservatoire, *n.m.* academy; conservation area.
conserve, *n.f.* canned food, pickle.
conserver, *vb.* keep; preserve, can.
considérable, *adj.* considerable.
considération, *n.f.* consideration.
considérer, *vb.* consider.
consigne, *n.f.* checkroom; (*mil.*) orders.
consigne automatique, *n.f.* (luggage) locker.
consigner, *vb.* consign.
consistance, *n.f.* consistency.
consistant, *adj.* consistent.
consister, *vb.* consist.
consœur, *n.f.* (female) colleague.
consolateur, *n.m.* comforter.
consolation, *n.f.* comfort, solace.
console, *n.f.* bracket.
consoler, *vb.* comfort, console.
consolider, *vb.* consolidate, strengthen.
consommateur, *n.m.* consumer.
consommation, *n.f.* consumption; end, consummation.
consommé, *adj.* consummate.
consommer, *vb.* consummate, complete; consume.
consomption, *n.f.* consumption.
consonne, *n.f.* consonant.
conspirateur, *n.m.* conspirator.
conspiration, *n.f.* conspiration.
conspirer, *vb.* conspire.
conspuer, *vb.* boo.
constamment, *adv.* continually, constantly.
constance, *n.f.* constancy, firmness.
constant, *adj.* constant, firm.
constat, *n.m.* certified report, statement.
constater, *vb.* observe, state as a fact.
constellation, *n.f.* constellation.
consternation, *n.f.* dismay.
consterné, *adj.* aghast.
consterner, *vb.* dismay.
constipation, *n.f.* constipation.
constipé, *adj.* constipated; tense.
constituant, *adj.* constituent.
constituer, *vb.* constitute.
constitution, *n.f.* constitution.
constitutionnel, *adj.* constitutional.

constructeur, *n.m.* builder.
constructif, *adj.* constructive.
construction, *n.f.* construction.
construire, *vb.* construct, build.
consul, *n.m.* consul.
consulat, *n.m.* consulate.
consultation, *n.f.* consultation.
consulter, *vb.* consult.
consumer, *vb.* consume.
contact (-kt), *n.m.* touch, contact.
contagieux, *adj.* contagious.
contagion, *n.f.* contagion.
contaminer, *vb.* contaminate.
conte, *n.m.* tale, story.
contemplation, *n.f.* contemplation.
contempler, *vb.* survey, observe, contemplate.
contemporain, *adj.* contemporary.
contenance, *n.f.* compass, capacity.
contenir, *vb.* hold, restrain, contain.
content de, *adj.* glad of, contented with. **c. de soi-même,** complacent.
contentement, *n.m.* content(ment), satisfaction. **c. de soi-même,** complacency.
contenter, *vb.* please, satisfy.
contentieux, *n.m.* litigation.
contenu, *n.m.* contents.
conter, *vb.* tell.
contestable, *adj.* questionable.
contestataire, *n.m.* protester.
contester, *vb.* challenge (dispute), object to, contest.
conteur, *n.m.* story-teller.
contexte, *n.m.* context.
contigu, *m.,* **contiguë** *f. adj.* adjoining.
continent, *n.m.* continent.
continental, *adj.* continental.
contigences, *n.f.pl.* contingencies.
contingent, *n.m.* quota.
continu, *adj.* continuous.
continuation, *n.f.* continuation, continuance.
continuel, *adj.* continual.
continuer, *vb.* carry on, keep on, go on, continue.
continuité, *n.f.* continuity.
contorsion, *n.f.* contortion.
contour, *n.m.* outline.
contourner, *vb.* go round.
contraceptif, *n.m.* contraceptive.

contracter, *vb.* contract.
contraction, *n.f.* contraction.
contractuel, *n.m.* traffic warden.
contradiction, *n.f.* discrepancy, contradiction.
contradictoire, *adj.* contradictory.
contraindre, *vb.* coerce, force.
contrainte, *n.f.* compulsion.
contraire, 1. *n.m.* reverse. **2.** *adj.* contrary. **au c.,** on the contrary.
contrarier, *vb.* thwart, vex, annoy, oppose, keep (from).
contrariété, *n.f.* annoyance.
contraste, *n.m.* contrast.
contraster, *vb.* contrast.
contrat, *n.m.* contract.
contravention, *n.f.* traffic ticket.
contre, *prep.* against.
contre-balancer, *vb.* counterbalance.
contrebande, *n.f.* smuggling; contraband.
contrecarrer, *vb.* thwart.
contre-cœur, *adv.* **à c.,** unwillingly.
contrecoup, *n.m.* consequence.
contredire, *vb.* contradict.
contrée, *n.f.* district, province.
contrefaire, *vb.* forge, counterfeit.
contrefort, *n.m.* buttress.
contremaître, *n.m.* foreman.
contre-partie, *n.f.* counterpart.
contrepoids (-pwä), *n.m.* counterbalance.
contresens, *n.m.* misinterpretation.
contretemps, *n.m.* mishap.
contribuer, *vb.* contribute.
contribution, *n.f.* share, contribution; tax.
contrôle, *n.m.* check.
contrôle des naissances, *n.m.* birth control, contraception.
contrôler, *vb.* control, check.
contrôleur, *n.m.* checker, collector.
controverse, *n.f.* controversy.
contusion, *n.f.* bruise, contusion.
convaincre, *vb.* convince.
convaincu, *adj.* positive.
convalescence, *n.f.* convalescence.
convalescent, *adj.* convalescent.
convenable, *adj.* becoming, appropriate, suitable, congenial.
convenance, *n.f.* convenience.
convenir à, *vb.* suit, fit, befit, agree.

convention, *n.f.* convention; contract.
conventionnel, *adj.* conventional.
convenu, *adj.* agreed.
converger, *vb.* converge.
conversation, *n.f.* talk, conversation.
converser, *vb.* talk, converse.
conversion, *n.f.* conversion, change.
convertir, *vb.* convert, transform.
convexe, *adj.* convex.
conviction, *n.f.* conviction.
convive, *n.m.* guest, companion.
convivial, *adj.* convivial, user-friendly.
convocation, *n.f.* summons.
convoi, *n.m.* convoy, funeral procession.
convoiter, *vb.* covet.
convoitise, *n.f.* covetousness.
convoquer, *vb.* summon, call.
convulsion, *n.f.* convulsion.
coopératif (kŏ ô-), *adj.* cooperative.
coopération (kŏ ô-), *n.f.* cooperation.
coopérative (kŏ ô-), *n.f.* cooperative.
coopérer (kŏ ô-), *vb.* cooperate.
coordonner (kŏ ôr-), *vb.* coordinate.
copain, *n.m.* pal, chum.
copie, *n.f.* copy; exercise.
copier, *vb.* copy.
copieux, *adj.* copious.
copine, *n.f.* (female) pal, chum.
coq (-k), *n.m.* rooster.
coque (-k), *n.f.* **œuf à la c.,** boiled egg.
coquet, *adj.* flirtatious, pretty.
coquille, *n.f.* shell.
coquin, *adj. and n.m.* rogue, rascal.
cor, *n.m.* horn; corn.
corail, *n.m., pl.* **coraux,** coral.
corbeau, *n.m.* raven, crow.
corbeille, *n.f.* basket.
corde, *n.f.* rope, string, cord.
cordial, *adj.* hearty, cordial.
cordon, *n.m.* rope.
cordonnier, *n.m.* shoemaker.
Corée, *n.f.* Korea.
coreligionnaire, *n.m.* member of the same religion.
corne, *n.f.* horn.
corneille, *n.f.* crow.

cornemuse, *n.f.* bagpipe.

cornet, *n.m.* cone.

cornichon, *n.m.* gherkin.

corporation, *n.f.* corporation.

corporel, *adj.* bodily.

corps, *n.m.* body.

corpulent, *adj.* burly.

corpuscule (-sk-), *n.m.* corpuscle.

correct (-kt), *adj.* right, correct.

correcteur, *n.m.* proofreader, examiner.

correction, *n.f.* correction, correctness; beating.

corrélation, *n.f.* correlation.

correspondance, *n.f.* (train) connection; similarity; correspondence.

correspondant, 1. *n.m.* correspondent. 2. *adj.* similar, corresponding.

correspondre, *vb.* correspond.

corriger, *vb.* mend, reclaim, correct.

corroborer, *vb.* corroborate.

corroder, *vb.* corrode.

corrompre, *vb.* bribe, corrupt.

corrompu, *adj.* corrupt.

corruption, *n.f.* bribery, graft, corruption.

corsage, *n.m.* bodice, blouse.

Corse, *n.f.* Corsica. *n.m.f.* Corsican.

corse, *adj.* Corsican.

corset, *n.m.* corset.

cortège, *n.m.* procession.

corvée, *n.f.* chore.

cosmétique, *adj. and n.m.* cosmetic.

cosmonaute, *n.m.* cosmonaut.

cosmopolite, *adj. and n.m.f.* cosmopolitan.

costaud, *adj.* strong, sturdy.

costume, *n.m.* attire, dress.

cote, *n.f.* quotation, rating.

côte, *n.f.* rib; coast.

côté, *n.f.* side, way. **mettre de c.,** put to one side (save; discard). **à c. de,** beside.

coteau, *n.m.* hill.

côtelette, *n.f.* chop, cutlet.

coton, *n.m.* cotton.

cou, *n.m.* neck.

couche, *n.f.* layer; bed; stratum; diaper.

coucher, *vb.* put to bed. **se c.,** lie down; set.

couchette, *n.f.* bunk, berth.

coucou, *n.m.* cuckoo.

coude, *n.m.* elbow.

coudoyer, *vb.* jostle.

coudre, *vb.* sew, stitch.

couette, *n.f.* duvet.

couler, *vb.* flow, sink, run; cast (metal).

couleur, *n.f.* hue, color; suit (cards).

couloir, *n.m.* corridor.

coup, *n.m.* blow, stroke, hit, bump, knock, cast. **c. de feu,** discharge (gun). **c. d'œil,** glance, look. **c. de pied,** kick. **c. de poing,** punch.

coupable, *adj.* guilty, to blame.

coupe, *n.f.* cut; goblet. **c. de cheveux,** haircut.

couper, *vb.* cut.

couple, *n.f.* couple, pair.

coupler, *vb.* couple.

coupole, *n.f.* dome.

coupon, *n.m.* remnant; coupon.

coupure, *n.f.* cut, clipping.

cour, *n.f.* court(yard).

courage, *n.m.* bravery, pluck, courage.

courageux, *adj.* brave.

couramment, *adv.* fluently.

courant, 1. *adj.* current. **peu c.,** unusual. **au c.,** well informed. 2. *n.m.* stream, current. **c. d'air,** draft.

courbe, *n.f.* curve, sweep.

courber, *vb.* bend, curve.

courbure, *n.f.* curvature.

coureur, *n.m.* runner; womanizer.

courgette, *n.f.* zucchini.

courir, *vb.* run.

couronne, *n.f.* crown, wreath.

couronnement, *n.m.* coronation.

couronner, *vb.* crown.

courrier, *n.m.* mail.

courroie, *n.f.* strap.

courroux, *n.m.* wrath.

cours, *n.m.* course.

course, *n.f.* race, errand.

coursier, *n.m.* messenger.

court, 1. *adj.* short. 2. *n.m.* (tennis) court.

courtepointe, *n.f.* quilt.

courtier, *n.m.* broker.

courtisan, *n.m.* courtier.
courtois, *adj.* courteous.
courtoisie, *n.f.* courtesy.
couscous, *n.m.* couscous.
cousin, *n.m.* cousin.
coussin, *n.m.* cushion.
coussinet, *n.m.* bearing.
coût, *n.m.* cost.
couteau, *n.m.* knife.
coutellerie, *n.f.* cutlery.
coûter, *vb.* cost.
coûteux, *adj.* expensive, costly.
coutume, *n.f.* custom.
couture, *n.f.* seam. **haute couture,** high fashion.
couturière, *n.f.* dressmaker.
couvée, *n.f.* brood.
couvent, *n.m.* convent.
couver, *vb.* brood, hatch; smolder.
couvercle, *n.m.* lid, cover.
couvert, 1, *n.m.* cover. **2.** *adj.* covered, cloudy.
couverture, *n.f.* blanket, cover; *(pl.)* bedclothes.
couvre-feu, *n.m.* curfew.
couvrir, *vb.* cover.
crabe, *n.m.* crab.
crachat, *n.m.* spit.
cracher, *vb.* spit.
craie, *n.f.* chalk.
craindre, *vb.* fear.
crainte, *n.f.* fear, dread, awe.
craintif, *adj.* fearful.
cramoisi, *adj.* and *n.m.* crimson.
crampe, *n.f.* cramp.
crampon, *n.m.* clamp, cramp iron.
cramponner, *vb.* **se c.,** cling.
crâne, *n.m.* skull.
crapaud, *n.m.* toad.
craquement, *n.m.* crack.
craquer, *vb.* crack, break down.
crasse, *n.f.* grime.
cratère, *n.m.* crater.
cravate, *n.f.* necktie.
crayon, *n.m.* pencil.
créance, *n.f.* belief. **lettres de c.,** credentials.
créancier, *n.m.* creditor.
créateur *m.,* **créatrice** *f.* **1.** *adj.* creative. **2.** *n.* creator.
création, *n.f.* creation.
créature, *n.f.* creature.
crèche, *n.f.* day-care center.
crédit, *n.m.* credit.
credo, *n.m.* creed.

crédule, *adj.* credulous.
créer, *vb.* create.
crème, *n.f.* cream, custard.
crémerie, *n.f.* dairy store.
créneau, *n.m.* slot.
Créole, *n.m.* Creole.
crêpe, *n.f.* pancake; crepe.
crépuscule (-sk-), *n.m.* dusk.
crête, *n.f.* ridge, crest.
crétin, *n.m.* dunce.
cretonne, *n.f.* cretonne.
creuser, *vb.* dig.
creuset, *n.m.* crucible.
creux, *adj.* and *n.m.* hollow.
crevasse, *n.f.* crevice.
crevé, *adj.* exhausted.
crever, *vb.* burst; die.
crevette, *n.f.* shrimp.
cri, *n.m.* cry, call.
criard, *adj.* garish.
crible, *n.m.* sieve.
crier, *vb.* yell, shout.
crime, *n.m.* crime.
criminel, *adj.* criminal.
crinière, *n.f.* mane.
crise, *n.f.* crisis.
crisper, *vb.* tense, clench.
cristal, *n.m.* crystal.
cristallin, *adj.* crystalline.
cristalliser, *vb.* crystallize.
critère, *n.m.* criterion.
critérium, *n.m.* criterion.
critique, 1. *n.m.f.* critic. **2.** *n.f.* criticism. **3.** *adj.* critical.
critiquer, *vb.* criticize.
croasser, *vb.* croak.
Croatie, *n.f.* Croatia.
croc (-ô), *n.m.* hook.
croche, *n.f.* quaver (music).
crochet, *n.m.* bracket, hook.
crochu, *adj.* hooked.
crocodile, *n.m.* crocodile.
croire, *vb.* believe.
croisade, *n.f.* crusade.
croisé, *n.m.* crusader.
croiser, *vb.* cross.
croiseur, *n.m.* cruiser.
croisière, *n.f.* cruise.
croissance, *n.f.* growth.
croissant, *n.m.* crescent; croissant (pastry).
croître, *vb.* grow.
croix, *n.f.* cross.

croquant, *adj.* crisp.
croque-monsieur, *n.m.* grilled ham and cheese sandwich.
croquer, *vb.* crunch; sketch.
croquet, *n.m.* croquet.
croquis, *n.m.* sketch.
crosse, *n.f.* (golf) club; butt (gun).
crotale, *n.m.* rattlesnake.
crouler, *vb.* fall apart.
croup, *n.m.* croup.
croupir, *vb.* wallow.
croustiller, *vb.* be crispy.
croûte, *n.f.* crust.
croûton, *n.m.* crouton.
croyable, *adj.* believable.
croyance, *n.f.* belief.
croyant, *vb.* believer.
cru, *adj.* raw.
cruauté, *n.f.* cruelty.
cruche, *n.f.* pitcher.
crucifier, *vb.* crucify.
crucifix, *n.m.* crucifix.
crudités, *n.f.pl.* raw vegetables.
cruel, *adj.* cruel.
cryochirurgie, *n.f.* cryosurgery.
Cuba, *n.m.* Cuba.
Cubain, *n.m.* Cuban.
cubain, *adj.* Cuban.
cube, *n.m.* cube.
cubique, *adj.* cubic.
cueillir, *vb.* pick.
cuiller, *n.f.* spoon. **c. à thé,** teaspoon. **c. à bouche,** tablespoon.
cuillerée, *n.f.* spoonful.
cuir, *n.m.* leather.
cuirassé, *n.m.* battleship.
cuire, *vb.* cook; sting, smart.
cuisine, *n.f.* kitchen, cooking.

cuisinier, *n.m.* cook.
cuisse, *n.f.* thigh.
cuisson, *n.m.* cooking.
cuivre, *n.m.* copper. **c. jaune,** brass.
cul-de-sac, *n.m.* blind alley.
culinaire, *adj.* culinary, cooking.
culotte, *n.f.* breeches, panties.
culpabilité, *n.f.* guilt.
culte, *n.m.* worship; cult.
cultivé, *adj.* cultured.
cultiver, *vb.* cultivate; grow, raise.
culture, *n.f.* culture, cultivation; farming.
culturel, *adj.* cultural.
cure, *n.f.* cure, treatment.
curé, *n.m.* (parish) priest.
curieux, *adj.* curious.
curiosité, *n.f.* curiosity, curio.
curseur, *n.m.* cursor.
cursif, *adj.* cursive.
cuticule, *n.f.* cuticle.
cuve, *n.f.* vat.
cuver, *vb.* ferment.
cuvette, *n.f.* (wash) basin.
cuvier, *n.m.* washtub.
cycle, *n.m.* cycle.
cycliste, *n.m.f.* cyclist.
cyclomoteur, *n.m.* moped.
cyclone, *n.m.* cyclone.
cygne, *n.m.* swan.
cylindre, *n.m.* cylinder.
cylindrique, *adj.* cylindrical.
cymbale, *n.f.* cymbal.
cynique, 1. *n.m.* cynic. 2. *adj.* cynical.
cynisme, *n.m.* cynicism.
cyprès, *n.m.* cypress.
czar, *n.m.* czar.

D

d'abord, *adv.* first, at first.
dactylo, *n.m.f.* typist.
dada, *n.m.* hobby-horse.
daigner, *vb.* design.
daim, *n.m.* buck.
daine, *n.f.* doe.
dais, *n.m.* canopy.
dalle, *n.f.* slab, flag(stone).
daltonien, *adj.* color-blind.
dame, *n.f.* lady.
damner (dä nã), *vb.* damn.
dancing, *n.m.* dance hall.
Danemark, *n.m.* Denmark.

danger, *n.m.* danger.
dangereux, *adj.* dangerous.
Danois, *n.m.* Dane.
danois, *adj. and n.m.* Danish (language).
dans, *prep.* in, into.
danse, *n.f.* dance.
danser, *vb.* dance.
danseur, *n.m.* dancer.
dard, *n.m.* dart.
date, *n.f.* date (calendar).
dater, *vb.* date.
datte, *n.f.* date (fruit).

dauphin, *n.m.* dolphin.
davantage, *adv.* more, further.
de, *prep.* of, from, by, about; some.
dé, *n.m.* die; thimble.
débâcle, *n.m.* downfall.
débarcadère, *n.m.* wharf.
débardeur, *n.m.* tank top.
débarquer, *vb.* land.
débarrasser, *vb.* rid.
débat, *n.m.* debate.
débattre, *vb.* canvass; debate.
débile, *adj.* weak, stupid.
débit, *n.m.* delivery (speech); sale;
debit.
débiter, *vb.* sell (retail).
débiteur, *n.m.* debtor.
déblayer, *vb.* clear.
débloquer, *vb.* overflow.
déboucher, *vb.* flow (into); un-
cork.
débourser, *vb.* disburse.
debout, *adv.* up. **être d.,** stand.
débrancher, *vb.* unplug.
débris, *n.m.pl.* wreck, debris.
débrouiller, *vb.* disentangle. **se d.,**
manage.
début, *n.m.* beginning, first appearance, debut.
débuter, *vb.* make one's first appearance; begin.
décadence, *n.f.* decay; decadence.
decaféiné, *adj.* decaffeinated.
décalage, *n.m.* gap.
décaler, *vb.* shift.
décapiter, *vb.* behead.
décéder, *vb.* die.
décembre, *n.m.* December.
décence, *n.f.* decency.
décennie, *n.f.* decade.
décent, *adj.* decent.
décentraliser, *vb.* decentralize.
déception, *n.f.* disappointment.
décerner, *vb.* award.
décès, *n.m.* death.
décevoir, *vb.* disappoint.
décharge, *n.f.* discharge.
décharger, *vb.* unload, discharge.
décharné, *adj.* gaunt.
déchausser, *vb.* take off shoes.
déchets (–ā), *n.m.pl.* waste.
déchets nucléaires, *n.m.pl.* nuclear waste.
déchiffrer, *vb.* decipher.
déchirer, *vb.* tear; rend.
déchirure, *n.f.* tear; rent.

décibel, *n.m.* decibel.
décider, *vb.* prevail upon, decide.
décimal, *adj.* decimal.
décisif, *adj.* decisive.
décision, *n.f.* decision.
déclamer, *vb.* recite.
déclaration, *n.f.* statement, declaration.
déclarer, *vb.* state, declare.
déclencher, *vb.* release, set off.
déclic, *n.m.* trigger.
déclin, *n.m.* ebb.
décliner, *vb.* decline.
décoller, *vb.* take off.
décolorer, *vb.* bleach, fade.
décomposer, *vb.* spoil, decompose.
déconcerter, *vb.* baffle, disconcert;
embarrass.
décongestionnant, *adj.* decongestant.
déconseiller, *vb.* advise against.
décontracté, *adj.* relaxed.
décor, *n.m.* scenery.
décoratif, *adj.* decorative.
décoration, *n.f.* decoration, trimming.
décorer, *vb.* decorate.
découper, *vb.* carve (meat).
découragé, *adj.* despondent.
découragement, *n.m.* discouragement.
décourager, *vb.* dishearten, discourage.
découverte, *n.f.* discovery.
découvreur, *n.m.* discoverer.
découvrir, *vb.* uncover, detect, discover.
décrépit, *adj.* decrepit.
décret, *n.m.* decree.
décréter, *vb.* enact.
décrire, *vb.* describe.
décrocher, *vb.* unhook.
dédaigneux, *adj.* scornful.
dédain, *n.m.* scorn, disdain.
dedans, *n.m.* inside, within.
dédicace, *n.f.* dedication.
dédier, *vb.* dedicate.
déduction, *n.f.* deduction.
déduire, *vb.* infer, deduce, deduct.
déesse, *n.f.* goddess.
défaillance, *n.f.* weakness.
défaire, *vb.* undo.
défaite, *n.f.* defeat.

défaut, *n.m.* flaw, fault, failure, lack. **à d. de,** for want of.
défavorable, *adj.* unfavorable.
défavoriser, *vb.* put at a disadvantage.
défectueux, *adj.* faulty, defective.
défendeur, *n.m.* defendant.
défendre, *vb.* forbid, defend.
défense, *n.f.* prohibition, plea, defense.
défenseur, *n.m.* advocate, defender.
défensif, *adj.* defensive.
déférer, *vb.* defer.
défi, *n.m.* challenge, defiance.
défiance, *n.f.* mistrust.
déficit (-t), *n.m.* deficit.
défier, *vb.* challenge, defy. **se d. de,** mistrust.
défigurer, *vb.* deface.
défiler, *vb.* march off.
défini, *adj.* definite.
définir, *vb.* define.
définitif, *adj.* final, definitive.
définition, *n.f.* definition.
déformer, *vb.* distort, deform.
défouler, *vb.* let off steam.
défraîchi, *adj.* dingy.
défricher, *vb.* reclaim; clear.
défunt, *adj. and n.m.* deceased.
dégagé, *adj.* breezy.
dégât, *n.m.* damage.
dégénérer, *vb.* degenerate.
dégoût, *n.m.* distaste, disgust.
dégoûtant, *adj.* foul, disgusting.
dégoûter, *vb.* disgust.
dégoutter, *vb.* drip.
dégradation, *n.f.* degradation.
dégrader, *vb.* degrade.
degré, *n.m.* degree, step.
déguisement, *n.m.* disguise.
déguiser, *vb.* disguise.
dehors, *adv.* outdoors, outside. **en d. de,** apart from.
déifier, *vb.* deify.
déité, *n.f.* deity.
déjà, *adv.* already.
déjeter, *vb.* make unsymmetrical.
déjeuner, *n.m. and vb.* lunch, breakfast. **petit d.,** breakfast.
déjouer, *vb.* foil, thwart.
delà, *adv.* beyond. **au d. de,** over, past, beyond.
délabrement, *n.m.* decay.
délabrer, *vb.* ruin, wreck.

délacer, *vb.* unlace.
délai, *n.m.* delay.
délaissement, *n.m.* desertion.
délaisser, *vb.* desert.
délassement, *n.m.* relaxation.
délasser, *vb.* refresh.
délateur, *n.m.* informer.
délavé, *adj.* faded, pallid.
délayer, *vb.* dilute with water.
délectable, *adj.* delicious.
délectation, *n.f.* enjoyment.
délecter, *vb.* delight.
délégation, *n.f.* delegation.
délégué, *n.m.* delegate.
déléguer, *vb.* delegate.
délester, *vb.* relieve of ballast.
délétère, *adj.* harmful; offensive.
délibératif, *adj.* deliberative.
délibération, *n.f.* deliberation.
délibéré, *adj.* deliberate.
délibérer, *vb.* deliberate.
délicat, *adj.* delicate, tactful.
délicatesse, *n.f.* delicacy.
délices, *n.f.pl.* delight.
délicieux, *adj.* delicious.
délié, *adj.* slender; keen.
délier, *vb.* untie.
délimiter, *vb.* mark the limits of.
délinéer, *vb.* delineate.
délinquant, 1. *n.m.* delinquent, offender. **2.** *adj.* delinquent.
délirant, *adj.* delirious.
délire, *n.m.* frenzy.
délirer, *vb.* rave.
délit, *n.m.* offense, crime.
délivrance, *n.f.* rescue, deliverance.
délivrer, *vb.* rescue, set free, deliver.
déloger, *vb.* dislodge.
déloyal, *adj.* disloyal.
déloyauté, *n.f.* disloyalty.
deltaplane, *n.m.* hang glider.
déluge, *n.m.* deluge.
déluré, *adj.* clever, cute.
démagogue, *n.m.* demagogue.
demain, *adv.* tomorrow.
demande, *n.f.* application, request, inquiry, claim. **d. en mariage,** proposal.
demander, *vb.* ask, request. **se d.,** wonder.
demandeur, *n.m.* plaintiff.
démangeaison, *n.f.* itch.
démanger, *vb.* itch.

démanteler, *vb.* dismantle.
démaquiller, *vb.* remove makeup.
démarcation, *n.f.* demarcation.
démarche, *n.f.* walk; bearing; step.
démarrage, *n.m.* start.
démarrer, *vb.* unmoor; start off.
démarreur, *n.m.* (self-)starter.
démasquer, *vb.* unmask; expose, reveal.
démêlant, *n.m.* conditioner.
démêler, *vb.* disentangle.
démembrement, *n.m.* dismemberment.
démembrer, *vb.* dismember.
déménagement, *n.m.* moving.
déménager, *vb.* move.
déménageur, *n.m.* furniture mover.
démence, *n.f.* insanity.
démener, *vb.* struggle.
dément, *adj.* insane.
démenti, *n.m.* denial.
démentir, *vb.* deny, refute.
démesuré, *adj.* measureless, immense.
démettre, *vb.* se d. (de), resign.
demeure, *n.f.* abode.
demeurer, *vb.* dwell.
demi, *n.m. and adj.* half.
demi-cercle, *n.m.* semicircle.
demi-dieu, *n.m.* demigod.
demi-frère, *n.m.* stepbrother.
demi-heure, *n.f.* half an hour.
démilitariser, *vb.* demilitarize.
demi-place, *n.f.* half price; half fare.
demi-saison, *adj.* between-season.
demi-sœur, *n.f.* stepsister.
demi-solde, *n.m.* half-pay.
démission, *n.f.* resignation.
démobilisation, *n.f.* demobilization.
démobiliser, *vb.* demobilize.
démocrate, *n.m.f.* democrat.
démocratie, *n.f.* democracy.
démocratique, *adj.* democratic.
démodé, *adj.* old-fashioned.
demoiselle, *n.f.* young lady. d. d'honneur, bridesmaid.
démolir, *vb.* demolish.
démolition, *n.f.* demolition.
démon, *n.m.* demon.
démonétiser, *vb.* demonetize.
démoniaque, *adj.* demonic.

démonstratif, *adj.* effusive; demonstrative.
démonstration, *n.f.* demonstration.
démonter, *vb.* take down; dismantle.
démontrable, *adj.* demonstrable.
démontrer, *vb.* demonstrate.
démoralisation, *n.f.* demoralization.
démoraliser, *vb.* demoralize.
démouler, *vb.* remove from a mold.
démuni, *adj.* lacking, impoverished.
dénationaliser, *vb.* denationalize.
dénaturer, *vb.* denature.
dénégation, *n.f.* denial.
dénigrer, *vb.* disparage.
dénivelé, *adj.* not level.
dénombrement, *n.m.* enumeration; census.
dénombrer, *vb.* count.
dénomination, *n.f.* denomination, designation.
dénommer, *vb.* name.
dénoncer, *vb.* report, denounce.
dénonciation, *n.f.* denunciation.
dénoter, *vb.* denote.
dénouement, *n.m.* result, outcome.
dénouer, *vb.* untie.
denrée, *n.f.* foodstuff, produce.
dense, *adj.* dense.
densité, *n.f.* density.
dent, *n.f.* tooth. mal de d.s, toothache. brosse à d.s, toothbrush.
dentaire, *adj.* dental.
denté, *adj.* cogged.
dentelle, *n.f.* lace.
dentifrice, *n.m.* tooth paste or powder.
dentiste, *n.m.* dentist.
dentition, *n.f.* dentition.
denture, *n.f.* set of natural teeth.
dénuder, *vb.* denude.
dénué, *adj.* destitute, bare.
dénuement, *n.m.* destitution.
dénuer, *vb.* divest.
déodorant, *n.m.* deodorant.
dépannage, *n.m.* emergency repairs.
dépanner, *vb.* repair; help out.
dépareillé, *adj.* odd (unmatched).
départ, *n.m.* departure.

département, *n.m.* department.
départir, *vb.* divide in shares.
dépassé, *adj.* outdated.
dépasser, *vb.* outrun, pass.
dépayser, *vb.* disorient, confuse.
dépêche, *n.f.* dispatch.
dépêcher, *vb.* **se d.,** hurry.
dépeindre, *vb.* portray.
dépendance, *n.f.* annex (to a building).
dépendant, *adj.* dependent.
dépendre, *vb.* depend.
dépens, *n.m.pl.* expenses.
dépense, *n.f.* expenditure, expense.
dépenser, *vb.* spend, expend.
dépérir, *vb.* waste away; decline.
dépeupler, *vb.* depopulate.
déphasé, *adj.* disoriented.
dépiécer, *vb.* dismember.
dépit, *n.m.* spite. **en d.,** despite.
déplacement, *n.m.* displacement.
déplacé, *adj.* out of place.
déplacer, *vb.* displace, move, shift.
déplaire à, *vb.* displease.
déplaisant, *adj.* displeasing.
déplanter, *vb.* transplant.
déplantoir, *n.m.* trowel.
dépliant, *n.m.* leaflet.
déplier, *vb.* unfold.
déploiement, *n.m.* deployment.
déplorable, *adj.* wretched, deplorable.
déplorer, *vb.* deplore.
déployer, *vb.* deploy.
déplumer, *vb.* pluck.
déportation, *n.f.* deportation.
déportements, *n.m.pl.* misconduct.
déporter, *vb.* deport.
déposant, *n.m.* depositor.
déposer, *vb.* deposit, set down, depose.
dépositaire, *n.m.f.* trustee.
déposséder, *vb.* oust; dispossess.
dépôt, *n.m.* deposit, depot. **d. de vivres,** commissary.
dépotoir, *n.m.* rubbish dump.
dépouille, *n.f.* hide, skin, pelt.
dépouiller, *vb.* strip. **se d. de,** shed.
dépourvu, *adj.* devoid; needy.
dépoussiéreur, *n.m.* vacuum cleaner.
dépravation, *n.f.* depravity.
dépraver, *vb.* deprave.
dépréciation, *n.f.* depreciation.

déprécier, *vb.* depreciate, cheapen.
déprédation, *n.f.* depredation.
dépression, *n.f.* depression.
déprimer, *vb.* depress.
depuis, *adv. and prep.* since. **d. que,** *conj.* since.
députation, *n.f.* delegation.
député, *n.m.* representative, deputy.
déraciné, *adj.* rootless.
déraciner, *vb.* uproot, eradicate.
dérailler, *vb.* derail; talk nonsense.
déraison, *n.f.* unreason.
déraisonnable, *adj.* unreasonable.
dérangement, *n.m.* disturbance.
déranger, *vb.* disturb, trouble.
déraper, *vb.* skid.
derechef, *adv.* once again.
dérégler, *vb.* upset, disorder.
dérider, *vb.* smooth; cheer up.
dérision, *n.f.* derision. **tourner en d.,** deride.
dérisoire, *adj.* ridiculous, derisory.
dérivation, *n.f.* derivation, etymology.
dérive, *n.f.* drift. **à la d.,** adrift.
dériver, *vb.* derive; drift.
dernier, *adj.* last, latter.
dernièrement, *adv.* lately.
dérober, *vb.* rob. **se d.,** steal away.
dérouiller, *vb.* remove the rust from.
dérouler, *vb.* unroll, unfold.
déroute, *n.f.* rout.
dérouter, *vb.* mislead; confuse.
derrière, *n.m., adv. and prep.* behind.
derviche, *n.m.* dervish.
dès, *prep.* since. **d. que,** *conj.* as soon as.
désabuser, *vb.* disillusion.
désaccord, *n.m.* disagreement.
désaccoutumer, *vb.* break of a habit.
désaffecté, *adj.* disused.
désaffecter, *vb.* close down.
désaffection, *n.f.* alienation.
désagréable, *adj.* nasty, distasteful.
désagrégation, *n.f.* disintegration.
désaligné, *adj.* out of alignment.
désaltérer, *vb.* quench (one's) thirst.
désapprobation, *n.f.* disapproval.
désapprouver, *vb.* disapprove.

désarçonner, *vb.* disconcert.
désarmement, *n.m.* disarmament.
désarmer, *vb.* disarm.
désarroi, *n.m.* disorder.
désastre, *n.m.* disaster.
désastreux, *adj.* disastrous.
désavantage, *n.m.* disadvantage.
désaveu, *n.m.* denial.
désavouer, *vb.* disown.
désaxé, *adj. and n.m.* unbalanced (person).
descendance, *n.f.* descent.
descendant, 1. *n.m.* offspring, descendant. **2.** *adj.* downward, descending.
descendre, *vb.* go down, come down, alight, descend.
descente, *n.f.* raid; descent.
descriptif, *adj.* descriptive.
description, *n.f.* description.
désembarquer, *vb.* disembark, unload.
désemparé, *adj.* distraught.
désenchanter, *vb.* disenchant.
désenivrer, *vb.* sober up.
déséquilibre, *n.m.* imbalance.
déséquilibrer, *vb.* throw off balance.
désert, *n.m.* wilderness, desert.
déserter, *vb.* desert.
déserteur, *n.m.* deserter.
désertion, *n.f.* desertion.
désespéré, *adj.* hopeless, forlorn, desperate.
désespérer, *vb.* despair.
désespoir, *n.m.* desperation, despair.
déshabiller, *vb.* undress.
déshériter, *vb.* disinherit.
déshonnête, *adj.* improper, indecent.
déshonneur, *n.m.* disgrace, dishonor.
déshonorant, *adj.* dishonorable.
déshonorer, *vb.* disgrace, dishonor.
déshydrater, *vb.* dehydrate.
désignation, *n.f.* nomination.
désigner, *vb.* appoint, nominate; point out; designate.
désillusion, *n.f.* disillusion.
désinfectant, *n.m.* disinfectant.
désinfecter, *vb.* disinfect, fumigate.
désinfection, *n.f.* disinfection.

désintégration, *n.f.* disintegration.
désintégrer, *vb.* disintegrate.
désintéressé, *adj.* unselfish.
désintéressement, *n.m.* unselfishness.
désintoxication, *n.f.* detoxication.
désinvolte, *adj.* casual.
désir, *n.m.* desire, wish.
désirable, *adj.* desirable.
désirer, *vb.* desire, wish.
désireux, *adj.* desirous.
désistement, *n.m.* withdrawal.
désobéissance, *n.f.* disobedience.
désobéir à, *vb.* disobey.
désobéissant, *adj.* disobedient.
désobligeant, *adj.* disagreeable.
désodorisant, *n.m.* air freshener, deodorant.
désœuvré, *adj.* idle.
désolation, *n.f.* desolation.
désolé, *adj.* disconsolate; desolate.
désoler, *vb.* desolate.
désopilant, *adj.* hilarious.
désordonné, *adj.* disorderly.
désordonner, *vb.* upset, confuse.
désordre, *n.m.* disorder.
désorganisation, *n.f.* disorganization.
désorganiser, *vb.* disorganize.
désorienté, *adj.* disoriented.
désormais, *adv.* henceforth.
despote, *n.m.* despot.
despotique, *adj.* despotic.
despotisme, *n.m.* despotism.
dessécher, *vb.* dry out, parch; drain.
dessein, *n.m.* plan, intent.
desserrer, *vb.* loosen.
dessert, *n.m.* dessert.
desservir, *vb.* serve; clear away.
dessin, *n.m.* drawing, design, sketch.
dessinateur, *n.m.* designer.
dessiner, *vb.* draw, design. **se d.,** loom.
dessous, *n.m.* underside. **en d., au-d. de,** beneath, underneath.
dessus, *n.m.* top. **en d., au-d. de,** above. **d. de lit,** bedspread.
déstabiliser, *vb.* destabilize.
destin, *n.m.* fate, destiny.
destinataire, *n.m./f.* addressee.
destination, *n.f.* destination. **à d. de,** bound for.

destinée, *n.f.* destiny.
destiner, *vb.* destine, intend.
destituer, *vb.* dismiss.
destructeur, *adj.* destructive.
destructif, *adj.* destructive.
destruction, *n.f.* destruction.
désuet, *adj.* obsolete.
désuétude, *n.f.* disuse.
désunion, *n.f.* disunion.
désunir, *vb.* disconnect.
détaché, *adj.* loose.
détachement, *n.m.* detachment.
détacher, *vb.* detach. **se d.,** stand
 out.
détail, *n.m.* item; particular, detail.
 au d., at retail.
détaillant, *n.m.* retailer.
détailler, *vb.* retail, itemize; detail.
détaxe, *n.f.* tax refund.
détaxer, *vb.* reduce the tax on.
détective, *n.m.* detective.
déteindre, *vb.* run (of colors).
détendre, *vb.* release; relax. **se d.,**
 relax.
détenir, *vb.* detain.
détente, *n.f.* 1. trigger. 2. (politics)
 détente.
détention, *n.f.* custody, detention.
détenu, *n.m.* prisoner.
détergent, *n.m.* detergent.
détérioration, *n.f.* deterioration.
détériorer, *vb.* deteriorate.
détermination, *n.f.* determination.
déterminer, *vb.* determine, fix.
détestable, *adj.* detestable, hateful.
détester, *vb.* abhor, loathe, detest.
détonation, *n.f.* detonation.
détoner, *vb.* detonate.
détour, *n.m.* turn; detour.
détourné, *adj.* devious.
détourner, *vb.* turn away; divert;
 avert; embezzle.
détracteur, *n.m.* critic.
détresse, *n.f.* trouble, distress.
détriment, *n.m.* detriment.
détritus, *n.m.pl.* rubbish.
détroit, *n.m.* strait.
détruire, *vb.* destroy.
dette, *n.f.* debt.
D.E.U.G., *n.m.* advanced (university) degree.
deuil, *n.m.* mourning.
deux, *adj. and n.m.* two. **tous les d.,**
 both.

deuxième, *adj.* second.
deux-points, *n.m.* colon.
dévaler, *vb.* hurtle down.
dévaliser, *vb.* rob.
dévaliseur, *n.m.* robber.
dévaloriser, *vb.* devalue.
dévaluation, *n.f.* devaluation.
devancer, *vb.* be ahead of.
devant, **1.** *n.m.* front. **2.** *prep.*
 before, in front of.
devanture, *n.f.* window, (shop)
 front.
dévastation, *n.f.* devastation.
dévaster, *vb.* devastate.
déveine, *n.f.* bad luck.
développement, *n.m.* development.
développer, *vb.* develop.
devenir, *vb.* become.
déverser, *vb.* divert.
dévêtir, *vb.* undress, disrobe.
déviation, *n.f.* deviation.
dévider, *vb.* unwind.
dévier, *vb.* turn away.
deviner, *vb.* guess.
devinette, *n.f.* puzzle, riddle.
devis, *n.m.* estimate.
dévisager, *vb.* stare at.
devise, *n.f.* motto; currency (finance).
dévisser, *vb.* unscrew.
dévoiler, *vb.* unveil, disclose, reveal.
devoir, *n.m.* duty.
devoir, *vb.* owe; be supposed to;
 have to; (conditional) ought.
dévorer, *vb.* devour.
dévot, *adj.* devout.
dévotion, *n.f.* devotion.
dévoué, *adj.* devoted.
dévouement, *n.m.* devotion.
dévouer, *vb.* dedicate, devote.
dextérité, *n.f.* dexterity.
diabète, *n.m.* diabetes.
diabétique, *adj. and n.m.f.* dia-
 betic.
diable, *n.m.* devil.
diablerie, *n.f.* mischief.
diabolique, *adj.* diabolic.
diacre, *n.m.* deacon.
diacritique, *adj.* diacritic.
diadème, *n.m.* diadem.
diagnostic, *n.m.* diagnosis.
diagnostiquer, *vb.* diagnose.
diagonal, *adj.* diagonal.

diagramme, *n.m.* diagram.

dialectal, *adj.* dialect.

dialecte, *n.m.* dialect.

dialogue, *n.m.* dialogue.

dialoguer, *vb.* converse, talk together.

diamant, *n.m.* diamond.

diamétral, *adj.* diametric.

diamètre, *n.m.* diameter.

diaphane, *adj.* diaphanous.

diaphragme, *n.m.* diaphragm.

diapositive, *n.f.* slide (photography).

diarrhée, *n.f.* diarrhea.

diathermie, *n.f.* diathermy.

diatribe, *n.f.* diatribe.

dictateur, *n.m.* dictator.

dictature, *n.f.* dictatorship.

dictée, *n.f.* dictation.

dicter, *vb.* dictate.

diction, *n.f.* diction.

dictionnaire, *n.m.* dictionary.

dicton, *n.m.* maxim, proverb.

didactique, *adj.* didactic.

dièse, *adj.* and *n.m.* sharp (music).

diesel, *adj* and *n.m.* diesel.

diète, *n.f.* diet.

diététique, *adj.* dietetic.

Dieu, *n.m.* God.

diffamant, *adj.* libelous.

diffamateur, *n.m.* libeler.

diffamation, *n.f.* libel.

diffamer, *vb.* defame.

différence, *n.f.* difference.

différenciation, *n.f.* differentiation.

différencier, *vb.* differentiate.

différend, *n.m.* difference, dispute.

différent, *adj.* different.

différer, *vb.* defer; differ.

difficile, *adj.* arduous, hard; difficult; fastidious.

difficilement, *adv.* with difficulty.

difficulté, *n.f.* trouble; difficulty.

difficulté psychologique, *n.f.* hangup.

difforme, *adj.* deformed.

difformité, *n.f.* deformity.

diffus, *adj.* diffuse.

diffuser, *vb.* diffuse, broadcast.

diffusion, *n.f.* spread, diffusion; broadcasting.

digérer, *vb.* digest.

digestible, *adj.* digestible.

digestif, 1. *adj.* digestive. 2. *n.m.* after-dinner liqueur.

digestion, *n.f.* digestion.

digital, *adj.* digital.

digitaline, *n.f.* digitalis.

digne, *adj.* worthy.

dignitaire, *n.m.* dignitary.

dignité, *n.f.* dignity.

digression, *n.f.* digression.

digue, *n.f.* dike, dam.

dilapidation, *n.f.* waste.

dilater, *vb.* expand, dilate.

dilemme, *n.m.* dilemma.

dilettante, *n.m.* amateur.

diligence, *n.f.* diligence.

diligent, *adj.* diligent.

diluer, *vb.* dilute.

dilution, *n.f.* dilution.

dimanche, *n.m.* Sunday.

dimension, *n.f.* dimension.

diminuer, *vb.* lessen, decrease, diminish.

diminutif, *adj.* and *n.m.* diminutive.

diminution, *n.f.* decrease.

dinde, *n.f.* turkey.

dindon, *n.m.* turkey.

dîner, 1. *n.m.* dinner. 2. *vb.* dine.

dîneur, *n.m.* diner.

dingue, *adj.* (colloquial) crazy.

diphtérie, *n.f.* diphtheria.

diphtongue, *n.f.* diphthong.

diplomate, *n.m.* diplomat.

diplomatie, *n.f.* diplomacy.

diplomatique, *adj.* diplomatic.

diplôme, *n.m.* diploma.

dipsomane, *n.m./f.* dipsomaniac.

dipsomanie, *n.f.* dipsomania.

dire, *vb.* say, tell. **vouloir d.,** mean. **c'est-à-d.,** namely; that is.

direct, *adj.* direct.

directement, *adv.* directly.

directeur, *n.m.* manager, director.

directif, *adj.* guiding.

direction, *n.f.* management, leadership, direction.

directive, *n.f.* instruction.

directorat, *n.m.* directorate.

dirigeable, *adj.* and *n.m.* dirigible.

dirigeant, *adj.* ruling.

diriger, *vb.* manage, boss; steer, direct.

dirigisme, *n.m.* interventionism.

discernable, *adj.* barely visible.

discernement, *n.m.* discernment, judgment.
discerner, *vb.* discern.
disciple, *n.m.* follower, disciple.
disciplinaire, *adj.* disciplinary.
discipline, *n.f.* discipline.
discipliner, *vb.* discipline.
disco, *adj.* disco.
discontinu, *adj.* intermittent.
discontinuer, *vb.* discontinue.
disconvenance, *n.f.* unsuitability.
discordance, *n.f.* discord.
discorde, *n.f.* discord.
discothèque, *n.f.* discotheque.
discourir, *vb.* speak one's views.
discours, *n.m.* speech, oration, talk, discourse.
discourtois, *adj.* discourteous.
discrédit, *n.m.* disrepute.
discréditer, *vb.* disparage.
discret, *adj.* discreet.
discrétion, *n.f.* discretion.
discrimination, *n.f.* discrimination.
disculper, *vb.* exonerate.
discursif, *adj.* discursive.
discussion, *n.f.* argument, discussion.
discutable, *adj.* debatable.
discuter, *vb.* argue, debate, discuss.
disette, *n.f.* famine.
diseur, *n.m.* talker.
disgrâce, *n.f.* disgrace.
disgracier, *vb.* put out of favor.
disjoindre, *vb.* sever, disjoint.
dislocation, *n.f.* dislocation.
disloquer, *vb.* dislocate.
disparaître, *vb.* disappear.
disparate, *adj.* unlike; badly matched.
disparition, *n.f.* disappearance.
disparu, *n.m.* missing person; dead person.
dispendieux, *adj.* expensive.
dispensaire, *n.m.* dispensary.
dispensation, *n.f.* dispensation.
dispense, *n.f.* military exemption.
dispenser, *vb.* dispense.
disperser, *vb.* scatter, disperse.
dispersion, *n.f.* dispersal.
disponible, *adj.* available.
disposé, *adj.* disposed. **d. d'avance,** predisposed. **peu d.,** reluctant.
disposer, *vb.* arrange.

dispositif, *n.m.* device.
disposition, *n.f.* arrangement, disposal, disposition.
disproportionné, *adj.* disproportionate.
dispute, *n.f.* row, fight, quarrel, dispute.
disputer, *vb.* dispute. **se d.,** quarrel.
disquaire, *n.m.* record dealer.
disqualifier, *vb.* disqualify.
disque, *n.m.* disk, record.
disquette, *n.f.* floppy disk, diskette.
dissemblable, *adj.* unlike.
dissemblance, *n.f.* dissimilarity.
disséminer, *vb.* scatter.
dissension, *n.f.* dissension.
dissentiment, *n.m.* dissent.
disséquer, *vb.* dissect.
dissertation, *n.f.* essay.
dissimulation, *n.f.* pretense.
dissimuler, *vb.* dissemble, pretend.
dissipation, *n.f.* dissipation.
dissiper, *vb.* dispel, waste, dissipate.
dissolu, *adj.* dissolute.
dissolution, *n.f.* dissolution.
dissonant, *adj.* discordant.
dissoudre, *vb.* dissolve.
dissuader, *vb.* dissuade.
distance, *n.f.* distance.
distancer, *vb.* outdistance.
distant, *adj.* distant.
distillation (-l-), *n.f.* distillation.
distiller (-l-), *vb.* distill.
distillerie (-l-), *n.f.* distillery.
distinct (-kt), *adj.* distinct.
distinctif, *adj.* distinctive.
distinction, *n.f.* distinction.
distingué, *adj.* distinguished.
distinguer, *vb.* discriminate; make out; distinguish.
distraction, *n.f.* distraction; pastime.
distraire, *vb.* distract, amuse. **se d.,** have fun.
distrait, *adj.* absentminded.
distribuer, *vb.* give out, deal out, distribute.
distributeur, *n.m.* distributor.
distribution, *n.f.* distribution; delivery; cast.
district (-trĕk), *n.m.* district.
dit, *adj.* called.

diurétique, *adj. and n.m.* diuretic.

diurne, *adj.* diurnal.

divaguer, *vb.* ramble.

divan, *n.m.* davenport, couch.

divergence, *n.f.* divergence.

diverger, *vb.* diverge.

divers, *adj.* various.

diversifier, *vb.* diversify.

diversion, *n.f.* diversion.

diversité, *n.f.* diversity.

divertir, *vb.* divert, entertain. **se d.,** enjoy oneself.

divertissement, *n.m.* diversion.

dividende, *n.m.* dividend.

divin, *adj.* divine.

divinateur, *n.m.* soothsayer.

divinité, *n.f.* divinity.

diviser, *vb.* part, divide.

divisible, *adj.* divisible.

division, *n.f.* division.

divorce, *n.m.* divorce.

divorcer, *vb.* divorce.

divulguer, *vb.* divulge.

dix (-s), *adj. and n.m.* ten.

dix-huit (-z-), *adj. and n.m.* eighteen.

dix-huitième (-z-), *adj. and n.m.f.* eighteenth.

dixième (-z-), *adj. and n.m.f.* tenth.

dix-neuf (-z-), *adj. and n.m.* nineteen.

dix-sept (-s-), *adj. and n.m.* seventeen.

dizaine, *n.f.* (group of) ten.

docile, *adj.* docile.

docilité, *n.f.* docility.

docte, *adj.* learned, wise.

docteur, *n.m.* doctor.

doctorat, *n.m.* doctorate.

doctrine, *n.f.* doctrine.

document, *n.m.* document.

documentaliste, *n.m.f.* researcher.

documenter, *vb.* document.

dodo, *n.m.* (colloquial) **faire d.,** go to sleep.

dodu, *adj.* plump.

dogmatique, *adj.* dogmatic.

dogma, *n.m.* dogma.

dogue, *n.m.* watchdog.

doigt (dwä), *n.m.* finger. **d. de pied,** toe.

doit, *n.m.* debit.

doléances, *n.f.pl.* grievances.

dollar, *n.m.* dollar.

domaine, *n.m.* domain, property.

dôme, *n.m.* dome.

domestique, 1. *n.m.f.* servant. **2.** *adj.* domestic.

domicile, *n.m.* residence.

dominant, *adj.* dominant.

domination, *n.f.* sway, domination, dominion.

dominer, *vb.* rule, dominate.

domino, *n.m.* domino.

dommage, *n.m.* injury; damage. **c'est d.,** that's too bad. **quel d.!,** what a pity!

dompter, *vb.* tame, subdue.

don, *n.m.* gift.

donateur, *n.m.* donor.

donation, *n.f.* donation.

donc (-k), *adv.* therefore.

donjon, *n.m.* dungeon.

donne, *n.f.* deal (cards).

donner, *vb.* give.

donneur, *n.m.* giver.

dont, *pron.* whose, of which.

dopage, *n.m.* doping.

doper, *vb.* dope.

dorénavant, *adv.* hereafter.

dorer, *vb.* gild.

dorloter, *vb.* coddle.

dormant, *adj.* dormant; asleep.

dormir, *vb.* sleep.

dortoir, *n.m.* dormitory.

dos, *n.m.* back.

dosage, *n.m.* mixture.

dose, *n.f.* dose.

doser, *vb.* decide the amount.

dossier, *n.m.* record.

dot (-t), *n.f.* dowry.

doter, *vb.* endow.

douaire, *n.m.* dowry.

douane, *n.f.* customs, custom house.

douanier, *n.m.* customs officer.

double, *adj. and n.m.* double. **faire le d. de,** duplicate.

doubler, *vb.* double.

doublure, *n.f.* lining.

doucement, *adv.* gently.

doucereux, *adj.* sugary; oversweet.

douceur, *n.f.* sweetness; gentleness, meekness.

douche, *n.f.* shower bath; douche.

doucher, *vb.* **se d.,** take a shower.

doudoune, *n.f.* anorak.

douer, *vb.* endow.

douille, *n.f.* socket.

douleur, *n.f.* pain, ache; sorrow, grief.

douloureux, *adj.* painful.

doute, *n.m.* doubt.

douter, *vb.* doubt. **se d. de,** suspect.

douteux, *adj.* dubious, doubtful, questionable.

douve, *n.f.* ditch.

doux *m.,* **douce** *f. adj.* soft, sweet, gentle, mild, meek.

douzaine, *n.f.* dozen.

douze, *adj. and n.m.* twelve.

douzième, *adj. and n.m.f.* twelfth.

doyen, *n.m.* dean.

dragée, *n.f.* sugar-coated pill.

dragon, *n.m.* dragon; dragoon.

draguer, *vb.* dredge; try to pick up.

drainage, *n.m.* drainage.

drainer, *vb.* drain.

dramatique, *adj.* dramatic.

dramatiser, *vb.* dramatize.

dramaturge, *n.m.* playwright.

drame, *n.m.* drama.

drap, *n.m.* sheet.

drapeau, *n.m.* flag.

draper, *vb.* drape.

draperie, *n.f.* drapery.

drapier, *n.m.* clothier.

dresser, *vb.* draw up.

dressoir, *n.m.* dresser.

drive, *n.m.* drive (tennis).

drogue, *n.f.* drug.

droguer, *vb.* drug.

droguerie, *n.f.* hardware store.

droguiste, *n.m.* owner or keeper of a hardware store.

droit, 1. *n.m.* right; law; claim. **2.** *adj. and adv.* (up)right, straight, fair. **d. d'auteur,** copyright.

droite, *n.f.* right. **à d.,** (to the) right.

droitier, *n.m.* right-handed person.

droiture, *n.f.* uprightness.

drôle, *adj.* funny.

du, *m.,* **de la,** *f.,* **des,** *pl. prep.* some, any.

dû *m.,* **due** *f. adj.* due.

duc, *n.m.* duke.

duché, *n.m.* dukedom.

duchesse, *n.f.* duchess.

ductile, *adj.* ductile.

duel, *n.m.* duel.

duelliste, *n.m.* duelist.

dûment, *adv.* duly.

dune, *n.f.* dune.

duo, *n.m.* duet.

dupe, *n.f.* dupe.

duper, *vb.* trick.

duperie, *n.f.* trickery.

duplicité, *n.f.* duplicity.

dur, *adj.* hard, tough.

durabilité, *n.f.* durability.

durable, *adj.* lasting, durable.

durant, *prep.* during.

durcir, *vb.* harden.

durcissement, *n.m.* hardening.

durée, *n.f.* duration.

durement, *adv.* hard, harshly, strongly.

durer, *vb.* last.

dureté, *n.f.* hardness.

duvet, *n.m.* down.

duveté, *adj.* downy.

dynamique, *adj.* dynamic.

dynamite, *n.f.* dynamite.

dynamo, *n.f.* dynamo.

dynastie, *n.f.* dynasty.

dynastique, *adj.* dynastic.

dysenterie, *n.f.* dysentery.

dyslexie, *n.f.* dyslexia.

dyspepsie, *n.f.* dyspepsia.

E

eau, *n.f.* water. **faire e.,** leak.

eau-de-vie, *n.f.* brandy.

eau-forte, *n.f.* nitric acid.

ébahir, *vb.* amaze.

ébahissement, *n.m.* amazement.

ébarber, *vb.* trim, clip.

ébattre, *vb.* **s'é.,** frolic.

ébauche, *n.f.* outline.

ébaucher, *vb.* outline.

ébène, *n.m.* ebony.

ébéniste, *n.m.* cabinetmaker.

ébénisterie, *n.f.* cabinet work.

éblouir, *vb.* dazzle.

éblouissement, *n.m.* dazzle, amazement.

éboulement, *n.m.* cave-in.

ébouriffer, *vb.* ruffle.

ébranler, *vb.* shake.

ébriété, *n.f.* drunkenness.

ébullition, *n.f.* boiling point.

écaille, *n.f.* scale.
écarlate, *adj. and n.f.* scarlet.
écart, *n.m.* separation. à l'é., aloof.
écarté, *adj.* isolated; lonely.
écartement, *n.m.* gap, separation.
écarter, *vb.* set aside.
ecclésiastique, *adj. and n.m.* ecclesiastique.
écervelé, *adj.* scatterbrained.
échafaud, *n.m.* scaffold.
échafaudage, *n.m.* scaffolding.
échalote, *n.f.* shallot.
échancrer, *vb.* scallop, notch.
échange, *n.m.* exchange.
échangeable, *adj.* exchangeable.
échanger, *vb.* exchange.
échantillon, *n.m.* sample.
échappatoire, *n.f.* loophole.
échappement, *n.m.* exhaust.
échapper, *vb.* escape.
écharde, *n.f.* splinter.
écharpe, *n.f.* scarf; sling.
échasse, *n.f.* stilt.
échauder, *vb.* scald.
échéance, *n.f.* maturity (finance).
échec, *n.m.* failure.
échecs (-shè), *n.m.pl.* chess.
échelle, *n.f.* ladder; scale.
échelon, *n.m.* step; echelon.
échevelé, *adj.* dishevelled.
échine, *n.f.* spine.
échiner, *vb.* work like a slave.
écho (-kō), *n.m.* echo.
échoir, *vb.* fall due.
échoppe, *n.f.* booth, stall.
échouer, *vb.* fail. faire é., frustrate.
éclabousser, *vb.* splash.
éclair, *n.m.* flash.
éclairage, *n.m.* lighting.
éclaircie, *n.f.* clearing.
éclaircir, *vb.* clear up.
éclairer, *vb.* (en)lighten, light, clear up, clarify.
éclaireur, *n.m.* scout.
éclat, *n.m.* chip, splinter; burst; brilliance, radiance, glamour.
éclatant, *adj.* bursting; loud; brilliant.
éclatement (de pneu), *n.m.* blowout.
éclater, *vb.* burst out.
éclectique, *adj.* eclectic.
éclipse, *n.f.* eclipse.
éclipser, *vb.* eclipse.

éclore, *vb.* hatch; open; blossom.
écluse, *n.f.* lock.
écœurant, *adj.* sickly, disgusting.
écœurer, *vb.* disgust.
école, *n.f.* school.
écolier, *n.m.* schoolboy.
écologie, *n.f.* ecology.
écologique, *adj.* ecological.
écologiste, *n.m.f.* ecologist; environmentalist.
économe, *adj.* economical.
économie, *n.f.* economy. é. politique, economics.
économique, *adj.* economic(al).
économiser, *vb.* economize.
économiste, *n.m.f.* economist.
écope, *n.f.* ladle.
écoper, *vb.* ladle or bail out.
écorce, *n.f.* bark.
écorcher, *vb.* skin.
écorchure, *n.f.* gall.
Écossais, *n.m.* Scotchman, Scotsman.
écossais, *adj.* Scotch, Scottish.
Écosse, *n.f.* Scotland.
écosystème, *n.m.* ecosystem.
écot, *n.m.* share.
écouler, *vb.* drain. s'é., flow, elapse.
écoute, *n.f.* listening.
écouter, *vb.* listen (to).
écouteur, *n.m.* listener.
écran, *n.m.* screen.
écraser, *vb.* crush.
écrémer, *vb.* skim.
écrevisse, *n.f.* crayfish.
écrier, *vb.* s'é., exclaim.
écrin, *n.m.* case, box.
écrire, *vb.* write. machine à é., typewriter.
écrit, *n.m.* written.
écriteau, *n.m.* notice.
écritoire, *n.f.* inkstand.
écriture, *n.f.* writing, scripture.
écrivain, *n.m.* writer.
écrou, *n.m.* nut.
écrouler, *vb.* s'é., fall to pieces.
écru, *adj.* natural, off-white.
écu, *n.m.* shield.
écueil, *n.m.* reef; pitfall.
écuelle, *n.f.* bowl, dish.
écume, *n.f.* lather, foam.
œcuménique, *adj.* ecumenical.
écureuil, *n.m.* squirrel.
écurie, *n.f.* stable.

écusson, *n.m.* escutcheon.

écuyer (-kwé-), *n.m.* squire.

édenté, *adj.* toothless.

édifice, *n.m.* building.

édifier, *vb.* build; edify.

édit, *n.m.* edict.

éditer, *vb.* publish.

éditeur, *n.m.* publisher.

édition, *n.f.* edition, publishing.

éditorial, *adj.* editorial.

éducateur, *n.m.* educator.

éducation, *n.f.* breeding, education.

éduquer, *vb.* educate, train.

effacer, *vb.* erase, efface.

effarant, *adj.* alarming.

effarer, *vb.* alarm.

effectif, *adj.* effective, actual.

effectivement, *adv.* effectively.

effectuer, *vb.* effect.

efféminé, *adj.* effeminate.

effet, *n.m.* effect; (*pl.*) belongings. **en e.,** as a matter of fact, indeed.

efficace, *adj.* effective.

efficacité, *n.f.* efficacy.

effigie, *n.f.* effigy.

effleurer, *vb.* skim, graze.

effluves, *n.m.pl.* exhalations.

effondrement, *n.m.* collapse.

effondrer, *vb.* s'e., collapse, sink.

efforcer, *vb.* s'e., endeavor, try hard.

effort, *n.m.* endeavor, strain, exertion, effort.

effrayant, *adj.* fearful.

effrayer, *vb.* frighten, scare, startle.

effréné, *adj.* unrestrained; frantic.

effriter, *vb.* s'e., crumble.

effroi, *n.m.* fright.

effronté, *adj.* brazen.

effronterie, *n.f.* effrontery.

effroyable, *adj.* appalling.

effusion, *n.f.* shedding.

égal, *adj.* even, equal, same.

également, *adv.* equally.

égaler, *vb.* equal.

égaliser, *vb.* equalize.

égalité, *n.f.* equality, evenness.

égard, *n.m.* regard, consideration, esteem. **à l'é. de,** as for. **plein d'é.s,** considerate.

égaré, *adj.* astray.

égarement, *n.m.* aberration.

égarer, *vb.* mislay, bewilder. **s'é.,** go astray, get lost.

égayer, *vb.* cheer up.

église, *n.f.* church.

égoïsme, *n.m.* selfishness, egoism.

égoïste, *adj.* selfish.

égorger, *vb.* kill.

égotisme, *n.m.* egotism.

égout, *n.m.* sewer.

égoutter, *vb.* drain; drip.

égratigner, *vb.* scratch.

égratignure, *n.f.* scratch.

Égypte, *n.m.* Egypt.

Égyptien, *n.m.* Egyptian.

égyptien, *adj.* Egyptian.

éhonté, *adj.* brazen, shameless.

éjecter, *vb.* eject.

élaboration, *n.f.* working out, elaboration; data processing.

élaborer, *vb.* draft, elaborate.

élan, *n.m.* elk; zest.

élancé, *adj.* slim.

élancer, *vb.* s'é., dash.

élargir, *vb.* widen, increase, enlarge.

élasticité, *n.f.* elasticity.

élastique, *adj. and n.m.* elastic.

électeur, *n.m.* voter.

électif, *adj.* elective.

élection, *n.f.* election.

électoral, *adj.* electoral.

électricien, *n.m.* electrician.

électricité, *n.f.* electricity.

électrique, *adj.* electric, electrical.

électrocardiogramme, *n. m.* electrocardiogram.

électrochoc, *n.m.* electric shock treatment.

électrocuter, *vb.* electrocute.

électroménager, *adj.* **appareils é.s,** household appliances.

électron, *n.m.* electron.

électronique, *adj.* electronic.

électrophone, *n.m.* record-player.

élégance, *n.f.* elegance.

élégant, *adj.* elegant, smart, stylish.

élégie, *n.f.* elegy.

élément, *n.m.* element.

élémentaire, *adj.* elementary.

éléphant, *n.m.* elephant.

élevage, *n.m.* breeding.

élévation, *n.f.* elevation.

élève, *n.m.f.* pupil.

élevé, *adj.* lofty.

élever, *vb.* raise. **s'é.**, arise; soar.

éleveur, *n.m.* breeder.

élider, *vb.* elide.

éligibilité, *n.f.* eligibility.

éligible, *adj.* eligible.

élimination, *n.f.* elimination.

éliminer, *vb.* eliminate.

élire, *vb.* elect.

élite, *n.f.* elite.

elle, *pron.f.* she, her; (*pl.*) they, them (*f.*).

elle-même, *pron.* herself.

ellipse, *n.m.* ellipse.

élocution, *n.f.* elocution.

éloge, *n.m.* praise.

éloigné, *adj.* remote.

éloignement, *n.m.* distance.

éloigner, *vb.* take away. **s'é.**, go away, recede.

élongation, *n.f.* pulled muscle.

éloquence, *n.f.* eloquence.

éloquent, *adj.* eloquent.

élu, *adj.* chosen.

éluder, *vb.* evade, elude.

émacié, *adj.* emaciated.

émail, *n.m.* enamel.

émancipation, *n.f.* emancipation.

émanciper, *vb.* emancipate.

émaner, *vb.* emanate.

emballage, *n.m.* wrapping.

emballer, *vb.* pack.

embarcadère, *n.m.* wharf.

embarcation, *n.f.* craft.

embargo, *n.m.* embargo.

embarquement, *n.m.* loading, boarding.

embarquer, *vb.* embark.

embarras, *n.m.* embarrassment; trouble, fix.

embarrassant, *adj.* embarrassing, awkward.

embarrasser, *vb.* embarrass.

embaucher, *vb.* hire.

embaumé, *adj.* balmy.

embaumer, *vb.* perfume; embalm.

embellir, *vb.* beautify.

embêter, *vb.* bore, irritate.

emblème, *n.m.* emblem.

embolie, *n.f.* embolism.

embouchure, *n.f.* mouth.

embourber, *vb.* bog.

embouteillage, *n.m.* traffic jam.

embranchement, *n.m.* junction.

embrasser, *vb.* embrace, kiss.

embrayage, *n.m.* clutch.

embrayer, *vb.* let in the clutch.

embrouillement, *n.m.* tangle, mix-up.

embrouiller, *vb.* perplex; entangle.

embrun, *n.m.* spray.

embuscade, *n.f.* ambush.

émeraude, *n.f.* emerald.

émerger, *vb.* emerge.

émerveiller, *vb.* astonish.

émetteur, *n.m.* transmitter.

émettre, *vb.* emit, send forth, issue.

émeute, *n.f.* riot.

émietter, *vb.* crumble.

émigrant, *n.m.* emigrant.

émigration, *n.f.* emigration.

émigré, *n.m.* political exile.

émigrer, *vb.* (e)migrate.

émincer, *vb.* cut into thin slices.

éminemment, *adv.* eminently.

éminence, *n.f.* eminence.

éminent, *adj.* eminent.

émission, *n.f.* issue.

emmagasinage, *n.m.* storage.

emmagasiner, *vb.* store.

emmener, *vb.* take away.

émoi, *n.m.* commotion.

émotif, *adj.* emotional.

émotion, *n.f.* emotion, feeling.

émoussé, *adj.* blunt.

émouvant, *adj.* moving.

émouvoir, *vb.* move.

empailler, *vb.* stuff.

empaler, *vb.* impale.

empan, *n.m.* span.

emparer, *vb.* **s'e. de**, take possession of.

empêchement, *n.m.* prevention.

empêcher, *vb.* prevent, stop, hinder, inhibit.

empereur, *n.m.* emperor.

empester, *vb.* stink.

empêtrer, *vb.* entangle.

emphase, *n.f.* emphasis.

emphatique, *adj.* emphatic.

empiéter, *vb.* encroach, trespass.

empire, *n.m.* empire.

empirer, *vb.* worsen.

empirique, *adj.* empirical.

emplette, *n.f.* purchase. **faire des e.s**, shop.

emplir, *vb.* fill.

emploi, *n.m.* employment, use; job.

employé, *n.m.* employee, clerk, (public) servant.
employer, *vb.* employ, use.
employeur, *n.m.* employer.
empoigner, *vb.* grab.
empois, *n.m.* starch.
empoisonné, *adj.* poisonous.
empoisonner, *vb.* poison.
emporter, *vb.* take away. s'e., get angry.
empreinte, *n.f.* print, impression.
empressé, *adj.* solicitous.
empressement, *n.m.* eagerness.
empresser, *vb.* s'e., be eager.
emprise, *n.f.* expropriation; influence.
emprisonnement, *n.m.* imprisonment.
emprisonner, *vb.* imprison.
emprunt, *n.m.* loan.
emprunter, *vb.* borrow from.
emprunteur, *n.m.* borrower.
ému, *adj.* touched, stirred.
émule, *n.* rival, competitor.
émulsion, *n.f.* lotion.
en, 1. *prep.* in, into. 2. *adv.* thence; of it; some, any.
encadrer, *vb.* frame.
encaisser, *vb.* cash; tolerate.
en-cas, *n.m.* reserve.
enceinte, *adj.f.* pregnant.
encens, *n.m.* incense.
enchaîner, *vb.* chain.
enchantement, *n.m.* enchantment.
enchanter, *vb.* delight, charm, enchant.
enchère, *n.f.* bid. **vente aux e.s,** auction.
enclore, *vb.* fence in, enclose.
enclos, 1. *n.m.* enclosure, 2. *adj.* shut in.
enclume, *n.f.* anvil.
encoche, *n.f.* notch.
encoignure, *n.f.* corner.
encoller, *vb.* paste.
encombrant, *adj.* cumbersome.
encombré, *adj.* crowded.
encombrement, *n.m.* congestion.
encombrer, *vb.* crowd, clutter, block up.
encontre, *adv.* à l'e., toward, counter (to).
encore, *adv.* still, yet, again.
encourageant, *adj.* encouraging.

encouragement, *n.m.* encouragement.
encourager, *vb.* encourage, urge, promote.
encourir, *vb.* incur.
encre, *n.f.* ink.
encrier, *n.m.* inkwell.
encyclopédie, *n.f.* encyclopedia.
endetté, *adj.* indebted.
endiguer, *vb.* dam up.
endimanché, *adj.* in one's Sunday best.
endive, *n.f.* endive, chicory.
endocrinologie, *n.f.* endocrinology.
endolori, *adj.* painful.
endommager, *vb.* damage.
endormi, *adj.* asleep.
endormir, *vb.* put to sleep. s'e., go to sleep.
endossement, *n.m.* endorsement.
endosser, *vb.* endorse; shoulder.
endroit, *n.m.* place.
enduire, *vb.* smear, daub.
endurance, *n.f.* endurance.
endurant, *adj.* patient.
endurcir, *vb.* harden.
endurcissement, *n.m.* hardening.
énergie, *n.f.* energy.
énergique, *adj.* energetic.
énervant, *adj.* enervating.
énervé, *adj.* nervous.
énerver, *vb.* irritate.
enfance, *n.f.* childhood. **première e.,** infancy.
enfant, *n.m.f.* child.
enfantement, *n.m.* childbirth.
enfanter, *vb.* bear (children).
enfantillage, *n.m.* childishness.
enfantin, *adj.* childish.
enfariner, *vb.* coat with flour.
enfer (-r), *n.m.* hell.
enfermer, *vb.* shut in.
enfiévrer, *vb.* excite, inspire.
enfin, *adv.* finally, at last.
enflammer, *vb.* inflame.
enfler, *vb.* swell.
enflure, *n.f.* swelling.
enfoncer, *vb.* sink.
enfouir, *vb.* bury.
enfourchure, *n.f.* bifurcation; crotch of a tree.
enfreindre, *vb.* violate.
enfuir, *vb.* s'e., run away, flee, elope.

enfumer, *vb.* fill or cover with smoke.

engagé, *adj.* committed.

engageant, *adj.* personable, charming.

engagement, *n.m.* pledge, agreement, engagement.

engager, *vb.* hire, engage. s'e., volunteer.

engelure, *n.f.* chilblain.

engendrer, *vb.* beget.

engin, *n.m.* machine; engine, motor.

englober, *vb.* include.

engloutir, *vb.* devour.

engorgement, *n.m.* choking.

engouement, *n.m.* infatuation.

engouffrer, *vb.* engulf.

engourdir, *vb.* dull.

engrais, *n.m.* fertilizer.

engraisser, *vb.* fatten.

engraver, *vb.* strand or ground (a ship).

engrenage, *n.m.* gear.

engrener, *vb.* engage (gears).

engueuler, *vb.* (colloquial) bawl out.

enhardir, *vb.* make bolder.

enième, *adj.* (colloquial) umpteenth.

énigmatique, *adj.* enigmatic.

énigme, *n.f.* riddle, puzzle, enigma.

enivrant, *adj.* intoxicating.

enivrement, *n.m.* intoxication.

enivrer, *vb.* intoxicate. s'e., get drunk.

enjambée, *n.f.* stride.

enjamber, *vb.* stride.

enjeu, *n.m.* stake.

enjoindre, *vb.* enjoin; call upon.

enjôlement, *n.m.* cajolery.

enjôler, *vb.* cajole.

enjoliver, *vb.* beautify.

enjoué, *adj.* playful.

enjouement, *n.m.* playfulness.

enlacer, *vb.* entwine; interlace; embrace.

enlaidir, *vb.* make or become ugly.

enlevable, *adj.* detachable.

enlèvement, *n.m.* removal, abduction.

enlever, *vb.* take away, remove, abduct.

enliser, *vb.* s'e., sink.

enneigé, *adj.* snow-covered.

ennemi, *adj. and n.m.* enemy.

ennoblir, *vb.* exalt; ennoble.

ennui (-nwē), *n.m.* nuisance, bore, bother; boredom.

ennuyer, *vb.* bore, annoy, vex, bother, irk.

ennuyeux, *adj.* boring, tedious, dull.

énoncer, *vb.* enunciate.

énonciation, *n.f.* enunciation.

énorme, *adj.* enormous.

énormité, *n.f.* enormity.

enquérir, *vb.* inquire.

enquête, *n.f.* inquiry.

enquiquiner, *vb.* irritate.

enraciner, *vb.* root. s'e., take root.

enragé, *adj.* rabid.

enrageant, *adj.* infuriating.

enrager, *vb.* be, go mad. s'e., get angry.

enregistrement, *n.m.* registration, recording; checking.

enregistrer, *vb.* record, register, list; check (luggage).

enrhumer, *vb.* s'e., catch a cold.

enrichir, *vb.* enrich.

enrober, *vb.* coat, envelop.

enrôlement, *n.m.* enlistment, enrollment.

enrôler, *vb.* enlist, enroll.

enroué, *adj.* hoarse.

enrouement, *n.m.* hoarseness.

enrouler, *vb.* s'e., roll up, twist, wind.

enseignant, *n.m.* teacher.

enseigne, *n.f.* sign, ensign.

enseignement, *n.m.* teaching, instruction.

enseigner, *vb.* teach.

ensemble, 1. *n.m.* set. **2.** *adv.* together.

ensevelir, *vb.* bury.

ensoleillé, *adj.* sunny.

ensommeillé, *adj.* sleepy.

ensorceler, *vb.* bewitch.

ensuite, *adv.* then, next, afterwards.

ensuivre, *vb.* s'e., ensue.

entablement, *n.m.* entablature.

entacher, *vb.* taint, besmirch.

entailler, *vb.* hack (notch).

entamer, *vb.* begin.

entassement, *n.m.* accumulation.

entasser, *vb.* heap up.

ente, *n.f.* scion (horticulture).
entendement, *n.m.* understanding, sense.
entendre, *vb.* hear; understand. **s'e.,** get on together.
entendu, *adj.* understood, agreed. **bien e.,** of course.
enténébré, *adj.* gloomy.
entente, *n.f.* understanding, agreement.
entériner, *vb.* ratify.
enterrement, *n.m.* burial.
enterrer, *vb.* bury.
entêté, *adj.* perverse.
entêtement, *n.m.* stubbornness.
entêter, s'e., be stubborn, insist.
enthousiasme, *n.m.* enthusiasm.
enthousiaste, 1. *n.m.f.* enthusiast. **2.** *adj.* enthusiastic. **e. de,** keen on.
entichement, *n.m.* infatuation.
entier, *adj.* whole, complete, entire.
entité, *n.f.* entity.
entonner, *vb.* start to sing.
entonnoir, *n.m.* funnel.
entorse, *n.f.* sprain.
entourage, *n.m.* circle of friends; surroundings.
entourer, *vb.* surround, encircle.
entournure, *n.f.* armhole.
entr'acte, *n.m.* intermission.
entr'aide, *n.f.* mutual assistance.
entrailles, *n.f.pl.* bowels.
entrain, *n.m.* zest.
entraînant, *adj.* rousing.
entraîner, *vb.* draw along; involve, entail; coach, train.
entraîneur, *n.m.* coach.
entrant, *adj.* incoming.
entrave, *n.f.* obstacle.
entraver, *vb.* clog.
entre, *prep.* among, between.
entre-clos, *adj.* ajar.
entre-deux, *n.m.* interval.
entrée, *n.f.* admission, entry; main course.
entreface, *n.f.* interface.
entregent, *n.m.* tact; spirit.
entrelacer, *vb.* interlace.
entremets (-mě), *n.m.* (side) dish; dessert.
entremetteur, *n.m.* intermediary.
entreposer, *vb.* store.
entreposeur, *n.m.* warehouseman.

entrepôt, *n.m.* warehouse.
entreprenant, *adj.* enterprising.
entreprendre, *vb.* undertake.
entrepreneur, *n.m.* contractor. **e. de pompes funèbres,** undertaker.
entreprise, *n.f.* concern, undertaking.
entrer (dans), *vb.* enter, come in, go in. **laisser e.,** admit.
entretenir, *vb.* entertain. **s'e.,** converse.
entretien, *n.m.* maintenance; conference; talk, conversation.
entrevoir, *vb.* glimpse.
entrevue, *n.f.* interview.
entr'ouvert, *adj.* ajar.
entr'ouvrir, *vb.* open halfway.
énumération, *n.f.* enumeration.
énumérer, *vb.* enumerate.
envahir, *vb.* invade.
envahissement, *n.m.* invasion.
enveloppe, *n.f.* envelope; wrapping.
envelopper, *vb.* envelop, wrap, enfold.
envergure, *n.f.* scope.
envers, 1. *n.m.* wrong side. **2.** *prep.* toward.
enviable, *adj.* enviable.
envie, *n.f.* envy, desire. **avoir e. de,** want, feel like.
envier, *vb.* envy.
envieux, *adj.* envious.
environ, *prep. and adv.* around, about; approximately.
environnement, *n.m.* surroundings.
environnementaliste, *n.m.f.* environmentalist.
environner, *vb.* surround.
environs, *n.m.pl.* surroundings.
envisager, *vb.* consider.
envol, *n.m.* shipment, sending.
envoler, s'e., fly away.
envoûter, *vb.* bewitch.
envoyé, *n.m.* envoy.
envoyer, *vb.* send.
enzyme, *n.f.* enzyme.
éon, *n.m.* con.
épais, *adj.* thick.
épaisseur, *n.f.* thickness.
épaissir, *vb.* thicken.
épancher, *vb.* shed (blood).
épanouir, *vb.* s'é., bloom.
épargne, *n.f.* savings.

épargner, vb. save, spare.

éparpiller, vb. scatter.

épars, adj. scattered, sparse.

éparvin, n.m. spavin.

épatant, adj. (colloq.) grand.

épate, n.f. swagger.

épatement, n.m. amazement.

épater, vb. amaze.

épaule, n.f. shoulder.

épaulette, n.f. epaulette.

épave, n.f. wreck.

épée, n.f. sword.

épeler, vb. spell.

épellation, n.f. spelling.

éperdu, adj. distracted.

éperlan, n.m. smelt.

éperon, n.m. spur.

éperonner, vb. spur.

épervier, n.m. hawk.

épeuré, adj. frightened.

éphémère, adj. ephemeral, fleeting.

épice, n.f. spice.

épicé, adj. spicy.

épicerie, n.f. grocery.

épicier, n.m. grocer.

épidémie, n.f. epidemic.

épiderme, n.m. epidermis.

épidermique, adj. epidermal.

épier, vb. spy.

épigramme, n.f. epigram.

épilatoire, adj. and n.m. depilatory.

épilepsie, n.f. epilepsy.

épileptique, adj. and n.m.f. epileptic.

épilogue, n.m. epilogue.

épinards (-nár), n.m.pl. spinach.

épine, n.f. spine, thorn. **é. dorsale,** spinal column.

épinet, n.f. spinet.

épineux, adj. thorny.

épingle, n.f. pin. **é. à cheveux,** hairpin. **é. anglaise,** safety pin.

épingler, vb. pin.

épique, adj. epic.

épiscopal, adj. Episcopal.

épisode, n.m. episode.

épisodique, adj. episodic.

épistolaire, adj. epistolary.

épitaphe, n.f. epitaph.

épithète, n.f. epithet.

épitomé, n.m. epitome.

épitre, n.f. epistle.

éploré, adj. tearful.

épluche-légumes, n.m. (potato) peeler.

éplucher, vb. peel.

épointé, adj. dull, blunted.

éponge, n.f. sponge.

éponger, vb. sponge up.

épopée, n.f. epic.

époque, n.f. epoch.

épouffé, adj. breathless, panting.

épouiller, vb. delouse.

épouse, n.f. wife.

épouser, vb. marry.

épouseur, n.m. suitor.

épousseter, vb. dust.

époussette, n.f. duster.

époustouflant, adj. staggering.

épouvantable, adj. terrible.

épouvante, n.f. fright.

épouvanter, vb. frighten.

époux, n.m. husband.

épreindre, vb. squeeze.

éprendre, vb. s'é., fall in love.

épreuve, n.f. trial, test; ordeal; proof.

éprouver, vb. experience.

éprouvette, n.f. test tube.

épuisant, adj. exhausting.

épuisement, n.m. exhaustion.

épuiser, vb. exhaust.

épuration, n.f. purification.

épurer, vb. purify.

équanimité (-kwá-), n.f. equanimity.

équateur (-kwá-), n.m. equator.

équation (-kwá-), n.f. equation.

équatorial (-kwá-), adj. equatorial.

équestre, adj. equestrian.

équidistant, adj. equidistant.

équilibre, n.m. poise.

équilibrer, vb. balance.

équilibriste, n. tightrope walker.

équinoxe, n.m. equinox.

équinoxial, adj. equinoctial.

équipage, n.m. crew.

équipe, n.f. team, crew, gang; shift.

équipement, n.m. equipment.

équiper, vb. equip.

équipier, n.m. team member.

équitable, adj. fair.

équitation, n.f. (horse) riding.

équité, n.f. equity.

équivalent, adj. and n.m. equivalent.

équivaloir, vb. equal in value.

équivoque, adj. equivocal.

érable, n.m. maple.
éradication, n.f. eradication.
éraflure, n.m. scratch; graze.
érailler, vb. unravel.
ère, n.f. era.
érection, n.f. erection; construction.
éreintant, adj. exhausting.
éreinter, vb. exhaust.
erg, n.m. erg.
ergoter, vb. quibble.
ériger, vb. erect.
ermitage, n.m. hermitage.
ermite, n.m. hermit.
éroder, vb. erode.
érosif, adj. erosive.
érosion, n.f. erosion.
érotique, adj. erotic.
errant, adj. wandering.
erratique, adj. erratic.
errer, vb. wander; err.
erreur, n.f. mistake, error.
erroné, adj. erroneous.
éructation, n.f. belch.
éructer, vb. belch.
érudit, adj. learned, scholarly.
érudition, n.f. learning.
éruption, n.f. rash, eruption.
érysipèle, n.m. erysipelas.
escabeau, n.m. stool.
escadrille, n.f. (ships) flotilla; (airplanes) squadron.
escadron, n.m. squadron.
escalade, n.f. climbing; escalation.
escalader, vb. scale; escalate.
escalator, n.m. escalator.
escale, n.f. stopover.
escalier, n.m. stairs.
escalope, n.f. cutlet.
escamotage, n.m. legerdemain.
escamoter, vb. evade, get around.
escamoteur, n.m. conjurer, magician.
escapade, n.f. escapade.
escarcelle, n.f. wallet.
escargot, n.m. snail.
escarmouche, n.f. skirmish.
escarole, n.f. chicory, endive.
escarpé, adj. abrupt.
escarpement, n.m. steepness.
eschare, n.f. scab; bedsore.
esclandre, n.m. slander.
esclavage, n.m. slavery.
esclave, n.m. slave.
escompte, n.m. discount.

escorte, n.f. escort.
escorter, vb. escort.
escouade, n.f. squad.
escrime, n.f. fencing.
escrimer, vb. fight.
escrimeur, n.m. swordsman.
escroc (-ō), n.m. swindler.
escroquer, vb. swindle.
escroquerie, n.f. swindle.
esculent, adj. esculent.
espace, n.m. space.
espacé, adj. at great intervals.
espacer, vb. space out.
espadon, n.m. swordfish.
espadrille, n.f. rope sandal.
Espagne, n.f. Spain.
Espagnol, n.m. Spaniard.
espagnol, adj. and n.m. Spanish.
espalier, n.m. espalier.
espèce, n.f. species, kind; (pl.) cash.
espérance, n.f. hope.
espéranto, n.m. Esperanto.
espérer, vb. hope.
espiègle, adj. mischievous.
espièglerie, n.f. mischief.
espion, n.m. spy.
espionnage, n.m. espionage.
espionner, vb. spy on.
esplanade, n.f. esplanade.
espoir, n.m. hope.
esprit, n.m. spirit, mind, wit. Saint-E., Holy Ghost.
esquif, n.m. skiff.
Esquimau, m., **Esquimaude**, f. n. Eskimo.
esquimau, adj. Eskimo.
esquinancie, n.m. quinsy.
esquinter, vb. exhaust, tire out.
esquisse, n.f. sketch.
esquisser, vb. sketch.
esquiver, vb. dodge.
essai, n.m. essay; attempt; experiment; assay.
essaim, n.m. swarm.
essaimer, vb. swarm.
essayer, vb. try; assay.
essence, n.f. gasoline; essence.
essentiel, adj. essential.
esseulement, n.m. solitude.
essieu, n.m. axle.
essor, n.m. flight; rapid expansion.
essorer, vb. dry.
essoufflé, adj. breathless.

essoufflement, *n.m.* breathlessness.

essuie-glace, *n.m.* windshield wiper.

essuyer, *vb.* wipe.

est (-t), *n.m.* east.

estacade, *n.f.* stockade.

estafette, *n.f.* courier.

estafier, *n.m.* bodyguard.

estagnon, *n.m.* oil drum.

estaminet, *n.m.* bar, taproom.

estampe, *n.f.* engraving.

estampille, *n.f.* trademark.

esthète, *n.m.* esthete.

esthéticienne, *n.f.* beautician.

esthétique, *adj.* aesthetic.

estimable, *adj.* estimable.

estimateur, *n.m.* estimator; appraiser.

estimatif, *adj.* estimated.

estimation, *n.f.* estimate.

estime, *n.f.* esteem; estimation.

estimer, *vb.* esteem; estimate, value, rate.

estival, *adj.* of summer.

estivant, *n.m.* summer tourist.

estiver, *vb.* spend the summer.

estoc, *n.m.* tree trunk.

estomac (mä), *n.m.* stomach.

estomper, *vb.* blur. **s'e.,** soften, become blurred.

estourbir, *vb.* kill.

estrade, *n.f.* platform; stage.

estragon, *n.m.* tarragon.

estropié, 1. *n.m.* cripple. **2.** *adj.* crippled.

estropier, *vb.* cripple.

estuaire, *n.m.* estuary.

estudiantin, *adj.* student.

esturgeon, *n.m.* sturgeon.

et, *conj.* and.

étable, *n.f.* barn.

établi, *n.m.* worktable.

établir, *vb.* settle; establish.

établissement, *n.m.* establishment.

étage, *n.m.* floor, story.

étagère, *n.f.* whatnot shelf.

étain, *n.m.* tin.

étal, *n.m.* stall.

étalage, *n.m.* display.

étalager, *vb.* display.

étaler, *vb.* display; spread.

étalon, *n.m.* standard.

étameur, *n.m.* tinsmith.

étamine, *n.f.* coarse muslin; stamen.

étampe, *n.f.* stamp.

étamper, *vb.* stamp.

étanche, *adj.* impervious.

étancher, *vb.* quench; stanch.

étang, *n.m.* pond.

étape, *n.f.* stage.

état, *n.m.* state.

étatisé, *adj.* state-controlled.

état-major, *n.m.* staff.

États-Unis, *n.m.pl.* United States.

été, *n.m.* summer.

éteindre, *vb.* extinguish, put out.

éteint, *adj.* extinct.

étendage, *n.m.* clotheslines.

étendard, *n.m.* standard.

étendre, *vb.* extend, spread, reach.

étendu, *adj.* extensive.

étendue, *n.f.* extent.

éternel, *adj.* everlasting.

éterniser, *vb.* perpetuate.

éternité, *n.f.* eternity.

éternuement, *n.m.* sneeze.

éternuer, *vb.* sneeze.

éther (-r), *n.m.* ether.

éthéré, *adj.* ethereal.

Éthiopie, *n.f.* Ethiopia.

éthique, *n.f.* ethics.

ethnie, *n.f.* ethnic group.

ethnique, *adj.* ethnic.

étinceler, *vb.* sparkle.

étincelle, *n.f.* spark, sparkle.

étincellement, *n.m.* sparkle, glitter.

étiolement, *n.m.* atrophy.

étioler, *vb.* blanch.

étiqueter, *vb.* label.

étiquette, *n.f.* label, tag; etiquette.

étirer, *vb.* stretch out.

étoffe, *n.f.* stuff, material, cloth.

étoffer, *vb.* stuff.

étoile, *n.f.* star.

étoiler, *vb.* bespangle.

étonnement, *n.m.* astonishment.

étonner, *vb.* astonish.

étouffé, *adj.* braised.

étouffer, *vb.* smother.

étourderie, *n.f.* thoughtlessness.

étourdi, *adj.* thoughtless.

étourdir, *vb.* daze.

étourdissant, *adj.* dazing.

étourdissement, *n.m.* dizziness.

étrange, *adj.* strange.

étranger, *n.m. and adj.* alien.

étranglement, *n.m.* strangulation.
étrangler, *vb.* strangle.
étrave, *n.f.* stem, bow.
être, 1. *n.m.* being. 2. *vb.* be.
étrécir, *vb.* shrink.
étreindre, *vb.* clasp.
étreinte, *n.f.* clasp; hug, embrace.
étrier, *n.m.* stirrup.
étrille, *n.f.* currycomb.
étroit, *adj.* narrow.
Étrusque, *n.m.f.* Etruscan.
étrusque, *adj.* Etruscan.
étude, *n.f.* study.
étudiant, *n.m.* student.
étudier, *vb.* study.
étui, *n.m.* 1. case. 2. needle case.
étuve, *n.f.* steam room.
étymologie, *n.f.* etymology.
étymologique, *adj.* etymological.
eucalyptus, *n.m.* eucalyptus.
eucharistie, *n.f.* eucharist.
eunuque, *n.m.* eunuch.
euphémique, *adj.* euphemistic.
euphémisme, *n.m.* euphemism.
euphonie, *n.f.* euphony.
euphonique, *adj.* euphonic.
euphorie, *n.f.* euphoria.
Europe, *n.f.* Europe.
Européen, *n.m.* European.
européen, *adj.* European.
euthanasie, *n.f.* euthanasia.
eux, *pron. m.pl.* them.
évacuable, *adj.* able to be evacuated.
évacuation, *n.f.* evacuation.
évacuer, *vb.* evacuate.
évader, *vb.* s'é., escape.
évaluateur, *n.m.* appraiser.
évaluation, *n.f.* appraisal.
évaluer, *vb.* evaluate, rate, assess.
évangélique, *adj.* evangelic.
évangéliste, *n.m.* evangelist.
évangile, *n.m.* gospel.
évanouir, *vb.* s'é., fade away; faint.
évanouissement, *n.m.* fainting fit.
évaporation, *n.f.* evaporation.
évaporer, *vb.* evaporate.
évasif, *adj.* evasive.
évasion, *n.f.* escape.
évêché, *n.m.* bishopric.
éveil, *n.m.* alertness.
éveillé, *adj.* sprightly.
éveiller, *vb.* wake.
événement, *n.m.* event.
éventail, *n.m.* fan.

éventrer, *vb.* disembowel.
éventualité, *n.f.* possibility.
éventuel, *adj.* possible.
éventuellement, *adv.* possibly.
évêque, *n.m.* bishop.
éviction, *n.f.* eviction.
évidemment, *adv.* evidently.
évidence, *n.f.* evidence. en é., conspicuous.
évident, *adj.* obvious, evident.
évider, *vb.* scoop out.
évier, *n.m.* sink.
évincer, *vb.* oust.
éviscérer, *vb.* eviscerate, disembowel.
évitable, *adj.* avoidable.
éviter, *vb.* avoid.
évocateur, *adj.* evocative.
évocation, *n.f.* evocation.
évolué, *adj.* mature.
évolution, *n.f.* evolution.
évoquer, *vb.* evoke.
exact (-kt), *adj.* exact, precise.
exactement, *adv.* exactly.
exactitude, *n.f.* precision.
exagération, *n.f.* exaggeration.
exagéré, *adj.* excessive.
exagérer, *vb.* exaggerate.
exaltant, *adj.* exciting.
exaltation, *n.f.* exaltation.
exalté, *adj.* impassioned.
exalter, *vb.* exalt, elate.
examen, *n.m.* examination.
examiner, *vb.* examine.
exaspération, *n.f.* exasperation.
exaspérer, *vb.* exasperate, aggravate.
exaucer, *vb.* grant.
excavateur, *n.m.* steam shovel.
excavation, *n.f.* excavation.
excaver, *vb.* excavate.
excédent, *n.m.* excess; overweight.
excéder, *vb.* exceed.
excellence, *n.f.* excellence; excellency, highness.
excellent, *adj.* excellent.
exceller, *vb.* excel.
excentrique, *adj.* eccentric.
excepté, *prep.* except.
excepter, *vb.* except.
exception, *n.f.* exception.
exceptionnel, *adj.* exceptional.
excès, *n.m.* excess.
excessif, *adj.* excessive, extreme.
exciser, *vb.* excise; cut out.

excitabilité, *n.f.* excitability.
excitable, *adj.* excitable.
excitant, 1. *n.m.* stimulant. **2.** *adj.* stimulating.
exciter, *vb.* excite.
exclamatif, *adj.* exclamatory.
exclamation, *n.f.* exclamation.
exclamer, *vb.* exclaim.
exclure, *vb.* exclude.
exclusif, *adj.* exclusive.
exclusion, *n.f.* exclusion.
excommunication, *n.f.* excommunication.
excommunier, *vb.* excommunicate.
excorier, *vb.* excoriate.
excrément, *n.m.* excrement.
excréter, *vb.* excrete.
excrétion, *n.f.* excretion.
excroissance, *n.f.* (out)growth.
excursion, *n.f.* excursion.
excursionniste, *n.m.f.* excursionist.
excusable, *adj.* excusable.
excuse, *n.f.* plea; excuse.
excuser, *vb.* excuse. s'e. de, apologize for.
exécrable, *adj.* atrocious.
exécrer, *vb.* loathe.
exécuter, *vb.* perform; enforce.
exécuteur, *n.m.* executor.
exécutif, *adj. and n.m.* executive.
exécution, *n.f.* performance; enforcement; execution.
exemplaire, 1. *n.m.* copy. **2.** *adj.* exemplary.
exemple, *n.m.* instance, example.
exempt, *adj.* exempt.
exempt de droits, *adj.* duty-free.
exempter, *vb.* exempt.
exemption, *n.f.* exemption.
exerçant, *adj.* practicing.
exercer, *vb.* exercise; drill, train. s'e., practice.
exercice, *n.m.* exercise; drill, practice.
exhalation, *n.f.* exhalation.
exhaler, *vb.* exhale.
exhaustion, *n.f.* exhaust.
exhiber, *vb.* show, present; exhibit.
exhibition, *n.f.* exhibition.
exhortation, *n.f.* exhortation.
exhorter, *vb.* exhort.
exhumer, *vb.* exhume.
exigeant, *adj.* demanding.

exigence, *n.f.* requirement.
exiger, *vb.* require, exact, demand.
exigu, *m.* **exiguë** *f. adj.* tiny.
exil (-l), *n.m.* exile.
exilé, *n.m.* exile.
exiler, *vb.* banish.
existant, *adj.* existent.
existence, *n.f.* existence.
exister, *vb.* exist.
exode, *n.m.* exodus.
exonération, *n.f.* exoneration.
exonérer, *vb.* exonerate.
exorbitant, *adj.* exorbitant.
exorciser, *vb.* exorcise.
exotique, *adj.* exotic.
expansible, *adj.* expansible.
expansif, *adj.* expansive.
expansion, *n.f.* expansion.
expatriation, *n.f.* expatriation.
expatrié, *n.* exile, expatriate.
expectorant, *adj. and n.m.* expectorant.
expectorer, *vb.* expectorate.
expédient, *n.m.* makeshift.
expédier, *vb.* dispatch.
expéditif, *adj.* expeditious.
expédition, *n.f.* dispatch; expedition, shipment.
expérience, *n.f.* experience; experiment.
expérimental, *adj.* experimental.
expérimentation, *n.f.* experimentation.
expérimenté, *adj.* experienced.
expert, *adj. and n.m.* expert.
expiable, *adj.* expiable.
expiation, *n.f.* atonement.
expier, *vb.* atone for.
expiration, *n.f.* expiration.
expirer, *vb.* expire.
explétif, *n.m. and adj.* expletive.
explicatif, *adj.* explanatory.
explication, *n.f.* explanation.
explicite, *adj.* explicit, clear.
expliquer, *vb.* explain.
exploit, *n.m.* feat, exploit.
exploitation, *n.f.* exploitation; working.
exploiter, *vb.* exploit.
explorateur, *n.m.* explorer.
exploratif, *adj.* exploratory.
exploration, *n.f.* exploration.
explorer, *vb.* explore.
exploser, *vb.* explode.
explosible, *adj.* explosive.

explosif, *adj. and n.m.* explosive.

explosion, *n.f.* blast, explosion.

exportation, *n.f.* export, exportation.

exporter, *vb.* export.

exposé, *n.m.* account, statement.

exposer, *vb.* expound; expose; exhibit.

exposition, *n.f.* exposition; exposure; show, display.

exprès, 1. *n.m.* special delivery. **2.** *adj.* express. **3.** *adv.* on purpose.

express, *n.m.* espresso.

expressif, *adj.* expressive.

expression, *n.f.* expression.

exprimable, *adj.* expressible.

exprimer, *vb.* express.

exproprier, *vb.* expropriate.

expulser, *vb.* expel.

expulsion, *n.f.* expulsion.

expurgation, *n.f.* expurgation.

expurger, *vb.* expurgate.

exquis, *adj.* exquisite.

exsangue, *adj.* bloodless.

exsuder, *vb.* exude.

extase, *n.f.* ecstasy.

extasier, *vb.* **s'e. sur,** rave about.

extatique, *adj.* ecstatic.

extensif, *adj.* extensive.

extension, *n.f.* extension.

exténuation, *n.f.* extenuation.

exténuer, *vb.* extenuate, exhaust.

extérieur, 1. *n.m.* exterior. **2.** *adj.* exterior, outer.

extérieurement, *adv.* externally.

extermination, *n.f.* extermination.

exterminer, *vb.* exterminate.

externat, *n.m.* day school.

externe, *adj.* external.

exterritorialité, *n.f.* extraterritoriality.

extincteur, *n.m.* fire extinguisher.

extinction, *n.f.* extinction.

extirper, *vb.* extirpate, root out.

extorquer, *vb.* extort.

extorsion, *n.f.* extortion.

extra, *adj.* first-rate.

extra-, *prefix* extra.

extraction, *n.f.* extraction; descent.

extrader, *vb.* extradite.

extradition, *n.f.* extradition.

extra-fin, *adj.* extremely fine.

extraire, *vb.* extract.

extrait, *n.m.* extract; abstract.

extraordinaire, *adj.* extraordinary, unusual.

extraordinairement, *adv.* extraordinarily.

extravagance, *n.f.* extravagance.

extravagant, *adj.* extravagant.

extraverti, *n.m.* extrovert.

extrême, *adj. and n.m.* extreme.

extrémiste, *n.m.f.* extremist.

extrémité, *n.f.* extremity.

extrinsèque, *adj.* extrinsic.

extroverti, *n.m.* extrovert.

extrusion, *n.f.* extrusion.

exubérance, *n.f.* exuberance.

exubérant, *adj.* exuberant.

exultation, *n.f.* exultation.

exulter, *vb.* exult.

F

fable, *n.f.* fable.

fabliau, *n.m.* fabliau.

fabricant, *n.m.* maker, manufacturer.

fabricateur, *n.m.* forger.

fabrication, *n.f.* make.

fabrique, *n.f.* factory.

fabriquer, *vb.* manufacture.

fabuleux, *adj.* fabulous.

fabuliste, *n.m.* fabulist.

fac, *n.f.* (colloquial) university.

façade, *n.f.* front.

face, *n.f.* face. **en f. de,** opposite. **faire f. à,** confront.

facétie, *n.f.* joke, prank.

facétieux, *adj.* facetious.

facette, *n.f.* facet.

fâché, *adj.* angry; sorry.

fâcher, *vb.* anger, offend; grieve. **se f.,** get angry.

fâcherie, *n.f.* quarrel, argument.

fâcheux, *adj.* upleasant.

facial, *adj.* facial.

facile, *adj.* easy.

facilité, *n.f.* fluency; ease.

faciliter, *vb.* facilitate, make easy.

façon, *n.f.* way, manner, fashion. **de f. à,** so as to.

faconde, *n.f.* glibness; fluency.

façonner, *vb.* shape, fashion.

facsimilé, *n.m.* facsimile.

facteur, *n.m.* factor, element; mail carrier.

factice, *adj.* artificial.

factieux, *adj.* factious; quarrelsome.

faction, *n.f.* faction, party.

factionnaire, *n.m.* sentry.

facture, *n.f.* invoice, bill.

facturer, *vb.* bill; send an invoice to.

facultatif, *adj.* optional.

faculté, *n.f.* faculty.

fadaise, *n.f.* nonsense.

fade, *adj.* insipid.

fadeur, *n.f.* insipidity.

fagot, *n.m.* bundle.

faible, *adj.* weak, faint, dim, feeble.

faiblement, *adv.* feebly, weakly.

faiblesse, *n.f.* weakness, frailty; dimness.

faiblir, *vb.* weaken.

faïence, *n.f.* earthenware.

faille, *n.f.* fault.

failli, *adj. and n.m.* bankrupt.

faillibilité, *n.f.* fallibility.

faillible, *adj.* fallible.

faillir, *vb.* fail.

faillite, *n.f.* bankruptcy.

faim, *n.f.* hunger.

fainéant, *n.m.* loafer.

faire, *vb.* make, do. **f. part,** inform. **f. mal à,** hurt. **f. voir,** show.

faire-part, *n.m.* announcement.

faisable, *adj.* feasible.

faisan, *n.m.* pheasant.

faisceau, *n.m.* bundle; beam.

fait, *n.m.* fact. **tout à f.,** wholly.

falaise, *n.f.* cliff.

fallacieux, *adj.* fallacious.

falloir, *vb.* be necessary. **comme il faut,** decent.

falot, *n.m.* lamp.

falsificateur, *n.* forger; falsifier.

falsification, *n.f.* falsification.

falsifier, *vb.* falsify.

famélique, *adj.* starving.

fameux, *adj.* famous.

familial, *adj.* family.

familiariser, *vb.* familiarize.

familiarité, *n.f.* familiarity.

familier, *adj.* familiar.

familièrement, *adv.* familiarly.

famille, *n.f.* family, household.

famine, *n.f.* famine.

fanatique, *adj. and n.m.f.* fanatic.

fanatisme, *n.m.* fanaticism.

faner, *vb.* fade.

fanfare, *n.f.* fanfare.

fanfaronnade, *n.f.* boast.

fange, *n.f.* filth; vice.

fantaisie, *n.f.* fancy, fantasy.

fantaisiste, *adj.* eccentric.

fantasme, *n.m.* fantasy.

fantastique, *adj.* fantastic.

fantoche, *n.m.* puppet.

fantôme, *n.m.* phantom, ghost; joke.

faon, *n.m.* fawn.

faramineux, *adj.* phenomenal.

farce, *n.f.* stuffing; farce.

farceur, *n.m.* jokester.

farcir, *vb.* stuff.

fard, *n.m.* facial makeup.

fardeau, *n.m.* burden.

farfelu, *adj.* weird.

farinacé, *adj.* farinaceous.

farine, *n.f.* meal, flour.

farniente, *n.m.* idleness.

farouche, *adj.* fierce; sullen, shy.

fascinant, *adj.* fascinating.

fascination, *n.f.* fascination.

fascine, *n.f.* faggot (of wood).

fasciner, *vb.* fascinate.

fascisme, *n.m.* fascism.

fasciste, *n.m.f.* fascist.

faste, *n.m.* ostentation.

fast-food, *n.m.* fast-food establishment.

fastidieux, *adj.* dull.

fat, *adj.* foppish.

fatal, *adj.* mortal, fatal.

fatalisme, *n.m.* fatalism.

fataliste, *n.m.f.* fatalist.

fatalité, *n.f.* fatality; misfortune.

fatidique, *adj.* fateful.

fatigant, *adj.* tiring.

fatigue, *n.f.* weariness.

fatiguer, *vb.* tire.

fatuité, *n.f.* smugness.

faubourg, *n.m.* suburb.

faubourien, *adj.* suburban.

fauché, *adj.* broke.

faucher, *vb.* mow.

faucheur, *n.m.* reaper, mower.

faucille, *n.f.* sickle.

faucon, *n.m.* hawk.

fauconneau, *n.m.* young falcon.

fauconnerie, *n.f.* falconry.

faufil, *n.m.* basting thread.
faufiler, *vb.* baste.
faune, *n.f.* fauna, wildlife.
faussaire, *n.m.f.* forger; liar.
faussement, *adv.* falsely.
fausser, *vb.* pervert, warp, distort.
fausset, *n.m.* falsetto; spigot, faucet.
fausseté, *n.f.* falseness.
faute, *n.f.* fault, mistake. **f. de,** for want of.
fauteuil, *n.m.* armchair.
fauteur, *n.m.* trouble-maker.
fautif, *adv.* faulty, wrong.
fauve, *adj.* wild.
faux, 1. *n.m.* forgery. **2.** *n.f.* scythe.
faux *m.,* **fausse** *f. adj.* false, wrong; spurious; counterfeit.
faux-filet, *n.m.* sirloin.
faveur, *n.f.* favor. **en f. de,** on behalf of.
favorable, *adj.* conducive, favorable.
favorablement, *adv.* favorably.
favori, *n.m.* whisker.
favori *m.,* **favorite** *f. adj. and n.* favorite.
favoriser, *vb.* favor.
favoritisme, *n.m.* favoritism.
fax, *n.m.* fax (machine).
faxer, *vb.* fax.
fayot, *n.m.* kidney bean.
féal, *adj.* faithful.
fébrile, *adj.* feverish.
fécal, *adj.* fecal.
fécond, *adj.* fertile.
féconder, *vb.* fertilize.
fécondité, *n.f.* fertility.
féculent, *adj.* starchy.
fédéral, *adj.* federal.
fédéraliser, *vb.* federalize.
fédéraliste, *n.m.f. and adj.* federalist.
fédération, *n.f.* confederacy, federation.
fédérer, *vb.* federate.
fée, *n.f.* fairy.
féerie, *n.f.* fairyland.
féerique, *adj.* fairylike.
feindre, *vb.* feign, pretend.
feinte, *n.f.* feint.
fêler, *vb.* crack.
félicitation, *n.f.* congratulation.
félicité, *n.f.* bliss.
féliciter, *vb.* congratulate.

félin, *adj.* feline.
félon, *adj.* disloyal.
fêlure, *n.f.* crack.
femelle, *adj. and n.f.* female.
féminin, *adj.* female, feminine.
féministe, *n.m.f.* feminist.
femme, *n.f.* woman, wife. **f. de chambre,** chambermaid.
fémoral, *adj.* femoral.
fémur, *n.m.* thighbone.
fendille, *n.f.* crack.
fendiller, se f., *vb.* crack.
fendoir, *n.m.* cleaver.
fendre, *vb.* split, rip.
fenêtre, *n.f.* window.
fenil, *n.m.* hayloft.
fenouil, *n.m.* fennel.
fente, *n.f.* crack; rip, split.
féodal, *adj.* feudal.
féodalité, *n.f.* feudalism.
fer (-r), *n.m.* iron. **chemin de f.,** railway. **fil de f.,** wire. **f. à cheval,** horseshoe.
fermail, *n.m.* brooch; clasp.
ferme, *n.f.* farm. **maison de f.,** farmhouse.
ferme, *adj.* firm, steady, fast.
fermement, *adv.* firmly.
ferment, *n.m.* ferment.
fermentation, *n.f.* fermentation.
fermenter, *vb.* ferment.
fermer, *vb.* close. **f. à clef,** lock.
fermeté, *n.f.* firmness.
fermeture, *n.f.* closing.
fermier, *n.m.* farmer.
féroce, *adj.* fierce.
férocité, *n.f.* ferocity.
ferraille, *n.f.* old iron.
ferreux, *adj.* ferrous.
ferrique, *adj.* ferric.
ferroviaire, *adj.* rail(way).
fertile, *adj.* fertile.
fertilisant, *n.m.* fertilizer.
fertilisation, *n.f.* fertilization.
fertiliser, *vb.* fertilize.
fertilité, *n.f.* fertility.
férule, *n.f.* cane, rod.
fervemment, *adv.* fervently.
fervent, *adj.* fervent.
ferveur, *n.f.* fervor.
fesse, *n.f.* buttock.
fessée, *n.f.* spanking.
fesser, *vb.* spank.
festin, *n.m.* feast.
festiner, *vb.* feast.

festival, *n.m.* festival.

feston, *n.m.* festoon.

fête, *n.f.* feast, party. **jour de f.,** holiday.

fêter, *vb.* fete.

fétiche, *n.m.* fetish.

fétide, *adj.* fetid.

feu, *n.m.* fire. **f. de joie,** bonfire. **f. d'artifice,** fireworks. **prendre f.,** catch fire. **coup de f.,** shot.

feu, *adj.* late (deceased).

feuillage, *n.m.* foliage.

feuille, *n.f.* leaf; sheet; foil.

feuillet, *n.m.* leaf.

feuilleter, *vb.* skim (book); roll and turn (pastry).

feuilleton, *n.m.* serial, TV series.

feutre, *n.m.* felt.

fève, *n.f.* bean.

février, *n.m.* February.

fez, *n.m.* fez.

fi, *interj.* fie!

fiable, *adj.* reliable.

fiacre, *n.m.* cab.

fiançailles, *n.f.pl.* engagement, betrothal.

fiancé, *n.m.* fiancé.

fiancer, *vb.* betroth.

fiasco, *n.m.* fiasco.

fibre, *n.f.* fiber.

fibreux, *adj.* fibrous.

ficeler, *vb.* tie up.

ficelle, *n.f.* string, twine.

fiche, *n.f.* slip (of paper).

ficher, *vb.* **se f. de,** care nothing about.

fichier, *n.m.* card index, file.

fichu, *adj.* ruined.

fictif, *adj.* fictitious.

fiction, *n.f.* fiction.

fidèle, *adj.* faithful.

fidélité, *n.f.* fidelity, loyalty, allegiance.

fief, *n.m.* fief.

fiel, *n.m.* gall.

fiente, *n.f.* dung.

fier (-r), *adj.* proud.

fier, *vb.* **se f.,** trust.

fierté, *n.f.* trust.

fièvre, *n.f.* fever.

fiévreux, *adj.* feverish.

fifre, *n.m.* fife(r).

figer, *vb.* coagulate.

figue, *n.f.* fig.

figurant, *n.m.* extra (film).

figuratif, *adj.* figurative.

figure, *n.f.* face; figure.

figurer, *vb.* figure, imagine. **se f.,** fancy.

fil (-), *n.m.* thread, string. **f. de fer,** wire.

filament, *n.m.* filament.

filature, *n.f.* spinning mill.

file, *n.f.* file.

filer, *vb.* spin.

filet, *n.m.* net.

filial, *adj.* filial.

filière, *n.f.* network.

filin, *n.m.* rope.

fille, *n.f.* daughter. **jeune f.,** girl. **vieille f.,** old maid.

fillette, *n.f.* little girl.

filleul, *n.m.* godson.

film, *n.m.* film.

filmer, *vb.* film.

filou, *n.m.* thief.

fils (fēs), *n.m.* son.

filtrant, *adj.* filtering.

filtration, *n.f.* filtration.

filtre, *n.m.* filter.

filtrer, *vb.* filter.

fin, **1.** *n.f.* end. **2.** *adj.* fine; sharp; clever.

final, *adj.* final.

finaliste, *n.m.f.* finalist.

finalité, *n.f.* finality.

finance, *n.f.* finance.

financer, *vb.* finance.

financier, **1.** *n.m.* financier. **2.** *adj.* financial.

finasser, *vb.* finesse.

finesse, *n.f.* fineness; slimness.

finir, *vb.* finish.

Finlande, *n.f.* Finland.

Finnois, *n.m.* Finn.

finnois, *adj. and n.m.* Finnish.

firmament, *n.m.* firmament.

firme, *n.f.* company.

fisc, *n.m.* tax authorities.

fiscal, *adj.* fiscal.

fissure, *n.f.* fissure.

fiston, *n.m.* (colloquial) son.

fixation, *n.f.* fixation.

fixe, *adj.* set, fixed.

fixer, *vb.* fix, settle; stare at.

fixité, *n.f.* fixity.

flaccidité, *n.f.* flabbiness.

flacon, *n.m.* bottle.

flagellation, *n.f.* flagellation.

flageller, *vb.* flog.

flageolet, *n.m.* kidney bean.

flagrant, *adj.* flagrant.

flair, *n.m.* flair.

flairer, *vb.* smell.

flamand, *adj.* Flemish.

flambant, *adj.* flaming.

flambeau, *n.m.* torch.

flambée, *n.f.* blaze.

flamber, *vb.* blaze.

flamboyant, *adj.* flaming; flamboyant.

flamboyer, *vb.* flame, flare.

flamme, *n.f.* flame.

flan, *n.m.* custard pie.

flanc, *n.m.* side, flank.

flanchet, *n.m.* flank (of beef).

flanelle, *n.f.* flannel.

flâner, *vb.* saunter, stroll; loiter, loaf.

flâneur, *n.m.* idler.

flanquer, *vb.* flank.

flaque, *n.f.* puddle.

flash, *n.m.* flash, news flash.

flasque, *adj.* flabby.

flatter, *vb.* flatter.

flatterie, *n.f.* flattery.

flatteur, *n.m.* flatterer.

fléau, *n.m.* scourge, plague.

flèche, *n.f.* arrow.

fléchir, *vb.* bend.

flegmatique, *adj.* phlegmatic.

flegme, *n.m.* phlegm.

flemmard, *n.m.* lazybones.

flemme, *n.f.* laziness.

flet, *n.m.* flounder.

flétan, *n.m.* halibut.

flétrir, *vb.* wilt, wither.

fleur, *n.f.* flower, blossom, bloom.

fleuret, *n.m.* foil.

fleuri, *adj.* flowery.

fleurir, *vb.* flower, bloom, blossom.

fleuriste, *n.m.f.* florist.

fleuve, *n.m.* river.

flexibilité, *n.f.* flexibility.

flexible, *adj.* flexible.

flic, *n.m.* (colloquial) cop.

flipper, *n.m.* pinball.

flirt (-t), *n.m.* flirtation.

flirter, *vb.* flirt.

flocon, *n.m.* flake.

flore, *n.f.* flora.

florissant, *adj.* prosperous, flourishing.

flot, *n.m.* wave. **à f.**, afloat.

flottant, *adj.* floating; irresolute.

flotte, *n.f.* fleet.

flottement, *n.m.* fluctuation; wavering.

flotter, *vb.* float.

flou, *adj.* hazy, indistinct.

fluctuation, *n.f.* fluctuation.

fluctuer, *vb.* fluctuate.

fluet, *m.* **fluette** *f.* *adj.* thin, delicate.

fluide, *adj. and n.m.* fluid, liquid.

fluidité, *n.f.* fluidity.

fluor, *n.m.* fluoride.

fluorescent, *adj.* fluorescent.

flûte, *n.f.* flute.

flûté, *adj.* soft; flutelike.

fluvial, *adj.* river.

flux, *n.m.* flow, flux.

fluxion, *n.f.* inflammation.

foi, *n.f.* faith; trust.

foie, *n.m.* liver.

foin, *n.m.* hay.

foire, *n.f.* fair.

fois, *n.f.* time. **à la f.**, at once.

foison, *n.f.* abundance.

foisonner, *vb.* abound.

folâtre, *adj.* frisky.

folâtrer, *vb.* frolic.

folichon, *adj.* playful.

folie, *n.f.* mania, madness, folly.

folklore, *n.m.* folklore.

follement, *adv.* foolishly.

follet, *adj.* merry, playful.

fomenter, *vb.* foment.

foncé, *adj.* dark.

foncer, *vb.* deepen.

fonction, *n.f.* function.

fonctionnaire, *n.m.* official, civil servant.

fonctionnement, *n.m.* operation, working.

fonctionner, *vb.* function, work.

fonctions, *n.f.pl.* office.

fond, *n.m.* bottom, (back)ground. **à f.**, thorough(ly). **au f.**, fundamentally.

fondamental, *adj.* basic, fundamental.

fondateur, *n.m.* founder.

fondation, *n.f.* foundation, establishment.

fondé, *adj.* authentic; (*comm.*) funded.

fondement, *n.m.* foundation.

fonder, *vb.* found.

fonderie, n.f. foundry.

fondre, vb. melt; fuse.

fondrière, n.f. bog.

fonds, n.m. fund.

fondu, adj. melted, molten.

fongus (-s), n.m. fungus.

fontaine, n.f. fountain.

fonte, n.f. melting.

fonts, n.m.pl. font.

foot, n.m. (colloquial) football.

football, n.m. football.

footing, n.m. walking; jogging.

forain, n.m. peddler.

forçat, n.m. convict.

force, n.f. strength, force; emphasis.

forcé, adj. forced; far-fetched.

forcément, adv. of necessity.

forcené, adj. frantic.

forceps, n.m. forceps.

forcer, vb. force, compel.

forcir, vb. thrive.

forer, vb. bore, drill.

forestier, n.m. forest ranger.

foret, n.m. drill.

forêt, n.f. forest.

foreuse, n.f. drill.

forfait, n.m. crime; forfeit; contract.

forfaiture, n.f. mishandling.

forfanterie, n.f. bragging.

forge, n.f. forge.

forger, vb. forge.

forgeron, n.m. blacksmith.

forgeur, n.m. forger; inventor.

formaliser, vb. formalize.

formaliste, adj. formal; precise.

formalité, n.f. formality, ceremony.

formater, vb. format.

formation, n.f. formation, training.

forme, n.f. shape, form.

formel, adj. formal.

former, vb. form, shape.

formidable, adj. tremendous; formidable.

formulaire, n.m. form.

formule, n.f. formula; form.

formuler, vb. formulate, draw up.

fort, 1. n.m. fort. **2.** adj. strong, loud. **3.** adv. hard.

forteresse, n.f. fort(ress).

fortifiant, adj. strengthening.

fortification, n.f. fortification.

fortifier, vb. strengthen.

fortuit, adj. accidental.

fortuité, n.f. fortuitousness.

fortune, n.f. fortune.

fortuné, adj. lucky, fortunate.

fosse, n.f. pit.

fossé, n.m. ditch; dike.

fossette, n.f. dimple.

fossile, n.m. fossil.

fossoyer, vb. dig a trench.

fou m., **folle** f. adj. mad, crazy, demented.

foudre, n.f. thunderbolt.

foudroyant, adj. terrifying, crushing.

foudroyer, vb. crush, blast.

fouet, n.m. whip, lash.

fouetter, vb. flog, whip.

fougère, n.f. fern.

fougue, n.f. ardor.

fougueux, adj. fiery, impetuous.

fouille, n.f. excavation.

fouiller, vb. ransack.

fouillis, n.m. litter, mess.

fouir, vb. dig, burrow.

foulard, n.m. scarf.

foule, n.f. crowd, mob.

fouler, vb. trample.

foulure, n.f. sprain; wrench.

four, n.m. oven.

fourbe, 1. n.m. knave. **2.** adj. scheming.

fourberie, n.f. knavery.

fourbir, vb. polish.

fourche, n.f. fork.

fourchette, n.f. fork.

fourgon, n.m. wagon.

fourmi, n.f. ant.

fourmillement, n.m. swarming; tingling.

fourmiller, vb. mill; swarm.

fourneau, n.m. stove, furnace.

fournée, n.f. batch.

fourniment, n.m. equipment.

fournir de, vb. supply, furnish.

fournisseur, n.m. tradesman.

fournitures, n.f.pl. supplies.

fourrage, n.m. fodder, forage.

fourrager, vb. forage.

fourré, adj. lined (of clothing); thick; wooded.

fourreau, n.m. sheath.

fourrer, vb. thrust in. **se f.,** interfere, meddle.

fourreur, n.m. furrier.

fourrure, *n.f.* fur.
fourvoyer, *vb.* (colloquial) mislead.
foutaise, *n.f.* (colloquial) rubbish.
foyer, *n.m.* focus; hearth. **f. domestique,** home.
frac, *n.m.* dress coat.
fracas, *n.m.* crash; rattle; noise; ado.
fracasser, se f., shatter.
fraction, *n.f.* fraction.
fracture, *n.f.* fracture.
fracturer, *vb.* break, fracture.
fragile, *adj.* brittle, delicate, frail, fragile.
fragilité, *n.f.* fragility.
fragment, *n.m.* fragment.
fragmenter, *vb.* divide up.
fraîcheur, *n.f.* freshness, coolness.
fraîchir, *vb.* freshen.
frais, *n.m.pl.* expense(s), cost, fee.
frais *m.*, **fraîche** *f.* fresh, cool.
fraise, *n.f.* strawberry; ruffle.
framboise, *n.f.* raspberry.
franc, 1. *n.m.* franc. **2.** *adj.m.*, **franche** *f.* frank, open.
Français, *n.m.* Frenchman.
français, *adj. and n.m.* French.
Française, *n.f.* Frenchwoman.
France, *n.f.* France.
franchement, *adv.* frankly.
franchir, *vb.* clear, cross.
franchise, *n.f.* frankness.
franciser, *vb.* make French.
franc-maçon, *n.m.* Freemason.
franco, *adv.* postage paid.
francophone, *adj.* French-speaking.
francophonie, *n.f.* French-speaking communities.
franc-parler, *n.m.* frankness.
franc-tireur, *n.m.* sniper; free-lancer.
frange, *n.f.* fringe.
frangible, *adj.* breakable.
frapper, *vb.* strike, hit, rap, knock. **f. du pied,** stamp.
frasque, *n.f.* prank.
fraternel, *adj.* brotherly.
fraterniser, *vb.* fraternize.
fraternité, *n.f.* brotherhood.
fraude, *n.f.* fraud.
frauder, *vb.* defraud.
fraudeur, *n.m.* smuggler.
frauduleux, *adj.* fraudulent.
frayer, *vb.* open up; rub.

frayeur, *n.f.* fright.
fredaine, *n.f.* prank.
fredonner, *vb.* hum.
frégate, *n.f.* frigate.
frein, *n.m.* brake; check.
freiner, *vb.* brake; restrain.
frelater, *vb.* adulterate.
frêle, *adj.* frail.
frelon, *n.m.* hornet.
frémir, *vb.* tremble. **faire f.,** thrill.
frémissement, *n.m.* shiver; thrill.
frêne, *n.m.* ash (tree).
frénésie, *n.f.* frenzy.
frénétique, *adj.* frantic.
fréquemment, *adv.* often.
fréquence, *n.f.* frequency.
fréquent, *adj.* frequent.
fréquenter, *vb.* frequent, associate with.
frère, *n.m.* brother.
fresque, *n.f.* fresco.
fret, *n.m.* freight.
fréter, *vb.* charter (ship); freight.
frétillant, *adj.* lively.
frétiller, *vb.* wag; quiver.
fretin, *n.m.* young fish.
frette, *n.f.* hoop.
friand, *adj.* dainty; fond (of).
friandise, *n.f.* love of delicacies; candy.
fric, *n.m.* (colloquial) money, dough, bread.
fricoter, *vb.* cook, stew.
friction, *n.f.* friction.
frictionner, *vb.* chafe.
frigidaire, *n.m.* (trademark) refrigerator.
frigide, *adj.* frigid.
frigo, *n.m.* frozen meat; fridge.
frigorifier, *vb.* freeze; refrigerate.
frileux, *adj.* chilly; susceptible to cold.
frime, *n.f.* pretense, sham.
frimer, *vb.* put on an act.
fringant, *adj.* lively, frisky.
fringuer, *vb.* crush, rumple.
fripier, *n.m.* secondhand clothing dealer.
fripon, 1. *adj.* knavish. **2.** *n.m.* rascal.
friponnerie, *n.f.* roguery.
fripouille, *n.f.* rascal.
frire, *vb.* fry.
frisé, *adj.* curly.

friser, *vb.* curl.

frisoir, *n.m.* (hair) curler.

frisson, *n.m.* shudder, shiver.

frissonnement, *n.m.* shudder, shivering.

frissonner, *vb.* shudder, shiver.

frites, *n.f.pl.* French fries.

friture, *n.f.* frying.

frivole, *adj.* frivolous.

frivolité, *n.f.* frivolity.

froc, *n.m.* (monk's) frock.

froid, *adj. and n.m.* cold. **un peu f.,** chilly. **avoir f.,** be cold.

froideur, *n.f.* coldness.

froissé, *adj.* bruised. **être f. de,** resent.

froissement, *n.m.* crumpling; rustling, jostling.

froisser, *vb.* crease, wrinkle; bruise, hurt.

frôler, *vb.* graze.

fromage, *n.m.* cheese.

froment, *n.m.* wheat.

froncement, *n.m.* puckering, contraction.

froncer, *vb.* pucker. **f. les sourcils,** frown.

frondaison, *n.f.* foliage.

fronde, *n.f.* sling.

fronder, *vb.* sling; censure.

front, *n.m.* forehead.

frontière, *n.f.* boundary, border; frontier.

frottement, *n.m.* rubbing.

frotter, *vb.* rub.

frou-frou, *n.m.* rustle.

fructueux, *adj.* fruitful.

frugal, *adj.* frugal.

frugalité, *n.f.* frugality.

fruit, *n.m.* fruit.

fruiterie, *n.f.* fruit store.

fruitier, *n.m.* fruit seller.

fruste, *adj.* uncultivated.

frustrer, *vb.* frustrate.

fugace, *adj.* fleeting.

fugitif, *adj.* fugitive.

fugue, *n.f.* flight, escape.

fuir, *vb.* flee; shun; leak.

fuite, *n.f.* escape, flight; leak.

fume-cigarette, *n.m.* cigarette holder.

fumée, *n.f.* smoke.

fumer, *vb.* smoke.

fumeur, *n.m.* one who smokes.

fumeux, *adj.* smoky.

fumier, *n.m.* dung.

fumiste, *n.m.* shirker.

fumisterie, *n.f.* con.

funèbre, *adj.* funereal.

funérailles, *n.f.pl.* funeral.

funeste, *adj.* disastrous.

fureter, *vb.* pry.

fureur, *n.f.* fury.

furibond, *adj.* furious.

furie, *n.f.* fury.

furieux, *adj.* furious.

furtif, *adj.* sly.

fuseau, *n.m.* spindle.

fusée, *n.f.* rocket.

fuser, *vb.* melt; spread.

fusible, *n.m.* fuse wire.

fusil, *n.m.* rifle.

fusiller (-zēl yā), *vb.* shoot.

fusion, *n.f.* merger; meltdown.

fusionner, *vb.* merge.

futé, *adj.* cunning, crafty.

futile, *adj.* futile.

futur, *adj. and n.m.* future.

futurologie, *n.f.* futurology.

fuyant, *adj.* passing, transitory; fugitive.

fuyard, *n.* fugitive.

G

gâcher, *vb.* mess.

gâchette, *n.f.* trigger.

gâchis, *n.m.* waste.

gadoue, *n.f.* sludge.

gaffe, *n.f.* blunder.

gage, *n.m.* pledge, wage.

gageure, *n.f.* bet.

gagnant, *n.m.* winner.

gagner, *vb.* earn, gain, win, beat (in a game).

gai, *adj.* cheerful, cheery, merry, gay.

gaieté, *n.f.* mirth, cheer, merriment, gaiety.

gaillard, *adj.* hearty, sound.

gain, *n.m.* gain, profit.

gaine, *n.f.* girdle.

galant, 1. *n.m.* beau. **2.** *adj.* gallant, civil, courteous. **g. homme,** gentleman.

galanterie, *n.f.* courtesy, compliment.

galaxie, *n.f.* galaxy.

galbe, *n.m.* outline, contour.

galère, *n.f.* galley, ship.

galerie, *n.f.* gallery; balcony (theater).

galet, *n.m.* boulder.

galette, *n.f.* flat cake.

Galles, *n.f.pl.* le pays de G., Wales.

Gallois, *n.m.* Welshman.

gallois, *adj. and n.m.* Welsh.

gallon, *n.m.* gallon.

galon, *n.m.* stripe, braid.

galop, *n.m.* gallop.

galoper, *vb.* gallop.

galvaudé, *adj.* worthless.

gambader, *vb.* frolic.

gamin, *n.m.* boy; urchin.

gamme, *n.f.* scale.

gangster (-r), *n.m.* gangster.

gant, *n.m.* glove.

ganterie, *n.f.* glove shop.

garage, *n.m.* garage.

garagiste, *n.m.f.* garage keeper, car mechanic.

garant, *n.m.* sponsor.

garantie, *n.f.* guarantee, pledge.

garantir, *vb.* guarantee, pledge; warrant.

garçon, *n.m.* boy; waiter; bachelor; flight attendant.

garçonnière, *n.f.* bachelor's apartment.

garde, *n.f.* watch, guard; custody. **prendre g. à,** beware of. **avant-g.,** vanguard. **g. du corps,** bodyguard.

garde-boue, *n.m.* fender.

garde-feu, *n.m.* fender (fireplace).

garde-manger, *n.m.* pantry.

garder, *vb.* guard, keep, mind.

garderie, *n.f.* nursery, day-care center.

garde-robe, *n.f.* wardrobe.

gardeur, *n.m.* keeper.

gardien, *n.m.* keeper, guard, watchman, guardian.

gare, 1. *n.f.* station. **2.** *interj.* look out!

garer, *vb.* garage, park.

gargariser, *vb.* se g., gargle.

gargarisme, *n.m.* gargle.

gargouille, *n.f.* gargoyle.

garnement, *n.m.* rascal.

garni, *adj.* furnished; garnished.

garnir, *vb.* trim, garnish.

garnison, *n.f.* garrison.

garniture, *n.f.* fittings.

gars, *n.m.* chap, guy.

gas-oil, *n.m.* diesel (oil).

gaspillage, *n.m.* waste.

gaspiller, *vb.* waste, squander.

gastronomique, *adj.* gastronomic.

gâteau, *n.m.* cake. **g. de miel,** honeycomb. **g. sec,** cookie.

gâter, *vb.* spoil.

gâterie, *n.f.* excessive indulgence.

gâteux, *adj.* senile.

gauche, *adj. and n.f.* left. **à g.,** on or to the left. *adj.* awkward, clumsy.

gaucher, *n.m.* left-handed person.

gaucherie, *n.f.* clumsiness.

gaufre, *n.f.* waffle.

gaule, *n.f.* pole.

gaulois, *adj.* Gallic; bawdy.

gausser, *vb.* se g. de, mock, banter.

gaver, *vb.* force-feed.

gaz (-z), *n.m.* gas.

gaze, *n.f.* gauze.

gazette, *n.f.* newspaper.

gazeux, *adj.* gassy, gaseous. **boisson gazeuse,** carbonated drink.

gazoduc, *n.m.* gas pipeline.

gazon, *n.m.* turf, lawn.

gazouillement, *n.m.* warble, twitter.

géant, *n.m.* giant.

geindre, *vb.* moan, whine.

gel, *n.m.* frost; gel.

gelé, *adj.* frozen.

gelée, *n.f.* jelly; frost.

geler, *vb.* freeze.

gélule, *n.f.* capsule.

gelures, *n.f.pl.* frostbite.

gémir, *vb.* groan, wail, moan.

gémissement, *n.m.* groan, moan.

gênant, *adj.* troublesome, bothersome.

gencive, *n.f.* gum.

gendarme, *n.m.* policeman.

gendarmerie, *n.f.* police force.

gendre, *n.m.* son-in-law.

gêne, *n.f.* trouble, uneasiness. **être à la g.,** be uneasy.

gêné, *adj.* uneasy.

généalogie, *n.f.* pedigree.

gêner, *vb.* hinder, be in the way; embarrass; bother.

général, *adj. and n.m.* general,

overhead (*comm.*). **quartier g.,** headquarters.

généraliser, *vb.* generalize.

généralissime, *n.m.* commander-in-chief.

généraliste, *n.m.f.* general practitioner.

généralité, *n.f.* generality.

génération, *n.f.* generation.

généreusement, *adv.* generously.

généreux, *adj.* generous, liberal.

générosité, *n.f.* generosity.

génial, *adj.* of genius, highly original; (colloquial) fantastic.

génie, *n.m.* genius; engineer corps. **soldat du g.,** engineer.

genièvre, *n.m.* gin.

génisse, *n.f.* heifer.

genou, *n.m.* knee; (*pl.*) lap.

genre, *n.m.* kind, gender.

gens, *n.m.f.pl.* people, persons, folk.

gentiane, *n.f.* gentian.

gentil *m.,* **gentille** *f. adj.* pleasant, nice.

gentilhomme, *n.m.* nobleman; peer.

gentillesse, *n.f.* prettiness, gracefulness.

géographie, *n.f.* geography.

géographique, *adj.* geographical.

géologie, *n.f.* geology.

géométrie, *n.f.* geometry.

géométrique, *adj.* geometric.

gérance, *n.f.* managership.

géranium, *n.m.* geranium.

gérant, *n.m.* manager, director, superintendent.

gerbe, *n.f.* sheaf.

gerçure, *n.f.* chap.

gérer, *vb.* manage.

germain, *adj.* first (of cousins).

germe, *n.f.* germ.

germer, *vb.* sprout.

gésir, *vb.* lie.

geste, *n.m.* gesture.

gesticuler, *vb.* gesticulate.

gestion, *n.f.* management.

ghetto, *n.m.* ghetto.

gibier, *n.m.* game.

giboulée, *n.f.* sudden storm.

gicler, *vb.* spurt.

gifler, *vb.* slap.

gigantesque, *adj.* great, huge.

gigot, *n.m.* leg (of meat).

gigue, *n.f.* leg; jig.

gilet, *n.m.* vest. **g. de dessous,** undershirt.

gingembre, *n.m.* ginger.

girafe, *n.f.* giraffe.

girofle, *n.m.* **clou de g.,** clove.

giron, *n.m.* lap.

gisement, *n.m.* deposit.

gitan, *n.m.* gypsy.

gîte, *n.m.* lodging, bed.

givre, *n.m.* frost.

glabre, *adj.* smooth-shaven.

glaçage, *n.m.* frosting.

glace, *n.f.* ice; ice cream; mirror.

glacé, *adj.* icy, frozen.

glacer, *vb.* freeze.

glacial, *adj.* icy.

glacier, *n.m.* glacier.

glacière, *n.f.* icebox.

glacis, *n.m.* slope.

glaçon, *n.m.* block of ice; ice cube.

glaise, *n.f.* clay.

gland, *n.m.* acorn.

glande, *n.f.* gland.

glaner, *vb.* glean.

glapir, *vb.* yelp; screech.

glas, *n.m.* knell.

glissade, *n.f.* slide, slip.

glissant, *adj.* slippery.

glisser, *vb.* slide, slip. **se g.,** creep, sneak.

global, *adj.* entire.

globe, *n.m.* globe. **g. de l'œil,** eyeball.

globule, *n.m.* corpuscle.

gloire, *n.f.* glory.

glorieux, *adj.* glorious.

glorifier, *vb.* glorify.

glose, *n.f.* criticism; gloss.

glossaire, *n.m.* glossary.

glousser, *vb.* cluck.

glouton, *adj.* gluttonous.

gluant, *adj.* sticky.

goal, *n.m.* goalkeeper.

gobelet, *n.m.* goblet.

gober, *vb.* swallow.

godasse, *n.f.* (colloquial) shoe.

goéland, *n.m.* seagull.

goinfre, *n.m.* glutton.

golfe, *n.m.* gulf.

gomme, *n.f.* gum; eraser.

gommeux, *adj.* gummy.

gond, *n.m.* hinge.

gonflé, *adj.* swollen; full of nerve.

gonfler, *vb.* inflate; swell.

gonfleur, *n.m.* tire pump.
gorge, *n.f.* throat; gorge.
gorger, *vb.* cram.
gosier, *n.m.* throat.
gosse, *n.m.f.* kid (child).
gothique, *adj.* Gothic.
goudron, *n.m.* tar.
gouffre, *n.m.* gulf, abyss.
goujat, *n.m.* boor, cad.
goulu, *adj.* gluttonous.
gourde, *n.f.* flask.
gourer, *vb.* (colloquial) **se g.,** make a mistake.
gourmand, 1. *n.m.* glutton. **2.** *adj.* greedy.
gourmander, *vb.* scold.
gourmandise, *n.f.* greediness.
gourmer, *vb.* curb.
gourmet, *n.m.* epicure.
gourmette, *n.f.* curb (horse).
gourou, *n.m.* guru.
gousse, *n.f.* shell, pod.
goût, *n.m.* taste, relish.
goûter, 1. *n.m.* snack. **2.** *vb.* taste, relish.
goutte, *n.f.* drop; gout.
goutteux, *adj.* gouty.
gouttière, *n.f.* gutter.
gouvernail, *n.m.* rudder, helm.
gouvernante, *n.f.* governess.
gouvernement, *n.m.* government.
gouverner, *vb.* govern, rule, steer.
gouverneur, *n.m.* governor.
grabuge, *n.m.* squabble.
grâce, *n.f.* grace. **faire g. de,** spare.
gracier, *vb.* pardon.
gracieux, *adj.* graceful, gracious.
grade, *n.m.* grade, rank.
gradé, *n.m.* non-commissioned officer.
gradin, *n.m.* step, tier.
graduel, *adj.* gradual.
graduer, *vb.* graduate.
graffiti, *nm.pl.* graffiti.
grain, *n.m.* grain, seed, berry, kernel. **g. de beauté,** mole.
graine, *n.f.* seed, berry.
graissage, *n.m.* greasing.
graisse, *n.f.* grease, fat.
graisser, *vb.* grease.
grammaire, *n.f.* grammar.
gramme, *n.m.* gram.
grand, *adj.* big, great, tall. **grand'chose,** much.
grandement, *adv.* grandly, greatly.

grandeur, *n.f.* size, height, greatness.
grandiose, *adj.* grand.
grandir, *vb.* grow.
grand-mère, *n.f.* grandmother.
grand-père, *n.m.* grandfather.
grange, *n.f.* barn.
granit (-t), *n.m.* granite.
graphique, *n.m.* chart.
grappe, *n.f.* bunch, cluster.
gras, grasse *f. adj.* fat, stout.
grassement, *adv.* plentifully.
grasset, *adj.* plump.
grassouillet, *adj.* plump.
gratification, *n.f.* bonus.
gratifier, *vb.* bestow.
gratin, *n.m.* cheese topping.
gratis (-s), *adv.* free.
gratitude, *n.f.* gratitude.
gratte-ciel, *n.m.* skyscraper.
gratter, *vb.* scrape, scratch.
gratuit, *adj.* free.
grave, *adj.* grave.
graveleux, *adj.* gritty.
graver, *vb.* engrave.
graveur, *n.m.* engraver.
gravier, *n.m.* gravel.
gravir, *vb.* climb.
gravité, *n.f.* gravity.
graviter, *vb.* gravitate.
gravure, *n.f.* engraving. **g. à l'eauforte,** etching.
gré, *n.m.* pleasure.
Grec *m.,* **Grecque** *f. n.* Greek (person).
grec, *n.m.* Greek (language).
grec *m.,* **grecque** *f. adj.* Greek.
Grèce, *n.f.* Greece.
gréement, *n.m.* rig.
gréer, *vb.* rig.
greffer, *vb.* graft, transplant.
greffier, *n.m.* clerk.
grêle, 1. *n.f.* hail. **2.** *adj.* thin, slight.
grêler, *vb.* hail.
grêlon, *n.m.* hailstone.
grelotter, *vb.* shiver.
grenade, *n.f.* grenade; pomegranate.
grenier, *n.m.* attic.
grenouille, *n.f.* frog.
grève, *n.f.* strike. **se mettre en g.,** strike.
gréviste, *n.m.f.* striker.

gribouiller, vb. scribble.
grief, n.m. grievance.
grièvement, adv. seriously.
griffe, n.f. claw, clutch.
griffer, vb. seize; scratch.
griffonner, vb. scribble.
grignoter, vb. nibble.
gril, n.m. grill.
grillade, n.f. broiling.
grille, n.f. grate, gate.
grille-pain, n.m. toaster.
griller, vb. broil, roast, toast.
grillon, n.m. cricket.
grimace, n.f. grimace.
grimacer, vb. make faces.
grimer, vb. make up.
grimper, vb. climb.
grincer, vb. creak, grate, grind.
grippe, n.f. flu.
gris, adj. gray; drab; drunk.
griser, vb. get drunk.
grive, n.f. thrush.
grogner, vb. growl, snarl, grumble.
grommeler, vb. mutter.
gronder, vb. scold, nag; roar, rumble.
gros m., **grosse** f. adj. overly large; gross, stout, rough. **en g.,** wholesale.
groseille, n.f. currant.
grossesse, n.f. pregnancy.
grosseur, n.f. size, thickness.
grossier, adj. coarse, crude, gross.
grossièreté, n.f. coarseness.
grossir, vb. magnify, grow.
grossiste, n.m. wholesaler.
grosso modo, adv. roughly.
grotesque, adj. grotesque.

grotte, n.f. cave, grotto.
grouiller, vb. stir, swarm.
groupe, n.m. group, party; cluster.
groupement, n.m. grouping.
grouper, vb. group.
grue, n.f. crane.
gruyère, n.m. Gruyère (cheese).
gué, n.m. ford. **traverser à g.,** wade.
guêpe, n.f. wasp.
guère, adv. hardly.
guérilla, n.f. guerrilla warfare.
guérir, vb. cure, heal.
guérison, n.f. cure.
guerre, n.f. war.
guerrier, adj. warlike.
guetter, vb. watch (for).
gueule, n.f. mouth, (colloquial) mouth, face.
gueuler, vb. bawl (out).
gueux, n.f. beggar, tramp.
guichet, n.m. ticket window.
guide, n.m. guide(book).
guider, vb. guide.
guidon, n.m. handlebars.
guignol, n.m. Punch and Judy show; puppet; clown.
guillemets, n.m.pl. quotation marks, inverted commas.
guillotine, n.f. guillotine.
guingan, n.m. gingham.
guirlande, n.f. garland.
guise, n.f. way, manner.
guitare, n.f. guitar.
gymnase, n.m. gymnasium.
gymnastique, n.f. gymnastics.
gynecologie, n.f. gynecology.
gynécologiste, n.m.f. gynecologist.

H

habile, adj. clever, skillful, smart, able.
habileté, n.f. craft, ability.
habillement, n.m. apparel.
habillements masculins, n.m.pl. menswear.
habiller, vb. dress.
habilleur n.m., **habilleuse** f. dresser.
habit, n.m. coat; attire; (pl.) clothes.
habitant, n.m. inhabitant, resident.

habitation, n.f. dwelling.
habiter, vb. inhabit, live.
habitude, n.f. habit, practice. **d'h.,** customarily. **avoir l'h. de,** be accustomed to.
habitué, n.m. regular visitor, regular (client).
habituel, adj. customary, usual.
habituer, vb. get used to.
hâbleur, n.m. boaster.
hache, n.f. ax.
hacher, vb. mince, chop, hack up.

hachette, *n.f.* hatchet.

hachis, *n.m.* hash.

hagard, *adj.* haggard.

haie, *n.f.* hedge.

haillon, *n.m.* rag.

haine, *n.f.* hatred.

haineux, *adj.* hating.

haïr, *vb.* hate.

haïssable, *adj.* hateful.

halage, *n.m.* towage.

hâle, *n.m.* tan; sunburn.

haleine, *n.f.* breath.

haler, *vb.* haul, tow.

hâler, *vb.* tan. **se h.,** become sunburned.

haleter, *vb.* pant, gasp.

hall, *n.m.* hall.

halle, *n.f.* market.

hallucination, *n.f.* hallucination.

halte, *n.f.* halt.

haltère, *n.m.* dumbbell.

hamac, *n.m.* hammock.

hamburger, *n.m.* hamburger.

hameau, *n.m.* hamlet.

hameçon, *n.m.* hook.

hampe, *n.f.* handle.

hanche, *n.f.* hip.

handicap, *n.m.* handicap.

handicapé, *n.m.* handicapped (person).

hangar, *n.m.* shed.

hanter, *vb.* haunt.

hantise, *n.f.* obsession.

happer, *vb.* snap.

harcèlement, *n.m.* hassle, harassment.

harceler, *vb.* worry, bother; hassle; harass.

hardes, *n.f.pl.* togs.

hardi, *adj.* bold.

hardiesse, *n.f.* boldness.

hareng, *n.m.* herring.

hargneux, *adj.* cross, snarling.

haricot, *n.m.* bean.

harmonie, *n.f.* harmony.

harmonieux, *adj.* harmonious.

harmoniser, *vb.* put in tune, harmonize.

harnacher, *vb.* harness.

harnais, *n.m.* harness.

harpe, *n.f.* harp.

harpin, *n.m.* boat hook.

hasard, *n.m.* chance. **au h.** *or* **par h.,** at random.

hasarder, *vb.* venture.

hasardeux, *adj.* hazardous, unsafe.

hâte, *n.f.* haste, hurry. **à la h.,** hastily.

hâter, *vb.* hasten, hurry.

hâtif, *adj.* early, hasty.

hausse, *n.f.* rise, increase.

haussement, *n.m.* raising; shrug.

hausser, *vb.* raise; shrug.

haussier, *n.m.* bull (stock exchange).

haut, 1. *n.m.* top. **2.** *adj.* high, loud. **à haute voix,** aloud. **en h.,** up, above.

hautain, *adj.* haughty, lofty, proud.

hautbois, *n.m.* oboe.

haute fidélité, *n.f.* high fidelity.

hautement, *adv.* highly.

hauteur, *n.f.* height; haughtiness. **être à la h. de,** be up to.

hauturier, *adj.* seagoing.

hâve, *adj.* wan, gaunt.

havre, *n.m.* haven.

havresac, *n.m.* knapsack.

hebdo, *n.m.* (colloquial) weekly.

hebdomadaire, *adj.* weekly.

héberger, *vb.* shelter.

hébété, *adj.* dull.

hébreu, 1. *n.m.* Hebrew (language). **2.** *adj.* Hebrew.

hécatombe, *n.f.* slaughter.

hectare, *n.m.* hectare.

hégémonie, *n.f.* hegemony.

hein, *interj.* huh?

hélas (-s), *interj.* alas!

héler, *vb.* call, hail.

hélice, *n.f.* propeller.

hélicoptère, *n.m.* helicopter.

helvétique, *adj.* Swiss.

hématome, *n.m.* bruise.

hémisphère, *n.m.* hemisphere.

hémorragie, *n.f.* hemorrhage.

hennir, *vb.* neigh.

hépatite, *n.f.* hepatitis.

héraut, *n.m.* herald.

herbe, *n.f.* grass, pasture.

herbe, *n.f.* grass, herb; marijuana. **mauvaise h.,** weed.

herbeux, *adj.* grassy.

héréditaire, *adj.* hereditary.

hérésie, *n.f.* heresy.

hérétique, 1. *n.m.f.* heretic. **2.** *adj.* heretic, heretical.

hérisser, *vb.* bristle.

hérisson, *n.m.* hedgehog.

héritage, *n.m.* inheritance.

hériter, *vb.* inherit.

héritier, *n.m.* heir.

hermétique, *adj.* (sealed) tight.

hermine, *n.f.* ermine.

hernie, *n.f.* hernia.

héroïne, *n.f.* heroine; heroin (drug).

héroïque, *adj.* heroic.

héroïsme, *n.m.* heroism.

héros, *n.m.* hero.

hertz, *n.m.* hertz.

hésitation, *n.f.* hesitation.

hésiter, *vb.* hesitate, waver, falter.

hétéroclite, *adj* heterogeneous.

hétérogène, *adj.* heterogeneous.

hétérosexuel, *adj.* heterosexual.

hêtre, *n.m.* beech.

heure, *n.f.* hour; time. **de bonne h.,** early.

heureusement, *adv.* happily, luckily.

heureux, *adj.* glad, happy; lucky, fortunate; successful.

heurt, *n.m.* blow, shock.

heurter, *vb.* collide (with).

heurtoir, *n.m.* (door) knocker.

hexagone, *n.m.* hexagon. **L'h.,** France.

hibou, *n.m.* owl.

hideux, *adj.* hideous.

hier (-r), *adv.* yesterday.

hiérarchie, *n.f.* hierarchy.

hi-fi, *adj. and n.m* hi-fi.

hilare, *adj.* hilarious.

hilarité, *n.f.* hilarity.

Hindou, *n.m.* Hindu.

hindou, *adj.* Hindu.

hippodrome, *n.m.* race course.

hippopotame, *n.m.* hippopotamus.

hirondelle, *n.f.* swallow.

hispanique, *adj.* Hispanic.

hisser, *vb.* hoist.

histoire, *n.f.* history; story; to-do, fuss.

historien, *n.m.* historian.

historique, *adj.* historic.

hiver (-r), *n.m.* winter.

hiverner, *vb.* **s'h.,** hibernate.

hocher, *vb.* shake, nod.

hochet, *n.m.* rattle.

hockey, *n.m.* hockey.

hoirie, *n.f.* inheritance.

hold-up, *n.m.* hold-up.

Hollandais, *n.m.* Hollander, Dutchman.

hollandais, *adj. and n.m.* Dutch.

Hollande, *n.f.* Holland; the Netherlands.

hologramme, *n.m.* hologram.

holographie, *n.f.* holography.

homard, *n.m.* lobster.

homicide, *n.m.* homicide.

hommage, *n.m.* homage.

hommasse, *adj.* mannish.

homme, *n.m.* man. **h. d'affaires,** businessman.

homogène, *adj.* of the same kind, homogeneous.

homologue, *n.m.* counterpart.

homonyme, *n.m.* namesake.

homosexuel, *adj.* homosexual.

Hongrie, *n.f.* Hungary.

Hongrois, *n.m.* Hungarian (person).

hongrois, 1. *n.m.* Hungarian (language). **2.** *adj.* Hungarian.

honnête, *adj.* honest.

honnêteté, *n.f.* honesty, fairness.

honneur, *n.m.* honor, credit.

honorable, *adj.* honorable.

honoraires, *n.m.pl.* fee.

honorer, *vb.* honor.

honorifique, *adj.* honorary.

honte, *n.f.* shame. **avoir h. de,** be ashamed of. **faire h. à.,** shame.

honteux, *adj.* ashamed; shameful.

hôpital, *n.m.* hospital.

hoquet, *n.m.* hiccup.

horaire, *n.m.* timetable.

horde, *n.f.* horde.

horizon, *n.m.* horizon.

horizontal, *adj.* horizontal.

horloge, *n.f.* clock.

horloger, *n.m.* watchmaker.

hormis, *prep.* except.

horreur, *n.f.* horror.

horrible, *adj.* horrible, ghastly.

horrifier, *vb.* horrify.

horrifique, *adj.* hair-raising.

horripiler, *vb.* annoy.

hors, *prep.* except (for).

hors-bord, *n.m.* outboard boat.

hors de, *prep.* out of, outside.

hors-taxe, *adj.* duty-free.

horticole, *adj.* horticultural.

hospice, *n.m.* refuge.

hospitalier, *adj.* hospitable.
hospitaliser, *vb.* hospitalize; shelter.
hospitalité, *n.f.* hospitality.
hostie, *n.f. (eccles.)* host.
hostile, *adj.* hostile.
hostilité, *n.f.* hostility.
hôte, *n.m.* host; guest.
hôtel, *n.m.* hotel; mansion. **h. de ville,** city hall.
hôtelier, *n.m.* innkeeper.
hôtesse, *n.f.* hostess.
hôtesse de l'air, *n.f.* stewardess, flight attendant.
hotte, *n.f.* basket carried on back.
houblon, *n.m.* hop (plant).
houe, *n.f.* hoe.
houer, *vb.* hoe.
houille, *n.f.* coal.
houillère, *n.f.* coal mine.
houle, *n.f.* surge.
houleux, *adj.* stormy, rough.
houppe, *n.f.* tuft; powder puff.
hourra, *n.m.* cheer.
housse, *n.f.* covering.
houx, *n.m.* holly.
hublot, *n.m.* porthole.
huer, *vb.* shout, hoot.
huile, *n.f.* oil.
huiler, *vb.* oil.
huileux, *adj.* oily.
huissier, *n.m.* usher.
huit, *adj.* and *n.m.* eight.
huitième, *adj.* and *n.m.f.* eighth.
huître, *n.f.* oyster.
humain, *adj.* human; humane.
humanitaire, *adj.* humanitarian.
humanité, *n.f.* humanity.
humble, *adj.* lowly, humble.
humecter, *vb.* moisten.

humer, *vb.* suck up, sniff up.
humeur, *n.f.* humor; mood, temper.
humide, *adj.* damp, humid.
humidité, *n.f.* moisture.
humiliation, *n.f.* humiliation.
humilier, *vb.* humiliate, humble.
humilité, *n.f.* humility.
humoristique, *adj.* humorous.
humour, *n.m.* humor.
hune, *n.f. (naut.)* top.
huppe, *n.f.* tuft, crest.
hurlement, *n.m.* noise, howling.
hurler, *vb.* howl, roar, yell.
hutte, *n.f.* hut, shed.
hybride, *adj.* and *n.m.* hybrid.
hydratant, *adj.* moisturizing.
hydravion, *n.m.* seaplane.
hydroélectrique, *adj.* hydroelectric.
hydrogène, *n.m.* hydrogen.
hyène, *n.f.* hyena.
hygiène, *n.f.* sanitation; hygiene.
hygiénique, *adj.* hygienic.
hymne, *n.m.* hymn; *n.f.* church hymn.
hypermarché, *n.m.* very large supermarket; hypermarket.
hypnotiser, *vb.* hypnotize.
hypocondriaque, *adj.* and *n.m.f.* hypochondriac.
hypocrisie, *n.f.* hypocrisy.
hypocrite, 1. *n.m.f.* hypocrite. **2.** *adj.* hypocritical.
hypothèque, *n.f.* mortgage.
hypothéquer, *vb.* mortgage.
hypothèse, *n.f.* hypothesis.
hystérectomie, *n.f.* hysterectomy.
hystérie, *n.f.* hysteria.
hystérique, *adj.* hysterical.

I

ici, *adv.* here. **d'i.,** hence.
ictère, *n.m.* jaundice.
idéal, *adj.* and *n.m.* ideal.
idéaliser, *vb.* idealize.
idéalisme, *n.m.* idealism.
idéaliste, *n.m.f.* idealist.
idée, *n.f.* idea, notion.
identification, *n.f.* identification.
identifier, *vb.* identify.
identique, *adj.* identical.
identité, *n.f.* identity.

idéologie, *n.f.* ideology.
idiome, *n.m.* idiom.
idiot, *adj.* and *n.m.* idiot(ic).
idiotie, *n.f.* idiocy.
idiotisme, *n.m.* idiom.
idolâtrer, *vb.* idolize.
idole, *n.f.* idol.
idyllique, *adj.* idyllic.
if, *n.m.* yew tree.
ignare, *adj.* ignorant.
ignoble, *adj.* ignoble.

ignorance, n.f. ignorance.

ignorant, adj. ignorant.

ignorer, vb. not know.

il (ēl), pron. he, it; (pl.) they.

île, n.f. island.

illégal (-l-), adj. illegal.

illégitime (-l-), adj. illegitimate.

illettré (-l-), adj. illiterate.

illicite (-l-), adj. illicit.

illimité (-l-), adj. boundless.

illogique (-l-), adj. illogical.

illuminer (-l-), vb. light, illuminate.

illusion (-l-), n.f. illusion; delusion.

illustration (-l-), n.f. illustration.

illustre (-l-), adj. illustrious, famous.

illustrer (-l-), vb. illustrate.

îlot, n.m. small island.

image, n.f. picture.

imaginaire, adj. fancied, imaginary.

imaginatif, adj. imaginative.

imagination, n.f. imagination.

imaginer, vb. imagine.

imam, n.m. imam.

imbattable, adj. unbeatable.

imbécile, 1. n.m.f. idiot. **2.** adj. idiotic.

imbécillité, n.f. imbecility; stupidity.

imberbe, adj. beardless.

imbiber, vb. soak; steep.

imbu, adj. imbued; steeped.

imitation, n.f. imitation, copy.

imiter, vb. imitate, copy; mimic.

immaculé, adj. immaculate.

immangeable, adj. uneatable.

immatériel, adj. incorporeal.

immatriculer, vb. matriculate.

immédiat, adj. immediate.

immense, adj. immense, great, huge.

immensité, n.f. immensity.

immerger, vb. immerse.

immeuble, n.m. real estate.

immigrer, v.b. immigrate.

imminent, adj. imminent.

immiscer, vb. s'i., meddle, interfere.

immixtion, n.f. mixing; interference.

immobile, adj. motionless.

immobilier, adj. property.

immodéré, adj. immoderate.

immoler, vb. sacrifice. s'i., sacrifice oneself.

immonde, adj. filthy.

immoral, adj. immoral.

immortaliser, vb. immortalize.

immortalité, n.f. immortality.

immortel, adj. and n.m. immortal.

immuable, adj. unchangeable.

immuniser, vb. immunize.

immunité, n.f. immunity.

impact, n.m. impact.

impair, adj. odd (number).

impalpable, adj. intangible.

impardonnable, adj. unforgivable.

imparfait, adj. and n.m. imperfect.

impartial, adj. impartial.

impasse, n.f. dead end.

impassible, adj. impassive.

impatience, n.f. impatience.

impatient, adj. impatient.

impatienter, vb. provoke.

impayable, adj. invaluable; very funny.

impeccable, adj. faultless.

impécunieux, adj. impecunious.

impénétrable, adj. impenetrable.

impératif, adj. and n.m. imperative.

impératrice, n.f. empress.

imperceptible, adj. imperceptible.

imperfection, n.f. imperfection.

impérial, adj. imperial.

impérialisme, n.m. imperialism.

impérieux, adj. domineering.

impérissable, adj. imperishable.

imperméabiliser, vb. waterproof.

imperméable, 1. n.m. raincoat. **2.** adj. waterproof.

impersonnel, adj. impersonal.

impertinence, n.f. impertinence.

impertinent, adj. saucy.

impétueux, adj. headlong, impetuous.

impie, adj. impious.

impitoyable, adj. merciless, pitiless, ruthless.

implanter, vb. establish; implant.

impliquer, vb. involve; imply.

implorer, vb. implore, beg.

impoli, adj. rude, impolite, discourteous.

impolitesse, n.f. discourtesy.

impopulaire, adj. unpopular.

importance, n.f. significance, importance.

important, *adj.* momentous, important.
importateur, *n.m.* importer.
importation, *n.f.* import.
importer, *vb.* matter; import.
importun, *adj.* tiresome, bothersome; importunate.
importuner, *vb.* pester, keep bothering.
importunité, *n.f.* importunity.
imposable, *adj.* taxable.
imposer, *vb.* impose; tax; enforce.
imposition, *n.f.* imposition.
impossibilité, *n.f.* impossibility.
 dans l'i. de, unable to.
impossible, *adj.* impossible.
imposteur, *n.m.* fraud (person), faker, impostor.
imposture, *n.f.* imposture, deception.
impôt, *n.m.* tax, tariff.
impotent, *adj.* weak, infirm.
impôt sur les ventes, *n.m.* sales tax.
imprécis, *adj.* imprecise.
imprégner, *vb.* impregnate, imbue.
imprenable, *adj.* impregnable.
impression, *n.f.* print, impression.
impressionnable, *adj.* sensitive, impressionable.
impressionnant, *adj.* impressive.
impressionner, *vb.* affect.
imprévisible, *adj.* unforseeable.
imprévoyance, *n.f.* improvidence.
imprévoyant, *adj.* not foresighted.
imprévu, *adj.* unexpected, unforeseen.
imprimante, *n.f.* printer.
imprimé, *n.m.* printed matter.
imprimer, *vb.* impress; print.
imprimerie, *n.f.* printery, printing.
imprimeur, *n.m.* printer.
improbable, *adj.* improbable.
improbité, *n.f.* dishonesty.
improductif, *adj.* unproductive.
impromptu, *adv., adj. and n.m.* impromptu.
impropre, *adv.* improper, unfit.
improviste, *adv.* **à l'i.,** all of a sudden.
imprudence, *n.f.* indiscretion.
impudence, *n.f.* impudence.
impudicité, *n.f.* lewdness.
impuissance, *n.f.* impotence.

impuissant, *adj.* impotent; powerless, helpless.
impulsif, *adj.* impulsive.
impulsion, *n.f.* impulse, spur.
impunément, *adv.* with impunity.
impunité, *n.f.* impunity.
impur, *adj.* impure.
impureté, *n.f.* impurity.
imputer, *vb.* impute.
inabordable, *adj.* inaccessible.
inaccessible, *adj.* inaccessible.
inaccoutumé, *adj.* unusual.
inachevé, *adj.* unfinished.
inactif, *adj.* inactive, indolent.
inadapté, *adj.* maladjusted.
inadmissible, *adj.* unacceptable.
inadvertance, *n.f.* oversight.
inanimé, *adj.* lifeless.
inanité, *n.f.* uselessness.
inaperçu, *adj.* unperceived.
inattaquable, *adj.* unassailable.
inattendu, *adj.* unexpected.
inaugurer, *vb.* inaugurate.
inavouable, *adj.* unavowable, shameful.
incalculable, *adj.* countless, incalculable.
incapable, *adj.* unable.
incapacité, *n.f.* incapacity.
incarcérer, *vb.* imprison.
incarnat, *adj.* flesh-colored, rosy.
incarner, *vb.* embody.
incartade, *n.f.* insult, prank.
incendie, *n.m.* fire.
incendier, *vb.* set fire to.
incertain, *adj.* uncertain.
incertitude, *n.f.* suspense.
incessamment, *adv.* incessantly; immediately.
incessant, *adj.* incessant.
inceste, *n.m.* incest.
incident, *n.m.* incident.
incinérer, *vb.* cremate; incinerate.
incisif, *adj.* incisive.
incision, *n.f.* incision.
inciter, *vb.* incite.
inclinaison, *n.f.* slope.
inclination, *n.f.* bow, nod; propensity.
incliner, *vb.* slant; nod, bow. **s'i.,** lean.
inclure, *vb.* include, enclose.
inclus, *adj.* included. **ci-inclus,** enclosed, herewith.
inclusif, *adj.* inclusive.

incohérent, *adj.* incoherent.
incolore, *adj.* colorless.
incomber, *vb.* devolve upon.
incombustible, *adj.* incombustible.
incommode, *adj.* uncomfortable, inconvenient.
incommoder, *vb.* inconvenience.
incomparable, *adj.* incomparable.
incompatible, *adj.* incompatible.
incompétence, *n.f.* incompetence.
incomplet, *adj.* imperfect, unfinished.
incompréhension, *n.m.* lack of understanding.
incompris, *adj.* unappreciated, not understood.
inconditionnel, *adj.* unquestioning.
inconduite, *n.f.* misconduct.
incongru, *adj.* unseemly.
inconnu, *adj.* unknown.
inconscient, *adj. and n.m.* unconscious.
inconséquent, *adj.* inconsistent.
inconsidéré, *adj.* thoughtless.
inconsistant, *adj.* weak, inconsistent.
inconstant, *adj.* fickle.
incontestable, *adj.* unquestionable.
incontesté, *adj.* unquestioned.
incontinent, 1. *adj.* incontinent. **2.** *adv.* immediately.
incontrôlable, *adj.* not verifiable.
inconvenance, *n.f.* impropriety.
inconvénient, *n.m.* inconvenience.
incorporer, *vb.* embody.
incorrect, *adj.* incorrect.
incrédule, *adj.* incredulous.
incriminer, *vb.* accuse.
incroyable, *adj.* incredible.
incroyant, *n.m.* unbeliever.
inculper, *vb.* charge, accuse.
inculquer, *vb.* instill.
inculte, *adj.* uncultivated; unkempt.
incurable, *adj.* incurable.
incurie, *n.f.* carelessness, neglect.
incursion, *n.f.* incursion.
Inde, *n.f.* India.
indécent, *adj.* indecent.
indécis, *adj.* doubtful, vague, dim.
indéfini, *adj.* indefinite.
indéfinissable, *adj.* nondescript.

indéfrisable, *n.f.* permanent wave.
indélicat, *adj.* indelicate.
indélicatesse, *n.f.* indelicacy; blunder.
indemne, *adj.* unharmed.
indemniser, *vb.* compensate for.
indemnité, *n.f.* indemnity.
indépendance, *n.f.* independence.
indépendant, *adj.* independent.
index (-ks), *n.m.* index; forefinger.
indicateur, *n.m.* timetable; informer.
indicatif, *adj. and n.m.* indicative.
indicatif interurbain, *n.m.* area code.
indication, *n.f.* indication.
indice, *n.m.* sign, proof.
indicible, *adj.* unspeakable, inexpressible.
Indien, *n.m.* Indian.
indien, *adj.* Indian.
indifférence, *n.f.* indifference.
indifférent, *adj.* indifferent.
indigène, *n.m.f.* native.
indigent, *adj.* destitute.
indigeste, *adj.* indigestible.
indignation, *n.f.* indignation, anger.
indigne, *adj.* worthless, unworthy.
indigné, *adj.* indignant.
indigner, *vb.* anger.
indiquer, *vb.* indicate, point out.
indirect, *adj.* indirect.
indiscret, *adj.* indiscreet.
indiscutable, *adj.* indisputable.
indispensable, *adj.* indispensable, essential.
indisposer, *vb.* indispose; set against.
indisposition, *n.f.* ailment.
indistinct, *adj.* indistinct.
individu, *n.m.* individual, person.
individuel, *adj.* individual.
indomptable, *adj.* adamant; unconquerable.
indu, *adj.* undue; not ordinary.
induire, *vb.* induce; infer.
indulgence, *n.f.* indulgence.
indulgent, *adj.* lenient; indulgent.
indûment, *adv.* unduly.
industrie, *n.f.* industry.
industriel, *adj.* industrial.
inébranlable, *adj.* immovable, firm.
inédit, *adj.* unpublished.

inefficace, *adj.* ineffectual.

inégal, *adj.* uneven, unequal.

inégalité, *n.f.* inequality; irregularity.

inepte, *adj.* inept; stupid.

ineptie, *n.f.* inept action.

inépuisable, *n.f.* inexhaustible.

inertie, *n.f.* inertia.

inestimable, *adj.* priceless.

inévitable, *adj.* inevitable.

inexact, *adj.* inexact.

inexécutable, *adj.* impracticable.

inexplicable, *adj.* inexplicable.

inexprimable, *adj.* inexpressible.

infaillible, *adj.* infallible.

infâme, *adj.* infamous.

infamie, *n.f.* infamy.

infanterie, *n.f.* infantry.

infarctus, *n.f.* coronary (thrombosis).

infatigable, *adj.* untiring.

infécond, *adj.* barren, sterile.

infect, *adj.* infected; rotten.

infecter, *vb.* infect.

infection, *n.f.* infection.

inférieur, *adj. and n.m.* inferior, low(er).

infériorité, *n.f.* inferiority.

infernal, *adj.* infernal.

infester, *vb.* infest.

infidèle, *adj.* disloyal, unfaithful, false.

infidélité, *n.f.* infidelity.

infime, *adj.* lowest; tiny.

infini, *adj. and n.m.* infinite.

infinité, *n.f.* infinity.

infinitif, *n.m.* infinitive.

infirme, *adj. and n.m.f.* invalid.

infirmer, *vb.* invalidate; weaken.

infirmière, *n.f.* nurse.

infirmité, *n.f.* infirmity.

inflammation, *n.f.* inflammation.

inflation, *n.f.* inflation.

infliger, *vb.* inflict.

influence, *n.f.* influence.

influent, *adj.* influential.

information, *n.f.* inquiry; (*pl.*) news.

informatique, *n.f.* computer science.

informatiser, *vb.* computerize.

informe, *adj.* shapeless.

informer, *vb.* inform. **i. de**, acquaint with.

infraction, *n.f.* breach.

infructueux, *adj.* fruitless.

infuser, *vb.* infuse. **faire i.**, brew.

ingambe, *adj.* nimble.

ingénieur, *n.m.* engineer.

ingénieux, *adj.* ingenious.

ingéniosité, *n.f.* ingenuity.

ingénu, *adj.* naive; ingenuous.

ingrat, *adj.* ungrateful.

ingrédient, *n.m.* ingredient.

inguérissable, *adj.* incurable.

inhabile, *adj.* awkward; incapable.

inhabituel, *adj.* unusual.

inhalation, *n.f.* inhalation.

inhiber, *vb.* inhibit.

inhospitalier, *adj.* inhospitable.

inhumain, *adj.* cruel, inhuman.

inimitié, *n.f.* enmity.

inique, *adj.* unfair.

initial, *adj.* initial.

initiale, *n.f.* initial.

initialiser, *vb.* format.

initiative, *n.f.* initiative.

initier, *vb.* initiate.

injecté, *adj.* **i. de sang**, bloodshot.

injecter, *vb.* inject.

injection, *n.f.* injection.

injonction, *n.f.* injunction.

injures, *n.f.pl.* abuse.

injurier, *vb.* abuse; insult.

injurieux, *adj.* abusive; insulting, offensive.

injuste, *adj.* unfair.

injustice, *n.f.* injustice.

inlassable, *adj.* untiring.

inné, *adj.* innate.

innocence, *n.f.* innocence.

innocent, *adj.* innocent.

innocenter, *vb.* declare innocent.

innombrable, *adj.* countless.

innovation, *n.f.* innovation.

inoccupé, *adj.* idle; unoccupied.

inoculer, *vb.* inoculate.

inodore, *adj.* odorless.

inoffensif, *adj.* innocuous, harmless.

inondation, *n.f.* flood.

inonder, *vb.* flood.

inopiné, *adj.* unexpected.

inoubliable, *adj.* unforgettable.

inouï, *adj.* unheard-of.

inox(ydable), *adj.* stainless.

inquiet, *adj.* restless, anxious, uneasy.

inquiéter, *vb.* trouble. **s'i.**, worry.

inquiétude, *n.f.* misgiving, worry.

insaisissable, *adj.* imperceptible.
insalubre, *adj.* unhealthy.
inscription, *n.f.* incription, entry.
inscrire, *vb.* inscribe; enter.
insecte, *n.m.* bug, insect.
insensé, *adj.* mad.
insensible, *adj.* insensible, unfeeling.
inséparable, *adj.* inseparable.
insérer, *vb.* insert.
insigne, *n.m.* badge, sign.
insignifiant, *adj.* petty, insignificant.
insinuer, *vb.* hint.
insipide, *adj.* tasteless; dull.
insistance, *n.f.* insistence.
insister, *vb.* insist.
insolation, *n.f.* sunstroke.
insolence, *n.f.* insolence.
insolite, *adj.* unusual.
insomnie, *n.f.* insomnia.
insondable, *adj.* bottomless.
insouciant, *adj.* casual, careless.
insoumis, *adj.* rebellious.
inspecter, *vb.* examine, survey.
inspecteur, *n.m.* inspector.
inspection, *n.f.* inspection.
inspiration, *n.f.* inspiration.
inspirer, *vb.* inspire.
instable, *adj.* temperamental; unsteady, unstable.
installer, *vb.* install.
instamment, *adv.* urgently.
instance, *n.f.* entreaty; instance; authority.
instant, *n.m.* instant. **à l'i.,** at once.
instantané, 1. *n.m.* snapshot. **2.** *adj.* instantaneous.
instinct, *n.m.* instinct.
instinctif, *adj.* instinctive.
instituer, *vb.* institute.
institut, *n.m.* institute.
instituteur, *n.m.* teacher.
institution, *n.f.* institution, institute.
institutrice, *n.f.* teacher.
instructeur, *n.m.* teacher.
instructif, *adj.* instructive.
instruction, *n.f.* education, instruction; (*pl.*) directions.
instruire, *vb.* educate, teach, instruct.
instrument, *n.m.* instrument.
instrumentation, *n.f.* orchestration.

insu, *n.m.* **à l'i. de,** unknown to.
insuccès, *n.m.* failure.
insuffisance, *n.f.* deficiency.
insuffisant, *adj.* deficient.
insulaire, 1. *n.m.* islander. **2.** *adj.* insular.
insuline, *n.f.* insulin.
insulte, *n.f.* affront, insult.
insulter, *vb.* affront, insult.
insurgé, *adj. and n.m.* insurgent.
insurger, *vb.* **s'i.,** revolt.
insurmontable, *adj.* insuperable.
intact (-kt), *adj.* intact.
intarissable, *adj.* inexhaustible.
intègre, *adj.* upright.
intégrisme, *n.m.* fundamentalism.
intégrité, *n.f.* integrity.
intellect, *n.m.* intellect.
intellectuel, *adj. and n.m.* intellectual.
intelligence, *n.f.* intelligence.
intelligent, *adj.* intelligent.
intelligible, *adj.* intelligible; audible.
intempérie, *n.f.* inclemency (of weather).
intempestif, *adj.* untimely.
intenable, *adj.* unbearable.
intendance, *n.f.* administration.
intendant, *n.m.* director.
intendante, *n.f.* matron.
intense, *adj.* intense.
intensif, *adj.* intensive.
intensité, *n.f.* intensity.
intention, *n.f.* intention.
intentionné, *adj.* intentioned.
intentionnel, *adj.* intentional.
interactif, *adj.* interactive.
intercéder, *vb.* intercede.
intercepter, *vb.* intercept.
interdiction, *n.f.* ban.
interdire, *vb.* forbid.
intéressant, *adj.* interesting.
intéresser, *vb.* interest, concern, affect.
intérêt, *n.m.* interest.
intérieur, *adj. and n.m.* interior.
interjection, *n.f.* interjection.
interlocuteur, *n.m.* speaker; person one is speaking to.
interloquer, *vb.* embarrass.
intermède, *n.m.* interlude.
intermédiaire, 1. *adj.* intermediate. **2.** *n.m.f.* intermediary.
interminable, *adj.* interminable.

internat, n.m. boarding school.
international, adj. international.
interne, 1. adj. internal. **2.** n.m.f. resident student.
interner, vb. intern.
interpellation, n.f. questioning.
interpeller, vb. ask.
interphone, n.m. intercom.
interposer, vb. interpose.
interprétation, n.f. interpretation.
interprète, n.m.f. interpreter.
interpréter, vb. interpret.
interrogateur, 1. n.m. examiner. **2.** adj. questioning.
interrogation, n.f. interrogation.
interrogatoire, n.m. cross-examination.
interroger, vb. question.
interrompre, vb. interrupt.
interrupteur, n.m. switch.
interruption, n.f. break, intermission, interruption.
interurbain, n.m. long-distance telephone service.
intervalle, n.m. interval.
intervenir, vb. interfere.
intervention, n.f. interference.
intervertir, vb. transpose.
interview, n.m. or f. interview.
interviewer, vb. interview.
intestin, n.m. bowels.
intimation, n.f. notification.
intime, adj. intimate.
intimer, vb. notify.
intimider, vb. daunt, intimidate.
intimité, n.f. intimacy.
intituler, vb. entitle.
intolérance, n.f. intolerance.
intonation, n.f. intonation.
intoxication, n.f. poisoning.
intoxiquer, vb. poison; brainwash.
intraitable, adj. intractable, difficult to deal with.
intrépide, adj. fearless.
intrigant, 1. adj. intriguing. **2.** n.m. schemer.
intrigue, n.f. plot, intrigue.
intriguer, vb. intrigue; puzzle.
intrinsèque, adj. intrinsic.
introduction, n.f. introduction.
introduire, vb. introduce, insert.
introuvable, adj. unfindable.
intrus, n.m. intruder.
introverti, n.m. introvert.
intrusion, n.f. intrusion; trespass.

intuitif, adj. intuitive.
intuition, n.f. intuition.
inusité, adj. unusual.
inutile, adj. useless, needless.
invalide, 1. n.m.f. invalid. **2.** adj. disabled, invalid.
invalider, vb. invalidate.
invasion, n.f. invasion.
invectiver, vb. abuse, revile.
inventaire, n.m. inventory.
inventer, vb. invent.
inventeur, n.m. inventor.
invention, n.f. invention.
inventorier, vb. inventory, catalogue.
inverse, adj. inverted, inverse.
investigateur, 1. adj. searching. **2.** n.m. investigator.
investigation, n.f. investigation, inquiry.
investir, vb. invest.
invétéré, adj. inveterate.
invincible, adj. invincible.
invisible, adj. invisible.
invitation, n.f. invitation.
invité, n.m. guest.
inviter, vb. invite, ask.
involontaire, adj. involuntary.
invoquer, vb. call upon.
invraisemblable, adj. improbable.
iode, n.m. iodine.
Irak, n.m. Iraq.
Iran, n.m. Iran.
iris (-s), n.m. iris.
irisé, adj. iridescent.
Irlandais, n.m. Irishman.
irlandais, adj. Irish.
Irlande, n.f. Ireland.
ironie, n.f. irony.
ironique, adj. ironical.
irradier, vb. radiate.
irraisonnable, adj. irrational.
irrationnel, adj. irrational.
irréel, adj. unreal.
irréfléchi, adj. thoughtless, rash.
irrégulier, adj. irregular.
irréligieux, adj. irreligious.
irrésistible, adj. irresistible.
irrésolu, adj. irresolute.
irrespectueux, adj. disrespectful.
irrévérence, n.f. disrespect.
irrigation, n.f. irrigation.
irriguer, vb. irrigate.
irritation, n.f. irritation.

irriter, *vb.* irritate, anger; provoke.

Islam, *n.m.* Islam.

islamique, *adj.* Islamic.

Islande, *n.f.* Iceland.

isolateur, *adj.* insulating.

isolement, *n.m.* isolation.

isoler, *vb.* isolate.

isoloire, *n.m.* polling booth.

Israël, *n.m.* Israel.

Israélien, *n.m.* Israeli.

israélien, *adj.* Israeli.

Israélite, *n.m.* Jew.

israélite, *adj.* Jewish.

issue, *n.f.* issue, outlet; outcome.

isthme, *n.m.* isthmus.

Italie, *n.f.* Italy.

Italien, *n.m.* Italian (person).

italien, 1. *n.m.* Italian (language). **2.** *adj.* Italian.

italique, 1. *n.m.* italics. **2.** *adj.* italic.

itinéraire, *n.m.* route, itinerary.

ivoire, *n.m.* ivory.

ivre, *adj.* drunk, intoxicated.

ivresse, *n.f.* drunkenness, intoxication.

ivrogne, *n.m./f.* drunkard.

ivrognerie, *n.f.* drunkenness.

J

jaboter, *vb.* prattle.

jacasser, *vb.* chatter.

jachère, *n.f.* fallow.

jacinthe, *n.f.* hyacinth.

jadis (-s), *adv.* formerly.

jaillir, *vb.* gush, spurt.

jaillissement, *n.m.* gush, spurt.

jais, *n.m.* jet (mineral).

jalon, *n.m.* staff; landmark.

jalonner, *vb.* mark out.

jalouser, *vb.* envy.

jalousie, *n.f.* jealousy.

jaloux, *adj.* jealous.

jamais, *adv.* ever; never.

jambe, *n.f.* leg.

jambière, *n.f.* legging.

jambon, *n.m.* ham.

jante, *n.f.* rim.

janvier, *n.m.* January.

Japon, *n.m.* Japan.

Japonais, *n.m.* Japanese (person).

japonais, 1. *n.m.* Japanese (language). **2.** *adj.* Japanese.

japper, *vb.* yelp.

jaquette, *n.f.* jacket.

jardin, *n.m.* garden.

jardinage, *n.m.* gardening.

jardinier, *n.m.* gardener.

jargon, *n.m.* jargon.

jarre, *n.f.* jar.

jarretière, *n.f.* garter.

jaser, *vb.* jabber.

jasmin, *n.m.* jasmine.

jatte, *n.f.* bowl.

jaunâtre, *adj.* yellowish.

jaune, 1. *adj.* yellow. **2.** *n.m.* yolk (of egg).

jaunir, *vb.* turn yellow.

jaunisse, *n.f.* jaundice.

jazz, *n.m.* jazz.

je (ja), *pron.* I.

jeans, *n.m.pl.* jeans.

jésuite, *n.m.* Jesuit.

jet, *n.m.* jet (water, gas).

jetable, *adj.* disposable.

jetée, *n.f.* pier.

jeter, *vb.* throw.

jeton, *n.m.* token.

jeu, *n.m.* play, game. **mettre en j.,** stake.

jeudi, *n.m.* Thursday.

jeune, *adj.* young, youthful.

jeûne, *n.m.* fast.

jeûner, *vb.* fast.

jeunesse, *n.f.* youth.

joaillerie, *n.f.* jewelry.

joaillier, *n.m.* jeweler.

job, *n.m.* (colloquial) job.

jobard, *n.m.* fool.

joie, *n.f.* joy.

joindre, *vb.* join.

joint, *n.m.* joint.

jointure, *n.f.* joint (esp. of the body).

joli, *adj.* pretty.

joliment, *adv.* prettily; awfully.

jonc, *n.m.* rush (plant).

joncher, *vb.* scatter.

jonction, *n.f.* junction.

jongler, *vb.* juggle.

jongleur, *n.m.* juggler.

jonquille, *n.f.* jonquil.

Jordanie, *n.f.* Jordan.

joue, *n.f.* cheek.

jouer, *vb.* play.

jouet, *n.m.* toy.

joueur, *n.m.* player.

joufflu, *adj.* chubby-cheeked, chubby.

joug (-g), *n.m.* yoke.

jouir, *vb.* enjoy.

jouissance, *n.f.* enjoyment.

jouisseur, *n.m.* pleasure-seeker.

jour, *n.m.* day, daylight. **j. de fête,** holiday. **point du j.,** dawn.

journal, *n.m.* newspaper; journal; diary.

journalier, *adj.* daily.

journalisme, *n.m.* journalism.

journaliste, *n.m.f.* journalist.

journée, *n.f.* day.

journellement, *adv.* daily.

joute, *n.f.* joust.

jovialité, *n.f.* jollity.

joyau, *n.m.* jewel.

joyeux, *adj.* joyful.

jubilé, *n.m.* jubilee.

jubiler, *vb.* exult.

judaïsme, *n.m.* Judaism.

judas, *n.m.* peephole.

judiciaire, *adj.* judicial; legal.

judicieux, *adj.* wise; judicious.

juge, *n.m.* judge.

jugement, *n.m.* judgment, reason. **mettre en j.,** try.

juger, *vb.* judge.

jugulaire, *adj.* jugular.

Juif *m.,* **Juive** *f. n.* Jew.

juif *m.,* **juive** *f. adj.* Jewish.

juillet, *n.m.* July.

juin, *n.m.* June.

jules, *n.m.* (colloquial) guy.

jumeau *m.,* **jumelle** *f. adj. and n.* twin.

jumeler, *vb.* couple, join.

jumelles, *n.f.pl.* opera glasses.

jument, *n.f.* mare.

jungle, *n.f.* jungle.

jupe, *n.f.* skirt.

jupon, *n.m.* petticoat.

jurer, *vb.* swear.

juridiction, *n.f.* jurisdiction.

juridique, *adj.* judicial, legal.

jurisconsulte, *n.m.f.* jurist; lawyer.

jurisprudence, *n.f.* jurisprudence.

juriste, *n.m.f.* jurist.

juron, *n.m.* oath.

jury, *n.m.* jury.

jus, *n.m.* juice; gravy.

jusque, *prep.* up to. **jusqu'à,** as far as; until. **jusqu'ici,** hitherto.

juste, **1.** *adj.* just, fair, right. **2.** *adv.* just.

justement, *adv.* precisely, exactly.

justesse, *n.f.* accuracy, precision.

justice, *n.f.* justice, fairness.

justifiant, *adj.* justifying.

justification, *n.f.* justification.

justifier, *vb.* justify.

juteux, *adj.* juicy.

juvénile, *adj.* juvenile.

K

kaki, *adj.* khaki.

kangourou, *n.m.* kangaroo.

karaté, *n.m.* karate.

kasher, *adj.* kosher.

képi, *n.m.* cap.

kermesse, *n.f.* fair.

kidnapper, *vb.* kidnap.

kif, *n.m.* marijuana.

kilogramme, *n.m.* kilogram.

kilohertz, *n.m.* kilohertz.

kilométrage, *n.m.* mileage.

kilomètre, *n.m.* kilometer.

kilométrique, *adj.* kilometric.

kinésithérapeute, *n.m.f.* physiotherapist.

kiosque, *n.m.* kiosk; newsstand; bandstand.

klaxon, *n.m.* car horn.

kyrielle, *n.f.* litany.

kyste, *n.m.* cyst.

L

la, *pron.* her; it (*f.*).

là, *adv.* there.

là-bas, *adv.* yonder, out there.

labeur, *n.m.* labor.

labo, *n.m.* (colloquial) lab.

laboratoire, *n.m.* laboratory.

laborieux, *adj.* industrious, laborious.

labour, *n.m.* plowing.

labourer, *vb.* plow.

labyrinthe, *n.m.* maze.

lac, *n.m.* lake.

lacérer, *vb.* lacerate; tear up.

lacet, *n.m.* shoelace; winding.

lâche, 1. *n.m.f.* coward. **2.** *adj.* cowardly; loose.

lâchement, *adv.* loosely; shamefully.

lâcher, *vb.* loosen; let go. **l. pied,** give ground, flee.

lâcheté, *n.f.* cowardice.

lacis, *n.m.* network.

laconique, *adj.* laconic.

lacrymogène, *adj.* gaz l., tear gas.

lacté, *adj.* milky.

lacune, *n.f.* gap, blank.

ladre, *adj.* stingy, mean.

lagune, *n.f.* lagoon.

laid, *adj.* ugly.

laideron, *n.m.* ugly person.

laideur, *n.f.* ugliness.

lainage, *n.m.* woolen goods.

laine, *n.f.* wool.

laineux, *adj.* woolly; downy.

laïque (lä ēk), *n.m.* layman.

laisse, *n.f.* leash.

laisser, *vb.* let; leave.

laisser-aller, *n.m.* freedom; negligence.

laissez-passer, *n.m.* pass.

lait, *n.m.* milk.

laitage, *n.m.* dairy foods.

laiterie, *n.f.* dairy.

laiteux, *adj.* milky.

laitier, *n.m.* milkman.

laiton, *n.m.* brass.

laitue, *n.f.* lettuce.

lambeau, *n.m.* rag.

lambin, *adj.* slow, dawdling.

lame, *n.f.* blade.

lamé, *adj.* gold- or silver-trimmed.

lamelle, *n.f.* (microscope) slide.

lamentable, *adj.* sad, grievous.

lamentation, *n.f.* lamentation.

lamenter, *vb.* mourn, lament.

laminer, *vb.* laminate.

lampadaire, *n.m.* lamp; street lamp.

lampe, *n.f.* lamp. **l. de poche,** flashlight.

lamper, *vb.* drink, gulp.

lampion, *n.m.* Chinese lantern.

lampiste, *n.m.* lamplighter.

lance, *n.f.* lance.

lancer, *vb.* hurl; launch.

lanceur, *n.m.* pitcher.

lancinant, *adj.* throbbing (of pain).

lande, *n.f.* wasteland; moor.

landeau, *n.m.* baby carriage.

langage, *n.m.* language.

langoureux, *adj.* languishing.

langouste, *n.f.* crayfish, crawfish.

langue, *n.f.* tongue; language.

languette, *n.f.* tonguelike strip.

langueur, *n.f.* languor.

languir, *vb.* pine, languish.

languissant, *adj.* languid.

lanière, *n.f.* strap, thong.

lanterne, *n.f.* lantern.

lapider, *vb.* stone; abuse.

lapin, *n.m.* rabbit.

laps, *n.m.* lapse of time.

lapsus (-sys), *n.m.* slip.

laquais, *n.m.* footman, lackey.

laque, *n.f.* shellac; hairspray.

larcin, *n.m.* larceny, theft.

lard, *n.m.* bacon, fat.

larder, *vb.* lard; pierce.

large, *adj.* wide.

largesse, *n.f.* generosity.

largeur, *n.f.* width.

larguer, *vb.* drop, let go.

larme, *n.f.* tear.

larmoyer, *vb.* weep, whimper.

larron, *n.m.* thief.

laryngite, *n.f.* laryngitis.

las, *adj.* weary.

lascif, *adj.* lewd, wanton.

laser, *n.m.* laser.

lasser, *vb.* weary.

lassitude, *n.f.* weariness.

latéral, *adj.* lateral.

Latin, *n.m.* Latin (person).

latin, 1. *n.m.* Latin (language). **2.** *adj.* Latin.

latitude, *n.f.* latitude.

latte, *n.f.* lath.

laurier, *n.m.* bay, laurel.

lavabo, *n.m.* lavatory.

lavage, *n.m.* washing.

lavande, *n.f.* lavender.

lavandière, *n.f.* laundress.

lavement, *n.m.* enema.

laver, *vb.* wash.

lavette, *n.f.* dishrag.

laxatif, *n.m.* laxative.

le (la) *m.,* **la** *f.,* **les** *pl.* 1. *art.* the. 2. *pron.* him, her, it.

lécher, *vb.* lick.

lèche-vitrines, *n.m.* window shopping.

leçon, *n.f.* lesson.

lecteur, *n.m.* reader.

lecture, *n.f.* reading.

légal, *adj.* lawful, legal.

légaliser, *vb.* legalize.

légalité, *n.f.* legality.

légataire, *n.m.* legatee.

légation, *n.f.* legation.

légendaire, *adj.* legendary.

légende, *n.f.* legend; inscription.

léger, *adj.* light.

légèreté, *n.f.* lightness.

légion, *n.f.* legion.

législateur, *n.m.* legislator.

législatif, *adj.* legislative.

législation, *n.f.* legislation.

législature, *n.f.* legislature.

légitime, *adj.* legitimate, lawful.

legs, *n.m.* bequest.

léguer, *vb.* bequeath.

légume, *n.m.* vegetable.

lendemain, *n.m.* the next day.

lent, *adj.* slow.

lenteur, *n.f.* slowness.

lentille, *n.f.* lentil; lens.

léopard, *n.m.* leopard.

lèpre, *n.f.* leprosy.

lépreux, 1. *adj.* leprous. 2. *n.m.* leper.

lequel, *pron.* which, who.

les, *pron.* them.

lesbien, *n.m.* lesbian.

lesbienne, *n.f.* lesbian.

léser, *vb.* wrong, hurt.

lésine, *n.f.* stinginess.

lésion, *n.f.* wrong; lesion.

lessive, *n.f.* laundry.

lessiveuse, *n.f.* washing machine.

lest (-t), *n.m.* ballast.

leste, *adj.* nimble, clever.

lettre, *n.f.* letter.

lettré, *adj.* lettered, literate.

leucémie, *n.f.* leukemia.

leur, 1. *pron.* to them; **le leur, la leur,** theirs. 2. **leur** *m.f.,* **leurs** *pl.* *adj.* their.

leurre, *n.m.* lure, trap.

leurrer, *vb.* lure.

levain, *n.m.* yeast; leaven.

levée, *n.m.* embankment, levee.

lever, *vb.* raise. **se l.,** get up.

levier, *n.m.* lever.

lèvre, *n.f.* lip.

lévrier, *n.m.* greyhound.

lexique, *n.m.* lexicon.

lézard, *n.m.* lizard.

lézarde, *n.f.* crevice.

liaison, *n.f.* connection, linkage.

liant, *adj.* supple; affable.

liasse, *n.f.* file; wad.

Liban, *n.m.* Lebanon.

libelle, *n.m.* libel.

libeller, *vb.* draw up, word.

libéral, *adj.* liberal.

libérateur, *n.m.* rescuer.

libérer, *vb.* free.

liberté, *n.f.* freedom, liberty.

libertin, 1. *adj.* wanton. 2. *n.* libertine.

libraire, *n.m.* bookseller.

librairie, *n.f.* bookstore.

libre, *adj.* free.

libre-échange, *n.m.* free trade.

Libye, *n.f.* Libya.

licence, *n.f.* license.

licencié, *n.m.* licensee; holder of university degree.

licencier, *v.b.* dismiss, lay off.

licencieux, *adj.* licentious.

licite, *adj.* lawful.

licorne, *n.f.* unicorn.

licou, *n.m.* halter.

lie, *n.f.* dreg.

liège, *n.m.* cork.

lien, *n.m.* bond, link, tie.

lier, *vb.* bind, tie, link.

lierre, *n.m.* ivy.

lieu, *n.m.* place. **au l. de,** instead of.

lieu-commun, *n.m.* commonplace.

lieue, *n.f.* league (distance).

lieutenant, *n.m.* lieutenant.

lièvre, *n.m.* hare.

ligne, *n.f.* line.

lignée, *n.f.* offspring.

ligoter, *vb.* bind up.

ligue, *n.f.* league.

liguer, *vb.* league.

lilas, *n.m.* lilac.

limaçon, *n.m.* snail.

lime, *n.f.* file; lime (fruit).

limer, *vb.* file.

limier, *n.m.* bloodhound.

limitation, *n.f.* limitation.

limitation des naissances, *n.f.* birth control, contraception.

limite, *n.f.* limit, border.
limiter, *vb.* limit, confine.
limoger, *vb.* dismiss.
limon, *n.m.* mud, slime.
limonade, *n.f.* lemon soda.
limoneux, *adj.* muddy.
limpide, *adj.* clear, limpid.
lin, *n.m.* flax.
linceul, *n.m.* shroud.
linéaire, *adj.* lineal.
linge, *n.m.* linen; wash.
lingerie, *n.f.* linen goods; underwear.
linguistique, *adj.* linguistic.
linon, *n.m.* lawn (sheer linen).
linteau, *n.m.* lintel.
lion, *n.m.* lion.
lippu, *adj.* thick-lipped.
liqueur, *n.m.* liquid; liqueur.
liquidation, *n.f.* liquidation; settling.
liquide, *adj. and n.m.* liquid, fluid.
liquider, *vb.* liquidate.
liquoreux, *adj.* sweet.
lire, *vb.* read.
lis (-s), *n.m.* lily.
liséré, *n.m.* piping, border.
liseur, *n.m.* reader.
liseuse, *n.f.* bookmark.
lisible, *adj.* legible.
lisière, *n.f.* edge.
lisse, *adj.* smooth.
lisser, *vb.* smooth.
liste, *n.f.* list, roll.
lit, *n.m.* bed.
litanie, *n.f.* litany.
lit-cage, *n.m.* (folding) cot.
lit de la mer, *n.m.* seabed.
literie, *n.f.* bedding.
litière, *n.f.* litter.
litige, *n.m.* litigation.
litigieux, *adj.* litigious.
litre, *n.m.* liter.
littéraire, *adj.* literary.
littéral, *adj.* literal.
littérature, *n.f.* literature.
littoral, *n.m.* coast.
liturgie, *n.f.* liturgy.
livide, *adj.* livid.
livraison, *n.f.* delivery. **l. contre remboursement,** C.O.D.
livre, *n.f.* pound.
livre, *n.m.* book.
livre de poche, *n.m.* paperback.
livrée, *n.f.* livery.

livrer, *vb.* deliver.
livresque, *adj.* bookish, from books.
livreur, *n.m.* delivery man.
local, *adj.* local.
localiser, *vb.* locate.
localité, *n.f.* locality.
locataire, *n.m.f.* tenant.
location, *n.f.* renting.
loch (-k), *n.m.* log.
locomotive, *n.f.* locomotive.
locuste, *n.f.* locust.
locution, *n.f.* locution, phrase.
loge, *n.f.* box.
logement, *n.m.* lodging.
loger, *vb.* lodge.
logiciel, *n.m.* software.
logique, 1. *n.f.* logic. **2.** *adj.* logical.
logis, *n.m.* dwelling.
loi, *n.f.* law.
loin, *adv.* far, away.
lointain, *adj.* distant.
loir, *n.m.* dormouse.
loisible, *adj.* optional, allowable.
loisir, *n.m.* leisure.
Londres, *n.m.* London.
long *m.*, **longue** *f.* *adj.* long.
longe, *n.f.* leash; loin (of veal).
longer, *vb.* go along.
longeron, *n.m.* beam, girder.
longitude, *n.f.* longitude.
longtemps, *adv.* long.
longueur, *n.f.* length.
look, *n.m.* (colloquial) look, image.
lopin, *n.m.* small piece, plot.
loquace, *adj.* talkative.
loque, *n.f.* morsel, rag.
loquet, *n.m.* latch.
loqueteux, *adj.* tattered.
lorgner, *vb.* glance at; ogle.
lorgnon, *n.m.* glasses.
loriot, *n.m.* oriole.
lors, *adv.* then. **l. de,** at the time of.
lorsque, *conj.* when.
losange, *n.m.* diamond, lozenge.
lot, *n.m.* lot, prize.
loterie, *n.f.* raffle, lottery.
lotion, *n.f.* lotion.
lotir, *vb.* divide, apportion.
loto, *n.m.* lotto, lottery.
louable, *adj.* praiseworthy.
louage, *n.m.* hire.
louange, *n.f.* praise.
louche, *adj.* shady.

loucher, *vb.* squint.
louer, *vb.* praise; hire, rent.
loueur, *n.m.* one who rents.
loup, *n.m.* wolf.
loupe, *n.f.* magnifying glass.
louper, *vb.* (colloquial) spoil, botch.
loup-garou, *n.m.* werewolf.
lourd, *adj.* heavy.
lourdaud, *n.m.* clod.
lourdeur, *n.f.* heaviness; dullness.
lorve, *n.f.* she-wolf.
loyal, *adj.* loyal.
loyauté, *n.f.* loyalty.
loyer, *n.m.* rent.
lubricité, *n.f.* lewdness.
lubrifier, *vb.* lubricate.
lucarne, *n.f.* attic window.
lucide, *adj.* lucid.
lucidité, *n.f.* clearness.
luciole, *n.f.* firefly.
lueur, *n.f.* gleam.
luge, *n.f.* sled.
lugubre, *adj.* doleful, dismal, lugubrious.
lui, *pron.* he; to him, to her.
lui-même, *pron.* himself, itself.
luire, *vb.* gleam.
luisant, *adj.* shiny.
lumière, *n.f.* light.
lumineux, *adj.* luminous.
lunaire, *adj.* lunar.
lunatique, *adj.* whimsical.
lunch, *n.m.* buffet lunch.
lundi, *n.m.* Monday.
lune, *n.f.* moon. **l. de miel,** honeymoon. **clair de l.,** moonlight.
lunetier, *n.m.* optician.
lunettes, *n.f.pl.* glasses.
lustre, *n.m.* chandelier; luster; five-year period.
lustrer, *vb.* polish, gloss.
luth, *n.m.* lute.
lutiner, *vb.* tease.
lutte, *n.f.* strife, struggle, contest.
lutter, *vb.* struggle, contend.
luxe, *n.m.* luxury.
Luxembourg, *n.m.* Luxembourg.
luxer, *vb.* dislocate.
luxueux, *adj.* luxurious.
luxure, *n.f.* lust.
luzerne, *n.f.* alfalfa.
lycée, *n.m.* high school.
lycéen, *n.m.* high-school student.
lymphatique, *adj.* lymphatic.
lynchage, *n.m.* lynching.
lyncher, *vb.* lynch.
lyre, *n.f.* lyre.
lyrique, *adj.* lyric.
lys, *n.m.* lily.

M

M. (abbr. for **Monsieur**), *n.m.* Mr.
macabre, *adj.* macabre, ghastly.
macadam, *n.m.* macadam.
macédoine, *n.f.* salad; mixture.
macérer, *vb.* macerate, soak.
mâcher, *vb.* chew.
machin, *n.m.* thing, gadget.
machinal, *adj.* mechanical.
machination, *n.f.* plot, scheme.
machine, *n.f.* machine. **m. à copier,** copier. **m. à écrire,** typewriter.
machiner, *vb.* plot.
machiniste, *n.m.f.* machinist.
macho, *adj.* (colloquial) macho.
mâchoire, *n.f.* jaw.
mâchonner, *vb.* mumble; munch.
maçon, *n.m.* mason.
maculer, *vb.* spot, blot.
Madame, *n.f.* Madam, Mrs.
madeleine, *n.f.* light cake.
Mademoiselle, *n.f.* Miss.
Madone, *n.f.* Madonna.
mafia, *n.f.* mafia.
magasin, *n.m.* store.
magazine, *n.m.* magazine.
mages, *n.m.pl.* Magi, Wise Men.
Maghreb, *n.m.* North Africa.
magicien, *n.m.* magician.
magie, *n.f.* magic.
magique, *adj.* magic.
magistral, *adj.* masterly, authoritative.
magistrat, *n.m.* magistrate.
magistrature, *n.f.* judiciary.
magnanime, *adj.* magnanimous.
magnat, *n.m.* magnate.
magnétique, *adj.* magnetic.
magnétophone, *n.m.* tape recorder.
magnétoscope, *n.m.* video-recorder.
magnificence, *n.f.* magnificence.

magnifique, *adj.* magnificent.
magouille, *n.f.* scheming.
mahométan, *adj.* Mohammedan.
mai, *n.m.* May.
maigre, *adj.* lean, thin, meager.
maigrir, *vb.* lose weight.
maille, *n.f.* stitch; mesh.
maillot, *n.m.* shorts; T-shirt. **m. de bain,** bathing suit.
main, *n.f.* hand. **sous la m.,** handy.
main-d'œuvre, *n.f.* manpower.
maintenant, *adv.* now. **dès m.,** henceforth.
maintenir, *vb.* maintain.
maintien, *n.m.* upkeep; behavior.
maire, *n.m.* mayor.
mairie, *n.f.* city hall.
mais, *conj.* but.
maïs (mä ēs), *n.m.* corn.
maison, *n.f.* house.
maisonnée, *n.f.* household.
maître, *n.m.* master, teacher.
maîtresse, *n.f.* mistress, teacher.
maîtrise, *n.f.* mastery.
maîtriser, *vb.* master, overcome.
majesté, *n.f.* majesty.
majestueux, *adj.* majestic.
majeur, *adj.* major.
majordome, *n.m.* majordomo.
majorer, *vb.* increase price, over- price.
majoritaire, *adj.* majority.
majorité, *n.f.* majority.
majuscule, *n.f.* capital.
mal, 1. *n.m.* harm, ill, evil. **2.** *adv.* badly. **faire m. à,** hurt. **avoir m. à,** have a pain in.
malade, 1. *n.m.f.* sick person, pa- tient. **2.** *adj.* sick.
maladie, *n.f.* disease, illness, sick- ness.
maladif, *adj.* sickly.
maladresse, *n.f.* awkwardness.
maladroit, *adj.* awkward.
malaise, *n.m.* discomfort.
malappris, *adj.* ill-bred.
malaria, *n.f.* malaria.
malavisé, *adj.* indiscreet, ill-ad- vised.
Malaisie, *n.f.* Malaysia.
malchance, *n.f.* bad luck, mishap.
maldonne, *n.f.* misdeal.
mâle, *adj.* and *n.m.* male.
malédiction, *n.f.* curse.
maléfice, *n.m.* witchery, evil spell.

malencontre, *n.f.* unlucky inci- dent.
malencontreux, *adj.* unlucky.
malentendu, *n.m.* misunderstand- ing.
malfaiteur, *n.m.* malefactor.
malfamé, *adj.* ill-famed.
malgré, *prep.* despite.
malhabile, *adj.* awkward, dull.
malheur, *n.m.* misfortune, acci- dent.
malheureux, *adj.* unfortunate; un- happy, miserable.
malhonnête, *adj.* dishonest.
malhonnêteté, *n.f.* dishonesty.
malice, *n.f.* mischief, malice.
malicieux, *adj.* malicious, roguish.
malin *m.,* **maligne** *f. adj.* sharp, sly; malignant.
malingre, *adj.* sickly, puny.
malintentionné, *adj.* ill-disposed.
malle, *n.f.* trunk.
mallette, *n.f.* small suitcase.
malnutrition, *n.f.* malnutrition.
malotru, *n.m.* boor, lout.
malpropre, *adj.* messy.
malpropreté, *n.f.* messiness.
malsain, *adj.* unhealthy.
malséant, *adj.* improper.
Malte, *n.f.* Malta.
maltraiter, *vb.* misuse.
malveillant, *adj.* malevolent.
malvenu, *adj.* without any right.
malversation, *n.f.* embezzlement.
maman, *n.f.* mamma.
mamelle, *n.f.* udder.
mamelon, *n.m.* nipple; hillock.
mamie, *n.f.* (colloquial) granny.
mammifère, *n.m.* mammal.
manche, *n.m.* handle. *f.* sleeve. **La M.,** the English Channel.
manchette, *n.f.* cuff.
manchon, *n.m.* muff.
manchot, *n.m.* one-armed person.
mandarine, *n.f.* tangerine.
mandat, *n.m.* warrant, writ, man- date. **m.-poste,** money order.
mandataire, *n.m.* agent, proxy.
mander, *vb.* send for, inform.
manège, *n.m.* horsemanship.
manette, *n.f.* handle, lever; joy- stick.
mangeable, *adj.* eatable.
mangeoire, *n.f.* manger.
manger, *vb.* eat.

maniable, *adj.* manageable; easygoing.
maniaque, 1. *n.m.f.* maniac. **2.** *adj.* maniac, maniacal.
manie, *n.f.* mania.
manier, *vb.* handle; wield.
manière, *n.f.* manner.
maniéré, *adj.* affected.
manière de vivre, *n.f.* life style.
manif (-f), *n.f.* (colloquial) demo.
manifestation, *n.f.* demonstration.
manifeste, 1. *n.m.* manifesto, petition. **2.** *adj.* manifest, evident, overt.
manifester, *vb.* manifest, show.
manigance, *n.f.* trick, intrigue.
manipuler, *adj.* manipulate.
manivelle, *n.f.* crank; winch.
mannequin, *n.m.* dummy; model.
manœuvre, *n.f.* maneuver.
manoir, *n.m.* country house, estate.
manquant, 1. *adj.* missing. **2.** *n.m.* absentee.
manque, *n.m.* lack.
manquer, *vb.* miss, lack; fail.
mansarde, *n.f.* attic.
mansuétude, *n.f.* mildness, kindness.
manteau, *n.m.* cloak, coat.
manucure, *n.m.f.* manicurist.
manuel, *adj. and n.m.* manual.
manufacture, *n.f.* manufacture.
manuscrit, *adj. and n.m.* manuscript.
manutention, *n.f.* management.
maquereau, *n.m.* mackerel; (colloquial) pimp.
maquette, *n.f.* preliminary sketch or model.
maquillage, *n.m.* makeup.
maquis, *n.m.* scrub land; Resistance fighters.
maquisard, *n.m.* Resistance fighter.
marais, *n.m.* marsh.
marasme, *n.m.* slump.
marâtre, *n.f.* stepmother.
maraude, *n.f.* marauding.
marbre, *n.m.* marble.
marchand, *n.m.* merchant.
marchander, *vb.* bargain, haggle.
marchandises, *n.f.pl.* goods.
marche, *n.f.* march, step.

marché, *n.m.* market, bargain. **bon m.,** cheap.
marchepied, *n.m.* runningboard.
marcher, *vb.* walk, step, march; run (machine).
marcheur, *n.m.* pedestrian.
mardi, *n.m.* Tuesday.
mare, *n.f.* pool.
marécage, *n.m.* bog.
marécageux, *adj.* marshy.
maréchal, *n.m.* marshal.
marée, *n.f.* tide.
mareyeur, *n.m.* fish seller.
margarine, *n.f.* margarine.
marge, *n.f.* margin.
margelle, *n.f.* edge, brink.
marguerite, *n.f.* daisy.
mari, *n.m.* husband.
mariage, *n.m.* marriage.
marié, 1. *n.m.* bridegroom. **2.** *adj.* married.
mariée, *n.f.* bride.
marie-jeanne, *n.f.* marijuana.
marier, *vb.* marry.
marijuana, *n.f.* marijuana.
marin, 1. *n.m.* sailor. **2.** *adj.* marine. **fusilier m.,** marine.
marinade, *n.f.* mixture for pickling.
marine, *n.f.* navy.
mariner, *vb.* pickle.
marionnette, *n.f.* puppet.
maritime, *adj.* marine.
marmite, *n.f.* pot.
marmiter, *vb.* blast (with gunfire).
marmonner, *vb.* mumble.
marmot, *n.m.* kid, brat.
marmotter, *vb.* mumble.
Maroc (-k), *n.m.* Morocco.
marocain, *adj. and n.m.* Moroccan.
maroquinerie, *n.f.* leather goods.
marotte, *n.f.* fad.
marque, *n.f.* brand, mark.
marquer, *vb.* mark.
marqueur, *n.m.* marker, scorekeeper.
marquis, *n.m.* marquis.
marraine, *n.f.* godmother; sponsor.
marrant, *adj.* funny.
marron, *n.m.* chestnut; brown.
marronier, *n.m.* chestnut tree.
mars (-s), *n.m.* March.
marteau, *n.m.* hammer.

marteler, vb. hammer.
martial, adj. warlike.
martre, n.f. marten.
martyr, n.m. martyr.
martyre, n.m. martyrdom.
marxisme, n.m. Marxism.
mascarade, n.f. masquerade.
mascotte, n.f. mascot.
masculin, adj. masculine.
maso, n.m. (colloquial) masochist.
masochiste, n.m.f. masochist.
masque, n.m. mask.
masquer, vb. mask.
massacre, n.m. slaughter.
massage, n.m. massage.
masse, n.f. mass.
masser, vb. mass; massage.
massif, adj. massive, solid.
massue, n.f. club.
mastiquer, vb. chew.
mat (-t), adj. dull.
mât (mä), n.m. mast.
matelas, n.m. mattress.
matelot, n.m. sailor.
matérialiser, vb. materialize.
matérialisme, n.m. materialism.
matérialiste, n.m.f. materialist.
    adj. materialistic.
matériaux, n.m.pl. stuff, materials.
matériel, adj. material, real.
maternel, adj. native; maternal.
maternité, n.f. maternity.
mathématique, adj. mathematical.
mathématiques, n.f.pl. mathematics.
maths, n.f.pl. (colloquial) math.
matière, n.f. matter. **table des m.s**,
    index.
matin, n.m. morning.
mâtin, n.m. big dog.
matinal, adj. early.
matinée, n.f. morning.
matineux, adj. rising early.
matois, adj. cunning, sly.
matou, n.m. tomcat.
matraque, n.f. heavy club.
matrice, n.f. womb.
matricule, n.f. roster, registration.
matriculer, vb. enroll, register.
matrimonial, adj. marital.
mâture, n.f. masts (of boats).
maturité, n.f. maturity.
maudire, vb. curse.
maudit, adj. cursed, miserable.
maugréer, vb. curse, grumble.

maussade, adj. glum, sullen, cross.
mauvais, adj. bad.
maxime, n.f. maxim.
maximum, n.m. maximum.
mayonnaise, n.f. mayonnaise.
mazout, n.m. (fuel) oil.
me (mə), pron. me; myself.
méandre, n.m. winding.
mec, n.m. (colloquial) guy.
mécanicien, n.m. mechanic, engineer.
mécanique, adj. mechanical.
mécaniser, vb. mechanize.
mécanisme, n.m. mechanism, machinery.
mécano, n.m. mechanic.
méchamment, adv. maliciously.
méchanceté, n.f. wickedness, malice.
méchant, adj. wicked, malicious.
mèche, n.f. lock (hair); wick, fuse.
mécompte, n.m. error; disappointment.
méconnaissable, adj. unrecognizable.
méconnaître, vb. fail to recognize.
mécontent, adj. discontented.
mécontentement, n.m. discontent.
mécontenter, vb. dissatisfy.
mécréant, n.m. unbeliever.
médaille, n.f. medal.
médaillon, n.m. locket.
médecin, n.m. physician.
médecine, n.f. medicine.
médiateur, n.m. mediator; ombudsman (in France).
médiation, n.f. mediation.
médiatique, adj. media.
médical, adj. medical.
médicament, n.m. medicine.
médicinal, adj. medicinal.
médiéval, adj. medieval.
médiocre, adj. mediocre.
médiocrité, n.f. mediocrity.
médire, vb. slander, defame.
médisance, n.f. slander.
méditation, n.f. meditation.
méditer, vb. meditate; muse, brood.
Méditerranée, n.f. the Mediterranean.
méditerranéen, adj. Mediterranean.
médium, n.m. medium.

méduse, *n.f.* jellyfish.
méduser, *vb.* stupefy.
méfait, *n.m.* crime, misdeed.
méfiance, *n.f.* distrust.
méfiant, *adj.* distrustful.
méfier, *vb.* **se m. de,** distrust.
mégarde, *n.f.* heedlessness.
mégère, *n.f.* vixen, shrew.
mégot, *n.m.* cigarette butt.
meilleur, *adj.* better, best.
mélancolie, *n.f.* melancholy.
mélancolique, *adj.* melancholy.
mélange, *n.m.* mixture.
mélasse, *n.f.* molasses.
mêlée, *n.f.* struggle.
mêler, *vb.* mix. **se m. de,** meddle in.
mélèze, *n.m.* larch.
melliflu, *adj.* sweet, honeyed.
mélo, 1. *n.m.* melodrama. 2. *adj.* melodramatic.
mélodie, *n.f.* melody.
mélodieux, *adj.* melodious.
mélodique, *adj.* melodic.
mélodrame, *n.m.* melodrama.
mélomane, *n.m.* lover of music.
melon, *n.m.* melon.
membrane, *n.f.* membrane.
membre, *n.m.* member, limb.
membrure, *n.f.* frame, limbs.
même, 1. *adj.* same, very; self. **moi-m.,** myself; **lui-m.,** himself, etc. 2. *adv.* even. **de m.,** likewise. **tout de m.,** notwithstanding. **mettre à m. de,** enable to.
mémé, *n.f.* (colloquial) granny.
mémento, *n.m.* memento, notebook.
mémoire, *n.f.* memory; memoir.
mémorable, *adj.* memorable.
mémorandum, *n.m.* memorandum.
mémorial, *n.m.* memorial; memoirs.
menaçant, *adj.* threatening.
menace, *n.f.* threat.
menacer, *vb.* threaten.
ménage, *n.m.* household.
ménagement, *n.m.* discretion.
ménager, 1. *n.m.* manager. 2. *vb.* manage.
ménagère, *n.f.* housewife, housekeeper.
ménagerie, *n.f.* menagerie.
mendiant, *n.m.* beggar.
mendicité, *n.f.* begging.

mendier, *vb.* beg.
menées, *n.f.pl.* schemes.
mener, *vb.* lead.
ménestrel, *n.m.* minstrel.
ménétrier, *n.m.* country fiddler.
meneur, *n.m.* leader, ringleader.
méningite, *n.f.* meningitis.
ménopause, *n.f.* menopause.
menottes, *n.f.pl.* handcuffs.
mensonge, *n.m.* falsehood, lie.
mensonger, *adj.* false, deceptive.
mensualité, *n.f.* remittance paid monthly.
mensuel, *adj.* monthly.
mensurable, *adj.* measurable.
mental, *adj.* mental.
mentalité, *n.f.* mentality.
menterie, *n.f.* lie.
menteur, *n.m.* liar.
menthe, *n.f.* mint.
mention, *n.f.* mention.
mentionner, *vb.* mention.
mentir, *vb.* lie.
menton, *n.m.* chin.
menu, 1. *n.m.* menu. 2. *adj.* little, minute.
menuet, *n.m.* minuet.
menuiserie, *n.f.* woodwork.
menuisier, *n.m.* carpenter.
méprendre, *vb.* **se m.,** be mistaken.
mépris, *n.m.* contempt, scorn.
méprisable, *adj.* mean, contemptible.
méprisant, *adj.* contemptuous.
méprise, *n.f.* mistake, misunderstanding.
mépriser, *vb.* scorn, despise.
mer (-r), *n.f.* sea. **mal de m.,** seasickness.
mercantile, *adj.* mercantile.
mercenaire, *adj. and n.m.* mercenary.
mercerie, *n.f.* haberdashery.
merci, *n.m.* thanks; mercy.
mercredi, *n.m.* Wednesday.
mercure, *n.m.* mercury.
mère, *n.f.* mother.
méridien, *n.m.* meridian.
méridional, *adj.* southern.
meringue, *n.f.* meringue.
méritant, *adj.* meritorious.
mérite, *n.m.* merit, desert.
mériter, *vb.* merit, deserve.
méritoire, *adj.* meritorious.
merle, *n.m.* blackbird.

merveille, *n.f.* marvel.

merveilleux, *adj.* wonderful, marvelous.

mésalliance, *n.f.* misalliance.

mésallier, *vb.* marry badly.

mésaventure, *n.f.* accident, mishap.

Mesdames, *pl.* of **Madame.**

Mesdemoiselles, *pl.* of **Mademoiselle.**

mésestime, *n.f.* low opinion or repute.

mésintelligence, *n.f.* difficulty, discord.

mesquin, *adj.* shabby, mean, stingy.

mesquinerie, *n.f.* meanness.

message, *n.m.* message.

messager, *n.m.* messenger.

messe, *n.f.* Mass.

Messie, *n.m.* Messiah.

Messieurs, *pl.* of **Monsieur.**

mesurage, *n.m.* measurement.

mesure, *n.f.* measure. **à m. que,** as.

mesuré, *adj.* measured, cautious.

mesurer, *vb.* measure.

métairie, *n.f.* small farm.

métal, *n.m.* metal.

métallique, *adj.* metallic.

métallurgie, *n.f.* metallurgy.

métamorphose, *n.f.* transformation.

métaphore, *n.f.* metaphor.

métaphysique, 1. *n.f.* metaphysics. **2.** *adj.* metaphysical.

métayer, *n.m.* small farmer.

météo, *n.f.* weather report.

météore, *n.m.* meteor.

météorologie, *n.f.* meteorology.

métèque, *n.m.f.* alien.

méthode, *n.f.* method.

méthodique, *adj.* methodical, systematic.

méticuleux, *adj.* meticulous.

métier, *n.m.* loom; craft, trade.

métis, *adj.* hybrid, crossbred.

métrage, *n.m.* measurement.

mètre, *n.m.* meter.

métrique, *adj.* metric.

métro, *n.m.* subway.

métropole, *n.f.* metropolis; native land.

métropolitain, *adj.* metropolitan.

mets, *n.m.* food, dish.

mettable, *adj.* wearable.

metteur, *n.m.* **m. en scène,** play director.

mettre, *vb.* put, place, set. **se m. à,** begin.

meuble, *n.m.* piece of furniture; (*pl.*) furniture.

meubler, *vb.* furnish, outfit.

meule, *n.f.* stack.

meunier, *n.m.* miller.

meurtre, *n.m.* murder.

meurtrier, *n.m.* murderer.

meurtrière, *n.f.* murderess.

meurtrir, *vb.* bruise.

meurtrissure, *n.f.* bruise.

meute, *n.f.* dog pack; mob.

Mexicain, *n.m.* Mexican.

mexicain, *adj.* Mexican.

Mexique, *n.m.* Mexico.

mezzanine, *n.f.* mezzanine.

mi, *adj.* mid, half.

miaou, *n.m.* mew.

miauler, *vb.* mew.

mica, *n.m.* mica.

miche, *n.f.* loaf of bread.

micro, *n.m.* microphone; mike; micro.

microbe, *n.m.* microbe.

microfiche, *n.f.* microfiche.

microforme, *n.f.* microform.

micro-ondes, *n.m.* microwave oven.

microphone, *n.m.* microphone.

microplaquette, *n.f.* (micro)chip.

microprocesseur, *n.m.* microprocessor.

microscope, *n.m.* microscope.

microscopique, *adj.* microscopic.

midi, *n.m.* noon; south.

midinette, *n.f.* young saleswoman.

mie, *n.f.* crumb.

miel, *n.m.* honey.

mielleux, *adj.* honeyed, sweet.

mien, *pron.* **le mien, la mienne,** mine.

miette, *n.f.* crumb.

mieux, *adv.* better, best.

mièvre, *adj.* affected.

mignard, *adj.* dainty, mincing.

mignon, 1. *adj.* delicate, dainty. **2.** *n.m.* darling.

migraine, *n.f.* headache.

migration, *n.f.* migration.

mijoter, *vb.* cook slowly, simmer.

mil (mēl), *n.m.* thousand.

milice, *n.f.* militia.

milieu, *n.m.* middle, center; environment.
militaire, *adj.* military.
militant, *adj.* militant.
militarisme, *n.m.* militarism.
militer, *vb.* militate.
mille (-l), 1. *n.m.* mile. **2.** *adj. and n.m.f.* thousand.
millénaire, *n.m.* millenium.
millet, *n.m.* millet.
milliard, *n.m.* billion.
millier (-l), *n.m.* thousand.
milligramme (-l), *n.m.* milligram.
millimètre, *n.m.* millimeter.
million (-l), *n.m.* million.
millionnaire (-l), *adj. and n.m.f.* millionaire.
mime, *n.m.* mime, mimic.
mimique, *adj.* mimic.
minable, *adj.* shabby, poor.
minauder, *vb.* simper.
mince, *adj.* slender, slight, thin.
minceur, *n.f.* slimness.
mine, *n.f.* mine; mien; lead.
miner, *vb.* mine; wear away; weaken.
minerai, *n.m.* ore.
minéral, *adj. and n.m.* mineral.
minet, *n.m.* (colloquial) kitty.
mineur, 1. *n.m.* miner. **2.** *adj. and n.m.* minor.
miniature, *n.f.* miniature.
miniaturiser, *vb.* miniaturize.
minibus, *n.m.* minibus.
minier, *adj.* of mines.
minime, *adj.* very small.
minimum, *n.m.* minimum.
mini-ordinateur, *n.m.* minicomputer.
ministère, *n.m.* ministry, department, board.
ministériel, *adj.* ministerial.
ministre, *n.m.* minister. **premier m.,** prime minister, premier.
Minitel, *n.m.* (trademark) Minitel (videotext terminal and service).
minorité, *n.f.* minority.
minotier, *n.m.* miller.
minuit, *n.m.* midnight.
minuscule, *adj.* minute.
minute, *n.f.* minute.
minuterie, *n.f.* time switch.
minutie, *n.f.* trifle; care with details.
minutieux, *adj.* minute.

mioche, *n.m.f.* urchin.
miracle, *n.m.* miracle.
miraculeux, *adj.* miraculous.
mirage, *n.m.* mirage.
mirer, *vb.* aim at, look at.
mirifique, *adj.* wonderful.
miroir, *n.m.* mirror.
miroiter, *vb.* glisten.
misanthrope, 1. *n.m.f.* misanthrope. **2.** *adj.* misanthropic.
mise, *n.f.* putting; mode. **m. en scène,** setting.
miser, *vb.* bid.
misérable, *adj.* miserable, wretched, squalid.
misère, *n.f.* misery.
miséreux, *adj.* poor, miserable.
miséricorde, *n.f.* mercy.
miséricordieux, *adj.* merciful.
misogyne, 1. *n.m.f.* misogynist. **2.** *adj.* woman-hating; misogynist.
missel, *n.m.* missal.
missile, *n.m.* missile.
mission, *n.f.* mission.
missionnaire, *adj. and n.m.f.* missionary.
missive, *n.f.* missive.
mistral, *n.m.* mistral wind.
mitaine, *n.f.* mitten.
mite, *n.f.* moth.
mi-temps, *n.f.* half-time, part-time.
miteux, *adj.* shabby.
mitiger, *vb.* moderate.
mitoyen, *adj.* midway; jointly owned.
mitrailleuse, *n.f.* machine gun.
mixage, *n.m.* (sound) mixing.
mixte, *adj.* mixed, joint.
Mlle. (abbr. for **Mademoiselle**), *n.f.* Miss.
Mme. (abbr. for **Madame**), *n.f.* Mrs.
mobile, *adj.* movable.
mobilier, *adj.* movable.
mobilisation, *n.f.* mobilization.
mobiliser, *vb.* mobilize.
mobilité, *n.f.* mobility; instability.
moche, *adj.* ugly.
modalité, *n.f.* mode.
mode, *n.f.* fashion, mode; mood; *pl.* millinery. **à la m.,** fashionable.
modèle, *n.m.* model, pattern.
modeler, *vb.* model, shape.
modelliste, *n.m.f.* dress designer.

modem, *n.m.* modem.
modérateur, *n.m.* moderator.
modération, *n.f.* moderation.
modéré, *adj.* moderate.
modérer, *vb.* check, moderate.
moderne, *adj.* modern.
moderniser, *vb.* modernize.
modernité, *n.f.* modernity.
modeste, *adj.* modest.
modestie, *n.f.* modesty.
modicité, *n.f.* small quantity.
modification, *n.f.* alteration.
modifier, *vb.* modify, qualify.
modique, *adj.* moderate, unimportant.
modiste, *n.f.* milliner.
modulation, *n.f.* modulation.
module, *n.m.* module.
moduler, *vb.* modulate.
moelle, *n.f.* marrow.
moelleux (mwä ly), *adj.* mellow, soft.
mœurs (-s), *n.f.pl.* manner(s), custom.
moi, **1.** *n.m.* ego. **2.** *pron.* me.
moignon, *n.m.* stump.
moi-même, *pron.* myself; I myself.
moindre, *adj.* less, lesser, least.
moine, *n.m.* monk.
moineau, *n.m.* sparrow.
moins, *adv.* less, least. **au m.**, at least. **à m. que**, unless.
moire, *n.f.* watered silk.
mois, *n.m.* month.
moisi, *adj.* moldy.
moisir, *vb.* mold.
moisissure, *n.f.* mold.
moisson, *n.f.* harvest, crop.
moissonner, *vb.* reap, harvest.
moissonneur, *n.m.* harvester.
moissonneuse, *n.f.* reaping machine.
moite, *adj.* moist.
moiteur, *n.f.* dampness.
moitié, *n.f.* half. **à m.**, half.
molaire, *adj. and n.f.* molar.
môle, *n.m.* pier.
molécule, *n.f.* molecule.
molester, *vb.* molest.
mollah, *n.m.* mullah.
mollasse, *adj.* flabby, soft.
mollesse, *n.f.* softness; weakness.
mollet, **1.** *adj.* soft. **œufs m.s**, soft-boiled eggs. **2.** *n.m.* calf of leg.
molletière, *n.f.* legging.

molleton, *n.m.* heavy flannel.
mollir, *vb.* soften, slacken.
mollusque, *n.m.* mollusk.
môme, *n.m.f.* (colloquial) kid.
moment, *n.m.* moment.
momentané, *adj.* momentary.
mon *m.*, **ma** *f.*, **mes** *pl. adj.* my.
monacal, *adj.* pertaining to monks.
Monaco, *n.m.* Monaco.
monarchie, *n.f.* monarchy.
monarchiste, *n.m.f.* monarchist.
monarque, *n.m.* monarch.
monastère, *n.m.* monastery.
monastique, *adj.* monastic.
monceau, *n.m.* pile.
mondain, *adj.* worldly.
monde, *n.m.* world; people. **tout le m.**, everybody, everyone. **mettre au m.**, bear.
mondial, *adj.* worldwide.
monétaire, *adj.* monetary.
moniteur, *n.m.* monitor.
monnaie, *n.f.* change; money, currency. **Hôtel de la M.**, mint.
monnayer, *vb.* mint.
monocle, *n.m.* monocle.
monogramme, *n.m.* monogram.
monologue, *n.m.* monologue.
monologuer, *vb.* soliloquize.
monoplan, *n.m.* monoplane.
monopole, *n.m.* monopoly.
monopoliser, *vb.* monopolize.
monosyllabe, *n.m.* monosyllable.
monosyllabique, *adj.* monosyllabic.
monotone, *adj.* monotonous.
monotonie, *n.f.* monotony, dullness.
monseigneur, *n.m.* title of honor; My Lord.
Monsieur, *n.m.*, gentleman, sir; Mr.
monstre, *n.m.* monster.
monstrueux, *adj.* monstrous.
monstruosité, *n.f.* monstrosity.
mont, *n.m.* mountain, hill.
montage, *n.m.* carrying up; setting; (film) editing.
montagnard, *n.m.* mountaineer.
montagne, *n.f.* mountain.
montagneux, *adj.* mountainous.
montant, *n.m.* amount.
mont-de-piété, *n.m.* pawnshop.
monté, *adj.* mounted; supplied.
montée, *n.f.* ascent, rise, climb.

monter, vb. go up, mount, climb, rise.
montre, n.f. watch; display. **m.-bracelet,** wristwatch.
montrer, vb. show.
montreur, n.m. showman.
montueux, adj. hilly.
monture, n.f. mount; setting.
monument, n.m. monument.
monumental, adj. monumental.
moquer, vb. se m. de, make fun of, mock, laugh at.
moquerie, n.f. mockery, ridicule.
moquette, n.f. wall-to-wall carpeting.
moqueur, adj. mocking.
moral, adj. ethical, moral.
morale, n.f. morals, morality. **m. morale.**
moraliser, vb. moralize.
moraliste, n.m.f. moralist.
moralité, n.f. morals, morality.
morbide, adj. morbid.
morceau, n.m. piece, bit, morsel. **gros m.,** lump, chunk.
morceler, vb. cut up.
mordant, adj. pointed.
mordiller, vb. nibble.
mordre, vb. bite.
morfondre, vb. chill.
morgue, n.f. morgue.
moribond, adj. dying.
morne, adj. bleak, dismal, dreary.
morose, adj. morose.
morosité, n.f. moroseness.
morphine, n.f. morphine.
morphinomane, n. drug addict.
morphologie, n.f. morphology.
mors, n.m. horse's bit.
morse, n.m. walrus.
morsure, n.f. bite.
mort, 1. n.m. dummy; dead man. **2.** n.f. death. **3.** adj. dead.
mortaise, n.f. mortise.
mortalité, n.f. mortality.
mortel, adj. deadly, mortal.
morte-saison, n.f. off season.
mortier, n.m. mortar.
mortifier, vb. mortify.
mort-né, adj. stillborn.
mortuaire, adj. mortuary.
morue, n.f. cod.
mosaïque (-ä ëk), n.f. mosaic.
Moscou (-ä ëk), Moscow.
mosquée, n.f. mosque.

mot, n.m. word; cue.
motard, n.m. biker; motorcycle cop.
motel, n.m. motel.
moteur, n.m. motor.
motif, n.m. motive.
motion, n.f. motion.
motiver, vb. motivate, justify.
motocyclette, n.f. motorcycle.
motocycliste, n.m. motorcyclist.
motorisé, adj. having transportation.
motte, n.f. clod.
mou m., molle f. adj. soft.
mouchard, n.m. spy.
moucharder, vb. spy.
mouche, n.f. fly.
moucher, vb. blow the nose.
moucheron, n.m. gnat.
moucheté, adj. spotted.
moucheture, n.f. spot.
mouchoir, n.m. handkerchief.
moudre, vb. grind.
moue, n.f. pout, wry face.
mouette, n.f. gull.
moufette, n.f. skunk.
moufle, n.f. mitten.
mouillage, n.m. wetting.
mouillé, adj. wet.
mouiller, vb. soak.
moulage, n.m. cast (from mold).
moule, 1. n.m. mold. **2.** n.f. mussel.
mouler, vb. mold.
mouleur, n.m. molder.
moulin, n.m. mill.
moulinette, n.f. vegetable shredder.
moulure, n.f. molding.
mourant, adj. dying.
mourir, vb. die.
mouron, n.m. pimpernel.
mousquetaire, n.m. musketeer.
mousse, n.f. moss; foam, lather.
mousseline, n.f. muslin.
mousser, vb. foam, froth.
mousseux, adj. foaming.
mousson, n.m. monsoon.
moustache, n.f. mustache, whisker.
moustiquaire, n.f. mosquito net.
moustique, n.m. mosquito.
moutarde, n.f. mustard.
mouton, n.m. sheep; mutton.
moutonner, vb. curl; make woolly.
mouture, n.f. grinding.

mouvant, *adj.* moving, shifting.
mouvement, *n.m.* movement, stir.
mouvoir, *vb.* move.
moyen, 1. *n.m.* means; medium. **2.** *adj.* middle, average.
moyennant, *prep.* by means of.
moyenne, *n.f.* average.
Moyen Orient, *n.m.* Middle East.
muabilité, *n.f.* changeability.
mucilage, *n.m.* mucilage.
mue, *n.f.* molting; changing (esp. of voice).
muer, *vb.* molt (animals); break, change (voice).
muet *m.,* **muette** *f. adj.* dumb, mute.
mufle, *n.m.* cad.
mugir, *vb.* roar, bellow.
mugissement, *n.m.* roaring, bellowing.
muguet, *n.m.* lily of the valley.
mulâtre, *adj. and n.m.f.* mulatto.
mulet, *n.m.* mule.
muletier, *n.m.* muleteer.
mulot, *n.m.* field mouse.
multinational, *adj.* multinational.
multiple, *adj.* multiple, manifold.
multiplicande, *n.m.* multiplicand.
multiplication, *n.f.* multiplication.
multiplicité, *n.f.* multiplicity.
multiplier, *vb.* multiply.
multitude, *n.f.* multitude.
municipal, *adj.* municipal.
municipalité, *n.f.* municipality.
munificence, *n.f.* munificence, liberality.
munificent, *adj.* very generous.
munir, *vb.* provide, supply.
munitionner, *vb.* provision, supply.
munitions, *n.f.pl.* ammunition.
muqueux, *adj.* mucous.
mur, *n.m.* wall.
mûr, *adj.* ripe, mature.
muraille, *n.f.* wall.
mural, *adj.* mural.
mûre, *n.f.* blackberry.
mûrier, *n.m.* mulberry tree.

mûrir, *vb.* ripen, mature.
murmure, *n.m.* murmur.
murmurer, *vb.* murmur.
musarder, *vb.* waste time, dawdle.
muscade, *n.f.* nutmeg.
muscle, *n.m.* muscle.
musculaire, *adj.* muscular.
musculeux, *adj.* muscular.
muse, *n.f.* muse.
museau, *n.m.* muzzle.
musée, *n.m.* museum.
museler, *vb.* muzzle; gag.
muselière, *n.f.* muzzle.
muser, *vb.* trifle, dawdle.
musette, *n.f.* lunchbag; accordion.
musical, *adj.* musical.
musicien, 1. *adj.* musical. **2.** *n.m.* musician.
musique, *n.f.* music.
musulman, *adj. and n.m.* Mohammedan.
mutabilité, *n.f.* mutability.
mutation, *n.f.* change, replacement.
mutilation, *n.f.* mutilation.
mutiler, *vb.* mutilate, mangle, mar.
mutin, *adj.* refractory, mutinous.
mutiner, *vb.* **se m.,** mutiny, revolt.
mutinerie, *n.f.* mutiny.
mutisme, *n.m.* muteness, lack of speech.
mutuel, *adj.* mutual.
myope, *adj.* nearsighted.
myopie, *n.f.* nearsightedness.
myosotis, *n.m.* forget-me-not.
myriade, *n.f.* myriad.
myrrhe, *n.f.* myrrh.
myrte, *n.m.* myrtle.
mystère, *n.m.* mystery.
mystérieux, *adj.* mysterious, weird.
mysticisme, *n.m.* mysticism.
mystification, *n.f.* hoax.
mystifier, *vb.* mystify.
mystique, *adj.* mystic.
mythe, *n.m.* myth.
mythique, *adj.* mythical.
mythologie, *n.f.* mythology.

N

nabot, *n.m.* dwarf.
nacre, *n.f.* mother-of-pearl.
nacré, *adj.* pearly.

nage, *n.f.* act of swimming.
nageoire, *n.f.* fin.
nager, *vb.* swim.

nageur, n.m. swimmer.

naguère, adv. a short time ago.

naïf (nä ēf) m., **naïve** f. adj. naive.

nain, adj. and n.m. dwarf.

naissance, n.f. birth.

naissant, adj. beginning; new-born.

naître, vb. be born.

naïveté (nä ēv-), n.f. simplicity.

nantir, vb. give as security; furnish.

nantis, n.m.pl. the well-to-do.

nantissement, n.m. pledge, guarantee.

naphte, n.m. naphtha.

nappe, n.f. tablecloth.

narcisse, n.m. daffodil.

narcotique, n.m. narcotic.

narguer, vb. defy, flout.

narine, n.f. nostril.

narrateur, n.m. narrator, story-teller.

narration, n.f. narrative, recital.

narrer, vb. narrate, relate.

nasal, adj. nasal.

naseau, n.m. nostril.

nasiller, vb. talk with a nasal voice.

nasse, n.f. fish trap.

natal, adj. native.

natalité, n.f. birthrate.

natation, n.f. swimming.

natif, adj. and n.m. native.

nation, n.f. nation.

national, adj. national.

nationalisation, n.f. nationalization.

nationaliser, vb. nationalize.

nationalisme, n.m. nationalism.

nationalité, n.f. nationality.

nativité, n.f. nativity.

naturaliser, vb. naturalize; (of animals) stuff.

naturalisme, n.m. naturalism, naturalness.

naturaliste, n.m.f. naturalist.

nature, n.f. nature.

naturel, 1. n.m. nature. 2. adj. natural.

naufrage, n.m. shipwreck.

naufragé, adj. shipwrecked.

nauséabond, adj. nauseous, offensive.

nausée, n.f. nausea.

nautique, adj. nautical.

nautisme, n.m. water sports.

naval, adj. naval.

navet, n.m. turnip.

navette spatiale, n.f. space shuttle.

navigable, adj. navigable.

navigateur, n.m. navigator, sea-man.

navigation, n.f. seafaring, navigation.

naviguer, vb. sail, navigate.

navire, n.m. ship.

navrant, adj. distressing, causing grief.

navrer, vb. wound; grieve.

né, adj. born.

néanmoins, adv. yet, nevertheless, however.

néant, n.m. nothing(ness).

nébuleux, adj. cloudy; worried.

nécessaire, adj. requisite, necessary.

nécessité, n.f. necessity. n. **préalable,** prerequisite.

nécessiter, vb. make necessary or imperative.

nécessiteux, adj. needy.

nécrologe, n.m. obituary.

néerlandais, adj. Dutch (language).

nef, n.f. nave.

néfaste, adj. ill-omened, unlucky.

négatif, adj. negative.

négation, n.f. negation; negative word.

négative, n.f. negative argument or opinion.

négligé, 1. adj. neglected, sloppy. 2. n.m. state of undress.

négligeable, adj. negligible.

négligence, n.f. neglect.

négligent, adj. negligent.

négliger, vb. overlook, neglect.

négoce, n.m. commerce, trade.

négociable, adj. negotiable.

négociant, n.m. merchant.

négociation, n.f. negotiation.

négocier, vb. negotiate.

nègre, adj. and n.m. black, Negro.

négresse, n.f. a black woman.

neige, n.f. snow.

neiger, vb. snow.

neigeux, adj. snowy.

néon, n.m. neon.

néophyte, n.m. neophyte, convert.

Néo-Zélandais, n. New Zealander.

néphrite, n.f. nephritis.

nerf (nĕr), n.m. nerve.

nerveux, *adj.* nervous.
nervosité, *n.f.* nervousness.
net (-t) *m.,* **nette** *f. adj.* net, clear; clean, neat.
netteté, *n.f.* clearness, neatness.
nettoyer, *vb.* clean, scour.
nettoyeur, *n.m.* one who or that which cleans.
neuf, *adj. and n.m.* nine.
neuf *m.,* **neuve** *f. adj.* brand-new.
neutraliser, *vb.* counteract.
neutralité, *n.f.* neutrality.
neutre, *adj. and n.m.* neutral.
neutron, *n.m.* neutron.
neuvième, *adj. and n.m.f.* ninth.
neveu, *n.m.* nephew.
névralgie, *n.f.* neuralgia.
névrite, *n.f.* neuritis.
névrose, *n.f.* neurosis.
névrosé, *adj. and n.m.* neurotic.
nez, *n.m.* nose.
ni, *conj.* nor. **ni . . . ni . . .,** neither . . . nor . . .
niais, *adj.* foolish.
niaiserie, *n.f.* silliness, trifle.
niche, *n.f.* alcove.
nichée, *n.f.* brood.
nicher, *vb.* **se n.,** nestle.
nickel, *n.m.* nickel.
nicotine, *n.f.* nicotine.
nid, *n.m.* nest.
nièce, *n.f.* niece.
nielle, *n.f.* wheat blight.
nier, *vb.* deny.
nigaud, *n.m.* fool, simpleton.
nihilisme, *n.m.* nihilism.
nimbe, *n.m.* halo.
n'importe, *interj.* never mind.
nippes, *n.f.pl.* old clothes.
nitrate, *n.m.* nitrate.
niveau, *n.m.* level. **au n. de,** level with.
niveler, *vb.* make level; survey.
nivellement, *n.m.* leveling; surveying.
noble, 1. *n.m.* nobleman, peer. **2.** *adj.* noble.
noblesse, *n.f.* nobility.
noce, *n.f.* wedding. **faire la n.,** revel.
noceur, *n.m.* gay blade.
nocif, *adj.* harmful.
noctambule, *n.m.f.* sleep-walker; noctambulist.
nocturne, *adj.* nocturnal.

Noël (nō ĕl), *n.m.* Christmas; carol.
nœud (nœ), *n.m.* knot.
noir, *adj. and n.m.* black.
noircir, *vb.* blacken.
noisetier, *n.m.* hazel (tree).
noisette, 1. *n.f.* hazelnut. **2.** *adj.* light reddish brown.
noix, *n.f.* nut, walnut.
nolis, *n.m.* freight.
nom, *n.m.* name; noun.
nomade, *adj.* wandering, roaming.
nombre, *n.m.* number.
nombrer, *vb.* number.
nombreux, *adj.* numerous, manifold.
nombril, *n.m.* navel.
nominal, *adj.* nominal.
nominatif, *adj. and n.m.* nominative.
nomination, *n.f.* nomination, appointment.
nommément, *adv.* particularly, namely.
nommer, *vb.* name; nominate, appoint.
non, *adv.* no. **n. plus,** neither.
non-aligné, *adj.,* non-aligned.
nonchalamment, *adv.* carelessly, nonchalantly.
nonchalant, *adj.* nonchalant.
non-combattant, *adj. and n.m.* non-combatant.
nonne, *n.f.* nun.
nonobstant, *prep.* in spite of, notwithstanding.
nonpareil, *adj.* unequaled.
non-sens, *n.m.* nonsense.
nord, *n.m.* north.
normal, *adj.* normal.
normand, *adj.* Norman; equivocal.
Normandie, *n.f.* Normandy.
norme, *n.f.* norm.
Norvège, *n.f.* Norway.
Norvégien, *n.m.* Norwegian (person).
norvégien, 1. *n.m.* Norwegian (language). **2.** *adj.* Norwegian.
nostalgie, *n.f.* nostalgia.
notabilité, *n.f.* notability.
notable, 1. *n.m.* notable. **2.** *adj.* remarkable, notable.
notaire, *n.m.* lawyer, notary.
notamment, *adv.* particularly.
notation, *n.f.* notation.
note, *n.f.* note, bill; grade.

noter, *vb.* note.
notice, *n.f.* notice, review.
notification, *n.f.* notification.
notifier, *vb.* notify.
notion, *n.f.* notion.
notoire, *adj.* notorious.
notoriété, *n.f.* notoriety.
notre *sg.,* **nos** *pl. adj.* our.
nôtre, *pron.* **le n.,** ours.
nouer, *vb.* tie.
noueux, *adj.* knotty.
nouilles, *n.f.pl.* noodles.
nounours, *n.m.* teddy bear.
nourrice, *n.f.* (wet) nurse.
nourricier, *adj.* nourishing; of nursing.
nourrir, *vb.* feed, nourish, foster.
nourrisson, *n.m.* infant.
nourriture, *n.f.* food, nourishment.
nous, *pron.* we, us, ourselves.
nouveau *m.,* **nouvelle** *f. adj.* new, fresh. **de n.,** anew.
nouveauté, *n.f.* novelty.
nouvel an, *n.m.* new year.
nouvelle, *n.f.* news.
nouvellement, *adv.* recently, newly.
Nouvelle-Zélande, *n.f.* New Zealand.
novembre, *n.m.* November.
novice, *n.m.f.* novice.

noviciat, *n.m.* novitiate.
noyade, *n.f.* drowning.
noyau, *n.m.* kernel, nucleus.
noyauter, *vb.* infiltrate.
noyer, *vb.* drown.
noyer, *n.m.* walnut (tree).
nu, *adj.* naked, bare.
nuage, *n.m.* cloud; gloom.
nuageux, *adj.* cloudy.
nuance, *n.m.* shade, degree.
nucléaire, *adj.* nuclear.
nudité, *n.f.* bareness.
nuée, *n.f.* cloud; swarm.
nuire, *vb.* injure, harm.
nuisible, *adj.* injurious, hurtful.
nuit, *n.f.* night.
nul, *adj.* no, none; void. **nulle part,** nowhere.
nullement, *adv.* not at all.
nullité, *n.f.* nonentity.
numéraire, *n.m.* cash.
numéral, *adj. and n.m.* numeral.
numérique, *adj.* numerical.
numéro, *n.m.* number.
nu-pieds, *adj.* barefoot.
nuptial, *adj.* bridal.
nuque, *n.f.* nape.
nu-tête, *adj.* bareheaded.
nutritif, *adj.* nutritious.
nutrition, *n.f.* nutrition.
nylon, *n.m.* nylon.
nymphe, *n.f.* nymph.

O

oasis (-s), *n.f.* oasis.
obéir, *vb.* obey.
obéissance, *n.f.* obedience.
obéissant, *adj.* obedient.
obélisque, *n.m.* obelisk.
obérer, *vb.* burden with debt.
obèse, *adj.* obese.
obésité, *n.f.* obesity.
objecter, *vb.* object.
objecteur, *n.m.* **o. de conscience,** conscientious objector.
objectif, *adj. and n.m.* objective.
objection, *n.f.* objection.
objet, *n.m.* object.
obligation, *n.f.* obligation.
obligatoire, *adj.* compulsory, mandatory, binding.
obligeance, *n.f.* obligingness.
obliger, *vb.* oblige, accommodate.

oblique, *adj.* slanting; devious.
oblitération, *n.f.* obliteration.
oblitérer, *vb.* obliterate.
oblong, *adj.* oblong.
obnubilé, *adj.* obsessed.
obscène, *adj.* filthy, obscene.
obscénité, *n.f.* obscenity.
obscur, *adj.* obscure, dark, dim.
obscurcir, *vb.* darken, obscure.
obscurcissement, *n.m.* darkening; state of being obscure.
obscurément, *adv.* obscurely.
obscurité, *n.f.* darkness, dimness, obscurity.
obséder, *vb.* harass, haunt.
obsèques, *n.f.pl.* funeral.
obséquieusement, *adv.* obsequiously.
obséquieux, *adj.* obsequious.

observance, *n.f.* observance.

observateur, *n.m.* observer.

observation, *n.f.* observation, remark.

observer, *vb.* observe, watch.

obsession, *n.f.* obsession.

obstacle, *n.m.* obstacle, bar.

obstétrical, *adj.* obstetrical.

obstétrique, *adj.* obstetrics.

obstination, *n.f.* stubbornness.

obstiné, *adj.* obstinate, stubborn.

obstiner, *vb.* s'o., persist.

obstruction, *n.f.* obstruction.

obstruer, *vb.* obstruct, stop up.

obtempérer, *vb.* obey.

obtenir, *vb.* obtain, get.

obtention, *n.f.* obtaining.

obtus, *adj.* obtuse, dull, stupid.

obus (-s), *n.m.* shell.

obusier, *n.m.* howitzer.

occasion, *n.f.* opportunity, chance; bargain.

occasionnel, *adj.* occasional.

occasionner, *vb.* cause, bring about.

occident, *n.m.* west.

occidental, *adj.* western.

occulte, *adj.* occult.

occupant, *n.m.* occupant, tenant.

occupation, *n.f.* pursuit; occupation.

occupé, *adj.* busy.

occuper, *vb.* occupy, busy. s'o. de, attend to.

occurrence, *n.f.* occurrence.

océan, *n.m.* ocean.

océanique, *adj.* oceanic.

ocre, *n.f.* ochre.

octane, *n.m.* octane.

octave, *n.f.* octave.

octobre, *n.m.* October.

octroyer, *vb.* grant.

oculaire, *adj.* ocular.

oculiste, *n.m.f.* oculist.

ode, *n.f.* ode.

odeur, *n.f.* odor, scent, perfume.

odieux, *adj.* hateful, obnoxious, odious.

odorant, *adj.* having a fragrant odor.

odorat, *n.m.* (sense of) smell.

œil, *n.m.* *pl.* **yeux,** eye. **coup d'o.,** glance.

œillade, *n.f.* wink, quick look.

œillère, *n.f.* eyetooth.

œillet, *n.m.* carnation.

œuf, *n.m.* egg.

œuvre, *n.f.* work.

offensant, *adj.* offensive.

offense, *n.f.* offense.

offenser, *vb.* offend.

offenseur, *n.m* offender.

offensif, *adj.* offensive.

offensive, *n.f.* offensive.

offensivement, *adv.* offensively.

office, *n.m.* office, pantry; (church) service.

officiant, *n.m.* one who officiates.

officiel, *adj.* official.

officier, 1. *n.m.* officer; mate. **2.** *vb.* officiate.

officieux, *adj.* officious.

offrande, *n.f.* offering.

offre, *n.f.* offer.

offrir, *vb.* offer, present.

offusquer, *vb.* obscure, shadow; irritate.

ogive, *n.f.* warhead.

ogre, *n.m.* ogre.

oie, *n.f.* goose.

oignon (ô nyôN), *n.m.* onion; bulb.

oindre, *vb.* anoint.

oiseau, *n.m.* bird.

oiselet, *n.m.* small bird.

oiseux, *adj.* idle, empty, useless.

oisif, *adj.* idle.

oisillon, *n.m.* young bird.

oisiveté, *n.f.* idleness.

oléagineux, *adj.* oily.

oléoduc, *n.m.* oil pipeline.

olivâtre, *adj.* olive-colored.

olive, *n.f.* olive.

olivier, *n.m.* olive tree.

olympique, *adj.* Olympic.

ombilical, *adj.* umbilical.

ombrage, *n.m.* shade.

ombragé, *adj.* shady.

ombrager, *vb.* shade.

ombrageux, *adj.* suspicious, doubtful.

ombre, *n.f.* shade, shadow.

ombrelle, *n.f.* parasol.

ombreux, *adj.* shady.

omelette, *n.f.* omelet.

omettre, *vb.* omit.

omission, *n.f.* omission.

omnibus (-s), *n.m.* bus.

omnipotent, *adj.* omnipotent.

omoplate, *n.f.* shoulder blade.

on, *pron.* one (indef. subj.).

once, *n.f.* ounce.
oncle, *n.m.* uncle.
onction, *n.f.* unction.
onctueux, *adj.* unctuous.
onde, *n.f.* wave.
ondé, *adj.* wavy.
on-dit, *n.m.* rumor.
ondoyer, *vb.* wave.
ondulation, *n.f.* wave. **o. permanente**, permanent wave.
onduler, *vb.* wave.
onéreux, *adj.* burdensome.
ongle, *n.m.* (finger)nail.
onglée, *n.f.* numb feeling.
onguent, *n.m.* salve, ointment.
onomatopée, *n.f.* onomatopœia.
onze, *adj. and n.m.* eleven.
onzième, *adj. and n.m.f.* eleventh.
opacité, *n.f.* opacity.
opale, *n.f.* opal.
opaque, *adj.* opaque.
opéra, *n.m.* opera.
opérateur, *n.m.* operator; cameraman.
opération, *n.f.* operation; transaction.
opératoire, *adj.* operative.
opéré, *n.m.* patient undergoing surgery.
opérer, *vb.* operate.
opérette, *n.f.* operetta.
opiner, *vb.* hold or express an opinion.
opiniâtre, *adj.* stubborn.
opiniâtreté, *n.f.* stubbornness.
opinion, *n.f.* opinion.
opium, *n.m.* opium.
opportun, *adj.* timely.
opportunité, *n.f.* timeliness.
opposant, *n.m.* opponent.
opposé, *adj.* opposite, averse.
opposer, *vb.* oppose. **s'o. à**, oppose, resist.
opposition, *n.f.* opposition.
oppresser, *vb.* weigh heavily on.
oppresseur, *n.m.* oppressor.
oppressif, *adj.* oppressive.
oppression, *n.f.* oppression.
opprimer, *vb.* oppress.
opprobre, *n.m.* disgrace, infamy.
opter, *vb.* select, decide.
opticien, *n.m.* optician.
optimisme, *n.m.* optimism.
optimiste, **1.** *adj.* optimistic. **2.** *n.m.f.* optimist.

option, *n.f.* option.
optique, *adj.* optic.
opulence, *n.f.* opulence, riches.
opuscule, *n.m.* small work.
or, **1.** *n.m.* gold. **2.** *conj.* now.
oracle, *n.m.* oracle.
orage, *n.m.* storm.
orageusement, *adv.* turbulently, stormily.
orageux, *adj.* stormy.
oraison, *n.f.* prayer, oration.
oral, *adj.* oral.
orange, *n.f.* orange.
oranger, *n.m.* orange tree.
orateur, *n.m.* speaker, orator.
oratoire, *adj.* oratorical. **art o.**, oratory.
orbe, *n.m.* orb, sphere.
orbite, *n.m.* orbit; socket (as of eye).
orchestre (-k-), *n.m.* orchestra, band.
orchestrer (-k-), *vb.* orchestrate.
orchidée, *n.f.* orchid.
ordinaire, *adj. and n.m.* ordinary.
ordinal, *adj. and n.m.* ordinal.
ordinateur, *n.m.* computer.
ordonnance, *n.f.* prescription; ordinance, decree.
ordonné, *adj.* orderly, tidy.
ordonner, *vb.* order, ordain, bid, command.
ordre, *n.m.* order. **de premier o.**, first-rate.
ordure, *n.f.* filth, garbage, refuse.
ordurier, *adj.* foul.
oreille, *n.f.* ear.
oreiller, *n.m.* pillow.
oreillons, *n.m.pl.* mumps.
orfèvrerie, *n.f.* gold or silver jewelry.
organdi, *n.m.* organdy.
organe, *n.m.* organ (body).
organigramme, *n.m.* flow chart, organization chart.
organique, *adj.* organic.
organisateur, **1.** *n.m.* organizer. **2.** *adj.* organizing.
organisation, *n.f.* organization, arrangement.
organiser, *vb.* organize.
organisme, *n.m.* organism.
organiste, *n.m.f.* organist.
orgasme, *n.m.* orgasm, climax.
orge, *n.f.* barley.

orgelet, *n.m.* sty (of eye).

orgie, *n.f.* orgy.

orgue, *n.m.* organ (instrument).

orgueil, *n.m.* pride.

orgueilleux, *adj.* proud, haughty.

Orient, *n.m.* Orient, East.

Oriental, *n.m.* Oriental.

oriental, *adj.* Oriental, eastern.

orientation, *n.f.* positioning.

orienté, *adj.* slanted.

orienter, *vb.* orient.

orifice, *n.m.* orifice, hole.

originaire, *adj.* original, native.

originairement, *adv.* originally.

original, 1. *n.m.* eccentric person. **2.** *adj.* original.

originalement, *adv.* originally; unusually.

originalité, *n.f.* originality.

origine, *n.f.* origin, source.

originel, *adj.* original.

oripeau, *n.m.* tinsel.

orme, *n.m.* elm.

orné, *adj.* ornate.

ornement, *n.m.* ornament, adornment, trimming.

ornemental, *adj.* ornamental.

ornementation, *n.f.* ornamentation.

orner, *vb.* adorn, trim.

ornière, *n.f.* rut, track.

ornithologie, *n.f.* ornithology.

orphelin, *n.m.* orphan.

orphelinat, *n.m.* orphanage.

orphéon, *n.m.* choral group.

orteil, *n.m.* toe.

orthodoxe, *adj.* orthodox.

orthodoxie, *n.f.* orthodoxy.

orthographe, *n.f.* spelling, orthography.

orthographier, *vb.* spell.

ortie, *n.f.* nettle.

os, *n.m.* bone.

oscillant, *adj.* oscillating.

oscillation, *n.f.* sway.

osciller, *vb.* fluctuate, oscillate.

osé, *adj.* attempted, bold.

oser, *vb.* dare.

osier, *n.m.* willow.

ossature, *n.f.* bony structure, skeleton.

ossements, *n.m.pl.* human remains.

osseux, *adj.* bony.

ossifier, *vb.* ossify.

ostensible, *adj.* ostensible.

ostentation, *n.f.* ostentation.

ostraciser, *vb.* ostracize.

otage, *n.m.* hostage.

ôter, *vb.* take off; take away.

otite, *n.f.* ear infection.

ou, *conj.* or. **ou . . . ou . . .,** either . . . or . . . .

où, *adv.* where.

ouailles, *n.f.pl.* religious congregation.

ouate, *n.f.* cotton; padding.

ouater (wä-), *vb.* pad.

oubli, *n.m.* forgetfulness; oblivion.

oublier, *vb.* forget.

oubliettes, *n.f.pl.* dungeon.

oublieux, *adj.* forgetful.

ouest (wĕst), *n.m.* west.

oui (wē), *adv.* yes.

ouï-dire, *n.m.* gossip, hearsay.

ouïe, *n.f.* hearing; gill.

ouïr, *vb.* hear.

ouragan, *n.m.* hurricane.

ourler, *vb.* hem.

ourlet, *n.m.* hem.

ours (-s), *n.m.* bear. **o. blanc,** polar bear.

ourson, *n.m.* bear cub.

outil, *n.m.* tool, implement.

outillage, *n.m.* quantity of tools, equipment.

outiller, *vb.* supply with tools.

outrage, *n.m.* outrage.

outrageant, *adj.* outrageous.

outrager, *vb.* outrage, affront.

outrance, *n.f.* extreme degree. **à o.** to the very end.

outre, *adv. and prep.* beyond. **en o.,** besides, furthermore.

outré, *adj.* excessive, extreme.

outrecuidant, *adj.* excessively bold and forward.

outre-mer, *adv.* across the seas.

outrer, *vb.* overdo, irritate.

ouvert, *adj.* open.

ouverture, *n.f.* opening, gap; overture.

ouvrable, *adj.* work, workable.

ouvrage, *n.m.* work.

ouvrer, *vb.* work.

ouvreuse, *n.f.* usher or usherette.

ouvrier, *n.m.* workman; *pl.* labor.

ouvrir, *vb.* open.
ouvroir, *n.m.* workroom or workshop.
ovaire, *n.m.* ovary.
ovale, *adj. and n.m.* oval.
ovation, *n.f.* ovation.

overdose, *n.f.* overdose.
ovni, *n.m.* UFO.
ovule, *n.f.* egg.
oxyder, *vb.* oxidize.
oxygène, *n.m.* oxygen.
ozone, *n.f.* ozone.

P

pacage, *n.m.* land used for pasture.
pacemaker, *n.m.* pacemaker.
pacificateur, 1. *adj.* pacifying. **2.** *n.m.* peacemaker.
pacification, *n.f.* peacemaking.
pacifier, *vb.* pacify, appease, soothe.
pacifique, *adj.* pacific, peaceful, peaceable.
pacifisme, *n.m.* pacifism.
pacotille, *n.f.* small wares.
pacte, *n.m.* covenant, pact.
pactiser, *vb.* make a pact, compromise.
pagaie, *n.f.* paddle.
pagaille, *n.f.* mess.
pagaie, *n.f.* disorder, rush.
paganisme, *n.m.* paganism.
pagayer, *vb.* paddle.
pagayeur, *n.m.* paddler.
page, 1. *n.m.* page (boy). **2.** *n.f.* page (in book).
pages centrales, *n.f.pl.* centerfold.
pagination, *n.f.* pagination.
paginer, *vb.* number pages.
pagode, *n.f.* pagoda.
paie, *n.f.* pay.
paiement, payement, *n.m.* payment.
païen, *adj. and n.m.* pagan, heathen.
paillard, *adj.* lewd, indecent.
paillasse, *n.f.* mattress of straw; ticking.
paillasson, *n.m.* (door)mat.
paille, *n.f.* straw; defect (in gems).
paillette, *n.f.* spangle; defect.
pain, *n.m.* bread, loaf. **petit p.,** roll.
pair, 1. *n.m.* peer. **2.** *adj.* even (number), equal.
paire, *n.f.* pair.
pairesse, *n.f.* peeress.
pairie, *n.f.* peerage.
paisible, *adj.* peaceful.
paître, *vb.* graze.

paix, *n.f.* peace.
Pakistan, *n.m.* Pakistan.
palabre, *n.f.* palaver.
palais, *n.m.* palace; palate.
palan, *n.m.* gear for hoisting.
palatal, *adj.* palatal.
pale, *n.f.* blade; paddle.
pâle, *adj.* pale.
palefrenier, *n.m.* groom.
Palestine, *n.f.* Palestine.
palet, *n.m.* quoit.
paletot, *n.m.* overcoat.
palette, *n.f.* palette.
pâleur, *n.f.* paleness.
palier, *n.m.* stair landing.
pâlir, *vb.* grow pale or dim.
palissade, *n.f.* paling, fence.
pâlissant, *adj.* becoming pale.
palliatif, *n.m.* palliative; stopgap measure.
palmarès, *n.m.* list of winners.
palme, *n.f.* palm.
palmier, *n.m.* palm (tree).
palpable, *adj.* palpable.
palper, *vb.* touch, feel.
palpitant, *adj.* fluttering, palpitating.
palpiter, *vb.* flutter, beat, palpitate.
paludéen, *adj.* marshy.
paludisme, *n.m.* malaria.
pâmer, *vb.* se p., faint.
pamphlet, *n.m.* pamphlet; satire.
pamphlétaire, *n.m.* pamphleteer.
pamplemousse, *n.m.* grapefruit.
pan, *n.m.* side, piece, flap.
panacée, *n.f.* panacea.
panache, *n.m.* plume; spirit.
panais, *n.m.* parsnip.
pancarte, *n.f.* sign, placard.
pandit, *n.m.* pundit.
pané, *adj.* dotted with bread crumbs.
panier, *n.m.* basket.
panique, *adj. and n.f.* panic.

panne, *n.f.* fat; accident, break-down.

panneau, *n.m.* panel.

panoplie, *n.f.* outfit; display.

panorama, *n.m.* panorama.

panse, *n.f.* paunch, cud.

pansement, *n.m.* dressing.

panser, *vb.* groom; dress.

pantalon, *n.m.* trousers.

panteler, *vb.* pant, gasp.

panthère, *n.f.* panther.

pantomime, *n.f.* pantomime.

pantoufle, *n.f.* slipper.

pantoufler, *vb.* act silly.

paon (pän), *n.m.* peacock.

papa, *n.m.* daddy.

papal, *adj.* papal.

papauté, *n.f.* papacy.

pape, *n.m.* pope.

paperasse, *n.f.* waste paper; official documents.

paperassier, *adj.* scribbling, petty.

papeterie, *n.f.* stationery.

papetier, *n.m.* stationer.

papier, *n.m.* paper.

papier à notes, *n.m.* notepaper.

papier à tapisser, *n.m.* wallpaper.

papier peint, *n.m.* wallpaper.

papillon, *n.m.* butterfly.

papillonner, *vb.* flutter, trifle.

papoter, *vb.* prate, prattle.

pâque, *n.f.* Passover.

paquebot, *n.m.* small liner, packet.

pâquerette, *n.f.* daisy.

Pâques, *n.m.* Easter.

paquet, *n.m.* package, parcel, bundle; deck (cards).

par, *prep.* by; through.

parabole, *n.f.* parabola; parable.

parachever, *vb.* perfect.

parachute, *n.m.* parachute.

parade, *n.f.* parade, procession.

parader, *vb.* parade, show off.

paradis, *n.m.* paradise.

paradoxal, *adj.* paradoxical.

paradoxe, *n.m.* paradox.

paraffine, *n.f.* paraffin.

parage, *n.m.* ancestry, descent; locality.

parages, *n.m.pl.* vicinity.

paragraphe, *n.m.* paragraph.

paraître, *vb.* appear, seem.

parallèle, *adj.* and *n.m.f.* parallel.

paralyser, *vb.* paralyze.

paralysie, *n.f.* paralysis.

paralytique, *adj.* and *n.m.f.* paralytic.

paramètre, *n.m.* parameter.

parangon, *n.m.* model, paragon.

paranoïa, *n.f.* paranoia.

paraphraser, *vb.* paraphrase.

parapluie, *n.m.* umbrella.

parasite, *n.m.* parasite.

parasol, *n.m.* parasol.

paratonnerre, *n.m.* lightning rod.

paravent, *n.m.* screen.

parc (-k), *n.m.* park.

parcelle, *n.f.* part, instalment.

parce que, *conj.* because.

parchemin, *n.m.* parchment.

parcimonie, *n.f.* parsimony.

parcomètre, *n.m.* parking meter.

parcourir, *vb.* run through.

parcours, *n.m.* course, journey.

par-dessous, *adv.* and *prep.* under(neath).

pardessus, *n.m.* overcoat.

par-dessus, *adv.* and *prep.* above, over.

pardon, 1. *n.m.* pardon, forgiveness. 2. *interj.* sorry!

pardonner, *vb.* forgive, pardon.

pardonneur, *n.m.* pardoner.

pare-balles, *adj.* bullet-proof.

pare-boue, *n.m.* mudguard.

pare-brise, *n.m.* windshield.

pare-chocs, *n.m.* bumper.

pareil, *adj.* like.

parent, *n.m.* relative; (*pl.*) parents.

parenté, *n.f.* relationship.

parenthèse, *n.f.* parenthesis.

parer, *vb.* attire, deck out; parry.

paresse, *n.f.* sloth.

paresser, *vb.* laze, waste time.

paresseux, *adj.* lazy.

parfaire, *vb.* complete, finish up.

parfait, *adj.* perfect.

parfois, *adv.* sometimes.

parfum, *n.m.* perfume.

parfumé, *adj.* fragrant..

parfumer, *vb.* perfume.

parfumerie, *n.f.* perfumery.

pari, *n.m.* bet.

paria, *n.m.* outcast.

parier, *vb.* bet.

parieur, *n.m.* one who bets.

Parisien, *n.m.* Parisian.

parisien, *adj.* Parisian.

parité, *n.f.* equality, parity.

parjure, *n.m.* perjury.

parjurer, vb. se p., commit perjury.
parking, n.m. parking lot.
parlant, adj. speaking, chatty.
parlement, n.m. parliament.
parlementaire, adj. parliamentary.
parlementer, vb. parley.
parler, vb. talk, speak.
parleur, n.m. one who speaks or talks.
parloir, n.m. parlor.
parmi, prep. among.
parodie, n.f. parody.
parodier, vb. parody, imitate.
paroi, n.f. wall lining.
paroisse, n.f. parish.
paroissial, adj. parochial.
parole, n.f. speech, word. **prendre la p.**, take the floor.
paroxysme, n.m. peak.
parquer, vb. park, enclose.
parquet, n.m. floor.
parqueterie, n.f. parquetry.
parrain, n.m. godfather.
parsemer, vb. spread, strew.
part, n.f. share, part. **de la p. de**, on behalf of. **quelque p.**, somewhere. **nulle p.**, nowhere. **faire p. à**, share; inform.
partage, n.m. partition, sharing, share.
partager, vb. share, divide.
partance, n.f. going, sailing.
partant, n.m. one who leaves.
partenaire, n.m.f. partner.
parti, n.m. party.
partial, adj. partial.
partialité, n.f. bias, partiality.
participant, adj. and n.m. participant.
participation, n.f. participation, share.
participe, n.m. participle.
participer, vb. partake, take part.
particularité, n.f. peculiarity.
particule, n.f. particle.
particulier, adj. particular; private; peculiar, special.
partie, n.f. part, party.
partiel, adj. partial.
partir, vb. depart, leave, go (come) away, sail.
partisan, n.m. partisan, follower.
partitif, adj. partitive.
partition, n.f. score (music).

partout, adv. everywhere, throughout. **p. où**, wherever.
parure, n.f. ornament.
parution, n.f. publication, appearance.
parvenir, vb. reach.
parvenu, n.m. upstart.
pas, 1. n.m. step, pace. **faux p.**, slip. **2.** adv. not. **p. du tout**, not at all.
passable, adj. fair.
passage, n.m. aisle, passage, alley.
passager, 1. n.m. passenger. **2.** adj. passing, fugitive.
passant, n.m. passer-by.
passavant, n.m. permit.
passe, n.f. passing, permit.
passé, adj. and n.m. past.
passe-partout, n.m. skeleton key; passport.
passeport, n.m. passport.
passer, vb. pass; go by; spend; strain. **se p. de**, go without.
passereau, n.m. sparrow.
passerelle, n.f. bridge.
passe-temps, n.m. pastime.
passible, adj. capable of feeling.
passif, adj. and n.m. passive.
passion, n.f. passion.
passionné, adj. passionate.
passionnel, adj. concerning or due to passion.
passionner, vb. interest, excite. **se p.**, be eager or excited over.
passoire, n.f. device for straining.
pastel, n.m. crayon.
pastèque, n.f. watermelon.
pasteur, n.m. pastor.
pasteuriser, vb. pasteurize.
pastille, n.f. lozenge, cough drop.
pastis, n.m. aniseed liquor.
pastoral, adj. pastoral.
pataud, adj. awkward.
patauger, vb. flounder.
pâte, n.f. paste, dough, batter.
pâté, n.m. block; pie.
patelin, n.m. (colloquial) village.
patenôtre, n.f. (Lord's) prayer.
patent, adj. patent, evident.
patente, n.f. license.
patenter, vb. license.
paterne, adj. paternal.
paternel, adj. paternal.
paternité, n.f. fatherhood.
pâteux, adj. pasty, thick, muddy.
pathétique, adj. pathetic.

pathologie, *n.f.* pathology.
patience, *n.f.* patience.
patient, *adj. and n.m.* patient.
patienter, *vb.* wait.
patin, *n.m.* skate.
patiner, *vb.* skate.
patineur, *n.m.* skater.
patinoire, *n.f.* skating rink.
pâtir, *vb.* suffer.
pâtisserie, *n.f.* pastry.
patois, *n.m.* dialect; gibberish.
pâtre, *n.m.* shepherd.
patriarche, *n.m.* patriarch.
patricien, *adj. and n.m.* patrician.
patrie, *n.f.* native country, homeland.
patrimoine, *n.m.* patrimony.
patriote, *n.m.f.* patriot.
patriotique, *adj.* patriotic.
patriotisme, *n.m.* patriotism.
patron, *n.m.* employer; boss;
model, pattern; patron.
patronat, *n.m.* management, em-
ployers.
patronner, *vb.* patronize, support.
patrouille, *n.f.* patrol
patrouiller, *vb.* patrol
patte, *n.f.* paw, leg; flap.
pâturage, *n.m.* pasture.
pâture, *n.f.* fodder; pasture.
paume, *n.f.* palm.
paumé, 1. *n.m.* loser. **2.** *adj.* lost.
paupière, *n.f.* eyelid.
pause, *n.f.* pause.
pauvre, *adj.* poor.
pauvreté, *n.f.* poverty.
pavaner, *vb.* se p., swagger, strut.
pavé, *n.m.* pavement.
paver, *vb.* pave.
pavillon, *n.m.* pavilion.
pavot, *n.m.* poppy.
payant, *adj.* paying, profitable.
paye, *n.f.* payment; salary
payement, *n.m.* payment.
payer, *vb.* pay, settle.
payeur, *n.m.* payer.
pays, *n.m.* country.
paysage, *n.m.* landscape, scenery.
paysager, *adj.* of the country,
rural.
paysan, *n.m.* peasant.
Pays-Bas, les, *n.m.pl.* Holland; the
Netherlands.
péage, *n.m.* toll, tollgate.
peau, *n.f.* skin, hide.

pêche, *n.f.* peach; fishing.
péché, *n.m.* sin.
pécher, *vb.* sin.
pêcher, 1. *vb.* fish. **2.** *n.m.* peach
tree.
pêcherie, *n.f.* fishing place.
pécheur *m.,* **pécheresse** *f.* **1.** *n.* sinner. **2.** *adj.* sinful.
pêcheur, *n.m.* fisherman.
pécule, *n.m.* savings.
pécuniaire, *adj.* pecuniary.
pédagogie, *n.f.* pedagogy.
pédale, *n.f.* pedal.
pédalo, *n.m.* pedal boat.
pédant, *adj. and n.m.* pedant, pe-
dantic.
pédanterie, *n.f.* pedantry.
pédé(raste), *n.m.* homosexual.
pédestre, *adj.* pedestrian.
pédiatre, *n.m.* pediatrician.
pédicure, *n.m.* podiatrist.
pègre, *n.f.* underworld.
peigne, *n.m.* comb.
peigner, *vb.* comb.
peignoir, *n.m.* dressing-gown.
peindre, *vb.* paint, portray, depict.
peine, *n.f.* pain; penalty. **à p.,**
hardly, barely; **faire de la p. à,**
pain, *vb.*; **valoir la p. de,** be worth
while to; **se donner la p.,** take the
trouble.
peiner, *vb.* labor; grieve.
peintre, *n.m.* painter.
peinture, *n.f.* paint, painting.
péjoratif, *adj.* pejorative.
pelage, *n.m.* coat.
pelé, *adj.* bald, uncovered.
pêle-mêle, *adv.* pell-mell.
peler, *vb.* peel, pare.
pèlerin, *n.m.* pilgrim.
pèlerinage, *n.m.* pilgrimage.
pèlerine, *n.f.* cape.
pélican, *n.m.* pelican.
pelle, *n.f.* shovel.
pelletier, *n.m.* furrier.
pellicule, *n.f.* film.
pelote, *n.f.* ball, pellet.
peloton, *n.m.* ball; group of sol-
diers.
pelouse, *n.f.* lawn.
peluche, *n.f.* **animal en p.,** stuffed
animal.
pelure, *n.f.* peel.
pénal, *adj.* penal.
pénalité, *n.f.* penalty.

penaud, *adj.* sheepish.

penchant, *n.m.* bent, liking, tendency.

pencher, *vb.* tilt, lean, droop. **se p.,** bend.

pendaison, *n.f.* hanging (execution).

pendant, *prep.* during; pending. **p. que, p. as,** while.

pendentatif, *n.m.* pendant.

penderie, *n.f.* wardrobe.

pendiller, *vb.* dangle.

pendre, *vb.* hang.

pendule, *n.m.* pendulum. *n.f.* clock.

pénétrable, *adj.* penetrable.

pénétrant, *adj.* keen.

pénétration, *n.f.* penetration.

pénétrer, *vb.* penetrate, pervade.

pénible, *adj.* painful.

pénicilline, *n.f.* penicillin.

péninsule, *n.f.* peninsula.

pénis, *n.m.* penis.

pénitence, *n.f.* penance.

pénitencier, *n.m.* penitentiary.

pénitent, *adj.* and *n.m.* penitent.

penne, *n.f.* feather.

pénombre, *n.f.* gloom, shadow.

pensée, *n.f.* thought; pansy.

penser, *vb.* think.

penseur, *n.m.* thinker.

pensif, *adj.* thoughtful, pensive.

pension, *n.f.* board; pension.

pensionnaire, *n.m.f.* boarder.

pensionnat, *n.m.* boarding school.

pente, *n.f.* slope, slant.

Pentecôte, *n.f.* Whitsun, Pentecost.

pénurie, *n.f.* penury, scarcity.

pépé, *n.m.* (colloquial) grandpa.

pépier, *vb.* chirp.

pépin, *n.m.* pip, kernel; (colloquial) problem.

pépinière, *n.f.* nursery (plants).

pépite, *n.f.* nugget.

perçant, *adj.* sharp.

perce, *n.f.* boring tool.

percée, *n.f.* opening; breakthrough.

perce-neige, *n.f.* snowdrop.

percepteur, *n.m.* tax collector.

perception, *n.f.* perception; collecting.

percer, *vb.* pierce, bore.

percevoir, *vb.* collect, amass; perceive.

perche, *n.f.* pole, perch.

percher, *vb.* **se p.,** perch.

perchoir, *n.m.* perch.

perclus, *adj.* lame, crippled.

percolateur, *n.m.* percolator.

percussion, *n.f.* percussion.

percuter, *vb.* hit, strike.

perdition, *n.f.* perdition.

perdre, *vb.* lose; waste.

perdrix, *n.f.* partridge.

père, *n.m.* father.

péremptoire, *adj.* peremptory.

perfection, *n.f.* perfection.

perfectionnement, *n.m.* improvement, finishing.

perfectionner, *vb.* perfect, finish.

perfectionniste, *adj.* and *n.m.f.* perfectionist.

perfide, *adj.* treacherous.

perfidie, *n.f.* treachery.

perforation, *n.f.* perforation.

perforer, *vb.* perforate, drill.

péricliter, *vb.* collapse.

péridural, *adj.* **anesthésie p.,** epidural.

péril (-l), *n.m.* peril, danger.

périlleux, *adj.* perilous, dangerous.

périmé, *adj.* outdated, expired.

périmètre, *n.m.* perimeter.

période, *n.f.* period, term, stage.

périodique, *adj.* periodic.

péripétie, *n.f.* shift of luck.

périphérique, *adj.* outlying, peripheral.

périr, *vb.* perish.

périscope, *n.m.* periscope.

périssable, *adj.* perishable.

perle, *n.f.* pearl, bead.

perlé, *adj.* pearly, perfect.

permanence, *n.f.* permanence.

permanent, *adj.* permanent.

perméable, *adj.* permeable.

permettre, *vb.* permit, allow.

permis, *n.m.* permit, license.

permission, *n.f.* permission; leave (of absence); furlough.

permissionnaire, *n.m.f.* one having a permit; one on leave.

permuter, *vb.* change, exchange.

pernicieux, *adj.* pernicious.

pérorer, *vb.* harangue, argue.

Pérou, *n.m.* Peru.

perpendiculaire, *adj.* perpendicular.

perpétrer, *vb.* commit.

perpétuel, *adj.* perpetual.

perpétuer, *vb.* perpetuate.

perplexe, *adj.* perplexed, undecided.

perplexité, *n.f.* perplexity.

perquisition, *n.f.* exploration, search.

perron, *n.m.* flight of steps.

perroquet, *n.m.* parrot.

perruque, *n.f.* wig.

persan, *adj. and n.m.* Persian.

perse, *adj.* Persian.

persécuter, *vb.* persecute.

persécution, *n.f.* persecution.

persévérance, *n.f.* perseverance.

persévérant, *adj.* persevering, resolute.

persévérer, *vb.* persevere.

persienne, *n.f.* blind, shutter.

persifler, *vb.* banter, ridicule.

persil, *n.m.* parsley.

Persique, *vb.* le golfe P., the Persian Gulf.

persistance, *n.f.* persistence.

persistant, *adj.* persistent.

persister, *vb.* persist.

personnage, *n.m.* personage; character.

personnalité, *n.f.* personality.

personne, 1. *n.f.* person. **2.** *pron.* nobody.

personnel, 1. *n.m.* personnel, staff. **2.** *adj.* personal.

personnifier, *vb.* personify.

perspective, *n.f.* perspective, prospect.

perspicace, *adj.* discerning.

perspicacité, *n.f.* insight.

persuader, *vb.* persuade, convince; induce.

persuasif, *adj.* persuasive.

perte, *n.f.* loss, waste; (*pl.*) casualties.

pertinence, *n.f.* pertinence.

pertinent, *adj.* relevant, pertinent.

perturbateur, *n.m.* agitator, disturber.

perturbation, *n.f.* disruption.

perturber, *vb.* disrupt.

pervenche, *n.f.* periwinkle.

pervers, *adj.* perverse, contrary.

pervertir, *vb.* pervert.

pesant, *adj.* heavy, ponderous.

pesanteur, *n.f.* weight, dullness.

peser, *vb.* weigh.

pessimisme, *n.m.* pessimism.

pessimiste, *n.m.f.* pessimist.

peste, *n.f.* pestilence; nuisance.

pester, *vb.* p. contre, curse against.

pestilence, *n.f.* pestilence, plague, nuisance.

pétale, *n.m.* petal.

pétanque, *n.f.* bowling.

pétiller, *vb.* twinkle, crackle.

petit, 1. *adj.* little, small, petty. **2.** *n.m.* cub.

petite-fille, *n.f.* granddaughter.

petitesse, *n.f.* smallness, pettiness.

petit-fils, *(-fès), n.m.* grandson.

petit-gris, *n.m.* fur of the squirrel.

pétition, *n.f.* petition.

pétitionner, *vb.* request, ask.

petits-enfants, *n.m.pl.* grandchildren.

petits-pois, *n.m.pl.* peas.

pétrifiant, *adj.* petrifying.

pétrifier, *vb.* petrify or (**se p.**) become petrified.

pétrin, *n.m.* (colloquial) jam, fix.

pétrir, *vb.* knead, mold.

pétrole, *n.m.* petroleum, kerosene.

pétulance, *n.f.* petulance.

peu, 1. *n.m.* little; few. **2.** *adv.* not. **p. à p.,** gradually.

peuplade, *n.f.* tribe, clan.

peuple, *n.m.* people.

peupler, *vb.* people.

peuplier, *n.m.* poplar.

peur, *n.f.* fear. **avoir p.,** be afraid. **de p. que … ne,** lest.

peureux, *adj.* shy, timid.

peut-être, *adv.* perhaps, maybe.

phallocrate, *adj.* macho.

phallocratie, *n.f.* machismo.

phantasme, *n.m.* fantasy.

phare, *n.m.* beacon, lighthouse; headlight.

pharmacie, *n.f.* drugstore, pharmacy.

pharmacien, *n.m.* druggist.

phase, *n.f.* phase.

phénix, *n.m.* phoenix; superior person.

phénoménal, *adj.* phenomenal.

phénomène, *n.m.* phenomenon; freak.

philanthrope, *n.m.* philanthropist.

philanthropie, *n.f.* philanthropy.
philatélie, *n.f.* stamp collecting.
Philippines, *n.f.pl.* the Philippines.
philosophe, *n.m.f.* philosopher.
philosophie, *n.f.* philosophy.
philosophique, *adj.* philosophical.
phobie, *n.f.* phobia.
phonéticien, *n.m.* phonetician.
phonétique, *adj. and n.f.* phonetic,
phonetics.
phonographe, *n.m.* phonograph.
phoque, *n.m.* seal.
phosphorescent, *adj.* luminous.
photo, *n.f.* photograph.
photocopie, *n.f.* photocopy.
photocopieur, *n.m.* photocopier.
photographe, *n.m.f.* photographer.
photographie, *n.f.* photograph;
photography.
phrase, *n.f.* sentence.
phtisie, *n.f.* consumption.
phtisique, *adj. and n.m.* consumptive.
physicien, *n.m.* physical scientist.
physionomie, *n.f.* looks, expression.
physique, 1. *n.f.* physics. **2.** *adj.*
physical.
piailler, *vb.* peep, squeal.
pianiste, *n.m.f.* pianist.
piano, *n.m.* piano.
pic, *n.m.* peak.
pichet, *n.m.* jug.
pick-up, *n.m.* phonograph.
picoter, *vb.* prick, peck.
pièce, *n.f.* piece; coin; patch; room.
p. de théâtre, play.
pied, *n.m.* foot. **aller à p.,** walk.
coup de p., kick.
pied-à-terre, *n.m.* temporary quarters.
piédestal, *n.m.* pedestal.
pied-noir, *n.m.* Algerian-born
French person.
piège, *n.m.* snare, trap.
pierre, *n.f.* stone.
pierreries, *n.f.pl.* jewelry, gems.
pierreux, *adj.* full of stone or grit.
pierrot, *n.m.* clown in pantomime.
piété, *n.f.* piety.
piétiner, *vb.* trample; mark time.
piéton, *n.m.* pedestrian.
piètre, *adj.* pitiful, mean,
wretched.

pieu, *n.m.* stake, pile.
pieuvre, *n.f.* octopus.
pieux, *adj.* pious.
pigeon, *n.m.* pigeon, dove.
piger, *vb.* (colloquial) understand.
pigiste, *n.m.f.* freelance(r).
pile, *n.f.* stack; battery.
piler, *vb.* crush; beat someone.
pilier, *n.m.* pillar, column.
pillage, *n.m.* plundering.
piller, *vb.* plunder.
pilotage, *n.m.* piloting; driving
piles.
pilote, *n.m.f.* pilot.
piloter, *vb.* pilot, lead.
pilule, *n.f.* pill.
piment, *n.m.* chili.
pimenter, *vb.* flavor, season.
pimpant, *adj.* stylish, smart.
pin, *n.m.* pine.
pinacle, *n.m.* pinnacle.
pinard, *n.m.* (colloquial) (cheap)
wine.
pince, *n.f.* clip; *(pl.)* pliers.
pinceau, *n.m.* paintbrush.
pince-nez, *n.m.* eyeglasses.
pincer, *vb.* pinch, nip.
pinte, *n.f.* pint.
pioche, *n.f.* pickax.
piocher, *vb.* dig.
piocheur, *n.m.* digger.
pion, *n.m.* pawn, peon.
pioncer, *vb.* nap, sleep.
pionnier, *n.m.* pioneer.
pipe, *n.f.* pipe.
pipeline, *n.m.* pipeline.
piper, *vb.* catch, decoy, trick.
piquant, *adj.* sharp. **mot p.,** quip.
pique, *n.m.* spade.
pique-nique, *n.m.* picnic.
piquer, *vb.* prick, sting.
piquet, *n.m.* picket, peg, stake.
piqûre, *n.f.* prick, sting, puncture.
pirate, *n.m.f.* pirate.
pirate de l'air, *n.m.f.* hijacker.
piraterie, *n.f.* piracy.
pire, *adj.* worse, worst.
pirouette, *n.f.* pirouette.
pis, *adv.* worse, worst.
piscine, *n.f.* pool.
pissenlit, *n.m.* dandelion.
pistache, *n.f.* pistachio.
piste, *n.f.* track.
pistolet, *n.m.* pistol.

piston, *n.m.* piston; strings (influence).

pistonner, *vb.* help, push; pull strings for.

pitance, *n.f.* meager amount, as of food.

piteux, *adj.* pitiful.

pitié, *n.f.* pity, mercy.

pitoyable, *adj.* pitiful, miserable.

pitre, *n.m.* clown.

pittoresque, *adj.* picturesque, colorful.

pivoine, *n.f.* peony.

pivot, *n.m.* pivot.

pivoter, *vb.* turn, pivot, revolve.

pizza, *n.f.* pizza.

placard, *n.m.* closet; poster.

placarder, *vb.* post, display.

place, *n.f.* place, room.

placement, *n.m.* investment; placing.

placer, *vb.* invest; place.

placet, *n.m.* petition, demand.

placide, *adj.* placid.

placidité, *n.f.* placidness.

plafond, *n.m.* ceiling.

plafonner, *vb.* reach one's ceiling.

plage, *n.f.* beach.

plagiaire, *n.m.f.* one who plagiarizes.

plagiat, *n.m.* plagiarism.

plagier, *vb.* plagiarize.

plaid, *n.m.* plaid.

plaider, *vb.* plead.

plaideur, *n.m.* pleader.

plaidoirie, *n.f.* lawyer's speech.

plaie, *n.f.* wound, sore.

plaignant, *n.m.* plaintiff.

plaindre, *vb.* pity. **se p.,** complain.

plaine, *n.f.* plain.

plainte, *n.f.* complaint.

plaintif, *adj.* mournful.

plaire, *vb.* please. **s'il vous plaît,** if you please.

plaisance, *n.f.* pleasure, ease.

plaisant, *adj.* joking.

plaisanter, *vb.* joke.

plaisanterie, *n.f.* joke.

plaisir, *n.m.* pleasure.

plan, *n.m.* plan; plane; schedule, scheme. **premier p.,** foreground.

planche, *n.f.* board, shelf, plank.

planche à roulettes, *n.f.* skateboard.

plancher, *n.m.* floor.

planer, *vb.* glide; hover.

planétaire, 1. *adj.* planetary. **2.** *n.m.* planetarium.

planète, *n.f.* planet.

planeur, *n.m.* glider (plane).

planifier, *vb.* plan.

plantation, *n.f.* plantation.

plante, *n.f.* plant; sole.

planter, *vb.* plant.

planteur, *n.m.* planter.

planton, *n.m.* military orderly.

plantureux, *adj.* fertile, rich.

plaque, *n.f.* plate, slab. **p. de projection,** lantern-slide.

plaquer, *vb.* plate; abandon.

plaquette, *n.f.* booklet; plaque.

plastic, *n.m.* plastic explosive.

plastique, *adj.* plastic.

plastiquer, *adj.* blow up.

plastronner, *vb.* pose, strut jauntily.

plat, 1. *n.m.* dish, platter. **2.** *adj.* flat. **œuf sur le p.,** fried egg.

platane, *n.m.* plane-tree.

plat-bord, *n.m.* gunwale.

plateau, *n.m.* plateau; tray.

plate-bande, *n.f.* flower bed.

plate-forme, *n.f.* platform.

platine, 1. *n.f.* platen, plate; turntable. **2.** *n.m.* platinum.

platitude, *n.f.* flatness.

plâtras, *n.m.* rubbish, rubble.

plâtre, *n.m.* plaster; cast (*med.*).

plausible, *adj.* plausible.

plébéien, *adj.* ignoble.

plébiscite, *n.m.* plebiscite.

plein, *adj.* full; crowded.

pleinement, *adv.* fully.

plénier, *adj.* complete, plenary.

plénitude, *n.f.* fullness.

pléthore, *n.f.* overabundance, plethora.

pleurer, *vb.* cry, weep, lament, mourn.

pleurésie, *n.f.* pleurisy.

pleurnicher, *vb.* complain, whine.

pleurs, *n.m.pl.* tears, weeping.

pleutre, *n.m.* cad, coward.

pleuvoir, *vb.* rain.

pli, *n.m.* envelope; fold, pleat, crease.

pliable, *adj.* pliable.

pliant, *n.m.* folding chair.

plier, *vb.* fold, bend.

plissement, *n.m.* fold, folding.

plisser, vb. pleat.

plomb, n.m. lead.

plomberie, n.f. plumbing.

plombier, n.m. plumber.

plongeoir, n.m. diving board.

plongeon, n.m. plunge, dive.

plonger, vb. plunge, dive, dip.

plongeur, n.m. diver; dishwasher.

plouf, interj. and n.m. splash, plop.

ploutocrate, n.m. plutocrat.

ployer, vb. incline, bend.

pluie, n.f. rain.

pluie radioactive, n.f. fallout.

plumage, n.m. feathers.

plume, n.f. pen; feather.

plumeau, n.m. feather duster.

plumer, vb. pluck.

plumet, n.m. plume.

plumeux, adj. feathery.

plumier, n.m. pen or pencil case.

plupart, n.f. greater part, majority.
pour la p., mostly.

pluralité, n.f. plurality.

pluriel, adj. and n.m. plural.

plus, adv. more, most. **ne . . . p.,** no
more. **non p.,** neither. **en p.,** extra.

plusieurs, adj. and pron. several.

plus-que-parfait, n.m. pluperfect.

plus-value, n.f. profit.

plutôt, adv. rather.

pluvieux, adj. rainy, wet.

pneu, n.m. tire.

pneumatique, abbr. **pneu,** n.m.
tire.

pneumonie, n.f. pneumonia.

pochade, n.f. hasty sketch.

poche, n.f. pocket.

pocher, vb. poach.

pocheter, vb. pocket.

pochette, n.f. little pocket; handkerchief.

pochoir, n.m. stencil.

poêle, n.m. stove.

poème, n.m. poem.

poésie, n.f. poem, poetry.

poète, n.m. poet.

poétique, adj. poetic.

poids (pwä), n.m. weight.

poignant, adj. poignant, keen.

poignard, n.m. dagger.

poignarder, vb. stab.

poigne, n.f. grip, power.

poignée, n.f. handful; handle.

poignet, n.m. wrist; cuff.

poil (pwäl), n.m. hair.

poilu, 1. adj. hairy. **2.** n.m. French
soldier.

poinçon, n.m. punch.

poing, n.m. fist.

point, n.m. point, dot, period;
stitch. **p. de vue,** point of view. **p.
du jour,** dawn. **ne . . . p.,** none. **être
sur le p. de,** be about to. **au p.,** in
focus. **deux p.s,** colon. **p. d'interrogation,** question mark.

pointage, n.m. pointing; (mil.)
sighting.

pointe, n.f. point, tip, touch (small
amount).

pointer, vb. point, aim; check in.

pointeur, n.m. pointer, checker.

pointillage, n.m. dotting.

pointiller, vb. dot; tease.

pointilleux, adj. fussy, precise.

pointu, adj. pointed.

pointure, n.f. size (shoe).

point-virgule, n.m. semicolon.

poire, n.f. pear.

poireau, n.m. leek.

poireauter, vb. hang around.

poirier, n.m. pear tree.

pois, n.m. pea; dot.

poison, n.m. poison.

poisser, vb. make gluey or sticky.

poisson, n.m. fish.

poissonnerie, n.f. fish store.

poissonneux, adj. filled with fish.

poissonnier, n.m. fish dealer.

poitrinaire, adj. and n.m.f. consumptive.

poitrine, n.f. chest.

poivre, n.m. pepper.

poivrer, vb. spice with pepper.

poivrier, n.m. pepper plant.

poivron, n.m. pepper.

poix, n.f. pitch.

polaire, adj. polar.

pôle, n.m. pole.

polémique, n.f. argument.

poli, 1. adj. civil, polite. **2.** n.m. polish.

police, n.f. police; (insurance) policy.

policer, vb. refine.

polichinelle, n.m. Punch (puppet).

policier, n.m. policeman. **roman p.,**
detective story.

polir, vb. polish.

polisseur, n.m. polisher.

polisson, 1. n.m. gamin, scamp. **2.** adj. running wild.
polissonnerie, n.f. naughty action or remark.
politesse, n.f. good manners.
politicien, n.m.f. politician, political schemer.
politique, 1. n.f. policy, politics. **2.** adj. politic, political.
polka, n.f. polka.
pollen, n.m. pollen.
polluer, vb. pollute.
pollution, n.f. pollution.
Pologne, n.f. Poland.
Polonais, n.m. Pole.
polonais, adj. and n.m. Polish.
poltron, 1. adj. craven, cowardly. **2.** n.m. coward.
poltronnerie, n.f. cowardly behavior.
polycopier, vb. duplicate.
polygame, 1. n.m.f. polygamist. **2.** adj. polygamous.
polygamie, n.f. polygamy.
polygone, n.m. polygon.
polyvalent, adj. varied, versatile.
pommade, n.f. pomade, salve.
pomme, n.f. apple. **p. de terre,** potato.
pommeau, n.m. pommel.
pommette, n.f. cheekbone.
pommier, n.m. apple tree.
pompe, n.f. pump; pomp.
pomper, vb. pump.
pompeux, adj. pompous.
pompier, n.m. fireman.
pompiste, n.m.f. gas station attendant.
pompon, n.m. pompom, tuft.
ponce, n.f. pumice.
ponctualité, n.f. punctuality.
ponctuation, n.f. punctuation.
ponctuel, adj. punctual.
ponctuer, vb. punctuate.
pondre, vb. lay (eggs).
poney, n.m. pony.
pont, n.m. bridge; deck.
pontife, n.m. pontiff.
pont-levis, n.m. drawbridge.
ponton, n.m. pontoon.
pop, adj. and n.m. pop (music).
popeline, n.f. poplin.
popote, n.f. mess (military).
populace, n.f. mob.
populaire, adj. popular.

populariser, vb. popularize.
popularité, n.f. popularity.
population, n.f. population.
populeux, adj. populous.
porc, n.m. pig, pork.
porcelaine, n.f. china.
porc-épic, n.m. porcupine.
porche, n.m. porch.
porcherie, n.f. pigpen.
pore, n.m. pore.
poreux, adj. porous.
porno, adj. porn.
pornographie, n.f. pornography.
port, n.m. port, harbor; carrying; postage.
portable, adj. wearable.
portail, n.m. portal.
portant, adj. **bien/mal p.,** in good/ill health.
portatif, adj. portable.
porte, n.f. door, gate.
porte-affiches, n.m. billboard.
porte-avions, n.m. aircraft carrier.
portée, n.f. range, import, scope, reach; litter. **hors de p.,** out of reach.
portefaix, n.m. porter.
portefeuille, n.m. wallet, case, portfolio.
portemanteau, n.m. cloak rack.
portement, n.m. carrying.
porte-monnaie, n.m. purse.
porte-parole, n.m. spokesman.
porter, vb. carry, bear; wear. **se p.,** be (in health).
porte-rame, n.m. oarlock.
porteur, n.m. porter, bearer.
portier, n.m. doorman, porter.
portière, n.f. door-curtain.
portion, n.f. portion, share.
portique, n.m. portico, porch.
porto, n.m. port wine.
portrait, n.m. portrait.
portraitiste, n.m.f. painter of portraits.
Portugais, n.m. Portuguese (person).
portugais, 1. n.m. Portuguese (language). **2.** adj. Portuguese.
Portugal, n.m. Portugal.
pose, n.f. pose, attitude.
posé, adj. poised, set.
poser, vb. place, stand, set, lay. **se p.,** settle, alight.

poseur, *n.m.* person or thing that places or applies; affected person.

positif, *adj. and n.m.* positive.

position, *n.f.* stand, place, position.

positiviste, *n.m.f.* positivist.

posologie, *n.f.* dosage.

posséder, *vb.* own, possess.

possesseur, *n.m.* possessor.

possessif, *adj. and n.m.* possessive.

possession, *n.f.* possession.

possibilité, *n.f.* possibility.

possible, *adj.* possible. **tout son p.,** one's utmost.

postal, *adj.* postal.

poste, *n.f.* mail. **mettre à la p.,** mail. **p. restante,** general delivery.

poste, *n.m.* post. **p. d'essence,** gas station. **p. de secours,** first-aid station.

poster, *vb.* post (letter); place.

postérieur, *adj.* rear, posterior.

postérité, *n.f.* posterity.

posthume, *adj.* posthumous.

postiche, *adj.* false, unnecessary.

postier, *n.m.* postal worker.

post-scriptum, *n.m.* postscript.

postulant, *n.m.* applicant.

postuler, *vb.* apply for.

posture, *n.f.* posture.

pot, *n.m.* pot, pitcher, jar.

potable, *adj.* drinkable.

potage, *n.m.* soup.

potager, *adj.* vegetable.

potasse, *n.f.* potash.

pot-au-feu, *n.m.* stew.

pot-de-vin, *n.m.* tip, bribe.

pote, *n.m.* (colloquial) buddy.

poteau, *n.m.* post.

potée, *n.f.* potful.

potelé, *adj.* chubby.

potence, *n.f.* gallows.

potentat, *n.m.* potentate.

potentiel, *adj. and n.m.* potential.

poterie, *n.f.* pottery.

poterne, *n.f.* postern.

potier, *n.m.* potter.

potins, *n.m.pl.* gossip.

potion, *n.f.* potion.

potiron, *n.m.* pumpkin.

pou, *n.m.* louse.

poubelle, *n.f.* garbage can.

pouce, *n.m.* thumb; inch.

pouding, *n.m.* pudding.

poudre, *n.f.* powder.

poudrer, *vb.* powder.

poudreux, *adj.* full of powder or dust.

poudrier, *n.m.* compact (cosmetic).

poudroyer, *vb.* be dusty.

pouilleux, *adj.* infested with lice.

poulailler, *n.m.* henhouse.

poulain, *n.m.* colt.

poule, *n.f.* hen, chicken.

poulet, *n.m.* chicken.

poulette, *n.f.* pullet.

poulie, *n.f.* pulley.

poulpe, *n.m.* octopus.

pouls, *n.m.* pulse.

poumon, *n.m.* lung.

poupe, *n.f.* poop (of ship).

poupée, *n.f.* doll.

poupin, *adj.* smart, chic.

pour, *prep.* for; in order to. **p. que,** so that.

pourboire, *n.m.* tip, gratuity.

pourceau, *n.m.* hog.

pour-cent, *n.m.* percent.

pourcentage, *n.m.* percentage.

pourchasser, *vb.* pursue.

pourfendeur, *n.m.* killer, bully.

pourparlers, *n.m.pl.* discussion, parley.

pourpoint, *n.m.* doublet.

pourpre, *adj.* purple.

pourquoi, *adv.* why.

pourri, *adj.* rotten.

pourrir, *vb.* rot, spoil.

pourriture, *n.f.* rot.

poursuite, *n.f.* pursuit.

poursuivant, *n.m.* one who sues or prosecutes.

poursuivre, *vb.* pursue; sue, prosecute.

pourtant, *adv.* however.

pourvoi, *n.m.* appeal (at court).

pourvoir, *vb.* provide, supply. **p. à,** cater to.

pourvoyeur, *n.m.* caterer, purveyor.

pourvu que, *conj.* provided that.

pousse, *n.f.* shoot, sprouting.

poussée, *n.f.* push.

pousser, *vb.* push, urge, drive; grow.

poussette, *n.f.* stroller.

poussier, *n.m.* coal dust.

poussière, *n.f.* dust.

poussiéreux, *adj.* dusty.

poussin, *n.m.* newly hatched chick.
poussoir, *n.m.* push-button.
poutre, *n.f.* beam.
pouvoir, 1. *vb.* be able, can, may. **2.** *n.m.* power.
prairie, *n.f.* meadow.
praline, *n.f.* burnt almond.
praticable, *adj.* practicable.
praticien, *n.m.* practitioner.
pratique, 1. *n.f.* practice, exercise. **2.** *adj.* practical.
pratiquement, *adv.* practically, virtually.
pratiquer, *vb.* practice, exercise.
pré, *n.m.* meadow.
préalable, *adj.* preliminary.
préambule, *n.m.* preamble.
préau, *n.m.* yard, as of a prison.
préavis, *n.m.* advance notice.
précaire, *adj.* precarious.
précaution, *n.f.* precaution, discretion.
précédent, *n.m.* precedent.
précéder, *vb.* precede; come (go) before.
précepte, *n.m.* precept.
précepteur, *n.m.* tutor.
prêche, *n.m.* sermon.
prêcher, *vb.* preach.
précieux, *adj.* precious, valuable.
préciosité, *n.f.* preciosity.
précipice, *n.m.* precipice.
précipitamment, *adv.* headlong.
précipitation, *n.f.* hurry.
précipité, *adj.* hasty.
précipiter, *vb.* precipitate. **se p.,** rush, hasten.
précis, *adj.* precise, exact, accurate.
précisément, *adv.* precisely, definitely, just so.
préciser, *vb.* specify.
précision, *n.f.* accuracy, precision.
précité, *adj.* previously cited.
précoce, *adj.* precocious.
précocité, *n.f.* precociousness.
précompter, *vb.* deduct in advance.
préconçu, *adj.* preconceived.
préconiser, *vb.* extol, praise.
préconnaissance, *n.f.* foreknowledge.
précurseur, *n.m.* precursor.
prédécesseur, *n.m.* predecessor.

prédestination, *n.f.* predestination.
prédicateur, *n.m.* preacher.
prédiction, *n.f.* prediction.
prédilection, *n.f.* preference, predilection.
prédire, *vb.* foretell, predict.
prédisposer, *vb.* predispose.
prédisposition, *n.f.* predisposition.
prédominant, *adj.* predominant.
prééminence, *n.f.* preeminence.
préfabriquer, *adj.* prefabricated.
préface, *n.f.* preface.
préfecture, *n.f.* prefecture, district.
préférable, *adj.* preferable.
préférence, *n.f.* preference.
préférer, *vb.* prefer.
préfet, *n.m.* prefect.
préfixe, *n.m.* prefix.
préfixer, *vb.* fix in advance.
prégnant, *adj.* pregnant.
préhistorique, *adj.* prehistoric.
préjudice, *n.m.* injury.
préjudiciel, *adj.* interlocutory (as in law).
préjugé, *n.m.* prejudice.
préjuger, *vb.* prejudge.
prélasser, *vb.* se p., bask, lounge.
prélat, *n.m.* prelate.
prélèvement, *n.m.* deduction in advance.
prélever, *vb.* deduct previously.
préliminaire, *adj.* preliminary.
prélude, *n.m.* prelude.
prématuré, *adj.* premature.
préméditation, *n.f.* premeditation.
préméditer, *vb.* premeditate.
prémices, *n.f.pl.* first fruits, first works.
premier, *adj.* first, foremost; early; former.
prémisse, *n.f.* premise.
prémonition, *n.f.* premonition.
prémunir, *vb.* warn, take precautions.
prendre, *vb.* take.
preneur, *n.m.* buyer.
prénom, *n.m.* given name.
prénommé, *adj.* previously named.
préoccupation, *n.f.* care, worry.
préoccuper, *vb.* worry.
prépaiement, *n.m.* prepayment.
préparatifs, *n.m.pl.* preparation.
préparation, *n.f.* preparation.

préparatoire, *adj.* preparatory.
préparer, *vb.* prepare.
prépondérance, *n.f.* preponderance.
prépondérant, *adj.* preponderant.
préposé, *n.m.* one in charge.
préposition, *n.f.* preposition.
préretraite, *n.f.* early retirement.
prérogative, *n.f.* prerogative.
près, 1. *adv.* near. **2.** *prep.* **p. de,** near. **de p.,** nearby.
présage, *n.m.* omen.
présager, *vb.* (fore)bode.
presbyte, *adj.* far-sighted.
presbytère, *n.m.* parsonage, presbytery.
prescription, *n.f.* prescription.
prescrire, *vb.* prescribe.
préséance, *n.f.* precedence.
présélection, *n.f.* triage.
présence, *n.f.* presence; attendance.
présent, *adj. and n.m.* present.
présentable, *adj.* presentable.
présentation, *n.f.* presentation, introduction.
présentement, *adv.* now, at present.
présenter, *vb.* present; introduce. **se p. à l'esprit,** come to mind.
préservatif, *n.m.* condom.
préservation, *n.f.* preservation.
préserver, *vb.* preserve.
présidence, *n.f.* presidency.
président, *n.m.* president, chairman.
présidente, *n.f.* chairwoman.
présidentiel, *adj.* presidential.
présider, *vb.* preside.
présomptif, *adj.* apparent, presumed.
présomptueux, *adj.* presumptuous.
presque, *adv.* almost, nearly.
presqu'île, *n.f.* peninsula.
pressage, *n.m.* pressing.
pressant, *adj.* urgent.
presse, *n.f.* press; crowd.
pressé, *adj.* hurried.
pressentiment, *n.m.* foreboding, misgiving.
pressentir, *vb.* foresee.
presse-papiers, *n.m.* paperweight.
presser, *vb.* press; urge; hurry.
pressing, *n.m.* dry cleaner.

pression, *n.f.* pressure.
pressoir, *n.m.* machine or device for squeezing.
pressurer, *vb.* squeeze, put pressure on.
prestance, *n.f.* imposing appearance.
prestation, *n.f.* allowance; performance.
preste, *adj.* dexterous, nimble.
prestesse, *n.f.* vivacity, nimbleness.
prestige, *n.m.* prestige; illusion.
prestigieux, *adj.* enchanting.
présumer, *vb.* presume.
présupposer, *vb.* presuppose.
prêt, 1. *n.m.* loan. **2.** *adj.* ready.
prêtable, *adj.* lendable.
prétendant, *n.m.* claimant.
prétendre, *vb.* claim.
prétendu, *adj.* supposed, so-called.
prétentieux, *adj.* pretentious.
prétention, *n.f.* claim.
prêter, *vb.* lend.
prêteur, *n.m.* lender.
prétexte, *n.m.* pretext.
prétexter, *vb.* pretend, feign.
prêtre, *n.m.* priest.
prêtresse, *n.f.* priestess.
preuve, *n.f.* proof.
preux, *adj. and n.m.* gallant, brave.
prévaloir, *vb.* prevail.
prévenance, *n.f.* attentiveness, obligingness.
prévenant, *adj.* considerate.
prévenir, *vb.* prevent; warn.
préventif, 1. *adj.* preventive. **2.** *n.m.* deterrent.
prévention, *n.f.* bias; prevention.
prévenu, *adj.* partial, biased.
prévision, *n.f.* forecast, expectation, prediction.
prévoir, *vb.* foresee.
prévôt, *n.m.* provost.
prévoyance, *n.f.* foresight.
prévoyant, *adj.* farseeing, prudent.
prier, *vb.* beg; pray.
prière, *n.f.* prayer.
prieur, *n.m.* prior.
prieuré, *n.m.* priory.
primaire, *adj.* primary.
primauté, *n.f.* preeminence, primacy.
prime, 1. *n.f.* premium; subsidy. **2.** *adj.* first; accented.

primé, *adj.* prize-winning.
primer, *vb.* outdo, excel.
primeur, *n.f.* freshness, earliness.
primitif, *adj.* primitive; original.
primordial, *adj.* primordial.
prince, *n.m.* prince.
princesse, *n.f.* princess.
princier, *adj.* princely.
principal, *adj.* chief, main, principal.
principauté, *n.f.* principality.
principe, *n.m.* principle.
printanier, *adj.* of spring.
printemps, *n.m.* spring.
priorité, *n.f.* priority.
prisable, *adj.* estimable.
prise, *n.f.* grasp, hold, grip. **p. de courant,** (electric) plug.
prisée, *n.f.* appraisal.
priser, *vb.* appraise; prize; take (drugs).
priseur, *n.m.* auctioneer, appraiser.
prisme, *n.m.* prism.
prison, *n.f.* jail, prison.
prisonnier, *n.m.* prisoner.
privation, *n.f.* privation, want, hardship.
privé, *adj.* private.
priver, *vb.* deprive.
privilège, *n.m.* privilege, license.
privilégier, *vb.* license.
prix, *n.m.* price, charge, fare; prize; award.
prix-courant, *n.m.* list of prices.
probabilité, *n.f.* probability, chances.
probable, *adj.* likely, probable.
probant, *adj.* convincing.
probité, *n.f.* probity.
problématique, *adj.* problematical.
problème, *n.m.* problem.
procédé, *n.m.* procedure, process.
procéder, *vb.* proceed.
procédure, *n.f.* proceeding.
procès, *n.m.* trial; (law)suit.
procession, *n.f.* procession.
processionnel, *adj.* processional.
processus, *n.m.* process.
procès-verbal, *n.m.* minutes (of meeting).
prochain, 1. *n.m.* neighbor. **2.** *adj.* next.
prochainement, *adv.* soon.

proche, *adj.* near, close.
Proche-Orient, *n.m.* Near East.
proclamation, *n.f.* proclamation.
proclamer, *vb.* proclaim.
procréation, *n.f.* procreation.
procurer, *vb.* procure, get.
procureur, *n.m.* prosecuting attorney.
prodigalement, *adv.* prodigally.
prodigalité, *n.f.* extravagance.
prodige, *n.m.* prodigy.
prodigieux, *adj.* wondrous.
prodigue, *adj.* extravagant, lavish, profuse.
prodiguer, *vb.* lavish.
producteur, *n.m.* producer.
productif, *adj.* productive.
production, *n.f.* production.
productivité, *n.f.* productivity.
produire, *vb.* produce, yield, breed.
produit, *n.m.* product, commodity.
proéminence, *n.f.* prominence.
proéminent, *adj.* prominent, standing out.
prof, *n.m.* teacher.
profane, *adj.* profane.
profaner, *vb.* misuse, debase, profane.
proférer, *vb.* say, utter.
professer, *vb.* profess.
professeur, *n.m.* professor, teacher.
profession, *n.f.* profession.
professionnel, *adj.* professional.
professoral, *adj.* professorial.
professorat, *n.m.* professorship; teaching.
profil (-1), *n.m.* profile.
profiler, *vb.* show a profile of.
profit, *n.m.* profit.
profitable, *adj.* profitable.
profiter, *vb.* profit.
profiteur, *n.m.* profiteer.
profond, *adj.* deep, profound; in-depth.
profondeur, *n.f.* depth.
profus, *adj.* profuse.
profusion, *n.f.* profusion, excess.
progéniture, *n.f.* offspring.
programmation, *n.f.* programming.
programme, *n.m.* program.
progrès, *n.m.* progress, advance.
progresser, *vb.* progress.

progressif, *adj.* progressive.
progressiste, *n.m.* progressive.
prohiber, *vb.* prohibit.
prohibitif, *adj.* prohibitive.
prohibition, *n.f.* prohibition.
proie, *n.f.* prey.
projecteur, *n.m.* projector.
projectile, *n.m.* missile.
projection, *n.f.* projection.
projet, *n.m.* project, plan. **p. de loi,** bill.
projeter, *vb.* project, plan.
prolétaire, *adj. and n.m.* proletarian.
prolétariat, *n.m.* proletariat.
prolifération, *n.f.* proliferation.
prolifique, *adj.* prolific.
prolixe, *adj.* verbose.
prologue, *n.m.* prologue.
prolongation, *n.f.* extension, prolongation.
prolonger, *vb.* extend, prolong.
promenade, *n.f.* excursion; walk; ride.
promener, *vb.* take out. **se p.,** take a walk (ride).
promeneur, *n.m.* walker.
promesse, *n.f.* promise.
promettre, *vb.* promise.
promiscuité, *n.f.* promiscuity; crowding.
promontoire, *n.m.* promontory.
promoteur, *n.m.* promoter.
promotion, *n.f.* promotion.
promouvoir, *vb.* promote.
prompt, *adj.* prompt.
promptitude, *n.f.* quickness.
promulguer, *vb.* promulgate.
prôner, *vb.* lecture to, praise.
pronom, *n.m.* pronoun.
prononcer, *vb.* pronounce, utter; deliver.
prononciation, *n.f.* pronunciation.
pronostic, *n.m.* prognosis; prediction.
propagande, *n.f.* propaganda.
propagandiste, *n.m.f.* propagandist.
propagateur, *n.m.* propagator.
propagation, *n.f.* propagation.
propager, *vb.* propagate.
propension, *n.f.* inclination, propensity.
prophète, *n.m.* prophet.
prophétie, *n.f.* prophecy.

prophétique, *adj.* prophetic.
prophétiser, *vb.* prophesy.
propice, *adj.* favorable. **peu p.,** unfavorable.
propitiation, *n.f.* propitiation, conciliation.
proportion, *n.f.* proportion.
proportionné, *adj.* proportionate.
proportionnel, *adj.* proportional.
proportionner, *vb.* keep in proportion.
propos, *n.m.* subject; discourse. **à p.,** relevant. **à p. de,** with regard to.
proposable, *adj.* suitable, appropriate.
proposer, *vb.* propose; move. **se p. de,** intend, mean.
proposition, *n.f.* proposal, proposition.
propre, *adj.* proper; clean, neat; own. **peu p.,** unfit.
propreté, *n.f.* cleanliness, neatness.
propriétaire, *n.m.f.* proprietor.
propriété, *n.f.* property (landed), estate.
propulser, *vb.* push, propel.
propulseur, *n.m.* propeller.
propulsion, *n.f.* propulsion.
proroger, *vb.* postpone, extend time limit.
prosaïque (-zä ěk), *adj.* prosaic.
prosaïsme, *n.m.* prosaicness, dullness.
prosateur, *n.m.* writer of prose.
proscription, *n.f.* proscription.
proscrire, *vb.* outlaw, proscribe.
proscrit, *adj. and n.m.* exile(d); forbidden.
prose, *n.f.* prose.
prosodie, *n.f.* prosody.
prospecter, *vb.* search, as for gold.
prospecteur, *n.m.* prospector.
prospectus (-s), *n.m.* leaflet, pamphlet.
prospère, *adj.* prosperous.
prospérer, *vb.* flourish, thrive, prosper.
prospérité, *n.f.* prosperity.
prosterner, *vb.* prostrate.
prostituée, *n.f.* prostitute.
prostitution, *n.f.* prostitution.
protagoniste, *n.m.f.* main character.

protecteur, 1. *n.m.* protector; patron. 2. *adj.* protective.

protecteur du citoyen, *n.m.* ombudsman (in Quebec).

protection, *n.f.* protection.

protectorat, *n.m.* protectorate.

protéger, *vb.* protect; patronize, foster.

protéine, *n.f.* protein.

protestant, *adj. and n.m.* Protestant.

protestantisme, *n.m.* Protestantism.

protestation, *n.f.* protest.

protester, *vb.* protest.

protêt, *n.m.* protest.

prothèse, *n.f.* artificial aid, as a denture.

protocole, *n.m.* protocol.

prototype, *n.m.* prototype.

protubérance, *n.f.* protuberance.

proue, *n.f.* prow, front.

prouesse, *n.f.* prowess.

prouver, *vb.* prove.

provenance, *n.f.* place of origin; product.

provençal, 1. *adj.* of Provence. 2. *n.m.* language of Provence.

provende, *n.f.* provender, foodstuffs.

provenir, *vb.* come from.

proverbe, *n.m.* proverb, saying.

proverbial, *adj.* proverbial.

providence, *n.f.* providence.

providentiel, *adj.* providential.

province, *n.f.* province.

provincial, *adj. and n.m.* provincial.

provincialisme, *n.m.* provincialism.

proviseur, *n.m.* principal, headmaster.

provision, *n.f.* supply, store, provision.

provisoire, *adj.* temporary.

provocateur, *n.m.* one who provokes action.

provocation, *n.f.* provocation.

provoquer, *vb.* provoke.

proximité, *n.f.* closeness, proximity.

prude, 1. *n.f.* prude. 2. *adj.* prudish.

prudence, *n.f.* caution, prudence.

prudent, *adj.* cautious, prudent.

pruderie, *n.f.* prudishness.

prune, *n.f.* plum.

pruneau, *n.m.* prune.

prunelle, *n.f.* pupil (of eye).

prunier, *n.m.* plum tree.

Prusse, *n.f.* Prussia.

Prussien, *n.m.* Prussian (person).

prussien, *adj.* Prussian.

psalmiste, *n.m.* psalmist.

psaume, *n.m.* psalm.

psautier, *n.m.* psalm book.

pseudonyme, *n.m.* pseudonym.

psychanalyse (-k-), *n.f.* psychoanalysis.

psychédélique (-k-), *adj.* psychedelic.

psychiatre (-k-), *n.m.* psychiatrist.

psychiatrie (-k-), *n.f.* psychiatry.

psychique (-k-), *adj.* psychic.

psychologie (-k-), *n.f.* psychology.

psychologique (-k-), *adj.* psychological.

psychologue (-k-), *n.m.f.* psychologist.

psychose (-k-), *n.f.* psychosis.

psychothérapie (-k-), *n.f.* psychotherapy.

puant, *adj.* foul; shameful.

pub, *n.f.* advertising; advertisement.

puberté, *n.f.* puberty.

public, 1. *adj. m.,* **publique** *f.* public. 2. *n.m.* public; audience (theater).

publication, *n.f.* publication.

publiciste, *n.m.f.* publicist.

publicité, *n.f.* publicity, advertisement(s).

publier, *vb.* publish, issue.

puce, *n.f.* flea.

pucelle, *n.f.* young girl, virgin.

pudeur, *n.f.* modesty.

pudibond, *adj.* prudish.

pudique, *adj.* modest.

puer, *vb.* smell, have an offensive odor.

puéril (-l), *adj.* childish.

pugiliste, *m.* boxer.

puîné, *adj.* younger (of a brother or sister).

puis, *adv.* then.

puisard, *n.m.* cesspool.

puisatier, *n.m.* well-digger.

puiser, *vb.* draw up, derive.

puisque, *conj.* since, as.

puissamment, *adv.* very, powerfully.

puissance, *n.f.* power.

puissant, *adj.* potent, powerful, mighty.

puits (pwē), *n.m.* well; shaft.

pull(-over), *n.m.* sweater.

pulluler, *vb.* breed abundantly, multiply.

pulmonaire, *adj.* pulmonary.

pulpe, *n.f.* pulp.

pulpeux, *adj.* pulpy.

pulsar, *n.m.* pulsar.

pulsation, *n.f.* pulsation, beating.

pulvérisateur, *n.m.* vaporizer, spray.

pulvériser, *vb.* spray; pulverize.

punaise, *n.f.* bedbug; thumbtack.

punir, *vb.* punish.

punitif, *adj.* punitive.

punition, *n.f.* punishment.

pupille (-l), *n.m.f.* ward; pupil (of the eye).

pupitre, *n.m.* desk.

pur, *adj.* pure.

purée, *n.f.* mash.

purement, *adv.* purely, solely.

pureté, *n.f.* purity.

purgatoire, *n.m.* purgatory.

purge, *n.f.* purge.

purger, *vb.* purge.

purification, *n.f.* purification.

purifier, *vb.* purify, cleanse.

puritain, *adj. and n.m.* Puritan.

pur-sang, *n.m.* thoroughbred.

purulent, *adj.* purulent.

pusillanime, *adj.* fainthearted.

pustule, *n.f.* pimple.

putain, *n.f.* (colloquial) whore.

putois, *n.m.* skunk; polecat.

putréfier, *vb.* corrupt, rot, spoil.

putride, *adj.* putrid.

putsch, *n.m.* putsch.

puzzle, *n.m.* jigsaw (puzzle).

pygmée, *n.m.* Pygmy.

pyjama, *n.m.* pajamas.

pyramidal, *adj.* pyramidal, overwhelming.

pyramide, *n.f.* pyramid.

Pyrénées, *n.f.pl.* the Pyrenees.

Q

quadragénaire (kw-), *n.m.* person in his forties.

quadrangle (kw-), *n.m.* quadrangle.

quadrillé, *adj.* checked, ruled off.

quadriphonique (kw-), *adj.* quadraphonic.

quadrupède (kw-), *n.m. and adj.* quadruped.

quadruple (kw-), *adj.* quadruple.

quai, *n.m.* pier, dock; (station) platform.

qualification, *n.f.* qualification.

qualifier, *vb.* qualify.

qualité, *n.f.* quality, nature, grade.

quand, *adv.* when.

quant à, *prep.* as to, as for.

quantité, *n.f.* amount, quantity.

quarantaine, *n.f.* quarantine.

quarante, *adj. and n.m.* forty.

quart, *n.m.* fourth, quarter.

quartier, *n.m.* district, quarter. **q. général,** headquarters.

quartz (kw-), *n.m.* quartz.

quasar (kw-), *n.m.* quasar.

quasi, *adv.* nearly, quasi.

quasiment, *adv.* almost.

quatorze, *adj. and n.m.* fourteen.

quatrain, *n.m.* quatrain.

quatre, *adj. and n.m.* four.

quatre-vingt-dix, *adj. and n.m.* ninety.

quatre-vingts, *adj. and n.m.* eighty.

quatrième, *adj. and n.m.f.* fourth.

quatuor (kw-), *n.m.* quartet.

que, 1. *pron.* whom, which, that. **2.** *conj.* that, than.

quel, *adj.* which, what; of what kind.

quelconque, *adj.* of any kind, ordinary.

quelque, *adj.* some, any. **q. chose,** something. **q. part,** somewhere.

quelquefois, *adv.* sometimes.

quelques, *adj.* a few.

quelques-uns, *pron.* a few.

quelqu'un, *pron.* somebody.

querelle, *n.f.* quarrel.

quereller, *vb.* quarrel (with); scold.

querelleur, 1. *n.m.* quarreler. **2.** *adj.* inclined to quarrel.

question, n.f. question; issue, matter.

questionner, vb. question.

quête, n.f. quest, seeking.

quêter, vb. seek, look for.

queue (kœ), n.f. tail; line. **faire la q.,** stand in line.

qui, 1. interr. pron. who, whom. **2.** rel. pron. who, which. **q. que,** whoever.

quiconque, pron. whoever.

quiétude, n.f. quiet, tranquility.

quignon, n.m. large piece of bread.

quincaillerie, n.f. hardware.

quinine, n.f. quinine.

quinquagénaire, n.m. person in his fifties.

quintal, n.m. unit of weight (100 kilograms).

quinte, n.f. **q. de toux,** coughing fit.

quintuple, n.m. five times.

quinze, adj. and n.m. fifteen.

quinzième, adj. and n.m.f. fifteenth.

quiproquo, n.m. misunderstanding.

quittance, n.f. receipt.

quitte, adj. free, quit, released.

quitter, vb. quit, leave.

quoi, pron. and interj. what.

quoique, conj. though.

quote-part, n.f. quota.

quotidien, adj. daily.

R

rabâcher, vb. keep repeating.

rabais, n.m. reduction.

rabaisser, vb. diminish, lower.

rabattre, vb. put down, suppress, quell.

rabbin, n.m. rabbi.

rabbinique, adj. rabbinical.

rabot, n.m. plane.

raboter, vb. plane, perfect.

raboteux, adj. rugged.

rabougri, adj. puny, stunted.

raccommodage, n.m. fixing, mending.

raccommoder, vb. mend.

raccompagner, vb. take back.

raccorder, vb. join, bring together.

raccourci, n.m. shortcut.

raccourcir, vb. shorten, curtail.

raccourcissement, n.m. shortening, curtailing.

raccrocher, vb. hook up, hang up; recover.

race, n.f. race.

rachat, n.m. redemption.

racheter, vb. redeem.

rachitique, adj. rickety, affected with rickets.

rachitisme, n.m. rickets.

racine, n.f. root.

raciste, n.m.f. racist.

racket, n.m. racketeering.

raclage, n.m. action of scraping.

racler, vb. scrape.

racoler, vb. recruit, esp. by fraud.

racontars, n.m.pl. gossip.

raconter, vb. tell, narrate, recount.

raconteur, n.m. story-teller.

radar, n.m. radar.

radeau, n.m. raft.

radiant, adj. radiant.

radiateur, n.m. radiator.

radiation, n.f. radiation.

radical, adj. and n.m. radical.

radier, vb. radiate; erase.

radieux, adj. radiant, beaming, glorious.

radio, n.f. radio; wireless; x-ray.

radio-actif, adj. radioactive.

radiocassette, n.f. radio and cassette player.

radiodiffuser, vb. broadcast.

radio-émission, n.f. broadcast.

radiogramme, n.m. radiogram.

radiographie, n.f. radiography.

radiophonique, adj. radio.

radis, n.m. radish.

radium, n.m. radium.

radoter, vb. babble, drivel.

radoub, n.m. refitting (of ship).

radoucir, vb. quiet, soften, appease.

rafale, n.f. blast, gust, squall.

raffermir, vb. make stronger or more secure.

raffinement, n.m. refinement.

raffiner, vb. refine.

raffinerie, n.f. refinery.

raffoler, vb. dote on, be mad about.

rafistoler, vb. mend, patch.

rafle, n.f. (police) raid.

rafler, vb. carry off.

rafraîchir, vb. refresh.

rafraîchissement, n.m. refreshment.

rage, n.f. rage, fury; rabies.

rager, vb. be angry, rage.

rageur, n.m. irritable person.

ragot, n.m. nasty gossip.

ragoût, n.m. stew.

ragoûtant, adj. tasty, pleasing.

ragréer, vb. refinish, renovate.

raid, n.m. raid.

raide, adj. stiff; taut; steep.

raideur, n.f. stiffness.

raidir, vb. stiffen.

raie, n.f. streak; part (in hair).

raifort, n.m. horseradish.

rail, n.m. rail.

railler, vb. make fun of.

raillerie, n.f. jesting.

railleur, n.m. scoffer, jester.

rainure, n.f. groove.

rais, n.m. ray, spoke.

raisin, n.m. grape(s). r. sec, raisin.

raison, n.f. reason, judgment. avoir r., be right.

raisonnable, adj. reasonable, rational.

raisonnement, n.m. reason; argument.

raisonner, vb. reason.

rajeunir, vb. rejuvenate.

rajuster, vb. readjust.

râle, n.m. rail (bird); rattle in throat.

ralentir, vb. slacken, slow down.

râler, vb. rattle (in dying); groan.

rallier, vb. rally.

rallonger, vb. make an addition to, lengthen.

rallye, n.m. rally.

ramadan, n.m. Ramadan.

ramage, n.m. flower pattern; chirping; babble.

ramassé, adj. thick-set, dumpy.

ramasser, vb. pick up.

ramasseur, n.m. collector.

rame, n.f. oar.

rameau, n.m. branch.

ramener, vb. bring (take) back.

rameneur, vb. restorer.

ramer, vb. row.

rameur, n.m. rower.

ramifier, vb. divide into branches, ramify.

ramille, n.f. twig.

ramollir, vb. soften; weaken.

rampe, n.f. banister; ramp.

ramper, vb. crawl, creep.

rance, 1. adj. rancid. 2. n.m. rancidness.

rancœur, n.f. rancor.

rançon, n.f. ransom.

rancune, n.f. grudge, spite, rancor. garder de la r., bear a grudge.

rancunier, adj. rancorous, bitter.

randonnée, n.f. walk, hike, ride.

rang, n.m. row; rank.

rangée, n.f. file, row.

ranger, vb. rank, array, (ar)range.

ranimer, vb. revive.

rapace, adj. predatory; greedy.

rapatrier, vb. repatriate.

râpe, n.f. file, rasp.

râper, vb. grate.

rapide, 1. n.m. rapid. 2. adj. rapid, fast, quick.

rapidité, n.f. rapidity.

rapiécer, vb. patch.

rapière, n.f. rapier.

rapin, n.m. art student, pupil.

rapiner, vb. plunder, rob.

rappel, n.m. recall, repeal; reminder.

rappeler, vb. recall, remind. se r., remember.

rapport, n.m. report; relation.

rapporter, vb. bring back; report. se r. à, relate to, refer to.

rapporteur, n.m. (court) reporter; tattle-tale.

rapprochement, n.m. bringing close, junction.

rapprocher, vb. bring together. se r. de, approximate.

rapt, n.m. rape, kidnapping.

raquette, n.f. racket; snowshoe.

rare, adj. scarce, rare.

raréfier, vb. rarefy.

rarement, adv. seldom.

rareté, n.f. rarity, uniqueness, scarcity.

ras, adj. smooth-shaven; open.

raser, vb. shave.

rasoir, n.m. razor.

rassasier, vb. cloy, sate.

rassemblement, *n.m.* rally.

rassembler, *vb.* gather, congregate; muster.

rasseoir, *vb.* reseat. **se r.,** be seated again.

rasséréner, *vb.* clear up (weather).

rassis, *adj.* stale.

rassurer, *vb.* reassure, comfort.

rat, *n.m.* rat.

ratatiner, *vb.* shrivel, shrink.

rate, *n.f.* spleen.

raté, *adj.* failed.

râteau, *n.m.* rake.

râteler, *vb.* rake.

râtelier, *n.m.* rack.

rater, *vb.* miss.

ratière, *n.f.* rat trap.

ratifier, *vb.* ratify.

ration, *n.f.* ration.

rationnel, *adj.* rational.

rationnement, *n.m.* rationing.

rationner, *vb.* ration.

ratissoire, *n.f.* scraper, rake.

rattacher, *vb.* fasten.

rattraper, *vb.* overtake, catch up with.

rature, *n.f.* erasure.

raturer, *vb.* erase, blot out.

rauque, *adj.* hoarse; raucous.

ravage, *n.m.* havoc.

ravager, *vb.* lay waste.

ravaler, *vb.* restore.

ravauder, *vb.* mend, patch.

ravi, *adj.* delighted.

ravigoter, *vb.* enliven, refresh.

ravin, *n.m.* ravine.

ravir, *vb.* ravish; delight.

ravissant, *adj.* ravishing, charming; ravenous.

ravissement, *n.m.* rapture.

ravisseur, *n.m.* ravisher, robber.

ravitailler, *vb.* resupply, refuel.

raviver, *vb.* revive.

rayé, *adj.* striped.

rayer, *vb.* streak; cross out.

rayon, *n.m.* ray, beam; shelf. **r. x,** x-ray.

rayonnant, *adj.* beaming.

rayonne, *n.f.* rayon.

rayonnement, *n.m.* radiation; radiance.

rayonner, *vb.* radiate, beam.

rayure, *n.f.* streak, blemish.

raz-de-marée, *n.m.* tidal wave.

re-, ré-, *prefix.* re-, again.

réabonnement, *n.m.* renewal of subscription.

réabonner, *vb.* renew, resubscribe.

réacteur, *n.m.* jet engine.

réaction, *n.f.* reaction. **avion à r.,** jet-plane.

reactionnaire, *adj. and n.m.f.* reactionary.

réadapter, *vb.* readjust.

réagir, *vb.* react.

réalisable, *adj.* realizable.

réalisateur, *n.m.* director; producer.

réalisation, *n.f.* attainment, carrying out.

réaliser, *vb.* realize; produce; direct. **se r.,** materialize.

réaliste, 1. *n.m.f.* realist. **2.** *adj.* realist, realistic.

réalité, *n.f.* reality.

réassurer, *vb.* reinsure.

rébarbatif, *adj.* forbidding.

rebattre, *vb.* repeat, beat again.

rebattu, *adj.* trite.

rebelle, 1. *n.m.f.* rebel. **2.** *adj.* rebel, rebellious.

rebeller, *vb.* **se r.,** rebel.

rébellion, *n.f.* rebellion.

rebondi, *adj.* plump.

rebondir, *vb.* bounce.

rebondissement, *n.m.* new development.

rebord, *n.m.* border, edge.

rebuffade, *n.f.* rebuff, rebuke.

rebut, *n.m.* trash, refuse, junk, rubbish.

rebuter, *vb.* rebuke, discard.

récalcitrant, *adj.* stubborn.

receler, *vb.* accept stolen goods; hide.

récemment, *adv.* recently.

recensement, *n.m.* census.

recenser, *vb.* make a census.

récent, *adj.* recent.

réceptacle, *n.m.* receptacle.

récepteur, *n.m.* receiver.

réceptif, *adj.* receptive.

réception, *n.f.* reception; receipt.

récession, *n.f.* recession.

recette, *n.f.* recipe; receipt; (*pl.*) returns.

receveur, *n.m.* conductor; receiver.

recevoir, *vb.* receive, get; entertain.

réchapper, *vb.* escape, get out.

recharge, *n.f.* refill.

réchaud, *n.m.* food warmer, chafing dish.
réchauffer, *vb.* warm again; excite.
recherche, *n.f.* inquiry, (re)search; quest.
rechercher, *vb.* seek again, investigate.
rechigner, *vb.* balk.
rechute, *n.f.* relapse.
récif, *n.m.* reef.
récipient, *n.m.* container.
réciproque, *adj.* mutual.
récit, *n.m.* account.
réciter, *vb.* recite, tell.
réclamation, *n.f.* complaint.
réclame, *n.f.* advertisement.
réclamer, *vb.* claim, demand.
reclus, 1. *adj.* withdrawn, secluded. **2.** *n.m.* recluse.
réclusion, *n.f.* (solitary) confinement.
recoin, *n.m.* recess, corner.
récolte, *n.f.* crop, harvest.
récolter, *vb.* harvest, gather.
recommandable, *adj.* advisable.
recommandation, *n.f.* recommendation.
recommander, *vb.* recommend; register (letter).
recommencer, *vb.* start again.
récompense, *n.f.* reward.
récompenser, *vb.* reward.
réconcilier, *vb.* reconcile.
reconduire, *vb.* accompany, show out, dismiss.
réconfort, *n.m.* comfort.
reconnaissance, *n.f.* recognition; gratitude.
reconnaissant, *adj.* grateful.
reconnaître, *vb.* recognize; admit, acknowledge.
reconstituer, *vb.* rebuild, restore.
recourir, *vb.* resort.
recours, *n.m.* resort, recourse. **avoir r. à,** resort to; appeal to.
recouvrement, *n.m.* recovery.
recouvrer, *vb.* recover, retrieve.
recouvrir, *vb.* re-cover, cover completely.
récréation, *n.f.* amusement.
récréer, *vb.* entertain. **se r.,** amuse oneself.
recroqueviller, *vb.* **se r.,** curl up, huddle up.

recrudescence, *n.f.* fresh outbreak.
recrue, *n.f.* recruit.
recruter, *vb.* recruit.
rectangle, *n.m.* rectangle.
recteur, *n.m.* rector.
rectificatif, *n.m.* correction.
rectifier, *vb.* rectify, correct.
reçu, *n.m.* receipt.
recueil, *n.m.* collection, compilation.
recueillir, *vb.* gather, collect, glean.
recul, *n.m.* kick, recoil.
reculade, *n.f.* backing, retreat.
reculer, *vb.* recoil, draw back, go back.
récupérer, *vb.* recover, get back; rehabilitate.
récuser, *vb.* challenge; reject.
recycler, *vb.* recycle.
rédacteur, *n.m.* editor.
rédaction, *n.f.* editorial staff.
reddition, *n.f.* surrendering.
rédemption, *n.f.* redemption.
redevance, *n.f.* rental charge, license fee.
rédiger, *vb.* draw up.
redingote, *n.f.* frock-coat.
redire, *vb.* repeat, echo, reveal.
redoubler, *vb.* intesify, increase; repeat (class).
redoutable, *adj.* redoubtable, alarming.
redouter, *vb.* dread.
redresser, *vb.* straighten.
réduction, *n.f.* reduction, decrease, cut.
réduire, *vb.* reduce. **se r. à,** amount to.
réduit, *n.m.* retreat, hovel.
réel, *adj.* real, actual.
réfection, *n.f.* reconstruction; refreshments.
réfectoire, *n.m.* dining-room.
référence, *n.f.* reference.
référer, *vb.* refer.
refermer, *vb.* close up or again.
réfléchir, *vb.* reflect, consider, ponder.
reflet, *n.m.* reflection.
refléter, *vb.* reflect.
réflexe, *adj. and n.m.* reflex.
réflexion, *n.f.* reflection, consideration, thought.

refluer, *vb.* return to source, ebb.

reflux, *n.m.* ebb.

refondre, *vb.* cast again; remodel, improve.

réformateur, 1. *adj.* reforming. **2.** *n.m.* reformer, crusader.

réforme, *n.f.* reform, reformation.

réformer, *vb.* reform.

refoulement, *n.m.* forcing back, retreat.

refouler, *vb.* drive back, repel.

réfractaire, *adj.* refractory.

réfrigérant, *n.m.* refrigerator.

réfrigérer, *vb.* put under refrigeration.

refroidir, *vb.* chill, cool.

refroidissement, *n.m.* cooling, refrigeration, chill.

refuge, *n.m.* refuge.

réfugié, *n.m.* refugee.

réfugier, se r., take refuge.

refus, *n.m.* refusal, denial.

refuser, *vb.* refuse, withhold, deny.

réfutation, *n.f.* rebuttal.

réfuter, *vb.* disprove, refute.

regagner, *vb.* regain, recover.

regain, *n.m.* regrowth, renewal.

régal, *n.m.* feast, repast.

régaler, *vb.* entertain, treat.

regard, *n.m.* look.

regarder, *vb.* look (at); concern.

régence, *n.f.* regency.

régénérer, *vb.* regenerate.

régent, *adj.* and *n.m.* regent.

régenter, *vb.* direct, dominate.

régie, *n.f.* management, control; control room.

régime, *n.m.* diet; government; direction.

régiment, *n.m.* regiment.

région, *n.f.* area, region.

régional, *adj.* regional.

régir, *vb.* rule.

régisseur, *n.m.* (stage) manager.

registre, *n.m.* register, record.

réglage, *n.m.* adjusting, tuning.

règle, *n.f.* rule; ruler.

règlement, *n.m.* regulation; settlement.

réglementaire, *adj.* according to regulations.

régler, *vb.* regulate; rule; settle.

règne, *n.m.* reign.

régner, *vb.* reign.

régression, *n.f.* regression.

regret, *n.m.* regret.

regrettable, *adj.* regrettable.

regretter, *vb.* regret, be sorry for.

régulariser, *vb.* regularize.

régularité, *n.f.* regularity.

régulateur, *n.m.* regulator.

régulier, *adj.* regular.

réhabiliter, *vb.* rehabilitate.

rehausser, *vb.* enhance.

rein, *n.m.* kidney; (*pl.*) loins; back.

reine, *n.f.* queen.

réinsertion, *n.f.* reintegration, rehabilitation.

réintégrer, *vb.* return to, reinstate.

réitérer, *vb.* reiterate.

rejet, *n.m.* rejection.

rejeter, *vb.* reject.

rejeton, *n.m.* plant shoot; offspring.

rejoindre, *vb.* rejoin; catch up with, overtake.

réjouir, *vb.* rejoice, delight, cheer up.

réjouissance, *n.f.* festivity.

relâche, *n.m.* respite; (theater) closing.

relâché, *adj.* loose.

relâcher, *vb.* relax, slacken.

relais, *n.m.* relay.

relance, *n.f.* boost.

relater, *vb.* relate.

relatif, *adj.* relative.

relation, *n.f.* relation, connection.

relaxation, *n.f.* relaxation, release.

relayer, *vb.* relay.

reléguer, *vb.* relegate, banish.

relève, *n.f.* (*mil.*) relief, replacement.

relèvement, *n.m.* bearing.

relever, *vb.* lift; relieve; point out.

relief, *n.m.* relief. **mettre en r.,** emphasize.

relier, *vb.* bind; link.

relieur, *n.m.* binder, esp. of books.

religieuse, *n.f.* nun.

religieux, *adj.* religious.

religion, *n.f.* religion.

reliquaire, *n.m.* receptacle for relic.

relique, *n.f.* relic.

relire, *vb.* reread.

reliure, *n.f.* binding.

reluire, *vb.* shine, glisten.

remanier, *vb.* redo, modify.

remarquable, *adj.* remarkable; noticeable.

remarque, n.f. remark.

remarquer, vb. remark; notice.

rembarrer, vb. drive back; put in one's place.

remblai, n.m. embankment.

rembourrer, vb. stuff.

remboursement, n.m. refund.

rembourser, vb. repay, refund.

remède, n.m. remedy, cure.

remédiable, adj. remediable.

remédier, vb. remedy.

remerciement, n.m. thanks.

remercier, vb. thank.

remettre, vb. put back; restore; remit; pardon; deliver. **se r.,** recover.

réminiscence, n.f. reminiscence.

remise, n.f. discount; delivery.

rémission, n.f. remission.

remontant, n.m. tonic.

remonte-pente, n.m. ski lift.

remontrance, n.f. remonstrance.

remontrer, vb. show anew, point out error.

remords (-môr), n.m. remorse.

remorquer, vb. tow.

remorqueur, n.m. tug(boat).

rémouleur, n.m. sharpener, grinder.

remous, n.m. eddy.

rempart, n.m. bulwark, rampart.

remplaçant, n.m. substitute.

remplacer, vb. replace, substitute.

rempli, n.m. tuck, hitch.

remplier, vb. take a tuck in.

remplir, vb. fill; carry out; crowd.

remporter, vb. take away, bring back; win.

remuer, vb. stir. **se r.,** bustle.

rémunérer, vb. pay.

renaissance, n.f. rebirth, revival.

renaître, vb. be reborn, get new life.

renard, n.m. fox; sly person.

rencontre, n.f. meeting. **aller à la r. de,** go to meet.

rencontrer, vb. meet; come across.

rendement, n.m. output.

rendez-vous, n.m. date, appointment.

rendre, vb. give back; repay; surrender. **se r. compte de,** realize.

rendu, adj. tired out, all in.

rêne, n.f. rein.

rené, adj. born-again.

renégat, adj. and n.m. renegade.

renfermé, adj. withdrawn.

renfermer, vb. enclose.

renfler, vb. swell, inflate.

renforcer, vb. reinforce.

renfort, n.m. reinforcement, aid.

renfrogner, vb. **se r.,** scowl, frown.

rengaine, n.f. often-told story.

renifler, vb. sniff.

renne, n.m. reindeer.

renom, n.m. renown, repute.

renommée, n.f. fame, renown.

renoncer, vb. renounce, give up, forego.

renonciation, n.f. renunciation.

renouement, n.m. renewing, retying.

renouer, vb. tie up (again).

renouveau, n.m. springtime.

renouveler, vb. renew, renovate.

renouvellement, n.m. renewal.

rénover, vb. renovate.

renseignements, n.m.pl. information.

renseigner, vb. inform. **se r.,** inquire.

rentable, adj. profitable.

rente, n.f. income; interest; annuity.

rentier, n.m. one who lives off interest on investments.

rentrée, n.f. return.

rentrer, vb. go back, go home.

renversant, adj. amazing, overwhelming.

renverser, vb. overthrow, overturn; reverse.

renvoi, n.m. dismissal; return.

renvoyer, vb. send back, return; dismiss.

repaire, n.m. den, animal's lair.

repaître, vb. feed, feast.

répandre, vb. diffuse, scatter, spill.

répandu, adj. prevalent, widespread.

reparaître, vb. reappear.

réparateur, n.m. restorer, repairer.

réparation, n.f. repair; amends.

réparer, vb. repair; make up for, make amends for.

repartie, n.f. reply, quick retort.

repartir, vb. leave again; retort.

répartir, vb. apportion, allot, distribute.

repas, n.m. meal.

repasser, *vb.* press; pass; look over.

repentir, 1. *n.m.* repentance. **2.** *vb.* se r., repent.

répercussion, *n.f.* repercussion.

répercuter, *vb.* reverberate, echo.

repère, *n.m.* guiding mark.

repérer, *vb.* spot, locate.

répertoire, *n.m.* list, repertory.

répéter, *vb.* repeat; rehearse.

répétition, *n.f.* repetition; rehearsal.

répit, *n.m.* respite.

replacer, *vb.* replace.

replier, *vb.* fold again or up.

réplique, *n.f.* rejoinder; cue.

répliquer, *vb.* rejoin.

répondant, *n.m.* respondent, bail.

répondeur, *n.m.* answering machine.

répondre, *vb.* answer, reply. **r. de,** vouch for.

réponse, *n.f.* answer, reply.

report, *n.m.* (in bookkeeping) amount brought forward.

reportage, *n.m.* reporting.

reporter, 1. *n.m.* reporter. **2.** *vb.* carry or take back.

repos, *n.m.* rest.

reposer, *vb.* rest, repose.

repousser, *vb.* push back, repel; spurn.

repoussoir, *n.m.* foil.

répréhensible, *adj.* objectionable.

répréhension, *n.f.* reprehension, censure.

reprendre, *vb.* take back; resume.

représailles, *n.f.pl.* retaliation.

représentant, *n.m.* representative.

représentatif, *adj.* representative.

représentation, *n.f.* representation, performance.

représenter, *adj.* represent.

répressif, *adj.* repressive.

répression, *n.f.* repression.

réprimande, *n.f.* reproof, rebuke, reprimand.

réprimander, *vb.* chide, reprove, reprimand.

réprimer, *vb.* quell.

reprise, *n.f.* recovery; turn; darn. à plusieurs r.s, repeatedly.

repriser, *vb.* darn.

réprobation, *n.f.* reprobation.

reproche, *n.m.* reproach.

reprocher, *vb.* reproach.

reproduction, *n.f.* reproduction.

reproduction exacte, *n.f.* clone.

reproduire, *vb.* reproduce.

réprouver, *vb.* censure.

reptile, *n.m.* reptile.

républicain, *adj. and n.m.* republican.

république, *n.f.* republic.

répudier, *vb.* repudiate.

répugnance, *n.f.* repugnance.

répulsion, *n.f.* repulsion.

réputation, *n.f.* reputation.

réputer, *vb.* consider, esteem.

requête, *n.f.* request, plea.

requin, *n.m.* shark.

requis, *adj.* required, necessary.

réquisition, *n.f.* requisition.

rescousse, *n.f.* rescue.

réseau, *n.m.* network.

réserve, *n.f.* reserve, reservation; qualification. **de r.,** spare, extra.

réservé, *adj.* aloof, reticent.

réserver, *vb.* reserve.

réserviste, *n.m.f.* reservist (mil.).

réservoir, *n.m.* tank, reservoir.

résidant, *adj.* resident.

résidence, *n.f.* residence, dwelling.

résider, *vb.* reside.

résidu, *n.m.* residue.

résignation, *n.f.* resignation.

résigner, *vb.* resign.

résiliation, *n.f.* cancelling.

résine, *n.f.* resin.

résistance, *n.f.* endurance, resistance.

résister, *vb.* resist.

résolu, *adj.* resolute.

résolument, *adv.* resolutely.

résolution, *n.f.* resolution.

résonnance, *n.f.* resonance.

résonnant, *adj.* resonant.

résonner, *vb.* resound.

résorber, *vb.* se r., be reduced, be absorbed.

résoudre, *vb.* resolve, solve.

respect (-spè), *n.m.* respect.

respectable, *adj.* decent, respectable.

respecter, *vb.* respect.

respectif, *adj.* respective.

respectueux, *adj.* respectful.

respiration, *n.f.* respiration, breathing.

respirer, *vb.* breathe.

resplendir, *vb.* gleam resplendently.

responsabilité, *n.f.* responsibility.

responsable, *adj.* responsible; accountable, liable.

ressaisir, *vb.* regain possession.

ressasser, *vb.* keep going over.

ressemblance, *n.f.* likeness.

ressembler, *vb.* resemble. **se r.,** look alike.

ressentiment, *n.m.* resentment.

ressentir, *vb.* feel, resent, show.

resserrer, *vb.* tighten, compress.

ressort, *n.m.* spring; elasticity.

ressortir, *vb.* stand out.

ressortissant, *n.m.* national, citizen.

ressource, *n.f.* resort, resource.

ressusciter, *vb.* revive, resuscitate.

restant, *n.m.* remainder.

restaurant, *n.m.* restaurant.

restaurateur, *n.m.* restorer; restaurant owner.

restauration, *n.f.* restoration; catering.

restaurer, *vb.* restore.

reste, *n.m.* remainder, rest, remnant.

rester, *vb.* remain, stay.

restituer, *vb.* give back, restore.

restoroute, *n.m.* restaurant along highway.

restreindre, *vb.* restrict.

restrictif, *adj.* restrictive.

restriction, *n.f.* restriction.

résultat, *n.m.* outcome, upshot, result.

résulter, *vb.* result.

résumé, *n.m.* summing up.

résumer, *vb.* sum up.

résurrection, *n.f.* resurrection; revival.

rétablir, *vb.* restore, reestablish. **se r.,** recover.

rétablissement, *n.m.* recovery.

retard, *n.m.* delay. **en r.,** late; slow.

retarder, *vb.* delay, retard; be slow.

retenir, *vb.* retain; keep; hold (back); detain. **se r. de,** refrain from.

rétentif, *adj.* retentive.

retentir, *vb.* resound.

retentissant, *adj.* reechoing.

retenue, *n.f.* deduction; detention; reticence.

réticence, *n.f.* silence, reticence.

retirer, *vb.* withdraw. **se r.,** retire, retreat.

retombées, *n.f.pl.* fallout.

rétorquer, *vb.* retort.

retoucher, *vb.* retouch, alter.

retour, *n.m.* return. **de r.,** back.

retourner, *vb.* go back, return; invert. **se r.,** turn around.

retrait, *n.m.* contraction, retraction.

retraite, *n.f.* retreat; privacy.

retrancher, *vb.* cut off, curtail.

retransmettre, *vb.* broadcast.

rétrécir, *vb.* shrink, contract.

rétribution, *n.f.* salary, recompense.

rétroactif, *adj.* retroactive; retrospective.

rétrograde, *adj.* reactionary; backward-looking.

retrousser, *vb.* turn up.

retrouver, *vb.* find; recover.

rétroviseur, *n.m.* rear-view mirror.

réunion, *n.f.* meeting, convention, reunion.

réunir, *vb.* unite. **se r.,** assemble.

réussi, *adj.* successful.

réussir, *vb.* succeed.

réussite, *n.f.* successful outcome.

revanche, *n.f.* revenge. **en r.,** in return.

rêve, *n.m.* dream.

réveil, *n.m.* awaking; revival.

réveille-matin, *n.m.* alarm clock.

réveiller, *vb.* wake (up), rouse, arouse.

réveillon, *n.m.* Christmas Eve; New Year's Eve.

révélateur, 1. *adj.* revealing. **2.** *n.m.* revealer.

révélation, *n.f.* revelation.

révéler, *vb.* disclose, reveal.

revenant, *n.m.* ghost, specter.

revendeur, *n.m.* retailer, old-clothes dealer.

revendication, *n.f.* claim, demand.

revendiquer, *vb.* claim.

revenir, *vb.* come back, return, recur; amount to.

revenu, *n.m.* income, revenue.

rêver, *vb.* dream.

réverbère, *n.m.* street lamp.

réverbérer, *vb.* reverberate.

révéremment, *adv.* reverently.

révérence, *n.f.* reverence; bow, curtsy.

révérend, *adj.* reverend.

révérer, *vb.* revere.

rêverie, *n.f.* dreaming, reverie.

revers, *n.m.* reverse, wrong side; lapel.

revêtir, *vb.* clothe; assume.

rêveur, 1. *n.m.* dreamer. **2.** *adj.* pensive.

revirement, *n.m.* change of mind, reversal.

réviser, *vb.* revise.

réviseur, *n.m.* reviser, inspector.

révision, *n.f.* revision, review.

revivre, *vb.* revive.

révocation, *n.f.* revocation, annulment.

revoir, *vb.* see again. **au r.,** goodbye.

révolte, *n.f.* revolt.

révolter, *vb.* **se r.,** revolt.

révolu, *adj.* past.

révolution, *n.f.* revolution, turn.

révolutionnaire, *adj.* and *n.m.f.* revolutionary.

revolver, *n.m.* revolver.

révoquer, *vb.* revoke.

revue, *n.f.* review, magazine.

rez-de-chaussée, *n.m.* ground floor.

rhétorique, *n.f.* rhetoric.

rhinocéros, *n.m.* rhinoceros.

Rhône, *n.m.* Rhone.

rhubarbe, *n.f.* rhubarb.

rhum, *n.m.* rum.

rhumatisme, *n.m.* rheumatism.

rhume, *n.m.* cold.

ricaner, *vb.* laugh objectionably.

riche, *adj.* rich, wealthy.

richesse, *n.f.* wealth.

ricocher, *vb.* ricochet, spring back.

rictus, *n.m.* grin; grimace.

ride, *n.f.* wrinkle, ripple.

rideau, *n.m.* curtain.

rider, *vb.* ripple, wrinkle.

ridicule, 1. *n.m.* ridicule. **2.** *adj.* ridiculous.

ridiculiser, *vb.* ridicule.

rien, *pron.* nothing.

rieur, *n.m.* laugher.

rigide, *adj.* rigid.

rigidité, *n.f.* rigidity.

rigole, *n.f.* ditch, gutter.

rigoler, *vb.* laugh.

rigolo *m.,* **rigolote** *f. adj.* funny.

rigoureux, *adj.* rigorous.

rigueur, *n.f.* rigor.

rime, *n.f.* rhyme.

rimer, *vb.* rhyme.

rince-doigts, *n.m.* finger bowl.

rincer, *vb.* rinse.

ringard, *adj.* old-fashioned.

ripaille, *n.f.* feasting, revelry.

riposte, *n.f.* retort.

rire, 1. *n.m.* laugh, laughter. **2.** *vb.* laugh.

ris, *n.m.* laugh; reef in a sail; sweetbread.

risée, *n.f.* laugh, mocking.

risible, *adj.* laughable.

risque, *n.m.* risk.

risquer, *vb.* risk.

risque-tout, *n.m.* daredevil.

rissoler, *vb.* brown, as in cooking.

rite, *n.m.* rite.

rituel, *adj.* ritual.

rivage, *n.m.* shore, bank.

rival, *adj.* and *n.m.* rival.

rivaliser, *vb.* compete, rival.

rivalité, *n.f.* rivalry.

rive, *n.f.* bank.

river, *vb.* clinch.

riverain, *n.m.* local resident.

rivet, *n.m.* rivet.

rivière, *n.f.* river.

rixe, *n.f.* brawl.

riz, *n.m.* rice.

rizière, *n.f.* rice field.

robe, *n.f.* dress, gown, frock, robe.

robinet, *n.m.* faucet, tap.

robot, *n.m.* robot.

robuste, *adj.* hardy, strong, robust.

roc, *n.m.* rock.

rocailleux, *adj.* rocky, rough.

roche, *n.f.* rock.

rocher, *n.m.* rock.

rocheux, *adj.* rocky.

rock, *adj.* rock (music).

rôder, *vb.* prowl.

rôdeur, *n.m.* prowler.

rogner, *vb.* pare, trim down.

rognon, *n.m.* kidney.

rogue, *adj.* proud, arrogant.

roi, *n.m.* king.

rôle, *n.m.* role, part.

Romain, *n.m.* Roman (person).

romain, *adj.* Roman.

roman, *n.m.* novel.

romance, *n.f.* ballad.
romancier, *n.m.* novelist.
romanesque, *adj.* romantic.
roman-feuilleton, *n.m.* serial.
romanichel, *n.m.* gypsy.
romantique, *adj.* romantic.
romarin, *n.m.* rosemary.
rompre, *vb.* break.
ronce, *n.f.* bramble.
rond, 1. *n.m.* round; circle. **2.** *adj.* round.
ronde, *n.f.* round, patrol.
rondelle, *n.f.* washer; slice.
rondeur, *n.f.* roundness.
rond-point, *n.m.* traffic circle.
ronflement, *n.m.* snoring, roar.
ronfler, *vb.* snore.
ronger, *vb.* gnaw; fret.
rongeur, *adj. and n.m.* rodent.
ronronner, *vb.* purr, murmur.
rosace, *n.f.* rose window.
rosaire, *n.m.* rosary.
rosbif, *n.m.* roast beef.
rose, 1. *n.f.* rose. **2.** *adj.* pink.
rosé, *adj.* pinkish.
roseau, *n.m.* reed.
rosée, *n.f.* dew.
rosier, *n.m.* rosebush.
rossignol, *n.m.* nightingale.
rôt, *n.m.* roast (meat).
rotation, *n.f.* rotation.
rotatoire, *adj.* rotary.
roter, *vb.* belch.
rôti, *n.m.* roast.
rôtir, *vb.* roast.
rôtisserie, *n.f.* grillroom.
rotondité, *n.f.* rotundity.
rotule, *n.f.* kneecap.
roturier, *adj.* commonplace, vulgar.
rouage, *n.m.* gearwheel, part, cog.
roublardise, *n.f.* cunningness.
roucouler, *vb.* coo.
roue, *n.f.* wheel.
roué, 1. *n.m.* rake, debauchee. **2.** *adj.* crafty.
rouge, 1. *n.m.* rouge. **2.** *adj.* red. **r. foncé,** maroon.
rouge-gorge, *n.m.* robin.
rougeole, *n.f.* measles.
rougeur, *n.f.* flush, blush.
rougir, *vb.* blush.
rouille, *n.f.* rust.
rouiller, *vb.* rust.
rouir, *vb.* soak.

rouleau, *n.m.* roll, roller, scroll, coil.
roulement, *n.m.* rolling, winding; rotation.
rouler, *vb.* roll, wind.
roulette, *n.f.* little wheel, caster.
roulis, *n.m.* roll.
Roumain, *n.m.* Romanian (person).
roumain, 1. *n.m.* Romanian (language). **2.** *adj.* Romanian.
Roumanie, *n.f.* Romania.
rouquin, *n.m.* redhead.
rousseur, *n.f.* redness. **tache de r.,** freckle.
roussir, *vb.* scorch.
route, *n.f.* road, way, course, route. **en r.,** under way. **en r. pour,** on the way to.
routine, *n.f.* routine.
routinier, *adj.* routine.
roux, *adj. and n.m.* red, reddish-brown.
royal, *adj.* royal, regal.
royaliste, *adj. and n.m.f.* royalist.
royaume, *n.m.* kingdom.
royauté, *n.f.* royalty.
ruban, *n.m.* ribbon, tape.
rubéole, *n.f.* German measles.
rubis, *n.m.* ruby.
rubrique, *n.f.* red ocher; heading.
ruche, *n.f.* hive.
rude, *adj.* rough, gruff, harsh; rugged.
rudement, *adv.* terribly (hard).
rudesse, *n.f.* harshness.
rudiment, *n.m.* rudiment, element.
rudimentaire, *adj.* rudimentary.
rudoyer, *vb.* bully.
rue, *n.f.* street, road.
ruée, *n.f.* rush.
ruelle, *n.f.* lane, alley.
ruer, *vb.* **se r.,** rush.
rugby, *n.m.* Rugby.
rugbyman, *n.m.* Rugby player.
rugir, *vb.* roar.
rugissement, *n.m.* roar.
rugueux, *adj.* rugged, harsh.
ruine, *n.f.* ruin.
ruiner, *vb.* ruin.
ruineux, *adj.* ruinous.
ruisseau, *n.m.* brook, creek; gutter.

ruisseler, vb. stream, flow.
rumeur, n.f. rumor; noise.
ruminant, adj. and n.m. ruminant.
ruminer, vb. chew the cud.
rupture, n.f. break, rupture.
rural, adj. rural.
ruse, n.f. trick; cunning.
rusé, adj. sly, cunning.
Russe, n.m.f. Russian (person).

russe, 1. n.m. Russian (language).
2. adj. Russian.
Russie, n.f. Russia.
rusticité, n.f. rusticity, uncouth-
ness.
rustique, adj. rustic.
rustre, adj. and n.m. boor, boorish.
rythme, n.m. rhythm.
rythmique, adj. rhythmical.

S

sabbat, n.m. Sabbath.
sable, n.m. sand.
sablé, n.m. shortbread biscuit.
sabler, vb. sand; quaff.
sablier, n.m. sandbox; sandman;
hourglass.
sablonneux, adj. sandy.
sablonnière, n.f. sand pit.
sabord, n.m. porthole.
sabot, n.m. hoof; wooden shoe.
sabotage, n.m. sabotage.
saboter, vb. sabotage.
saboteur, n.m. saboteur; awkward
bungler.
sabre, n.m. saber.
sac, n.m. sack, bag. **s. à main,**
pocketbook. **s. à air,** airbag.
saccade, n.f. jerk.
saccager, vb. ransack, sack, plunder.
saccharine, n.f. saccharin.
sacerdoce, n.m. priesthood.
sachet, n.m. sachet; packet.
sacre, n.m. consecration, coronation.
sacré, adj. sacred.
sacrement, n.m. sacrament.
sacrer, vb. crown, consecrate;
curse.
sacrifice, n.m. sacrifice.
sacrifier, vb. sacrifice.
sacrilège, n.m. sacrilege.
sacristain, n.m. sexton.
sac tyrolien, n.m. backpack.
sadique, adj. sadistic.
sadisme, n.m. sadism.
sagace, adj. shrewd.
sagacité, n.f. sagacity.
sage, 1. n.m. sage. **2.** adj. wise,
good.
sage-femme, n.f. midwife.
sagesse, n.f. wisdom.

Sahara, n.m. Sahara (desert).
saignant, adj. rare (meat).
saignée, n.f. bleeding.
saigner, vb. bleed.
saillant, adj. prominent, project-
ing.
saillie, n.f. projection.
saillir, vb. protrude.
sain, adj. healthy, sound, wholesome. **s. d'esprit,** sane.
saindoux, n.m. lard.
saint, 1. n.m. saint. **2.** adj. holy.
Saint-Esprit, n.m. Holy Ghost.
sainteté, n.f. holiness.
saisie, n.f. seizure.
saisir, vb. seize, grasp, snatch,
grab.
saisissement, n.m. chill; seizure.
saison, n.f. season.
salade, n.f. salad.
saladier, n.m. salad bowl or dish.
salaire, n.m. wages, earnings, pay.
salarié, 1. adj. salaried. **2.** n.m. person earning a salary.
sale, adj. dirty.
salé, adj. salty.
saler, vb. salt.
saleté, n.f. dirt.
salière, n.f. saltcellar.
salin, adj. salt, salty.
salir, vb. get dirty.
salive, n.f. saliva.
salle, n.f. (large) room, hall, auditorium, (hospital) ward. **s. de
classe,** classroom. **s. de bain,** bathroom.
salon, n.m. parlor.
salopette, n.f. overalls.
saltimbanque, n.m.f. charlatan;
buffoon, acrobat.
salubre, adj. healthful.
salubrité, n.f. healthfulness.

saluer, *vb.* bow, greet, salute.
salut, *n.m.* bow, salute; salvation.
salutaire, *adj.* wholesome, beneficial.
salutation, *n.f.* greeting.
salve, *n.f.* salvo, salute.
samedi, *n.m.* Saturday.
SAMU, *n.m.* paramedics.
sanctifier, *vb.* hallow.
sanction, *n.f.* sanction.
sanctionner, *vb.* sanction, countenance.
sanctuaire, *n.m.* sanctuary.
sandale, *n.f.* sandal.
sang, *n.m.* blood.
sang-froid, *n.m.* calmness, composure.
sanglant, *adj.* bloody.
sangler, *vb.* strap, fasten.
sanglier, *n.m.* (wild) boar.
sanglot, *n.m.* sob.
sangloter, *vb.* sob.
sangsue, *n.f.* leech.
sanguin, *adj.* pertaining to blood.
sanguinaire, *adj.* bloodthirsty.
sanitaire, *adj.* sanitary.
sans, *prep.* without, out of. **s. doute**, without doubt. **s. plomb**, unleaded. **s. repos**, restless. **s. valeur**, worthless. **s. nom**, nameless.
sans-souci, *adj.* carefree, careless.
santé, *n.f.* health.
Saoudien, *n.m.* Saudi (person).
Saoudien, *adj.* Saudi Arabian.
saoul (soo), *adj.* drunk.
saper, *vb.* sap, weaken.
saphir, *n.m.* sapphire.
sapin, *n.m.* fir.
sarcasme, *n.m.* sarcasm.
sarcastique, *adj.* sarcastic.
sarcler, *vb.* weed, root out.
Sardaigne, *n.f.* Sardinia.
sardine, *n.f.* sardine.
sardonique, *adj.* sardonic.
satanique, *adj.* satanic.
satellite, *n.m.* satellite.
satin, *n.m.* satin.
satire, *n.f.* satire.
satiriser, *vb.* satirize.
satisfaction, *n.f.* satisfaction.
satisfaire, *vb.* satisfy.
satisfaisant, *adj.* satisfactory.
saturer, *vb.* saturate.
satyre, *n.m.* satyr.

sauce, *n.f.* sauce. **s. piquante**, hot sauce.
saucisse, *n.f.* sausage.
saucisson, *n.m.* (slicing) sausage.
sauf, **1.** *prep.* but. **2.** *adj.* safe. **sain et s.**, safe and sound.
sauf-conduit, *n.m.* safe-conduct.
sauge, *n.f.* sage.
saugrenu, *adj.* absurd, preposterous.
saule, *n.f.* willow.
saumon, *n.m.* salmon.
saumure, *n.f.* brine.
saut, *n.m.* spring, jump.
saute, *n.f.* wind shift.
sauter, *vb.* spring, jump, leap, skip. **faire s.**, blow up.
sauterelle, *n.f.* grasshopper.
sautiller, *vb.* hop.
sauvage, **1.** *n.m.f.* savage. **2.** *adj.* wild, savage.
sauvegarde, *n.f.* safeguard.
sauvegarder, *vb.* safeguard; (computers) save, back up.
sauve-qui-peut, *n.m.* stampede, panic.
sauver, *vb.* save. **se s.**, run away.
sauvetage, *n.m.* salvage.
sauveteur, *n.m.* rescuer, saver.
sauveur, *n.m.* savior; Savior.
savane, *n.f.* prairie.
savant, **1.** *n.m.* scholar. **2.** *adj.* learned.
saveur, *n.f.* flavor, savor, zest.
savoir, **1.** *vb.* know, be aware, have knowledge. **vouloir s.**, wonder. **2.** *n.m.* knowledge.
savoir-faire, *n.m.* poise, ability.
savoir-vivre, *n.m.* breeding, manners.
savon, *n.m.* soap.
savonner, *vb.* soap, lather.
savourer, *vb.* relish.
savoureux, *adj.* tasty.
saxo(phone), *n.m.* sax(ophone).
scabreux, *adj.* improper; risky.
scalper, *vb.* scalp.
scandale, *n.m.* scandal.
scandaleux, *adj.* scandalous.
scandaliser, *vb.* shock.
scander, *vb.* scan.
Scandinave, *n.m.f.* Scandinavian (person).
scandinave, *adj.* Scandinavian.
Scandinavie, *n.f.* Scandinavia.

scaphandre, *n.m.* diving suit; space suit.
scarabée, *n.m.* beetle.
scarlatine, *n.f.* scarlet fever.
sceau, *n.m.* seal.
scélérat, *n.m.* villain, criminal, knave, ruffian.
sceller, *vb.* seal.
scénario, *n.m.* scenario.
scène, *n.f.* scene; stage.
scénique, *adj.* scenic.
scepticisme, *n.m.* skepticism.
sceptique, 1. *n.m.f.* skeptic. **2.** *adj.* skeptical.
sceptre, *n.m.* scepter.
schéma, *n.m.* diagram.
schématique, *adj.* digrammatic; oversimplified.
schisme, *n.m.* schism.
schizophrène (sk-), *adj.* schizophrenia.
sciatique, *n.f.* sciatica.
scie, *n.f.* saw.
science, *n.f.* science.
science-fiction, *n.f.* science fiction.
scientifique, 1. *adj.* scientific. **2.** *n.m.f.* scientist.
scier, *vb.* saw.
scinder, *vb.* divide.
scintiller, *vb.* twinkle.
scission, *n.f.* cutting, division.
sclérose, *n.f.* sclerosis.
scolaire, *adj.* scholastic. **système s.,** school system.
scolastique, *adj.* scholastic.
scooter, *n.m.* (motor) scooter.
score, *n.m.* score.
Scotch, *n.m.* Scotish whisky; (trademark) Scotch tape.
scout (-t), *n.m.* scout.
scrofule, *n.f.* scrofula.
scrupule, *n.m.* scruple.
scrupuleux, *adj.* scrupulous.
scruter, *vb.* scan, scrutinize.
scrutin, *n.m.* ballot, poll.
sculpter (-lt-), *vb.* carve.
sculpteur (-lt-), *n.m.* sculptor.
sculpture (-lt-), *n.f.* sculpture.
se (sa), *pron.* himself, herself, itself, oneself, themselves, each other.
séance, *n.f.* sitting; session; meeting.
séant, *adj.* sitting, proper.
seau, *n.m.* pail, bucket.

sec *m.,* **sèche** *f.* *adj.* dry.
sécession, *n.f.* secession.
sèche-cheveux, *n.m.* hair dryer.
sécher, *vb.* dry.
sécheresse, *n.f.* dryness, drought.
séchoir, *n.m.* dryer.
second (-g-), *adj.* second.
secondaire (-g-), *adj.* secondary.
seconde (-g-), *n.f.* second.
seconder (-g-), *vb.* second, help.
secouer, *vb.* shake, rouse.
secourir, *vb.* relieve, succor, help.
secours, *n.m.* help, relief. **premiers s.,** first aid. **poste de s.,** first-aid station. **au s.!,** help!
secousse, *n.f.* jar, shock.
secret, *adj.* and *n.m.* secret.
secrétaire, *n.m.f.* secretary.
secréter, *vb.* secrete.
sécrétion, *n.f.* secretion.
sectaire, *adj.* sectarian.
secte, *n.f.* sect.
secteur, *n.m.* district, sector.
section, *n.f.* section.
sectionner, *vb.* cut into sections.
Sécu, *n.f.* Social Security.
séculaire, *adj.* secular.
séculier, *adj.* secular, lay.
sécuriser, *vb.* make (someone) feel secure.
sécurité, *n.f.* safety.
sédatif, *adj.* and *n.m.* sedative.
sédentaire, *adj.* sedentary, stationary.
séditieux, *adj.* seditious.
sédition, *n.f.* sedition.
séduction, *n.f.* seduction.
séduire, *vb.* seduce, attract, allure.
séduisant, *adj.* attractive.
segment, *n.m.* segment.
ségrégation, *n.f.* segregation.
seigle, *n.m.* rye.
seigneur, *n.m.* lord, peer.
seigneurie, *n.f.* lordship.
sein, *n.m.* bosom, breast.
séisme, *n.m.* earthquake.
seize, *adj.* and *n.m.* sixteen.
seizième, *adj.* and *n.m.f.* sixteenth.
séjour, *n.m.* stay. **lieu de s.,** resort.
séjourner, *vb.* stay, sojourn.
sel, *n.m.* salt.
sélection, *n.f.* selection.
self(-service), *n.m.* self-service.
selle, *n.f.* saddle.
seller, *vb.* saddle.

sellette, *n.f.* little stool or saddle.

selon, *prep.* according to.

seltz, *n.m.* eau de s., soda water.

semailles, *n.f.pl.* sowing.

semaine, *n.f.* week; weekly pay.

semblable, *adj.* similar, alike.

semblant, *n.m.* show; appearance. **faire s.,** make believe.

sembler, *vb.* seem, appear.

semelle, *n.f.* sole (shoe).

semence, *n.f.* seed.

semer, *vb.* sow.

semestre, *n.m.* semester.

semeur, *n.m.* sower.

sémillance, *n.f.* briskness, liveliness.

séminaire, *n.m.* seminar; seminary.

semi-remorque, *n.f.* semitrailer.

sémitique, *adj.* Semitic.

semoncer, *vb.* lecture, scold.

semoule, *n.f.* semolina.

sénat, *n.m.* senate.

sénateur, *n.m.* senator.

sénile, *adj.* senile.

sénilité, *n.f.* senility.

sens (-s), *n.m.* meaning, sense; direction.

sensation, *n.f.* sensation, feeling.

sensationnel, *adj.* sensational.

sensé, *adj.* sensible.

sensibiliser, *vb.* make sensitive.

sensibilité, *n.f.* sensitivity.

sensible, *adj.* sensitive; conscious (of).

sensitif, *adj.* oversensitive.

sensualisme, *n.m.* sensualism.

sensualité, *n.f.* sensuality.

sensuel, *adj.* sensual.

sentence, *n.f.* sentence.

sentencieux, *adj.* sententious.

senteur, *n.f.* smell.

sentier, *n.m.* path.

sentiment, *n.m.* feeling.

sentimental, *adj.* sentimental.

sentimentalité, *n.f.* sentimentality.

sentinelle, *n.f.* sentry.

sentir, *vb.* feel; smell.

séparable, *adj.* separable.

séparation, *n.f.* separation, parting.

séparatiste, *adj.* separatist.

séparé, *adj.* separate.

séparer, *vb.* separate, segregate. **se s.,** part.

sept (sĕt), *adj. and n.m.* seven.

septembre, *n.m.* September.

septième (sĕt-), *adj. and n.m.f.* seventh.

septique, *adj.* septic.

sépulcre, *n.m.* sepulcher.

sépulture, *n.f.* burial (place).

sequelles, *n.f.pl.* after-effects, aftermath.

séquence, *n.f.* sequence.

séquestrer, *vb.* withdraw.

serein, *adj.* serene, placid.

sérénade, *n.f.* serenade.

sérénité, *n.f.* serenity.

serf, 1. *n.m.* serf. **2.** *adj.* in serfdom or the like.

sergent, *n.m.* sergeant.

série, *n.f.* series.

sérieux, 1. *adj.* serious, sober, grave. **2.** *n.m.* gravity.

serin, *n.m.* canary.

seringue, *n.f.* syringe.

serment, *n.m.* oath.

sermon, *n.m.* sermon.

sermonner, *vb.* lecture, preach.

séropostif, *adj.* HIV-positive.

serpent, *n.m.* snake, serpent.

serpenter, *vb.* wind, wander.

serpillière, *n.f.* floor-cloth.

serre, *n.f.* greenhouse; claw.

serré, *adj.* tight.

serre-joint, *n.m.* clamp.

serrer, *vb.* tighten, squeeze, press; crowd; shake (hands). **s. dans ses bras,** hug.

serrure, *n.f.* lock.

sérum, *n.m.* serum.

servage, *n.m.* servitude.

servant, 1. *adj.* serving. **2.** *n.m.* server; gunner.

servante, *n.f.* maid.

serveuse, *n.f.* waitress.

serviable, *adj.* helpful.

service, *n.m.* service, favor. **être de s.,** be on duty.

serviette, *n.f.* napkin; towel; briefcase.

servile, *adj.* menial.

servilité, *n.f.* servility.

servir, *vb.* serve. **se s. de,** use. **ne s. à rien,** be of no use.

serviteur, *n.m.* attendant, servant.

servitude, *n.f.* slavery.

session, *n.f.* session.

seuil, *n.m.* threshold.

seul, *adj.* alone, only, single.

seulement, *adv.* only, solely.
sève, *n.f.* sap.
sévère, *adj.* severe, stern.
sévérité, *n.f.* severity, rigor.
sévir, *vb.* punish, rage.
sevrer, *vb.* wean, withhold.
sexe, *n.m.* sex; sex organ(s).
sexisme, *n.m.* sexism.
sexiste, *adj.* sexist.
sexuel, *adj.* sexual.
seyant, *adj.* becoming, suitable.
shampooing, *n.m.* shampoo.
short, *n.m.* (pair of) shorts.
shrapnel, *n.m.* shrapnel.
si, 1. *adv.* so, so much; yes. **si . . .
que,** however (+*adj.*). **2.** *conj.* if,
whether.
Sicile, *n.f.* Sicily.
sida, SIDA, *n.m.* AIDS.
sidérurgie, *n.f.* iron and steel industry.
siècle, *n.m.* century.
siège, *n.m.* seat; siege.
siéger, *vb.* sit, convene, reside.
sien, *pron.* **le sien, la sienne,** his,
hers, its.
sieste, *n.f.* siesta.
siffler, *vb.* whistle, hiss.
sifflerie, *n.f.* hissing, whistling.
sifflet, *n.m.* whistle.
sigle, *n.m.* abbreviation, acronym.
signal, *n.m.* signal.
signalement, *n.m.* description, details.
signaler, *vb.* point out.
signataire, *n.m.f.* signatory.
signature, *n.f.* signature.
signe, *n.m.* sign. **s. de la tête,** nod.
faire s. à, beckon.
signer, *vb.* sign. **se s.,** cross oneself.
significatif, *adj.* significant, meaningful.
signification, *n.f.* significance,
meaning.
signifier, *vb.* signify, mean.
silence, *n.m.* silence.
silencieux, *adj.* noiseless, silent.
silex, *n.m.* flint.
silhouette, *n.f.* outline, silhouette.
silicium, *n.m.* silicon.
sillage, *n.m.* wake, course.
sillon, *n.m.* furrow.
sillonner, *vb.* plow.
similaire, *adj.* similar.

simple, *adj.* plain, simple, mere;
no-frills.
simplicité, *n.f.* simplicity.
simplifier, *vb.* simplify.
simpliste, *adj.* simplistic.
simulacre, *n.m.* pretense, sham.
simulation, *n.f.* simulation.
simuler, *vb.* pretend.
simultané, *adj.* simultaneous.
sincère, *adj.* candid, sincere.
sincérité, *n.f.* candor, sincerity.
singe, *n.m.* monkey; imitator.
singer, *vb.* imitate, ape.
singularité, *n.f.* singularity; peculiar trait.
singulier, *adj. and n.m.* singular;
peculiar, strange.
sinistre, 1. *n.m.* disaster, damage.
2. *adj.* sinister.
sinistré, 1. *n.m.* disaster victim. **2.**
adj. disaster-stricken.
sinon, *conj.* otherwise.
sinueux, *adj.* winding, sinuous.
sirène, *n.f.* siren; mermaid.
sirop, *n.m.* syrup.
siroter, *vb.* sip.
site, *n.m.* site.
sitôt, *adv.* as soon (as).
situation, *n.f.* situation; position,
location, office.
situer, *vb.* situate, locate.
six (sēs), *adj. and n.m.* six.
sixième (-z-), *adj. and n.m.f.* sixth.
ski, *n.m.* ski. **faire du s.,** ski.
skieur, *n.m.* skier.
Slave, 1. *adj.* Slavonic. **2.** *n.m.f.*
Slav.
slip, *n.m.* underpants, panties.
SMIC, *n.m.* minimum wage.
smoking, *n.m.* dinner jacket, tux-
edo.
snak(-bar), *n.m.* snackbar.
snob, *n.m.* snob.
sobre, *adj.* temperate, sober.
sobriété, *n.f.* moderation, temperance.
sobriquet, *n.m.* nickname.
soc, *n.m.* plowshare.
sociable, *adj.* sociable.
social, *adj.* social.
socialisme, *n.m.* socialism.
socialiste, *adj. and n.m.f.* socialist.
société, *n.f.* society; company.
sociologie, *n.f.* sociology.
sociologue, *n.m.f.* sociologist.

sœur, *n.f.* sister.

sofa, *n.m.* sofa.

soi-disant, *adj.* so-called.

soie, *n.f.* silk; bristle.

soierie, *n.f.* silk goods.

soif, *n.f.* thirst. **avoir s.,** be thirsty.

soigné, *adj.* trim. **mal s.,** sloppy.

soigner, *vb.* tend, look after, take care of.

soigneux, *adj.* careful.

soi-même, *pron.* oneself.

soin, *n.m.* care. **prendre s. de,** take care of.

soir, *n.m.* evening. **hier s.,** last night. **ce s.,** tonight. **le s.,** at night.

soirée, *n.f.* evening.

soit, *vb.* so be it. **s . . . . s.,** whether . . . or. **s. que,** whether.

soixantaine, *n.f.* about sixty.

soixante (-s-), *adj. and n.m.* sixty.

soixante-dix, *adj. and n.m.* seventy.

sol, *n.m.* earth, soil, ground.

solaire, *adj.* solar.

soldat, *n.m.* soldier.

solde, *n.m.* balance.

sole, *n.f.* sole (fish).

solécisme, *n.m.* solecism.

soleil, *n.m.* sun, sunshine. **coucher du s.,** sunset. **lever du s.,** sunrise.

solennel, *adj.* solemn.

solenniser, *vb.* solemnize.

solennité, *n.f.* solemnity.

solex, *n.m.* (trademark) moped.

solidaire, *adj.* jointly binding.

solidariser, *vb.* **se s.,** unite, join together.

solidarité, *n.f.* joint responsibility.

solide, *adj. and n.m.* solid.

solidifier, *vb.* solidify.

solidité, *n.f.* solidity.

soliloque, *n.m.* soliloquy.

soliste, *n.m.f.* soloist.

solitaire, *adj.* lonely, lonesome.

solitude, *n.f.* solitude.

solliciter, *vb.* solicit, ask, apply.

sollicitude, *n.f.* solicitude.

soluble, *adj.* soluble.

solution, *n.f.* solution.

solvable, *adj.* solvent.

sombre, *adj.* dark, dim, gloomy, somber.

sombrer, *vb.* sink.

sommaire, *n.m.* summary.

sommation, *n.f.* appeal, summons.

somme, 1. *n.f.* amount, sum. **2.** *n.m.* nap.

sommeil, *n.m.* sleep. **avoir s.,** be sleepy.

sommeiller, *vb.* doze, slumber.

sommer, *vb.* summon.

sommet, *n.m.* top, peak, summit.

somnifère, *n.m.* sleeping pill.

somnolence, *n.f.* drowsiness.

somnolent, *adj.* drowsy, sleepy.

somptueux, *adj.* lavish, sumptuous.

son *m.,* **sa** *f.,* **ses** *pl. adj.* his, her, its.

son, *n.m.* sound, ring; bran.

sonate, *n.f.* sonata.

sondage, *n.m.* (opinion) poll.

sonde, *n.f.* sounding line; probe; catheter; feeding tube.

sonder, *vb.* fathom; probe.

songe, *n.m.* dream.

songer, *vb.* think of, dream.

songeur, 1. *adj.* dreamy, thoughtful. **2.** *n.m.* dreamer.

sonner, *vb.* sound, ring, strike.

sonnerie, *n.f.* ringing.

sonnette, *n.f.* bell.

sonore, *adj.* sonorous.

sonorisation, *n.f.* public address system.

sophiste, *n.m.f.* sophist.

sophistiqué, *adj.* sophisticated.

soprano, *n.m.* soprano.

sorbet, *n.m.* sorbet.

sorcellerie, *n.f.* sorcery.

sorcier, *n.m.* wizard.

sorcière, *n.f.* witch.

sordide, *adj.* sordid.

sort, *n.m.* lot.

sorte, *n.f.* sort, kind. **de s. que,** so that.

sortie, *n.f.* exit, way out.

sortilège, *n.m.* sorcery.

sortir, *vb.* go (come, get) out.

sot *m.,* **sotte** *f. adj.* silly, stupid, foolish, dumb.

sottise, *n.f.* foolishness.

sou, *n.m.* cent. **sans le s.,** penniless.

soubassement, *n.m.* basement.

soubresaut, *n.m.* bound, jerk.

souche, *n.f.* stub, stump.

souci, *n.m.* care, worry, concern.

soucier, *vb.* **se s. (de),** care, worry (about).

soucieux, *adj.* anxious.

soucoupe, *n.f.* saucer. **s. volante,** flying saucer.

soudain, *adj.* sudden.

soudaineté, *n.f.* suddenness.

soude, *n.f.* soda.

souder, *vb.* solder, fuse.

souffle, *n.m.* breath.

souffler, *vb.* blow.

soufflet, *n.m.* bellows; blow, slap.

souffleter, *vb.* slap one's face.

souffrance(s), *n.f. (pl.)* misery, pain, suffering.

souffrir, *vb.* suffer, bear.

soufre, *n.m.* sulphur.

souhait, *n.m.* wish.

souhaiter, *vb.* wish for.

souiller, *vb.* soil, defile.

souillure, *n.f.* stain, dirt.

soûl (soo), *adj.* drunk.

soulager, *vb.* relieve, alleviate.

soûler, *vb.* fill with food and drink, inebriate.

soulèvement, *n.m.* uprising.

soulever, *vb.* lift, raise, arouse.

soulier, *n.m.* shoe.

souligner, *vb.* underline.

soumettre, *vb.* submit, subdue.

soumis, *adj.* obedient, submissive.

soumission, *n.f.* submission.

soupape, *n.f.* valve.

soupçon, *n.m.* suspicion.

soupçonner, *vb.* suspect.

soupçonneux, *adj.* suspicious.

soupe, *n.f.* soup.

souper, *n.m.* supper.

soupir, *n.m.* sigh.

soupirant, *n.m.* suitor.

soupirer, *vb.* sigh. **s. après,** yearn for.

souple, *adj.* flexible.

souplesse, *n.f.* suppleness, pliability.

source, *n.f.* source; spring.

sourcil, *n.m.* eyebrow.

sourciller, *vb.* frown.

sourcilleux, *adj.* haughty, disdainful.

sourd, *adj.* deaf.

sourd-muet, *n.m.* deaf mute.

souriant, *adj.* cheerful.

souricière, *n.f.* (mouse)trap.

sourire, *n.m. and vb.* smile.

souris, *n.f.* mouse.

sournois, *adj.* sly.

sous, *prep.* under.

souscription, *n.f.* subscription.

souscrire, *vb.* subscribe.

sous-entendre, *vb.* imply.

sous-estimer, *vb.* underestimate.

sous-louer, *vb.* sublet.

sous-marin, *n.m.* submarine.

sous-produit, *n.m.* by-product.

soussigné, *adj.* undersigned.

sous-sol, *n.m.* basement.

sous-titre, *n.m.* subtitle.

soustraction, *n.f.* subtraction.

soustraire, *vb.* subtract.

sous-traitant, *n.m.* subcontractor.

sous-vêtements, *n.m.pl.* underwear.

soutane, *n.f.* cassock.

soute, *n.f.* storeroom.

soutenir, *vb.* support, uphold, maintain; claim; back up.

soutenu, *adj.* steady.

souterrain, *adj.* underground.

soutien, *n.m.* support.

soutien-gorge, *n.m.* brassiere.

souvenance, *n.f.* recall, recollection.

souvenir, 1. *n.m.* remembrance, memory. **2.** *vb.* **se s. de,** remember.

souvent, *adv.* often.

souverain, *n.m.* ruler, sovereign.

souveraineté, *n.f.* sovereignty.

Soviétique, *n.m.f.* Soviet citizen.

soviétique, *adj.* Soviet.

soyeux, *adj.* silky.

spacieux, *adj.* spacious.

spasme, *n.m.* spasm.

spatial, *adj.* space.

spatule, *n.f.* spatula.

spécial, *adj.* special.

spécialiser, *vb.* specialize.

spécialiste, *n.m.f.* specialist.

spécialité, *n.f.* specialty.

spécifier, *vb.* specify.

spécifique, *adj.* specific.

spécimen, *n.m.* specimen.

spectacle, *n.m.* sight, show.

spectaculaire, *adj.* spectacular.

spectateur, *n.m.* spectator.

spectre, *n.m.* ghost; spectrum.

spéculation, *n.f.* speculation.

spéculer, *vb.* speculate.

sphère, *n.f.* sphere.

spinal, *adj.* spinal.

spiral, *adj.* spiral.

spirale, *n.f.* spiral.

spirite, *n.m.f.* spiritualist.
spiritisme, *n.m.* spiritualism.
spirituel, *adj.* spiritual; witty.
spiritueux, *adj.* pertaining to alcohol.
splendeur, *n.f.* splendor.
splendide, *adj.* splendid.
spolier, *vb.* plunder, pillage.
spontané, *adj.* spontaneous.
spontanéité, *n.f.* spontaneity.
sporadique, *adj.* sporadic.
sport, *n.m.* sport.
sportif, *adj.* sporting, athletic, sports.
spot, *n.m.* spot(light).
squatter, 1. *n.m.* squatter. 2. *vb.* squat in.
squelette, *n.m.* skeleton.
stabiliser, *vb.* stabilize.
stabilité, *n.f.* stability.
stable, *adj.* stable, steady.
stage, *n.m.* training or instruction period.
stagflation, *n.f.* stagflation.
stagiaire, *n.m.f.* trainee.
stagnant, *adj.* stagnant.
stalle, *n.f.* stall.
stance, *n.f.* stanza.
standard, *n.m.* switchboard.
standardiste, *n.m.f.* phone operator.
starter, *n.m.* (car) choke.
station, *n.f.* stand, stop, station (subway).
stationnaire, *adj.* stationary.
stationnement, *n.m.* parking.
stationner, *vb.* park.
station-service, *n.f.* gas/service station.
statique, *adj.* static.
statistique, *n.f.* statistics.
statue, *n.f.* statue.
statuer, *vb.* decree, decide.
stature, *n.f.* stature.
statut, *n.m.* statute.
steak, *n.m.* steak.
sténographe, *n.m.f.* stenographer.
sténographie, *n.f.* stenography.
stéréo, *n.f.* and *adj.* stereo.
stéréophonique, *adj.* stereophonic.
stérile, *adj.* barren.
stérilet, *n.m.* coil, IUD.
stériliser, *vb.* sterilize.
stéthoscope, *n.m.* stethoscope.

stigmatiser, *vb.* mark, stigmatize.
stimulant, *n.m.* stimulus.
stimuler, *vb.* stimulate.
stipuler, *vb.* stipulate.
stoïque, *adj.* and *n.m.f.* stoic.
stop, *n.m.* stop sign; hitchhiking.
store, *n.m.* (window) shade, blind.
strapontin, *n.m.* folding seat.
stratagème, *n.m.* stratagem.
stratégie, *n.f.* strategy.
stratégique, *adj.* strategic.
stressant, *adj.* stressful.
strict (-kt), *adj.* severe, strict.
strier, *vb.* mark, streak, groove.
structure, *n.f.* structure.
stuc, *n.m.* stucco.
studieux, *adj.* studious.
stupéfait, *adj.* astounded.
stupéfiant, *n.m.* narcotic, dope.
stupéfier, *vb.* astound.
stupeur, *n.f.* amazement.
stupide, *adj.* stupid.
stupidité, *n.f.* stupidity.
style, *n.m.* style.
styler, *vb.* train, teach.
stylet, *n.m.* stiletto.
stylographe, stylo, *n.m.* fountain pen.
suavité, *n.f.* suavity.
subalterne, *adj.* and *n.m.f.* junior (rank).
subdiviser, *vb.* subdivide.
subir, *vb.* undergo, bear.
subit, *adj.* sudden.
subjectif, *adj.* subjective.
subjonctif, *adj.* and *n.m.* subjunctive.
subjuguer, *vb.* subdue, overcome.
sublime, *adj.* sublime, exalted.
submerger, *vb.* submerge, flood.
subordonné, *adj.* and *n.m.* subordinate.
subordonner, *vb.* subordinate.
subornation, *n.f.* bribing.
subreptice, *adj.* surreptitious.
subséquent, *adj.* subsequent.
subside, *n.m.* subsidy.
subsister, *vb.* subsist, live.
substance, *n.f.* substance.
substantiel, *adj.* substantial.
substantif, *n.m.* noun.
substituer, *vb.* substitute.
substitution, *n.f.* substitution.
subtil (-l), *adj.* subtle.
subtilité, *n.f.* subtlety.

subvenir, vb. provide.
subvention, n.f. grant, subsidy.
subventionner, vb. subsidize.
subversif, adj. subversive.
suc, n.m. juice.
succéder à, vb. succeed, follow.
succès, n.m. success, hit.
successeur, n.m. successor.
successif, adj. successive.
succession, n.f. succession.
succion, n.f. suction.
succomber, vb. succumb.
succursale, n.f. branch office.
sucer, vb. suck.
sucre, n.m. sugar.
sucrer, vb. add sugar.
sucreries, n.f.pl. sweets.
sud (-d), n.m. south.
sudation, n.f. sweating.
sud-est, n.m. southeast.
sud-ouest, n.m. southwest.
Suède, n.f. Sweden.
Suédois, n.m. Swede (person).
suédois, adj. and n.m. Swedish.
suer, vb. sweat.
sueur, n.f. sweat.
suffire, vb. suffice.
suffisance, n.f. adequacy; conceit.
suffisant, adj. sufficient, adequate; conceited.
suffixe, n.m. suffix.
suffoquer, vb. suffocate.
suffrage, n.m. suffrage.
suggérer, vb. suggest.
suggestion, n.f. suggestion.
suicide, n.m. suicide.
suicider, vb. se s., kill oneself.
suie, n.f. soot.
suif, n.m. tallow.
suinter, vb. seep.
Suisse, 1. n.m. Swiss (person). 2. n.f. Switzerland.
suisse, adj. Swiss.
suite, n.f. sequence; retinue; (pl.) results, aftermath. **et ainsi de s.,** and so on. **tout de s.,** at once.
suivant, 1. n.m. follower. 2. adj. next, following, subsequent. 3. prep. by, according to.
suivi, adj. followed, coherent.
suivre, vb. follow; attend. **faire s.,** forward.
sujet, 1. n.m. subject; topic. 2. adj. subject. **s. à,** liable to.

sujétion, n.f. subjection, slavery.
superbe, adj. superb, magnificent.
super(carburant), n.m. high-octane gasoline.
superette, n.f. small supermarket.
superficie, n.f. surface.
superficiel, adj. superficial, shallow.
superflu, adj. superfluous.
supérieur, adj. and n.m. superior, higher, upper; senior.
supériorité, n.f. superiority.
superlatif, adj. and n.m. superlative.
supermarché, n.m. supermarket.
superpuissance, n.f. superpower.
superstar, n.f. superstar.
superstitieux, adj. superstitious.
superstition, n.f. superstition.
suppléant, adj. and n.m. assistant, substitute.
suppléer, vb. substitute.
supplément, n.m. supplement.
supplémentaire, adj. extra. **heures s.s,** overtime.
supplice, n.m. punishment, torture.
supplier, vb. beseech, entreat, beg, supplicate.
support, n.m. support, stand.
supportable, adj. tolerable.
supporter, vb. support; bear, stand, endure.
supposer, vb. suppose, assume.
supposition, n.f. assumption, conjecture, supposition.
suppôt, n.m. implement, tool, agent.
suppression, n.f. suppression.
supprimer, vb. suppress, put down; take out.
supputation, n.f. computation.
supputer, vb. compute.
suprématie, n.f. supremacy.
suprême, adj. supreme.
sur, prep. on, upon, over.
sûr, adj. safe, sure, secure.
surabonder, vb. be very abundant.
suranné, adj. out-of-date.
surcharge, n.f. excess load.
surcharger, vb. overload.
surcroît, n.m. addition.
surdité, n.f. deafness.
suret, adj. sour.

sureté, *n.f.* safety, security, reliability.

surf, *n.m.* surf.

surface, *n.f.* surface, area.

surgélateur, *n.m.* deep freeze.

surgir, *vb.* spring up, arise.

surhumain, *adj.* superhuman.

surintendant, *n.m.* superintendent.

sur-le-champ, *adv.* at once, immediately.

surlendemain, *n.m.* two days later.

surmener, *vb.* overwork.

surmonter, *vb.* overcome, surmount.

surnager, *vb.* float.

surnaturel, *adj. and n.m.* supernatural.

surnom, *n.m.* nickname.

surpasser, *vb.* surpass.

surpeuplé, *adj.* overpopulated.

surplis, *n.m.* surplice.

surplomber, *vb.* overhang.

surplus, *n.m.* surplus, excess.

surprendre, *vb.* surprise.

surprise, *n.f.* surprise.

sursaut, *n.m.* start.

sursauter, *vb.* give a start.

sursis, *n.m.* delay, putting off.

surtaxe, *n.f.* surtax.

surtout, 1. *n.m.* overcoat. **2.** *adv.* above all.

surveillance, *n.f.* supervision, watch.

surveillant, *n.m.* superintendent.

surveiller, *vb.* supervise, watch over.

survenir, *vb.* happen.

survêtement, *n.m.* track suit.

survie, *n.f.* survival.

survivance, *n.f.* survival.

survivre, *vb.* survive.

susceptible, *adj.* susceptible; liable.

susciter, *vb.* arouse, provoke.

suspect (-kt), *adj.* suspicious.

suspecter, *vb.* suspect.

suspendre, *vb.* suspend, hang, sling.

suspens, *adv.* **en s.,** in suspense.

suspense, *n.m.* suspense.

suspension, *n.f.* suspension.

suspicion, *n.f.* suspicion.

sustenter, *vb.* sustain, bulwark.

svelte, *adj.* slender, slim.

sweat-shirt (swĕt shœrt), *n.m.* sweatshirt.

syllabe, *n.f.* syllable.

sylphide, *n.f.* sylph.

sylvestre, *adj.* sylvan, woody.

sylviculture, *n.f.* forestry.

symbole, *n.m.* symbol.

symboliser, *vb.* symbolize.

symétrie, *n.f.* symmetry.

sympa, *adj.* nice.

sympathie, *n.f.* sympathy. **avoir de la s. pour,** like.

sympathique, *adj.* congenial, likeable.

sympathiser, *vb.* sympathize.

symphonie, *n.f.* symphony.

symptôme, *n.m.* symptom.

synchroniser, *vb.* synchronize.

syncape, *n.f.* blackout.

syndic, *n.m.f.* association/union representative.

syndical, *adj.* of a trade union.

syndicat, *n.m.* syndicate. **s. ouvrier,** trade union.

syndiqué, *n.m.* (trade) union member.

syndrome, *n.m.* syndrome.

synonyme, *n.m.* synonym.

syntaxe, *n.f.* syntax.

synthèse, *n.f.* synthesis.

synthétique, *adj.* synthetic.

Syrie, *n.f.* Syria.

Syrien, *n.m.* Syrian (person).

syrien, *adj.* Syrian.

systématique, *adj.* systematic.

système, *n.m.* system.

T

tabac (-bă), *n.m.* tobacco.

tabagie, *n.f.* smoking.

tabernacle, *n.m.* tabernacle.

table, *n.f.* table. **t. des matières,** index.

tableau, *n.m.* picture. **t. noir,** blackboard.

tabler, *vb.* count on, depend.

tablette, *n.f.* tablet.

tableur, *n.m.* spreadsheet.

tablier, *n.m.* apron.
tabou, *n.m.* taboo.
tabouret, *n.m.* stool.
tache, *n.f.* spot, stain, blot, smear.
tâche, *n.f.* task; assignment.
tacher, *vb.* spot, stain, blot.
tâcher, *vb.* try.
tacite, *adj.* tacit, silent.
taciturne, *adj.* unspeaking.
tact (-kt), *n.m.* tact.
tacticien, *n.m.* tactician.
tactique, 1. *adj.* of tactics, tactical. **2.** *n.f.* tactics.
taffetas, *n.m.* taffeta.
taie, *n.f.* **t. d'oreiller,** pillowcase.
taillade, *n.f.* slash.
taille, *n.f.* waist; figure; size.
tailler, *vb.* trim, cut.
tailleur, *n.m.* tailor.
taire, *vb.* keep quiet. **se t.,** be silent.
talent, *n.m.* ability, talent.
talon, *n.m.* heel; (check) stub.
talus, *n.m.* slope.
tambour, *n.m.* drum.
tambourin, *n.m.* tambourine.
tamis, *n.m.* sieve.
tampon, *n.m.* plug, pad. **t. hygié-nique,** tampon.
tamponner, *vb.* plug; run together.
tan, *n.m.* tan (leather).
tandis que, *conj.* while, whereas.
tangible, *adj.* tangible.
tanguer, *vb.* cover with pitch.
tant, *adv.* so much, so many. **t. que,** as long as.
tante, *n.f.* aunt.
tantième, *n.m.* part, percentage.
tantôt, *adv.* presently, soon.
tapage, *n.m.* din.
tapageur, *adj.* rowdy.
taper, *vb.* pat, knock, tap; type.
tapir, *vb.* **se t.,** squat, cower, lurk.
tapis, *n.m.* carpet, rug.
tapisserie, *n.f.* tapestry.
tapissier, *n.m.* upholsterer.
taquiner, *vb.* tease.
taquinerie, *n.f.* teasing.
tard, *adv.* late.
tarder, *vb.* delay.
tardif, *adj.* slow, tardy, late.
tare, *n.f.* defect.
tarière, *n.f.* auger.
tarif, *n.m.* scale of charges; rate; fare. **t. douanier,** tariff.
tartan, *n.m.* plaid.

tarte, *n.f.* pie.
tartine, *n.f.* slice of bread.
tartre, *n.m.* tartar.
tas, *n.m.* heap, pile.
tasse, *n.f.* cup.
tasser, *vb.* pack, fill up.
tâter, *vb.* feel.
tâtonner, *vb.* grope.
taudis, *n.m.* hovel, slum.
taupe, *n.f.* mole.
taureau, *n.m.* bull.
taux, *n.m.* rate.
taverne, *n.f.* tavern.
taxe, *n.f.* tax. **t. (à la) valeur ajoutée,** value-added tax.
taxer, *vb.* tax, assess.
taxi, *n.m.* cab, taxi.
Tchécoslovaquie, *n.f.* Czechoslovakia.
te (ta), *pron.* you, yourself.
technicien, *n.m.* technician.
technique, 1. *n.f.* technique. **2.** *adj.* technical.
technologie, *n.f.* technology.
teindre, *vb.* dye.
teint, *n.m.* complexion.
teinte, *n.f.* tint, shade.
teinter, *vb.* tint, stain.
teinture, *n.f.* dye.
teinturier, *n.m.* dry-cleaner; dyer.
tel, *adj.* such.
télé, *n.f.* TV.
télécommande, *n.f.* remote control.
télécommunitions, *n.f.pl.* telecommunications.
télécopie, *n.f.* fax.
télécopieur, *n.m.* fax machine.
télédistribution, *n.f.* cable TV.
télégramme, *n.m.* telegram.
télégraphe, *n.m.* telegraph.
télégraphie, *n.f.* telegraphy. **t. sans fil,** *abbr.* T.S.F., radio, wireless.
télégraphir, *vb.* telegraph.
téléguider, *vb.* operate by remote control, radio-control.
télématique, *n.f.* computer communications.
téléphone, *n.m.* telephone. **coup de t.,** telephone call.
téléphoner, *vb.* telephone.
télescope, *n.m.* telescope.
télescoper, *vb.* crash, run together.
téléspectateur, *n.m.* TV viewer.

téléviseur, n.m. TV set.

télévision, n.f. television.

télex, n.m. telex.

tellement, adv. so much.

téméraire, adj. rash.

témoignage, n.m. testimony; token.

témoigner, vb. testify.

témoin, n.m. witness.

tempe, n.f. temple (anatomy).

tempérament, n.m. temper, temperament.

tempérance, n.f. temperance.

tempérant, adj. temperate.

température, n.f. temperature.

tempéré, adj. temperate.

tempérer, vb. moderate, calm, lessen.

tempête, n.f. storm, tempest.

tempétueux, adj. tempestuous.

temple, n.m. temple.

temporaire, adj. temporary.

temporiser, vb. temporize, evade.

temps (tän), n.m. time; weather.

tenace, adj. tenacious.

ténacité, n.f. tenacity.

tenailles, n.f.pl. tongs.

tendance, n.f. tendency, trend, leaning.

tendre, 1. adj. tender, fond, loving. **2.** vb. tend, extend.

tendresse, n.f. tenderness, fondness.

tendu, adj. tense; uptight.

ténèbres, n.f.pl. gloom, darkness.

ténébreux, adj. dismal.

teneur, n.m. **t. de livres,** bookkeeper.

tenir, vb. hold.

tennis (-s), n.m. tennis.

ténor, n.m. tenor.

tension, n.f. strain; stress.

tentacule, n.m. tentacle.

tentatif, adj. tentative.

tentation, n.f. temptation.

tentative, n.f. attempt.

tente, n.f. tent; awning.

tenter, vb. tempt, try, attract.

tenture, n.f. wallcovering.

tenue, n.f. rig; conduct, manners.

ténuité, n.f. tenuity, unimportance.

térébenthine, n.f. turpentine.

terme, n.m. term, period; end.

terminaison, n.f. ending.

terminal, adj. and n.m. terminal.

terminer, vb. end.

terminologie, n.f. terminology.

terminus, n.m. terminus.

terne, adj. drab, dull, dim, dingy.

ternir, vb. tarnish, dull.

terrain, n.m. ground(s).

terrasse, n.f. terrace.

terrasser, vb. heap up, embank; knock down, conquer.

terre, n.f. earth, ground, land. **pomme de t.,** potato. **à t.,** ashore.

terrestre, adj. earthly.

terreur, n.f. terror, fright, fear.

terrible, adj. terrible, awful; (colloquial) terrific.

terrifier, vb. terrify.

terrine, n.f. terrine, pâté.

territoire, n.m. territory.

terroir, n.m. soil.

terroriser, vb. terrorize.

terrorisme, n.m. terrorism.

tertre, n.m. mound.

tesson, n.m. broken piece, fragment.

testament, n.m. testament, will.

testateur, n.m. testator.

tester, vb. test.

testicule, n.m. testicle.

tête, n.f. head. **tenir t. à,** cope with.

téter, vb. suck.

téton, n.m. breast.

têtu, adj. stubborn.

texte, n.m. text.

textile, adj. textile.

textuel, adj. textual.

texture, n.f. texture.

Thaïlande, n.f. Thailand.

thé, n.m. tea.

théâtral, adj. theatrical.

théâtre, n.m. theater.

théière, n.f. teapot.

thème, n.m. theme.

théologie, n.f. theology.

théorie, n.f. theory.

théorique, adj. theoretical.

thérapie, n.f. therapy.

thermomètre, n.m. thermometer.

thermostat, n.m. thermostat.

thésauriser, vb. hoard.

thèse, n.f. thesis.

thon, n.m. tuna.

thym, n.m. thyme.

ticket, n.m. check, ticket, coupon.

tiède, adj. lukewarm.

tiédir, vb. make or become cool.

tien, pron. **le tien, la tienne,** yours.

tiers, n.m. third.

Tiers Monde, n.m. Third World.

tige, n.f. stem, stalk.

tigre, n.m. tiger.

tilleul, n.m. linden, lime tree.

timbre, n.m. stamp. **t.-poste,** postage stamp.

timbrer, vb. stamp.

timide, adj. timid, shy, coy, bashful.

timidité, n.f. timidity.

timoré, adj. timorous.

tintamarre, n.m. racket.

tinter, vb. ring, knell, tinkle.

tir, n.m. shooting, firing.

tirage, n.m. printing, print; circulation, edition.

tirailleur, n.m. sharpshooter.

tire, n.f. pull, yank.

tire-bouchon, n.m. corkscrew.

tirer, vb. draw, pull; shoot.

tiret, n.m. blank; dash.

tiroir, n.m. drawer.

tisane, n.f. drink, herbal tea.

tisser, vb. weave.

tisserand, n.m. weaver.

tissu, n.m. web; cloth, fabric.

titre, n.m. title, right.

titrer, vb. invest with a title.

titulaire, adj. incumbent.

toast (-t), n.m. toast.

toaster, vb. toast.

toi, pron. you.

toile, n.f. web; canvas; linen.

toilette, n.f. toilet; dressing, dress.

toison, n.f. fleece.

toit, n.m. roof.

toiture, n.f. roofing.

tolérance, n.f. tolerance.

tolérer, vb. tolerate, bear.

tomate, n.f. tomato.

tombe, n.f. grave.

tombeau, n.m. tomb.

tombée, n.f. fall, decline.

tomber, vb. fall. **laisser t.,** drop.

tome, n.m. volume.

ton, n.m. tone, pitch.

ton m., **ta** f., **tes** pl. adj. your.

tonalité, n.f. dial tone, tone, key.

tondeuse, n.f. (lawn) mower.

tondre, vb. shear; mow.

tonique, adj. and n.m. tonic.

tonne, n.f. ton; barrel.

tonneau, n.m. cask, barrel.

tonner, vb. thunder.

tonnerre, n.m. thunder.

topaze, n.f. topaz.

topographie, n.f. topography.

torche, n.f. torch.

tordre, vb. twist, wrench, wring. **se t.,** writhe.

torpeur, n.f. torpor.

torpille, n.f. torpedo.

torrent, n.m. torrent.

torride, adj. torrid.

torse, n.m. torso.

tort, n.m. wrong. **avoir t.,** be wrong.

tortiller, vb. twist, wiggle.

tortionnaire, n.m.f. torturer.

tortu, adj. crooked.

tortue, n.f. turtle, tortoise.

torture, n.f. torture.

torturer, vb. torture.

tôt, adv. soon, early.

total, adj. and n.m. total.

totalisateur, n.m. adding machine.

totaliser, vb. total, add up.

totalitaire, adj. totalitarian.

totalité, n.f. entirety.

toubib (-b) n.m. (colloquial) doctor.

touchant, prep. concerning.

touche, n.f. key.

toucher, 1. n.m. touch. 2. vb. touch; collect; affect; border on.

touffe, n.f. tuft, bunch.

touffu, adj. bushy.

toujours, adv. always, still, ever, yet.

toupie, n.f. top (child's toy).

tour, 1. n.m. turn; trick; stroll. **faire le t. de,** go around. 2. n.f. tower.

tourbe, n.f. rabble.

tourbillon, n.m. whirl. **t. d'eau,** whirlpool. **t. de vent,** whirlwind.

tourbillonner, vb. whirl.

tourelle, n.f. turret.

touriste, n.m.f. tourist.

tourment, n.m. torment.

tourmenter, vb. torment.

tournage, n.m. (film) shooting.

tourne-disques, n.m. record player.

tournedos, n.f. beefsteak.

tournée, n.f. round.

tourner, vb. turn, revolve, spin.

tournesol, n.m. sunflower.

tournevis, *n.m.* screwdriver.

tournoi, *n.m.* tournament.

tournure, *n.f.* figure; turn of phrase.

tousser, *vb.* cough.

tout, 1. *adj.m.,* **toute** *f.,* **tous** *m.pl.,* **toutes** *f.pl.* all, each, every. **2.** *pron.* everything. **tous les deux,** both. **t. d'un coup,** all at once. **t. de même,** all the same. **pas du t.,** not at all.

toutefois, *adv.* however.

tout-puissant, *adj.* almighty.

toux, *n.f.* cough.

toxicomane, *n.m.f.* drug addict.

toxique, *adj.* toxic.

tracasser, *vb.* worry.

trace, *n.f.* trace, step, track, footprint.

tracer, *vb.* outline, trace.

tracteur, *n.m.* tractor.

traction, *n.f.* traction.

tradition, *n.f.* tradition.

traditionnel, *adj.* traditional.

traducteur, *n.m.* translator.

traduction, *n.f.* translation.

traduire, *vb.* translate.

trafic, *n.m.* traffic.

trafiquer, *vb.* traffic; carry on dealings.

tragédie, *n.f.* tragedy.

tragique, *adj.* tragic.

trahir, *vb.* betray.

trahison, *n.f.* treason.

train, *n.m.* train.

traînard, *n.m.* loiterer, dawdler.

traîne, *n.f.* train of dress.

traîneau, *n.m.* sled, sleigh.

traîner, *vb.* drag, haul.

traire, *vb.* milk.

trait, *n.m.* feature; draft; shot. **t. d'union,** hyphen.

traité, *n.m.* treaty.

traitement, *n.m.* treatment. **t. de données,** data processing. **t. de texte,** word processing.

traiter, *vb.* treat, deal; process.

traiteur, *n.m.* caterer.

traître, *n.m.* traitor.

traîtrise, *n.f.* treachery.

trajet, *n.m.* crossing.

trame, *n.f.* web (woof); plan, plot.

tramer, *vb.* devise.

tramway, *n.m.* streetcar.

tranchant, *adj.* sharp, crisp.

tranche, *n.f.* slice.

tranchée, *n.f.* trench.

trancher, *vb.* cut.

tranquille (-l-), *adj.* quiet. **laisser t.,** leave alone.

tranquilliser (-l-), *vb.* soothe, make tranquil.

tranquillité (-l-), *n.f.* quiet, stillness.

transaction, *n.f.* transaction.

transe, *n.f.* fright, fear.

transférer, *vb.* transfer.

transfert, *n.m.* transfer.

transformer, *vb.* transform.

transfuser, *vb.* transfuse.

transfusion, *n.f.* transfusion.

transitif, *adj.* transitive.

transition (-z-), *n.f.* transition.

transitoire (-z-), *adj.* transitory.

transmettre, *vb.* transmit, convey, send.

transmetteur, *n.m.* transmitter.

transmission, *n.f.* transmission.

transparent, *adj.* transparent.

transpiration, *n.f.* perspiration.

transpirer, *vb.* perspire.

transplanter, *vb.* transplant.

transport, *n.m.* transfer, transport, transportation; bliss, ecstasy. **t.s en commun,** mass transport.

transporter, *vb.* transport, transfer, convey.

transposer, *vb.* transpose.

transsexuel, *adj.* transsexual.

traumatiser, *vb.* traumatize.

travail, *n.m.* work, job, labor.

travailler, *vb.* work.

travailleur, 1. *n.m.* worker, laborer. **2.** *adj.* industrious.

travée, *n.f.* span.

travers, *n.m.* breadth. **à t.,** across, through. **de t.,** askance, awry.

traversée, *n.f.* crossing.

traverser, *vb.* cross.

traversin, *n.m.* bolster.

travesti, *adj.* transvestite.

travestir, *vb.* disguise.

trébucher, *vb.* stumble, trip.

trèfle, *n.m.* clover; club (cards).

treillis, *n.m.* denim.

treize, *adj. and n.m.* thirteen.

tréma, *n.m.* dieresis.

tremblement, *n.m.* trembling. **t. de terre,** earthquake.

trembler, *vb.* tremble, shake, quake.

trembloter, *vb.* quiver.

trémousser, *vb.* flutter.

trempe, *n.f.* temper, cast.

tremper, *vb.* soak, drench, temper.

trentaine, *n.f.* about thirty.

trente, *adj. and n.m.* thirty.

trépasser, *vb.* die.

trépied, *n.m.* tripod, trivet.

très, *adv.* very.

trésor, *n.m.* treasure, treasury; darling.

trésorier, *n.m.* treasurer.

tressaillement, *n.m.* thrill; start.

tressaillir, *vb.* thrill; start.

tresse, *n.f.* braid.

tresser, *vb.* braid.

tréteau, *n.m.* trestle.

trêve, *n.f.* truce.

tri, *n.m.* sorting, selection.

triangle, *n.m.* triangle.

tribade, *n.f.* lesbian.

tribu, *n.f.* tribe.

tribulation, *n.f.* tribulation.

tribut, *n.m.* tribute.

tributaire, *adj.* tributary.

tricher, *vb.* cheat.

tricherie, *n.f.* cheating.

tricolore, *adj.* three-colored; (French) blue, white, red; *(fig.)* France.

tricot, *n.m.* knitting; undershirt; sweater.

tricoter, *vb.* knit.

trier, *vb.* sort.

trimestre, *n.m.* term.

trimestriel, *adj.* quarterly.

trinquer, *vb.* touch glasses in making a toast.

triomphant, *adj.* triumphant.

triomphe, *n.m.* triumph.

triompher, *vb.* triumph.

triple, *adj. and n.m.* triple.

tripoter, *vb.* fiddle with, dabble in; bother.

triste, *adj.* sad.

tristesse, *n.f.* sadness.

trivial, *adj.* trivial.

trivialité, *n.f.* triviality.

troc, *n.m.* barter.

trois, *adj. and n.m.* three.

troisième, *adj. and n.m.f.* third.

trompe, *n.f.* horn, trumpet; elephant's trunk.

trompe l'œil, *n.m.* trompe l'œil style of painting.

tromper, *vb.* deceive, cheat. **se t.,** be wrong, make a mistake.

tromperie, *n.f.* deceit.

trompette, *n.f.* trumpet.

trompeur, *adj.* deceitful.

tronc, *n.m.* trunk.

trône, *n.m.* throne.

trop, *adv.* too; too much, too many.

trophée, *n.m.* trophy.

tropical, *adj.* tropical.

tropique, *n.m.* tropic.

troquer, *vb.* barter, dicker, trade.

trot, *n.m.* trot.

trotter, *vb.* trot.

trottiner, *vb.* trot, jog.

trottoir, *n.m.* sidewalk.

trou, *n.m.* hole.

trouble, *n.m.* disturbance, riot.

troublé, *adj.* anxious, worried.

troubler, *vb.* perturb.

trouer, *vb.* pierce, bore.

trouille, *n.f.* (colloquial) **avoir la t.,** be scared to death.

troupe, *n.f.* troop.

troupeau, *n.m.* herd, flock, drove.

troupier, *n.m.* soldier, trooper.

trousseau, *n.m.* bunch; outfit.

trousser, *vb.* truss up, turn up.

trouvaille, *n.f.* discovery; find.

trouver, *vb.* find. **se t.,** be located.

truc, *n.m.* trick; thing.

truelle, *n.f.* trowel.

truite, *n.f.* trout.

truquer, *vb.* fake.

trust, *n.m.* trust.

T.S.F., *n.f.* radio.

tu, *pron.* you.

tube, *n.m.* tube, pipe.

tuberculeux, *adj.* tuberculous.

tuberculose, *n.f.* tuberculosis.

tuer, *vb.* kill.

tuerie, *n.f.* slaughter, massacre.

tueur, *n.m.* killer.

tuile, *n.f.* tile.

tulipe, *n.f.* tulip.

tuméfier, *vb.* make swollen.

tumulte, *n.m.* tumult, turmoil, uproar.

tunique, *n.f.* tunic.

Tunisie, *n.f.* Tunisia.

Tunisien, *n.m.* Tunisian (person).

tunisien, *adj.* Tunisian.

tunnel, *n.f.* tunnel.

Turc *m.*, **Turque** *f. n.* Turk.
turc, *n.m.* Turkish (language).
turc *m.*, **turque** *f. adj.* Turkish.
Turquie, *n.f.* Turkey.
tutelle, *n.f.* tutelage, protection.
tuteur, *n.m.* guardian.
tutoyer, *vb.* address familiarly as "tu."

tuyau, *n.f.* pipe; hose.
tympan, *n.m.* eardrum.
type, *n.m.* type; fellow, guy.
typique, *adj.* typical.
tyran, *n.m.* tyrant.
tyrannie, *n.f.* tyranny.
tyranniser, *vb.* tyrannize.
tzigane, *n.m.f.* gypsy.

U

ubiquité, *n.f.* ubiquity.
ulcère, *n.m.* ulcer.
ultérieur, *adj.* ulterior, further.
ultime, *adj.* ultimate, last.
un *m.*, **une** *f.* **1.** *art.* a. **2.** *adj. and n.* one.
unanime, *adj.* unanimous.
unanimité, *n.f.* unanimity.
uni, *adj.* united; plain; even.
unifier, *vb.* unify.
uniforme, *adj. and n.m.* uniform.
union, *n.f.* union.
unique, *adj.* unique; only.
unir, *vb.* unite.
unisexuel, *adj.* unisex.
unisson, *n.m.* unison.
unité, *n.f.* unit, unity.
univers, *n.m.* universe.
universel, *adj.* universal.
université, *n.f.* university, college.
urbain, *adj.* urban.

urbanisme, *n.m.* city planning.
urgence, *n.f.* urgency, emergency.
urgent, *adj.* urgent, pressing.
urine, *n.f.* urine.
urne, *n.f.* urn; ballot box.
urticaire, *n.f.* hives.
usage, *n.m.* use; custom.
usager, *adj.* for daily use.
usé, *adj.* shabby, worn-out.
user, *vb.* wear out.
usine, *n.f.* factory.
ustensile, *n.f.* utensil.
usuel, *adj.* usual.
usure, *n.f.* wear and tear; usury; interest.
usurper, *vb.* usurp.
utile, *adj.* helpful, useful.
utilisation, *n.f.* use.
utiliser, *vb.* use.
utilité, *n.f.* utility.
utopie, *n.f.* utopia.

V

vacance, *n.f.* vacancy; *(pl.)* vacation.
vacarme, *n.m.* uproar.
vaccin, *n.m.* vaccine.
vacciner, *vb.* vaccinate.
vache, *n.f.* cow.
vaciller (-l-), *vb.* waver.
vacuité, *n.f.* emptiness, vacuity.
vagabond, *n.m.* vagrant.
vagabonder, *vb.* roam, tramp.
vagin, *n.m.* vagina.
vague, 1. *n.f.* wave. **2.** *adj.* vague.
vaguer, *vb.* wander.
vaillant, *adj.* valiant, brave, gallant.
vain, *adj.* idle; vain, futile.
vaincre, *vb.* defeat.
vainqueur, *n.m.* victor.

vaisseau, *n.m.* ship.
vaisselle, *n.f.* dishes.
valable, *adj.* valid; worthwhile.
valeur, *n.f.* valor; value, worth; *(pl.)* securities.
valeureux, *adj.* brave, valorous.
valide, *adj.* valid.
valise, *n.f.* suitcase.
vallée, *n.f.* valley.
vallon, *n.m.* valley, vale.
valoir, *vb.* be worth. **v. mieux,** be better.
valorisé, *adj.* valued.
valoriser, *vb.* add value to.
valse, *n.f.* waltz.
vandale, *n.m.f.* vandal.
vanille, *n.f.* vanilla.
vanité, *n.f.* conceit, vanity.

vaniteux, *adj.* vain.

vantard, *adj.* boastful.

vanter, *vb.* extol. **se v.**, boast, brag.

vapeur, 1. *n.m.* steamship. 2. *n.f.* vapor, steam.

vaporisateur, *n.f.* vaporizer, spray.

variation, *n.f.* variation, change.

varicelle, *n.f.* chicken pox.

varier, *vb.* vary.

variété, *n.f.* variety.

variole, *n.f.* smallpox.

vase, *n.m.* vase, jar, pot.

vasectomie, *n.f.* vasectomy.

vaseux, *adj.* slimy; hazy.

vassal, *n.m.* vassal.

vaste, *adj.* vast, spacious.

vaurien, *n.m.* worthless person, idler.

veau, *n.m.* calf.

vedette, *n.f.* (movie) star.

végéter, *vb.* vegetate.

véhicule, *n.m.* vehicle.

veille, *n.f.* eve, day before.

veiller, *vb.* watch over, sit up.

veine, *n.f.* vein; luck.

véliplanchiste, *n.m.f.* windsurfer.

vélo, *n.m.* bike.

vélomoteur, *n.m.* moped.

velours, *n.m.* velvet. **v. côtelé**, corduroy.

velouté, *adj.* like velvet.

velu, *adj.* hairy.

vendange, *n.f.* vintage.

vendeur, *n.m.* seller; clerk, salesman.

vendre, *vb.* sell.

vendredi, *n.m.* Friday.

vénéneux, *adj.* poisonous.

vénérer, *vb.* venerate.

vengeance, *n.f.* revenge.

venger, *vb.* avenge. **se v.**, get revenge.

venimeux, *adj.* poisonous.

venin, *n.m.* poison.

venir, *vb.* come. **v. de**, have just. **. . . à v.**, forthcoming.

vent, *n.m.* wind.

vente, *n.f.* sale.

venteux, *adj.* windy.

ventilateur, *n.m.* fan.

ventiler, *vb.* ventilate.

ventre, *n.m.* belly.

venue, *n.f.* advent, arrival.

vêpres, *n.f.pl.* vespers.

ver (-r), *n.m.* worm.

véracité, *n.f.* veracity.

véranda, *n.f.* porch.

verbe, *n.m.* verb.

verbeux, *adj.* wordy, verbose.

verdeur, *n.f.* greenness, sharpness; vigor.

verdict (-kt), *n.m.* verdict.

verdir, *vb.* make or become green.

verdure, *n.f.* greenery.

verge, *n.f.* rod.

verger, *n.m.* orchard.

verglas, *n.m.* sleet.

vérification, *n.f.* check.

vérifier, *vb.* check, confirm.

véritable, *adj.* genuine, real.

vérité, *n.f.* truth.

vermine, *n.f.* vermin.

vermouth, *n.m.* vermouth.

vernir, *vb.* varnish.

vernis, *n.m.* varnish.

vérole, *n.f.* **petite v.**, smallpox.

verre, *n.m.* glass.

verrou, *n.m.* bolt.

verrouiller, *vb.* bolt.

vers, 1. *n.m.* verse. 2. *prep.* toward.

verse, *adj.* **tomber à v.**, pour.

verser, *vb.* pour; shed.

versifier, *vb.* versify.

version, *n.f.* version, translation.

vert, *adj.* green.

vertèbre, *n.f.* vertebra.

vertical, *adj.* upright, vertical.

vertige, *n.m.* dizziness.

vertigineux, *adj.* dizzy.

vertu, *n.f.* virtue.

vertueux, *adj.* virtuous.

verveux, *adj.* lively, animated.

vessie, *n.f.* bladder.

veste, *n.f.* jacket.

vestiaire, *n.m.* cloak-room.

vestibule, *n.m.* hall, lobby.

vestige, *n.m.* vestige, remains.

veston, *n.m.* jacket, coat.

vêtement, *n.m.* garment; *(pl.)* clothes.

vétéran, *n.m.* veteran.

vétérinaire, *n.m.f.* veterinary.

vêtir, *vb.* clothe.

véto, *n.m.* veto.

veuf, *n.m.* widower.

veuve, *n.f.* widow.

vexation, *n.f.* vexation.

vexer, *vb.* vex.

viaduc, *n.m.* viaduct.

viande, *n.f.* meat.
vibrant, *adj.* vibrant, vibrating.
vibration, *n.f.* vibration.
vibrer, *vb.* vibrate.
vicaire, *n.m.* vicar.
vice, *n.m.* vice.
vice-roi, *n.m.* viceroy.
vicieux, *adj.* depraved, wrong.
vicomte, *n.m.* viscount.
victime, *n.f.* victim.
victoire, *n.f.* victory.
victorieux, *adj.* victorious.
victuailles, *n.f.pl.* provisions.
vidange, *n.f.* emptying, cleaning.
vide, 1. *n.m.* emptiness, vacuum, blank, gap. **2.** *adj.* empty, void, vacant, blank.
vidéocassette, *n.f.* videocassette.
vidéodisque, *n.m.* videodisc.
vider, *vb.* empty, drain.
vie, *n.f.* life.
vieil, *adj.* old.
vieillard, *n.m.* old man.
vieille, 1. *n.f.* old woman. **2.** *adj.f.* old.
vieillesse, *n.f.* old age.
vieillir, *vb.* age.
Vienne, *n.f.* Vienna.
vierge, *n.f.* virgin.
Viêt-nam, Vietnam, *n.m.* Vietnam.
Vietnamien, *(m.),* **Vietnamienne** *(f)* *n.* Vietnamese (person).
vietnamien, *n.m.* and *adj.* Vietnamese.
vieux, *adj.m.* old.
vif *m.,* **vive** *f.* *adj.* lively, quick, brisk, bright, vivacious.
vif-argent, *n.m.* quicksilver.
vigie, *n.f.* lookout man or station.
vigilance, *n.f.* vigilance.
vigilant, *adj.* watchful.
vigne, *n.f.* vine; vineyard.
vigneron, *n.m.* wine grower.
vignoble, *n.m.* vineyard.
vigoureux, *adj.* lusty, hardy, vigorous.
vigueur, *n.f.* vigor, force.
vil (-l), *adj.* vile.
vilain, *adj.* ugly, mean, wicked.
village (-l-), *n.m.* village.
ville (-l-), *n.f.* city, town.
villégiature (-l-), *n.f.* country holiday.

vin, *n.m.* wine.
vinaigre, *n.m.* vinegar.
vindicatif, *adj.* vindictive.
vingt (văn), *adj. and n.m.* twenty.
vingtaine (văn-), *n.f.* score; about twenty.
vingtième (văn-), *adj. and n.m.f.* twentieth.
viol, *n.m.* rape, violation.
violateur, *n.m.* violator.
violation, *n.f.* violation.
violemment, *adj.* violently.
violence, *n.f.* violence.
violent, *adj.* violent.
violer, *vb.* violate.
violet, *adj.* purple, violet.
violette, *n.f.* violet.
violon, *n.m.* violin.
violoncelle, *n.m.* cello.
vipère, *n.f.* viper.
virement, *n.m.* transfer.
virgule, *n.f.* comma.
viril (-l), *adj.* manly.
virilité, *n.f.* manhood.
virtuel, *adj.* virtual.
virtuose, *n.m.f.* virtuoso.
virus (-s), *n.m.* virus.
vis (-s), *n.f.* screw.
visa, *n.m.* visa.
visage, *n.m.* face.
vis-à-vis, *adv.* opposite, across from.
viser, *vb.* aim.
visibilité, *n.f.* visibility.
visible, *adj.* visible.
visière, *n.f.* visor; keenness.
vision, *n.f.* vision.
visionnaire, *adj. and n.m.f.* visionary.
visite, *n.f.* call, visit.
visiter, *vb.* visit.
visiteur, *n.m.* visitor.
visqueux, *adj.* viscous, sticky.
visser, *vb.* screw.
visuel, *adj.* visual.
vital, *adj.* vital.
vitalité, *n.f.* vitality.
vitamine, *n.f.* vitamin.
vite, *adv.* quick, fast.
vitesse, *n.f.* speed, rate; gear.
changer de v., shift gears.
viticole, *adj.* wine.
viticulteur, *n.m.* wine grower.
vitrail, *n.m.* (church) window.

vitre, *n.f.* pane.

vitrine, *n.f.* display case, shop window.

vitupération, *n.f.* vituperation.

vivace, *adj.* long-lived; perennial (of plant).

vivacité, *n.f.* vivacity.

vivant, *adj.* alive.

vivement, *adv.* quickly, smartly, vividly.

vivre, *vb.* live.

vocabulaire, *n.m.* vocabulary.

vocal, *adj.* vocal.

vocation, *n.f.* vocation.

vodka, *n.f.* vodka.

vœu (vœ), *n.m.* vow.

vogue, *n.f.* vogue.

voguer, *vb.* sail.

voici, *vb.* here is, behold.

voie, *n.f.* track, road. **v. d'eau,** leak.

voilà, *vb.* there is; behold.

voile, *n.m.* veil; sail.

voiler, *vb.* veil, hide.

voilure, *n.f.* sails.

voir, *vb.* see. **faire v.,** show.

voirie, *n.m.* dump; highway maintenance.

voisin, 1. *n.m.* neighbor. **2.** *adj.* nearby, adjoining.

voisinage, *n.m.* neighborhood.

voisiner, *vb.* act like a neighbor.

voiture, *n.f.* car; carriage. **en v.!,** all aboard!

voix, *n.f.* voice.

vol, *n.m.* flight; theft, robbery; rip-off.

volage, *adj.* fickle.

volaille, *n.f.* fowl, poultry.

volant, *n.m.* steering wheel.

volatil, *adj.* volatile.

volcan, *n.m.* volcano.

volcanique, *adj.* volcanic.

volée, *n.f.* flight, covey; herd.

voler, *vb.* fly; steal, rob; rip off.

volet, *n.m.* shutter, blind.

voleur, *n.m.* thief, robber.

vol frété, *n.m.* charter flight.

volontaire, 1. *n.m.f.* volunteer. **2.** *adj.* voluntary, volunteer.

volonté, *n.f.* will.

volontiers, *adv.* gladly, willingly.

voltigement, *n.m.* flutter.

voltiger, *vb.* flutter; hover.

volubilité, *n.f.* volubility, glibness.

volume, *n.m.* volume.

volumineux, *adj.* bulky.

volupté, *n.f.* pleasure, voluptuousness.

vomir, *vb.* vomit.

vorace, *adj.* voracious.

votant, *n.m.* voter.

vote, *n.m.* vote.

voter, *vb.* vote.

votre *sg.,* **vos** *pl. adj.* your.

vôtre, *pron.* **le v.,** yours.

vouer, *vb.* vow.

vouloir, *vb.* want, wish, will. **v. dire,** mean. **v. savoir,** wonder. **v. bien,** be willing. **en v. à,** bear a grudge against.

vous, *pron.* you, yourself.

voûte, *n.f.* vault.

voûter, *vb.* arch.

vouvoyer, *vb.* address politely as "vous."

voyage, *n.m.* journey, trip.

voyager, *vb.* travel.

voyageur, *n.m.* traveler, passenger.

voyageur de banlieue, *n.m.* commuter.

voyant, 1. *n.m.* clairvoyant. **2.** *adj.* gaudy, flashy.

voyelle, *n.f.* vowel.

vrai, *adj.* true, real.

vraisemblable, *adj.* probable, likely.

vraisemblance, *n.f.* probability.

vue, *n.f.* view, sight.

vue d'ensemble, *n.f.* overview.

vulcaniser, *vb.* vulcanize.

vulgaire, *adj.* vulgar, rude.

vulgariser, *vb.* popularize.

vulgarité, *n.f.* vulgarity.

vulnérable, *adj.* vulnerable.

W, X, Y, Z

wagon, *n.m.* coach, car.

wagon-lits, *n.m.* sleeping car.

wagon-restaurant, *n.m.* diner, dining-car.

walkman, *n.m.* (trademark) Walkman.

Wallon, *n.m. and adj.* Walloon.

watt, *n.m.* watt.

week-end, *n.m.* weekend.

whisky, *n.m.* whiskey.

xénophobe (ks-), *n.m.f. and adj.* xenophobic (person).

xérès (ks-), *n.m.* sherry.

xylophone (ks-), *n.m.* xylophone.

y, *adv.* there, in it, to it.

yacht, *n.m.* yacht.

yaourt, *n.m.* yogurt.

yoga, *n.m.* yoga.

Yougoslave, *n.m.f.* Yugoslav (person).

yougoslave, *adj.* Yugoslav.

Yougoslavie, *n.f.* Yugoslavia.

yuppie, *n.m.f.* yuppie.

zèbre, *n.m.* zebra.

zèle, *n.m.* zeal.

zélé, *adj.* zealous.

zénith, *n.m.* zenith.

zéro, *n.m.* zero.

zeste, *n.m.* peel, zest.

zézayer, *vb.* lisp.

zibeline, *n.f.* sable.

zigzaguer, *vb.* zigzag.

zinc, *n.m.* zinc; (bar) counter.

zodiaque, *n.m.* zodiac.

zone, *n.f.* zone, district; slum.

zoologie, *n.f.* zoology.

zoologique, *adj.* zoological. **jardin z.,** zoo.

A

a, *art.* un *m.*, une *f.*

aardvark, *n.* aardvark *m.*

aback, *adv.* déconcerté.

abacus, *n.* abaque *m.*

abandon, *vb.* abandonner.

abandon, *n.* abandon *m.*

abandoned, *adj.* abandonné.

abandonment, *n.* abandon *m.*

abase, *vb.* abaisser, avilir.

abasement, *n.* abaissement *m.*, avilissement *m.*

abash, *vb.* déconcerter.

abate, *vb.* diminuer.

abatement, *n.* diminution *f.*

abbess, *n.* abbesse *f.*

abbey, *n.* abbaye *f.*

abbot, *n.* abbé *m.*

abbreviate, *vb.* abréger.

abbreviation, *n.* abréviation *f.*

abdicate, *vb.* abdiquer.

abdication, *n.* abdication *f.*

abdomen, *n.* abdomen *m.*

abdominal, *adj.* abdominal.

abduct, *vb.* enlever.

abduction, *n.* enlèvement *m.*

abductor, *n.* ravisseur *m.*

aberrant, *adj.* aberrant, égaré.

aberration, *n.* égarement *m.*

abet, *vb.* aider, encourager, appuyer.

abetment, *n.* encouragement *m.*, appui *m.*

abettor, *n.* aide *m.*, complice *m.*

abeyance, *n.* suspension *f.*

abhor, *vb.* détester.

abhorrence, *n.* aversion extrême *f.*, horreur *f.*

abhorrent, *adj.* odieux, répugnant (à).

abide, *vb.* (tolerate) supporter; (remain) demeurer; **(a. by the law)** respecter la loi.

abiding, *adj.* constant, durable.

ability, *n.* talent *m.*

abject, *adj.* abject.

abjuration, *n.* abjuration *f.*

abjure, *vb.* abjurer, renoncer à.

abjurer, *n.* personne *(f.)* qui abjure.

ablative, *adj. and n.* ablatif *m.*

ablaze, *adj.* en feu, en flammes.

able, *adj.* capable; **(to be a.)** pouvoir.

able-bodied, *adj.* fort, robuste.

able-bodied seaman, *n.* marin (*m.*) de première classe.

ablution, *n.* ablution *f.*

ably, *adv.* capablement.

abnegate, *vb.* nier.

abnegation, *n.* abnégation *f.*

abnormal, *adj.* anormal.

abnormality, *n.* irrégularité *f.*

abnormally, *adv.* anormalement.

aboard, 1. *adv.* *(naut.)* à bord; **(all a.)** en voiture. **2.** *prep.* à bord de.

abode, *n.* demeure *f.*

abolish, *vb.* abolir.

abolishment, *n.* abolissement *m.*

abolition, *n.* abolition *f.*

abominable, *adj.* abominable.

abominate, *vb.* abominer.

abomination, *n.* abomination *f.*

aboriginal, *adj.* aborigène, primitif.

aborigines, *n.* aborigènes *m.pl.*

abort, *vb.* faire avorter.

abortion, *n.* avortement *m.*

abortive, *adj.* abortif, manqué.

abound, *vb.* abonder (en).

about, 1. *adv.* (approximately) à peu près; (around) autour; **(to be a. to)** être sur le point de. **2.** *prep.* (concerning) au sujet de; (near) auprès de; (around) autour de.

about-face, *n.* volte-face *f.*

above, 1. *adv.* au-dessus. **2.** *prep.* (higher than) au-dessus de; (more than) plus de.

aboveboard, 1. *adj.* ouvert, franc. **2.** *adv.* ouvertement, franchement.

abrasion, *n.* abrasion *f.*

abrasive, *adj.* abrasif.

abreast, *adv.* de front.

abridge, *vb.* abréger.

abridgment, *n.* abrégé *m.*, réduction *f.*

abroad, *adv.* à l'étranger.

abrogate, *vb.* abroger.

abrogation, *n.* abrogation *f.*

abrupt, *adj.* brusque; (steep) escarpé.

abruptly, *adv.* brusquement, subitement.

abruptness, *n.* brusquerie *f.*, précipitation *f.*

abscess, *n.* abcès *m.*

abscond, *vb.* disparaître, se dérober.

absence, *n.* absence *f.*

absent, *adj.* absent.

absentee, *n.* absent *m.*, manquant *m.*

absinthe, *n.* absinthe *f.*

absolute, *adj.* absolu.

absolutely, *adv.* absolument.

absoluteness, *n.* pouvoir absolu *m.*; arbitraire *m.*

absolution, *n.* absolution *f.*

absolutism, *n.* absolutisme *m.*

absolve, *vb.* absoudre.

absorb, *vb.* absorber.

absorbed, *adj.* absorbé, préoccupé.

absorbent, *n. and adj.* absorbant *m.*

absorbing, *adj.* absorbant, préoccupant.

absorption, *n.* absorption *f.*

abstain from, *vb.* s'abstenir de.

abstemious, *adj.* abstème.

abstinence, *n.* abstinence *f.*

abstract, 1. *n.* (book) extrait *m.* **2.** *adj.* abstrait.

abstracted, *adj.* détaché, pensif.

abstraction, *n.* abstraction *f.*

abstruse, *adj.* caché, abstrus.

absurd, *adj.* absurde.

absurdity, *n.* absurdité *f.*

absurdly, *adv.* absurdement.

abundance, *n.* abondance *f.*

abundant, *adj.* abondant.

abundantly, *adv.* abondamment.

abuse, 1. *n.* (misuse) abus *m.*; (insult) injures *f.pl.* **2.** *vb.* abuser de, injurier.

abusive, *adj.* (insulting) injurieux.

abusively, *adv.* abusivement, injurieusement.

abut, *vb.* s'embrancher (sur), aboutir (à).

abutment, *n.* contrefort *m.*; (of a bridge) culée *f.*

abysmal, *adj.* exécrable.

abyss, *n.* abîme *m.*

academic, *adj.* académique.

academic freedom, *n.* liberté (*f.*) de l'enseignement.

academy, *n.* académie *f.*

acanthus, *n.* acanthe *f.*

accede, *vb.* consentir.

accelerate, *vb.* accélérer.

acceleration, *n.* accélération *f.*

accelerator, *n.* accélérateur *m.*

accent, *n.* accent *m.*

accentuate, *vb.* accentuer.

accept, *vb.* accepter.

acceptability, *n.* acceptabilité *f.*

acceptable, *adj.* acceptable.

acceptably, *adv.* agréablement.

acceptance, *n.* acceptation *f.*

access, *n.* accès *m.*

accessible, *adj.* accessible.

accession, *n.* accession *f.*

accessory, *n. and adj.* accessoire *m.*

accident, *n.* accident *m.*

accidental, *adj.* accidentel.

accidentally, *adv.* accidentellement, par hasard.

acclaim, *vb.* acclamer.

acclamation, *n.* acclamation *f.*

acclimate, *vb.* acclimater.

acclivity, *n.* montée *f.*, rampe *f.*

accolade, *n.* accolade *f.*

accommodate, *vb.* (lodge) loger; (oblige) obliger.

accommodating, *adj.* accommodant, obligeant.

accommodation, *n.* (lodging) logement *m.*

accompaniment, *n.* accompagnement *m.*

accompanist, *n.* accompagnateur *m.*, accompagnatrice *f.*

accompany, *vb.* accompagner.

accomplice, *n.* complice *m.f.*

accomplish, *vb.* accomplir.

accomplished, *adj.* accompli, achevé.

accord, *n.* accord *m.*

accordance, *n.* conformité *f.*

accordingly, *adv.* (correspondingly) à l'avenant; (therefore) donc.

according to, *prep.* selon.

accordion, *n.* accordéon *m.*

accost, *vb.* aborder.

account, *n.* (*comm.*) compte *m.*; (narrative) récit *m.*

accountable for, *adj.* responsable de.

accountant, *n.* comptable *m.*

account for, *vb.* rendre compte de.

accounting, *n.* comptabilité *f.*

accouter, vb. habiller, équiper.

accouterments, n. équipements m.pl., accoutrements m.pl.

accredit, vb. accréditer.

accretion, n. accroissement m.

accrual, n. accroissement m.

accrue, vb. provenir.

accrued interest, n. intérêt (m.) cumulé.

accumulate, vb. entasser.

accumulation, n. entassement m.

accumulative, adj. (thing) qui s'accumule, (person) qui accumule.

accumulator, n. accumulateur m., accumulatrice f.

accuracy, n. précision f.

accurate, adj. précis.

accursed, adj. maudit, exécrable.

accusation, n. accusation f.

accusative, n. and adj. accusatif m.

accuse, vb. accuser.

accused, n. and adj. accusé m., accusée f.

accuser, n. accusateur m., accusatrice f.

accustom, vb. accoutumer.

accustomed, adj. accoutumé, habituel.

ace, n. as m.

acerbity, n. acerbité f., âpreté f.

acetate, n. acétate m.

acetic acid, n. acide (m.) acétique.

acetylene, n. acétylène m.

ache, 1. n. douleur f. 2. vb. faire mal à.

achieve, vb. accomplir.

achievement, n. accomplissement m.

acid, adj. and n. acide m.

acidify, vb. acidifier.

acidity, n. acidité f.

acidosis, n. acidose f.

acid test, n. épreuve (f.) concluante.

acidulous, adj. acidulé.

acknowledge, vb. reconnaître; (a. receipt of) accuser réception de.

acme, n. comble m., apogée m.

acne, n. acné f.

acolyte, n. acolyte m.

acorn, n. gland m.

acoustics, n. acoustique f.

acquaint, vb. informer (de); (be a.ed with) connaître.

acquaintance, n. connaissance f.

acquainted, adj. connu, familier (avec).

acquiesce in, vb. acquiescer à.

acquiescence, n. acquiescement m.

acquire, vb. acquérir.

acquirement, n. acquis m., acquisition f.

acquisition, n. acquisition f.

acquisitive, adj. porté à acquérir.

acquit, vb. acquitter.

acquittal, n. acquittement m.

acre, n. arpent m., acre f.

acreage, n. superficie f.

acrid, adj. âcre.

acrimonious, adj. acrimonieux.

acrimony, n. acrimonie f., aigreur f.

acrobat, n. acrobate m.f.

across, 1. prep. à travers; (on the other side of) de l'autre côté de. 2. adv. en travers.

acrostic, n. acrostiche m.

acrylic, n. acrylique m.

act, 1. n. acte m. 2. vb. (do) agir; (play) jouer; (behave) se conduire.

acting, 1. n. (theater) jeu m.; feinte f. 2. adj. (taking the place of) suppléant; (comm.) gérant.

actinism, n. actinisme m.

actinium, n. actinium m.

action, n. action f.

activate, vb. activer.

activation, n. activation f.

activator, n. activateur m.

active, adj. actif.

activity, n. activité f.

actor, n. acteur m.

actress, n. actrice f.

actual, adj. réel.

actuality, n. réalité f., actualité f.

actually, adv. réellement, véritablement, en effet.

actuary, n. actuaire m.

actuate, vb. mettre en action, animer.

acumen, n. finesse f., pénétration f.

acupuncture, n. acuponcture f.

acute, adj. (geom.) aigu m., aiguë f.; (mind) fin.

acutely, adv. vivement, d'une manière poignante.

acuteness, n. finesse f., vivacité f.

ad, n. annonce f.

adage, n. adage m., proverbe m.

adamant, *adj.* indomptable.

Adam's apple, *n.* pomme (*f.*) d'Adam.

adapt, *vb.* adapter.

adaptability, *n.* faculté (*f.*) d'adaptation.

adaptable, *adj.* adaptable.

adaptation, *n.* adaptation *f.*

adapter, *n.* qui adapte.

adaptive, *adj.* adaptable.

add, *vb.* (join) ajouter; (*arith.*) additionner.

adder, *n.* vipère *f.*

addict, *n.* toxicomane, *m.f.*

addicted, *adj.* adonné (à).

addition, *n.* addition *f.*

additional, *adj.* additionel.

additive, *n.* additif *m.*

addle, **1.** *vb.* corrompre, rendre couvi (of eggs). **2.** *adj.* couvi, pourri.

address, **1.** *n.* (on letters, etc.) adresse *f.*; (speech) discours *m.* **2.** *vb.* (a letter) adresser; (a person) adresser la parole à.

addressee, *n.* destinataire *m.f.*

adduce, *vb.* alléguer, avancer.

adenoid, *adj. and n.* adénoïde *f.*

adeptly, *adv.* habilement, adeptement.

adeptness, *n.* habileté *f.*

adequacy, *n.* suffisance *f.*

adequate, *adj.* suffisant.

adequately, *adv.* suffisamment, convenablement.

adhere, *vb.* adhérer.

adherence, *n.* adhérence *f.*, attachement *m.*

adherent, *n.* adhérent *m.*

adhesion, *n.* adhésion *f.*

adhesive, *adj.* adhésif.

adhesiveness, *n.* propriété d'adhérer *f.*

ad hoc, *adj.* improvisé.

adieu, *n. and adv.* adieu *m.*

adjacent, *adj.* adjacent.

adjective, *n.* adjectif *m.*

adjoin, *vb.* adjoindre, être contigu (à).

adjourn, *vb.* ajourner, *tr.*; s'ajourner, *intr.*

adjournment, *n.* ajournement *m.*

adjudicate, *vb.* juger.

adjunct, *n. and adj.* adjoint *m.*, accessoire *m.*

adjust, *vb.* ajuster, arranger, régler.

adjuster, *n.* ajusteur *m.*

adjustment, *n.* ajustement *m.*, accommodement *m.*

adjutant, *n.* capitaine (*m.*) adjudant major.

ad-lib, *vb.* improviser.

administer, *vb.* administrer.

administration, *n.* administration *f.*

administrative, *adj.* administratif.

administrator, *n.* administrateur *m.*

admirable, *adj.* admirable.

admirably, *adv.* admirablement.

admiral, *n.* amiral *m.*

admiralty, *n.* amirauté *f.*

admiration, *n.* admiration *f.*

admire, *vb.* admirer.

admirer, *n.* admirateur *m.*

admiringly, *adv.* avec admiration.

admissible, *adj.* admissible.

admission, *n.* (entrance) entrée *f.*; (confession) aveu *m.*

admit, *vb.* (let in) laisser entrer; (confess) avouer.

admittance, *n.* entrée *f.*

admittedly, *adv.* de l'aveu de tout le monde.

admixture, *n.* mélange *m.*

admonish, *vb.* réprimander.

admonition, *n.* admonition *f.*, avertissement *m.*

ad nauseam, *adv.* à n'en plus finir.

ado, *n.* fracas *m.*

adolescence, *n.* adolescence *f.*

adolescent, *adj. and n.* adolescent *m.f.*

adopt, *vb.* adopter.

adoption, *n.* adoption *f.*

adorable, *adj.* adorable.

adoration, *n.* adoration *f.*

adore, *vb.* adorer.

adorn, *vb.* orner.

adornment, *n.* ornement *m.*

adrenal glands, *n.pl.* capsules (*f.pl.*) surrénales.

adrenalin, *n.* adrénaline *f.*

Adriatic (Sea), *n.* Adriatique *f.*

adrift, *adv.* (*naut.*) à la dérive.

adroit, *adj.* adroit.

adulate, *vb.* aduler.

adulation, *n.* adulation *f.*

adult, *adj. and n.* adulte *m.f.*

adulterant, *n.* adultérant *m.*

adulterate, *vb.* adultérer; (of wines, milk, etc.) frelater.

adulterer, *n.* adultère *m.*

adulteress, *n.* femme adultère *f.*

adultery, *n.* adultère *m.*

advance, 1. *n.* (motion forward) avancement *m.;* (progress) progrès *m.;* (pay) avances *f.pl.;* (in a.) d'avance. **2.** *vb.* avancer.

advanced, *adj.* avancé.

advancement, *n.* avancement *m.,* progrès *m.*

advantage, *n.* avantage *m.*

advantageous, *adj.* avantageux.

advantageously, *adv.* avantageusement.

advent, *n.* venue *f.;* (eccles.) Avent *m.*

adventitious, *adj.* adventice, fortuit.

adventure, *n.* aventure *f.*

adventurer, *n.* aventurier *m.*

adventurous, *adj.* aventureux.

adventurously, *adv.* aventureusement.

adverb, *n.* adverbe *m.*

adverbial, *adj.* adverbial.

adversary, *n.* adversaire *m.*

adverse, *adj.* adverse.

adversely, *adv.* défavorablement, d'une manière hostile.

adversity, *n.* adversité *f.*

advert, *vb.* faire allusion (à).

advertise, *vb.* annoncer; (**a. a product**) faire de la réclame pour un produit.

advertisement, *n.* publicité *f.,* réclame *f.;* (in a paper) annonce *f.;* (on a wall) affiche *f.*

advertiser, *n.* annonceur *m.*

advertising, *n.* publicité *f.,* annonce (newspaper) *f.*

advice, *n.* conseil *m.;* (comm.) avis *m.*

advisability, *n.* convenance *f.,* utilité *f.*

advisable, *adj.* recommandable.

advisably, *adv.* convenablement.

advise, *vb.* conseiller.

advisedly, *adv.* de propos délibéré.

advisement, *n.* délibération.

advocacy, *n.* défense *f.,* plaidoyer *m.*

advocate, 1. *n.* (law) avocat *m.;*

(supporter) défenseur *m.* **2.** *vb.* appuyer.

aegis, *n.* égide *f.*

aerate, *vb.* aérer.

aeration, *n.* aération *f.*

aerial, *adj.* aérien.

aerially, *adv.* d'une manière aérienne.

aerie, *n.* aire *f.*

aerobics, *n.* aérobic *m.*

aerodynamic, *adj.* aérodynamique.

aerogram, *n.* aérogramme *m.*

aeronautics, *n.* aéronautique *f.*

aerosol, *n.* atomiseur *m.*

aerospace, *n.* aérospatial.

aesthetic, *adj.* esthétique.

afar, *adv.* loin, de loin.

affability, *n.* affabilité *f.*

affable, *adj.* affable.

affably, *adv.* affablement.

affair, *n.* affaire *f.*

affect, *vb.* (move) toucher; (concern) intéresser; (pretend) affecter.

affectation, *n.* affectation *f.*

affected, *adj.* maniéré.

affecting, *adj.* touchant, émouvant.

affection, *n.* affection *f.*

affectionate, *adj.* affectueux.

affectionately, *adv.* affectueusement.

afferent, *adj.* afférent.

affiance, *vb.* fiancer.

affidavit, *n.* attestation (sous serment) *f.*

affiliate, *vb.* affilier.

affiliation, *n.* affiliation *f.*

affinity, *n.* affinité *f.*

affirm, *vb.* affirmer.

affirmation, *n.* affirmation *f.*

affirmative, *adj.* affirmatif.

affirmatively, *adv.* affirmativement.

affix, *vb.* apposer.

afflict, *vb.* affliger (de).

affliction, *n.* affliction *f.*

affluence, *n.* affluence *f.,* opulence *f.*

affluent, *adj.* affluent, opulent.

afford, *vb.* (have the means to) avoir les moyens de.

affray, *n.* bagarre *f.,* tumulte *m.*

affront, 1. *n.* affront *m.* **2.** *vb.* insulter.

afield, adv. aux champs, en campagne; **(go far a.)** aller très loin.

afire, adv. en feu.

afloat, adv. à flot, en train.

aforementioned, adj. mentionné plus haut, susdit.

aforesaid, adj. susdit; ledit.

afraid, pred. adj. **(be afraid)** avoir peur.

afresh, adv. de nouveau.

Africa, n. Afrique f.

African, 1. n. Africain m. 2. adj. africain.

aft, adv. à l'arrière.

after, 1. adv. and prep. après. 2. conj. après que.

aftereffect, n. effet m.

aftermath, n. suites f. pl.

afternoon, n. après-midi m. or f.

aftershave, n. lotion après-rasage f.

afterthought, n. réflexion (f.) tardive.

afterward, adv. ensuite.

again, adv. de nouveau, encore; **(a. and a.)** maintes et maintes fois.

against, prep. contre.

agape, adv. bouche bée.

agate, n. agate f.

age, 1. n. âge m. 2. vb. vieillir.

aged, adj. vieux, âgé.

ageism, n. attitude (f.) discriminative basée sur l'âge.

ageless, adj. qui ne vieillit jamais.

agency, n. (comm.) agence f.

agenda, n. ordre du jour m.; agenda m.

agent, n. agent m.

agglutinate, vb. agglutiner.

agglutination, n. agglutination f.

aggrandize, vb. agrandir.

aggrandizement, n. agrandissement m.

aggravate, vb. (intensify) aggraver; (exasperate) exaspérer.

aggravation, n. aggravation f., agacement m.

aggregate, n. masse f.

aggregation, n. agrégation f., assemblage m.

aggression, n. agression f.

aggressive, adj. agressif.

aggressively, adv. agressivement.

aggressiveness, n. caractère (m.) agressif.

aggressor, n. agresseur m.

aggrieved, adj. affligé.

aghast, adj. consterné.

agile, adj. agile.

agility, n. agilité f.

agitate, vb. agiter.

agitation, n. agitation f.

agitator, n. agitateur m.

agnostic, n. and adj. agnostique m.

ago, adv. il y a (always precedes).

agonized, adj. torturé, déchirant.

agony, n. (anguish) angoisse f.; (death agony) agonie f.

agrarian, adj. agraire, agrarien.

agree, vb. être d'accord.

agreeable, adj. agréable.

agreeably, adv. agréablement.

agreement, n. accord m.

agriculture, n. agriculture f.

ahead, 1. adv. and interj. en avant. 2. prep. (a. of) en avant de.

aid, 1. n. aide f.; (first a.) premiers secours; (first-a.station) poste de secours. 2. vb. aider.

aide, n. aide m., assistant m.

AIDS, n. SIDA m.

ail, vb. intr. être souffrant.

ailing, adj. malade.

ailment, n. indisposition f.

aim, 1. n. (fig.) but m. 2. vb. viser.

aimless, adj. sans but.

aimlessly, adv. sans but, à la dérive.

air, 1. n. air m.; (a. force) aviation f.; (by a. mail) par avion; (in the open a.) en plein air. 2. vb. aérer.

airbag, n. (in automobiles) sac à air m.

air base, n. champ (m.) d'aviation.

airborne, adj. par voie de l'air.

air-condition, vb. climatiser.

air conditioner, n. climatiseur m.

air conditioning, n. climatisation f.

aircraft, n. avions m.pl.; (a. carrier) porte-avions m.

air gun, n. fusil à vent.

airing, n. aérage m., tour m.

airline, n. ligne (f.) aérienne.

airliner, n. avion m.

air mail, n. poste (f.) aérienne.

airplane, n. avion m.

air pollution, n. pollution (f.) de l'air.

airport, n. aéroport m.

air pressure, *n.* pression (*f.*) d'air.

air raid, *n.* raid (*m.*) aérien.

airsick, *adj.* **(to be a.)** avoir le mal d'air.

airtight, *adj.* imperméable à l'air, étanche.

air-traffic controller, *n.* aiguilleur (*m.*) du ciel.

airy, *adj.* **(well-aired)** aéré; **(light)** léger.

aisle, *n.* **(passageway)** passage *m.;* **(arch.)** bas côté *m.*

ajar, *adj.* entr'ouvert.

akin, *adj.* allié (à), parent (de).

alacrity, *n.* empressement *m.*

alarm, *n.* alarme *f.*

alarmist, *n.* alarmiste *m.*

alas, *interj.* hélas.

albeit, *conj.* bien que.

albino, *n.* albinos *m.*

album, *n.* album *m.*

alcohol, *n.* alcool *m.*

alcoholic, *adj.* alcoolique, alcoolisé.

alcove, *n.* **(recess)** niche *f.;* **(sleeping alcove)** alcôve *f.*

ale, *n.* bière *f.*

alert, *adj.* alerte.

alfalfa, *n.* luzerne *f.*

algebra, *n.* algèbre *f.*

Algeria, *n.* Algérie *f.*

algorithm, *n.* algorithme *m.*

alias, 1. *n.* nom d'emprunt *m.* **2.** *adv.* autrement nommé, dit.

alibi, *n.* alibi *m.*

alien, *adj.* étranger.

alienate, *vb.* aliéner.

alight, *vb.* **(descend)** descendre; **(stop after descent)** s'abattre.

align, *vb.* aligner.

alike, 1. *adj.* semblable; **(be a.)** se ressembler. **2.** *adv.* également.

alimentary canal, *n.* canal (*m.*) alimentaire.

alimony, *n.* pension (*f.*) alimentaire.

alive, *adj.* vivant.

alkali, *n.* alcali *m.*

alkaline, *adj.* alcalin.

all, 1. *adj.* tout *m.sg.,* toute *f.sg.,* tous *m.pl.,* toutes *f.pl.* **2.** *adv. and pron.* **(everything)** tout; **(above a.)** surtout; **(a. at once)** tout d'un coup; **(a. the same)** tout de même; **(that's a.)** c'est tout; **(not at a.)** pas du tout; **(everybody)** tous; **(a. of you)** vous tous.

allay, *vb.* apaiser.

allegation, *n.* allégation *f.*

allege, *vb.* alléguer.

allegiance, *n.* fidélité *f.*

allegory, *n.* allégorie *f.*

allergy, *n.* allergie *f.*

alleviate, *vb.* soulager.

alley, *n.* **(in town)** ruelle *f.;* **(blind a.)** cul-de-sac *m.*

alliance, *n.* alliance *f.*

allied, *adj.* allié.

alligator, *n.* alligator *m.*

all-night, *adj.* qui dure toute la nuit.

allocate, *vb.* assigner.

allot, *vb.* **(grant)** accorder; **(distribute)** répartir.

allotment, *n.* partage *m.,* lot *m.*

all-out, 1. *adj.* total. **2.** *adv.* à fond.

allow, *vb.* **(permit)** permettre; **(admit)** admettre; **(grant)** accorder; **(a. for)** tenir compte de.

allowance, *n.* **(money granted)** allocation *f.;* **(food)** ration *f.;* **(tolerance)** tolérance *f.;* **(pension)** rente *f.;* **(weekly a.)** semaine *f.*

alloy, *n.* alliage *m.*

all right, *adv.* très bien.

allude to, *vb.* faire allusion à.

allure, *vb.* séduire.

allusion, *n.* allusion *f.*

ally, 1. *n.* allié *m.* **2.** *vb.* allier.

almanac, *n.* almanach *m.*

almighty, *adj.* tout-puissant.

almond, *n.* amande *f.*

almost, *adv.* presque.

alms, *n.* aumône *f.*

aloft, *adv.* en haut.

alone, *adj.* seul; **(let a.)** laisser tranquille.

along, 1. *prep.* le long de. **2.** *adv.* **(come a.!)** venez donc!

alongside, *prep.* le long de.

aloof, 1. *adv.* à l'écart. **2.** *adj.* réservé.

aloud, *adv.* à haute voix.

alpaca, *n.* alpaga **(fabric)** *m.;* alpaca **(animal)** *m.*

alphabet, *n.* alphabet *m.*

alphabetical, *adj.* alphabétique.

alphabetize, *vb.* alphabétiser.

Alps, *n.pl.* Alpes *f.pl.*

already, *adv.* déjà.

also, adv. aussi.

altar, n. autel m.

alter, vb. changer.

alteration, n. modification f.

altercation, n. altercation f., dispute f.

alternate, 1. n. remplaçant m. **2.** adj. alternatif. **3.** vb. alterner.

alternative, n. alternative f.

alternator, n. alternateur m.

although, conj. bien que.

altitude, n. altitude f.

altogether, adv. tout à fait.

altruism, n. altruisme m.

alum, n. alun m.

aluminum, n. aluminium m.

Alzheimer's (disease), n. maladie (f.) d'Alzheimer.

always, adv. toujours.

amalgam, n. amalgame n.

amalgamate, vb. amalgamer; (computer) fusionner.

amass, vb. amasser.

amateur, n. amateur m.

amaze, vb. étonner.

amazement, n. stupeur f.

amazing, adj. étonnant.

ambassador, n. ambassadeur m., ambassadrice f.

amber, n. ambre m.

ambidextrous, adj. ambidextre.

ambiguity, n. ambiguïté f.

ambiguous, adj. ambigu m., ambiguë f.

ambition, n. ambition f.

ambitious, adj. ambitieux.

ambivalent, adj. ambigu, ambivalent.

amble, vb. errer.

ambulance, n. ambulance f.

ambulatory, adj. ambulatoire.

ambush, n. embuscade f.

ameliorate, vb. améliorer.

amenable, adj. responsable, soumis (à), sujet (à).

amend, vb. amender.

amendment, n. amendement m.

amenity, n. aménité f., agrément m.

America, n. Amérique f.; (North A.) A. du Nord; (South A.) A. du Sud.

American, 1. n. Américain m. **2.** adj. américain.

amethyst, n. améthyste f.

amiable, adj. aimable.

amicable, adj. amical.

amid, prep. au milieu de.

amidships, adv. par le travers.

amiss, adv. de travers.

amity, n. amitié f.

ammonia, n. ammoniaque f.

ammunition, n. munitions (f.pl.) de guerre.

amnesia, n. amnésie f.

amnesty, n. amnistie f.

amniocentesis, n. amniocentèse f.

amoeba, n. amibe f.

among, prep. parmi, entre.

amoral, adj. amoral.

amorous, adj. amoureux.

amorphous, adj. amorphe.

amortize, vb. amortir.

amount, 1. n. (sum) somme f.; (quantity) quantité f. **2.** vb. (a. to) (sum) se monter à; (summary) se réduire à.

amp, n. (colloquial) amp(ère) m.

ampere, n. ampère m.

amphibian, n. amphibie m.

amphibious, adj. amphibie.

amphitheater, n. amphithéâtre m.

ample, adj. ample.

amplify, vb. amplifier.

amplifier, n. amplificateur m.

amputate, vb. amputer.

amputee, n. amputé m.

amuse, vb. amuser.

amusement, n. amusement m.

an, art. un m., une f.

anachronism, n. anachronisme m.

analog, adj. analogique.

analogous, adj. analogue.

analogy, n. analogie f.

analysis, n. analyse f.

analyst, n. analyste m.f.

analytic, adj. analytique.

analyze, vb. analyser.

anarchy, n. anarchie f.

anathema, n. anathème m.

anatomy, n. anatomie f.

ancestor, n. ancêtre m.

ancestral, adj. d'ancêtres, héréditaire.

ancestry, n. aïeux, m.pl.

anchor, n. vb. ancrer. **2.** n. ancre f.

anchorperson, n. présentateur m., présentatrice f.

anchorage, n. mouillage m., ancrage m.

anchovy, n. anchois m.

ancient, adj. ancien m., ancienne f.

and, conj. et.

anecdote, n. anecdote f.

anemia, n. anémie f.

anesthetic, adj. and n. anesthésique m.

anesthetist, n. anesthésiste m.f.

anew, adv. de nouveau.

angel, n. ange m.

anger, n. colère f.

angle, 1. n. angle m.; **(at an a.)** en biais. **2.** vb. (fish) pêcher à la ligne.

Anglican, adj. and n. anglican.

angry, adj. fâché; **(to get a.)** se fâcher.

anguish, n. angoisse f.

angular, adj. anguleux.

aniline, n. aniline f.

animal, n. and adj. animal m.

animate, vb. animer.

animated, adj. animé.

animated cartoon, n. dessin animé m.

animation, n. animation f.

animosity, n. animosité f.

anise, n. anis m.

ankle, n. cheville f.

annals, n.pl. annales f.pl.

annex, n. (to a building) dépendance f.

annexation, n. annexion f.

annihilate, vb. anéantir.

anniversary, n. anniversaire m.

annotate, vb. annoter.

annotation, n. annotation f.

announce, vb. annoncer.

announcement, n. annonce f.

announcer, n. speaker m.

annoy, vb. (vex) contrarier; (bore) ennuyer.

annoyance, n. contrariété f.

annual, adj. annuel.

annuity, n. annuité f., rente annuelle f.

annul, vb. annuler.

anode, n. anode f.

anoint, vb. oindre.

anomalous, adj. anomal, irrégulier.

anonymous, adj. anonyme.

another, adj. and pron. un autre m., une autre f.; **(one a.)** l'un l'autre.

answer, 1. vb. répondre. **2.** n. réponse f.

answerable, adj. responsable (de), susceptible de réponse.

ant, n. fourmi f.

antacid, adj. antiacide.

antagonism, n. antagonisme m.

antagonist, n. antagoniste m.

antagonistic, adj. en opposition (à), hostile (à), opposé (à).

antagonize, vb. s'opposer à.

antarctic, adj. antarctique.

antecedent, adj. and n. antécédent m.

antedate, vb. antidater.

antelope, n. antilope f.

antenna, n. antenne f.

anterior, adj. antérieur.

anteroom, n. antichambre m. or f.

anthem, n. (national) hymne national m.

anthology, n. anthologie f.

anthracite, n. anthracite m.

anthrax, n. anthrax m.

anthropology, n. anthropologie f.

antiaircraft, adj. contre-avion, antiaérien.

antibiotic, n. antibiotique m.

antibody, n. anticorps m.

antic, n. bouffonerie f.

anticipate, vb. (advance) anticiper; (expect) s'attendre à; (foresee) prévoir.

anticipation, n. anticipation f.

anticlerical, adj. anticlérical.

anticlimax, n. anticlimax m.

antidote, n. antidote m.

antifreeze, n. antigel m.

antihistamine, n. antihistaminique m.

antimony, n. antimoine f.

antinuclear, adj. antinucléaire.

antipathy, n. antipathie f.

antiquated, adj. desuet, vieilli.

antique, n. antique m.; **(a. dealer)** antiquaire m.

antiquity, n. antiquité f.

anti-Semite, n. antisémite m.

anti-Semitic, adj. antisémite.

antiseptic, adj. and n. antiseptique m.

antisocial, adj. antisocial.

antithesis, n. antithèse f.

antitoxin, n. antitoxine f.

antler, n. andouiller m.

anus, *n.* anus *m.*

anvil, *n.* enclume *f.*

anxiety, *n.* anxiété *f.*

anxious, *adj.* inquiet *m.*, inquiète *f.*

any, **1.** *adj.* (in questions, for "some") du *m.sg.*, de la *f.sg.*, des *pl.*; (not . . . a.) ne . . . pas de; (no matter which) n'importe quel; (every) tout. **2.** *pron.* (**a. of it or them**, with verb) en.

anybody, *pron.* (somebody) quelqu'un; (somebody, implying negation) personne; (no matter who) n'importe qui.

anyhow, *adv.* en tout cas; d'une manière quelconque.

anyone, *pron. see* **anybody.**

anything, *pron.* (something) quelque chose; (something, implying negation) rien; (not . . . a.) ne . . . rien; (no matter what) n'importe quoi.

anyway, *adv. see* **anyhow.**

anywhere, *adv.* n'importe où.

apart, **1.** *adv.* à part. **2.** *prep.* (**a. from**) en dehors de.

apartheid, *n.* apartheid *m.*

apartment, *n.* appartement *m.*

apathetic, *adj.* apathique.

apathy, *n.* apathie *f.*

ape, **1.** *n.* singe *m.* **2.** *vb.* singer.

aperture, *n.* ouverture *f.*

apex, *n.* sommet *m.*

aphorism, *n.* aphorisme *m.*

aphrodisiac, *n. and adj.* aphrodisiaque.

apiary, *n.* rucher *m.*

apiece, *adv.* chacun.

apocalypse, *n.* apocalypse *f.*

apogee, *n.* apogée *m.*

apologetic, *adj. use verb* s'excuser.

apologist, *n.* apologiste *m.*

apologize for, *vb.* s'excuser de.

apology, *n.* excuses *f.pl.*

apoplectic, *adj.* apoplectique.

apoplexy, *n.* apoplexie *f.*

apostate, *n.* apostat *m.*

apostle, *n.* apôtre *m.*

apostolic, *adj.* apostolique.

apostrophe, *n.* apostrophe *f.*

appall, *vb.* épouvanter.

apparatus, *n.* appareil *m.*

apparel, *n.* habillement *m.*

apparent, *adj.* apparent.

apparition, *n.* apparition *f.*

appeal, **1.** *n.* appel *m.* **2.** *vb.* (**a. to**) en appeler à.

appear, *vb.* (become visible) apparaître; (seem) sembler.

appearance, *n.* (apparition) apparition *f.*; (semblance) apparence *f.*; (aspect) aspect *m.*

appease, *vb.* apaiser.

appeaser, *n.* personne qui apaise.

appellant, *n.* appelant *m.*

appellate, *adj.* d'appel.

append, *vb.* attacher; apposer; ajouter.

appendage, *n.* accessoire *m.*, apanage *m.*

appendectomy, *n.* appendéctomie *f.*

appendicitis, *n.* appendicite *f.*

appendix, *n.* appendice *f.*

appetite, *n.* appétit *m.*

appetizer, *n.* (drink) apéritif *m.*

appetizing, *adj.* appétissant.

applaud, *vb.* applaudir.

applause, *n.* applaudissements *m.pl.*

apple, *n.* pomme *f.*

applesauce, *n.* compote *(f.)* de pommes.

appliance, *n.* appareil *m.*

applicable, *adj.* applicable.

applicant, *n.* postulant *m.*

application, *n.* (request) demande *f.*

applied, *adj.* appliqué.

apply, *vb.* (**a. to somebody**) s'adresser à; (**a. for a job**) solliciter; (put on) appliquer; (**a. oneself**) s'appliquer.

appoint, *vb.* (**a. person**) nommer; (time, place) désigner.

appointment, *n.* (meeting) rendezvous *m.*; (**make an a. with**) donner un rendezvous à; (nomination) nomination *f.*

apportion, *vb.* répartir.

apposition, *n.* apposition *f.*

appraisal, *n.* évaluation *f.*

appraise, *vb.* priser.

appreciable, *adj.* appréciable.

appreciate, *vb.* apprécier.

appreciation, *n.* appréciation *f.*

apprehend, *vb.* saisir.

apprehension, *n.* (seizure) arresta-

tion *f.*; (understanding) compréhension *f.*; (fear) appréhension *f.*
apprehensive, *adj.* craintif.
apprentice, *n.* apprenti *m.*
apprenticeship, *n.* stage *m.*
apprise, *vb.* prévenir, informer.
approach, 1. *n.* approche *f.*; (make a.s to) faire des avances à. 2. *vb.* s'approcher.
approachable, *adj.* abordable, accessible.
approbation, *n.* approbation *f.*
appropriate, 1. *adj.* convenable. 2. *vb.* s'approprier.
appropriation, *n.* appropriation *f.*
approval, *n.* approbation *f.*
approve, *vb.* approuver.
approximate, 1. *adj.* approximatif. 2. *vb.* se rapprocher (de).
approximately, *adv.* approximativement, à peu près.
approximation, *n.* approximation *f.*
appurtenance, *n.* appartenance *f.*, dépendance *f.*
apricot, *n.* abricot *m.*
April, *n.* avril *m.*
apron, *n.* tablier *m.*
apropos, *adj.* à propos.
apse, *n.* abside *f.*
apt, *adj.* (likely to) sujet à; (suitable for) apte à; (appropriate) à propos; (clever) habile.
aptitude, *n.* aptitude *f.*
aqualung, *n.* scaphandre autonome *m.*
aquarium, *n.* aquarium *m.*
Aquarius, *n.* le Verseau.
aquatic, *adj.* aquatique.
aqueduct, *n.* aqueduc *m.*
aqueous, *adj.* aqueux.
aquiline, *adj.* aquilin.
Arab, 1. *n.* Arabe *m.f.* 2. *adj.* arabe.
Arabic, *adj. and n.* arabe *m.*
arable, *adj.* arable, labourable.
arbiter, *n.* arbitre *m.*
arbitrary, *adj.* arbitraire.
arbitrate, *vb.* arbitrer.
arbitration, *n.* arbitrage *m.*
arbitrator, *n.* arbitre *m.*
arbor, *n.* (bower) berceau *m.*
arboreal, *adj.* arboricole.
arc, *n.* arc *m.*
arcade, *n.* arcade *f.*

arch, 1. *n.* arc *m.*; (of bridge) arche *f.* 2. *adj.* espiègle.
archaeology, *n.* archéologie *f.*
archaic, *adj.* archaïque.
archbishop, *n.* archevêque *m.*
archdiocese, *n.* archidiocèse *m.*
archduke, *n.* archiduc *m.*
archenemy, *n.* ennemi (*m.*) de toujours.
archer, *n.* archer *m.*
archery, *n.* tir à l'arc *m.*
archetype, *n.* achétype *m.*, modèle *m.*
archipelago, *n.* archipel *m.*
architect, *n.* architecte *m.*
architectural, *adj.* architectural.
architecture, *n.* architecture *f.*
archives, *n.* archives *f.*
archway, *n.* voûte *f.*, passage (sous une voûte) *m.*
arctic, *adj.* arctique.
ardent, *adj.* ardent.
ardor, *n.* ardeur *f.*
arduous, *adj.* difficile.
area, *n.* (geom.) aire *f.*; (locality) région *f.*; (surface) surface *f.*
area code, *n.* indicatif (*m.*) interurbain.
arena, *n.* arène *f.*
Argentina, *n.* Argentine *f.*
argentine, *adj.* argentin.
argue, *vb.* (reason) argumenter; (indicate) prouver; (discuss) discuter.
argument, *n.* (reasoning) argument *m.*; (dispute) discussion *f.*
argumentative, *adj.* disposé à argumenter, raisonneur.
aria, *n.* air *m.*, chanson *f.*
arid, *adj.* aride.
arise, *vb.* (move upward) s'élever; (originate from) provenir de.
aristocracy, *n.* aristocratie *f.*
aristocrat, *n.* aristocrate *m.f.*
aristocratic, *adj.* aristocratique.
arithmetic, *n.* arithmétique *f.*
ark, *n.* arche *f.*
arm, 1. *n.* (limb) bras *m.*; (weapon) arme *f.* 2. *vb.* armer.
armament, *n.* armement *m.*
armchair, *n.* fauteuil *m.*
armed forces, *n.* forces armées *f.pl.*
armed robbery, *n.* vol (*m.*) à main armée.

armful, *n.* brassée *f.*

armhole, *n.* emmanchure *f.,* entournure *f.*

armistice, *n.* armistice *m.*

armor, *n.* armure *f.*

armory, *n.* (drill hall) salle *(f.)* d'exercice.

armpit, *n.* aisselle *f.*

armrest, *n.* accoudoir *m.*

arms, *n.* armes *f.pl.*

army, *n.* armée *f.*

arnica, *n.* arnica *f.*

aroma, *n.* arome *m.*

aromatic, *adj.* aromatique.

around, 1. *adv.* autour. **2.** *prep.* autour de.

arouse, *vb.* (stir) soulever; (awake) réveiller; (anger, passion) exciter.

arraign, *vb.* accuser, poursuivre en justice.

arrange, *vb.* arranger.

arrangement, *n.* arrangement *m.*

array, 1. *n.* (military) rangs *m.pl.;* (display) étalage *m.* **2.** *vb.* ranger.

arrear, *n.* arriéré *m.*

arrest, 1. *n.* (capture) arrestation *f.;* (military) arrêts *m.pl.;* (halt) arrêt *m.* **2.** *vb.* arrêter.

arrival, *n.* arrivée *f.*

arrive, *vb.* arriver.

arrogance, *n.* arrogance *f.*

arrogant, *adj.* arrogant.

arrogate, *vb.* usurper; **(a. to oneself)** s'arroger.

arrow, *n.* flèche *f.*

arrowhead, *n.* pointe *(f.)* de flèche; (plant) sagittaire *f.*

arsenal, *n.* arsenal *m.*

arsenic, *n.* arsenic *m.*

arson, *n.* crime d'incendie *m.*

art, *n.* art *m.;* **(fine a.s)** beaux-arts.

artefact, *n.* objet fabriqué *m.*

arterial, *adj.* artériel.

arteriosclerosis, *n.* artériosclérose *f.*

artery, *n.* artère *f.*

artesian well, *n.* puits artésien *m.*

artful, *adj.* (crafty) artificieux; (skillful) adroit.

arthritis, *n.* arthrite *f.*

artichoke, *n.* artichaut *m.*

article, *n.* article *m.*

articulate, *vb.* articuler.

articulation, *n.* articulation *f.*

artifice, *n.* artifice *m.*

artificial, *adj.* artificiel.

artificiality, *n.* nature artificielle *f.*

artillery, *n.* artillerie *f.*

artisan, *n.* artisan *m.*

artist, *n.* artiste *m.*

artistic, *adj.* artistique.

artistry, *n.* habileté *f.*

artless, *adj.* ingénu, naïf.

as, 1. *adv.* comme; **(as . . . as)** aussi . . . que; **(as much as)** autant que; **(such as)** tel que. **2.** *conj.* **(so . . . as)** de façon à; (while) pendant que; (since) puisque; (progress) à mesure que. **3.** *prep.* **(as to)** quant à.

asbestos, *n.* asbeste *m.*

ascend, *vb.* monter.

ascendancy, *n.* ascendant *m.*

ascendant, *adj.* ascendant, supérieur.

ascent, *n.* montée *f.;* (of a mountain) ascension *f.*

ascertain, *vb.* s'assurer (de).

ascetic, *n.* ascétique.

ascribe, *vb.* attribuer.

ash, *n.* cendre *f.;* (tree) frène *m.*

ashamed, *adj.* honteux; **(be a. of)** avoir honte de.

ashen, *adj.* cendré, gris pâle.

ashore, *adv.* à terre; **(go a.)** débarquer.

ashtray, *n.* cendrier *m.*

Ash Wednesday, *n.* mercredi *(m.)* des cendres.

Asia, *n.* Asie *f.*

Asian, 1. *n.* Asiatique *m.f.* **2.** *adj.* asiatique.

aside, *adv.* de côté.

ask, *vb.* demander à; (invite) inviter.

askance, *adv.* de travers, obliquement.

askew, *adv. and adj.* de travers.

asleep, *adj.* endormi.

asp, *n.* aspic *m.*

asparagus, *n.* asperges *f.pl.*

aspect, *n.* aspect *m.*

asperity, *n.* aspérité *f.,* rudesse *f.*

aspersion, *n.* aspersion *f.*

asphalt, *n.* asphalte *m.*

asphyxia, *n.* asphyxie *f.*

asphyxiate, *vb.* asphyxier.

aspirant, *n.* aspirant *m.*

aspirate, *vb.* aspirer.

aspiration, *n.* aspiration *f.*

aspirator, *n.* aspirateur *m.*

aspire, vb. aspirer.

aspirin, n. aspirine f.

ass, n. âne m., ânesse f.

assail, vb. assaillir.

assailable, adj. attaquable.

assailant, n. assaillant m.

assassin, n. assassin m.

assassinate, vb. assassiner.

assassination, n. assassinat m.

assault, n. assaut m.

assay, 1. n. essai m., vérification f., épreuve f. **2.** vb. essayer.

assemblage, n. assemblage m.

assemble, vb. assembler, tr.; s'assembler, intr.

assembly, n. assemblée f.

assent, 1. n. assentiment m. **2.** vb. consentir.

assert, vb. affirmer.

assertion, n. assertion f.

assertive, adj. assertif.

assertiveness, n. qualité d'être assertif.

assess, vb. (tax) taxer; (evaluate) évaluer.

assessor, n. assesseur m.

assets, n.pl. (comm.) actif m.; (property) biens m.pl.

asseverate, vb. affirmer solennellement.

asseveration, n. affirmation f.

assiduous, adj. assidu.

assiduously, adv. assidûment.

assign, vb. assigner.

assignable, adj. assignable, transférable.

assignation, n. assignation f., rendez-vous m.

assignment, n. (law) cession f.; (school) tâche f., devoir m.

assimilate, vb. assimiler, tr.; s'assimiler, intr.

assimilation, n. assimilation f.

assimilative, adj. assimilatif, assimilateur.

assistance, n. aide f.

assistant, n. aide m.f.

assist in, vb. aider à.

associate, vb. associer, tr.; s'associer, intr.

association, n. association f.

assonance, n. assonance f.

assort, vb. assortir.

assorted, adj. assorti.

assortment, n. assortiment m.

assuage, vb. adoucir, apaiser.

assume, vb. (take) prendre; (appropriate) s'arroger; (feign) simuler; (suppose) supposer.

assuming, adj. prétentieux, arrogant.

assumption, n. supposition f.; (eccles.) Assomption f.

assurance, n. assurance f.

assure, vb. assurer.

assured, adj. assuré.

assuredly, adv. assurément.

aster, n. aster m.

asterisk, n. astérisque m.

astern, adv. à l'arrière, de l'arrière.

asteroid, n. astéroïde m.

asthma, n. asthme m.

astigmatism, n. astigmatisme m.

astir, adj. agité, debout.

astonish, vb. étonner.

astonishment, n. étonnement m.

astound, vb. stupéfier.

astral, adj. astral.

astray, adj. égaré; (go a.) s'égarer.

astride, adv. à califourchon.

astringent, n. and adj. astringent m.

astrology, n. astrologie f.

astronaut, n. astronaute m.

astronomy, n. astronomie f.

astute, adj. fin.

asunder, adv. (apart) écartés; (to pieces) en morceaux.

asylum, n. asile m.

asymmetry, n. asymétrie f.

at, prep. (time, place, price) à; (someone's house, shop, etc.) chez.

ataxia, n. ataxie f.

atheist, n. athée m.f.

athlete, n. athlète m.f.

athletic, adj. athlétique.

athletics, n. sports m.pl.

athwart, adv. de travers.

Atlantic, adj. atlantique.

Atlantic Ocean, n. océan Atlantique m.

atlas, n. atlas m.

atmosphere, n. atmosphère f.

atmospheric, adj. atmosphérique.

atoll, n. atoll m.

atom, n. atome m.

atomic, adj. atomique.

atomic bomb, n. bombe atomique f.

atomic energy, *n.* énergie atomique *f.*

atomic theory, *n.* théorie atomique *f.*

atomic warfare, *n.* guerre atomique *f.*

atomic weight, *n.* poids atomique *m.*

atonal, *adj.* atonal.

atone for, *vb.* expier.

atonement, *n.* expiation *f.*

atrocious, *adj.* atroce.

atrocity, *n.* atrocité *f.*

atrophy, *n.* atrophie *f.*

atropine, *n.* atropine *f.*

attach, *vb.* attacher.

attaché, *n.* attaché *m.*

attaché case, *n.* mallette *f.*, attaché-case *m.*

attachment, *n.* attachement *m.*; (device) accessoire *m.*

attack, 1. *n.* attaque *f.* **2.** *vb.* attaquer.

attacker, *n.* agresseur *m.*

attain, *vb.* atteindre.

attainable, *adj.* qu'on peut atteindre.

attainment, *n.* (realization) réalisation *f.*; (knowledge) connaissance *f.*

attempt, *n.* tentative *f.*

attend, *vb.* (give heed to) faire attention à; (medical) soigner; (serve) servir; (meeting) assister à; (lectures) suivre; (see to) s'occuper de.

attendance, *n.* service *m.*; présence *f.*

attendant, *n.* serviteur *m.*; (retinue) suite *f.*

attention, *n.* attention *f.*; (pay a. to) faire attention à.

attentive, *adj.* attentif.

attentively, *adv.* attentivement.

attenuate, *vb.* atténuer.

attest, *vb.* attester.

attic, *n.* grenier *m.*

attire, 1. *n.* costume *m.* **2.** *vb.* parer, *tr.*; se parer, *intr.*

attitude, *n.* attitude *f.*

attorney, *n.* avoué *m.*

attract, *vb.* attirer.

attraction, *n.* attraction *f.*

attractive, *adj.* attrayant.

attributable, *adj.* attribuable, imputable.

attribute, 1. *n.* attribut *m.* **2.** *vb.* attribuer, imputer (à).

attrition, *n.* attrition *f.*; (war of a.) guerre (*f.*) d'usure.

attune, *vb.* accorder, mettre à l'unisson.

auburn, *adj.* châtain roux.

auction, *n.* vente (*f.*) aux enchères.

auctioneer, *n.* commissaire-priseur *m.*

audacious, *adj.* audacieux.

audacity, *n.* audace *f.*

audible, *adj.* intelligible.

audience, *n.* (listeners) auditoire *m.*; (interview) audience *f.*

audiovisual, *adj.* audiovisuel.

audiovisual aids, *n.* supports audiovisuels *m.pl.*

audit, 1. *vb.* vérifier (des comptes). **2.** *n.* vérification (des comptes) *f.*

audition, *n.* audition *f.*

auditor, *n.* vérificateur *m.*, censeur *m.*

auditorium, *n.* salle *f.*

auditory, *adj.* auditif.

auger, *n.* tarière *f.*

augment, *vb.* augmenter.

augur, *vb.* augurer.

August, *n.* août *m.*

aunt, *n.* tante *f.*

au pair, *n.* jeune fille (*f.*) au pair.

aura, *n.* atmosphère *f.*

auspice, *n.* auspice *m.*

auspicious, *adj.* de bon augure.

austere, *adj.* austère.

austerity, *n.* austérité *f.*

Australia, *n.* Australie *f.*

Australian, 1. *n.* Australien *m.* **2.** *adj.* australien.

Austria, *n.* Autriche *f.*

Austrian, 1. *n.* Autrichien *m.* **2.** *adj.* autrichien.

authentic, *adj.* authentique.

authenticate, *vb.* authentiquer, valider.

authenticity, *n.* authenticité *f.*

author, *n.* auteur *m.*

authoritarian, *adj.* autoritaire.

authoritative, *adj.* autoritaire.

authoritatively, *adv.* avec autorité, en maître.

authority, n. autorité f.
authorization, n. autorisation f.
authorize, vb. autoriser.
austistic, adj. autistique.
auto, n. auto f.
autobiography, n. autobiographie f.
autocracy, n. autocratie f.
autocrat, n. autocrate m.
autograph, 1. n. autographe m. **2.** vb. autographier.
autoimmune, adj. auto-immune.
automatic, adj. automatique.
automatically, adv. automatiquement.
automation, n. automatisation f.
automobile, n. automobile f.
automotive, adj. automoteur.
autonomously, adv. d'une manière autonome.
autonomy, n. autonomie f.
autopsy, n. autopsie f.
autumn, n. automne m.
auxiliary, adj. auxiliaire.
avail, vb. servir; **(be of no a.)** ne servir à rien.
available, adj. disponible.
avalanche, n. avalanche f.
avarice, n. avarice f.
avariciously, adv. avec avarice.
avenge, vb. venger.
avenger, n. vengeur m., vengeresse f.
avenue, n. avenue f.
average, 1. n. moyenne f. **2.** adj. moyen.
averse, adj. opposé.
aversion, n. aversion f.
avert, vb. détourner.
aviary, n. volière f.
aviation, n. aviation f.

aviator, n. aviateur m.
aviatrix, n. aviatrice f.
avid, adj. avide.
avocado, n. avocat m.
avocation, n. distraction f., profession f., métier m.
avoid, vb. éviter.
avoidable, adj. évitable.
avoidance, n. action d'éviter f.
avow, vb. avouer.
avowal, n. aveu m.
avowed, adj. avoué, confessé.
avowedly, adj. de son propre aveu, ouvertement.
await, vb. attendre.
awake, vb. éveiller, tr.; s'éveiller, intr.
awaken, vb. see awake.
award, 1. n. (prize) prix m.; (law) sentence f. **2.** vb. décerner.
aware, adj. **(be a.)** savoir; **(not to be a.)** ignorer.
awash, adj. dans l'eau.
away, adv. loin; **(go a.)** s'en aller; **(a. from)** absent de.
awe, n. crainte f.
awesome, adj. inspirant du respect.
awful, adj. affreux.
awhile, adv. pendant quelque temps.
awkward, adj. (clumsy) gauche; (embarrassing) embarrassant.
awning, n. tente f.
awry, adv. de travers.
ax, n. hache f.
axiom, n. axiome m.
axis, n. axe m.
axle, n. essieu m.
ayatollah, n. ayatollah m.
azure, 1. n. azur m. **2.** adj. azuré.

B

babble, vb. babiller.
babbler, n. babillard m.
babe, n. enfant m.f.
baboon, n. babouin m.
baby, n. bébé m.
babyish, adj. enfantin.
baby-sit, vb. garder les enfants.
baby-sitter, n. baby-sitter m.f.
bachelor, n. célibataire m.; **(B. of**

Arts/Science) licencié(e) ès lettres/ sciences.
bacillus, n. bacille m.
back, 1. n. dos m. **2.** vb. **(b. up, go b.)** reculer; (uphold) soutenir. **3.** adv. en arrière.
backache, n. mal de/aux reins m.
backbone, n. épine dorsale f.
backer, n. partisan m.

backfire, *vb.* (car) pétarader; (plans) mal tourner.

background, *n.* fond *m.*, arrière-plan *m.*

backhand, *adj.* donné avec le revers de la main.

backing, *n.* soutien *m.*

backlash, *n.* contrecoup *m.*, répercussion *f.*

backlog, *n.* réserve *f.*

back out, *vb.* se retirer.

backpack, *n.* sac à dos *m.*

backside, *n.* derrière *m.*

backstage, *adv.* dans les coulisses.

backup, (computer) **1.** *n.* sauvegarde *f.* **2.** *adj.* de sauvegarde.

backward, *adj.* en arrière.

backwardness, *n.* retard *m.*

backwards, *adv.* en arrière.

backwater, 1. *n.* eau stagnante *f.* **2.** *vb.* aller en arrière (dans l'eau).

backwoods, *n.* forêts vierges *f.pl.*

backyard, *n.* arrière-cour *f.*

bacon, *n.* porc (*m.*) salé et fumé, lard *m.*

bacteria, *n.* bactéries *f.pl.*

bacteriologist, *n.* bactériologue *m.f.*

bacteriology, *n.* bactériologie *f.*

bacterium, *n.* bactérie *f.*

bad, *adj.* mauvais; (wicked) méchant.

badge, *n.* insigne *m.*

badger, *vb.* ennuyer.

badly, *adv.* mal.

badness, *n.* mauvaise qualité *f.*; (wickedness) méchanceté *f.*

baffle, *vb.* déconcerter.

bafflement, *n.* confusion *f.*

bag, *n.* sac *m.*; (suitcase) valise *f.*

baggage, *n.* bagage *m.*

baggage cart, *n.* (airport) chariot *m.*

baggage claim, *n.* bulletin (*m.*) de bagage.

baggy, *adj.* bouffant.

bagpipe, *n.* cornemuse *f.*

Bahamas, *n.* les Bahamas *f.pl.*

bail, 1. *n.* (law) caution *f.* **2.** *vb.* (b. out water) vider (l'eau).

bailiff, *n.* huissier *m.*

bait, *n.* appât *m.*

bake, *vb.* faire cuire au four, *tr.*

baker, *n.* boulanger *m.*

bakery, *n.* boulangerie *f.*

baking, *n.* boulangerie *f.*

baking powder, *n.* levure *f.*

baking soda, *n.* bicarbonate (*m.*) de sodium.

balance, 1. *n.* (equilibrium) équilibre *m.*; (bank) solde *m.* (account, scales) balance *f.* **2.** *vb.* balancer, *tr.*

balance sheet, *n.* bilan *m.*

balcony, *n.* balcon *m.*; (theater) galerie *f.*

bald, *adj.* chauve.

baldness, *n.* calvitie *f.*; *(fig.)* sécheresse *f.*

bale, *n.* balle *f.*

balk, *vb.* frustrer.

balky, *adj.* regimbe.

ball, *n.* (games, bullet) balle *f.*; (round object) boule *f.*; (dance) bal *m.*

ballad, *n.* (song) romance *f.*; (poem) ballade *f.*

ball bearing, *n.* roulement (*m.*) à billes.

ballerina, *n.* ballerine *f.*

ballet, *n.* ballet *m.*

ballistic, *adj.* balistique; (b. missile) engin (*m.*) balistique.

balloon, *n.* ballon *m.*

ballot, *n.* scrutin *m.*; (b. box) urne *f.*

ballpoint pen, *n.* stylo (*m.*) à bille.

ballroom, *n.* salon de bal *m.*

balm, *n.* baume *m.*

balmy, *adj.* embaumé; doux.

balsa, *n.* balsa *f.*

balsam, *n.* baume *m.*

balustrade, *n.* balustrade *f.*

bamboo, *n.* bambou *m.*

ban, 1. *n.* ban *m.* **2.** *vb.* mettre au ban, *tr.*

banal, *adj.* banal.

banana, *n.* banane *f.*

band, *n.* bande *f.*; (music) orchestre *m.*

bandage, *n.* bandage *m.*

Band-Aid, *n.* pansement adhésif *m.*

bandanna, *n.* foulard *m.*

bandbox, *n.* carton (de modiste) *m.*

bandit, *n.* bandit *m.*

bandmaster, *n.* chef de musique *m.*

bandsman, *n.* musicien *m.*

bandstand, *n.* kiosque *m.*

bandwagon, *n.* (jump on the b.)

(fig.) monter dans le train en marche.

baneful, *adj.* pernicieux.

bang, 1. *n.* coup *m.;* **(b.s)** frange *f.* **2.** *vb.* frapper.

banish, *vb.* bannir.

banishment, *n.* bannissement *m.*

banister, *n.* rampe *f.*

banjo, *n.* banjo *m.*

bank, *n.* banque *f.;* (river) rive *f.*

bank account, *n.* compte *(m.)* en banque.

bankbook, *n.* livret de banque *m.*

banker, *n.* banquier *m.*

banking, *n.* banque *f.,* affaires de banque *f.pl.*

bank note, *n.* billet de banque *m.*

bankrupt, *adj. and n.* failli *m.*

bankruptcy, *n.* faillite *f.*

bank statement, *n.* relevé *(m.)* de compte.

banner, *n.* bannière *f.*

banquet, *n.* banquet *m.*

banter, 1. *n.* badinage *m.* **2.** *vb.* badiner, railler.

baptism, *n.* baptême *m.*

baptismal, *adj.* baptismal.

Baptist, *n.* Baptiste *m.*

baptistery, *n.* baptistère *m.*

baptize, *vb.* baptiser.

bar, *n.* (drinks) bar *m.;* (metal) barre *f.;* (law) barreau *m.*

barb, *n.* barbillon *m.*

barbarian, barbarous, *adj. and n.* barbare *m.f.*

barbarism, *n.* barbarie *f.; (gramm.)* barbarisme *m.*

barbecue, *n.* barbecue *m.*

barbed wire, *n.* fil *(m.)* de fer barbelé.

barbell, *n.* haltère *m.*

barber, *n.* coiffeur *m.*

barbiturate, *n.* barbiturique *m.*

bar code, *n.* code *(m.)* à barres.

bare, 1. *adj.* nu. **2.** *vb.* découvrir.

bareback, *adv.* à dos nu.

barefoot, *adv.* nu-pieds.

barely, *adv.* à peine.

bareness, *n.* nudité *f.*

bargain, 1 *n.* marché *m.* **2.** *vb.* marchander.

barge, *n.* chaland *m.*

barium, *n.* barium *m.*

bark, 1. *n.* (tree) écorce *f.;* (dog) aboiement *m.* **2.** *vb.* (dog) aboyer.

barley, *n.* orge *f.*

barmaid, *n.* serveuse *f.*

barman, *n.* barman *m.*

barn, *n.* (grain) grange *f.;* (livestock) étable *f.*

barnacle, *n.* (shellfish) anatife *m.;* (goose) barnache *f.*

barnyard, *n.* basse-cour *f.*

barometer, *n.* baromètre *m.*

barometric, *adj.* barométrique.

baron, *n.* baron *m.*

baroness, *n.* baronne *f.*

baronial, *adj.* baronnial, seigneurial.

baroque, *adj.* baroque.

barracks, *n.* caserne *f.*

barrage, *n.* barrage *m.*

barred, *adj.* barré, empêché, exclus, défendu.

barrel, *n.* tonneau *m.*

barren, *adj.* stérile.

barrenness, *n.* stérilité *f.*

barricade, *n.* barricade *f.*

barrier, *n.* barrière *f.*

barring, *prep.* sauf.

barroom, *n.* buvette *f.,* comptoir *m.,* bar *m.*

bartender, *n.* barman *m.*

barter, 1. *n.* troc *m.* **2.** *vb.* échanger, troquer.

base, 1. *n.* base *f.* **2.** *adj.* bas *m.,* basse *f.* **3.** *vb.* baser, fonder.

baseball, *n.* baseball *m.*

baseboard, *n.* moulure de base *f.*

basement, *n.* sous-sol *m.*

baseness, *n.* bassesse *f.*

bash, *vb.* frapper.

bashful, *adj.* timide.

bashfully, *adv.* timidement, modestement.

bashfulness, *n.* timidité *f.,* modestie *f.*

basic, *adj.* fondamental.

basil, *n.* basilic *m.*

basin, *n.* (wash) cuvette *f.;* (river) bassin *m.*

basis, *n.* base *f.*

bask, *se chauffer, intr.*

basket, *n.* (with handle) panier *m.;* (without handle) corbeille *f.*

basketball, *n.* basket(ball) *m.*

Basque, 1. *n.* Basque *m.f.* **2.** *adj.* basque.

bass, *n.* (music) basse *f.;* (fish) bar *m.*

bassinet, n. bercelonnette f.
bassoon, n. basson m.
bastard, n. bâtard m., (law) enfant naturel m.; (vulgar) salaud m.
baste, vb. (cooking) arroser; (sewing) faufiler.
bat, n. (animal) chauve-souris f.; (baseball) batte f.
batch, n. fournée f.
bate, vb. rabattre, diminuer.
bath, n. bain m.
bathe, vb. se baigner.
bather, n. baigneur m.
bathing, n. baignade f.
bathing cap, n. bonnet (m.) de bain.
bathing suit, n. maillot (m.) de bain.
bathrobe, n. peignoir (m.) de bain.
bathroom, n. salle (f.) de bain.
bathtub, n. baignoire f.
baton, n. bâton m.
battalion, n. bataillon m.
batter, n. (cooking) pâte f.
battery, n. (military) batterie f.; (electric) pile f.
battle, 1. n. bataille f. 2. vb. lutter.
battlefield, n. champ (m.) de bataille.
battleship, n. cuirassé m.
bauxite, n. bauxite f.
bawdy, adj. paillard.
bawl, vb. brailler.
bay, n. (geography) baie f.; (plant) laurier m.
bayonet, n. baïonnette f.
bazaar, n. bazar m.
be, vb. être.
beach, n. plage f.
beachhead, n. (haut de) plage f.
beacon, n. phare m.
bead, n. perle f.
beading, n. ornement de grains m.
beady, adj. comme un grain, couvert de grains.
beak, n. bec m.
beaker, n. gobelet m., coupe f.
beam, 1. n. (construction) poutre f.; (light) rayon m. 2. vb. rayonner.
beaming, adj. rayonnant.
bean, n. haricot m.
bear, 1. n. ours m.; (teddy b.) our-

son m. 2. vb. (carry) porter; (endure) supporter; (birth) enfanter.
bearable, adj. supportable.
beard, n. barbe f.
bearded, adj. barbu.
beardless, adj. imberbe.
bearer, n. porteur m.
bearing, n. (person) maintien m.; (machinery) coussinet m.; (naut.) relèvement m.
bearskin, n. peau (f.) d'ours.
beast, n. bête f.
beat, 1. vb. battre. 2. n. battement m.
beaten, adj. battu.
beatify, vb. béatifier.
beating, n. battement m., rossée f.
beau, n. galant m.
beautician, n. esthéticien(ne) m.(f.).
beautiful, adj. beau (bel) m., belle f.
beautifully, adv. admirablement.
beautify, vb. embellir.
beauty, n. beauté f.
beauty mark, n. grain (m.) de beauté.
beauty parlor, n. salon (m.) de beauté.
beaver, n. castor m.
becalm, vb. calmer, apaiser; (naut.) abriter.
because, conj. parce que.
beckon, vb. faire signe (à).
become, vb. devenir.
becoming, adj. convenable; (dress) seyant.
bed, n. lit m.
bedbug, n. punaise f.
bedclothes, n. couvertures f.pl.
bedding, n. literie f.
bedfellow, n. camarade de lit m.
bedizen, vb. parer, attifer.
bedlam, n. chahut m.
bedraggled, adj. débraillé.
bedridden, adj. alité.
bedrock, n. roche solide f.
bedroom, n. chambre (f.) à coucher.
bedside, n. bord du lit m.
bedspread, n. dessus (m.) de lit.
bedstead, n. bois de lit m.
bedtime, n. heure (f.) de se coucher.
bee, n. abeille f.

beef, n. bœuf m.

beefsteak, n. bifteck m.

beefy, adj. musclé, costaud.

beehive, n. ruche f.

beeper, n. récepteur (m.) de poche

beer, n. bière f.

beeswax, n. cire jaune f.

beet, n. betterave f.

beetle, n. scarabée m.

befall, vb. arriver (à).

befit, vb. convenir (à).

befitting, adj. convenable.

before, 1. adv. (place) en avant; (time) avant. **2.** prep. (place) devant; (time) avant. **3.** conj. avant que.

beforehand, adv. d'avance.

befriend, vb. aider; traiter en ami.

befuddle, vb. embrouiller, déconcerter.

beg, vb. (of beggar) mendier; (ask) prier.

beget, vb. engendrer, produire.

beggar, n. mendiant m.

beggarly, adj. chétif, misérable.

begin, vb. commencer.

beginner, n. commençant m.

beginning, n. commencement m.

begrudge, vb. envier, donner à contrecœur.

beguile, vb. tromper, séduire.

behalf, n. (on b. of) de la part de; (in b. of) en faveur de.

behave, vb. se conduire.

behavior, n. conduite f.

behead, vb. décapiter.

behind, 1. adv. and prep. derrière. **2.** n. derrière m.

behold, vb. voir. 2. interj. voici.

beige, adj. beige.

being, n. être m.

bejewel, vb. orner de bijoux.

belated, adj. attardé.

belch, vb. éructer, roter.

belfry, n. clocher m., beffroi m.

Belgian, 1. n. Belge m.f. **2.** adj. belge.

Belgium, n. Belgique f.

belie, vb. démentir.

belief, n. croyance f.; (confidence) confiance f.

believable, adj. croyable.

believe, vb. croire.

believer, n. croyant m.

belittle, vb. rabaisser.

bell, n. (house) sonnette f.; (church) cloche f.

bellboy, n. chasseur m.

bell buoy, n. bouée sonore f.

belligerence, n. belligérance f.

belligerent, adj. and n. belligérant m.

belligerently, adv. d'une manière belligérante.

bellow, vb. mugir.

bellows, n. soufflet m.

bell-tower, n. clocher m.

belly, n. ventre m.

belongings, n. effets m.pl., affaires f.pl.

belong to, vb. appartenir à.

beloved, adj. and n. chéri m.

below, 1. adv. en bas. **2.** prep. au-dessous de.

belt, n. ceinture f.

beltway, n. périphérique m.

bemused, adj. perplexe.

bemoan, vb. lamenter.

bench, n. banc m.

bend, vb. plier; (curve) courber, tr.

beneath, see below.

benediction, n. bénédiction f.

benefactor, n. bienfaiteur m.

benefactress, n. bienfaitrice f.

beneficent, adj. bienfaisant.

beneficial, adj. salutaire.

beneficiary, n. bénéficiaire m.

benefit, n. (favor) bienfait m.; (advantage) bénéfice m.

Benelux, n. Bénélux m.

benevolence, n. bienveillance f.

benevolent, adj. bienveillant.

benevolently, adv. bénévolement.

benign, adj. bénin m., bénigne f.

benignity, n. bénignité f.

bent, n. penchant m.

benzene, n. benzène m.

benzine, n. benzine f.

bequeath, vb. léguer.

bequest, n. legs m.

berate, vb. gronder.

bereave, vb. priver (de).

bereavement, n. privation f., perte f., deuil m.

beriberi, n. béribéri m.

Bermuda, n. Bermudes f.pl.

berry, n. baie f.

berserk, adj. fou m., folle f.

berth, n. couchette f.

beseech, vb. supplier.

beseechingly, *adv.* en suppliant.

beset, *vb.* attaquer, presser, assiéger.

beside, *prep.* à côté de.

besides, *adv.* en outre.

besiege, *vb.* assiéger.

besieged, *adj.* assiégé.

besieger, *n.* assiégeant *m.*

besmirch, *vb.* tacher, salir.

best, 1. *adj.* (le) meilleur. **2.** *adv.* (le) mieux.

bestial, *adj.* bestial.

bestir, *vb.* remuer.

best man, *n.* garçon d'honneur (at weddings) *m.*

bestow, *vb.* accorder.

bestowal, *n.* dispensation *f.*

best-seller, *n.* best-seller *m.*, succès de librairie.

bet, 1. *n.* pari *m.* **2.** *vb.* parier.

betake (oneself), *vb.* se rendre.

betray, *vb.* trahir.

betroth, *vb.* fiancer.

betrothal, *n.* fiançailles *f.pl.*

better, 1. *adj.* meilleur. **2.** *adv.* mieux.

between, *prep.* entre.

bevel, 1. *adj.* en biseau. **2.** *vb.* biaiser.

beverage, *n.* boisson *f.*

bevy, *n.* essaim *m.*

bewail, *vb.* lamenter, pleurer.

beware of, *vb.* prendre garde à.

bewilder, *vb.* égarer.

bewildered, *adj.* égaré, dérouté(e).

bewildering, *adj.* déconcertant.

bewilderment, *n.* égarement *m.*

bewitch, *vb.* ensorceler.

beyond, 1. *adv.* au delà. **2.** *prep.* au delà de.

biannual, *adj.* semestriel.

bias, *n.* (slant) biais *m.*; (prejudice) prévention *f.*

bib, *n.* bavette *f.*

Bible, *n.* Bible *f.*

biblical, *adj.* biblique.

bibliography, *n.* bibliographie *f.*

bicarbonate, *n.* bicarbonate *m.*

bicentennial, *n. and adj.* bicentenaire *m.*

biceps, *n.* biceps *m.*

bicker, *vb.* se quereller, se chamailler.

bicycle, 1 *n.* bicyclette *f.* **2.** *vb.* faire de la bicyclette.

bicyclist, *n.* cycliste *m.*

bid, 1. *n.* (auction) enchère *f.*; (bridge) appel *m.* **2.** *vb.* (order) ordonner; (invite) inviter; (auction) faire une offre.

bidder, *n.* enchérisseur *m.*

bide, *vb.* (live) demeurer; (wait) attendre.

biennial, *adj.* biennal.

bier, *n.* corbillard *m.*, civière *f.*

bifocal, 1. *adj.* bifocal. **2.** *n.* lunettes bifocales *f.pl.*

big, *adj.* grand.

bigamy, *n.* bigamie *f.*

big business, *n.* les grandes affaires *f.pl.*

bigot, *n.* bigot *m.*

bigotry, *n.* bigoterie *f.*

bike, *n.* vélo *m.*

bilateral, *adj.* bilatéral.

bile, *n.* bile *f.*

bilingual, *adj.* bilingue.

bilious, *adj.* bilieux.

bill, *n.* (restaurant) addition *f.*; (hotel, profession) note *f.*; (shop, public utility, etc.) facture *f.*; (money) billet *(m.)* de banque; (poster) affiche *f.*; (politics) projet *(m.)* de loi; **(b. of fare)** carte *(f.)* du jour; (bird) bec *m.*

billboard, *n.* panneau *(m.)* d'affichage.

billet, *n.* (mil.) billet de logement *m.*

billfold, *n.* portefeuille *m.*

billiard balls, *n.* billes *f.pl.*

billiards, *n.* billard *m.*

billion, *n.* (U.S.) milliard *m.*, (Britain) billion *m.*

bill of health, *n.* patente *(f.)* de santé.

bill of lading, *n.* connaissement *m.*

bill of sale, *n.* lettre de vente *f.*, acte *(m.)* de propriété.

billow, *n.* grande vague *f.*, lame *f.*

billy-goat, *n.* bouc *m.*

bimetallic, *adj.* bimétallique.

bimonthly, *adj. and adv.* bimensuel.

bin, *n.* coffre *m.*

bind, *vb.* lier; (books) relier.

bindery, *n.* atelier de reliure *m.*

binding, 1. *n.* (book) reliure *f.* **2.** *adj.* obligatoire.

binoculars, *n.* jumelles *f.pl.*

biochemistry, n. biochimie f.

biodegradable, adj. sujet à la putréfaction.

biofeedback, n. biofeedback m., information (f.) reçue par un organisme pendant un processus biologique.

biographer, n. biographe m.

biographical, adj. biographique.

biography, n. biographie f.

biological, adj. biologique.

biologically, adv. biologiquement.

biology, n. biologie f.

biorhythm, n. biorythme m.

bipartisan, adj. représentant les deux partis.

biped, n. bipède m.

birch, n. bouleau m.

bird, n. oiseau m.

birdlike, adj. comme un oiseau.

bird of prey, n. oiseau de proie m.

bird's-eye view, n. vue (f.) à vol d'oiseau.

birth, n. naissance f.

birth certificate, n. acte (m.) de naissance.

birth control, n. contrôle (m.) des naissances.

birthday, n. anniversaire (m.) de naissance, fête f.

birthmark, n. tache (f.) de naissance.

birthplace, n. lieu (m.) de naissance.

birth rate, n. natalité f.

birthright, n. droit (m.) d'aînesse.

biscuit, n. (hard) biscuit m.; (soft) petit pain (m.) au lait.

bisect, vb. couper en deux.

bisexual, adj. bis(s)exuel.

bishop, n. évêque m.

bishopric, n. évêché m.

bismuth, n. bismuth m.

bison, n. bison m.

bit, n. (piece) morceau m.; (a b. of) un peu (de); (harness) mors m.; (computer) unité unique d'information f.

bitch, n. chienne f.; (vulgar) garce f., salope f.

bite, 1. n. morsure f. **2.** vb. mordre.

biting, adj. mordant.

bitter, adj. amer.

bitterly, adv. amèrement, avec amertume.

bitterness, n. amertume f.

bivouac, n. bivouac m.

biweekly, adj. and adv. tous les quinze jours.

blab, vb. jaser.

black, adj. noir.

Black, n. and adj. (for person) noir m.; noire f.

blackberry n. mûre (f.) de ronce.

blackbird, n. merle m.

blackboard, n. tableau (m.) noir.

black currant, n. cassis m.

blacken, vb. noircir.

black eye, n. œil poché m.

blackguard, n. gredin m., polisson m., salaud m.

blackmail, 1. n. chantage m. **2.** vb. faire chanter.

black market, n. marché noir m.

blackout, n. panne (f.) d'électricité; (med.) syncope f.

blacksmith, n. forgeron m.

bladder, n. vessie f.

blade, n. (sword, knife) lame f.; (grass) brin m.

blame, 1. n. blâme m. **2.** vb. blâmer.

blameless, adj. innocent, sans tache.

blanch, vb. blanchir, pâlir.

bland, adj. doux m., douce f.; (insipid) fade.

blank, 1. n. (space) blanc m.; (void) vide m.; (printing) tiret m. **2.** adj. (page) blanc m., blanche f.; (empty) vide.

blanket, n. couverture f.

blare, 1. n. son (de la trompette) m.; rugissement m. **2.** vb. retentir, intr.

blaspheme, vb. blasphémer.

blasphemer, n. blasphémateur m.

blasphemous, adj. blasphématoire.

blasphemy, n. blasphème m.

blast, n. (wind) rafale f.; (mine) explosion f.

blatant, adj. criard, bruyant.

blaze, 1. n. flambée f. **2.** vb. flamber.

blazer, n. blazer m.

blazing, adj. enflammé, flamboyant.

bleach, vb. décolorer, tr.

bleak, adj. morne.

bleakness, n. froideur f.

bleat, vb. bêler.

bleed, vb. saigner.

blemish, n. défaut m.

blend, 1. n. mélange m. **2.** vb. mêler, tr.

blended, adj. mélangé.

blender, n. mixeur m., mixer m.

bless, vb. bénir.

blessed, adj. béni.

blessing, n. bénédiction f.

blight, 1. vb. flétrir, détruire, nieller, brouir. **2.** n. brouissure f., flétrissure f.

blind, 1. n. store m. **2.** adj. aveugle; **(b. alley)** cul-de-sac m.

blindfold, adj. and adv. les yeux bandés.

blinding, adj. aveuglant.

blindly, adv. aveuglément.

blindness, n. cécité f.

blink, vb. clignoter.

bliss, n. béatitude f.

blissful, adj. bienheureux.

blissfully, adv. heureusement.

blister, n. ampoule f.

blithe, adj. gai, joyeux.

blizzard, n. tempête (f.) de neige.

bloat, vb. boursoufler.

bloated, adj. gonflé.

bloc, n. bloc m.

block, 1. n. bloc m.; (houses) pâté m. **2.** vb. bloquer.

blockade, n. blocus m.

blond, adj. and adv. blond m.

blood, n. sang m.

blood-curdling, adj. à tourner le sang.

bloodhound, n. limier m.

bloodless, adj. exsangue, sans effusion de sang.

blood plasma, n. plasma (m.) du sang.

blood poisoning, n. empoisonnement (m.) du sang.

blood pressure, n. tension artérielle f.

bloodshed, n. effusion (f.) de sang.

bloodshot, adj. injecté de sang.

bloodthirsty, adj. sanguinaire.

bloody, adj. sanglant.

bloom, n. fleur f. **2.** vb. fleurir.

blooming, 1. n. floraison f. **2.** adj. fleurissant.

blossom, see bloom.

blot, 1. n. tache f. **2.** vb. (spot) tacher; (dry ink) sécher l'encre.

blotch, n. tache f.

blotchy, adj. couvert de taches.

blotter, n. buvard m.

blouse, n. blouse f.

blow, 1. n. coup m. **2.** vb. souffler; **(b. out)** éteindre; **(b. over)** passer; **(b. up)** faire sauter, tr.

blowout, n. éclatement (m.) de pneu.

blowtorch, n. chalumeau m.

blubber, 1. vb. pleurer comme un veau. **2.** n. graisse de baleine f.

bludgeon, 1. n. matraque f. **2.** vb. donner des coups de matraque.

blue, adj. bleu; **(have the b.s)** avoir le cafard.

blue jeans, n. blue jeans m.pl.

blueprint, n. dessin négatif m.

bluff, n. bluff m.

bluffer, n. bluffeur m.

blunder, n. bévue f.

blunderer, n. maladroit m.

blunt, adj. (blade) émoussé; (person) brusque.

bluntly, adv. brusquement.

bluntness, n. brusquerie f.

blur, vb. (smear) barbouiller.

blurb, n. résumé (m.) publicitaire.

blurt, vb. **(b. out)** lâcher, dire.

blush, 1. n. rougeur f. **2.** vb. rougir.

bluster, n. fanfaronnade f.

boar, n. (wild) sanglier m.

board, 1. n. (plank) planche f.; (daily meals) pension f.; (boat) bord m.; (politics) ministère m.; (administration) conseil m.

boarder, n. pensionnaire m.f.

boarding house, n. pension f.

boarding pass, n. carte (f.) d'embarquement.

boarding school, n. internat m., pensionnat m.

boast (of), vb. se vanter (de).

boaster, n. vantard m.

boastful, adj. vantard.

boastfulness, n. vantardise f.

boat, n. bateau m.

boathouse, n. abri (m.) à bateaux.

boatswain, n. maître d'équipage m.

bob, vb. (hair) couper court.

bobbin, n. bobine f.

bode, vb. présager.
bodice, n. corsage m.
bodily, adj. corporel.
body, n. corps m.
bodyguard, n. garde (f.) du corps.
bog, 1. n. marécage m. 2. vb. embourber.
bogus, adj. bidon.
Bohemia, n. (geographical) Bohème f.; (fig.) bohème f.
Bohemian, 1. n. (geographical) Bohémien m.; (fig.) bohème m.f. 2. adj. (geographical) bohémien; (fig.) bohème.
boil, 1. vb. bouillir, intr.; faire bouillir, tr. 2. n. (med.) furoncle m., clou m.
boiler, n. chaudière f.
boisterous, adj. (person) bruyant.
boisterously, adv. bruyamment.
bold, adj. hardi.
boldface, adj. (type) caractères gras m.pl.
boldly, adv. hardiment, avec audace.
boldness, n. hardiesse f.
Bolivia, n. Bolivie f.
bologna, n. saucisson (m.) de Bologne.
bolster, n. traversin m.
bolster up, vb. soutenir.
bolt, 1. n. verrou m. 2. vb. verrouiller.
bomb, n. bombe f.
bombard, vb. bombarder.
bombardier, n. bombardier m.
bombardment, n. bombardement m.
bombastic, adj. pompeux.
bomber, n. avion (m.) de bombardement; bombardier m.
bombproof, adj. à l'épreuve des bombes.
bombshell, n. bombe f.
bombsight, n. viseur (m.) de lancement.
bona fide, adj. véritable.
bonbon, n. bonbon m.
bond, n. lien m.; (law, finance) obligation f.
bondage, n. servitude f.
bonded, adj. entreposé.
bone, n. os m.
boneless, adj. sans os.
bonfire, n. feu (m.) de joie.

bonnet, n. chapeau m.
bonus, n. gratification f.
bony, adj. osseux.
boo, vb. huer.
book, 1. n. livre m. 2. vb. (ticket) prendre, (space) réserver.
bookbindery, n. atelier (m.) de reliure.
bookcase, n. bibliothèque f.
bookkeeper, n. teneur (m.) de livres.
bookkeeping, n. comptabilité f.
booklet, n. opuscule m., brochure f.
bookseller, n. libraire m.; (secondhand) bouquiniste m.
bookstore, bookshop, n. librairie f.
boom, 1. n. grondement m.; (in numbers) forte augmentation. 2. vb. gronder; prospérer.
boon, n. bienfait m., don m.
boor, n. rustre m.
boorish, adj. rustre.
boost, vb. (push) pousser; (praise) louer.
boot, 1. n. bottine f., botte f. 2. vb. initialiser.
bootblack, n. cireur m.
booth, n. (fair) baraque f.; (telephone) cabine f.
booty, n. butin m.
booze, n. boissons (f.pl.) alcooliques.
border, n. bord m.; (of country) frontière f.
borderline, adj. touchant (à), avoisinant.
bore, vb. (make a hole) forer; (annoy) ennuyer.
boredom, n. ennui m.
boric acid, n. acide borique m.
boring, adj. ennuyeux.
born, 1. adj. né. 2. vb. (be b.) naître.
born-again, adj. rené.
borough, n. (administration) circonscription électorale f.; (large village) bourg m.
borrower, n. emprunteur m.
borrow from, vb. emprunter à.
Bosnia, n. Bosnie f.
bosom, n. sein m.
boss, 1. n. patron m. 2. vb. diriger.
bossy, adj. comme un patron, impérieux.

botanical, *adj.* botanique.
botany, *n.* botanique *f.*
botch, 1. *n.* ravaudage *m.* **2.** *vb.* ravauder, faire une mauvaise besogne.
both, *adj. and pron.* tous (les) deux *m.,* toutes (les) deux *f.*
bother, 1. *n.* ennui *m.* **2.** *vb.* gêner.
bothersome, *adj.* gênant.
bottle, *n.* bouteille *f.*
bottleneck, *n.* (traffic) bouchon.
bottom, *n.* fond *m.*
bottomless, *adj.* sans fond.
bough, *n.* branche *f.*
bouillon, *n.* bouillon *m.*
boulder, *n.* galet *m.*
boulevard, *n.* boulevard *m.*
bounce, *vb.* (ball) rebondir.
bound, 1. *n.* (limit) borne *f.;* (jump) bond *m.* **2.** *vb.* (limit) borner; (jump) bondir.
boundary, *n.* frontière *f.*
bound for, *adj.* en route pour.
boundless, *adj.* sans bornes, illimité.
boundlessly, *adv.* sans bornes.
bounteous, *adj.* généreux, bienfaisant.
bounty, *n.* largesse *f.;* (premium) prime *f.*
bouquet, *n.* bouquet *m.*
bourgeois, *adj.* bourgeois.
bout, *n.* (fever) accès *m.*
bovine, *n.* bovine *f.; adj.* bovin.
bow, *n.* (weapon) arc *m.;* (violin) archet *m.;* (curtsy) révérence *f.;* (ship) avant *m.*
bow, *vb.* incliner, *tr.*
bowels, *n.* entrailles *f.pl.*
bowl, 1. *n.* bol *m.* **2.** *vb.* jouer aux boules.
bowlegged, *adj.* à jambes arquées.
bowler, *n.* joueur (*m.*) de boule.
bowling, *n.* jeu (*m.*) de boules.
box, 1. *n.* boîte *f.;* (theater) loge *f.* **2.** *vb.* boxer.
boxcar, *n.* wagon (*m.*) de marchandises.
boxer, *n.* boxeur *m.*
boxing, *n.* boxe *f.*
box office, *n.* bureau (*m.*) de location.
boy, *n.* garçon *m.*
boycott, *vb.* boycotter.
boyfriend, *n.* (petit) ami *m.*

boyhood, *n.* première jeunesse *f.*
boyish, *adj.* enfantin, puéril.
boyishly, *adv.* comme un gamin.
bra, *n.* soutien-gorge *m.*
brace, 1. *vb.* fortifier. **2.** *n.* vilebrequin (tool) *m.,* paire *f.,* couple *m.*
bracelet, *n.* bracelet *m.*
bracket, *n.* (wall) console *f.;* (printing) crochet *m.*
brag, *vb.* se vanter.
braggart, *n.* fanfaron *m.*
braid, *n.* (hair) tresse *f.;* (sewing) galon *m.*
Braille, *n.* braille *m.*
brain, *n.* cerveau *m.;* **(b.s)** cervelle *f.*
brainwash, *vb.* faire un lavage de cerveau à.
brainy, *adj.* intelligent.
brake, *n.* frein *m.*
bramble, *n.* ronce *f.*
bran, *n.* son *m.*
branch, *n.* branche *f.*
brand, *n.* marque *f.*
brandish, *vb.* brandir.
brand-new, *adj.* tout neuf.
brandy, *n.* eau-de-vie *f.*
brash, *adj.* impertinent.
brass, *n.* cuivre *m.;* (color) jaune.
brassiere, *n.* soutien-gorge *m.*
brat, *n.* gosse *m.f.*
bravado, *n.* bravade *f.*
brave, *adj.* courageux.
bravery, *n.* courage *m.*
brawl, *n.* rixe *f.*
brawn, *n.* partie charnue *f.,* muscles *m.pl.*
bray, *vb.* braire.
brazen, *adj.* (person) effronté.
Brazil, *n.* Brésil *m.*
breach, *n.* infraction *f.;* (mil.) brèche *f.*
bread, *n.* pain *m.*
breadcrumbs, *n.* chapelure *f.*
breadth, *n.* largeur *f.*
breadwinner, *n.* soutien (*m.*) de la famille.
break, 1. *n.* rupture *f.;* (pause) interruption *f.;* (rest) pause *f.* **2.** *vb.* rompre, briser, casser.
breakable, *adj.* cassable.
breakage, *n.* cassure *f.,* rupture *f.*
breakdown, *n.* panne *f.;* dépression *f.;* analyse *f.*

breakfast, *n.* (petit) déjeuner *m.*

breakwater, *n.* brise-lames *m.*, jetée *f.*

breast, *n.* poitrine *f.*, sein *m.*

breath, *n.* haleine *f.*; *(fig., wind)* souffle *m.*

Breathalyzer, *n.* alcootest *m.*

breathe, *vb.* respirer.

breathless, *adj.* (out of breath) essoufflé.

breathlessly, *adv.* hors d'haleine.

breathtaking, *adj.* à vous couper le souffle.

bred, *adj.* élevé.

breeches, *n.* pantalon *m.sg.*

breed, *vb.* produire; (livestock) élever.

breeder, *n.* (raiser) éleveur *m.*

breeding, *n.* (manners) éducation *f.*; (animals) élevage *m.*

breeze, *n.* brise *f.*

breezy, *adj.* (windy) venteux; (manner) dégagé.

Breton, 1. *n.* Breton *m.* **2.** *adj.* breton.

brevity, *n.* brièveté *f.*

brew, *vb.* (beer) brasser; (tea) faire infuser, *tr.*

brewery, *n.* brasserie *f.*

briar, *n.* ronce *f.*

bribe, *vb.* corrompre.

briber, *n.* corrupteur *m.*

bribery, *n.* corruption *f.*

brick, *n.* brique *f.*

bricklaying, *n.* maçonnerie *f.*

bricklike, *adj.* comme une brique.

bridal, *adj.* nuptial.

bride, *n.* mariée *f.*

bridegroom, *n.* marié *m.*

bridesmaid, *n.* demoiselle *(f.)* d'honneur.

bridge, *n.* pont *m.*; (boat) passerelle *f.*; (cards) bridge *m.*

bridged, *adj.* lié.

bridgehead, *n.* tête de pont *f.*

bridle, *n.* bride *f.*

brief, 1. *adj.* bref *m.*, brève *f.* **2.** *n.* dossier *m.* **3.** *vb.* donner des instructions à.

briefcase, *n.* serviette *f.*

briefly, *adv.* brièvement.

briefness, *n.* brièveté *f.*

brier, *n.* bruyère *f.*, ronces *f.pl.*

brig, *n.* brick *m.*

brigade, *n.* brigade *f.*

bright, *adj.* vif *m.*, vive *f.*; intelligent.

brighten, *vb.* faire briller, *tr.*

brightness, *n.* éclat *m.*

brilliance, *n.* éclat *m.*

brilliant, *adj.* brillant.

brim, *n.* bord *m.*

brine, *n.* saumure *f.*

bring, *vb.* (thing) apporter; (person) amener; (**b. about**) amener, causer; (**b. up**) élever.

brink, *n.* bord *m.*

briny, *adj.* salé.

brisk, *adj.* vif *m.*, vive *f.*

brisket, *n.* (meat) poitrine *f.*

briskly, *adv.* vivement.

briskness, *n.* vivacité *f.*

bristle, *n.* soie *f.*

bristly, *adj.* hérissé (de), poilu.

British, *adj.* britannique.

British Empire, *n.* Empire Britannique *m.*

British Isles, *n.* Iles Britanniques *f.pl.*

brittle, *adj.* fragile.

broad, *adj.* large.

broadcast, 1. *vb.* diffuser. **2.** *n.* émission *f.*

broadcaster, *n.* speaker *m.*

broadcloth, *n.* drap (*m.*) fin.

broaden, *vb.* élargir.

broadly, *adv.* largement.

broadminded, *adj.* large d'esprit.

broadside, *n.* côté *f.*, bordée *f.*

brocade, *n.* brocart *m.*

brocaded, *adj.* de brocart.

broccoli, *n.* brocoli *m.*

brochure, *n.* brochure *f.*

broil, *vb.* griller.

broiler, *n.* gril *m.*

broke, *adj.* fauché.

broken-hearted, *adj.* qui a le coeur brisé.

broker, *n.* courtier *m.*; (stock-b.) agent (*m.*) de change.

brokerage, *n.* courtage *m.*

bronchial, *adj.* bronchique.

bronchitis, *n.* bronchite *f.*

bronze, *n.* bronze *m.*

brooch, *n.* broche *f.*

brood, 1. *n.* couvée *f.* **2.** *vb.* couver.

brook, *n.* ruisseau *m.*

broom, *n.* balai *m.*

broomstick, *n.* manche *(m.)* à balai.

broth, n. bouillon m.
brothel, n. bordel m., maison mal famée f.
brother, n. frère m.
brotherhood, n. fraternité f.
brother-in-law, n. beau-frère m.
brotherly, adj. fraternel.
brow, n. front m.
browbeat, vb. intimider.
brown, adj. brun.
browse, vb. (animals) brouter; (books) feuilleter (des livres).
bruise, 1. n. meurtrissure f. **2.** vb. meurtrir.
bruised, adj. couvert de bleus.
brunette, adj. and n. brune f.
brunt, n. choc m.
brush, 1. n. brosse f.; (paint-b.) pinceau m. **2.** vb. brosser.
brushwood, n. broussailles f.pl.
brusque, adj. brusque.
brusquely, adv. brusquement.
Brussels, n. Bruxelles, f.
brutal, adj. brutal.
brutality, n. brutalité f.
brutalize, vb. abrutir.
brute, n. brute f.
bubble, 1. n. bulle f. **2.** vb. bouillonner.
buck, n. daim m.; (male) mâle m.; (colloquial) dollar m.
bucket, n. seau m.
buckle, n. boucle f.
buckram, n. bougran m.
buckshot, n. chevrotine f.
buckwheat, n. sarrasin m., blé noir m.
bud, 1. n. bourgeon m. **2.** vb. bourgeonner.
budding, adj. en herbe.
buddy, n. copain m., pote m.
budge, vb. bouger.
budget, n. budget m.
buffalo, n. buffle m.
buffer, n. tampon m.; (computer) mémoire (f.) tampon.
buffet, n. (sideboard) buffet m.
buffoon, n. bouffon m.
bug, 1. n. insecte m.; (computer) erreur f. **2.** vb. embêter; mettre des micros dans.
bugle, n. clairon m.
build, vb. bâtir.
builder, n. (buildings) entrepreneur m.; (ships) constructeur m.

building, n. bâtiment m.
bulb, n. (electricity) ampoule f.; (botany) bulbe m.
Bulgaria, n. Bulgarie f.
bulge, n. bosse f.
bulimia, n. boulimie f.
bulk, n. masse f.
bulkhead, n. cloison étanche f.
bulky, adj. volumineux.
bull, n. taureau m.
bulldog, n. bouledogue m.
bulldozer, n. machine à refouler f.
bullet, n. balle f.
bulletin, n. bulletin m.
bulletproof, adj. à l'épreuve des balles.
bullfight, n. corrida f.
bullfighting, n. tauromachie f.
bullfinch, n. bouvreuil m.
bullion, n. lingot m.
bully, 1. n. brute f., tyran m. **2.** vb. rudoyer.
bulwark, n. rempart m.
bum, n. fainéant m.
bumblebee, n. bourdon m.
bump, 1. n. (blow) coup m.; (protuberance) bosse f. **2.** vb. cogner.
bumper, n. (auto) pare-chocs m.
bumpy, adj. cahoteux.
bun, n. brioche f.
bunch, n. (flowers) bouquet m.; (grapes) grappe f.; (keys) trousseau m.
bundle, n. paquet m.
bungalow, n. bungalow m.
bungle, vb. bousiller.
bunion, n. cor m.
bunk, n. couchette f.; (colloquial) foutaises f.pl.
bunny, n. lapin m.
bunting, n. drapeaux m.pl.
buoy, n. bouée f.
buoyant, adj. qui a du ressort.
burden, n. fardeau m.
burdensome, adj. onéreux.
bureau, n. (office) bureau m.; (chest of drawers) commode f.
bureaucracy, n. bureaucratie f.
bureaucrat, n. bureaucrate m.f.
burglar, n. cambrioleur m.
burglarize, vb. cambrioler.
burglary, n. vol (m.) avec effraction, cambriolage.
Burgundy, n. Bourgogne f.
burial, n. enterrement m.

burlap, n. gros canevas m.

burly, adj. corpulent.

Burma, n. Birmanie f.

burn, vb. brûler.

burner, n. bec m.

burning, adj. brûlant.

burnish, vb. brunir, polir.

burp, vb. roter.

burrow, n. terrier m.

burst, vb. éclater.

bury, vb. enterrer.

bus, n. autobus m.

bush, n. buisson m.; (land) brousse f.

bushel, n. boisseau m.

bushy, adj. buissonneux; (hair) touffu.

busily, adv. activement.

business, n. affaire f.; (comm.) affaires f.pl.

businesslike, adj. pratique.

businessman, n. homme (m.) d'affaires.

businesswoman, n. femme (f.) d'affaires.

bust, n. buste m.

bustle, vb. se remuer.

busy, adj. occupé.

busybody, n. officieux m.

but, conj. mais; (only) ne . . . que; (except) sauf.

butane, n. butane m.

butcher, n. boucher m.

butchery, n. tuerie f., massacre m.

butler, n. maître (m.) d'hôtel.

butt, n. bout m.; (of jokes) plastron m.; (of cigarette) mégot m.; (colloquial) derrière m.

butter, n. beurre m.

buttercup, n. bouton (m.) d'or.

butterfly, n. papillon m.

buttermilk, n. babeurre m.

butterscotch, n. caramel (m.) au beurre.

buttock, n. fesse f.

button, n. bouton m.

buttonhole, n. boutonnière f.

buttress, n. contrefort m.; (flying b.) arc-boutant m.

buxom, adj. (of women) aux formes rebondies.

buy, vb. acheter.

buyer, n. acheteur m.

buzz, 1. n. bourdonnement m. 2. vb. bourdonner.

buzzard, n. buse f.

buzzer, n. trompe f., sirène f.

by, prep. (through) par; (near) près de.

by-and-by, adv. bientôt.

bye(-bye), interj. au revoir, salut.

bygone, adj. passé, d'autrefois.

bylaw, n. règlement local m.

by-pass, 1. n. route (f.) d'évitement. 2. vb. faire un détour.

by-product, n. sous-produit m.

bystander, n. spectateur m.

byte, n. unité fondamentale de données f.; octet m.

byway, n. sentier détourné m.

C

cab, n. (taxi) taxi m.; (horse) fiacre m.

cabaret, n. cabaret m.

cabbage, n. chou m.

cabin, n. (hut) cabane f.; (boat) cabine f.

cabinet, n. cabinet m.

cabinetmaker, n. ébéniste m.

cable, 1. n. câble m. 2. vb. câbler.

cable car, n. téléphérique m.

cablegram, n. câblogramme m.

caboose, n. fourgon m.

cachet, n. cachet m.

cackle, 1. n. caquet m. 2. vb. caqueter.

cacophony, n. cacophonie f.

cactus, n. cactus m.

cad, n. mufle m.

cadaver, n. cadavre m.

cadaverous, adj. cadavérique.

cadence, n. cadence f.

cadet, n. cadet m.

cadmium, n. cadmium f.

cadre, n. cadre m.

Caesarean (section), n. césarienne f.

café, n. café, (-restaurant) m.

cafeteria, n. restaurant m.

caffeine, n. caféine f.

cage, n. cage f.

caged, adj. mis en cage.

cagey, adj. méfiant.

caisson, n. caisson m.

cajole, vb. cajoler.

cake, n. gâteau m.

calamitous, adj. calamiteux, désastreux.

calamity, n. calamité f.

calcify, vb. calcifier.

calcium, n. calcium m.

calculable, adj. calculable.

calculate, vb. calculer.

calculating, adj. qui fait des calculs.

calculation, n. calcul m.

calculator, n. calculatrice f.

calculus, n. calcul m.

caldron, n. chaudron m.

calendar, n. calendrier m.

calender, n. calandre f.

calf, n. veau m.

calfskin, adj. en peau de veau.

caliber, n. calibre m.

calico, n. calicot m.

calisthenic, adj. callisthénique.

calisthenics, n. callisthénie f.

calk, vb. ferrer à glace.

call, 1. n. appel m.; (visit) visite f. 2. vb. appeler; (c. on) faire visite à.

calligraphy, n. calligraphie f.

calling, n. vocation f., profession f.

calling card, n. carte de visite f.

callously, adv. d'une manière insensible.

callousness, n. insensibilité f.

callow, adj. blanc-bec.

callus, n. callosité f.

calm, 1. adj. calme. 2. vb. calmer.

calmly, adv. calmement.

calmness, n. calme m., tranquillité f.

caloric, adj. calorique.

calorie, n. calorie f.

calorimeter, n. calorimètre m.

calumniate, vb. calomnier.

calumny, n. calomnie f.

Calvary, n. Calvaire m.

calve, vb. vêler.

calyx, n. calice m.

camaraderie, n. camaraderie f.

Cambodia, n. Cambodge m.

cambric, n. batiste f.

camcorder, n. camescope m.

camel, n. chameau m.

camellia, n. camélia m.

camel's hair, n. poil (m.) de chameau.

cameo, n. camée m.

camera, n. appareil photographique m.

Cameroons, n. la République fédérale du Cameroun.

camouflage, vb. camoufler.

camouflaged, adj. camouflé.

camouflaging, adj. camouflant.

camp, 1. n. camp m.; (holiday camp) camping m. 2. vb. camper.

campaign, n. campagne f.

camper, n. qui fait du camping; (vehicle) camping-car m.

camphor, n. camphre m.

camphor ball, n. balle (f.) de camphre.

campsite, n. (terrain m. de) camping.

campus, n. terrains (m.pl.) de l'université.

can, 1. n. (food) boîte f.; (general) bidon m. 2. vb. (be able) pouvoir; (put in a can) conserver.

Canada, n. Canada m.

Canadian, 1. n. Canadien m. 2. adj. canadien.

canal, n. canal m.

canalize, vb. canaliser.

canapé, n. canapé m.

canard, n. canard m.

canary, n. serin m.

Canary Islands, n. Îles Canaries f.pl.

cancel, vb. annuler; (erase) biffer.

cancellation, n. annulation f.

cancer, n. cancer m.

candelabrum, n. candélabre m.

candid, adj. sincère.

candidacy, n. candidature f.

candidate, n. candidat m.

candidly, adv. franchement.

candidness, n. candeur f.

candied, adj. candi.

candle, n. bougie f.; (church) cierge m.

candler, n. fabricant (m.) de chandelles.

candlestick, n. chandelier m.

candor, n. sincérité f.

candy, n. bonbon m.

cane, n. canne f.

canine, adj. canin.

canister, n. boîte à thé f.

canker, n. chancre m.

cankerworm, n. ver rongeur m.

canned, adj. conservé en boîtes (de fer blanc).

canner, n. travailleur dans une conserverie m.

cannery, n. conserverie f.

cannibal, adj. and n. cannibale m.f.

canning, n. mise en conserve, en boîtes (de fer blanc) f.

cannon, n. canon m.

cannonade, n. canonnade f.

cannoneer, n. canonier m.

cannot, vb. ne peut pas.

canoe, n. canot m.

canon, n. chanoine m.; (rule) canon m.

canonical, adj. canonique.

canonize, vb. canoniser.

can opener, n. ouvre-boîte m.

canopy, n. dais m.

cant, n. hypocrisie f.

can't, vb. ne peut pas.

cantaloupe, n. melon m., cantaloup m.

cantankerous, adj. grincheux.

canteen, n. cantine f.; bidon m.

canter, 1. n. petit galop f. 2. vb. aller au petit galop.

cantonment, n. cantonnement m.

canvas, n. toile f.

canvass, 1. n. sollicitation f. 2. vb. solliciter; (discuss) débattre.

canyon, n. gorge f., défilé m.

cap, n. bonnet m.; (peaked) casquette f.

capability, n. capacité f.

capable, adj. capable.

capably, adv. capablement.

capacious, adj. ample, spacieux.

capacity, n. capacité f.

caparison, 1. n. caparaçon m. 2. vb. caparaçonner.

cape, n. (geography) cap m.; (cloak) cape f.

caper, 1. n. bond m.; (plant) câpre f. 2. vb. bondir.

capillary, adj. capillaire.

capital, 1. n. (finance) capital m.; (city) capitale f.; (letter) majuscule f.; (architecture) chapiteau m. 2. adj. capital.

capitalism, n. capitalisme m.

capitalist, n. capitaliste m.f.

capitalistic, adj. capitaliste.

capitalization, n. capitalisation f.

capitalize, vb. capitaliser.

capitulate, vb. capituler.

capon, n. chapon m.

caprice, n. caprice m.

capricious, adj. capricieux.

capriciously, adv. capricieusement.

capriciousness, n. caractère capricieux m., humeur fantasque f.

capsize, vb. chavirer, intr.; faire chavirer, tr.

capsule, n. capsule f.

captain, n. capitaine m.

caption, n. en-tête m.

captious, adj. chicaneur.

captivate, vb. captiver.

captivating, adj. séduisant.

captive, adj. and n. captif m.

captivity, n. captivité f.

captor, n. capteur m.

capture, 1. n. capture f. 2. vb. capturer.

car, n. (auto) voiture f.; (train) wagon m.

caracul, n. caracul m.

carafe, n. carafe f.

caramel, n. caramel m.

carat, n. carat m.

caravan, n. caravane f.

caraway, n. carvi m., cumin (m.) (des prés).

carbide, n. carbure m.

carbine, n. carabine f.

carbohydrate, n. carbohydrate m.

carbon, n. carbone m.

carbon dioxide, n. acide carbonique m.

carbon monoxide, n. oxyde de carbone m.

carbon paper, n. papier carbone m.

carbuncle, n. escarboucle f., (med.) charbon m.

carburetor, n. carburateur m.

carcass, n. carcasse f.

carcinogenic, adj. cancérogène.

card, n. carte f.

cardboard, n. carton m.

cardiac, adj. cardiaque.

cardigan, n. gilet de tricot m.

cardinal, n. cardinal m.

care, 1. n. (worry) souci m.; (attention) attention f.; (take c.!) faites attention!; (charge) soin m.; (take c. of) prendre soin de. 2. vb. (c.

about) se soucier de; **(c. for)** aimer; (look after) soigner.

careen, vb. caréner.

career, n. carrière f.

carefree, adj. insouciant.

careful, adj. soigneux.

carefully, adv. soigneusement, attentivement.

carefulness, n. soin m., attention f.

careless, adj. insouciant.

carelessly, adv. nonchalamment, négligement.

carelessness, n. insouciance f., négligence f.

caress, 1. n. caresse f. **2.** vb. caresser.

caretaker, n. concierge m.f.

cargo, n. cargaison f.

Caribbean, n. **the C.** (sea) la mer des Caraïbes; **the C.** (islands) les Antilles.

caricature, n. caricature f.

caries, n. carie f.

carillon, n. carillon m.

carload, n. voiturée f.

carnage, n. carnage m.

carnal, adj. charnel.

carnation, n. œillet m.

carnival, n. carnaval m.

carnivorous, adj. carnivore.

carol, n. **(Xmas c.)** noël m.

carouse, vb. faire la fête.

carousel, n. carrousel m.

carpenter, n. charpentier m.

carpet, n. tapis m.

carpeting, n. pose de tapis f.

car pool, n. groupe (m.) de personnes qui voyagent régulièrement ensemble en auto.

carriage, n. (vehicle) voiture f.; (bearing) maintien m.; (transport) transport m.

carrier, n. porteur m., messager m.

carrier pigeon, n. pigeon voyageur m.

carrot, n. carotte f.

carry, vb. porter; **(c. on)** continuer; **(c. out)** exécuter; **(c. through)** mener à bonne fin.

cart, n. charrette f.

cartage, n. charriage m., transport m.

cartel, n. cartel m.

carter, n. charretier m.

cartilage, n. cartilage m.

carton, n. carton m.

cartoon, n. dessin satirique m., (cinema) dessin (m.) animé.

cartoonist, n. caricaturiste m.

cartridge, n. cartouche f.

carve, vb. (art) sculpter; (meat) découper.

carver, n. découpeur m., sculpteur m.

carving, n. découpage m., sculpture f.

cascade, n. cascade f.

case, n. (instance, state of things) cas m.; (law) cause f.; (packing) caisse f.; (holder) étui m.; **(in any c.)** en tout cas.

cash, 1. n. espèces f.pl.; (C.O.D.) livraison (f.) contre remboursement. **2.** vb. **(c. a check)** toucher.

cashew, n. noix (f.) de cajou.

cashier, n. caissier m.

cashmere, n. cachemire m.

cash register, n. caisse f.

casing, n. revêtement m., enveloppe f.

casino, n. casino m.

cask, n. tonneau m.

casket, n. cassette f.

casserole, n. casserole f.

cassette, n. cassette f.

cast, 1. n. (throw) coup m.; (characteristic) trempe f.; (theater) distribution f.; **(c. from mold)** moulage m.; (hue) nuance f.; (med.) plâtre m. **2.** vb. (throw) jeter; (metal) couler.

castaway, n. naufragé m.; rejeté m.

caste, n. caste f.

caster, n. fondeur m.

castigate, vb. châtier, punir.

cast iron, n. fonte f.

castle, n. château m.

castoff, adj. abandonné.

castrate, vb. châtrer.

casual, adj. (accidental) casuel; (person) insouciant.

casually, adv. fortuitement, en passant.

casualness, n. nonchalance f.

casualties, n. (mil.) pertes f.pl.

cat, n. chat m., chatte f.

cataclysm, n. cataclysme m.

catacomb, n. catacombe f.

catalogue, n. catalogue m.

catalyst, n. catalyseur m.

catapult, n. catapulte m.

cataract, n. cataracte f.

catarrh, n. catarrhe m.

catastrophe, n. catastrophe f.

catch, vb. attraper; (seize, understand) saisir; **(c. up)** se rattraper.

catcher, n. qui attrape.

catchword, n. mot d'ordre m.

catchy, adj. (musical air) facile à retenir; (question) insidieuse.

catechism, n. catéchisme m.

catechize, vb. catéchiser.

categorical, adj. catégorique.

category, n. catégorie f.

cater, vb. pourvoir à.

caterpillar, n. chenille f.

catgut, n. corde (f.) à boyau.

catharsis, n. catharsis f., (med.) purgation f.

cathartic, adj. cathartique, purgatif.

cathedral, n. cathédrale f.

cathode, n. cathode f.

Catholic, adj. catholique.

Catholic Church, n. Église catholique f.

Catholicism, n. catholicisme m.

cat nap, n. somme m.

catsup, n. sauce piquante f.

cattle, n. bétail m., bestiaux m.pl.

cattleman, n. éleveur de bétail m.

catty, adj. méchant.

catwalk, n. coursive f.

caucus, n. comité (m.) local ou electoral.

cauliflower, n. chou-fleur m.

causation, n. causation f.

cause, n. cause f.

causeway, n. chaussée f.

caustic, adj. caustique.

cauterize, vb. cautériser.

cautery, n. cautère m.

caution, 1. n. prudence f. 2. vb. avertir.

cautious, adj. prudent.

cavalcade, n. cavalcade f.

cavalier, adj. and n. cavalier m.

cavalry, n. cavalerie f.

cave, n. caverne f.

cave-in, n. effondrement m.

cavern, n. caverne f.

caviar, n. caviar m.

cavity, n. cavité f.

cavort, vb. cabrioler.

CD, n. compact disc m.

cease, vb. cesser (de).

ceaseless, adj. incessant, continuel.

cedar, n. cèdre m.

cede, vb. céder.

cedilla, n. cédille f.

ceiling, n. plafond m.

celebrant, n. célébrant m.

celebrate, vb. célébrer.

celebration, n. célébration f.

celebrity, n. célébrité f.

celerity, n. célérité f., vitesse f.

celery, n. céleri m.

celestial, adj. céleste.

celibacy, n. célibat m.

celibate, adj. célibataire.

cell, n. cellule f.

cellar, n. cave f.

cellist, n. violoncelliste m.f.

cello, n. violoncelle m.

cellophane, n. cellophane f.

cellular, adj. cellulaire.

celluloid, n. celluloïd m.

cellulose, n. cellulose f.

Celtic, adj. celtique.

cement, 1. n. ciment m. 2. vb. cimenter.

cemetery, n. cimetière m.

censor, 1. n. censeur m. 2. vb. censurer.

censorious, adj. critique, hargneux.

censorship, n. censure f.

censure, n. censure f.

census, n. recensement m.

cent, n. cent m.; **(per c.)** pour cent.

centenary, centennial, adj. and n. centenaire m.

center, n. centre m.

centerfold, n. pages centrales f.pl.

centerpiece, n. pièce de milieu f.

centigrade, adj. centigrade.

centigrade thermometer, n. thermomètre centigrade m.

centipede, n. mille-pattes m.

central, adj. central.

Central America, n. Amérique (f.) Centrale.

central heating, n. chauffage (m.) central.

centralize, vb. centraliser.

century, n. siècle m.

century plant, n. agave (m.) d'Amérique.

ceramic, adj. céramique.

ceramics, n. céramique f.

cereal, adj. and n. céréale f.

cerebral, adj. cérébral.

ceremonial, adj. and n. cérémonial m.

ceremonious, adj. cérémonieux.

ceremony, n. cérémonie f.

certain, adj. certain.

certainly, adv. certainement.

certainty, n. certitude f.

certificate, n. certificat m.; (**birth c.**) acte (m.) de naissance.

certification, n. certification f.

certified, adj. certifié, diplômé, breveté.

certifier, n. (personne) qui certifie.

certify, vb. certifier.

certitude, n. certitude f.

cervical, adj. cervical.

cervix, n. col (de l'utérus) m.

cessation, n. cessation f., suspension f.

cession, n. cession f.

cesspool, n. fosse (f.) d'aisances.

Chad, n. Tchad m.

chafe, vb. frictionner.

chaff, 1. n. menue paille f.; (colloquial) blague f. 2. vb. blaguer.

chafing dish, n. réchaud f.

chagrin, n. chagrin m.

chain, n. chaîne f.

chain reaction, n. réaction caténaire f.

chain store, n. succursale (f.) de grand magasin.

chair, n. chaise f.; (**arm-c.**) fauteuil m.

chairman, n. président m.

chairmanship, n. présidence f.

chairperson, n. président m., présidente f.

chairwoman, n. présidente f.

chalice, n. calice f.

chalk, n. craie f.

chalky, adj. de craie, calcaire.

challenge, 1. n. défi m. 2. vb. défier; (dispute) contester.

challenger, n. qui fait un défi, prétendant m.

chamber, n. chambre f.

chamberlain, n. chambellan m.

chambermaid, n. femme de chambre f.

chamber music, n. musique de chambre f.

chameleon, n. caméléon m.

chamois, n. chamois m.

champ, vb. ronger, mâcher.

champagne, n. champagne m.

champion, n. champion m.

championship, n. championnat m.

chance, n. chance f.; (**by c.**) par hasard; (**take a c.**) prendre un risque.

chancel, n. sanctuaire m., choeur m.

chancellery, n. chancellerie f.

chancellor, n. chancelier m.

chancy, adj. risqué.

chandelier, n. lustre m.

change, 1. n. changement m.; (money) monnaie f.; (exchange) change m. 2. vb. changer.

changeability, n. variabilité f.

changeable, adj. changeant.

changer, n. changeur m.

channel, n. canal m.; (**the English C.**) la Manche f.; (television) chaîne f.

chant, 1. n. chant m. 2. vb. chanter.

chaos, n. chaos m.

chaotic, adj. chaotique.

chap, n. (on skin) gerçure f.; (young man) gars m.

chapel, n. chapelle f.

chaperon, n. (person) duègne f., chaperon m.

chaplain, n. aumônier m.

chapman, n. colporteur m.

chapped, adj. gercé.

chapter, n. chapitre m.

char, vb. carboniser.

character, n. caractère m.; (in fiction) personnage m.; (role) rôle m.

characteristic, 1. n. trait caractéristique m. 2. adj. caractéristique.

characteristically, adv. d'une manière caractéristique.

characterization, n. action de caractériser f.

characterize, vb. caractériser.

charcoal, n. charbon (m.) de bois.

charge, 1. n. (guns, legal, electric) charge f.; (price) prix m.; (care) soin m. 2. vb. charger; (c. with) charger de; (price) demander.

charger, n. grand plat m.; cheval de bataille m.

chariot, n. char m., chariot m.

charioteer, n. conducteur de chariot m.

charisma, n. charisme m.

charitable, adj. charitable.

charitableness, n. bienveillance f.

charitably, adv. charitablement.

charity, n. charité f.

charlatan, n. charlatan m.

charlatanism, n. charlatanisme m.

charm, 1. n. charme m. **2.** vb. charmer.

charmer, n. charmeur m., enchanteur m.

charming, adj. charmant.

charred, adj. carbonisé.

chart, n. (map) carte f.; (graph) graphique m.

charter, 1. n. charte f. **2.** vb. (boat) affréter.

charter flight, n. vol frété m.; charter m.

charwoman, n. femme (f.) de journée; femme (f.) de ménage.

chase, 1. n. chasse f. **2.** vb. chasser.

chaser, n. chasseur m.; ciseleur m.

chasm, n. abîme m.

chassis, n. chassis m.

chaste, adj. chaste.

chasten, vb. châtier, corriger.

chasteness, n. pureté f.

chastise, vb. châtier.

chastisement, n. châtiment m.

chastity, n. chasteté f.

chat, 1. n. causette f. **2.** vb. causer.

chateau, n. château m.

chattel, n. bien m., meuble m.

chatter, 1. n. bavardage m. **2.** vb. bavarder.

chatterbox, n. bavard m.

chatty, adj. bavard.

chauffeur, n. chauffeur m.

chauvinist, adj. (male) phallocrate; (nationalist) chauvin m.

cheap, adj. (inexpensive) bon marché; (mean) de peu de valeur.

cheapen, vb. déprécier.

cheaply, adv. à bon marché.

cheapness, n. bon marché m., bas prix m.; basse qualité f.

cheat, vb. tromper; (at games) tricher.

cheater, n. tricheur m., trompeur m.

check, 1. n. (restraint) frein m.; (verification) vérification f.; (stub) ticket m.; (bill) addition f.; (bank draft) chèque m. **2.** vb. (stop) arrêter; (restrain) modérer; (verify) vérifier; (luggage) enregistrer.

checker, n. enregistreur m., contrôleur m.

checkbook, n. chéquier m., carnet (m.) de chèques.

checkers, n. jeu de dames m.

checkmate, 1. n. échec et mat m. **2.** vb. mater.

checkroom, n. vestiaire m.

cheek, n. joue f.

cheer, 1. n. (applause) hourra m. **2.** vb. (acclaim) acclamer; (c. up, tr.) réjouir.

cheerful, adj. gai.

cheerfully, adv. gaiement, de bon cœur.

cheerfulness, n. gaieté f., bonne humeur f.

cheerless, adj. triste, morne, sombre.

cheery, adj. gai, joyeux.

cheese, n. fromage m.

cheesecloth, n. gaze f.

cheesy, adj. fromageux.

cheetah, n. guépard m.

chef, n. chef m.

chemical, adj. chimique.

chemically, adv. chimiquement.

chemist, n. chimiste m.f.

chemistry, n. chimie f.

chemotherapy, n. chimiothérapie f.

chenille, n. chenille f.

cherish, vb. chérir.

cherry, n. cerise f.

cherub, n. chérubin m.

chess, n. échecs m.pl.

chessman, n. pièce f.

chest, n. (box) coffre m.; (body) poitrine f.; (c. of drawers) commode f.

chestnut, n. châtaigne f.

chevron, n. chevron m.

chew, vb. mâcher.

chewer, n. mâcheur m.

chic, adj. chic, élégant, smart.

chicanery, n. chicane f., chicanerie f.

chick, n. poussin m.

chicken, n. poulet m.

chicken-hearted, adj. peureux.

chicken-pox, n. varicelle f.

chickpea, n. pois (m.) chiche.
chicle, n. chiclé m.
chicory, n. chicorée f.
chide, vb. gronder, réprimander.
chief, 1. n. chef m. **2.** adj. principal; (c. executive) directeur général.
chiefly, adv. surtout, principalement.
chieftain, n. chef de clan m.
chiffon, n. chiffon m.
chilblain, n. engelure f.
child, n. enfant m.f.
childbirth, n. enfantement m.; accouchement m.
childhood, n. enfance f.
childish, adj. enfantin.
childishness, n. puérilité f., enfantillage m.
childless, adj. sans enfant.
childlessness, n. l'état d'être sans enfants.
childlike, adj. comme un enfant, en enfant.
Chile, n. Chili m.
Chilean, 1. n. Chilien m. **2.** adj. chilien.
chili, n. piment m.
chill, 1. n. froid m.; (shiver) frisson m. **2.** vb. refroidir.
chilliness, n. froid m., frisson m.
chilly, adj. un peu froid.
chime, 1. n. carillon m. **2.** vb. carillonner.
chimney, n. cheminée f.
chimney sweep, n. ramoneur m.
chimpanzee, n. chimpanzé m.
chin, n. menton m.
China, n. Chine f.
china, n. (ware) porcelaine f.
chinchilla, n. chinchilla m.
Chinese, 1. n. (person) Chinois m.; (language) chinois m. **2.** adj. chinois.
chink, n. fente f., crevasse f.
chintz, n. perse f.
chip, 1. n. éclat m.; (potato c.s) chips m.pl. **2.** vb. ébrecher.
chipmunk, n. tamias m.
chiropractor, n. chiropracteur m.
chirp, n. pépier, gazouiller.
chisel, 1. vb. ciseler. **2.** n. ciseau m.
chitchat, n. bavardage m.
chivalrous, adj. chevaleresque.
chivalry, n. chevalerie f.
chive, n. ciboulette f.

chloride, n. chlorure m.
chlorine, n. chlore m.
chloroform, n. chloroforme m.
chlorophyll, n. chlorophylle m.
chockfull, adj. plein comme un œuf.
chocolate, n. chocolat m.
choice, n. choix m.
choir, n. chœur m.
choke, vb. étouffer.
choker, n. foulard m.
cholera, n. choléra m.
choleric, adj. cholérique.
cholesterol, n. cholestérol m.
choose, vb. choisir.
choosy, adj. exigeant.
chop, 1. n. (meat) côtelette f. **2.** vb. couper.
chopper, n. couperet m.
choppy, adj. (sea) clapoteux.
chopstick, n. baguette f., bâtonnet m.
choral, adj. choral.
chord, n. (music) accord m.
chore, n. travail (m.) de ménage.
choreography, n. chorégraphie f.
chorister, n. choriste m., enfant de chœur m.
chortle, vb. glousser de joie.
chorus, n. chœur m.; (of song) refrain m.
chowder, n. (sorte de) bouillabaisse f.
Christ, n. le Christ m.
christen, vb. baptiser.
Christendom, n. chrétienté f.
christening, n. baptême m.
Christian, 1. n. Chrétien m. **2.** adj. chrétien.
Christianity, n. christianisme m.
Christmas, n. Noël m.; (C. Day) jour (m.) de Noël; (C. Eve) veille (f.) de Noël; (C. tree) sapin (m.) de Noël.
chromatic, adj. chromatique.
chromium, n. chrome m.
chromosome, n. chromosome m.
chronic, adj. chronique.
chronically, adv. d'une manière chronique.
chronicle, n. chronique f.
chronological, adj. chronologique.
chronologically, adv. chronologiquement.
chronology, n. chronologie f.

chrysalis, n. chrysalide f.

chrysanthemum, n. chrysanthème m.

chubby, adj. joufflu.

chuck, n. petite tape f., gloussement (de volaille) m.

chuckle, vb. rire tout bas.

chug, 1. n. souffle m. (d'une machine à vapeur). **2.** vb. souffler.

chum, n. camarade m., copain m.

chummy, adj. familier, intime.

chunk, n. gros morceau m.

chunky, adj. en gros morceaux.

church, n. église f.

churchman, n. homme (m.) d'église, ecclésiastique m.

churchyard, n. cimetière m.

churn, vb. baratter.

chute, n. glissière f.

chutney, n. chutney m.

cicada, n. cigale f.

cider, n. cidre m.

cigar, n. cigare m.

cigarette, n. cigarette f.

cilia, n. cils m.pl.

ciliary, adj. ciliaire.

cinch, n. (it's a c.) c'est facile.

cinchona, n. quinquina m.

Cinderella, n. Cendrillon f.

cinema, n. cinéma m.

cinematic, adj. cinématographique.

cinnamon, n. cannelle f.

cipher, n. chiffre m.; (nought) zéro m.

circle, 1. n. cercle m. **2.** vb. entourer (de).

circuit, n. circuit m.

circuitous, adj. détourné, sinueux.

circuitously, adv. d'une manière détournée, par des détours.

circular, adj. circulaire.

circularize, vb. envoyer des circulaires.

circulate, vb. circuler, intr.; faire circuler, tr.

circulation, n. circulation f.; (newspaper) tirage m.

circulator, n. circulateur m.

circulatory, adj. circulaire, circulatoire.

circumcise, vb. circoncire.

circumcision, n. circoncision f.

circumference, n. circonférence f.

circumflex, n. accent (m.) circonflexe.

circumlocution, n. circonlocution f.

circumscribe, vb. circonscrire.

circumspect, adj. circonspect.

circumstance, n. (condition) circonstance f.; (financial) moyens m.pl.

circumstantial, adj. circonstancié.

circumstantially, adv. en détail.

circumvent, vb. circonvenir.

circumvention, n. circonvention f.

circus, n. cirque m.

cirrhosis, n. cirrhose f.

cistern, n. citerne f.

citadel, n. citadelle f.

citation, n. citation f.

cite, vb. citer.

citizen, n. citoyen m.

citizenry, n. tous les citoyens m.pl.

citizenship, n. droit (m.) de cité.

citric acid, n. acide citrique m.

citrus fruit, n. agrume m.

city, n. ville f.; cité f.

city hall, n. hôtel (m.) de ville.

city planning, n. urbanisme m.

civic, adj. civique.

civics, n. instruction (f.) civique.

civil, adj. civil; (polite) poli; (c. servant) fonctionnaire m.

civilian, n. civil m.

civility, n. civilité f., politesse f.

civilization, n. civilisation f.

civilize, vb. civiliser.

civilized, adj. civilisé.

civil rights, n. droits (m.pl.) de l'homme.

civil servant, n. fonctionnaire m.

civil service, n. administration (civile) f.

civil war, n. guerre civile f.

clad, adj. habillé, vêtu.

claim, 1. n. (demand) demande f.; (right) droit m. **2.** vb. (demand) réclamer, prétendre; (insist) soutenir.

claimant, n. réclamateur m., prétendant m.

clairvoyance, n. clairvoyance f.

clairvoyant, n. voyant m.

clam, n. palourde f., mollusque m.

clamber, vb. grimper.

clammy, adj. visqueux, moite.

clamor, n. clameur f.

clamorous, adj. bruyant.

clamp, 1. n. (metal) crampon m.; (carpentry) serre-joint m. **2.** vb. cramponner, serrer.

clan, n. clan m., clique f., coterie f.

clandestine, adj. clandestin.

clandestinely, adv. clandestinement.

clang, 1. n. cliquetis m., son métallique m. **2.** vb. résonner.

clangor, n. cliquetis m.

clannish, adj. de clan.

clap, vb. (applaud) applaudir.

clapboard, n. bardeau m.

clapper, n. claqueur m., battant (of a bell) m.

claque, n. claque f.

claret, n. vin rouge (m.) de Bordeaux.

clarification, n. clarification f.

clarify, vb. (lit.) clarifier; (fig.) éclaircir.

clarinet, n. clarinette f.

clarinetist, n. clarinettiste m.f.

clarion, n. clairon m.

clarity, n. clarté f.

clash, 1. n. vb. choquer, tr.; s'entrechoquer, intr. **2.** n. choc m.

clasp, 1. n. agrafe f.; (embrace) étreinte f. **2.** vb. agrafer, étreindre.

class, n. classe f.

classic, classical, adj. classique.

classicism, n. classicisme m.

classifiable, adj. classifiable.

classification, n. classification f.

classified, adj. (information) secret.

classified ad, n. petite annonce f.

classify, vb. classifier, classer.

classmate, n. camarade (m.) de classe.

classroom, n. salle (f.) de classe.

clatter, n. bruit m.

clause, n. clause f.

claustrophobia, n. claustrophobie f.

claw, n. griffe f.

claw-hammer, n. marteau à dent m.

clay, n. argile f., glaise f.

clean, 1. adj. propre. **2.** vb. nettoyer.

clean-cut, adj. net, fin.

cleaner, n. (dry-c.) teinturier m.

cleaning, n. nettoyage m.

cleanliness, cleanness, n. propreté f.

cleanse, vb. nettoyer, curer.

cleanser, n. chose qui nettoie f., détersif m., cureur m.

clear, 1. adj. clair. **2.** vb. (c. up) déblayer; (profit) gagner; (get over) franchir; (weather, intr.) s'éclaircir.

clearance sale, n. vente f., liquidation f.

clear-cut, adj. nettement dessiné.

clearing, n. (open place) clairière f., éclaircissement f., (comm.) acquittement m., (woods) éclaircie f.

clearing house, n. banque de virement f., chambre de compensation f.

clearly, adv. clairement, nettement, évidemment.

clearness, n. clarté f., netteté f.

cleat, n. fer m., (naut.) taquet m.

cleavage, n. fendage m., scission f.

cleave, vb. (split) fendre; (adhere) adhérer.

cleaver, n. fendeur (person) m.; fendoir m., couperet (instrument) m.

cleft, n. fente f.

clemency, n. clémence f.

clench, vb. serrer.

clergy, n. clergé m.

clergyman, n. ecclésiastique m.

clerical, adj. (clergy) clérical; (business) de bureau.

clericalism, n. cléricalisme m.

clerk, n. (business) employé m.; (store) commis m.; (law, eccles.) clerc m.

clerkship, n. place de clerc f., place de commis f.

clever, adj. habile.

cleverly, adv. habilement.

cleverness, n. adresse f.

clew, n. fil m.

cliché, n. cliché m.

click, 1. n. cliquetis m., déclic m.; (computer) clic m. **2.** vb. cliqueter; (computer) clicquer.

client, n. client m.

clientele, n. clientèle f.

cliff, n. falaise f.

climactic, adj. arrivé à son apogée.

climate, n. climat m.

climatic, *adj.* climatique.

climax, *n.* comble *m.*

climb, 1. *n.* montée *f.* **2.** *vb.* monter, grimper.

climber, *n.* grimpeur *m.*, ascensioniste *m.*

clinch, *vb.* river; (settle) conclure.

cling, *vb.* s'accrocher.

clinging, *adj.* qui se crampone, qui s'accroche (à).

clinic, *n.* clinique *f.*

clinical, *adj.* clinique.

clinically, *adv.* d'une manière clinique.

clink, *vb.* tinter, cliqueter.

clip, 1. *vb.* couper. **2.** *n.* pince *f.*; **(paper c.)** trombone *m.*

clipper, *n.* rogneur *m.*, tondeuse (instrument) *f.*, (naut.) fin voilier *m.*

clipping, *n.* coupure *f.*

clique, *n.* clique *f.*

cloak, *n.* manteau *m.*; **(c. room)** vestiaire *m.*

clobber, *vb.* rosser.

clock, *n.* horloge *f.*; **(two o'c.)** deux heures.

clockwise, *adv.* dans le sens des aiguilles d'une montre.

clockwork, *n.* mouvement *(m.)* d'horlogerie.

clod, *n.* motte *(f.)* de terre; (person) lourdaud *m.*

clog, 1. *vb.* entraver. **2.** *n.* sabot *m.*

cloister, *n.* cloître *m.*

clone, *n.* reproduction exacte *f.*

close, 1. *adj.* (closed) fermé; (narrow) étroit; (near) proche; (secret) réservé. **2.** *vb.* fermer. **3.** *adv.* tout près. **4.** *prep.* **(c. to)** près de.

closely, *adv.* de près, étroitement.

closeness, *n.* proximité *f.*, lourdeur (of weather) *f.*, réserve *f.*

closet, *n.* (room) cabinet *m.*; (clothes) placard *m.*

close-up, *n.* gros plan *m.*

closure, *n.* fermeture *f.*

clot, *n.* (blood) caillot *m.*

cloth, *n.* étoffe *f.*

clothe, *vb.* vêtir (de); habiller *m.*

clothes, *n.* habits *m.pl.*

clothes hanger, *n.* cintre *m.*

clothespin, *n.* pince *f.*

clothier, *n.* drapier *m.*, tailleur *m.*

clothing, *n.* vêtements *m.pl.*

cloud, *n.* nuage *m.*

cloudburst, *n.* trombe *f.*, rafale (f.) de pluie.

cloudiness, *n.* état nuageux *m.*, obscurité *f.*

cloudless, *adj.* sans nuage.

cloudy, *adj.* nuageux, couvert.

clout, 1. *n.* gifle *f.*; tape *f.*; (power) pouvoir *m.* **2.** *vb.* gifler, taper.

clove, *n.* clou *(m.)* de girofle; **(c. of garlic)** gousse *(f.)* d'ail.

clover, *n.* trèfle *m.*

clown, *n.* bouffon *m.*

clownish, *adj.* rustre, grossier, de paysan.

cloy, *vb.* rassasier.

cloying, *adj.* écœurant.

club, 1. *n.* (society) club *m.*, société *f.*, cercle *m.*; (stick) massue *f.*; (golf) crosse *f.*; (cards) trèfle *m.* **2.** *vb.* matraquer.

clubfoot, *n.* pied bot *m.*

clue, *n.* fil *m.*

clump, *n.* (trees) bosquet *m.*; massif *m.*

clumsiness, *n.* gaucherie *f.*, maladresse *f.*

clumsy, *adj.* gauche.

cluster, 1. *n.* (people) groupe *m.*; (fruit) grappe *f.*; (flowers, trees) bouquet *m.* **2.** *vb.* se grouper.

clutch, 1. *n.* (claw) griffe *f.*; (auto) embrayage *m.* **2.** *vb.* saisir.

clutter, 1. *vb.* encombrer. **2.** *n.* désordre *m.*

coach, 1. *n.* (carriage) carrosse *m.*; (train) wagon *m.*; (sports) entraîneur *m.* **2.** *vb.* (sports) entraîner; (school) donner des leçons particulières à.

coachman, *n.* cocher *m.*

coagulate, *vb.* se coaguler.

coagulation, *n.* coagulation *f.*

coal, *n.* charbon *m.* de terre, houille *f.*

coalesce, *vb.* se fondre, se fusionner, s'unir.

coalition, *n.* coalition *f.*

coal tar, *n.* goudron *(m.)* de houille.

coarse, *adj.* grossier.

coarsen, *vb.* rendre plus grossier.

coarseness, *n.* grossièreté *f.*

coast, 1. *n.* côte *f.* **2.** *vb.* (bicycle) descendre en roue libre.

coastal, *adj.* de la côte, littoral.

coaster, *n.* caboteur *m.,* dessous de carafe *m.*

coast guard, *n.* garde-côtes *m.*

coastline, *n.* littoral *m.*

coat, 1. *n.* (man) pardessus *m.;* (woman) manteau *m.;* (paint) couche *f.* **2.** *vb.* **(c. with)** revêtir de.

coating, *n.* couche *f.,* enduit *m.,* étoffe pour habits *f.*

coat of arms, *n.* écusson *m.*

coax, *vb.* cajoler.

cob, *n.* épi *m.*

cobalt, *n.* cobalt *m.*

cobbler, *n.* savetier *m.,* cordonnier *m.*

cobblestone, *n.* pavé *m.*

cobra, *n.* cobra *m.*

cobweb, *n.* toile (*f.*) d'araignée.

cocaine, *n.* cocaïne *f.*

cock, 1. *n.* (fowl) coq *m.;* (male) mâle *m.* **2.** *vb.* faire de l'œil.

cocker spaniel, *n.* épagneul cocker *m.*

cockeyed, *adj.* louche.

cockhorse, *n.* dada *m.*

cockpit, *n.* poste (*m.*) de pilotage.

cockroach, *n.* blatte *f.,* cafard *m.*

cocksure, *adj.* sûr et certain.

cocktail, *n.* cocktail *m.;* **(fruit c.)** macédoine *f.* (de fruits).

cocky, *adj.* suffisant.

cocoa, *n.* cacao *m.*

coconut, *n.* noix (*f.*) de coco.

cocoon, *n.* cocon *m.*

cod, *n.* morue *f.*

coddle, *vb.* dorloter.

code, *n.* code *m.*

codeine, *n.* codéine *f.*

codfish, *n.* morue *f.*

codify, *vb.* codifier.

cod-liver oil, *n.* huile (*f.*) de foie de morue.

coeducation, *n.* enseignement mixte *m.*

coequal, *adj.* égal.

coerce, *vb.* contraindre.

coercion, *n.* coercition *f.,* contrainte *f.*

coercive, *adj.* coercitif.

coexist, *vb.* coexister.

coffee, *n.* café *m.*

coffee break, *n.* pause-café *f.*

coffee pot, *n.* cafetière *f.*

coffee shop, *n.* cafétéria *f.*

coffee table, *n.* table (*f.*) basse.

coffer, *n.* coffre *m.*

coffin, *n.* cercueil *m.*

cog, *n.* dent *f.*

cogent, *adj.* puissant, fort.

cogitate, *vb.* méditer, penser.

cognac, *n.* cognac *m.*

cognizance, *n.* connaissance *f.*

cognizant, *adj.* instruit, (law) compétent.

cogwheel, *n.* roue (*f.*) d'engrenage.

cohabit, *vb.* vivre en concubinage.

coherent, *adj.* cohérent.

cohesion, *n.* cohésion *f.*

cohesive, *adj.* cohésif.

cohort, *n.* cohorte *f.*

coiffure, *n.* coiffure *f.*

coil, *n.* rouleau *m.*

coin, *n.* pièce (*f.*) de monnaie.

coinage, *n.* monnayage *m.,* monnaie *f.*

coincide, *vb.* coïncider.

coincidence, *n.* coïncidence *f.*

coincident, *adj.* coïncident.

coincidental, *adj.* coïncident, d'accord (avec).

coincidentally, *adv.* par coïncidence.

colander, *n.* passoire *f.*

cold, 1. *n.* (temperature) froid *m.;* (med.) rhume *m.* **2.** *adj.* froid; **(it is c.)** il fait froid; **(feel c.)** avoir froid; **(catch c.)** attraper un rhume.

cold-blooded, *adj.* de sang froid.

coldly, *adv.* froidement.

coldness, *n.* froideur *f.*

cold sore, *n.* bouton (*m.*) de fièvre.

colic, *n.* colique *f.*

collaborate, *vb.* collaborer.

collaboration, *n.* collaboration *f.*

collaborator, *n.* collaborateur *m.*

collapse, 1. *n.* effondrement *m.;* (med.) affaissement *m.* **2.** *vb.* s'effondrer; (med.) s'affaisser.

collapsible, *adj.* pliant.

collar, *n.* col *m.;* (dog) collier *m.*

collarbone, *n.* clavicule *f.*

collate, *vb.* collationner, comparer.

collateral, *adj. and n.* collatéral *m.*

collation, *n.* collation *f.,* comparaison *f.,* repas froid *m.*

colleague, n. collègue m.f.

collect, vb. rassembler.

collection, n. collection f.; (money) collecte f.

collective, adj. collectif.

collectively, adv. collectivement.

collector, n. (art) collectionneur m.; (tickets) contrôleur m.

college, n. collège m.; (higher education) université f.

collegiate, adj. de collège, collégial.

collide, vb. se heurter (contre).

collie, n. colley m.

colliery, n. houillère f., mine (f.) de charbon.

collision, n. collision f.

colloquial, adj. familier.

colloquialism, n. expression de style familier f.

colloquially, adv. en style familier.

colloquy, n. colloque m., entretien m.

collusion, n. collusion f., connivence f.

colon, n. (gramm.) deux points m.pl.

colonel, n. colonel m.

colonial, adj. colonial.

colonist, n. colon m.

colonization, n. colonisation f.

colonize, vb. coloniser.

colony, n. colonie f.

color, 1. n. couleur f. 2. vb. colorer, tr.

color-blind, adj. daltonien.

coloration, n. coloris m.

colored, adj. coloré, de couleur, colorié.

colorful, adj. coloré, pittoresque.

coloring, n. coloris m., couleur f.; (skin) teint m.

colorless, adj. sans couleur, incolore, terne.

colossal, adj. colossal.

colt, n. poulain m.

colter, n. coutre m.

column, n. colonne f.

columnist, n. journaliste (qui a sa rubrique à lui) m.

coma, n. coma m.

comb, 1. n. peigne m. 2. vb. peigner.

combat, 1. n. combat m. 2. vb. combattre.

combatant, adj. and n. combattant m.

combative, adj. combatif.

combination, n. combinaison f.

combination lock, n. serrure (f.) à combinaisons.

combine, vb. combiner, tr.

combustible, adj. and n. combustible m.

combustion, n. combustion f.

come, vb. venir; (c. about) arriver; (c. across) rencontrer; (c. away) partir; (c. back) revenir; (c. down) descendre; (c. in) combler; (c. off) se détacher; (c. out) sortir; (c. up) monter; (c. upon) tomber sur.

comedian, n. comédien m.

comedienne, n. comédienne f.

comedy, n. comédie f.

comely, adj. avenant.

comet, n. comète f.

comfort, 1. n. (mental) consolation f.; (material) confort m. 2. vb. consoler.

comfortable, adj. commode.

comfortably, adv. confortablement, commodément.

comforter, n. consolateur m.; (quilt) édredon m.

comfortingly, adv. d'une manière réconfortante.

comfortless, adj. sans consolation, inconsolable, désolé.

comic, comical, adj. comique.

comic strip, n. bande (f.) dessinée.

coming, n. venue f., arrivée f., approche f.

comma, n. virgule f.

command, 1. n. commandement m. 2. vb. commander (à).

commandeer, vb. réquisitionner.

commander, n. commandant m.

commander in chief, n. généralissime m.

commandment, n. commandement m.

commando, n. commando m.

commemorate, vb. commémorer.

commemoration, n. célébration f., commémoration f.

commemorative, adj. commémoratif.

commence, vb. commencer.

commencement, n. (school) distribution (f.) des diplômes.

commend, vb. (entrust) recommander; (praise) louer.

commendable, adj. louable, recommandable.

commendably, adv. d'une manière louable.

commendation, n. louange f.

commensurate, adj. proportionné.

comment, 1. n. commentaire m. **2.** vb. commenter.

commentary, n. commentaire m.; reportage m.

commentator, n. commentateur m.

commerce, n. commerce m.

commercial, 1. adj. commercial. **2.** n. annonce (f.) publicitaire; spot m.

commercialism, n. commercialisme m.

commercialize, vb. commercialiser.

commercially, adv. commercialement.

commiserate, vb. plaindre, avoir pitié de.

commissary, n. (person) commissaire m.; (supply store) dépôt (m.) de vivres.

commission, n. (assignment) commande f.; (officer) brevet m.; (committee, percentage) commission f.

commissioner, n. commissaire m.

commit, vb. commettre; (**c. oneself**) s'engager.

commitment, n. engagement m.

committee, n. comité m.

commodious, adj. spacieux.

commodity, n. produit m., commodité f., denrée f.

common, adj. commun; (vulgar) vulgaire.

common law, n. droit coutumier m.

commonly, adv. communément, ordinairement.

Common Market, n. Marché (m.) commun.

commonness, n. vulgarité f.

commonplace, 1. n. lieu-commun m. **2.** adj. banal.

common sense, n. bon sens m.

commonwealth, n. état m.

commotion, n. agitation f.

communal, adj. communal.

commune, n. commune f.

communicable, adj. communicable.

communicant, n. communiant m.

communicate, vb. communiquer.

communication, n. communication f.

communicative, adj. communicatif.

communion, n. communion f.

communiqué, n. communiqué m.

communism, n. communisme m.

communist, adj. and n. communiste m.f.

communistic, adj. communiste.

community, n. communauté f.

commutation, n. commutation f.

commutation ticket, n. carte (f.) d'abonnement.

commute, vb. changer; (law) commuer; faire la navette.

commuter, n. voyageur (m.) de banlieue.

compact, 1. n. (agreement) accord m.; (cosmetic) poudrier m. **2.** adj. compact.

compact disc, n. disque (m.) compact.

compact disc player, n. lecteur (m.) de disque compact.

compactness, n. compacité f.

companion, n. compagnon m., compagne f.

companionable, adj. sociable.

companionship, n. camaraderie f.

company, n. compagnie f.

comparable with, adj. comparable à.

comparative, adj. and n. comparatif m.

comparatively, adv. comparativement, relativement.

compare, vb. comparer.

comparison, n. comparaison f.

compartment, n. compartiment m.

compass, n. (naut.) boussole f.; (geom.) compas m.

compassion, n. compassion f.

compassionate, adj. compatissant.

compassionately, adv. avec compassion.

compatible, adj. compatible.

compatriot, n. compatriote m.f.

compel, vb. forcer.

compelling, adj. irrésistible.

compendium, n. abrégé m., résumé m.

compensate, vb. compenser.

compensation, n. compensation f.

compensatory, adj. compensateur.

compete, vb. rivaliser.

competence, n. compétence f.

competent, adj. capable.

competently, adv. convenablement, avec compétence.

competition, n. concurrence f.

competitive, adj. concurrentiel; de compétition.

competitor, n. concurrent m.

compile, vb. compiler.

complacency, n. contentement (m.) de soi-même.

complacent, adj. content de soi-même.

complacently, adv. avec un air (un ton) suffisant.

complain, vb. se plaindre.

complainer, n. plaignant m., réclameur m.

complainingly, adv. d'une manière plaignante.

complaint, n. plainte f.

complement, n. complément m.

complementary, adj. complémentaire.

complete, adj. complet.

completely, adv. complètement, tout à fait.

completeness, n. état complet m., perfection f.

completion, n. achèvement m.

complex, adj. and n. complexe m.

complexion, n. teint m.

complexity, n. complexité f.

compliance, n. acquiescement m.

compliant, adj. complaisant, accommodant.

complicate, vb. compliquer.

complicated, adj. compliqué.

complication, n. complication f.

complicity, n. complicité f.

compliment, n. compliment m.

complimentary, adj. flatteur, de félicitation; (ticket) de faveur.

comply with, vb. se conformer à.

component, n. composant m., élément m.

comport, vb. s'accorder (avec), convenir (à).

compose, vb. composer; (c. oneself) se calmer.

composed, adj. composé, calme, tranquille.

composer, n. compositeur m.

composite, adj. composé.

composition, n. composition f.

compost, n. compost m., terreau m.

composure, n. calme m., tranquillité f., sang-froid m.

compote, n. compote f.

compound, 1. adj. and n. composé m. **2.** vb. aggraver.

compound fracture, n. fracture (f.) compliquée.

compound interest, n. intérêt (m.) composé.

comprehend, vb. comprendre.

comprehensible, adj. compréhensible, intelligible.

comprehension, n. compréhension f.

comprehensive, adj. compréhensif.

compress, 1. n. compresse f. **2.** vb. comprimer, tr.

compressed, adj. comprimé.

compression, n. compression f.

compressor, n. compresseur m.

comprise, vb. comprendre.

compromise, 1. n. compromis m. **2.** vb. compromettre.

compromiser, n. comprometteur m.

compulsion, n. contrainte f.

compulsive, adj. coercitif, obligatoire; (psychological) compulsif; (liar, smoker) invétéré.

compulsory, adj. obligatoire.

compunction, n. componction f., scrupule m.

computation, n. supputation f.

compute, vb. supputer.

computer, n. ordinateur m.

computerize, vb. informatiser.

computer programmer, n. programmeur m.

computer science, n. informatique f.

comrade, n. camarade m.f.

comradeship, n. camaraderie f.

con, vb. rouler, escroquer.

concave, *adj.* concave.
conceal, *vb.* cacher.
concealment, *n.* action (*f.*) de cacher.
concede, *vb.* concéder.
conceit, *n.* vanité *f.*
conceited, *adj.* vaniteux, suffisant.
conceivable, *adj.* concevable.
conceivably, *adv.* d'une manière concevable.
conceive, *vb.* concevoir.
concentrate, *vb.* concentrer, *tr.*
concentration, *n.* concentration *f.*
concentration camp, *n.* camp (*m.*) de concentration.
concept, *n.* concept *m.*
conception, *n.* conception *f.*
concern, 1. *n.* (what pertains to one) affaire *f.*; (*comm.*) entreprise *f.*; (solicitude) souci *m.* **2.** *vb.* concerner; (**c. oneself with**) s'intéresser à; (**be c.ed about**) s'inquiéter de.
concerning, *prep.* concernant.
concert, *n.* concert *m.*
concerted, *adj.* concerté.
concerto, *n.* concerto *m.*
concession, *n.* concession *f.*
conciliate, *vb.* concilier.
conciliation, *n.* conciliation *f.*
conciliator, *n.* conciliateur *m.*
conciliatory, *adj.* conciliant, conciliatoire.
concise, *adj.* concis.
concisely, *adv.* avec concision, succinctement.
conciseness, *n.* concision *f.*
conclave, *n.* conclave *m.*
conclude, *vb.* conclure.
conclusion, *n.* conclusion *f.*
conclusive, *adj.* concluant.
conclusively, *adv.* d'une manière concluante.
concoct, *vb.* préparer.
concoction, *n.* mélange *m.*
concomitant, 1. *adj.* concomitant. **2.** *n.* accessoire *m.*
concord, *n.* concorde *f.*
concordat, *n.* concordat *m.*
concourse, *n.* concours *m.*, affluence *f.*
concrete, 1. *n.* béton *m.* **2.** *adj.* concret.
concretely, *adv.* d'une manière concrète.

concreteness, *n.* état concret *m.*
concubine, *n.* concubine *f.*
concur, *vb.* (events) concourir; (persons) être d'accord.
concurrence, *n.* assentiment *m.*, concours *m.*
concurrent, *adj.* concourant.
concussion, *n.* secousse *f.*, ébranlement *m.*
condemn, *vb.* condamner.
condemnable, *adj.* condamnable.
condemnation, *n.* condamnation *f.*
condensation, *n.* condensation *f.*
condense, *vb.* condenser, *tr.*
condenser, *n.* condenseur *m.*
condescend, *vb.* condescendre.
condescendingly, *adv.* avec condescendance.
condescension, *n.* condescendance *f.*
condiment, *n.* condiment *m.*, assaisonnement *m.*
condition, 1. *n.* condition *f.* **2.** *vb.* conditionner.
conditional, *adj. and n.* conditionnel *m.*
conditionally, *adv.* conditionnellement.
conditioner, *n.* (hair) après-shampooing *m.*
condolence, *n.* condoléance *f.*
condole with, *vb.* faire ses condoléances à.
condom, *n.* préservatif *m.*
condominium, *n.* condominium *m.*
condone, *vb.* approuver (tacitement).
conducive, *adj.* favorable.
conduct, 1. *n.* conduite *f.* **2.** *vb.* conduire.
conductivity, *n.* conductivité *f.*
conductor, *n.* conducteur *m.*; (bus) receveur *m.*; (rail) chef (*m.*) de train; (music) chef (*m.*) d'orchestre.
conduit, *n.* conduit *m.*, tuyau *m.*
cone, *n.* cône *m.*
confection, *n.* confection *f.*; (sweet) bonbon *m.*
confectioner, *n.* confiseur *m.*
confectionery, *n.* confiserie *f.*
confederacy, confederation, *n.* confédération *f.*

confederate, *adj. and n.* confédéré *m.*

confer, *vb.* conférer.

conference, *n.* (meeting) entretien *m.*; (congress) congrès *m.*

confess, *vb.* avouer; *(eccles.)* confesser, *tr.*

confession, *n.* confession *f.*

confessional, *n.* confessional *m.*

confessor, *n.* confesseur *m.*

confetti, *n.* confetti *m.*

confidant, *n.* confident *m.*

confidante, *n.* confidente *f.*

confide, *vb.* confier (à), *tr.*

confidence, *n.* (trust) confiance *f.*; (secret) confidence *f.*

confident, *adj.* confiant.

confidential, *adj.* confidentiel.

confidentially, *adv.* confidentiellement.

confidently, *adv.* avec confiance.

configure, *vb.* (computer) configurer.

confine, *vb.* (banish) confiner; (limit) limiter.

confinement, *n.* détention *f.*

confirm, *vb.* confirmer.

confirmation, *n.* confirmation *f.*

confirmed, *adj.* invétéré, incorrigible.

confiscate, *vb.* confisquer.

confiscation, *n.* confiscation *f.*

conflagration, *n.* conflagration *f.*, incendie *m.*

conflict, *n.* conflit *m.*

conflicting, *adj.* contradictoire.

conform, *vb.* conformer, *tr.*

conformation, *n.* conformation *f.*, conformité *f.*

conformer, *n.* conformiste *m.*

conformist, *n.* conformiste *m.*

conformity, *n.* conformité *f.*

confound, *vb.* confondre; **(c. him!)** que le diable l'emporte!

confront, *vb.* confronter.

confrontation, *n.* confrontation *f.*

confuse, *vb.* confondre.

confusing, *adj.* peu clair.

confusion, *n.* confusion *f.*

congeal, *vb.* congeler, *tr.*

congealment, *n.* congélation *f.*

congenial, *adj.* (person) sympathique; (thing) convenable.

congenital, *adj.* congénital.

congenitally, *adv.* d'une manière congénitale.

congested, *adj.* (area) surpeuplé; (road) bloqué; (medical) congestionné.

congestion, *n.* *(med.)* congestion *f.*; (traffic) encombrement *m.*

conglomerate, *adj.* congloméré.

conglomeration, *n.* conglomération *f.*

congratulate, *vb.* féliciter (de).

congratulation, *n.* félicitation *f.*

congratulatory, *adj.* de félicitation.

congregate, *vb.* rassembler, *tr.*

congregation, *n.* assemblée *f.*

congress, *n.* congrès *m.*

congressional, *adj.* congressionnel.

congressman, -woman, *n.* membre *(m.)* du congrès.

conic, *adj.* conique.

conjecture, *n.* conjecture *f.*

conjugal, *adj.* conjugal.

conjugate, *vb.* conjuguer.

conjugation, *n.* conjugaison *f.*

conjunction, *n.* conjonction *f.*

conjunctive, *adj.* conjonctif.

conjunctivitis, *n.* conjonctivite *f.*

conjure, *vb.* conjurer.

conk, *vb.* **(c. out)** (colloquial) tomber en panne.

con man, *n.* arnaqueur *m.*

connect, *vb.* joindre.

connection, *n.* connexion *f.*; (social) relations *f.pl.*; (train) correspondance *f.*

connivance, *n.* connivence *f.*

connive, *vb.* conniver (à).

connoisseur, *n.* connaisseur *m.*

connotation, *n.* connotation *f.*

connote, *vb.* signifier, vouloir dire.

connubial, *adj.* conjugal, du mariage.

conquer, *vb.* conquérir.

conquerable, *adj.* qui peut être vaincu, domptable.

conqueror, *n.* conquérant *m.*

conquest, *n.* conquête *f.*

conscience, *n.* conscience *f.*

conscientious, *adj.* consciencieux.

conscientiously, *adv.* consciencieusement.

conscious, *adj.* conscient.

consciously, *adv.* sciemment, en parfaite connaissance.

consciousness, *n.* conscience *f.*

conscript, *adj. and n.* conscrit *m.*

conscription, *n.* conscription *f.*

consecrate, *vb.* consacrer.

consecration, *n.* consécration *f.*

consecutive, *adj.* consécutif.

consecutively, *adv.* consécutivement, de suite.

consensus, *n.* consensus *m.*, assentiment général *m.*

consent, 1. *n.* consentement *m.* **2.** *vb.* consentir.

consequence, *n.* conséquence *f.*

consequent, *adj.* conséquent.

consequential, *adj.* conséquent, logique.

consequently, *adv.* par conséquent.

conservation, *n.* conservation *f.*; **(c. area)** zone *(f.)* classée.

conservationist, *n.* défenseur *(m.)* de l'environnement.

conservatism, *n.* conservatisme *m.*

conservative, *adj.* (politics) conservateur; *(comm.)* prudent.

conservatively, *adv.* d'une manière conservatrice.

conservatory, *n.* conservatoire *m.*

conserve, *vb.* conserver.

consider, *vb.* considérer.

considerable, *adj.* considérable.

considerably, *adv.* considérablement.

considerate, *adj.* prévenant, attentionné.

considerately, *adv.* avec égards, avec indulgence.

consideration, *n.* considération *f.*

considering, *prep.* vu que, attendu que.

consign, *vb.* consigner.

consignment, *n.* expédition *f.*, consignation *f.*

consistency, *n.* consistance *f.*

consistent, *adj.* consistant; **(c. with)** conforme à.

consist of, *vb.* consister en.

consolation, *n.* consolation *f.*

console, *vb.* consoler.

consolidate, *vb.* consolider.

consommé, *n.* consommé *m.*

consonant, *n.* consonne *f.*

consort, 1. *n.* compagnon *m.*, époux *m.* **2.** *vb.* s'associer (à).

conspicuous, *adj.* en évidence.

conspicuously, *adv.* visiblement, éminemment.

conspicuousness, *n.* éclat *m.*, position éminente *f.*

conspiracy, *n.* conspiration *f.*

conspirator, *n.* conspirateur *m.*

conspire, *vb.* conspirer.

conspirer, *n.* conspirateur *m.*

constancy, *n.* constance *f.*, fermeté *f.*

constant, *adj.* constant.

constantly, *adv.* constamment.

constellation, *n.* constellation *f.*

consternation, *n.* consternation *f.*

constipate, *vb.* constiper.

constipation, *n.* constipation *f.*

constituency, *n.* circonscription électorale *f.*

constituent, *adj.* constituant.

constitute, *vb.* constituer.

constitution, *n.* constitution *f.*

constitutional, *adj.* constitutionnel.

constrain, *vb.* contraindre.

constrained, *adj.* contraint.

constraint, *n.* contrainte *f.*, gêne *f.*

constrict, *vb.* resserrer.

constriction, *n.* resserrement *f.*

construct, *vb.* construire.

construction, *n.* construction *f.*

constuction worker, *n.* ouvrier *(m.)* de bâtiment.

constructive, *adj.* constructif.

constructively, *adv.* constructivement, par induction.

constructor, *n.* constructeur *m.*

construe, *vb.* interpréter.

consul, *n.* consul *m.*

consular, *adj.* consulaire.

consulate, *n.* consulat *m.*

consult, *vb.* consulter.

consultant, *n.* conseiller *m.*, consultant *m.*

consultation, *n.* consultation *f.*

consume, *vb.* consommer.

consumer, *n.* consommateur *m.*

consumer goods, *n.* biens *(m.pl.)* de consommation.

consumerism, *n.* protection *(f.)* des consommateurs.

consummate, 1. *adj.* consommé. **2.** *vb.* consommer.

consummation, n. consommation f.

consumption, n. consommation f.; (med.) phtisie f.

consumptive, adj. poitrinaire, tuberculeux.

contact, n. contact m.

contact lenses, n. lentilles (f.pl.) (de contact), verres (m.pl.) de contact.

contagion, n. contagion f.

contagious, adj. contagieux.

contain, vb. contenir.

container, n. récipient m.

contaminate, vb. contaminer.

contaminated, adj. contaminé.

contamination, n. contamination f.

contemplate, vb. contempler.

contemplation, n. contemplation f.

contemplative, adj. contemplatif.

contemporary, adj. contemporain.

contempt, n. mépris m.

contemptible, adj. méprisable.

contemptuous, adj. méprisant.

contemptuously, adv. avec mépris, dédaigneusement.

contend, vb. (struggle) lutter; (maintain) soutenir.

contender, n. compétiteur m.

content, n. (satisfaction) contentement m.; (c.s) contenu m.

contented with, adj. content de.

contention, n. contention f., lutte f.

contentment, n. contentement m.

contents, n.pl. (of text) contenu m.; (table of c.) table (f.) des matières.

contest, 1. n. (struggle) lutte f.; (competition) concours m. **2.** vb. contester.

contestable, adj. contestable.

contestant, n. concurrent m., disputant m.

context, n. contexte m.

contiguous, adj. contigu m., contiguë f.

continence, n. continence f., retenue f.

continent, adj. and n. continent m.

continental, adj. continental.

contingency, n. contingence f.; (c. plan) plan (m.) d'urgence.

contingent, adj. contingent; (be c. upon) dépendre de.

continual, adj. continuel.

continuance, n. continuation f.

continuation, n. continuation f.; (of story) suite f.; (after interruption) reprise f.

continue, vb. continuer.

continuity, n. continuité f.

continuous, adj. continu.

continuously, adv. continûment, sans interruption.

contort, vb. tordre, défigurer.

contortion, n. torsion f.; contorsion f.

contortionist, n. contortionniste m.f.

contour, n. contour m.

contraband, n. contrebande f.

contraception, n. limitation des naissances f., contraception f.

contraceptive, n. contraceptif m.

contract, 1. n. contrat m. **2.** vb. contracter, tr.

contracted, adj. contracté, resserré.

contraction, n. contraction f.

contractor, n. entrepreneur m.

contradict, vb. contredire.

contradictable, adj. qui peut être contredit.

contradiction, n. contradiction f., démenti m.

contradictory, adj. contradictoire.

contraption, n. machin m.

contrary, adj. and n. contraire m.; (on the c.) au contraire.

contrast, 1. n. contraste m. **2.** vb. mettre en contraste, tr.; contraster, intr.

contravene, vb. contrevenir à.

contribute, vb. contribuer.

contribution, n. contribution f.

contributive, adj. contributif.

contributor, n. contribuant m.

contributory, adj. contribuant.

contrite, adj. contrit, pénitent.

contrition, n. contrition f.

contrivance, n. combinaison f., invention f., artifice m.

contrive, vb. inventer, imaginer, arranger.

control, 1. n. autorité f.; (machinery) commande f. **2.** vb. gouverner; (check) contrôler.

controllable, adj. vérifiable, gouvernable.

controller, n. contrôleur m.

control panel, n. tableau (m.) de commande.

control room, n. salle (f.) des commandes.

controversial, adj. de controverse, polémique.

controversy, n. controverse f.

contusion, n. contusion f.

conundrum, n. devinette f., énigme f.

convalescence, n. convalescence f.

convalescent, adj. convalescent.

convector, n. radiateur m. (à convexion).

convene, vb. assembler, tr.

convenience, n. convenance f.; (comfort) commodité f.

convenient, adj. commode.

conveniently, adv. commodément.

convent, n. couvent m.

convention, n. convention f.

conventional, adj. conventionnel.

conventionally, adv. par convention.

converge, vb. converger.

convergence, n. convergence f.

convergent, adj. convergent.

conversant, adj. versé (dans), familier (avec).

conversation, n. conversation f.

conversational, adj. de conversation.

conversationalist, n. causeur m.

converse, 1. vb. converser. **2.** adj. and n. inverse.

conversely, adv. réciproquement.

conversion, n. conversion f.

convert, vb. convertir, tr.

converter, n. convertisseur m.

convertible, adj. convertible (of things), convertissable (of persons), décapotable (of car).

convex, adj. convexe.

convey, vb. (transport) transporter; (transmit) transmettre.

conveyance, n. transport m.

conveyor, n. transporteur m., conducteur électrique m.; (c. belt) tapis (m.) roulant.

convict, 1. n. forçat m. **2.** vb. condamner.

conviction, n. (condemnation)

condamnation f.; (persuasion) conviction f.

convince, vb. convaincre.

convincing, adj. convaincant.

convincingly, adv. d'une manière convaincante.

convivial, adj. jovial, joyeux.

convocation, n. convocation f.

convoke, vb. convoquer.

convoluted, adj. compliqué.

convoy, n. convoi m.

convulse, vb. convulser, bouleverser.

convulsion, n. convulsion f.

convulsive, adj. convulsif.

coo, vb. roucouler.

cook, 1. n. cuisinier m. **2.** vb. cuire, intr.; faire cuire, tr.

cookbook, n. livre (m.) de cuisine.

cookie, n. gâteau sec m.

cooking, n. cuisine f.

cool, 1. adj. frais m., fraîche f. **2.** vb. rafraîchir.

cooler, n. rafraîchissoir m., réfrigérant m., (motor) radiateur m.

coolness, n. fraîcheur f.

coop, 1. n. cage (f.) à poules. **2.** vb. (c. up) enfermer.

cooperate, vb. coopérer.

cooperation, n. coopération f.

cooperative, 1. n. coopérative f. **2.** adj. coopératif.

cooperatively, adj. d'une manière coopérative.

co-opt, vb. coopter.

coordinate, vb. coordonner.

coordination, n. coordination f.

coordinator, n. coordinateur m.

co-ownership, n. copropriété f.

cop, 1. n. (slang) flic m. **2.** vb. (colloquial) attraper, pincer.

cope with, vb. tenir tête à.

copier, n. machine à copier f.

copious, adj. copieux.

copiously, adv. copieusement.

copiousness, n. abondance f.

copper, n. cuivre m.

copperplate, n. cuivre plané m.; taille-douce f.

copulate, vb. s'accoupler.

copy, 1. n. (duplicate) copie f.; (book) exemplaire m. **2.** vb. copier.

copyist, n. copiste m., imitateur m.

copyright, n. droit (m.) d'auteur.

coquetry, n. coquetterie f.

coquette, n. coquette f.

coral, n. corail m.; pl. coraux.

cord, n. corde f.

cordial, adj. and n. cordial m.

cordiality, n. cordialité f.

cordially, adv. cordialement.

cordon, n. cordon m.

cordovan, adj. cordovan.

corduroy, n. velours côtelé m.

core, n. cœur m.

coriander, n. coriandre.

cork, n. (botany) liège m.; (stopper) bouchon m.

corkscrew, n. tire-bouchon m.

corn, n. maïs m.; (c. on the cob) épi (m.) de maïs.

cornea, n. cornée f.

corner, n. coin m.

cornerstone, n. pierre angulaire f.

cornet, n. cornet m.

cornetist, n. cornettiste m.

cornstarch, n. farine (f.) de maïs.

cornice, n. corniche f.

cornucopia, n. corne (f.) d'abondance.

corny, adj. rebattu.

corollary, n. corollaire m.

coronary, adj. coronaire.

coronation, n. couronnement m.

coroner, n. coroner m.

coronet, n. (petite) couronne f.

corporal, n. (mil.) caporal m.

corporate, adj. de corporation.

corporation, n. société f. (anonyme).

corps, n. corps m.

corpse, n. cadavre m.

corpulent, adj. corpulent, gros.

corpuscle, n. corpuscule m.

corral, n. corral m.

correct, 1. adj. correct. 2. vb. corriger.

correction, n. correction f.

corrective, 1. adj. correctif. 2. n. correctif m.

correctly, adv. correctement, justement.

correctness, n. correction f.

correlate, vb. être en corrélation, intr.; mettre en corrélation, tr.

correlation, n. corrélation f.

correspond, vb. correspondre.

correspondence, n. correspondance f.

correspondent, n. correspondant m.

corridor, n. couloir m.

corroborate, vb. corroborer.

corroboration, n. corroboration f., confirmation f.

corroborative, adj. corroboratif.

corrode, vb. corroder.

corrosion, n. corrosion f.

corrosive, adj. corrosif.

corrugate, vb. rider, plisser.

corrugated, adj. ondulé.

corrupt, 1. adj. corrompu. 2. vb. corrompre.

corruptible, adj. corruptible.

corruption, n. corruption f.

corruptive, adj. corruptif.

corsage, n. corsage m.

corset, n. corset m.

Corsica, n. Corse f.

cortege, n. cortège m.

cortisone, n. cortisone f.

corvette, n. corvette f.

cosmetic, adj. and n. cosmétique m.

cosmic, adj. cosmique.

cosmic rays, n. rayons cosmiques m.pl.

cosmonaut, n. cosmonaute m.f.

cosmopolitan, adj. and n. cosmopolite m.f.

cosmos, n. cosmos m.

Cossack, n. cosaque f.

cost, 1. n. coût m. 2. vb. coûter.

costliness, n. haut prix m., somptuosité f.

cost-effective, adj. rentable.

cost price, n. prix (m.) de revient.

co-star, n. partenaire m.f.

costly, adj. coûteux.

costume, n. costume m.

costume jewelry, n. bijoux (m.pl.) de fantaisie.

costumer, n. costumier m.

cot, n. (berth) couchette f.; (folding) lit-cage m.

coterie, n. coterie f., clique f.

cotillion, n. cotillon m.

cottage, n. chaumière f.

cottage industry, n. activité (f.) artisanale.

cotton, n. coton m.

cottonseed, n. graine (f.) de coton.

couch, n. divan m.

cougar, *n.* couguar *m.*

cough, 1. *n.* toux *f.* **2.** *vb.* tousser.

could, *vb.* pouvait, pourrait.

council, *n.* conseil *m.*

councilman, -woman, *n.* conseiller *m.*, conseillère *f.*

counsel, 1. *n.* conseil *m.* **2.** *vb.* conseiller.

counselor, *n.* conseiller *m.*

count, 1. *n.* (calculation) compte *m.*; (title) comte *m.* **2.** *vb.* compter; (c. on) compter sur.

countenance, *n.* expression *f.*

counter, 1. *n.* (shop) comptoir *m.* **2.** *adv.* (c. to) à l'encontre de.

counteract, *vb.* neutraliser.

counteraction, *n.* action contraire *f.*

counterattack, 1. *n.* contre-attaque *f.* **2.** *vb.* contreattaquer.

counterbalance, 1. *n.* contrepoids *m.* **2.** *vb.* contre-balancer.

counterclockwise, *adj. and adv.* dans le sens inverse des aiguilles d'une montre.

counterfeit, 1. *adj.* (money) faux *m.*, fausse *f.* **2.** *vb.* contrefaire.

countermand, *vb.* contremander.

counteroffensive, *n.* contre-offensive *f.*

counterpart, *n.* contre-partie *f.*, homologue *m.*

counterproductive, *adj.* qui produit l'effet contraire.

countersign, *vb.* contresigner.

countess, *n.* comtesse *f.*

countless, *adj.* innombrable.

country, 1. *n.* (nation) pays *m.*; (opposed to town) campagne *f.*; (native c.) patrie *f.*

countryman, *n.* (of same c.) compatriote *m.f.*; (rustic) campagnard *m.*

countryside, *n.* campagne *f.*

county, *n.* comté *m.*

coupé, *n.* coupé *m.*

couple, 1. *n.* couple *f.* **2.** *vb.* coupler.

coupon, *n.* coupon *m.*

courage, *n.* courage *m.*

courageous, *adj.* courageux.

courier, *n.* courrier *m.*

course, *n.* cours *m.*; (of c.) bien entendu; (route) route *f.*; (meal) service *m.*

court, 1. *n.* cour *f.*; (tennis) court. **2.** *vb.* faire la cour à.

courteous, *adj.* courtois.

courtesy, *n.* courtoisie *f.*

courthouse, *n.* palais (*m.*) de justice.

courtier, *n.* courtisan *m.*

courtly, *adj.* de cour, élégant, courtois.

courtmartial, *n.* conseil (*m.*) de guerre.

courtroom, *n.* salle (*f.*) d'audience.

courtship, *n.* cour *f.*

courtyard, *n.* cour *f.*

cousin, *n.* cousin *m.*, cousine *f.*

cove, *n.* anse *f.*, crique *f.*

covenant, *n.* pacte *m.*

cover, 1. *n.* (book, comm.) blanket) couverture *f.*; (pot) couvercle *m.*; (shelter) abri *m.*; (envelope) pli *m.*; (mil.) couvert *m.* **2.** *vb.* couvrir.

coverage, *n.* couverture *f.*

coveralls, *n.* bleus (*m.pl.*) de travail.

cover charge, *n.* couvert *m.*

covering, *n.* couverture *f.*, enveloppe *f.*

covert, *adj.* secret; voilé.

cover-up, *n.* tentative (*f.*) pour étouffer une affaire.

covet, *vb.* convoiter.

covetous, *adj.* avide, avaricieux.

cow, *n.* vache *f.*

coward, *adj. and n.* lâche *m.f.*

cowardice, *n.* lâcheté *f.*

cowardly, *adv.* lâche.

cowboy, *n.* cowboy *m.*

cower, *vb.* se blottir.

cow hand, *n.* cowboy *m.*

cowhide, *n.* peau (*f.*) de vache.

cowshed, *n.* étable *f.*

coxswain, *n.* patron (*m.*) de chaloupe, barreur *m.*

coy, *adj.* faussement timide.

cozy, *adj.* confortable, douillet.

crab, 1. *n.* crabe *m.* **2.** *vb.* rouspéter.

crab apple, *n.* pomme sauvage *f.*

crack, 1. *n.* (fissure) fente *f.*; (noise) craquement *m.* **2.** *vb. tr.* (glass, china) fêler; (nuts) casser; (noise) faire craquer. **3.** *vb. intr.* (split) se fendiller; (noise) craquer.

cracked, *adj.* fendu, fêlé.

cracker, *n.* biscuit *m.*

cracking, *n.* craquement *m.*, claquement *m.*

crackle, 1. *n.* crépitement *m.* **2.** *vb.* crépiter.

crackup, *n.* crach *m.*

cradle, *n.* berceau *m.*

craft, *n.* (skill) habileté *f.*; (trade) métier *m.*; (boat) embarcation *f.*

craftsman, *n.* artisan *m.*

craftsmanship, *n.* habileté *f.*, technique *f.*, art *m.*

crafty, *adj.* rusé, astucieux.

crag, *n.* rocher à pic *m.*, rocher escarpé *m.*

cram, *vb.* remplir, farcir.

cramp, *n.* (*med.*) crampe *f.*; (mechanical) crampon *m.*

cranberry, *n.* canneberge *f.*, airelle *f.*

crane, *n.* grue *f.*

cranium, *n.* crâne *m.*

crank, *n.* manivelle *f.*

cranky, *adj.* d'humeur difficile.

cranny, *n.* crevasse *f.*, fente *f.*

craps, *n.* (slang) jeu de dés *m.*

crapshooter, *n.* (slang) joueur aux dés *m.*

crash, 1. *n.* (noise) fracas *m.*; (accident) accident *m.* **2.** *vb.* tomber avec fracas, *intr.*

crash landing, *n.* atterrissage *(m.)* forcé.

crass, *adj.* grossier.

crate, *n.* caisse *f.*

crater, *n.* cratère *m.*

crave, *vb.* désirer ardemment.

craven, *adj.* lâche, poltron.

craving, *n.* désir ardent *m.*, besoin impérieux *m.*

crawl, *vb.* (reptiles) ramper; (persons) se traîner.

crayfish, *n.* (freshwater) écrevisse *f.*; (saltwater) langouste *f.*

crayon, *n.* pastel *m.*, crayon *m.*

craze, *n.* engouement *m.*

crazed, *adj.* fou, dément.

crazy, *adj.* fou *m.*, folle *f.*

creak, *vb.* grincer.

creaky, *adj.* qui crie, qui grince.

cream, *n.* crème *f.*

cream cheese, *n.* fromage *(m.)* frais.

creamery, *n.* crêmerie *f.*

creamy, *adj.* crémeux, de crème.

crease, 1. *n.* pli *m.* **2.** *vb.* froisser, *tr.*

create, *vb.* créer.

creation, *n.* création *f.*

creative, *adj.* créateur *m.*, créatrice *f.*

creator, *n.* créateur *m.*, créatrice *f.*

creature, *n.* créature *f.*

credence, *n.* créance *f.*, croyance *f.*

credentials, *n.* lettres *(f.pl.)* de créance; (student, servant) certificat *m.*

credibility, *n.* crédibilité *f.*

credible, *adj.* croyable.

credit, *n.* crédit *m.*; (merit) honneur *m.*

creditable, *adj.* estimable.

creditably, *adv.* honorablement.

credit card, *n.* carte *(f.)* de crédit.

creditor, *n.* créancier *m.*

credo, *n.* credo *m.*

credulity, *n.* crédulité *f.*

credulous, *adj.* crédule.

creed, *n.* (belief) croyance *f.*, (theology) credo *m.*

creek, *n.* ruisseau *m.*

creep, *vb.* (reptiles, insects, plants) ramper; (persons) se glisser.

creepy, *adj.* qui fait frissonner.

cremate, *vb.* incinérer.

crematorium, *n.* four *(m.)* crématoire.

crematory, *n.* crématorium *m.*

Creole, *n.* créole *m.f.*

creosote, *n.* créosote *f.*

crepe, *n.* crêpe *m.*

crescent, *n.* croissant *m.*

crest, *n.* crête *f.*

crestfallen, *adj.* abattu, découragé.

Crete, *n.* Crète *f.*

cretin, *n.* crétin *m.*

cretonne, *n.* cretonne *f.*

crevice, *n.* crevasse *f.*

crew, *n.* (boat) équipage *m.*; (gang) équipe *f.*

crew cut, *n.* les cheveux *(m.pl.)* en brosse.

crib, *n.* (child's bed) lit *(m.)* d'enfant; (manger) mangeoire *f.*

cricket, *n.* (insect) grillon *m.*; (game) cricket *m.*

crier, *n.* crieur *m.*, huissier *m.*

crime, *n.* crime *m.*

criminal, *adj.* criminel.

criminologist, *n.* criminologue *m.f.*

criminology, *n.* criminologie *f.*

crimson, *adj. and n.* cramoisi *m.*

cringe, *vb.* faire des courbettes, se tapir, s'humilier.

crinkle, 1. *n.* pli *m.*, sinuosité *f.* **2.** *vb.* serpenter, former en zigzag.

cripple, 1. *n.* estropié *m.* **2.** *vb.* estropier.

crisis, *n.* crise *f.*

crisp, *adj.* (food) croquant; (manner) tranchant.

crispness, *n.* frisure *f.*

crisscross, 1. *adj. and adv.* entrecroisé. **2.** *vb.* (s')entrecroiser.

criterion, *n.* critérium *m.*

critic, *n.* critique *m.*

critical, *adj.* critique.

criticism, *n.* critique *f.*

criticize, *vb.* critiquer.

critique, *n.* critique *f.*

croak, *vb.* (frogs) coasser; (crows, persons) croasser.

Croatia, *n.* Croatie *f.*

crochet, 1. *vb.* broder au crochet. **2.** *n.* crochet *m.*

crock, *n.* pot *(m.)* de terre.

crockery, *n.* faïence *f.*

crocodile, *n.* crocodile *m.*

crocodile tears, *n.* larmes *(f.pl.)* de crocodile.

croissant, *n.* croissant *m.*

crone, *n.* vieille femme *f.*

crony, *n.* vieux camarade *m.*, compère *m.*

crook, *n.* escroc *m.*; (thief) voleur *m.*

crooked, *adj.* tortu.

croon, *vb.* chantonner, fredonner.

crop, 1. *n.* (farming) récolte *f.* **2.** *vb.* (c. up) surgir.

croquet, *n.* (jeu de) croquet *m.*

croquette, *n.* croquette *f.*

cross, 1. *n.* croix *f.* **2.** *adj.* maussade. **3.** *vb.* croiser, *tr.*; (c. oneself) se signer; (c. out) rayer; (go across) traverser.

crossbreed, *n.* race croisée *f.*

cross-examine, *vb.* contreexaminer.

cross-eyed, *adj.* louche.

cross-fertilization, *n.* croisement *m.*

crossfire, *n.* feux croisés *m.pl.*

cross-purpose, *n.* opposition *f.*, contradiction *f.*, malentendu *m.*

cross section, *n.* coupe *(f.)* en travers.

crossword puzzle, *n.* mots croisés *m.pl.*

crotch, *n.* (tree) fourche *f.*; (trousers) fourchet *m.*

crouch, *vb.* s'accroupir.

croup, *n.* croupe *f.*; *(med.)* croup *m.*

croupier, *n.* croupier *m.*

crouton, *n.* crouton *m.*

crow, 1. *n.* (bird) corneille *f.*; (cock-c.) chant *(m.)* du coq. **2.** *vb.* chanter.

crowd, 1. *n.* foule *f.* **2.** *vb.* serrer, *tr.*; (c. with) remplir de.

crowded, *adj.* (streets, etc.) encombré.

crown, 1. *n.* couronne *f.*; (of head) sommet *m.*; (of hat) calotte *f.* **2.** *vb.* couronner.

crown prince, *n.* prince héritier *m.*

crow's-foot, *n.* patte d'oie (near the eye) *f.*; *(naut.)* araignée *f.*

crucial, *adj.* crucial.

crucible, *n.* creuset *m.*

crucifix, *n.* crucifix *m.*

crucifixion, *n.* crucifixion *f.*, crucifiement *m.*

crucify, *vb.* crucifier.

crude, *adj.* (unpolished) grossier; (metals, etc.) brut.

crudeness, *n.* crudité *f.*

cruel, *adj.* cruel.

cruelty, *n.* cruauté *f.*

cruet, *n.* burette *f.*

cruise, *n.* croisière *f.*

cruiser, *n.* croiseur *m.*

crumb, *n.* (small piece) miette *f.*; (not crust) mie *f.*

crumble, *vb.* émietter, *tr.*

crumple, *vb.* chiffonner, *tr.*

crunch, 1. *vb.* croquer, broyer. **2.** *n.* grincement *m.*

crusade, *n.* croisade *f.*

crusader, *n.* croisé *m.*

crush, 1. *vb.* écraser. **2.** *n.* presse *f.*, foule *f.*; (a c. on) le béguin pour.

crust, *n.* croûte *f.*

crustacean, *adj.* crustacé.

crusty, *adj.* couvert d'une croûte; *(fig.)* bourru, maussade.

crutch, *n.* béquille *f.*

cry, **1.** *n.* cri *m.* **2.** *vb.* (shout) crier; (weep) pleurer.

crybaby, *n.* pleurnicheur *m.*

crying, *adj.* criant.

cryosurgery, *n.* cryochirurgie *f.*

crypt, *n.* crypte *f.*

cryptic, *adj.* occulte, secret.

cryptography, *n.* cryptographie *f.*

crystal, *n.* cristal *m.*

crystalline, *adj.* cristallin.

crystallize, *vb.* cristalliser, *tr.*

cub, *n.* petit *m.* (d'un animal).

Cuba, *n.* Cuba *m.*

Cuban, **1.** *n.* Cubain *m.* **2.** *adj.* cubain.

cubbyhole, *n.* retraite *f.,* cachette *f.,* placard *m.*

cube, *n.* cube *m.*

cubic, *adj.* cubique.

cubicle, *n.* compartiment *m.,* cabine *f.*

cubic measure, *n.* mesures (*f.pl.*) de volume.

cubism, *n.* cubisme *m.*

cuckold, **1.** *n.* cocu *m.* **2.** *vb.* cocufier, faire cocu.

cuckoo, *n.* coucou *m.; (fig.)* niais *m.*

cucumber, *n.* concombre *m.*

cud, *n.* bol alimentaire *m.,* panse *f.,* chique (of tobacco) *f.*

cuddle, *vb.* serrer (dans ses bras), *tr.*

cudgel, **1.** *n.* bâton *m.,* gourdin *m.,* trique *f.* **2.** *vb.* bâtonner.

cue, *n.* (theater) réplique *f.;* (hint) mot *m.*

cuff, *n.* poignet *m.*

cuff link, *n.* bouton (*m.*) de manchette.

cuisine, *n.* cuisine *f.*

cul-de-sac, *n.* cul de sac *m.,* impasse *f.*

culinary, *adj.* culinaire, de cuisine.

cull, *vb.* cueillir, recueillir.

culminate, *vb.* culminer.

culmination, *n.* point culminant *m.*

culpable, *adj.* coupable.

culprit, *n.* coupable *m.f.*

cult, *n.* culte *m.*

cultivate, *vb.* cultiver.

cultivated, *adj.* cultivé.

cultivation, *n.* culture *f.*

cultivator, *n.* cultivateur *m.*

cultural, *adj.* culturel.

culture, *n.* culture *f.*

cumbersome, *adj.* encombrant.

cumulative, *adj.* cumulatif.

cunning, **1.** *n.* (guile) ruse *f.;* (skill) adresse *f.* **2.** *adj.* rusé; (attractive) charmant.

cup, *n.* tasse *f.*

cupboard, *n.* armoire *f.*

cupidity, *n.* cupidité *f.*

curable, *adj.* guérissable.

curator, *n.* conservateur *m.*

curb, **1.** *n.* (horse) gourmette *f.;* (pavement) bord *m.* **2.** *vb.* (horse) gourmer; *(fig.)* border.

curbstone, *n.* garde-pavé *m.*

curd, *n.* lait caillé *m.*

curdle, *vb.* cailler.

cure, **1.** *n.* (healing) guérison *f.;* (remedy) remède *m.* **2.** *vb.* guérir.

curfew, *n.* couvre-feu *m.*

curio, *n.* curiosité *f.*

curiosity, *n.* curiosité *f.*

curious, *adj.* curieux.

curl, **1.** *n.* boucle *f.* **2.** *vb.* friser.

curler, *n.* bigoudi *m.*

curly, *adj.* frisé.

currant, *n.* groseille *f.*

currency, *n.* monnaie *f.*

current, *adj. and n.* courant *m.*

current affairs, *n.* actualités *f.pl*

currently, *adv.* actuellement.

curriculum, *n.* programme (*m.*) d'études, plan (*m.*) d'études.

curry, **1.** *n.* (food) cari *m.* **2.** *vb.* (c. favor with) chercher à s'attirer des bonnes grâces de.

curse, **1.** *n.* (malediction) malédiction *f.;* (oath) juron *m.;* (scourge) fléau *m.* **2.** *vb.* maudire; (swear) jurer.

cursed, *adj.* maudit.

cursor, *n.* curseur *m.*

cursory, *adj.* rapide, superficiel.

curt, *adj.* brusque.

curtail, *vb.* raccourcir.

curtain, *n.* rideau *m.*

curtsy, *n.* révérence *f.*

curvature, *n.* courbure *f.*

curve, **1.** *n.* courbe *f.* **2.** *vb.* courber, *tr.*

cushion, *n.* coussin *m.*

cuspidor, *n.* crachoir *m.*

custard, *n.* crème *f.*

custodian, *n.* gardien *m.*

custody, *n.* (care) garde *f.*; (arrest) détention *f.*

custom, *n.* coutume *f.*

customary, *adj.* habituel.

customer, *n.* client *m.*

customize, *vb.* personnaliser.

customized, *adj.* fait sur demande.

custom-made, *adj.* fait sur mesure.

customs, *n.* douane *f.*

customs-officer, *n.* douanier *m.*

cut, **1.** *n.* (wound) coupure *f.*; (clothes, hair) coupe *f.*; (reduction) réduction *f.* **2.** *vb.* couper.

cutaneous, *adj.* cutané.

cute, *adj.* gentil *m.*, gentille *f.*

cut glass, *n.* cristal *m.*

cuticle, *n.* cuticule *f.*

cutlery, *n.* coutellerie *f.*

cutlet, *n.* côtelette *f.*

cutout, *n.* découpage *m.*, coupe *f.*

cutter, *n.* coupeur *m.*, coupeuse *f.*

cutthroat, *n.* coupe-jarret *m.*

cutting, **1.** *n.* incision *f.* **2.** *adj.* incisif, tranchant.

cyanide, *n.* cyanure *m.*

cybernetics, *n.* cybernétique *f.*

cyclamate, *n.* cyclamate *m.*

cycle, **1.** *n.* cycle *m.* **2.** *vb.* faire de la bicyclette.

cyclist, *n.* cycliste *m.*

cyclone, *n.* cyclone *m.*

cyclotron, *n.* cyclotron *m.*

cylinder, *n.* cylindre *m.*

cylindrical, *adj.* cylindrique.

cymbal, *n.* cymbale *f.*

cynic, *n.* cynique *m.*

cynical, *adj.* cynique.

cynicism, *n.* cynisme *m.*

cypress, *n.* cyprès *m.*

czar, *n.* tsar *m.*

Czechoslovakie, *n.* Tchécoslovaquie *f.*

cyst, *n.* kyste *m.*

D

dab, **1.** *n.* coup léger *m.*, tape *f.* **2.** *vb.* toucher légèrement.

dabble, *vb.* humecter, faire l'amateur.

dad, *n.* papa *m.*

daddy, *n.* papa *m.*

daffodil, *n.* narcisse *m.*

daffy, *adj.* niais, sot.

dagger, *n.* poignard *m.*

dahlia, *n.* dahlia *m.*

daily, *adj.* quotidien.

dainty, *n.* laiterie *f.*

dairyman, *n.* crémier *m.*

dais, *n.* estrade *f.*

daisy, *n.* marguerite *f.*

dale, *n.* vallon *m.*, vallée *f.*

dam, *n.* digue *f.*

damage, **1.** *n.* dommage *m.* **2.** *vb.* endommager.

damaging, *adj.* nuisible.

damask, *n.* damas *m.*

damnation, *n.* damnation *f.*

damp, *adj.* humide.

dampen, *vb.* humecter.

dampness, *n.* humidité *f.*, moiteur *f.*

damsel, *n.* demoiselle *f.*, jeune fille *f.*

dance, **1.** *n.* danse *f.* **2.** *vb.* danser.

dancer, *n.* danseur *m.*

dandelion, *n.* pissenlit *m.*

dandruff, *n.* pellicules *f.pl.*

dandy, **1.** *n.* dandy *m.* **2.** *adj.* élégant.

Dane, *n.* Danois *m.*

danger, *n.* danger *m.*

dangerous, *adj.* dangereux.

dangle, *vb.* pendiller, *intr.*

Danish, **1.** *n.* Danois *m.* **2.** *adj.* danois.

dank, *adj.* humide et froid.

dapper, *adj.* pimpant, petit et vif.

dappled, *adj.* pommelé.

dare, *vb.* oser.

daredevil, *n.* casse-cou *m.*

daring, *adj.* audacieux.

dark, *adj.* sombre.

darken, *vb.* obscurcir, *tr.*

dark horse, *n.* tocard *m.*

darkness, *n.* obscurité *f.*

darkroom, *n.* chambre noire *f.*

darling, *adj. and n.* chéri *m.*

darn, **1.** *n.* reprise *f.* **2.** *vb.* repriser.

darning needle, *n.* aiguille à repriser *f.*

dart, 1. *n.* dard *m.;* (sewing) pince *f.* **2.** *vb.* se précipiter.

dash, 1. *n.* (energy) fougue *f.;* (pen trait *m.* **2.** *vb.* (throw) lancer; (destroy) détruire; (rush) se précipiter.

dashboard, *n.* tableau (*m.*) de bord.

dashing, *adj.* fougueux, brillant, superbe.

data, *n.* données *f.pl.*

database, *n.* base (*f.*) de données.

data processing, *n.* élaboration *f.,* traitement (*m.*) de données.

date, 1. *n.* date *f.;* (appointment) rendez-vous *m.;* (fruit) datte *f.* **2.** *vb.* dater.

dated, *adj.* démodé.

date line, *n.* ligne (*f.*) de changement de date.

daub, 1. *n.* barbouillage *m.* **2.** *vb.* barbouiller.

daughter, *n.* fille *f.*

daughter-in-law, *n.* belle-fille *f.*

daunt, *vb.* intimider.

dauntless, *adj.* intrépide, indomptable.

dauntlessly, *adv.* d'une manière intrépide.

davenport, *n.* divan *m.*

dawdle, *vb.* flâner, muser.

dawn, *n.* aube *f.*

day, *n.* jour *m.;* (span of day) journée *f.*

day care, *n.* garderie *f.*

daydream, *n.* rêverie *f.*

daylight, *n.* lumière (*f.*) du jour.

daylight-saving time, *n.* l'heure (*f.*) d'été.

daytime, *n.* jour *m.* journée *f.*

daze, *vb.* étourdir.

dazzle, *vb.* éblouir.

deacon, *n.* diacre *m.*

dead, *adj.* mort.

deaden, *vb.* amortir.

dead end, *n.* cul-de-sac *m.,* impasse *f.*

dead letter, *n.* lettre morte *f.*

deadline, *n.* ligne (*f.*) de délimitation, date (*f.*) de limite.

deadlock, *n.* impasse *f.*

deadly, *adj.* mortel.

deadpan, *adj.* impassible.

deadwood, *n.* bois mort *m.*

deaf, *adj.* sourd.

deafen, *vb.* assourdir.

deaf-mute, *adj.* sourd-muet.

deafness, *n.* surdité *f.*

deal, 1. *n.* (business) affaire *f.;* **(great d.)** beaucoup; (cards) donne *f.* **2.** *vb.* (throw) lancer; **(d. with)** traiter; **(d. out)** distribuer.

dealer, *n.* marchand *m.*

dealings, *n.* relations *f.pl.*

dean, *n.* doyen *m.*

dear, *adj. and n.* cher *m.*

dearly, *adv.* chèrement.

death, *n.* mort *f.*

death certificate, *n.* acte (*m.*) de décès.

deathless, *adj.* impérissable.

deathly, *adj.* mortel.

death penalty, *n.* peine (*f.*) de mort.

debacle, *n.* débâcle *f.*

debase, *vb.* avilir.

debatable, *adj.* discutable.

debate, 1. *n.* débat *m.* **2.** *vb.* discuter.

debater, *n.* orateur parlementaire *m.,* argumentateur *m.*

debauch, 1. *n.* débauche *f.* **2.** *vb.* débaucher, corrompre.

debenture, *n.* obligation *f.*

debilitate, *vb.* débiliter, affaiblir.

debility, *n.* débilité *f.*

debit, *n.* débit *m.*

debonair, *adj.* courtois et jovial.

debris, *n.* débris *m.pl.*

debt, *n.* dette *f.*

debtor, *n.* débiteur *m.*

debunk, *vb.* dégonfler.

debut, *n.* début *m.*

debutante, *n.* débutante *f.*

decade, *n.* décennie *f.*

decadence, *n.* décadence *f.*

decadent, *adj.* décadent.

decaffeinated, *adj.* décaféiné.

decalcomania, *n.* décalcomanie *f.*

decanter, *n.* carafe *f.*

decapitate, *vb.* décapiter.

decay, 1. *n.* décadence *f.;* (state of ruin) délabrement *m.;* (teeth) carie *f.* **2.** *vb.* tomber en décadence.

deceased, *adj.* défunt.

deceit, *n.* tromperie *f.*

deceitful, *adj.* trompeur.

deceive, *vb.* tromper.

deceiver, *n.* imposteur *m.*

December, n. décembre m.
decency, n. décence f.
decent, adj. décent.
decentralization, n. décentralisation f.
decentralize, vb. décentraliser.
deception, n. tromperie f., duperie f.
deceptive, adj. décevant, trompeur.
decibel, n. décibel m.
decide, vb. décider.
decided, adj. décidé, prononcé.
decidedly, adv. décidément.
deciduous, adj. à feuillage caduc.
decimal, adj. décimal.
decimal point, n. virgule f.
decimate, vb. décimer.
decipher, vb. déchiffrer.
decision, n. décision f.
decisive, adj. décisif.
deck, n. (boat) pont m.; (cards) jeu m.
deck chair, n. chaise (f.) longue.
deck hand, n. matelot (m.) de pont.
declaim, vb. déclamer.
declamation, n. déclamation f.
declaration, n. déclaration f.
declarative, adj. explicatif, (law) déclaratif.
declare, vb. déclarer.
declension, n. déclinaison f.
decline, vb. décliner.
decode, vb. déchiffrer, décoder.
decoder, n. décodeur m.
décolleté, adj. décolleté.
decompose, vb. décomposer, tr.
decongestant, n. décongestionnant.
decor, n. décor m.
decorate, vb. décorer.
decoration, n. décoration f.
decorative, adj. décoratif.
decorator, n. décorateur m.
decorous, adj. bienséant, convenable.
decorum, n. décorum m.
decoy, 1. n. leurre m. 2. vb. leurrer.
decrease, 1. n. diminution f. 2. vb. diminuer.
decree, n. décret m.
decrepit, adj. décrépit.
decry, vb. décrier, dénigrer.
dedicate, vb. dédier.

dedication, n. dédicace f.
deduce, vb. déduire.
deduct, vb. déduire.
deduction, n. déduction f.
deductive, adj. déductif.
deed, n. action f.; (law) acte (m.) notarié.
deem, vb. juger.
deep, adj. profond.
deepen, vb. approfondir, tr.
deep freeze, n. surgélateur m.
deeply, adv. profondément.
deep-rooted, adj. enraciné.
deep-seated, adj. profond.
deer, n. cerf m.
deerskin, n. peau (f.) de daim.
deface, vb. défigurer.
defamation, n. diffamation f.
defame, vb. diffamer.
default, n. défaut m.
defeat, 1. n. défaite f. 2. vb. vaincre.
defeatism, n. défaitisme m.
defect, 1. n. défaut m. 2. vb. passer à l'ennemi.
defection, n. défection f.
defective, adj. défectueux.
defend, vb. défendre.
defendant, n. défendeur m.; (in court) accusé m., prévenu m.
defender, n. défenseur m.
defense, n. défense f.
defenseless, adj. sans défense.
defensible, adj. défendable, soutenable.
defensive, adj. défensif.
defer, vb. (put off) différer; (show deference) déférer.
deference, n. déférence f.
deferential, adj. plein de déférence, respectueux.
defiance, n. défi m.
defiant, adj. de défi.
deficiency, n. insuffisance f.
deficient, adj. insuffisant.
deficit, n. déficit m.
defile, vb. souiller.
define, vb. définir.
definite, adj. défini.
definitely, adv. d'une manière déterminée.
definition, n. définition f.
definitive, adj. définitif.
deflate, vb. dégonfler.
deflation, n. dégonflement m.

deflect, vb. faire dévier, détourner.
deforestation, n. déforestation f.
deform, vb. déformer.
deformity, n. difformité f.
defraud, vb. frauder.
defray, vb. payer.
defrost, vb. déglacer.
defroster, n. déglaceur m.
deft, adj. adroit.
defunct, adj. défunt.
defy, vb. défier.
degenerate, vb. dégénérer.
degeneration, n. dégénérescence f.
degradation, n. dégradation f.
degrade, vb. dégrader.
degree, n. degré m.; (university) diplôme m.
dehydrate, vb. déshydrater.
de-ice, vb. dégivrer.
deify, vb. déifier.
deign, vb. daigner.
deity, n. divinité f.
dejected, adj. abattu.
dejection, n. abattement m.
delay, 1. n. retard m. 2. vb. retarder, tr.; tarder, intr.
delectable, adj. délectable.
delegate, 1. n. délégué m. 2. vb. déléguer.
delegation, n. délégation f.
delete, vb. rayer, biffer; (computer) effacer.
deletion, n. suppression f., rature f.
deliberate, 1. adj. délibéré. 2. vb. délibérer.
deliberately, adv. (carefully) de propos délibéré; (on purpose) exprès.
deliberation, n. délibération f.
deliberative, adj. délibératif.
delicacy, n. délicatesse f.
delicate, adj. délicat.
delicatessen, n. charcuterie f.
delicious, adj. délicieux.
delight, 1. n. délices f.pl. 2. vb. enchanter.
delightful, adj. charmant.
delineate, vb. esquisser, dessiner.
delinquency, n. délit m.
delinquent, adj. and n. délinquant m.
delirious, adj. délirant.
delirium, n. délire m.

deliver, vb. délivrer; (speech) prononcer.
deliverance, n. délivrance f.
delivery, n. (child) accouchement m.; (speech) débit m.; (goods) livraison f.; (letters) distribution f.; (general d.) poste restante f.
delouse, vb. épouiller.
delta, n. delta m.
delude, vb. tromper.
deluge, n. déluge m.
delusion, n. illusion f.
deluxe, adv. de luxe.
delve, vb. creuser, pénétrer.
demagogue, n. démagogue m.
demand, 1. n. demande f. 2. vb. demander; (as right) exiger.
demanding, adj. exigeant.
demarcation, n. démarcation f.
demean, vb. (d. oneself) s'avilir, s'abaisser.
demeanor, n. maintien m.
demented, adj. fou m., folle f.
demerit, n. démérite m.
demigod, n. demi-dieu m.
demilitarize, vb. démilitariser.
demise, n. décès m., mort f.
demo, n. démonstration f.
demobilization, n. démobilisation f.
demobilize, vb. démobiliser.
democracy, n. démocratie f.
democrat, n. démocrate m.f.
democratic, adj. démocratique.
demolish, vb. démolir.
demolition, n. démolition f.
demon, n. démon m.
demonstrable, adj. démonstrable.
demonstrate, vb. démontrer.
demonstration, n. démonstration f.
demonstrative, adj. démonstratif.
demonstrator, n. démonstrateur m.
demoralize, vb. démoraliser.
demote, vb. réduire à un grade inférieur.
demur, vb. hésiter, s'opposer à.
demure, adj. posé, d'une modestie affectée.
den, n. antre m., repaire m.
denaturalize, vb. dénaturaliser.
denature, vb. dénaturer.
denial, n. dénégation f.; (refusal) refus m.

denim, n. treillis m.

Denmark, n. Danemark m.

denomination, n. dénomination f.; (religion) confession f.

denominator, n. dénominateur m.

denote, vb. dénoter.

denouement, n. dénouement m.

denounce, vb. dénoncer.

dense, adj. dense; (stupid) bête.

density, n. densité f.

dent, n. bosselure f.

dental, adj. dentaire; (gramm.) dental.

dentifrice, n. dentifrice m.

dentist, n. dentiste m.

dentistry, n. art (m.) du dentiste, dentisterie f.

denture, n. dentier m., râtelier m.

denude, vb. dénuder.

denunciation, n. dénonciation f.

deny, vb. nier.

deodorant, n. désodorisant m.

deodorize, vb. désodoriser, désinfecter.

depart, vb. partir, s'en aller, quitter.

department, n. département m.; (government) ministère m.; (d. store) grand magasin m.

departmental, adj. départemental.

departure, n. départ m.

dependability, n. confiance (f.) que l'on inspire.

dependable, adj. digne de confiance.

dependence, n. dépendance f., confiance f.

dependent, 1. adj. dépendant. **2.** n. personne (f.) à charge.

depend on, vb. dépendre de; (rely) compter sur.

depict, vb. peindre.

depiction, n. description f.

deplete, vb. épuiser.

deplorable, adj. déplorable.

deplore, vb. déplorer.

depopulate, vb. dépeupler.

deport, vb. déporter.

deportation, n. déportation f.

deportment, n. maintien m.

depose, vb. déposer.

deposit, 1. n. dépôt m. **2.** vb. déposer.

depositor, n. déposant m.

depository, n. dépôt m., dépositaire m.

depot, n. dépôt m., gare f.

deprave, vb. dépraver, corrompre.

depravity, n. dépravation f., corruption f.

deprecate, vb. désapprouver, s'opposer à.

depreciate, vb. déprécier.

depreciation, n. dépréciation f.

depredation, n. déprédation f., pillage m.

depress, vb. (lower) abaisser; (fig.) abattre.

depressed, adj. abattu, bas.

depression, n. dépression f.; (personal) abattement m.; (comm.) crise f.

deprivation, n. privation f.

deprive, vb. priver.

depth, n. profondeur f.

depth charge, n. grenade (f.) sous-marine.

deputy, n. délégué m.; (politics) député m.

derail, vb. dérailler.

derange, vb. déranger.

deranged, adj. dérangé, troublé.

derelict, 1. n. vaisseau abandonné m., épave f. **2.** adj. abandonné, délaissé.

dereliction, n. abandon m.

deride, vb. tourner en dérision.

derision, n. dérision f.

derisive, adj. dérisoire.

derisory, adj. dérisoire.

derivation, n. dérivation f., origine f.

derivative, n. dérivatif m.

derive, vb. dériver.

dermatology, n. dermatologie f.

derogatory, adj. dérogatoire.

derrick, n. grue f.

descend, vb. descendre.

descendant, n. descendant m.

descent, n. descente f.

describe, vb. décrire.

description, n. description f.

descriptive, adj. descriptif.

desecrate, vb. profaner.

desensitize, vb. désensibiliser.

desert, 1. n. (place) désert m.; (merit) mérite m. **2.** vb. déserter.

deserter, n. déserteur m.

desertion, n. abandon m.; (military) désertion f.

deserve, vb. mériter.

deserving, adj. méritoire, de mérite.

design, 1. n. (project) dessein m.; (architecture) projet m. **2.** vb. dessiner; (d. for) destiner à.

designate, vb. désigner.

designation, n. désignation f.

designedly, adv. à dessein.

designer, n. dessinateur m.

designing, adj. intrigant, artificieux.

desirable, adj. désirable.

desire, 1. n. désir m. **2.** vb. désirer.

desirous, adj. désireux.

desist, vb. cesser.

desk, n. (office) bureau m.; (school) pupitre m.

desolate, adj. désolé.

desolation, n. désolation f.

despair, 1. n. désespoir m. **2.** vb. désespérer.

desperado, n. désespéré m., cerveau brûlé m.

desperate, adj. désespéré.

desperation, n. désespoir m.

despicable, adj. méprisable.

despise, vb. mépriser.

despite, prep. en dépit de.

despondent, adj. découragé.

despot, n. despote m.

despotic, adj. despotique.

despotism, n. despotisme m.

dessert, n. dessert m.

destination, n. destination f.

destine, vb. destiner.

destiny, n. destin m.

destitute, adj. (deprived) dénué; (poor) indigent.

destitution, n. destitution f.

destroy, vb. détruire.

destroyer, n. destructeur m.; (naval) contre-torpilleur m.

destructible, adj. destructible.

destruction, n. destruction f.

destructive, adj. destructif.

desultory, adj. à bâtons rompus, décousu.

detach, vb. détacher.

detachment, n. détachement m.

detail, n. détail m.

detain, vb. retenir; (in prison) détenir.

detect, vb. découvrir.

detection, n. découverte f.

detective, n. agent (m.) de la police secrète; **(d. novel)** roman policier.

detente, n. détente f.

detention, n. détention f.

deter, vb. détourner, empêcher (de), dissuader (de).

detergent, n. détersif m.

deteriorate, vb. détériorer, tr.

deterioration, n. détérioration f.

determination, n. détermination f.

determine, vb. déterminer.

determined, adj. déterminé.

determinism, n. déterminisme m.

deterrence, n. préventif m.

deterrent, n. and adj. préventif m.

detest, vb. détester.

dethrone, vb. détrôner.

detonate, vb. détoner.

detour, n. détour m.

detract, vb. enlever, ôter (à), dénigrer, déroger (à).

detriment, n. détriment m., préjudice m.

detrimental, adj. préjudiciable, nuisible (à).

devaluate, vb. dévaluer, déprécier.

devaluation, n. dévaluation f.

devastate, vb. dévaster.

devastating, adj. dévastateur, (news) accablant.

develop, vb. développer, tr.

developer, n. (photography) révélateur m.

developing nation, n. nation (f.) en voie de développement.

development, n. développement m.

deviant, 1. adj. anormal. **2.** n. déviant m.

deviate, vb. dévier, s'écarter (de).

deviation, n. déviation f., écart m.

device, n. expédient m.

devil, n. diable m.

devilish, adj. diabolique.

devious, adj. détourné.

devise, vb. (plan) combiner; (plot) tramer.

devitalize, vb. dévitaliser.

devoid, adj. dépourvu.

devolution, n. décentralisation f.

devote, vb. consacrer.

devoted, *adj.* dévoué.
devotee, *n.* dévot *m.,* dévote *f.,* adepte *m.f.*
devotion, *n.* (religious) dévotion *f.;* (to person or thing) dévouement *m.*
devour, *vb.* dévorer.
devout, *adj.* dévot.
dew, *n.* rosée *f.*
dewy, *adj.* de rosée.
dexterity, *n.* dextérité *f.*
dexterous, *adj.* adroit.
diabetes, *n.* diabète *m.*
diabolic, *adj.* diabolique.
diadem, *n.* diadème *m.*
diagnose, *vb.* diagnostiquer.
diagnosis, *n.* diagnose *f.*
diagnostic, *adj.* diagnostique.
diagonal, *adj.* diagonal.
diagonally, *adv.* diagonalement.
diagram, *n.* diagramme *m.*
dial, 1. *n.* cadran *m.* **2.** *vb.* **(d. a number)** composer.
dialect, *n.* dialecte *m.*
dialogue, *n.* dialogue *m.*
dial tone, *n.* tonalité *f.*
diameter, *n.* diamètre *m.*
diametrical, *adj.* diamétral.
diamond, *n.* diamant *m.;* (shape) losange *m.;* (cards) carreau *m.*
diaper, *n.* (babies) couche *f.*
diaphragm, *n.* diaphragme *m.*
diarrhea, *n.* diarrhée *f.*
diary, *n.* journal *m.*
diathermy, *n.* diathermie *f.*
diatribe, *n.* diatribe *f.*
dice, *n.* dés *m.pl.*
dicker, *vb.* marchander.
dictaphone, *n.* machine à dicter *f.*
dictate, *vb.* dicter.
dictation, *n.* dictée *f.*
dictator, *n.* dictateur *m.*
dictatorial, *adj.* dictatorial.
dictatorship, *n.* dictature *f.*
diction, *n.* diction *f.*
dictionary, *n.* dictionnaire *m.*
didactic, *adj.* didactique.
die, 1. *n.* dé *m.* **2.** *vb.* mourir.
die-hard, *n.* intransigeant *m.,* ultra *m.*
diesel, *n.* diesel *m.*
diet, *n.* régime *m.*
dietary, *adj.* diététique.
dietetics, *n.* diététique *f.*

dietitian, *n.* diététicien *m.*
differ, *vb.* différer.
difference, *n.* différence *f.*
different, *adj.* différent.
differential, *adj.* différentiel.
differentiate (between), *vb.* faire une différence (entre).
difficult, *adj.* difficile.
difficulty, *n.* difficulté *f.*
diffident, *adj.* hésitant, timide.
diffuse, *adj.* diffus.
diffusion, *n.* diffusion *f.*
dig, *vb.* bêcher; (hole) creuser.
digest, *vb.* digérer.
digestible, *adj.* digestible.
digestion, *n.* digestion *f.*
digestive, *adj. and n.* digestif *m.*
digit, *n.* chiffre *m.*
digital, *adj.* (in watches, etc.) digital, numérique.
digitalis, *n.* digitaline *f.*
dignified, *adj.* plein de dignité.
dignify, *vb.* honorer, élever.
dignitary, *n.* dignitaire *m.*
dignity, *n.* dignité *f.*
digress, *vb.* faire une digression.
digression, *n.* digression *f.*
dike, *n.* (ditch) fossé *m.;* (dam) digue *f.*
dilapidated, *adj.* délabré.
dilapidation, *n.* délabrement *m.*
dilate, *vb.* dilater, *tr.*
dilatory, *adj.* dilatoire, lent, négligent.
dilemma, *n.* dilemme *m.*
dilettante, *n.* dilettante *m.,* amateur *m.*
diligence, *n.* diligence *f.*
diligent, *adj.* diligent.
dill, *n.* aneth *m.*
dilute, *vb.* diluer.
dim, 1. *adj.* (light, sight) faible; (color) terne. **2.** *vb.* réduire, baisser.
dime, *n.* un dixième de dollar *m.*
dimension, *n.* dimension *f.*
diminish, *vb.* diminuer.
diminution, *n.* diminution *f.*
diminutive, 1. *adj.* tout petit. **2.** *n.* (gramm.) diminutif *m.*
dimness, *n.* (weakness) faiblesse *f.;* (darkness) obscurité *f.*
dimple, *n.* (face) fossette *f.*
din, *n.* tapage *m.*
dine, *vb.* dîner.

diner, dining-car, n. wagon-restaurant m.

dingy, adj. défraîchi.

dining room, n. salle (f.) à manger.

dinner, n. dîner m.; (d. jacket) smoking m.

dinosaur, n. dinosaurie m.

diocese, n. diocèse m.

dint, n. (by d. of) à force de.

dip, vb. plonger.

diphtheria, n. diphtérie f.

diphthong, n. diphtongue f.

diploma, n. diplôme m.

diplomacy, n. diplomatie f.

diplomat, n. diplomate m.

diplomatic, adj. diplomatique.

dipper, n. cuiller (f.) à pot.

dire, adj. affreux.

direct, 1. vb. (guide) diriger; (address) adresser; (film) réaliser; (play) mettre en scène. **2.** adj. direct.

direct current, n. courant continu m.

direction, n. direction f.; (orders) instructions f.pl.

directional, adj. de direction.

directive, 1. n. directif m. **2.** adj. dirigeant.

directly, adv. directement.

directness, n. rectitude f.; (frankness) franchise f.

director, n. directeur m., (theater) metteur (m.) en scène, (cinema, TV) réalisateur f.

directorate, n. conseil (m.) d'administration.

directory, n. annuaire m.

dirge, n. chant funèbre m.

dirigible, adj. and n. dirigeable m.

dirt, n. saleté f.

dirty, 1. adj. sale. **2.** vb. salir.

disability, n. incapacité f.

disable, vb. mettre hors de combat, tr.

disabled, adj. invalide.

disabuse, vb. désabuser.

disadvantage, n. désavantage m.

disagree, vb. être en désaccord.

disagreeable, adj. désagréable.

disagreement, n. désaccord m.

disappear, vb. disparaître.

disappearance, n. disparition f.

disappoint, vb. désappointer.

disappointing, adj. décevant.

disappointment, n. déception f.

disapproval, n. désapprobation f.

disapprove, vb. désapprouver.

disarm, vb. désarmer.

disarmament, n. désarmement m.

disarray, n. désarroi m., désordre m.

disassemble, vb. démonter, désassembler.

disaster, n. désastre m.

disastrous, adj. désastreux.

disavow, vb. désavouer.

disavowal, n. désaveu m.

disband, vb. congédier, tr.; se débander, intr.

disbar, vb. rayer du tableau des avocats.

disbelief, n. incrédulité f.

disbelieve, vb. ne pas croire, refuser de croire.

disburse, vb. débourser.

disc, n. disque m.

discard, vb. mettre de côté.

discern, vb. discerner.

discerning, adj. judicieux, éclairé.

discernment, n. discernement m.

discharge, 1, n. décharge f.; (mil.) congé m. **2.** vb. décharger; (mil.) congédier.

disciple, n. disciple m.

disciplinarian, n. disciplinaire m.

disciplinary, adj. disciplinaire.

discipline, n. discipline f.

disclaim, vb. désavouer, nier.

disclaimer, n. désaveu m.

disclose, vb. révéler.

disclosure, n. révélation f.

disco, adj. disco.

discolor, vb. décolorer.

discoloration, n. décoloration f.

discomfiture, n. défaite f., déroute f.

discomfort, n. malaise m.

disconcert, vb. déconcerter.

disconnect, vb. désunir; (electric) débrancher.

disconnected, adj. (electricity) hors circuit.

disconsolate, adj. désolé.

discontent, n. mécontentement m.

discontented, adj. mécontent.

discontinue, vb. discontinuer.

discord, n. discorde f.

discordant, adj. discordant, en désaccord.

discotheque, n. discothèque f.

discount, 1. n. escompte m.; (reduction) remise f. **2.** vb. ne pas tenir compte de.

discourage, vb. décourager.

discouragement, n. découragement m.

discourse, n. discours m.

discourteous, adj. impoli.

discourtesy, n. impolitesse f.

discover, vb. découvrir.

discoverer, n. découvreur f.

discovery, n. découverte f.

discredit, 1. n. discrédit m. **2.** vb. discréditer.

discreditable, adj. déshonorant, peu honorable.

discreet, adj. discret.

discrepancy, n. contradiction f.

discretion, n. discrétion f.

discriminate, vb. distinguer.

discrimination, n. discernement m., jugement m.

discursive, adj. discursif, sans suite.

discuss, vb. discuter.

discussion, n. discussion f.

disdain, n. dédain m.

disdainful, adj. dédaigneux.

disease, n. maladie f.

diseased, adj. malade.

disembark, vb. débarquer.

disembody, vb. dépouiller du corps.

disenchantment, n. désenchantement m.

disengage, vb. dégager.

disentangle, vb. démêler.

disfavor, n. défaveur f.

disfigure, vb. défigurer, enlaidir.

disfranchise, vb. priver du droit de vote.

disgorge, vb. dégorger.

disgrace, n. disgrâce f.

disgraceful, adj. honteux.

disgruntled, adj. mécontent, de mauvaise humeur.

disguise, 1. n. déguisement m. **2.** vb. dégoûter.

disgust, 1. n. dégout m. **2.** vb. dégoûter.

disgusting, adj. dégoûtant.

dish, n. plat m.; **(wash the d.s)** laver la vaisselle.

dishcloth, n. torchon m.

dishearten, vb. décourager.

disheveled, adj. échevelé.

dishonest, adj. malhonnête.

dishonesty, n. malhonnêteté f.

dishonor, n. déshonneur m.

dishonorable, adj. (action) déshonorant.

dishwasher, n. lave-vaisselle m.

disillusion, n. désillusion f.

disinclined, adj. **(be d. to)** décourager.

disinfect, vb. désinfecter.

disinfectant, n. désinfectant m.

disinherit, vb. déshériter.

disintegrate, vb. désagréger.

disinterested, adj. désintéressé.

disjointed, adj. désarticulé, disloqué.

disk, n. disque m.; **(floppy d.)** disquette f.; **(d. drive)** lecteur (m.) de disquettes.

diskette, n. disquette f.

dislike, 1, n. aversion f. **2.** vb. ne pas aimer.

dislocate, vb. disloquer.

dislodge, vb. déloger.

disloyal, adj. infidèle.

disloyalty, n. infidélité f., perfidie f.

dismal, adj. sombre.

dismantle, vb. dépouiller (de).

dismay, n. consternation f.

dismember, vb. démembrer.

dismiss, vb. congédier.

dismissal, n. renvoi m.

dismount, vb. descendre.

disobedience, n. désobéissance f.

disobedient, adj. désobéissant.

disobey, vb. désobéir à.

disorder, n. désordre m.

disorderly, adj. désordonné.

disorganize, vb. désorganiser.

disorient, vb. désorienter.

disown, vb. désavouer.

disparage, vb. déprécier, dénigrer.

disparaging, adj. désobligeant.

disparate, adj. disparate.

disparity, n. inégalité f.

dispassionate, adj. calme.

dispatch, 1. n. (business) expédition f.; (speed) promptitude f.; (message) dépêche f. **2.** vb. expédier.

dispatcher, n. expéditeur m.

dispel, vb. dissiper.

dispensable, adj. dont on peut se passer.

dispensary, n. dispensaire m.

dispensation, n. dispensation f.

dispense, vb. distribuer, dispenser.

dispersal, n. dispersion f.

disperse, vb. disperser.

dispirited, adj. découragé.

displace, vb. déplacer.

displaced person, n. réfugié m.

displacement, n. déplacement m.

display, 1. n. (show) exposition f.; (shop, ostentation) étalage m. **2.** vb. étaler.

display window, n. vitrine f.

displease, vb. déplaire à.

disposable, adj. disponible, jetable.

disposal, n. disposition f.

dispose, vb. disposer.

disposition, n. disposition f.; (character) caractère m.

dispossess, vb. déposséder, exproprier.

disproportion, n. disproportion f.

disproportionate, adj. disproportionné.

disprove, vb. réfuter.

disputable, adj. contestable, disputable.

dispute, 1. n. (discussion) discussion f.; (quarrel) dispute f. **2.** vb. (se) disputer.

disqualify, vb. (sports) disqualifier.

disregard, vb. ne tenir aucun compte de.

disrepair, n. délabrement m.

disreputable, adj. déshonorant, honteux.

disrespect, n. irrévérence f.

disrespectful, adj. irrespectueux.

disrobe, vb. déshabiller, dévêtir.

disrupt, vb. faire éclater, rompre.

dissatisfaction, n. mécontentement m.

dissatisfy, vb. mécontenter.

dissect, vb. disséquer.

dissemble, vb. dissimuler.

disseminate, vb. disséminer.

dissension, n. dissension f.

dissent, 1. vb. différer. **2.** n. dissentiment m.

dissertation, n. dissertation f., discours m.

disservice, n. mauvais service rendu m.

dissimilar, adj. dissemblable.

dissipate, vb. dissiper.

dissipated, adj. dissipé.

dissipation, n. dissipation f.

dissociate, vb. désassocier, dissocier.

dissolute, adj. dissolu.

dissolution, n. dissolution f.

dissolve, vb. dissoudre, tr.

dissonance, n. dissonance f., désaccord m.

dissonant, adj. dissonant.

dissuade, vb. dissuader.

distance, n. distance f.

distant, adj. distant.

distaste, n. dégoût m.

distasteful, adj. désagréable.

distemper, 1. n. maladie (f.) des chiens. **2.** vb. peindre en détrempe.

distend, vb. dilater, gonfler.

distended, adj. dilaté.

distill, vb. distiller.

distillation, n. distillation f.

distiller, n. distillateur m.

distillery, n. distillerie f.

distinct, adj. distinct.

distinction, n. distinction f.

distinctive, adj. distinctif.

distinctly, adv. distinctement, clairement.

distinguish, vb. distinguer.

distinguished, adj. distingué.

distort, vb. déformer.

distract, vb. (divert) distraire; (upset) affoler.

distracted, adj. affolé, bouleversé.

distraction, n. (diversion) distraction f.; (madness) folie f.

distraught, adj. affolé, éperdu, hors de soi.

distress, 1. n. détresse f. **2.** vb. affliger.

distressing, adj. affligeant, pénible, désolant.

distribute, vb. distribuer.

distribution, n. distribution f.

distributor, n. distributeur m.

district, n. (region) contrée f.; (administration) district m.; (town) quartier m.

district attorney, n. procureur (m.) de la République.

distrust, 1. n. méfiance f. **2.** vb. se méfier de.

distrustful, adj. méfiant.

distribute, vb. déranger.

disturbance, n. dérangement m.

disunite, vb. désunir.

disuse, n. désuétude f.

ditch, n. fossé m.

ditto, adv. idem, de même.

diva, n. diva f.

divan, n. divan m.

dive, vb. plonger.

dive bomber, n. avion (m.) de bombardement qui fait des vols piqués.

diver, n. plongeur m.

diverge, vb. diverger.

divergence, n. divergence f.

divergent, adj. divergent.

diverse, adj. divers.

diversion, n. (amusement) divertissement m.; (turning aside) détournement m.

diversity, n. diversité f.

divert, vb. (turn aside) détourner; (amuse) divertir.

divest, vb. ôter, dépouiller, priver.

divide, vb. diviser.

divided, adj. divisé, séparé.

dividend, n. dividende m.

divine, adj. divin.

diving, n. plongée f.; **(d. board)** plongeoir m.; **(d. suit)** tenue (f.) de plongée.

divinity, n. divinité f.

divisible, adj. divisible.

division, n. division f.

divisive, adj. qui divise, qui sépare.

divorce, 1. n. divorce m. **2.** vb. divorcer.

divorcee, n. divorcé m., divorcée f.

divulge, vb. divulguer.

dizziness, n. vertige m.

dizzy, adj. pris de vertige.

do, vb. faire; **(how d. you d.?)** comment allez-vous?

docile, adj. docile.

dock, n. bassin m.

docket, n. registre m., bordereau m.

dockyard, n. chantier (m.) de construction de navires.

doctor, n. (academic) docteur m.; (med.) médecin m.

doctorate, n. doctorat m.

doctrinaire, adj. doctrinaire.

doctrine, n. doctrine f.

document, n. document m.

documentary, adj. documentaire.

documentation, n. documentation f.

dodge, vb. esquiver, éluder.

doe, n. daine f., biche f.

doeskin, n. peau (f.) de daim.

dog, n. chien m.

dogfight, n. combat (m.) de chiens, mêlée générale f.

dogged, adj. obstiné, tenace.

doggerel, n. poésie burlesque f.

doghouse, n. chenil m.

dogma, n. dogme m.

dogmatic, adj. dogmatique.

dogmatism, n. dogmatisme m.

doily, n. petit napperon m.

do-it-yourself, n. bricolage m.

doldrum, n. (naut.) zone des calmes f.; cafard m.

dole, 1. n. pitance f.; aumône f. **2.** vb. distribuer parcimonieusement.

doleful, adj. lugubre.

doll, n. poupée f.

dollar, n. dollar m.

dolorous, adj. douloureux.

dolphin, n. dauphin m.

domain, n. domaine m.

dome, n. dôme m.

domestic, adj. domestique.

domesticate, vb. domestiquer, apprivoiser.

domicile, n. domicile m.

dominance, n. dominance f., prédominance f.

dominant, adj. dominant.

dominate, vb. dominer.

domination, n. domination f.

domineer, vb. se montrer tyrannique.

domineering, adj. impérieux.

dominion, n. domination f.; (territory) possessions f.pl.

domino, n. domino m.

don, vb. endosser, revêtir.

donate, vb. donner.

donation, n. donation f.

done, vb. fait.

donkey, n. âne m.

don't, vb. ne faites pas!, ne fais pas!

doodle, vb. griffonner.

doom, vb. condamner.

doomsday, n. (jour du) jugement dernier m.

door, n. porte f.; (**d.-keeper**) concierge m.f.

doorbell, n. sonnette f.

doorman, n. portier m.

doorstep, n. seuil m., pas (m.) de la porte.

doorway, n. (baie de) porte f., encadrement (m.) de la porte.

dope, 1. n. stupéfiant m. 2. vb. doper.

dormant, adj. endormi, assoupi.

dormer, n. lucarne f.

dormitory, n. maison (f.) d'étudiants.

dosage, n. dosage m.

dose, n. dose f.

dossier, n. dossier m.

dot, n. point m.

dotage, n. radotage m.

dote, vb. radoter; (**d. on**) aimer excessivement.

dot-matrix printer, n. imprimante (f.) matricielle.

double, 1. adj. and n. double m. 2. vb. doubler.

double-bass, n. contre basse f.

double-breasted, adj. croisé.

double-cross, vb. duper, tromper.

double-dealing, n. duplicité f.

double room, n. chambre (f.) pour deux personnes.

double time, n. pas gymnastique m.

doubly, adv. doublement.

doubt, 1. n. doute m. 2. vb. douter (de).

doubtful, adj. douteux.

doubtless, adv. sans doute.

dough, n. pâte f.; (colloquial) fric m.

doughnut, n. pet (m.) de nonne, baignet m.

dour, adj. austère.

douse, vb. plonger, tremper.

dove, n. colombe f.

dowager, n. douairière f.

dowdy, adj. sans élégance, qui manque de chic.

dowel, 1. n. goujon m. 2. vb. goujonner.

down, 1. n. duvet m. 2. adv. en bas. 3. prep. (along) le long de.

downcast, adj. (look) baissé.

downfall, n. chute f.

downgrade, vb. déclasser.

downhearted, adj. découragé, déprimé.

downhill, 1. n. descente f. 2. adj. en pente, incliné.

downpour, n. averse f.

downright, adv. tout à fait.

downstairs, adv. en bas.

downtown, adv. en ville.

downtrodden, adj. opprimé, piétiné.

downward, adj. descendant.

downy, adj. duveteux.

dowry, n. dot f.

doze, vb. sommeiller.

dozen, n. douzaine f.

drab, adj. (color) gris; (dull) terne.

draft, 1. n. (drawing) dessin m.; (mil.) conscription f.; (air) courant (m.) d'air. 2. vb. (mil.) appeler sous le drapeau.

draftee, n. conscrit m.

draftsman, n. dessinateur m.

drafty, adj. plein de courants d'air.

drag, vb. traîner.

dragnet, n. drague f., seine f., chalut m.

dragon, n. dragon m.

dragon-fly, n. libellule f.

drain, vb. drainer, tr.; s'écouler, intr.

drainage, n. drainage m.

dram, n. drachme f., goutte f.

drama, n. drame m.

dramatic, adj. dramatique.

dramatics, n. théâtre m.

dramatist, n. dramaturge m.

dramatize, vb. dramatiser.

dramaturgy, n. dramaturgie f.

drape, vb. draper.

drapery, n. draperie f.

drastic, adj. drastique.

draw, vb. (pull) tirer; (sketch) dessiner.

drawback, n. inconvénient m.

drawbridge, m. pont-levis m.

drawer, n. tiroir m.

drawing, n. dessin m.

drawl, 1. n. voix (f.) traînante. 2. vb. traîner la voix.

dray, n. camion m.

drayman, n. camionneur m.

dread, 1. n. crainte f. **2.** vb. redouter.

dreadful, adj. affreux.

dreadfully, adv. terriblement, affreusement.

dream, n. rêve m.

dreamer, n. rêveur m.

dreamy, adj. rêveur m., rêveuse f.

dreary, adj. morne.

dredge, vb. draguer.

dreg, n. lie f.

drench, vb. tremper.

dress, 1. n. robe f. **2.** vb. habiller, tr.; s'habiller, intr.

dresser, n. commode f.

dressing, n. toilette f.; (surgical) pansement m.

dressing gown, n. robe (f.) de chambre. peignoir m.

dressmaker, n. couturière f.

dress rehearsal, n. répétition générale f.

dressy, adj. chic.

dribble, vb. baver.

drier, n. sécheur m., dessécheur m.

drift, vb. (boat) dériver; (person) se laisser aller.

drifter, n. personne (f.) sans but.

driftwood, n. bois flottant m.

drill, 1. n. (tool) foret m.; (exercise) exercice m. **2.** vb. (hole) forer; (exercise) exercer, tr.; faire l'exercice, intr.

drink, 1. n. boisson f. **2.** vb. boire.

drinkable, adj. potable.

drip, 1. n. dégoutter. **2.** n. goutte f.

dripping, 1. n. dégouttement m. **2.** adj. ruisselant.

drive, 1. n. promenade (f.) en voiture; (energy) énergie f. **2.** vb. (auto, animals) conduire; (force) pousser.

drivel, n. bave f.

driver, n. (auto) chauffeur m.

driver's license, n. permis (m.) de conduire.

driveway, n. allée f.

driving, n. conduite f.

drizzle, 1. n. bruine f. **2.** vb. bruiner.

dromedary, n. dromadaire m.

drone, 1. n. abeille mâle f.; bourdonnement m. **2.** vb. bourdonner.

drool, vb. baver.

droop, vb. pencher.

drop, 1. n. goutte f.; (fall) chute f. **2.** vb. tomber, intr.; laisser tomber, tr.

dropout, n. étudiant qui quitte l'école avant de recevoir son diplôme m.

dropper, n. compte-gouttes m.

dropsy, n. hydropisie f.

drought, n. sécheresse f.

drove, n. troupeau m.

drown, vb. noyer, tr.

drowse, vb. s'assoupir.

drowsiness, n. somnolence f.

drowsy, adj. somnolent.

drudge, vb. s'éreinter.

drudgery, n. corvée f.

drug, n. drogue f.

drug addict, n. toxicomane m.f.

druggist, n. pharmacien m.

drugstore, n. pharmacie f.

drum, n. tambour m.; (ear) tympan m.

drum major, n. tambour-major m.

drummer, n. tambour m.

drumstick, n. baguette (f.) de tambour.

drunk, adj. ivre.

drunkard, n. ivrogne m.

drunkenness, n. ivresse f.; (habitual) ivrognerie f.

dry, 1. adj. sec m., sèche f. **2.** vb. sécher.

dry-clean, vb. nettoyer à sec.

dry cleaner, n. teinturier m.

dry dock, n. cale sèche f. **2.** vb. mettre en cale sèche.

dry goods, n. articles (m.pl.) de nouveauté.

dryness, n. sécheresse f.

dual, adj. double.

dualism, n. dualisme m.

dubbed, adj. doublé.

dubious, adj. douteux.

duchess, n. duchesse f.

duchy, n. duché m.

duck, n. canard m.

duckling, n. caneton m.

duct, n. conduit m.

ductile, adj. ductile.

dud, 1. adj. incapable. **2.** n. obus qui a raté m.

due, adj. dû m., due f.

duel, n. duel m.

duelist, n. duelliste m.

duet, n. duo m.

duffel bag, n. sac (m.) pour les vêtements de rechange.

duffel coat, n. duffel-coat m.

dugout, n. abri-caverne m.

duke, n. duc m.

dukedom, n. duché m.

dulcet, adj. doux, suave.

dull, adj. (boring) ennuyeux; (blunt) émoussé.

dullard, n. lourdaud m.

dullness, n. (monotony) monotonie f.

duly, adv. dûment.

dumb, adj. muet m., muette f.; (stupid) sot m., sotte f.

dumbfound, vb. abasourdir, interdire.

dumbfounded, adj. sidéré.

dumbwaiter, n. monte-plats m.

dummy, n. (dressmaking) mannequin m.; (cards) mort m.

dump, 1. n. voirie f. 2. vb. déposer; (computer) vider, transférer.

dumpling, n. boulette (de pâte) m.

dumpy, adj. boulot.

dun, vb. importuner, talonner.

dunce, n. crétin m.

dunce cap, n. bonnet d'âne m.

dune, n. dune f.

dung, n. fiente f.; (agriculture) fumier m.

dungaree, n. salopette f., bleus m.pl.

dungeon, n. cachot m.

dupe, 1. n. dupe f. 2. vb. duper.

duplex, adj. double.

duplicate, 1. n. double m. 2. vb. faire le double de.

duplication, n. duplication f.

duplicity, n. duplicité f.

durability, n. durabilité f.

durable, adj. durable.

duration, n. durée f.

duress, n. contrainte f., coercition f.

during, prep. pendant.

dusk, n. crépuscule m.

dusky, adj. sombre.

dust, 1. n. poussière f. 2. vb. épousseter.

dustpan, n. ramasse-poussière m.

dust storm, n. tourbillon (m.) de poussière.

dusty, adj. poussiéreux.

Dutch, adj. and n. hollandais m.

Dutchman, n. Hollandais m.

dutiful, adj. respectueux, fidèle.

dutifully, adv. avec soumission.

duty, n. (moral, legal) devoir m.; (tax) droit m.; (be on d.) être de service.

duty-free, adj. exempt de droits, hors-taxe.

dwarf, adj. and n. nain m.

dwell, vb. demeurer.

dwindle, vb. diminuer.

dye, 1. n. teinture f. 2. vb. teindre.

dyer, n. teinturier m.

dyestuff, n. matière colorante f.

dynamic, adj. dynamique.

dynamics, n. dynamique f.

dynamite, n. dynamite f.

dynamo, n. dynamo f.

dynasty, n. dynastie f.

dysentery, n. dysenterie f.

dyslexia, n. dyslexie f.

dyspepsia, n. dyspepsie f.

dyspeptic, adj. dyspeptique.

E

each, 1. adj. chaque. 2. pron. chacun m., chacune f.; (e. other) l'un l'autre.

eager, adj. ardent.

eagerly, adv. ardemment, avidement.

eagerness, n. empressement m.

eagle, n. (bird) aigle m.; (mil.) aigle f.

eaglet, n. aiglon m.

ear, n. oreille f.

earache, n. mal d'oreille m.

eardrum, n. tympan m.

earl, n. comte m.

early, 1. adj. (of morning) matinal; (first) premier. 2. adv. de bonne heure; tôt.

earmark, 1. n. marque distinctive f. 2. vb. marquer, assigner.

earn, vb. gagner.

earnest, adj. sérieux.

earnestly, *adv.* sérieusement, sincèrement.

earnestness, *n.* gravité *f.*, sérieux *m.*

earnings, *n.* salaire *m.*

earphone, *n.* casque (téléphonique) *m.*

earring, *n.* boucle (*f.*) d'oreille.

earshot, *n.* portée de voix *f.*

earth, *n.* terre *f.*

earthenware, *n.* poterie *f.*, argile cuite *f.*, faïence *f.*

earthly, *adj.* terrestre.

earthquake, *n.* tremblement (*m.*) de terre.

earthworm, *n.* ver de terre *m.*

earthy, *adj.* terreux.

ease, 1. *n.* aise *f.*; (with e.) avec facilité. 2. *vb.* calmer, détendre.

easel, *n.* chevalet *m.*

easily, *adv.* facilement.

easiness, *n.* facilité *f.*

east, *n.* est *m.*; (the E.) l'Orient *m.*

Easter, *n.* Pâques *m.*

easterly, *adj.* d'est, vers l'est.

eastern, *adj.* de l'est, oriental.

eastward, *adv.* vers l'est.

easy, *adj.* facile; (of manners) aisé.

easy chair, *n.* fauteuil *m.*

easygoing, *adj.* insouciant, peu exigeant, accommodant.

eat, *vb.* manger.

eaves, *n.* avant-toit *m.*

eavesdrop, *vb.* écouter aux portes.

ebb, *n.* (water) reflux *m.*; (decline) déclin *m.*

ebony, *n.* ébène *f.*

ebullient, *adj.* bouillonnant.

eccentric, *adj.* excentrique.

eccentricity, *n.* excentricité *f.*

ecclesiastic, *adj. and n.* ecclésiastique *m.*

ecclesiastical, *adj.* ecclésiastique.

echelon, *n.* échelon *m.*

echo, *n.* écho *m.*

eclipse, *n.* éclipse *f.*

ecological, *adj.* écologique.

ecology, *n.* écologie *f.*

economic, *adj.* économique.

economical, *adj.* (person) économe.

economics, *n.* économie (*f.*) politique.

economist, *n.* économiste *m.f.*

economize, *vb.* économiser.

economy, *n.* économie *f.*

ecosystem, *n.* écosystème *m.*

ecru, *n.* écru *m.*

ecstasy, *n.* (religious) extase *f.*; (fig.) transport *m.*

ecumenical, *adj.* œcuménique.

eczema, *n.* eczéma *m.*

eddy, *n.* remous *m.*

edge, *n.* bord *m.*; (blade) fil *m.*

edging, *n.* pose *f.*, bordure *f.*

edgy, *adj.* d'un air agacé.

edible, *adj.* comestible.

edict, *n.* édit *m.*

edifice, *n.* édifice *m.*

edify, *vb.* édifier.

edit, *vb.* (text) corriger; (report) préparer; (film) monter.

edition, *n.* édition *f.*

editor, *n.* (text) correcteur *m.*, éditeur *m.*; (paper) rédacteur *m.*

editorial, *n.* éditorial *m.*

educate, *vb.* (upbringing) élever; (knowledge) instruire.

education, *n.* éducation *f.*; (schooling) instruction *f.*

educational, *adj.* pédagogique; scolaire.

educator, *n.* éducateur *m.*

eel, *n.* anguille *f.*

eerie, *adj.* inquiétant.

efface, *vb.* effacer.

effect, 1. *n.* effet *m.* 2. *vb.* effectuer.

effective, *adj.* (having effect) efficace; (in effect) effectif.

effectively, *adv.* efficacement, effectivement.

effectiveness, *n.* efficacité *f.*

effectual, *adj.* efficace.

effeminate, *adj.* efféminé.

effervesce, *vb.* être en effervescence, pétiller d'animation.

effervescent, *adj.* gazeux.

effete, *adj.* epuisé, caduc.

efficacious, *adj.* efficace.

efficacy, *n.* efficacité *f.*

efficiency, *n.* (person) compétence *f.*; (machine) rendement *m.*

efficient, *adj.* (person) capable.

efficiently, *adv.* efficacement, avec compétence.

effigy, *n.* effigie *f.*

effort, *n.* effort *m.*

effortless, *adj.* sans effort.

effrontery, *n.* effronterie *f.*

effulgent, *adj.* resplendissant.

effusive, *adj.* démonstratif.

egalitarian, *adj.* égalitaire.

egg, *n.* œuf *m.;* **(boiled e.)** œuf à la coque; **(fried e.)** œuf sur le plat; **(poached e.)** œuf poché; **(scrambled e.)** œuf brouillé.

eggplant, *n.* aubergine *f.*

egg shell, *n.* coquille *(f.)* d'œuf.

ego, *n.* moi *m.*

egoism, *n.* égoïsme *m.*

egotism, *n.* égotisme *m.*

egotist, *n.* égotiste *m.*

Egypt, *n.* Égypte *m.*

Egyptian, 1. *n.* Égyptien *m.* **2.** *adj.* égyptien.

eiderdown, *n.* édredon *m.*

eight, *adj. and n.* huit *m.*

eighteen, *adj. and n.* dix-huit *m.*

eighteenth, *adj. and n.* dix-huitième *m.f.*

eighth, *adj. and n.* huitième *m.f.*

eightieth, *adj. and n.* quatre-vingtième *m.f.*

eighty, *adj. and n.* quatre-vingts *m.*

Eire, *n.* République *(f.)* d'Irlande.

either, 1. *adj.* (each of two) chaque; (one or other) l'un ou l'autre. **2.** *pron.* chacun; l'un ou l'autre. **3.** *conj.* **(e. . . . or)** ou . . . ou . . .

ejaculate, *vb.* éjaculer, prononcer.

eject, *vb.* (throw) jeter.

ejection, *n.* jet *m.,* éjection *f.,* expulsion *f.*

eke, *vb.* suppléer à, subsister pauvrement.

elaborate, 1. *adj.* minutieux. **2.** *vb.* élaborer.

elapse, *vb.* (time) s'écouler.

elastic, *adj. and n.* élastique *m.*

elasticity, *n.* élasticité *f.*

elate, *vb.* exalter, transporter.

elated, *adj.* exalté.

elation, *n.* exaltation *f.*

elbow, *n.* coude *m.*

elbowroom, *n.* aisance *(f.)* des coudes.

elder, *adj. and n.* aîné *m.*

elderberry, *n.* baie de sureau *f.*

elderly, *adj.* d'un certain âge.

eldest, *adj.* aîné.

elect, 1. *vb.* élire. **2.** *adj.* **(the president e.)** le président élu.

election, *n.* élection *f.*

electioneer, *vb.* faire une campagne électorale.

elective, *adj.* électif.

electorate, *n.* électorat *m.,* les votants *m.pl.*

electric, electrical, *adj.* électrique.

electric chair, *n.* fauteuil électrique *m.*

electric eel, *n.* anguille électrique *f.*

electrician, *n.* électricien *m.*

electricity, *n.* électricité *f.*

electrocardiogram, *n.* électrocardiogramme *m.*

electrocute, *vb.* électrocuter.

electrode, *n.* électrode *f.*

electrolysis, *n.* électrolyse *f.*

electron, *n.* électron *m.*

electronic, *adj.* électronique.

electronics, *n.* électronique *f.*

electroplate, 1. *vb.* plaquer **2.** *adj.* plaqué.

elegance, *n.* élégance *f.*

elegant, *adj.* élégant.

elegiac, *adj.* élégiaque.

elegy, *n.* élégie *f.*

element, *n.* élément *m.*

elemental, elementary, *adj.* élémentaire.

elephant, *n.* éléphant *m.*

elephantine, *adj.* éléphantin.

elevate, *vb.* élever.

elevation, *n.* élévation *f.*

elevator, *n.* ascenseur *m.*

eleven, *adj. and n.* onze *m.*

eleventh, *adj. and n.* onzième *m.f.*

elf, *n.* elfe *m.,* lutin *m.*

elfin, *adj.* d'elfe.

elicit, *vb.* tirer, faire jaillir.

eligibility, *n.* éligibilité *f.*

eligible, *adj.* éligible.

eliminate, *vb.* éliminer.

elimination, *n.* élimination *f.*

elixir, *n.* élixir *m.*

elk, *n.* élan *m.*

ellipse, *n.* ellipse *f.*

elm, *n.* orme *m.*

elocution, *n.* élocution *f.*

elongate, *vb.* allonger, étendre.

elope, *vb.* s'enfuir.

eloquence, *n.* éloquence *f.*

eloquent, *adj.* éloquent.

eloquently, *adv.* d'une manière éloquente.

else, 1. *adj.* autre; **(someone e.)**

quelqu'un d'autre; (everyone e.) tous les autres. 2. adv. autrement.
elsewhere, adv. ailleurs.
elucidate, vb. élucider, éclaircir.
elude, vb. éluder.
elusive, adj. évasif, insaisissable.
emaciated, adj. émacié.
emanate, vb. émaner.
emancipate, vb. émanciper.
emancipation, n. émancipation f.
emancipator, n. émancipateur m.
emasculate, vb. émasculer.
embalm, vb. embaumer.
embankment, n. levée f.
embargo, n. embargo m.
embark, vb. embarquer, tr.
embarkation, n. embarquement m.
embarrass, vb. embarrasser.
embarrassing, adj. embarrassant.
embarrassment, n. embarras m.
embassy, n. ambassade f.
embed, vb. encastrer.
embellish, vb. embellir.
embellishment, n. embellissement m.
ember, n. braise f., charbon ardent m.
embezzle, vb. détourner.
embitter, vb. aigrir, envenimer.
emblazon, vb. blasonner.
emblem, n. emblème m.
emblematic, adj. emblématique.
embody, vb. incarner, incorporer.
emboss, vb. graver en relief, travailler en bosse.
embrace, 1. n. étreinte f. 2. vb. embrasser.
embroider, vb. broder.
embroidery, n. broderie f.
embroil, vb. embrouiller.
embryo, n. embryon m.
embryology, n. embryologie f.
embryonic, adj. embryonnaire.
emerald, n. émeraude f.
emerge, vb. émerger.
emergency, n. circonstance (f.) critique; (e. exit) sortie (f.) de secours; (e. landing) atterrissage (m.) forcé.
emergent, adj. émergent.
emery, n. émeri m.
emetic, n. émétique m.
emigrant, n. émigrant m.
emigrate, vb. émigrer.
emigration, n. émigration f.

eminence, n. éminence f.
eminent, adj. éminent.
emissary, n. émissaire m.
emission control, n. appareil (m.) pour limiter l'émission de vapeurs nuisibles.
emit, vb. émettre.
emollient, adj. émollient.
emolument, n. traitement m.
emotion, n. émotion f.
emotional, adj. émotif; (excitable) émotionnable.
emperor, n. empereur m.
emphasis, n. (impressiveness) force f.; (stress) accent m.
emphasize, vb. mettre en relief, souligner.
emphatic, adj. (manner) énergique.
empire, n. empire m.
empirical, adj. empirique.
employ, vb. employer.
employee, n. employé m.
employer, n. patron m.
employment, n. emploi m.
employment agency, n. agence (f.) de placement.
empower, vb. autoriser.
empress, n. impératrice f.
emptiness, n. vide m.
empty, 1. adj. vide. 2. vb. vider.
emulate, vb. émuler.
emulsion, n. émulsion f.
enable, vb. mettre à même (de).
enact, vb. (law) décréter; (play) jouer.
enactment, n. promulgation f., acte législatif m.
enamel, n. émail m., pl. émaux.
enamored, adj. (be e. of) être épris de.
encamp, vb. camper, faire camper.
encampment, n. campement m.
encased, adj. (e. in) enfermé dans.
encephalitis, n. encéphalite f.
encephalon, n. encéphale m.
enchant, vb. enchanter.
enchanting, adj. ravissant.
enchantment, n. enchantement m.
encircle, vb. entourer.
enclose, vb. enclore; (in letter) joindre.
enclosure, n. enclos m.; (in letter) pièce (f.) jointe.
encompass, vb. entourer.

encounter, vb. rencontrer.
encourage, vb. encourager.
encouragement, n. encouragement m.
encroach, vb. empiéter.
encumber, vb. encombrer.
encyclical, n. encyclique f.
encyclopedia, n. encyclopédie f.
end, 1. n. fin f.; (extremity) bout m.; (aim) but m. **2.** vb. finir.
endanger, vb. mettre en danger.
endear, vb. rendre cher.
endearing, adj. attachant.
endearment, n. charme m., attrait m.
endeavor, 1. n. effort m. **2.** vb. s'efforcer.
endemic, adj. endémique.
ending, n. terminaison f.
endive, n. chicorée f., endive f.
endless, adj. sans fin.
endocrine gland, n. glande endocrine f.
endorse, vb. (sign) endosser; (support) appuyer.
endorsement, n. (signing) endossement m.; (approval) approbation f.
endow, vb. doter.
endowment, n. dotation f., fondation f.
endurance, n. résistance f.
endure, vb. supporter.
enduring, adj. durable.
enema, n. lavement m.
enemy, n. adj. and n. ennemi m.
energetic, adj. énergique.
energy, n. énergie f.
enervate, vb. énerver, affaiblir.
enervation, n. affaiblissement m.
enfold, vb. envelopper.
enforce, vb. imposer; (law) exécuter.
enforcement, n. exécution f.
enfranchise, vb. affranchir, accorder le droit de vote.
engage, vb. engager, tr.; (**become e.d,** to be married) se fiancer.
engaged, adj. occupé, pris; fiancé.
engagement, n. engagement m.; (marriage) fiançailles f.pl.
engaging, adj. attrayant, séduisant.
engender, vb. engendrer.

engine, n. machine f.; (train) locomotive f.; (motor) moteur m.
engineer, n. (profession) ingénieur m.; (engine operator) mécanicien m.; (mil.) soldat (m.) du génie.
engineering, n. génie m., ingénierie f.
England, n. Angleterre f.
English, adj. and n. anglais m.
Englishman, n. Anglais m.
Englishwoman, n. Anglaise f.
engrave, vb. graver.
engraver, n. graveur m.
engraving, n. gravure f.
engross, vb. (absorb) absorber.
engrossing, adj. absorbant.
engulf, vb. engouffrer.
enhance, vb. rehausser.
enigma, n. énigme f.
enigmatic, adj. énigmatique.
enjoin, vb. enjoindre.
enjoy, vb. jouir de; (**e. oneself**) s'amuser.
enjoyable, adj. agréable.
enjoyment, n. plaisir m.
enlace, vb. enlacer.
enlarge, vb. agrandir, tr.
enlargement, n. agrandissement m.
enlarger, n. agrandisseur m., amplificateur m.
enlighten, vb. éclairer.
enlightenment, n. éclaircissement m.; (**the E.**) le Siècle (m.) des Lumières.
enlist, vb. enrôler, tr.
enlisted man, n. gradé m.
enlistment, n. enrôlement m.
enliven, vb. animer.
enmesh, vb. engrener, embarrasser.
enmity, n. inimitié f.
ennoble, vb. anoblir.
ennui, n. ennui m.
enormity, n. énormité f.
enormous, adj. énorme.
enough, adj. and adv. assez (de).
enrage, vb. faire enrager.
enrapture, vb. ravir, enchanter.
enrich, vb. enrichir.
enroll, vb. enrôler, s'inscrire.
enrollment, n. inscription f.
ensemble, n. ensemble m.
enshrine, vb. enchâsser.
ensign, n. (navy) enseigne m.

enslave, vb. asservir.

ensnare, vb. prendre au piège.

ensue, vb. s'ensuivre.

entail, vb. (involve) entraîner; (law) substituer.

entangle, vb. empêtrer.

enter, vb. entrer (dans).

enterprise, n. entreprise f.

enterprising, adj. entreprenant.

entertain, vb. (amuse) amuser; (receive) recevoir.

entertainment, n. amusement m.

enthrall, vb. captiver, ensorceler.

enthusiasm, n. enthousiasme m.

enthusiast, n. enthousiaste m.f.

enthusiastic, adj. enthousiaste.

entice, vb. attirer.

entire, adj. entier.

entirely, adv. entièrement.

entirety, n. totalité f.

entitle, vb. donner droit à; (book) intituler.

entity, n. entité f.

entomb, vb. enterrer, ensevelir.

entrails, n. entrailles f.pl.

entrain, vb. embarquer en chemin de fer.

entrance, 1. n. entrée f. **2.** vb. enchanter.

entrant, n. débutant m., inscrit m.

entrap, vb. attraper, prendre au piège.

entreat, vb. supplier.

entreaty, n. instance f.

entrench, vb. retrancher.

entrust to, vb. confier à.

entry, n. (entrance) entrée f.; (recording) inscription f.

enumerate, vb. énumérer.

enumeration, n. énumération f.

enunciate, vb. énoncer.

enunciation, n. énonciation f.

envelop, vb. envelopper.

envelope, n. enveloppe f.

enviable, adj. enviable.

envious, adj. envieux.

environment, n. milieu m.; (ecology) environnement m.

environmentalist, n. écologiste m.f.; environnementaliste m.

environmental protection, n. protection (f.) de l'environnement.

environs, n. environs m.pl., alentours m.pl.

envisage, vb. envisager.

envoy, n. envoyé m.

envy, 1. n. envie f. **2.** vb. envier.

enzyme, n. enzyme m.

eon, n. éon m.

ephemeral, adj. éphémère.

epic, 1. n. épopée f. **2.** adj. épique.

epicure, n. gourmet m.

epidemic, n. épidémie f.

epidermis, n. épiderme m.

epigram, n. épigramme f.

epilepsy, n. épilepsie f.

epilogue, n. épilogue m.

episode, n. épisode m.

epistle, n. épître f.

epitaph, n. épitaphe f.

epithet, n. épithète f.

epitome, n. épitomé m., résumé m.

epitomize, vb. résumer, abréger.

epoch, n. époque f.

equable, adj. uniforme, régulier.

equal, 1. adj. égal; **2.** vb. égaliser.

equality, n. égalité f.

equalize, vb. égaliser, tr.

equanimity, n. tranquillité (f.) d'esprit, équanimité f., sérénité f.

equate, vb. égaler, mettre en équation.

equation, n. équation f.

equator, n. équateur m.

equatorial, adj. équatorial.

equestrian, adj. équestre.

equidistant, adj. équidistant.

equilateral, adj. équilatéral.

equilibrium, n. équilibre m.

equinox, n. équinoxe m.

equip, vb. équiper.

equipment, n. équipement m.

equitable, adj. équitable, juste.

equity, n. équité f., action f.

equivalent, adj. and n. équivalent m.

equivocal, adj. équivoque.

equivocate, vb. équivoquer.

era, n. ère f.

eradicate, vb. déraciner.

eradicator, n. effaceur m., grattoir m.

erase, vb. effacer.

eraser, n. gomme f.

erasure, n. rature f.

erect, adj. droit.

erection, n. érection f., construction f.

erectness, n. attitude droite f.

ermine, n. hermine f.

erode, vb. éroder, ronger.
erosion, n. érosion f.
erosive, adj. érosif.
erotic, adj. érotique.
err, vb. errer.
errand, n. course f.
errant, adj. errant.
erratic, adj. irrégulier, excentrique.
erring, adj. égaré, dévoyé.
erroneous, adj. erroné.
error, n. erreur f.
erudite, adj. érudit.
erudition, n. érudition f.
erupt, vb. entrer en éruption.
eruption, n. éruption f.
escalate, vb. escalader.
escalator, n. escalier roulant m.
escapade, n. escapade f.
escape, 1. n. fuite f. **2.** vb. échapper.
escapism, n. évasion f., échappement m.
eschew, vb. éviter, s'abstenir.
escort, 1. n. (mil.) escorte f.; (to a lady) cavalier m. **2.** vb. escorter.
esculent, adj. comestible.
escutcheon, n. écusson m.
Eskimo, 1. n. Esquimau m., Esquimaude f. **2.** adj. esquimau m., esquimaude f.
esoteric, adj. ésotérique.
especially, adj. surtout, particulièrement.
espionage, n. espionnage m.
espousal, n. adoption f., adhésion (à) f.
espouse, vb. épouser, embrasser (une cause).
esquire, n. écuyer m.; titre honorifique d'un "gentleman".
essay, 1. n. essai m.; (school) composition f. **2.** vb. essayer.
essayist, n. essayiste m.
essence, n. essence f.
essential, adj. essentiel.
essentially, adv. essentiellement.
establish, vb. établir.
establishment, n. établissement m.; (the E.) l'ordre (m.) établi.
estate, n. (condition, class) état m.; (wealth) biens m.pl.; (land) propriété f.
esteem, 1. n. estime f. **2.** vb. estimer.
estimable, adj. estimable.

estimate, 1. n. estimation f.; (comm.) devis m. **2.** vb. estimer.
estimation, n. (opinion) jugement m., estimation f.
estrange, vb. aliéner.
estuary, n. estuaire m.
etching, n. gravure (f.) à l'eau-forte.
eternal, adj. éternel.
eternity, n. éternité f.
ether, n. éther m.
ethereal, adj. éthéré.
ethical, adj. moral.
ethics, n. éthique f.
Ethiopia, n. Éthiopie f.
ethnic, adj. ethnique.
etiquette, n. étiquette f.
Etruscan, 1. n. Étrusque m.f. **2.** adj. étrusque.
etymology, n. étymologie f.
eucalyptus, n. eucalyptus m.
eugenic, adj. eugénésique.
eugenics, n. eugénisme m., eugénique f.
eulogize, vb. faire l'éloge de.
eulogy, n. panégyrique m.
eunuch, n. eunuque m.
euphonious, adj. mélodieux, euphonique.
euphoria, n. euphorie f.
eurocheque, n. eurochèque m.
Europe, n. Europe f.
European, 1. n. Européen m. **2.** adj. européen.
European Community, n. Communauté (f.) européenne.
euthanasia, n. euthanasie f.
evacuate, vb. évacuer.
evacuee, n. évacué m.-e f.
evade, vb. éluder.
evaluate, vb. évaluer.
evaluation, n. évaluation f.
evanescent, adj. évanescent, éphémère.
evangelist, n. évangéliste m.
evaporate, vb. évaporer, tr.
evaporation, n. évaporation f.
evasion, n. subterfuge f.
evasive, adj. évasif.
eve, n. veille f.
even, 1. adj. égal; (number) pair. **2.** adv. même.
evening, n. soir m.; (span of e.) soirée f.
evenness, n. égalité f.

event, n. événement m.; (eventuality) cas m.

eventful, adj. mouvementé.

eventual, adj. (ultimate) définitif; (contingent) éventuel.

eventually, adv. en fin de compte, un jour ou l'autre.

ever, adv. (at all times) toujours; (at any time) jamais.

everglade, n. région marécageuse (de la Floride) f.

evergreen, adj. à feuilles persistantes, toujours vert.

everlasting, adj. éternel.

every, adj. (each) chaque; (all) tous les m.; toutes les f.

everybody, everyone, pron. tout le monde; chacun.

everyday, adj. de tous les jours.

everything, pron. tout.

everywhere, adv. partout.

evict, vb. évincer.

eviction, n. éviction f., expulsion f.

evidence, n. évidence f.; (proof) preuve f.

evident, adj. évident.

evidently, adv. évidemment.

evil, 1. n. mal m. **2.** adj. mauvais.

evince, vb. démontrer.

eviscerate, vb. éviscérer.

evoke, vb. évoquer.

evolution, n. évolution f.

evolutionist, n. évolutionniste m.f.

evolve, vb. évoluer, développer.

ewe, n. agnelle f.

exacerbate, vb. exacerber.

exact, adj. exact.

exacting, adj. (person) exigeant.

exactly, adv. exactement.

exaggerate, vb. exagérer.

exaggerated, adj. exagéré.

exaggeration, n. exagération f.

exalt, vb. exalter; (raise) élever.

exaltation, n. exaltation f.

examination, n. examen m.

examine, vb. examiner.

example, n. exemple m.

exasperate, vb. exaspérer.

exasperation, n. exaspération f.

excavate, vb. creuser.

exceed, vb. excéder.

exceedingly, adv. extrêmement.

excel, vb. exceller, intr.

excellence, excellency, n. excellence f.

excellent, adj. excellent.

excelsior, n. copeaux (m.pl.) d'emballage.

except, 1. vb. excepter. **2.** prep. excepté, sauf.

exception, n. exception f.

exceptional, adj. exceptionnel.

excerpt, n. extrait m.

excess, n. excès m.; (surplus) excédent m.

excessive, adj. excessif.

exchange, 1. n. échange m.; (money) change m. **2.** vb. échanger.

exchangeable, adj. échangeable.

excise, n. contribution indirecte f., régie f.

excitable, adj. émotionnable, excitable.

excite, vb. exciter.

excitement, n. agitation f.

exciting, adj. passionnant.

exclaim, vb. s'écrier.

exclamation, n. exclamation f.

exclamation point or **mark,** n. point (m.) d'exclamation.

exclude, vb. exclure.

exclusion, n. exclusion f.

exclusive, adj. exclusif; (stylish) sélect.

excommunicate, vb. excommunier.

excommunication, n. excommunication f.

excoriate, vb. excorier, écorcher.

excrement, n. excrément m.

excruciating, adj. atroce, affreux.

exculpate, vb. disculper, exonérer.

excursion, n. excursion f.

excusable, adj. excusable.

excuse, 1. n. excuse f. **2.** vb. excuser.

execrable, adj. exécrable, abominable.

execute, vb. exécuter.

execution, n. exécution f.

executioner, n. bourreau m.

executive, adj. and n. exécutif m., cadre m.

executive mansion, n. maison présidentielle f.

executor, n. exécuteur m.

exemplary, adj. exemplaire.

exemplify, vb. expliquer par des exemples.

exempt, 1. *adj.* exempt. 2. *vb.* exempter.
exercise, 1. *n.* exercice *m.* 2. *vb.* exercer.
exercise bike, *n.* vélo (*m.*) d'appartement.
exert, *vb.* employer; (**e. oneself**) s'efforcer de.
exertion, *n.* effort *m.*
exhale, *vb.* exhaler.
exhaust, 1. *n.* (machines) échappement *m.* 2. *vb.* épuiser.
exhausted, *adj.* épuisé.
exhaustion, *n.* épuisement *m.*
exhaustive, *adj.* complet, approfondi.
exhibit, *vb.* (pictures, etc.) exposer; (show) montrer.
exhibition, *n.* exposition *f.*
exhibitionism, *n.* exhibitionnisme *m.*
exhilarate, *vb.* égayer.
exhort, *vb.* exhorter.
exhortation, *n.* exhortation *f.*
exhume, *vb.* exhumer.
exigency, *n.* exigence *f.*
exile, 1. *n.* exil *m.;* (person) exilé *m.* 2. *vb.* exiler.
exist, *vb.* exister.
existence, *n.* existence *f.*
existent, *adj.* existant.
exit, 1. *n.* sortie *f.* 2. *vb.* sortir.
exit ramp, *n.* bretelle (*f.*) d'accès.
exodus, *n.* exode *m.*
exonerate, *vb.* exonérer.
exorbitant, *adj.* exorbitant.
exorcise, *vb.* exorciser.
exotic, *adj.* exotique.
expand, *vb.* étendre, *tr.;* (dilate) dilater, *tr.*
expanse, *n.* étendue *f.*
expansion, *n.* expansion *f.*
expansive, *adj.* expansif.
expatiate, *vb.* discourir.
expatriate, *vb.* expatrier.
expect, *vb.* s'attendre à; (await) attendre.
expectancy, *n.* attente *f.*
expectant, *adj.* (**e. mother**) future maman *f.*
expectation, *n.* attente *f.;* (hope) espérance *f.*
expectorate, *vb.* expectorer.
expediency, *n.* convenance *f.*
expedient, *n.* expédient *m.*

expedite, *vb.* activer, accélérer.
expedition, *n.* expédition *f.*
expel, *vb.* expulser.
expend, *vb.* (money) dépenser; (use up) épuiser.
expenditure, *n.* dépense *f.*
expense, *n.* dépense *f.;* (expenses) frais *m.pl.*
expensive, *adj.* coûteux, cher.
expensively, *adv.* coûteusement.
experience, 1. *n.* expérience *f.* 2. *vb.* éprouver.
experienced, *adj.* expérimenté.
experiment, *n.* expérience *f.*
experimental, *adj.* expérimental.
expert, *adj. and n.* expert *m.*
expiate, *vb.* expier.
expiration, *n.* expiration *f.*
expire, *vb.* expirer.
explain, *vb.* expliquer.
explanation, *n.* explication *f.*
explanatory, *adj.* explicatif.
expletive, *n.* explétif *m.*
explicit, *adj.* explicite.
explode, *vb.* (burst) éclater, *intr.*
exploit, 1. *n.* exploit *m.* 2. *vb.* exploiter.
exploitation, *n.* exploitation *f.*
exploration, *n.* exploration *f.*
exploratory, *adj.* exploratif.
explore, *vb.* explorer.
explorer, *n.* explorateur *m.*
explosion, *n.* explosion *f.*
explosive, *adj. and n.* explosif *m.*
exponent, *n.* interprète *m.*
export, 1. *n.* (exportation) exportation *f.;* (exported object) article (*m.*) d'exportation. 2. *vb.* exporter.
exportation, *n.* exportation *f.*
expose, *vb.* exposer.
exposé, *n.* exposé *m.*
exposition, *n.* exposition *f.*
expository, *adj.* expositoire.
expostulate, *vb.* faire des remontrances à.
exposure, *n.* exposition *f.*
expound, *vb.* exposer.
express, 1. *adj.* exprès. 2. *vb.* exprimer.
expression, *n.* expression *f.*
expressive, *adj.* expressif.
expressly, *adv.* expressément.
expressman, *n.* agent (*m.*) de messageries.

expropriate, vb. exproprier.
expulsion, n. expulsion f.
expunge, vb. effacer, rayer.
expurgate, vb. expurger, épurer.
exquisite, adj. exquis.
extant, adj. existant.
extemporaneous, adj. improvisé, impromptu.
extend, vb. étendre; (prolong) prolonger.
extension, n. extension f.
extensive, adj. étendu.
extensively, adv. largement, considérablement.
extent, n. étendue f.; **(to some e.)** jusqu'à un certain point.
extenuate, vb. (tire out) exténuer; (diminish) atténuer.
extenuating circumstances, n. circonstances (f.pl.) atténuantes.
exterior, adj. and n. extérieur m.
exterminate, vb. exterminer.
extermination, n. extermination f.
external, adj. externe.
extinct, adj. éteint.
extinction, n. extinction f.
extinguish, vb. éteindre.
extol, vb. vanter.
extort, vb. extorquer.
extortion, n. extorsion f.
extortioner, n. extorqueur m.
extra, adj. (additional) supplémentaire; (spare) de réserve.

extra-, prefix. (outside of) en dehors de; (intensive) extra-.
extract, 1. n. extrait m. 2. vb. extraire.
extraction, n. extraction f.
extradite, vb. extrader.
extramarital, adj. extra-conjugal.
extraneous, adj. étranger à.
extraordinary, adj. extraordinaire.
extravagance, n. extravagance f.; (money) prodigalité f.
extravagant, adj. extravagant; (money) prodigue.
extravaganza, n. œuvre fantaisiste f.
extreme, adj. and n. extrême m.
extremity, n. extrémité f.
extricate, vb. dégager, tirer.
extrovert, n. extroverti m.
exuberant, adj. exubérant.
exude, vb. exsuder.
exult, vb. exulter.
exultant, adj. exultant, joyeux.
eye, n. œil m., pl. yeux.
eyeball, n. globe (m.) de l'œil.
eyebrow, n. sourcil m.
eyeglass, n. lorgnon m.
eyeglasses, n. lunettes f.pl.
eyelash, n. cil m.
eyelet, n. œillet m.
eyelid, n. paupière f.
eye shadow, n. fard (m.) à paupières.
eyesight, n. vue f.
eyewitness, n. témoin oculaire m.

F

fable, n. fable f.
fabric, n. (structure) édifice m.; (cloth) tissu m.
fabricate, vb. fabriquer.
fabrication, n. fabrication f.
fabulous, adj. fabuleux.
façade, n. façade f.
face, 1. n. figure f. 2. vb. faire face à.
facet, n. facette f.
facetious, adj. facétieux.
face value, n. valeur nominale f.
facial, adj. facial.
facile, adj. facile.
facilitate, vb. faciliter.
facility, n. facilité f.

facing, n. revêtement m., revers m.
facsimile, n. fac-similé m.; (document) télécopie f., fax m.; **(f. machine)** télécopieur m.
fact, n. fait m.; **(as a matter of f.)** en effet.
faction, n. faction f.
factor, n. facteur m.
factory, n. fabrique f., usine f.
factual, adj. effectif, positif.
faculty, n. faculté f.
fad, n. marotte f.
fade, vb. intr. se faner; (color) se décolorer; **(f. away)** s'évanouir.
fail, vb. manquer; (not succeed) échouer.

failing, 1. n. manquement m. **2.** adj. faiblissant. **3.** prep. au défaut de.

faille, n. faille f.

failure, n. (lack) défaut m.; (want of success) insuccès m.

faint, 1. adj. faible. **2.** vb. s'évanouir.

faintly, adv. faiblement, timidement, légèrement.

fair, 1. n. foire f. **2.** adj. (beautiful) beau m., belle f.; (blond) blond; (honest) juste; (pretty good) passable.

fairly, adv. honnêtement, impartialement.

fairness, n. (honesty) honnêteté f.

fairy, n. fée f.

fairyland, n. pays (m.) des fées.

fairy tale, n. conte (m.) de fées.

faith, n. foi f.

faithful, adj. fidèle.

faithless, adj. infidèle.

fake, vb. truquer.

faker, n. truqueur m.

falcon, n. faucon m.

falconry, n. fauconnerie f.

fall, 1. n. chute f.; (autumn) automne m. **2.** vb. tomber.

fallacious, adj. fallacieux.

fallacy, n. fausseté f.

fallen, adj. tombé, déchu.

fallible, adj. faillible.

fallout, n. pluie radioactive f.

fallow, adj. en jachère.

false, adj. faux m., fausse f.

falsehood, n. mensonge m.

falseness, n. fausseté f.

falsetto, n. and adj. fausset m.

falsification, n. falsification f.

falsify, vb. falsifier.

falter, vb. hésiter.

fame, n. renommée f.

famed, adj. célèbre, renommé, fameux.

familiar, adj. familier.

familiarity, n. familiarité f.

familiarize, vb. familiariser.

family, n. famille f.

famine, n. (food) disette f.; (general) famine f.

famished, adj. affamé.

famous, adj. célèbre.

fan, n. éventail m.; (mechanical) ventilateur m.; (of person) admirateur m.

fanatic, adj. and n. fanatique m.

fanatical, adj. fanatique.

fanaticism, n. fanatisme m.

fan belt, n. courroie (f.) de ventilateur.

fanciful, adj. fantastique, fantaisiste.

fancy, 1. n. fantaisie f. **2.** vb. se figurer; avoir envie de.

fanfare, n. fanfare f.

fang, n. croc (of a dog) m., crochet (of a snake) m.

fantastic, adj. fantastique.

fantasy, n. fantaisie f.

far, adv. loin; (so f.) jusqu'ici; (as f. as) autant que; (much) beaucoup; (by f.) de beaucoup.

faraway, adj. lointain.

farce, n. farce f.

farcical, adj. bouffon.

fare, 1. n. (price) prix m.; (food) chère f. **2.** vb. aller.

Far East, n. Extrême-Orient m.

farewell, interj. and n. adieu m.

far-fetched, adj. forcé.

far-flung, adj. très étendu, vaste.

farina, n. farine f.

farm, n. ferme f.

farmer, n. fermier m.

farmhouse, n. maison (f.) de ferme.

farming, n. culture f.

farmyard, n. cour de ferme f.

far-reaching, adj. de grande envergure.

far-sighted, adj. clairvoyant.

farther, 1. adj. plus éloigné. **2.** adv. plus loin.

farthest, adj. and adv. le plus lointain.

fascinate, vb. fasciner.

fascination, n. fascination f.

fascism, n. fascisme m.

fashion, n. mode f.; (manner) manière f.

fashionable, adj. à la mode.

fast, 1. n. jeûne m. **2.** adj. (speedy) rapide; (firm) ferme; (of clock) en avance. **3.** vb. jeûner. **4.** adv. (quickly) vite; (firmly) ferme.

fasten, vb. attacher, tr.

fastener, n. fermeture f.

fastening, n. attache f.

fastidious, *adj.* difficile.
fat, *adj.* gras *m.*, grasse *f.*
fatal, *adj.* fatal; (deadly) mortel.
fatality, *n.* fatalité *f.*
fatally, *adv.* fatalement, mortellement.
fate, *n.* destin *m.*
fateful, *adj.* fatal.
father, *n.* père *m.*
fatherhood, *n.* paternité *f.*
father-in-law, *n.* beau-père *m.*
fatherland, *n.* patrie *f.*
fatherless, *adj.* sans père.
fatherly, *adj.* paternel.
fathom, **1.** *n.* (naut.) brasse *f.* **2.** *vb.* sonder.
fatigue, *n.* fatigue *f.*
fatten, *vb.* engraisser.
fatty, *adj.* graisseux.
fatuous, *adj.* sot.
faucet, *n.* robinet *m.*
fault, *n.* (mistake) faute *f.*; (defect) défaut *m.*
faultfinding, *n.* disposition (*f.*) à critiquer.
faultless, *adj.* sans défaut.
faultlessly, *adv.* d'une manière impeccable.
faulty, *adj.* défectueux.
fauna, *n.* faune *f.*
favor, **1.** *n.* faveur *f.* **2.** *vb.* favoriser.
favorable, *adj.* favorable.
favored, *adj.* favorisé.
favorite, *adj. and n.* favori *m.*, favorite *f.*
favoritism, *n.* favoritisme *m.*
fawn, *n.* faon *m.*
fax, **1.** *n.* (document) télécopie *f.*, fax *m.*; (**f. machine**) télécopieur *m.* **2.** *vb.* télécopier, faxer.
faze, *vb.* bouleverser.
fear, **1.** *n.* crainte *f.* **2.** *vb.* craindre.
fearful, *adj.* (person) craintif; (thing) effrayant.
fearless, *adj.* intrépide.
fearlessness, *n.* intrépidité *f.*
fearsome, *adj.* redoutable.
feasible, *adj.* faisable.
feast, *n.* fête *f.*; (banquet) festin *m.*
feat, *n.* exploit *m.*
feather, *n.* plume *f.*
feathered, *adj.* emplumé.
featherweight, *n.* poids (*m.*) plume.

feathery, *adj.* plumeux.
feature, *n.* trait *m.*
February, *n.* février *m.*
fecund, *adj.* fécond.
federal, *adj.* fédéral.
federation, *n.* fédération *f.*
fedora, *n.* chapeau mou *m.*
fee, *n.* (for professional services) honoraires *m.pl.*; (school) frais *m.pl.*
feeble, *adj.* faible.
feeble-minded, *adj.* d'esprit faible.
feebleness, *n.* faiblesse *f.*
feed, **1.** *n.* nourriture *f.* **2.** *vb.* nourrir, *tr.*
feedback, *n.* action (*f.*) de contrôle en retour.
feel, *vb.* sentir, *tr.*; (touch) tâter.
feeling, *n.* sentiment *m.*
feign, *vb.* feindre.
feint, *n.* feinte *f.*
felicitate, *vb.* féliciter.
felicitous, *adj.* heureux.
felicity, *n.* félicité *f.*
feline, *adj.* félin.
fell, *adj.* funeste.
fellow, *n.* (general) homme *m.*, garçon *m.*; (companion) compagnon *m.*
fellowship, *n.* camaraderie *f.*; (university) bourse (*f.*) universitaire.
fellow traveler, *n.* compagnon (*m.*) de route.
felon, *n.* criminel *m.*
felony, *n.* crime *m.*
felt, *n.* feutre *m.*
female, **1.** *n.* (person) femme *f.*; (animals, plants) femelle *f.* **2.** *adj.* féminin, femelle.
feminine, *adj.* féminin.
femininity, *n.* féminité *f.*
fence, **1.** *n.* (enclose) enclore; (sword, foil) faire de l'escrime.
fencer, *n.* escrimeur *m.*
fencing, *n.* escrime *f.*
fender, *n.* garde-boue *m.*; (fireplace) garde-feu *m.*
ferment, *vb.* fermenter.
fermentation, *n.* fermentation *f.*
fern, *n.* fougère *f.*
ferocious, *adj.* féroce.
ferociously, *adv.* d'une manière féroce.
ferocity, *n.* férocité *f.*

ferry, *n.* passage *(m.)* en bac; (f. **boat**) bac *m.*

fertile, *adj.* fertile.

fertility, *n.* fertilité *f.*

fertilization, *n.* fertilisation *f.*

fertilize, *vb.* fertiliser.

fervency, *n.* ardeur *f.*

fervent, *adj.* fervent.

fervently, *adv.* ardemment.

fervid, *adj.* fervent.

fervor, *n.* ferveur *f.*

fester, *vb.* suppurer.

festival, *n.* fête *f.*

festive, *adj.* de fête.

festivity, *n.* réjouissance *f.*

festoon, 1. *n.* feston *m.* 2. *vb.* festonner.

fetal, *adj.* foetal.

fetch, *vb.* (go and get) aller chercher; (bring) apporter.

fetching, *adj.* attrayant.

fete, *vb.* fêter.

fetid, *adj.* fétide.

fetish, *n.* fétiche *m.*

fetlock, *n.* fanon *m.*

fetter, 1. *n.* lien *m.*, chaîne *f.* 2. *vb.* enchaîner.

fetus, *n.* fœtus *m.*

feud, *n.* inimitié *f.*; (historical) fief *m.*

feudal, *adj.* féodal.

feudalism, *n.* régime féodal *m.*

fever, *n.* fièvre *f.*

feverish, *adj.* fiévreux.

feverishly, *adv.* fébrilement, fiévreusement.

few, 1. *adj.* peu de; (a f.) quelques. 2. *pron.* peu; (a f.) quelques-uns.

fiancé, *n.* fiancé *m.*

fiasco, *n.* fiasco *m.*

fiat, *n.* décret *m.*

fib, *n.* petit mensonge *m.*

fiber, *n.* fibre *f.*

fiberboard, *n.* fibre *(m.)* de bois.

fiberglass, *n.* fibre *(m.)* de verre.

fibrous, *adj.* fibreux.

fickle, *adj.* volage.

fickleness, *n.* inconstance *f.*

fiction, *n.* fiction *f.*; (literature) romans *m.pl.*

fictional, *adj.* de romans.

fictitious, *adj.* fictif, imaginaire.

fictitiously, *adv.* d'une manière factice.

fiddle, 1. *n.* violon *m.* 2. *vb.* jouer du violon.

fiddlesticks, *interj.* quelle blague!

fidelity, *n.* fidélité *f.*

fidget, *vb.* se remuer.

field, *n.* champ *m.*

fiend, *n.* démon *m.*

fiendish, *adj.* diabolique, infernal.

fierce, *adj.* féroce.

fiery, *adj.* ardent.

fiesta, *n.* fête *f.*

fife, *n.* fifre *m.*

fifteen, *adj. and n.* quinze *m.*

fifteenth, *adj. and n.* quinzième *m.f.*

fifth, *adj. and n.* cinquième *m.f.*

fifty, *adj. and n.* cinquante *m.*

fig, *n.* figue *f.*

fight, 1. *n.* combat *m.*; (struggle) lutte *f.*; (quarrel) dispute *f.* 2. *vb.* combattre; se disputer.

fighter, *n.* combattant *m.*

figment, *n.* invention *f.*

figurative, *adj.* figuré.

figuratively, *adv.* au figuré.

figure, 1. *n.* figure *f.*; (of body) ligne *f.*; (math.) chiffre *m.* 2. *vb.* figurer; calculer.

figured, *adj.* à dessin.

figurehead, *n.* homme de paille *m.*

figure of speech, *n.* façon *(f.)* de parler.

figurine, *n.* figurine *f.*

filament, *n.* filament *m.*

filch, *vb.* escamoter.

file, 1. *n.* (tool) lime *f.*; (row) file *f.*; (papers) liasse *f.*; (for papers, etc.) classeur *m.*; (computer) fichier *m.*; (f.s) archives *f.pl.* 2. *vb.* (tool) limer; (papers) classer; (f. off) défiler.

filial, *adj.* filial.

filigree, *n.* filigrane *m.*

filing cabinet, *n.* classeur *m.*

filings, *n.* limaille *f.*

fill, *vb.* remplir, *tr.*

fillet, *n.* (band) bandeau *m.*; (meat, fish) filet *m.*

filling, *n.* remplissage *m.*, (food) farce *f.*; (tooth) plombage *m.*

filling station, *n.* station-service *f.*

film, *n.* (cinema) film *m.*; (photo) pellicule *f.*

filmy, *adj.* couvert d'une pellicule.

filter, 1. *n.* filtre *m.* 2. *vb.* filtrer.

filth, n. ordure f.

filthy, adj. immonde; obscène.

fin, n. nageoire f.

final, adj. final.

finale, n. finale m.

finalist, n. finaliste m.

finality, n. finalité f.

finalize, vb. mettre au point.

finally, adv. finalement, enfin.

finance, 1. n. finance f. **2.** vb. financer.

financial, adj. financier.

financier, n. financier m.

find, vb. trouver.

findings, n. conclusions f.pl., verdict m.

fine, 1. n. amende f. **2** adj. (beautiful) beau m., belle f.; (pure, thin) fin. **3.** vb. mettre à l'amende.

fine arts, n. beaux arts m.pl.

finery, n. parure f.

finesse, 1. n. finesse f. **2.** vb. finasser.

finger, n. doigt m.

finger bowl, n. rince-bouche m.

fingernail, n. ongle m.

fingerprint, n. empreinte digitale f.

finicky, adj. affété.

finish, vb. finir.

finished, adj. fini, achevé.

finite, adj. fini.

Finland, n. Finlande f.

Finn, n. Finlandais, Finnois m.

Finnish, 1. n. finnois m. **2.** adj. finlandais, finnois.

fir, n. sapin m.

fire, 1. n. feu m.; (burning of house, etc.) incendie m. **2.** vb. (weapon) tirer.

fire alarm, n. avertisseur (m.) d'incendie.

firearm, n. arme (f.) à feu.

firecracker, n. pétard m.

firedamp, n. grisou m.

fire engine, n. pompe (f.) à incendie.

fire escape, n. échelle (f.) de sauvetage.

fire extinguisher, n. extincteur m.

firefly, n. luciole f.

fireman, n. pompier m.

fireplace, n. cheminée f.

fireproof, adj. à l'épreuve du feu.

fireside, n. coin du feu m.

firewood, n. bois (m.) de chauffage.

fireworks, n. feu (m.) d'artifice.

firing squad, n. peloton (m.) d'exécution.

firm, 1. n. maison (f.) de commerce. **2.** adj. ferme.

firmness, n. fermeté f.

first, 1. adj. premier. **2.** adv. d'abord.

first aid, n. premiers secours m.pl.

first-class, adj. de premier ordre.

firsthand, adj. de première main.

first-rate, adj. de premier ordre.

fiscal, adj. fiscal.

fish, 1. n. poisson m. **2.** vb. pêcher.

fisherman, n. pêcheur m.

fishery, n. pêcherie f.

fishhook, n. hameçon m.

fishing, n. pêche f.

fishmonger, n. marchand (m.) de poisson.

fishwife, n. marchande (f.) de poisson.

fishy, adj. de poisson; (slang) louche.

fission, n. fission f.

fissure, n. fente f.

fist, n. poing m.

fistic, adj. au poing.

fit, 1. n. accès m. **2.** adj. (suitable) convenable; (capable) capable; (f. for) propre à. **3.** vb. (befit) convenir à; (clothes) aller à; (adjust) ajuster, tr.

fitful, adj. agité, irrégulier.

fitness, n. à-propos m.; (person) aptitude f.; (medical) forme (f.) physique.

fitting, 1. n. ajustage m. **2.** adj. convenable.

five, adj. and n. cinq m.

fix, 1. n. embarras m. **2.** vb. fixer; (repair) réparer.

fixation, n. fixation f.

fixed, adj. fixe.

fixture, n. object (m.) d'attache.

fizzy, adj. pétillant, gazeux.

flabbergasted, adj. sidéré.

flabby, adj. flasque.

flaccid, adj. flasque.

flag, 1. n. drapeau m.; (stone) dalle f. **2.** vb. flagging, 1.

flagellate, vb. flageller.

flagging, 1. n. relâchement m. **2.** adj. qui s'affaiblit.

flagon, n. flacon m.

flagpole, n. mât de drapeau m.

flagrant, adj. flagrant.

flagrantly, adv. d'une manière flagrante.

flagship, n. vaisseau amiral m.

flagstone, n. dalle f.

flail, 1. n. fléau m. **2.** vb. battre au fléau.

flair, n. flair m.

flake, 1. n. (snow) flocon m. **2.** vb. s'écailler.

flamboyant, adj. flamboyant.

flame, 1. n. flamme f. **2.** vb. flamboyer.

flame thrower, n. lanceur (m.) de flammes.

flaming, adj. flamboyant.

flamingo, n. flamant m.

flank, n. flanc m.

flannel, n. flanelle f.

flap, 1. n. (wing) coup m.; (pocket) patte f.; (table) battant m. **2.** vb. battre.

flare, vb. flamboyer.

flare-up, 1. n. emportement m. **2.** vb. s'emporter.

flash, 1. n. éclair m. **2.** vb. briller, clignoter.

flashback, n. retour (m.) en arrière.

flashcube, n. flash-cube m.

flashiness, n. faux brillant m., éclat superficiel m.

flashlight, n. (lighthouse) feu (m.) à éclats; (pocket) lampe (f.) de poche.

flashy, adj. voyant.

flask, n. gourde f.

flat, 1. n. appartement m.; (tire) pneu (m.) crevé. **2.** adj. plat m., platte f.

flatcar, n. wagon en plateforme m.

flatness, n. (evenness) égalité f.; (dullness) platitude f.

flatten, vb. aplatir.

flatter, vb. flatter.

flatterer, n. flatteur m.

flattery, n. flatterie f.

flattop, n. porte-avion m.

flaunt, vb. étaler, étaler.

flautist, n. flûtiste m.f.

flavor, n. (taste) saveur f.; (fragrance) arome m.

flavoring, n. assaisonnement m.

flavorless, adj. fade.

flaw, n. défaut m.

flawless, adj. sans défaut, parfait.

flawlessly, adv. d'une manière impeccable.

flax, n. lin m.

flay, vb. écorcher.

flea, n. puce f.

fleck, 1. n. tache f. **2.** vb. tacheter.

fledgling, n. oisillon m.

flee, vb. s'enfuir.

fleece, 1. n. toison f. **2.** vb. voler.

fleecy, adj. laineux, moutonneux.

fleet, n. flotte f.

fleeting, adj. fugitif.

Flemish, adj. flamand.

flesh, n. chair f.

fleshy, adj. charnu.

flex, vb. fléchir.

flexibility, n. flexibilité f.

flexible, adj. flexible.

flick, 1. n. petit coup m. **2.** vb. donner un petit coup à.

flicker, 1. n. lueur (f.) vacillante. **2.** vb. trembloter.

flier, n. aviateur m.

flight, n. (flying) vol m.; (fleeing) fuite f.

flight attendant, n. hôtesse (f.) de l'air.

flighty, adj. étourdi.

flimsy, adj. sans solidité.

flinch, vb. reculer, broncher.

fling, 1. vb. jeter. **2.** n. (have a f.) faire la fête.

flint, n. (lighter) pierre (f.) à briquet; (mineral) silex m.

flip, vb. donner un petit coup à.

flippant, adj. léger.

flippantly, adv. légèrement.

flirt, vb. flirter.

flirtation, n. flirt m.

float, vb. flotter.

flock, 1. n. troupeau m. **2.** vb. accourir.

flog, vb. fouetter.

flood, n. inondation f.

floodgate, n. écluse f.

floodlight, n. lumière (f.) à grand flots.

floor, n. plancher m.; **(take the f.)** prendre la parole; (story) étage m.

flooring, n. plancher m., parquet m.

floorwalker, *n.* inspecteur du magasin *m.*

flop, 1. *vb.* faire plouf, s'effondrer. **2.** *n.* fiasco *m.*

floral, *adj.* floral.

florid, *adj.* fleuri, vermeil.

florist, *n.* fleuriste *m.f.*

flounce, 1. *n.* volant *m.* **2.** *vb.* se démener.

flounder, *n.* flet *m.*

flour, *n.* farine *f.*

flourish, *vb.* prospérer.

flow, *vb.* couler.

flower, 1. *n.* fleur *f.* **2.** *vb.* fleurir.

flowerpot, *n.* pot à fleurs *m.*

flowery, *adj.* fleuri.

flu, *n.* grippe *f.*

fluctuate, *vb.* osciller.

fluctuation, *n.* fluctuation *f.*

flue, *n.* tuyau *(m.)* de cheminée.

fluency, *n.* facilité *f.*

fluent, *adj.* (be a f. speaker of . . .) parler . . . couramment.

fluid, *adj* and *n.* fluide *m.*

fluidity, *n.* fluidité *f.*

flunk, *vb.* coller, recaler.

flunkey, *n.* laquais *m.*

fluorescent lamp, *n.* lampe fluorescente *f.*

fluoride, *n.* fluorure *f.*

fluoroscope, *n.* fluoroscope *m.*

flurry, 1. *n.* agitation *f.* **2.** *vb.* agiter.

flush, *n.* (redness) rougeur *f.;* (plumbing) chasse *f.*

flustered, *adj.* énervé.

flute, *n.* flûte *f.*

flutter, 1. *n.* (bird) voltigement *m.;* (agitation) agitation *f.* **2.** *vb.* s'agiter; (heart) palpiter.

flux, *n.* flux *m.*

fly, 1. *n.* mouche *f.;* (on pants) braguette *f.* **2.** *vb.* voler.

foam, *n.* écume *f.*

focal, *adj.* focal.

focus, 1. *n.* foyer *m.;* (in f.) au point. **2.** *vb.* (photo) mettre au point.

fodder, *n.* fourrage *m.*

foe, *n.* ennemi *m.*

fog, *n.* brouillard *m.*

foggy, *adj.* brumeux.

foil, *n.* (sheet) feuille *f.;* (set-off) repoussoir *m.;* (fencing) fleuret *m.*

foist, *vb.* fourrer.

fold, 1. *n.* pli *m.* **2.** *vb.* plier.

folder, *n.* (booklet) prospectus *m.*

foliage, *n.* feuillage *m.*

folio, *n.* in-folio *m.*

folk, *n.* gens *m.f.pl.*

folklore, *n.* folk-lore *m.*

folksong, *n.* chanson *(f.)* folklorique.

follicle, *n.* follicule *m.*

follow, *vb.* suivre.

follower, *n.* disciple *m.*

folly, *n.* folie *f.*

foment, *vb.* fomenter.

fond, *adj.* tendre; (be f. of) aimer.

fondant, *n.* fondant *m.*

fondle, *vb.* caresser.

fondly, *adv.* tendrement.

fondness, *n.* tendresse *f.*

font, *n.* fonte *f.*

food, *n.* nourriture *f.*

foodstuff, *n.* comestible *m.*

fool, *n.* sot *m.,* sotte *f.;* (jester) bouffon *m.*

foolhardiness, *n.* témérité *f.*

foolhardy, *adj.* téméraire.

foolish, *adj.* sot *m.,* sotte *f.*

foolproof, *adj.* infaillible.

foolscap, *n.* papier écolier *m.*

foot, *n.* pied *m.*

footage, *n.* métrage *m.*

football, *n.* football *m.,* ballon *m.*

foothill, *n.* colline basse *f.*

foothold, *n.* point d'appui *m.*

footing, *n.* pied *m.,* point d'appui *m.*

footlights, *n.* rampe *f.*

footnote, *n.* note *f.*

footprint, *n.* empreinte de pas *f.*

footsore, *adj.* aux pieds endoloris.

footstep, *n.* pas *m.*

footstool, *n.* tabouret *m.*

footwork, *n.* jeu de pieds *m.*

fop, *n.* fat *m.*

for, 1. *prep.* pour. **2.** *conj.* car.

forage, 1. *n.* fourrage *m.* **2.** *vb.* fourrager.

foray, *n.* razzia *f.*

forbear, *vb.* (avoid) s'abstenir de; (be patient) montrer de la patience.

forbearance, *n.* patience *f.*

forbid, *vb.* défendre (à).

forbidding, *adj.* menaçant.

force, 1. *n.* force *f.* **2.** *vb.* forcer.

forced, *adj.* forcé.

forceful, *adj.* énergique.

forcefulness, *n.* énergie *f.*, vigueur *f.*

forceps, *n.* forceps *m.*

forcible, *adj.* forcé.

ford, 1. *n.* gué *m.* **2.** *vb.* traverser à gué.

fore, 1. *adj.* antérieur, de devant. **2.** *n.* avant *m.*

fore and aft, *adv.* de l'avant à l'arrière.

forearm, *n.* avant-bras *m.*

forebears, *n.* ancêtres *m.pl.*

forebode, *vb.* présager.

foreboding, 1. *n.* mauvais augure *m.*; pressentiment *m.* **2.** *adj.* qui présage le mal.

forecast, 1. *n.* prévision *f.* **2.** *vb.* prévoir.

forecaster, *n.* pronostiqueur *m.*

forecastle, *n.* gaillard *m.*

foreclose, *vb.* exclure, forclore.

forefather, *n.* ancêtre *m.*

forefinger, *n.* index *m.*

forefront, *n.* premier rang *m.*

foregone, *adj.* décidé d'avance.

foreground, *n.* premier plan *m.*

forehead, *n.* front *m.*

foreign, *adj.* étranger.

foreign aid, *n.* aide *(f.)* aux pays étrangers.

foreigner, *n.* étranger *m.*

foreleg, *n.* jambe antérieure *f.*

foreman, *n.* contremaître *m.*

foremost, *adj.* premier.

forenoon, *n.* matinée *f.*

forensic, *adj.* judiciaire.

forerunner, *n.* avant-coureur *m.*

foresee, *vb.* prévoir.

foreseeable, *adj.* prévisible.

foreshadow, *vb.* présager.

foresight, *n.* prévoyance *f.*

forest, *n.* forêt *f.*

forestall, *vb.* anticiper, devancer.

forester, *n.* forestier *m.*

forestry, *n.* sylviculture *f.*

foretaste, *n.* avant-goût *m.*

foretell, *vb.* prédire.

forever, *adv.* pour toujours.

forevermore, *adv.* à jamais.

forewarn, *vb.* prévenir.

foreword, *n.* avant-propos *m.*

forfeit, *vb.* forfaire.

forfeiture, *n.* perte *(f.)* par confiscation, forfaiture *f.*

forgather, *vb.* se réunir.

forge, 1. *n.* forge *f.* **2.** *vb.* forger; (signature, money) contrefaire.

forger, *n.* faussaire *m.*, falsificateur *m.*

forgery, *n.* faux *m.*

forget, *vb.* oublier.

forget-me-not, *n.* myosotis *m.*

forgetful, *adj.* oublieux.

forgive, *vb.* pardonner (à).

forgiveness, *n.* pardon *m.*

forgo, *vb.* renoncer à.

fork, *n.* fourchette *f.*; (tool, road) fourche *f.*

forlorn, *adj.* (hopeless) désespéré; (forsaken) abandonné.

form, 1. *n.* forme *f.*; (blank) formule *f.* **2.** *vb.* former.

formal, *adj.* formel.

formaldehyde, *n.* formaldéhyde *f.*

formality, *n.* formalité *f.*

formally, *adv.* formellement.

format, 1. *n.* format *m.* **2.** *vb.* formater.

formation, *n.* formation *f.*

formative, *adj.* formatif.

former, 1. *adj.* précédent; (with latter) premier. **2.** *pron.* le premier.

formerly, *adv.* autrefois, jadis, auparavant.

formidable, *adj.* formidable.

formless, *adj.* informe.

formula, *n.* formule *f.*

formulate, *vb.* formuler.

formulation, *n.* formulation *f.*

forsake, *vb.* abandonner.

forsythia, *n.* forsythie *f.*

fort, *n.* fort *m.*

forte, *n.* fort *m.*

forth, *adv.* en avant; **(and so f.)** et ainsi de suite.

forthcoming, *adj.* à venir.

forthright, 1. *adj.* tout droit. **2.** *adv.* carrément, nettement.

forthwith, *adv.* sur-le-champ, tout de suite.

fortieth, *adj.* and *n.* quarantième *m.f.*

fortification, *n.* fortification *f.*

fortify, *vb.* fortifier, renforcer.

fortissimo, *adv.* fortissimo.

fortitude, *n.* courage *m.*

fortnight, *n.* quinzaine *f.*

fortress, *n.* forteresse *f.*

fortuitous, *adj.* fortuit.

fortunate, *adj.* heureux.
fortune, *n.* fortune *f.*
fortuneteller, *n.* diseur *(m.)* de bonne aventure.
forty, *adj. and n.* quarante *m.*
forum, *n.* (Roman) forum *m.*
forward, 1. *adj.* en avant; (advanced) avancé; (bold) hardi. **2.** *adv.* en avant. **3.** *vb.* (letter) faire suivre.
forwardness, *n.* empressement *m.*, effronterie *f.*
fossil, *n.* fossile *m.*
fossilize, *vb.* fossiliser.
foster, *vb.* nourrir.
foster child, *n.* enfant *(m.)* adopté.
foul, *adj.* (dirty) sale; (disgusting) dégoûtant; (obscene) ordurier; (abominable) infâme.
found, *vb.* fonder.
foundation, *n.* fondation *f.*; (theory) fondement *m.*
founder, *n.* fondateur *m.*
foundling, *n.* enfant trouvé.
foundry, *n.* fonderie *f.*
fountain, *n.* fontaine *f.*
fountainhead, *n.* source *f.*
fountain pen, *n.* stylo(-graphe) *m.*
four, *adj. and n.* quatre *m.*
four-in-hand, *n.* attelage à quatre *m.*
fourscore, *adj.* quatre-vingts.
foursome, *n.* à quatre.
fourteen, *adj. and n.* quatorze *m.*
fourth, *adj. and n.* quatrième *m.f.*; (fraction) quart *m.*
fourth estate, *n.* quatrième état *m.*
fowl, *n.* volaille *f.*
fox, *n.* renard *m.*
foxglove, *n.* digitale *f.*
foxhole, *n.* renardière *f.*
fox terrier, *n.* fox-terrier *m.*
fox trot, *n.* fox-trot *m.*
foxy, *adj.* rusé.
foyer, *n.* foyer *m.*
fracas, *n.* fracas *m.*
fraction, *n.* fraction *f.*
fracture, *n.* fracture *f.*
fragile, *adj.* fragile.
fragment, *n.* fragment *m.*
fragmentary, *adj.* fragmentaire.
fragrance, *n.* parfum *m.*
fragrant, *adj.* parfumé.
frail, *adj.* frêle.

frailty, *n.* faiblesse *f.*
frame, *n.* (picture) cadre *m.*; (structure) structure *f.*
frame-up, 1. *n.* coup monté **2.** *vb.* monter un coup.
framework, *n.* charpente *f.*
France, *n.* France *f.*
franchise, *n.* droit *(m.)* électoral.
frank, *adj.* franc *m.*, franche *f.*
frankfurter, *n.* saucisse *(f.)* de Francfort.
frankincense, *n.* encens *m.*
frankly, *adv.* franchement.
frankness, *n.* franchise *f.*
frantic, *adj.* frénétique.
fraternal, *adj.* fraternel.
fraternally, *adv.* fraternellement.
fraternity, *n.* fraternité *f.*
fraternization, *n.* fraternisation *f.*
fraternize, *vb.* fraterniser.
fratricide, *n.* fratricide *m.*
fraud, *n.* fraude *f.*; (person) imposteur *m.*
fraudulent, *adj.* frauduleux.
fraudulently, *adv.* frauduleusement.
fraught, *adj.* chargé (de), plein, gros.
fray, 1. *n.* bagarre *f.* **2.** *vb.* érailler.
freak, *n.* (whim) caprice *m.*; (abnormality) phénomène *m.*
freckle, *n.* tache de rousseur *f.*
freckled, *adj.* taché de rousseur.
free, 1. *adj.* libre; (without cost) gratuit. **2.** *vb.* libérer, affranchir.
freedom, *n.* liberté *f.*
freelance, 1. *n.* journaliste ou politicien indépendant **2.** *vb.* faire du journalisme indépendant.
freestone, *n.* pêche *(f.)* dont la chair n'adhère pas au noyau.
free verse, *n.* vers libre *m.*
free will, *n.* libre arbitre *m.*
freeze, *vb.* geler; (food) surgeler.
freezer, *n.* glacière *f.*; congélateur *m.*
freezing point, *n.* point *(m.)* de congélation.
freight, *n.* fret *m.*
freightage, *n.* frètement *m.*
freighter, *n.* affréteur *m.*
French, *adj. and n.* français *m.*
French fries, *n.* frites *f.pl.*
French leave, *n.* filer à l'anglaise.
Frenchman, *n.* Français *m.*

French toast, *n.* tranche de pain frite *f.*

Frenchwoman, *n.* Française *f.*

frenzied, *adj.* affolé, frénétique.

frenzy, *n.* frénésie *f.*

frequency, *n.* fréquence *f.*

frequent, 1. *adj.* fréquent. **2.** *vb.* fréquenter.

frequently, *adv.* fréquemment.

fresco, *n.* fresque *f.*

fresh, *adj.* frais *m.*, fraîche *f.*; (new, recent) nouveau; nouvel *m.*, nouvelle *f.*; (impudent) culotté.

freshen, *vb.* rafraîchir.

freshman, *n.* étudiant (*m.*) de première année.

freshness, *n.* fraîcheur *f.*

fresh-water, *adj.* d'eau douce.

fret, *vb.* ronger, *tr.*

fretful, *adj.* chagrin.

fretfully, *adv.* avec irritation.

fretfulness, *n.* irritabilité *f.*

friar, *n.* moine *m.*, frère religieux *m.*

fricassee, *n.* fricassée *f.*

friction, *n.* friction *f.*

Friday, *n.* vendredi *m.*

fridge, *n.* frigo *m.*

friend, *n.* ami *m.*, amie *f.*

friendless, *adj.* sans amis.

friendliness, *n.* disposition (*f.*) amicale.

friendly, *adj.* amical.

friendship, *n.* amitié *f.*

fright, *n.* effroi *m.*

frighten, *vb.* effrayer.

frightening, *adj.* effrayant.

frightful, *adj.* affreux.

frigid, *adj.* glacial.

Frigid Zone, *n.* zone glaciale *f.*

frill, 1. *n.* volant *m.*; affectation *f.* **2.** *vb.* plisser.

frilly, *adj.* froncé, ruché.

fringe, *n.* frange *f.*

fringe benefits, *n.* avantages (*m.pl.*) sociaux.

frisk, *vb.* fouiller.

frisky, *adj.* folâtre.

frivolity, *n.* frivolité *f.*

frivolous, *adj.* frivole.

frivolousness, *n.* frivolité *f.*

frizzy, *adj.* crépu.

frock, *n.* robe *f.*; (monk's) froc *m.*

frog, *n.* grenouille *f.*

frolic, *vb.* folâtrer.

from, *prep.* de; (time) depuis.

front, *n.* front *m.*; (front part) devant *m.*; **(in f. of)** devant.

frontage, *n.* étendue de devant *f.*

frontal, *adj.* frontal, de face.

frontier, *n.* frontière *f.*

frost, *n.* gelée *f.*

frostbite, *n.* gelure *f.*

frosting, *n.* glaçage *m.*

frosty, *adj.* gelé, glacé.

froth, 1. *n.* écume *f.* **2.** *vb.* écumer.

frown, *vb.* froncer les sourcils.

frowzy, *adj.* mal tenu, peu soigné.

frozen, *adj.* gelé; (food) surgelé.

fructify, *vb.* fructifier.

frugal, *adj.* frugal.

frugality, *n.* frugalité *f.*

fruit, *n.* fruit *m.*

fruitful, *adj.* fructueux.

fruition, *n.* réalisation *f.*, fructification *f.*

fruitless, *adj.* infructueux.

frustrate, *vb.* faire échouer.

frustration, *n.* frustration *f.*

fry, *vb.* frire, *intr.*; faire frire, *tr.*

fryer, *n.* casserole *f.*

fuchsia, *n.* fuchsia *m.*

fudge, 1. *n.* espèce de fondant américain. **2.** *interj.* bah!

fuel, *n.* combustible *m.*

fugitive, *adj.* fugitif.

fugue, *n.* fugue *f.*

fulcrum, *n.* pivot *m.*, point d'appui *m.*

fulfill, *vb.* accomplir.

fulfillment, *n.* accomplissement *m.*

full, *adj.* plein.

fullback, *n.* arrière *m.*

full dress, *adj.* en tenue de cérémonie.

fullness, *n.* plénitude *f.*

fully, *adv.* pleinement.

fulminate, *vb.* fulminer.

fulmination, *n.* fulmination *f.*

fumble, *vb.* tâtonner.

fume, *n.* fumée *f.*

fumigate, *vb.* désinfecter.

fumigator, *n.* fumigateur *m.*

fun, *n.* (amusement) amusement *m.*; **(have f.)** s'amuser; (joke) plaisanterie *f.*; **(make f. of)** se moquer de.

function, *n.* fonction *f.*; (social occasion) cérémonie *f.*

functional, *adj.* fonctionnel.

functionary, *n.* fonctionnaire *m.*

fund, *n.* fonds *m.*

fundamental, *adj.* fondamental.

fundamentalist, *n.* intégriste *m.*

fundamentalism, *n.* intégrisme *m.*

funeral, *n.* funérailles *f.pl.*

funereal, *adj.* funèbre, funéraire.

fungicide, *n.* fongicide *m.*

fungus, *n.* fongus *m.*

funk, *n.* (be in a f.) être déprimé.

funnel, *n.* entonnoir *m.;* (smoke-stack) cheminée *f.*

funny, *adj.* drôle.

fur, *n.* fourrure *f.*

furious, *adj.* furieux.

furlong, *n.* furlong *m.*

furlough, *n.* permission *f.*

furnace, *n.* fourneau *m.*

furnish, *vb.* fournir; (house) meubler.

furnishings, *n.* ameublement *m.*

furniture, *n.* meubles *m.pl.*

furor, *n.* fureur *f.*

furred, *adj.* fourré.

furrier, *n.* fourreur *m.*

furrow, *n.* sillon *m.*

furry, *adj.* qui ressemble à la fourrure.

further, 1. *adj.* ultérieur. **2.** *adv.* (distance) plus loin; (extent) davantage.

furtherance, *n.* avancement *m.*

furthermore, *adv.* en outre.

fury, *n.* furie *f.*

fuse, *vb.* fondre.

fuselage, *n.* fuselage *m.*

fusillade, *n.* fusillade *f.*

fusion, *n.* fusion *f.,* fusionnement *m.*

fuss, *n.* (make a f.) faire des histoires.

fussy, *adj.* difficile.

futile, *adj.* futile.

futility, *n.* futilité *f.*

future, 1. *n.* avenir *m.; (gramm.)* futur *m.* **2.** *adj.* futur.

futurity, *n.* avenir *m.*

futurology, *n.* futurologie *f.*

fuzz, *n.* duvet *m.,* flou *m.*

fuzzy, *adj.* flou, frisotté.

G

gab, *vb.* jaser.

gabardine, *n.* gabardine *f.*

gable, *n.* pignon *m.*

gadabout, *n.* coureur *m.*

gadfly, *n.* taon *m.*

gadget, *n.* truc *m.*

Gaelic, *adj.* gaélique.

gaffe, *n.* gaffe *f.*

gag, 1. *vb.* bâillonner. **2.** *n.* blague *f.,* bobard *m.;* bâillon *m.*

gaiety, *n.* gaieté *f.*

gaily, *adv.* gaiement.

gain, 1. *n.* gain *m.* **2.** *vb.* gagner.

gainful, *adj.* profitable, rémunérateur.

gainfully, *adv.* profitablement.

gainsay, *vb.* contredire.

gait, *n.* allure *f.*

gal, *n.* (colloquial) femme *f.*

gala, *n.* fête de gala *f.*

galaxy, *n.* galaxie *f.,* assemblée brillante *f.*

gale, *n.* grand vent *m.*

gall, *n.* (bile) fiel *m.;* (sore) écorchure *f.*

gallant, *adj.* (brave) vaillant; (with ladies) galant.

gallantly, *adv.* gallamment.

gallantry, *n.* vaillance *f.,* galanterie *f.*

gall bladder, *n.* vésicule biliaire *f.*

galleon, *n.* galion *m.*

gallery, *n.* galerie *f.*

galley, *n.* galère *f.,* (naut.) cuisine *f.,* (typographic) galée *f.*

galley proof, *n.* épreuve en première *f.*

Gallic, *adj.* gaulois, français.

gallivant, *vb.* courailler.

gallon, *n.* gallon *m.*

gallop, 1. *n.* galop *m.* **2.** *vb.* galoper.

gallows, *n.* potence *f.*

gallstone, *n.* calcul biliaire *m.*

galore, *adv.* à foison, à profusion.

galosh, *n.* galoche *f.,* caoutchouc *m.*

galvanize, *vb.* galvaniser.

Gambia, *n.* Gambie *f.*

gamble, 1. *n.* jeu *(m.)* de hasard. **2.** *vb.* jouer.

gambler, *n.* joueur *m.*

gambling, *n.* jeu *m.*

gambol, 1. *n.* gambade *f.* **2.** *vb.* gamboler.

game, *n.* jeu *m.*; (hunting) gibier *m.*

gamely, *adv.* courageusement, crânement.

gameness, *n.* courage *m.*, crânerie *f.*

gamin, *n.* gamin *m.*

gamut, *n.* gamme *f.*

gamy, *adj.* giboyeux.

gander, *n.* jars *m.*

gang, *n.* bande *f.*; (workers) équipe *f.*

gangling, *adj.* dégingandé.

gangplank, *n.* passerelle *f.*

gangrene, *n.* gangrène *f.*

gangrenous, *adj.* gangreneux.

gangster, *n.* gangster *m.*

gangway, *n.* passage *m.*

gap, *n.* (opening) ouverture *f.*; (empty space) vide *m.*

gape, *vb.* rester bouche bée.

garage, *n.* garage *m.*

garb, 1. *n.* vêtement *m.*, costume *m.* **2.** *vb.* vêtir, habiller.

garbage, *n.* ordures *f.pl.*

garble, *vb.* tronquer, altérer.

garden, *n.* jardin *m.*

gardener, *n.* jardinier *m.*

gardenia, *n.* gardénia *m.*

gargle, 1. *n.* gargarisme *f.* **2.** *vb.* se gargariser.

gargoyle, *n.* gargouille *f.*

garish, *adj.* voyant.

garland, *n.* guirlande *f.*

garlic, *n.* ail *m.*

garment, *n.* vêtement *m.*

garner, *vb.* mettre en grenier.

garnet, *n.* grenat *m.*

garnish, *vb.* garnir.

garnishee, *n.* tiers-saisi *m.*

garnishment, *n.* saisie-arrêt *f.*

garret, *n.* mansarde *f.*

garrison, *n.* garnison *f.*

garrote, 1. *n.* garrotte *f.* **2.** *vb.* garrotter.

garrulous, *adj.* bavard, loquace.

garter, *n.* jarretière *f.*

gas, *n.* gaz *m.*; (auto) essence *f.* **(g. station)** station-service *f.*

gaseous, *adj.* gazeux.

gash, 1. *n.* coupure *f.*, entaille *f.* **2.** *vb.* couper, entailler.

gasket, *n.* garcette *f.*

gasless, *adj.* sans gaz.

gas mask, *n.* masque à gaz *m.*

gasohol, *n.* essence (*f.*) fabriquée avec de l'alcool.

gasoline, *n.* essence *f.*

gasp, *vb.* (astonishment) sursauter; (lack of breath) haleter.

gassy, *adj.* gazeux; (talkative) bavard.

gastric, *adj.* gastrique.

gastric juice, *n.* suc gastrique *m.*

gastritis, *n.* gastrite *f.*

gastronomically, *adv.* d'une manière gastronomique.

gastronomy, *n.* gastronomie *f.*

gate, *n.* (city) porte *f.*; (with bars) barrière *f.*; (wrought-iron) grille *f.*

gateway, *n.* porte *f.*, entrée *f.*

gather, *vb.* rassembler, *tr.*; recueillir, *tr.*

gathering, *n.* rassemblement *m.*

gaudily, *adv.* de manière voyante.

gaudiness, *n.* éclat criard *m.*, ostentation *f.*

gaudy, *adj.* voyant.

gaunt, *adj.* décharné.

gauntlet, *n.* gantelet *m.*

gauze, *n.* gaze *f.*

gavel, *n.* marteau *m.*

gavotte, *n.* gavotte *f.*

gawky, *adj.* dégingandé.

gay, 1. *adj.* gai; (homosexual) homosexuel. **2.** *n.* homosexuel *m.*

gaze, *vb.* regarder fixement.

gazelle, *n.* gazelle *f.*

gazette, *n.* gazette *f.*

gazetteer, *n.* gazetier *m.*, répertoire géographique *m.*

gear, *n.* (implements, device) appareil *m.*; (machines) engrenage *m.*; **(in g.)** engrené; **(g. change)** changement (*m.*) de vitesse.

gearing, *n.* engrenage *m.*

gearshift, *n.* changement (*m.*) de vitesse.

gel, *n.* gel *m.*

gelatin, *n.* gélatine *f.*

gelatinous, *adj.* gélatineux.

geld, *vb.* châtrer.

gelding, *n.* animal châtré *m.*

gem, *n.* pierre (*f.*) précieuse.

gender, *n.* genre *m.*

gene, *n.* gène *m.*

genealogical, *adj.* généalogique.

genealogy, n. généalogie f.
general, adj. and n. général m.
generality, n. généralité f.
generalization, n. généralisation f.
generalize, vb. généraliser.
generally, adv. généralement.
general practioner, n. généraliste m.
generalship, n. stratégie f.
generate, vb. engendrer, générer.
generation, n. génération f.
generator, n. (electricity) groupe (m.) électrogène.
generic, adj. générique.
generosity, n. générosité f.
generous, adj. généreux.
generously, adv. généreusement.
genetic, adj. génétique.
genetics, n. génétique f.
genial, adj. sympathique.
geniality, n. jovialité f., bienveillance f.
genially, adv. affablement.
genital, adj. génital.
genitals, n. organes génitaux m.pl.
genitive, n. and adj. génitif m.
genius, n. génie m.
genocide, n. génocide m.
genre, n. genre m.
genteel, adj. de bon ton.
gentian, n. gentiane f.
gentile, n. gentil m.
gentility, n. prétention (f.) à la distinction.
gentle, adj. doux m., douce f.
gentleman, n. monsieur m., pl. messieurs; (character) galant homme m.
gentlemanly, adj. comme il faut, bien élevé.
gentlemen's agreement, n. convention verbale f.
gentleness, n. douceur f.
gently, adv. doucement.
gentry, n. petite noblesse f.
genuflect, vb. faire des génuflexions.
genuine, adj. véritable.
genuinely, adv. véritablement.
genuineness, n. authenticité f.
genus, n. genre m.
geographer, n. géographe m.
geographical, adj. géographique.
geography, n. géographie f.
geometric, adj. géométrique.

geometry, n. géométrie f.
geopolitics, n. géopolitique f.
geranium, n. géranium m.
geriatric, adj. gériatrique.
germ, n. germe m.
German, 1. n. (person) Allemand m.; (language) allemand m. **2.** adj. allemand.
germane, adj. approprié.
Germanic, adj. allemand, germanique.
German measles, n. rougeole bénigne f.
Germany, n. Allemagne f.
germicide, n. microbicide m.
germinal, adj. germinal.
germinate, vb. germer.
gestate, vb. enfanter.
gestation, n. gestation f.
gesticulate, vb. gesticuler.
gesticulation, n. gesticulation f.
gesture, n. geste m.
get, vb. (obtain) obtenir; (receive) recevoir; (take) prendre; (become) devenir; (arrive) arriver; (g. in) entrer; (g. off) descendre; (g. on, agree) s'entendre; (g. on, go up) monter; (g. out) sortir; (g. up) se lever.
getaway, n. fuite f.
geyser, n. geyser m.
Ghana, n. Ghana m.
ghastly, adj. horrible.
ghetto blaster, n. stéréo (f.) portable.
ghost, n. (specter) revenant m.; (Holy G.) Saint-Esprit m.
ghost writer, n. collaborateur anonyme m., nègre m.
ghoul, n. goule f., vampire m.
giant, n. géant m.
gibberish, n. baragouin m.
gibbon, n. gibbon m.
gibe, 1. n. raillerie f. **2.** vb. railler.
giblet, n. abatis (de volaille) m.
Gibraltar, n. Gibraltar.
giddy, adj. étourdi.
gift, n. don m.; (present) cadeau m.
gifted, adj. doué.
gigantic, adj. géant, gigantesque.
giggle, vb. rire nerveusement, glousser.
gigolo, n. gigolo m.
gild, vb. dorer.
gill, n. (of fish) ouïes f.pl.

gilt, 1. n. dorure f. 2. adj. doré.
gilt-edged, adj. doré sur tranche.
gimcrack, 1. n. camelote f. 2. adj. de camelote.
gimlet, n. vrille f.
gimmick, n. truc m.
gin, n. genièvre m.
ginger, n. gingembre m.
ginger ale, n. boisson (f.) gazeuse au gingembre.
gingerly, adv. avec précaution.
gingersnap, n. biscuit (m.) au gingembre.
gingham, n. guingan m.
giraffe, n. girafe f.
gird, vb. ceindre.
girder, n. support m.
girdle, n. gaine f.
girl, n. jeune fille f.
girlfriend, n. petite amie f.
girlish, adj. de jeune fille.
girth, n. sangle f., circonférence f., corpulence f.
gist, n. fond m., essence f.
give, vb. donner; (**g. back**) rendre; (**g. in**) céder; (**g. out**) distribuer; (**g. up**) renoncer à.
give-and-take, adv. donnant donnant.
given, adj. donné.
given name, n. prénom m.
giver, n. donneur m.
gizzard, n. gésier m.
glace, adj. glacé.
glacial, adj. glaciaire.
glacier, n. glacier m.
glad, adj. heureux.
gladden, vb. réjouir.
glade, n. clairère f., éclaircie f.
gladiolus, n. glaïeul m.
gladly, adv. volontiers.
gladness, n. joie f.
Gladstone bag, n. sac américain m.
glamour, n. éclat m.
glance, 1. n. coup (m.) d'œil. 2. vb. jeter un coup d'œil.
gland, n. glande f.
glandular, adj. glandulaire.
glare, 1. n. (light) clarté f.; (stare) regard (m.) enflammé. 2. vb. (shine) briller; (look) jeter des regards enflammés.
glaring, adj. éclatant, flagrant, voyant, manifeste.
glass, n. verre m.

glass-blowing, n. soufflage m.
glasses, n. lunettes f.pl.
glassful, n. verre m., verrée f.
glassware, n. verrerie f.
glassy, adj. vitreux.
glaucoma, n. glaucome m.
glaze, 1. n. lustre m. 2. vb. vitrer.
glazier, n. vitrier m.
gleam, 1. n. lueur f. 2. vb. luire.
glean, vb. glâner.
glee, n. allégresse f.
glee club, n. chœur d'hommes m.
gleeful, adj. joyeux, allègre.
glen, n. vallon m., ravin m.
glib, adj. spécieux, facile.
glide, vb. glisser; (plane) planer.
glider, n. planeur m.
glimmer, 1. n. faible lueur f. 2. vb. jeter une faible lueur.
glimmering, adj. faible, vacillant.
glimpse, 1. vb. entrevoir. 2. n. aperçu m.
glint, 1. n. éclair m., reflet m. 2. vb. entreluire, étinceler.
glisten, vb. briller.
glitter, vb. étinceler.
gloat, vb. se régaler de.
global, adj. global.
globe, n. globe m.
globetrotter, n. globe trotter m.
globular, adj. globulaire, globuleux.
globule, n. globule m.
glockenspiel, n. glockenspiel m.
gloom, n. (darkness) ténèbres f.pl.; (sadness) tristesse f.
gloomy, adj. sombre.
glorification, n. glorification f.
glorify, vb. glorifier.
glorious, adj. glorieux; (weather) radieux.
glory, n. gloire f.
gloss, 1. n. lustre m., vernis m., glose f. 2. vb. lustrer, glacer.
glossary, n. glossaire m.
glossy, adj. lustré, glacé.
glove, n. gant m.
glow, 1. n. (light) lumière f.; (heat) chaleur f. 2. vb. briller.
glower, vb. (**g. at**) lancer des regards mauvais à.
glowing, adj. embrasé, rayonnant.
glowingly, adv. en termes chaleureux.
glowworm, n. ver luisant m.

glucose, *n.* glucose *f.*

glue, 1. *n.* colle (*f.*) forte. **2.** *vb.* coller.

glum, *adj.* maussade.

glumness, *n.* air maussade *m.*, tristesse *f.*

glut, 1. *n.* assouvissement *m.*, excès *m.*, pléthore *f.* **2.** *vb.* assouvir, rassasier, gorger.

glutinous, *adj.* glutineux.

glutton, *n.* gourmand *m.*

gluttonous, *adj.* gourmand, goulu.

glycerin, *n.* glycérine *f.*

gnarl, *n.* loupe *f.*, nœud *m.*

gnash, *vb.* grincer.

gnat, *n.* moucheron *m.*

gnaw, *vb.* ronger.

gnu, *n.* gnou *m.*

go, *vb.* aller; (g. away) s'en aller; (g. back) retourner; (g. by) passer; (g. down) descendre; (g. in) entrer; (g. on) continuer; (g. out) sortir; (g. up) monter; (g. without) se passer de.

goad, 1. *n.* aiguillon *m.* **2.** *vb.* aiguillonner, piquer.

goal, *n.* but *m.*

goat, *n.* chèvre *f.*

goatee, *n.* barbiche *f.*

goatherd, *n.* chevrier *m.*

goatskin, *n.* peau (*f.*) de chèvre.

gobble, *vb.* avaler goulûment, dévorer.

gobbler, *n.* avaleur *m.*; dindon *m.*

go-between, *n.* intermédiaire *m.*

goblet, *n.* gobelet *m.*

goblin, *n.* gobelin *m.*, lutin *m.*

God, *n.* Dieu *m.*

godchild, *n.* filleul *m.*

goddess, *n.* déesse *f.*

godfather, *n.* parrain *m.*

godless, *adj.* athée, impie, sans Dieu.

godlike, *adj.* comme un dieu, divin.

godly, *adj.* dévot, pieux, saint.

godmother, *n.* marraine *f.*

godsend, *n.* aubaine *f.*, bienfait du ciel *m.*

Godspeed, *interj.* bon voyage!

go-getter, *n.* homme (*m.*) d'affaires énergique, arriviste *m.*

goggles, *n.* lunettes (*f.pl.*) protectrices.

goiter, *n.* goitre *m.*

gold, *n.* or *m.*

gold brick, *n.* attrape-niais *m.*

golden, *adj.* d'or.

goldenrod, *n.* solidage *m.*

golden rule, *n.* règle (*f.*) par excellence.

gold-filled, *adj.* aurifié, en (or) doublé.

goldfinch, *n.* chardonneret *m.*

goldfish, *n.* poisson rouge *m.*

gold leaf, *n.* feuille d'or *f.*, or battu *m.*

gold-plated, *adj.* plaqué d'or.

goldsmith, *n.* orfèvre *m.*

gold standard, *n.* étalon or *m.*

golf, *n.* golf *m.*

gondola, *n.* gondole *f.*

gondolier, *n.* gondolier *m.*

gone, *adj.* disparu, parti.

gong, *n.* gong *m.*

gonorrhea, *n.* gonorrhée *f.*, blennorrhagie *f.*

good, 1. *adj.* bon *m.*, bonne *f.* **2.** *n.* bien *m.*; (goods) marchandises *f.pl.*

good-bye, *n. and interj.* adieu *m.*

Good Friday, *n.* Vendredi Saint *m.*

good-hearted, *adj.* qui a bon cœur, compatissant.

good-humored, *adj.* de bonne humeur, plein de bonhomie.

good-looking, *adj.* beau, joli.

good-natured, *adj.* au bon naturel, accommodant.

goodness, *n.* bonté *f.*

good will, *n.* bonne volonté *f.*

goody-goody, *n.* petit saint *m.*

goose, *n.* oie *f.*

gooseberry, *n.* groseille verte *f.*

gooseflesh, *n.* chair (*f.*) de poule.

gooseneck, *n.* col (*m.*) de cygne.

goose step, *n.* pas (*m.*) d'oie.

gore, 1. *n.* (dress) chanteau *m.*, soufflet *m.*; (blood) sang coagulé *m.* **2.** *vb.* corner.

gorge, *n.* gorge *f.*

gorgeous, *adj.* splendide.

gorilla, *n.* gorille *m.*

gory, *adj.* sanglant, ensanglanté.

gosh, *interj.* mince (alors).

gosling, *n.* oison *m.*

gospel, *n.* évangile *m.*

gossamer, *n.* filandre *f.*, gaze légère *f.*

gossip, 1. n. bavardage m. 2. vb. bavarder.
Gothic, adj. gothique.
gouge, 1. n. gouge f. 2. vb. gouger.
gourd, n. gourde f., courge f.
gourmand, n. gourmand m.
gourmet, n. gourmet m.
govern, vb. gouverner.
governess, n. gouvernante f.
government, n. gouvernement m.
governmental, adj. gouvernemental.
governor, n. gouvernant m.
governorship, n. fonctions de gouverneur f.pl., temps de gouvernement m.
gown, n. robe f.
grab, vb. saisir.
grace, n. grâce f.
graceful, adj. gracieux.
gracefully, adv. avec grâce.
graceless, adj. sans grâce, gauche.
gracious, adj. gracieux; (merciful) miséricordieux.
grackle, n. mainate m.
gradation, n. gradation f.
grade, 1. n. grade m.; (quality) qualité f. 2. vb. classer.
grade crossing, n. passage (m.) à niveau.
gradual, adj. graduel, progressif.
gradually, adv. graduellement.
graduate, vb. graduer; (school) obtenir son diplôme; prendre ses grades.
graduation, n. remise (f.) des diplômes.
graft, n. corruption f.
grail, n. graal m.
grain, n. grain m.
gram, n. gramme m.
grammar, n. grammaire f.
grammarian, n. grammairien m.
grammar school, n. école primaire f.
grammatical, adj. grammatical.
gramophone, n. phonographe.
granary, n. grenier m.
grand, adj. grandiose; (in titles) grand; (fine, collog.) épatant.
grandchild, n. petit-fils m.; petite-fille f.; petits-enfants m.pl.
granddaughter, n. petite-fille f.
grandee, n. grand m.
grandeur, n. grandeur f.

grandfather, n. grand-père m.
grandiloquent, adj. grandiloquent.
grandiose, adj. grandiose.
grand jury, n. jury d'accusation m.
grandly, adv. grandement, magnifiquement.
grandmother, n. grand'mère f.
grand opera, n. grand opéra m.
grandson, n. petit-fils m.
grandstand, n. grande tribune f.
granger, n. régisseur m.
granite, n. granit m.
granny, n. bonne-maman f.
grant, 1. n. concession f.; (money) subvention f. 2. vb. accorder; (admit) admettre.
granular, adj. en grains, granulé.
granulate, vb. granuler, grener.
granulation, n. granulation f.
granule, n. granule m.
grape, n. raisin m.
grapefruit, n. pamplemousse f.
grapeshot, n. mitraille f.
grapevine, n. treille f.
graph, n. courbe f.
graphic, adj. graphique, pittoresque, explicite.
graphite, n. graphite m.
graphology, n. graphologie f.
grapple, 1. n. grappin m.; lutte f. 2. vb. accrocher; en venir aux prises.
grasp, 1. n. (hold) prise f. 2. vb. saisir.
grasping, adj. avide, cupide.
grass, n. herbe f.
grasshopper, n. sauterelle f.
grass-roots, adj. de la base, du people.
grassy, adj. herbeux, verdoyant.
grate, 1. n. grille f. 2. vb. (cheese, etc.) râper; (make noise) grincer.
grateful, adj. reconnaissant.
gratify, vb. contenter, satisfaire.
grating, 1. n. grille f. 2. vb. grinçant, discordant.
gratis, adv. gratis, gratuitement.
gratitude, n. gratitude f.
gratuitous, adj. gratuit.
gratuity, n. (tip) pourboire m.
grave, 1. n. tombe f. 2. adj. grave.
gravel, n. gravier m.
gravely, adv. gravement, sérieusement.

gravestone, n. pierre sépulcrale f., tombe f.

graveyard, n. cimetière m.

gravitate, vb. graviter.

gravitation, n. gravitation f.

gravity, n. gravité f.

gravure, n. gravure f.

gravy, n. jus m.

gray, adj. gris.

grayish, adj. grisâtre.

gray matter, n. substance grise f., cendrée f.

graze, vb. paître.

grazing, n. pâturage m.

grease, 1. n. graisse f. **2.** vb. graisser.

great, adj. grand.

Great Dane, n. grand Danois m.

greatness, n. grandeur f.

Greece, n. Grèce f.

greediness, n. gourmandise f.

greedy, adj. gourmand.

Greek, 1. n. (person) Grec m., Grecque f.; (language) grec m. **2.** adj. grec m., grecque f.

green, adj. vert.

greenery, n. verdure f.

greenhouse, n. serre f.

greet, vb. saluer.

greeting, n. salutation f.; (reception) accueil m.

gregarious, adj. grégaire.

grenade, n. grenade f.

grenadine, n. grenadine f.

greyhound, n. lévrier m.

grid, n. gril m.

griddle, n. gril m.

gridiron, n. gril m.

grief, n. chagrin m.

grievance, n. grief m.

grieve, vb. affliger, tr.; chagriner, tr.

grievous, adj. douloureux.

grill, 1. n. gril m. **2.** vb. griller.

grillroom, n. grill-room m.

grim, adj. sinistre.

grimace, n. grimace f.

grime, n. saleté f., noirceur f.

grimy, adj. sale, noirci, encrassé.

grin, n. large sourire m.

grind, vb. (crush) moudre; (sharpen) aiguiser.

grindstone, n. meule f.

gringo, n. Anglo-américain m.

grip, n. prise f.

gripe, vb. saisir, empoigner; grogner.

grisly, adj. hideux, horrible.

grist, n. blé à moudre m., mouture f.

gristle, n. cartilage m.

grit, n. grès m., sable m.; (fig.) cran m., courage m.

grizzled, adj. grison, grisonnant.

groan, 1. n. gémissement m. **2.** vb. gémir.

grocer, n. épicier m.

grocery, n. épicerie f.

grog, n. grog m.

groggy, adj. gris, titubant.

groin, n. aine f.

groom, 1. n. (horses) palefrenier m.; (bridegroom) nouveau marié m. **2.** vb. (horses) panser.

groove, n. rainure f.

grope, vb. tâtonner.

grosgrain, adj. de grosgrain.

gross, adj. (bulky) gros m., grosse f.; (coarse) grossier; (comm.) brut.

grossly, adv. grossièrement.

grossness, n. grossièreté f., énormité f.

grotesque, adj. and n. grotesque m.

grotto, n. grotte f.

grouch, 1. n. maussaderie f.; grogneur m. **2.** vb. grogner.

ground, n. (earth) terre f.; (territory) terrain m.; (reason) raison f.; (background) fond m.

ground hog, n. marmotte d'Amérique f.

groundless, adj. sans fondement.

ground swell, n. houle f., lame de fond f.

groundwork, n. fondement m., fond m., base f.

group, 1. n. groupe m. **2.** vb. grouper, tr.

groupie, n. groupie f.; membre (m.) d'un groupe de jeunes filles.

grouse, 1. n. tétras m. **2.** vb. grogner.

grove, n. bocage m., bosquet m.

grovel, vb. ramper, se vautrer.

grow, vb. croître; (persons) grandir; (become) devenir; (cultivate) cultiver.

growl, vb. grogner.

grown, adj. fait, grand.

grownup, adj. and n. grand m., adulte m.f.

growth, n. croissance f.; (increase) accroissement m.

grub, 1. n. larve f., ver blanc m.; (slang) nourriture f. **2.** vb. défricher, fouiller.

grubby, adj. véreux, (fig.) sale.

grudge, n. rancune f.

gruel, n. gruau m.

gruesome, adj. lugubre, terrifiant.

gruff, adj. bourru.

grumble, vb. grommeler.

grumpy, adj. bourru, morose.

grunt, 1. n. grognement m. **2.** vb. grogner.

guarantee, 1. n. garantie f. **2.** vb. garantir.

guarantor, n. garant m.

guaranty, n. garantie f.

guard, 1. n. garde f. **2.** vb. garder.

guarded, adj. prudent, circonspect, réservé.

guardhouse, n. corps de garde m., poste m.

guardian, n. gardien m.; (law) tuteur m.

guardianship, n. tutelle f.

guardsman, n. garde m.

guava, n. goyave f.

gubernatorial, adj. du gouverneur, du gouvernement.

guerrilla, n. guérilla f.

guess, 1. n. conjecture f. **2.** vb. deviner.

guesswork, n. conjecture f.

guest, n. invité m.

guffaw, 1. n. gros rire m. **2.** vb. s'esclaffer.

guidance, n. direction f.

guide, 1. n. guide m. **2.** vb. guider.

guidebook, n. guide m.

guided missile, n. missile (m.) téléguidé.

guidepost, n. poteau indicateur m.

guild, n. corporation f., corps de métier m.

guile, n. astuce f., artifice m.

guillotine, n. guillotine f.

guilt, n. culpabilité f.

guiltily, adv. criminellement.

guiltless, adj. innocent.

guilty, adj. coupable.

guimpe, n. guimpe f.

guinea fowl, n. pintade f.

guinea pig, n. cobaye m.

guise, n. guise f., façon f.

guitar, n. guitare f.

gulch, n. ravin m.

gulf, n. (geog.) golfe m.; (fig.) gouffre m.

gull, n. mouette f.

gullet, n. gosier m.

gullible, adj. crédule, facile à duper.

gully, n. ravin m.

gulp, 1. n. goulée f., gorgée f., trait m. **2.** vb. avaler, gober.

gum, n. gomme f.; (teeth) gencive f.

gumbo, n. gombo m.

gummy, adj. gommeux.

gumption, n. initiative f., audace f.

gun, n. (cannon) canon m.; (rifle) fusil m.

gunboat, n. canonnière f.

gunman, n. partisan armé m., voleur armé m., bandit m.

gunner, n. artilleur m.

gunpowder, n. poudre (f.) à canon.

gunshot, n. portée (f.) de fusil.

gunwale, n. plat-bord m.

gurgle, vb. faire glouglou, gargouiller.

guru, n. gourou m.

gush, 1. n. jaillissement m. **2.** vb. jaillir.

gusher, n. source jaillissante f., personne exubérante f.

gusset, n. gousset m., soufflet m.

gust, n. (wind) rafale f.

gustatory, adj. gustatif.

gusto, n. goût m., délectation f., verve f.

gusty, adv. venteux, orageux.

gut, 1. n. boyau m., intestin m. **2.** vb. éventrer, vider.

gutter, n. (roof) gouttière f.; (street) ruisseau m.

guttural, adj. guttural.

guy, 1. n. type m., individu m. **2.** vb. se moquer de.

guzzle, vb. ingurgiter, boire avidement.

gym, n. gymnase m.

gymnasium, n. gymnase m.

gymnast, n. gymnaste m.

gymnastic, adj. gymnastique.

gymnastics, n. gymnastique f.

gynecology, n. gynécologie f.

gypsum, n. gypse m.

gypsy, n. gitan m.

gyrate, vb. tournoyer.

gyroscope, n. gyroscope m.

H

habeas corpus, n. habeas corpus m.

haberdasher, n. chemisier m., mercier m.

haberdashery, n. chemiserie f., mercerie f.

habiliment, n. habillement m., apprêt m.

habit, n. habitude f.

habitable, adj. habitable.

habitat, n. habitat m.

habitation, n. habitation f.

habitual, adj. habituel.

habituate, vb. habituer, accoutumer.

habitué, n. habitué m.

hack, 1. n. (tool) pioche f.; (horse) cheval (m.) de louage; (vehicle) voiture (f.) de louage. **2.** vb. (h. up) hacher; (notch) entailler.

hackneyed, adj. banal, rebattu.

hacksaw, n. scie (f.) à métaux.

haddock, n. aigle fin m.

haft, n. manche m., poignée f.

hag, n. vieille sorcière f.

haggard, adj. hagard.

haggle, vb. marchander.

hagridden, adj. tourmenté par le cauchemar.

Hague (The), n. La Haye f.

hail, 1. n. grêle f. **2.** vb. (weather) grêler; (salute) saluer; (come from) venir de. **3.** interj. salut.

Hail Mary, n. Ave Maria m.

hailstone, n. grêlon m.

hailstorm, n. tempête (f.) de grêle.

hair, n. cheveux m.pl.; (single, on head) cheveu m.; (on body, animals) poil m.

haircut, n. coupe (f.) de cheveux.

hairdo, n. coiffure f.

hairdresser, n. coiffeur m.

hairline, n. délié m.

hairpin, n. épingle (f.) à cheveux.

hair-raising, adj. horripilant, horrifique.

hair's-breadth, n. l'épaisseur d'un cheveu f.

hairspray, n. laque f.

hairy, adj. velu, poilu.

halcyon, 1. n. alcyon m. **2.** adj. calme.

hale, adj. sain.

half, 1. n. moitié f. **2.** adj. demi. **3.** adv. à moitié.

half-and-half, n. moitié de l'un, moitié de l'autre f.

halfback, n. demi-arrière m.

half-baked, adj. à moitié cuit, inexpérimenté, incomplet.

half-breed, n. métis m.

half brother, n. frère de père m., frère de mère m.

half dollar, n. demi-dollar m.

half-hearted, adj. sans enthousiasme.

half-mast, adv. à mi-mât.

halfpenny, n. petit sou m.

halfway, adv. à mi-chemin.

half-wit, n. niais m., sot m.

halibut, n. flétan m.

hall, n. (large room) salle f.; (entrance) vestibule m.

hallmark, n. contrôle m.

hallow, vb. sanctifier.

Halloween, n. la veille (f.) de la Toussaint.

hallucination, n. hallucination f.

hallway, n. corridor m., vestibule m.

halo, n. auréole f.

halt, 1. n. halte f. **2.** vb. arrêter, tr.

halter, n. licou m., longe f., corde f.

halve, vb. diviser en deux, partager en deux.

halyard, n. drisse f.

ham, n. jambon m.

hamburger, n. hamburger n.

hamlet, n. hameau m.

hammer, 1. n. marteau m. **2.** vb. marteler.

hammock, n. hamac m.

hamper, 1. n. pannier m. **2.** vb. embarrasser, gêner.

hamstring, vb. couper le jarret à, couper les moyens à.

hand, n. main f.

handbag, n. sac (m.) à main.

handball, n. balle f.

handbook, n. manuel m.

handcuff, 1. n. menotte f. 2. vb. mettre les menottes à.

handful, n. poignée f.

handicap, n. handicap m., désavantage m.

handicraft, n. artisanat m.

handiwork, n. main-d'œuvre f.

handkerchief, n. mouchoir m.

handle, 1. n. manche m. 2. vb. manier.

handlebar, n. guidon m.

handmade, adj. fait à la main, fabriqué à la main.

handmaid, n. servante f.

hand organ, n. orgue portatif m., orgue de Barbarie f.

handout, n. aumône f.; compte rendu (m.) communiqué à la presse.

hand-pick, vb. trier à la main, éplucher à la main.

handsome, adj. beau m., belle f.

hand-to-hand, adj. corps à corps.

handwriting, n. écriture f.

handy, adj. (person) adroit; (thing) commode; (at hand) sous la main.

handyman, n. homme (m.) à tout faire, bricoleur m., factotum.

hang, vb. pendre.

hangar, n. hangar m.

hangdog, adj. avec une mine patibulaire, avec un air en dessous.

hanger-on, n. dépendant m., parasite m.

hang glider, n. glisseur (m.) duquel l'usager pend.

hanging, 1. n. suspension f., pendaison f. 2. adj. suspendu, pendant.

hangman, n. bourreau m.

hangnail, n. envie f.

hangout, n. repaire m., nid m.

hangover, n. gueule (f.) de bois.

hang-over, n. reste m., reliquat m.

hangup, n. difficulté psychologique f.

hank, n. écheveau m., torchette f.

hanker, vb. désirer vivement, convoiter.

haphazard, adv. au hasard.

happen, vb. (take place) arriver; (chance to be) se trouver.

happening, n. événement m.

happily, adv. heureusement.

happiness, n. bonheur m.

happy, adj. heureux.

happy-go-lucky, adj. sans souci, insouciant.

harakiri, n. hara-kiri m.

harangue, 1. n. harangue f. 2. vb. haranguer.

harass, vb. harceler, tracasser.

harbinger, n. avant-coureur m., précurseur m.

harbor, 1. n. (refuge) asile m.; (port) port m. 2. vb. héberger.

hard, 1. adj. dur; (difficult) difficile. 2. adv. fort.

hard-bitten, adj. tenace, dur à cuire.

hard-boiled, adj. dur, tenace, boucané.

hard coal, n. anthracite m.

hard disk, n. disque (m.) dur.

harden, vb. durcir.

hard-headed, adj. pratique, positif.

hard-hearted, adj. insensible, impitoyable, au cœur dur.

hardiness, n. robustesse f., vigueur f.

hardly, adv. (in a hard manner) durement; (scarcely) à peine; (h. ever) presque jamais.

hardness, n. dureté f.; (difficulty) difficulté f.

hardship, n. privation f.

hardtack, n. galette f., biscuit de mer m.

hardware, n. quincaillerie f., matériel m.

hardwood, n. bois dur m.

hardy, adj. robuste.

hare, n. lièvre m.

harebrained, adj. écervelé, étourdi.

harelip, n. bec-de-lièvre m.

harem, n. harem m.

hark, 1. vb. prêter l'oreille à. 2. interj. écoutez!

Harlequin, n. Arlequin m.

harlot, n. prostituée f., fille de joie f.

harm, 1. n. mal m. 2. vb. nuire à.

harmful, adj. nuisible.

harmless, adj. inoffensif.

harmonic, adj. harmonique.

harmonica, n. harmonica m.

harmonious, *adj.* harmonieux.

harmonize, *vb.* harmoniser.

harmony, *n.* harmonie *f.*

harness, 1. *n.* harnais *m.* **2.** *vb.* harnacher.

harp, *n.* harpe *f.*

harpoon, 1. *n.* harpon *m.* **2.** *vb.* harponner.

harpsichord, *n.* clavecin *m.*

harridan, *n.* vieille sorcière *f.*, vieille mégère *f.*

harrowing, *adj.* déchirant.

harry, *vb.* harceler.

harsh, *adj.* rude.

harshness, *n.* rudesse *f.*

harvest, 1. *n.* moisson *f.* **2.** *vb.* moissoner.

hash, 1. *n.* hachis *m.*, émincé *m.* **2.** *vb.* hacher (de la viande).

hashish, *n.* hachisch *m.*

hasn't, *vb.* n'a pas.

hassle, 1. *vb.* harceler. **2.** *n.* harcèlement *m.*

hassock, *n.* agenouilloir *m.*

haste, *n.* hâte *f.*

hasten, *vb.* hâter, *tr.*

hastily, *adv.* à la hâte.

hasty, *adj.* précipité.

hat, *n.* chapeau *m.*

hatch, *vb.* (hen) couver; (egg) éclore.

hatchback, *adj.* (auto) avec hayon arrière.

hatchery, *n.* établissement *(m.)* de pisciculture.

hatchet, *n.* hachette *f.*

hate, *vb.* haïr.

hateful, *adj.* odieux.

hatred, *n.* haine *f.*

haughtiness, *n.* arrogance *f.*, hauteur *f.*

haughty, *adj.* hautain.

haul, *vb.* traîner.

haunch, *n.* hanche *f.*, cuissot *m.*

haunt, *vb.* hanter.

have, *vb.* avoir; (**h. to,** necessity) devoir.

haven, *n.* havre *m.*; (refuge) asile *m.*

haven't, *vb.* n'ont pas.

havoc, *n.* ravage *m.*

hawk, 1. *n.* faucon *m.* **2.** *vb.* colporter.

hawker, *n.* colporteur *m.*, marchand ambulant *m.*

hawser, *n.* haussière *f.*, amarre *f.*

hawthorn, *n.* aubépine *f.*

hay, *n.* foin *m.*

hay fever, *n.* fièvre *(f.)* des foins.

hayfield, *n.* champs *(m.)* de foin.

hayloft, *n.* fenil *m.*, grenier *m.*

haystack, *n.* meule *(f.)* de foin.

hazard, 1. *n.* hasard *m.* **2.** *vb.* hasarder, risquer.

hazardous, *adj.* hasardeux.

haze, *n.* brume *(f.)* légère.

hazel, *n.* noisetier *m.*; couleur de noisette *f.*

hazy, *adj.* brumeux, nébuleux.

he, *pron.* il; (alone, stressed, with another subject) lui.

head, *n.* tête *f.*

headache, *n.* mal *(m.)* de tête.

headband, *n.* bandeau *m.*

headfirst, *adv.* la tête la première.

headgear, *n.* garniture *(f.)* de tête, coiffure *f.*

head-hunting, *n.* chasse *(f.)* aux têtes.

heading, *n.* rubrique *f.*

headlight, *n.* phare *m.*, projecteur *m.*

headline, *n.* titre *m.*

headlong, *adv.* la tête la première.

headman, *n.* chef *m.*

headmaster, *n.* directeur *m.*

head-on, *adj. and adv.* de front.

headquarters, *n.* *(mil.)* quartier *(m.)* général; *(comm.)* bureau *(m.)* principal.

headstone, *n.* pierre angulaire *f.*

headstrong, *adj.* volontaire, têtu, entêté.

headwaters, *n.* cours supérieur (d'une rivière) *m.*, eau d'amont *f.*

headway, *n.* progrès *m.*

headwork, *n.* travail de tête *m.*, travail intellectuel *m.*

heady, *adj.* impétueux, capiteux.

heal, *vb.* guérir.

health, *n.* santé *f.*

health foods, *n.* aliments *(m.pl.)* diététiques.

healthful, *adj.* salubre.

healthy, *adj.* sain.

heap, 1. *n.* tas *m.* **2.** *vb.* entasser.

hear, *vb.* entendre.

hearing, *n.* audition *f.*; ouïe *f.*

hearsay, *n.* ouï-dire *m.*

hearse, n. catafalque m., corbillard m.

heart, n. cœur m.

heartache, n. chagrin m.

heart attack, n. crise (f.) cardiaque.

heartbreak, n. déchirement de cœur m.

heartbroken, adj. avec le cœur brisé, navré.

heartburn, n. brûlures (f.pl.) d'estomac. aigreur f.

heartfelt, adj. sincère, qui va au cœur.

hearth, n. foyer m., âtre m.

heartless, adj. sans cœur, insensible, sans pitié.

heart-rending, adj. à fendre le cœur, navrant, déchirant.

heartsick, adj. écœuré.

heart-stricken, adj. frappé au cœur, navré.

heart-to-heart, adj. à cœur ouvert, intime.

hearty, adj. cordial.

heat, 1. n. chaleur f. 2. vb. chauffer.

heated, adj. chaud, chauffé, animé.

heath, n. bruyère f., lande f.

heathen, adj. and n. païen m., païenne f.

heather, n. bruyère f., brande f.

heatstroke, n. coup (m.) de chaleur.

heat wave, n. vague (f.) de chaleur, canicule f.

heave, vb. (lift) lever; (utter) pousser; (rise) se soulever, intr.

heaven, n. ciel m., pl. cieux.

heavenly, adj. céleste.

heavy, adj. lourd.

heavyweight, n. poids lourd m.

Hebrew, 1. n. (language) hébreu m. 2. adj. hébreu.

Hebrides, n. les Hébrides f.pl.

heckle, vb. poser des questions embarrassantes.

hectare, n. hectare m.

hectic, adj. (restless) agité.

hectograph, 1. n. hectographe m., autocopiste m. 2. vb. hectographier, autocopier.

hedge, n. haie f.

hedgehog, n. hérisson m.

hedgehop, vb. voler à ras de terre.

hedgerow, n. bordure de haies f.

hedonism, n. hédonisme m.

heed, 1. n. attention f. 2. vb. faire attention à.

heedless, adj. étourdi, imprudent, insouciant.

heel, n. talon m.

hefty, adj. fort, solide, costaud.

hegemony, n. hégémonie f.

heifer, n. génisse f.

height, n. hauteur f.

heighten, vb. rehausser, augmenter.

heinous, adj. odieux, atroce, abominable.

heir, n. héritier m.

heir apparent, n. héritier présomptif m.

heirloom, n. meuble m. (or bijou m.) de famille.

heir presumptive, n. héritier présomptif m.

helicopter, n. hélicoptère m.

heliocentric, adj. héliocentrique.

heliograph, n. héliographe m.

heliotrope, n. héliotrope m.

heliport, n. héliport m.

helium, n. hélium m.

hell, n. enfer m.

Hellenism, n. hellénisme m.

hellish, adj. infernal, diabolique.

hello, interj. (telephone) allô.

helm, n. barre (f.) du gouvernail.

helmet, n. casque m.

helmsman, n. homme de barre m., timonier m.

help, 1. n. aide f. 2. vb. aider; (at table) servir. 3. interj. au secours!

helper, n. aide m.f.

helpful, adj. (person) serviable; (thing) utile.

helpfulness, n. serviabilité f., utilité f.

helping, 1. n. portion f. 2. adj. secourable.

helpless, adj. (forlorn) délaissé; (powerless) impuissant.

helter-skelter, adv. pêle-mêle, en désordre.

hem, 1. n. ourlet m. 2. vb. ourler.

hematite, n. hématite f.

hemisphere, n. hémisphère m.

hemlock, n. ciguë f.

hemoglobin, n. hémoglobine f.

hemophilia, n. hémophilie f.

hemorrhage, n. hémorragie f.

hemorrhoid, n. hémorroïde f.

hemp, n. chanvre m.

hemstitch, 1. n. ourlet m. **2.** vb. ourler.

hen, n. poule f.

hence, adv. (time, place) d'ici; (therefore) de là.

henceforth, adv. désormais.

henchman, n. homme de confiance m., acolyte m., satellite m.

henequen, n. henequen m.

henna, 1. n. henné m. **2.** vb. teindre au henné.

henpeck, vb. mener par le bout du nez.

hepatic, adj. hépatique.

hepatica, n. hépatique f.

hepatitis, n. hépatite f.

her, 1. adj. son m., sa f., ses pl. **2.** pron. (direct) la; (indirect) lui; (alone, stressed, with prep.) elle.

herald, n. héraut m.

heraldic, adj. héraldique.

heraldry, n. l'héraldique f.

herb, n. herbe f.

herbaceous, adj. herbacé.

herbarium, n. herbier m.

herculean, adj. herculéen.

herd, n. troupeau m.

here, adv. ici; (h. is) voici.

hereabout, adv. par ici, près d'ici.

hereafter, adv. dorénavant.

hereby, adv. par ceci, par ce moyen, par là.

hereditary, adj. héréditaire.

heredity, n. hérédité f.

herein, adv. ici; (h. enclosed) ci-enclus.

heresy, n. hérésie f.

heretic, n. hérétique m.f.

heretical, adj. hérétique.

hereto, adv. ci-joint.

heretofore, adv. jusqu'ici.

herewith, adv. avec ceci, ci-joint.

heritage, n. héritage m., patrimoine m.

hermetic, adj. hermétique.

hermit, n. ermite m.

hermitage, n. ermitage m.

hernia, n. hernie f.

hero, n. héros m.

heroic, adj. héroïque.

heroically, adv. héroïquement.

heroin, n. héroïne f.

heroine, n. héroïne f.

heroism, n. héroïsme m.

heron, n. héron m.

herpes, n. herpès m.

herring, n. hareng m.

herringbone, n. arête (f.) de hareng.

hers, pron. le sien m., la sienne f.

herself, pron. elle-même; (reflexive) se.

hertz, n. hertz m.

hesitancy, n. hésitation f., incertitude f.

hesitant, adj. hésitant, irrésolu.

hesitate, vb. hésiter.

hesitation, n. hésitation f.

heterodox, adj. hétérodoxe.

heterodoxy, n. hétérodoxie f.

heterogeneous, adj. hétérogène.

heterosexual, adj. hétérosexuel.

hew, vb. couper, tailler.

hexagon, n. hexagone m.

heyday, n. apogée m., beaux jours m.pl.

hi, interj. salut!

hiatus, n. lacune f.

hibernate, vb. hiberner, hiverner.

hibernation, n. hibernation f.

hibiscus, n. hibiscus m.

hiccup, 1. n. hoquet m. **2.** vb. hoqueter.

hickory, n. noyer (blanc) d'Amérique m.

hide, 1. vb. cacher, tr. **2.** n. peau f.

hideous, adj. hideux.

hide-out, n. cachette f., lieu (m.) de retraite.

hierarchical, adj. hiérarchique.

hierarchy, n. hiérarchie f.

hieroglyphic, adj. hiéroglyphique.

hi-fi, 1. n. hi-fi f. **2.** adj. hi-fi.

high, adj. haut.

highbrow, n. intellectuel m.

high fidelity, n. haute fidélité f.

high-handed, adj. arbitraire, tyrannique.

high-hat, vb. traiter de haut en bas.

highland, n. haute terre f.

highlight, 1. n. clou m. **2.** vb. mettre en relief.

highly, adv. extrêmement.

high-minded, adj. à l'esprit élevé, généreux.

Highness, n. (title) Altesse f.

high school, n. lycée m.

high seas, n. haute mer f.

high-strung, *adj.* nerveux, impressionable.

high-tech, *n. and adj.* de pointe.

high tide, *n.* marée haute *f.*

highway, *n.* grande route *f.*

hijack, *vb.* détourner.

hijacker, *n.* pirate de l'air *m.*

hike, *n.* excursion (*f.*) à pied.

hilarious, *adj.* hilare.

hilariousness, *n.* hilarité *f.*

hilarity, *n.* hilarité *f.*

hill, *n.* colline *f.*

hilt, *n.* poignée *f.*, garde *f.*

him, *pron.* (direct) le; (indirect) lui; (alone, stressed, with prep.) lui.

himself, *pron.* lui-même; (reflexive) se.

hinder, *vb.* (impede) gêner; (prevent) empêcher.

hindmost, *adj.* dernier.

hindquarter, *n.* arrière-main *m.*, arrière-train *m.*

hindrance, *n.* empêchement *m.*, obstacle *m.*, entrave *f.*

hindsight, *n.* (with h.) avec du recul.

Hindu, 1. *n.* Hindou *m.* 2. *adj.* hindou.

hinge, *n.* gond *m.*

hint, 1. *n.* allusion *f.* 2. *vb.* insinuer.

hinterland, *n.* hinterland *m.*, arrière-pays *m.*

hip, *n.* hanche *f.*

hippie, *n.* hippie *m.f.*

hippodrome, *n.* hippodrome *m.*

hippopotamus, *n.* hippopotame *m.*

hire, *vb.* louer; (servant) engager.

hireling, *n.* mercenaire *m.*, stipendié *m.*

hirsute, *adj.* hirsute, velu.

his, 1. *adj.* son *m.*, sa *f.*, ses *pl.* 2. *pron.* le sien *m.*, la sienne *f.*

Hispanic, *adj.* hispanique.

hiss, *vb.* siffler.

historian, *n.* historien *m.*

historic, *adj.* historique.

historical, *adj.* historique.

history, *n.* histoire *f.*

histrionic, *adj.* histrionique, théâtral.

histrionics, *n.* parade d'émotions *f.*, démonstration peu sincère *f.*

hit, 1. *n.* coup *m.*; (success) succès *m.* 2. *vb.* frapper.

hitch, 1. *n.* (obstacle) anicroche *f.* 2. *vb.* (fasten) accrocher, *tr.*

hitchhike, *vb.* faire de l'auto-stop.

hither, 1. *adv.* ici. 2. *adj.* le plus rapproché.

hitherto, *adj.* jusqu'ici.

hive, *n.* ruche *f.*

hives, *n.* éruption *f.*, varicelle pustuleuse *f.*, urticaire *f.*

hoard, 1. *n.* amas *m.* 2. *vb.* amasser; (money) thésauriser.

hoarse, *adj.* enroué.

hoax, *n.* mystification *f.*

hobble, *vb.* boitiller, clopiner, entraver.

hobby, *n.* marotte *f.*

hobbyhorse, *n.* dada *m.*, cheval de bois *m.*

hobgoblin, *n.* lutin *m.*, esprit follet *m.*

hobnail, 1. *n.* caboche *f.*, clou (*n.*) à ferrer. 2. *vb.* ferrer.

hobnob, *vb.* boire avec, fréquenter.

hobo, *n.* vagabond *m.*, clochard *m.*, ouvrier ambulant *m.*

hock, 1. *n.* jarret *m.* 2. *vb.* mettre au clou.

hockey, *n.* hockey *m.*

hocuspocus, *n.* passe-passe *m.*

hod, *n.* auge *f.*

hodgepodge, *n.* mélange confus *m.*

hoe, 1. *n.* houe *f.* 2. *vb.* houer.

hog, *n.* porc *m.*

hogshead, *n.* tonneau *m.*, barrique *f.*

hog-tie, *vb.* lier les quatre pattes.

hoist, 1. *n.* treuil *m.*, grue *f.* 2. *vb.* hisser.

hold, 1. *n.* prise *f.*; (ship) cale *f.* 2. *vb.* tenir; (contain) contenir; (h. back) retenir; (h. up) arrêter, détenir, entraver.

holdup, *n.* arrêt *m.*, suspension *f.*; coup (*m.*) à main armée.

hole, *n.* trou *m.*

holiday, *n.* jour (*m.*) de fête; fête *f.*; (h.s) vacances *f.pl.*

holiness, *n.* sainteté *f.*

holistic, *adj.* holistique.

Holland, *n.* les Pays-Bas *m.pl.*, Hollande *f.*

hollow, *adj. and n.* creux *m.*

holly, *n.* houx *m.*

hollyhock, n. passe-rose f., rose-trémière f.

holocaust, n. holocauste m.

hologram, n. hologramme m.

holography, n. holographie f.

holster, n. étui m.

holy, adj. saint.

Holy See, n. Saint-Siège m.

Holy Spirit, n. Saint-Esprit m.

Holy Week, n. semaine sainte f.

homage, n. hommage m.

home, n. maison f: (hearth) foyer (m.) domestique; (at h.) à la maison, chez soi.

homeland, n. patrie f.

homeless, 1. adj. sans asile, sans abri. **2.** n. sans abri m.

homelike, adj. qui resemble au foyer domestique.

homely, adj. laid.

homemade, adj. fait à la maison.

home rule, n. autonomie f.

homesick, adj. (be h.) avoir le mal du pays.

homespun, adj. (étoffe) de fabrication domestique, fait à la maison, simple.

homestead, n. ferme f., bien de famille m.

homeward, adj. de retour.

homework, n. travail fait à la maison m., devoirs m.pl.

homicide, n. homicide m.

homily, n. homélie f.

homing pigeon, n. pigeon messager m.

hominy, n. bouillie (f.) de farine de maïs, semoule (f.) de maïs.

homogeneous, adj. homogène.

homonym, n. homonyme m.

homosexual, adj. and adj. homosexuel m., homosexuelle f.

Honduras, n. Honduras m.

hone, vb. aiguiser, affiler.

honest, adj. honnête.

honestly, adv. honnêtement, de bonne foi.

honesty, n. honnêteté f.

honey, n. miel m.

honeybee, n. abeille domestique f.

honeycomb, 1. n. rayon de miel m. **2.** vb. cribler, affouiller.

honeydew melon, n. melon m.

honeymoon, n. lune (f.) de miel.

honeysuckle, n. chèvre-feuille m.

honor, 1. n. honneur m. **2.** vb. honorer.

honorable, adj. honorable.

honorary, adj. honoraire.

hood, n. capuchon m.; (vehicle) capote f.

hoodlum, n. voyou m.

hoodwink, vb. tromper, bander les yeux à.

hoof, n. sabot m.

hook, 1. n. croc m.; (fishing) hameçon m. **2.** vb. accrocher.

hooked, adj. crochu, recourbé; (be h. on) (drugs) se droguer à; (hobbies, etc.) être fana de.

hooked rug, n. tapis (m.) à points noués simples.

hooker, n. (colloquial) prostituée f.

hookworm, n. ankylostome m.

hoop, n. cercle m.

hoop skirt, n. jupe (f.) à paniers, vertugadin m.

hoot, 1. n. ululation f., hululement m., huée f. **2.** vb. hululer, huer.

hop, 1. n. (plant) houblon m. **2.** vb. sautiller.

hope, 1. n. espérance f., espoir m. **2.** vb. espérer.

hopeful, adj. plein d'espoir.

hopeless, adj. désespéré.

hopelessness, n. désespoir m., état désespéré m.

hopscotch, n. marelle f.

horde, n. horde f.

horizon, n. horizon m.

horizontal, adj. horizontal.

hormone, n. hormone f.

horn, n. corne f.; (music) cor m.; (auto) klaxon m.

hornet, n. frelon m., guêpe-frelon f.

horny, adj. corné, calleux.

horoscope, n. horoscope m.

horrendous, adj. horrible, horripilant.

horrible, adj. horrible.

horrid, adj. affreux.

horrify, vb. horrifier.

horror, n. horreur f.

horror film, n. film (m.) d'horreur.

horse, n. cheval m.

horseback, n. **(on h.)** à cheval.

horsefly, n. taon m.

horsehair, n. crin m.

horseman, n. cavalier m.

horsemanship, n. équitation f., manège m.

horseplay, n. jeu (m.) de mains, badinerie grossière f.

horsepower, n. puissance (f.) en chevaux.

horse-racing, n. courses (f.pl.) de chevaux.

horseradish, n. raifort m.

horseshoe, n. fer à cheval m.

horsewhip, 1. n. cravache f. 2. vb. cravacher, sangler.

hortatory, adj. exhortatif.

horticulture, n. horticulture f.

hose, n. (pipe) tuyau m.; (stockings) bas m.pl.

hosiery, n. bonneterie f.

hospice, n. hospice m.

hospitable, adj. hospitalier.

hospital, n. hôpital m.

hospitality, n. hospitalité f.

hospitalization, n. hospitalisation f.

hospitalize, vb. hospitaliser.

host, n. hôte m.; (show) animateur m.; (religion) hostie f.

hostage, n. otage m.

hostel, n. hôtellerie f., auberge f.

hostelry, n. hôtellerie f., auberge f.

hostess, n. hôtesse f.

hostile, adj. hostile, agressif, contre.

hostility, n. hostilité f.

hot, adj. chaud.

hotbed, n. couche f., foyer ardent m.

hot dog, n. saucisse chaude f.

hotel, n. hôtel m.

hot-headed, adj. impétueux, exalté, emporté.

hothouse, n. serre f.

hound, n. chien (m.) de chasse. 2. vb. poursuivre, pourchasser.

hour, n. heure f.

hourglass, n. sablier m.

hourly, adv. à chaque heure, à l'heure.

house, 1. n. maison f.; (legislature) chambre f. 2. vb. loger; abriter.

housecoat, n. peignoir m.

housefly, n. mouche domestique f.

household, n. (house, family) ménage, m., (family) famille f.; (servants) domestiques m.pl.

housekeeper, n. gouvernante f.

housekeeping, n. ménage m., économie domestique f.

housemaid, n. fille (f.) de service, bonne f., femme de chambre f.

housewarming (party), n. pendaison (f.) de la crémaillère f.

housewife, n. ménagère f., femme (f.) au foyer.

housework, n. ménage m.

housing, n. logement m.

hovel, n. taudis m., bicoque f.

hover, vb. planer.

hovercraft, n. aéroglisseur m.

how, adv. comment; (h. are you) comment allez-vous?; (h. much) combien (de); (in exclamation) comme.

however, adv. (in whatever way) de quelque manière que; (with adj.) si . . . que; (nevertheless) cependant.

howitzer, n. obusier m.

howl, vb. hurler.

hub, n. moyeu m., centre m.

hubbub, n. vacarme m., tintamarre m.

huckleberry, n. airelle f.

huddle, 1. n. tas confus m., fouillis m. 2. vb. entasser.

hue, n. couleur f.

huff, 1. n. emportement m., accès de colère m. 2. vb. gonfler, enfler.

hug, 1. n. étreinte f. 2. vb. serrer dans ses bras.

huge, adj. énorme.

hulk, n. carcasse f., ponton m.

hull, n. coque f., corps m.

hullabaloo, n. vacarme m.

hum, vb. (insect) bourdonner; (sing) fredonner.

human, humane, adj. humain.

human being, n. être (m.) humain.

humanism, n. humanisme m.

humanitarian, adj. humanitaire.

humanities, n. humanités f.pl.

humanity, n. humanité f.

humanly, adv. humainement.

humble, adj. humble.

humbug, n. blague f., tromperie f., fumisterie f.

humdrum, *adj.* monotone, assommant.

humid, *adj.* humide.

humidify, *vb.* humidifier.

humidor, *n.* boîte à cigares *f.*

humiliate, *adj.* humilier.

humiliation, *n.* humiliation *f.*

humility, *n.* humilité *f.*

humor, 1. *n.* (wit) humour *m.*; (medical, mood) humeur *f.* 2. *vb.* se prêter aux caprices de.

humorous, *adj.* (witty) humoristique; (funny) drôle.

hump, *n.* bosse *f.*

humpback, *n.* bossu *m.*

humus, *n.* humus *m.*; terreau *m.*

hunch, 1. *n.* bosse *f.*; pressentiment *m.* 2. *vb.* arrondir, voûter.

hunchback, *n.* bossu *m.*

hundred, *adj. and n.* cent *m.*

hundredth, *n. and adj.* centième *m.f.*

Hungarian, 1. *n.* (person) Hongrois *m.*; (language) hongrois *m.* 2. *adj.* hongrois.

Hungary, *n.* Hongrie *f.*

hunger, *n.* faim *f.*

hunger strike, *n.* grève *(f.)* de la faim.

hungry, *adj.* affamé; (**be h.**) avoir faim.

hunk, *n.* gros morceau *m.*

hunt, *vb.* chasser.

hunter, *n.* chasseur *m.*

hunting, *n.* chasse *f.*

huntress, *n.* chasseuse *f.*, chasseresse *f.*

hurdle, *n.* claie *f.*

hurl, *vb.* lancer.

hurrah, hurray, *interj.* houra!

hurricane, *n.* ouragan *m.*

hurry, 1. *n.* hâte *f.*; (**in a h.**) à la hâte. 2. *vb.* presser, *tr.*; se presser, *intr.*

hurt, *vb.* faire mal (à).

hurtful, *adj.* nuisible, pernicieux, préjudiciable.

hurtle, *vb.* se choquer, se heurter.

husband, *n.* mari *m.*

husbandry, *n.* agriculture *f.*, économie *f.*

hush, 1. *interj.* chut! paix! 2. *vb.* taire, imposer silence à.

husk, 1. *n.* cosse *f.*, gousse *f.* 2. *vb.* écosser, éplucher.

husky, 1. *adj.* (body) cossu; (voice) rauque, enroué. 2. *n.* chien *(m.)* de traineau.

hustle, *vb.* bousculer, se presser.

hut, *n.* cabane *f.*

hutch, *n.* huche *f.*, clapier *m.*

hyacinth, *n.* jacinthe *f.*

hybrid, *n.* hybride *m.*

hydrangea, *n.* hortensia *m.*

hydrant, *n.* prise d'eau *f.*, bouche d'incendie *f.*

hydraulic, *adj.* hydraulique.

hydrochloric acid, *n.* acide *(m.)* chlorhydrique.

hydroelectric, *adj.* hydroélectrique.

hydrofoil, *n.* hydroptère *m.*

hydrogen, *n.* hydrogène *m.*

hydrophobia, *n.* hydrophobie *f.*

hydroplane, *n.* hydroplane *m.*

hydrotherapy, *n.* hydrothérapie *f.*

hyena, *n.* hyène *f.*

hygiene, *n.* hygiène *f.*

hygienic, *adj.* hygiénique.

hymn, *n.* (song, anthem) hymne *m.*; (church) hymne *f.*

hymnal, *n.* hymnaire *m.*, recueil d'hymnes *m.*

hype, 1. *n.* tapage *(m.)* publicitaire. 2. *vb.* faire du tapage autour de.

hyperacidity, *n.* hyperacidité *f.*

hyperbole, *n.* hyperbole *f.*

hypercritical, *adj.* hypercritique.

hypermarket, *n.* hypermarché *m.*

hypersensitive, *adj.* hypersensible.

hypertension, *n.* hypertension *f.*

hyphen, *n.* trait *(m.)* d'union.

hyphenate, *vb.* mettre un trait d'union à.

hypnosis, *n.* hypnose *f.*

hypnotic, *adj.* hypnotique.

hypnotism, *n.* hypnotisme *f.*

hypnotize, *vb.* hypnotiser.

hypochondria, *n.* hypocondrie *f.*

hypochondriac, *n. and adj.* hypocondriaque *m.*

hypocrisy, *n.* hypocrisie *f.*

hypocrite, *n.* hypocrite *m.f.*

hypocritical, *adj.* hypocrite.

hypodermic, *adj.* hypodermique.

hypotenuse, *n.* hypoténuse *f.*

hypothermia, *n.* hypothermie *f.*

hypothesis, *n.* hypothèse *f.*

hypothetical, *adj.* hypothétique.

hysterectomy, n. hystérectomie f.

hysteria, n. hystérie f.

hysterical, adj. hystérique.

hysterics, n.pl. crise (f.) de nerfs.

I

I, pron. je; (alone, stressed, with another subject) moi.

iambic, adj. iambique.

Iberia, n. Ibérie f.

ice, n. glace f.

iceberg, n. iceberg m., gros bloc de glace m.

ice-box, n. glacière f.

ice cream, n. glace f.

ice cube, n. glaçon m.

Iceland, n. Islande f.

ice skate, 1. n. patin à glace m. **2.** vb. patiner.

ichthyology, n. ichtyologie f.

icicle, n. glaçon m.

icing, n. glacé m.

icon, n. icône f.

icy, adj. glacial.

idea, n. idée f.

ideal, adj. and n. idéal m.

idealism, n. idéalisme m.

idealist, n. idéaliste m.f.

idealistic, adj. idéaliste.

idealize, vb. idéaliser.

ideally, adv. idéalement, en idée.

identical (with), adj. identique (à).

identifiable, adj. identifiable.

identification, n. identification f.

identify, vb. identifier.

identity, n. identité f.

ideology, n. idéologie f.

idiocy, n. idiotie f., idiotisme m.

idiom, n. (language) idiome m.; (peculiar expression) idiotisme m.

idiot, adj. and n. idiot m.

idiotic, adj. idiot.

idle, adj. (unoccupied) désœuvré; (lazy) paresseux; (futile) vain.

idleness, n. oisiveté f.

idol, n. idole f.

idolatry, n. idolâtrie f.

idolize, vb. idolâtrer.

idyl, n. idylle f.

idyllic, adj. idyllique.

if, conj. si.

ignite, vb. allumer, mettre en feu.

ignition, n. ignition f., allumage m.

ignoble, adj. ignoble; (low birth) plébéien.

ignominious, adj. ignominieux.

ignoramus, n. ignorant m., ignare m.

ignorance, n. ignorance f.

ignorant, adj. ignorant; (be i. of) ignorer.

ignore, vb. feindre d'ignorer.

ill, 1. n. mal m. **2.** adj. (sick) malade; (bad) mauvais. **3.** adv. mal.

illegal, adj. illégal.

illegible, adj. illisible.

illegibly, adv. illisiblement.

illegitimacy, n. illégitimité f.

illegitimate, adj. illégitime.

illicit, adj. illicite.

illiteracy, n. analphabétisme m.

illiterate, adj. illettré, analphabète.

illness, n. maladie f.

illogical, adj. illogique.

illuminate, vb. illuminer.

illumination, n. illumination f., enluminure f.

illusion, n. illusion f.

illusive, adj. illusoire.

illustrate, vb. illustrer.

illustration, n. illustration f.; (example) exemple m.

illustrative, adj. explicatif, qui éclaircit.

illustrious, adj. illustre.

ill will, adj. mauvais vouloir m., malveillance f.

image, n. image f.

imagery, n. images f.pl., langage figuré m.

imaginable, adj. imaginable.

imaginary, adj. imaginaire.

imagination, n. imagination f.

imaginative, adj. imaginatif.

imagine, vb. imaginer, tr.

imam, n. imam m.

imbalance, n. déséquilibre m.

imbecile, n. imbécile m.

imbue, vb. imprégner.

imitate, vb. imiter.

imitation, n. imitation f.

imitative, adj. imitatif.

immaculate, adj. immaculé, sans tache.

immanent, *adj.* immanent.

immaterial, *adj.* immatériel, incorporel, sans conséquence.

immature, *adj.* pas mûr, prématuré.

immediate, *adj.* immédiat.

immediately, *adv.* immédiatement, tout de suite.

immense, *adj.* immense.

immerse, *vb.* immerger, plonger.

immigrant, *n.* immigrant *m.,* immigré *m.*

immigrate, *vb.* immigrer.

imminent, *adj.* imminent.

immobile, *adj.* fixe, immobile.

immobilize, *vb.* immobiliser.

immoderate, *adj.* immodéré, intempéré, outré.

immodest, *adj.* immodeste, impudique, présomptueux.

immoral, *adj.* immoral.

immorality, *n.* immoralité *f.*

immorally, *adv.* immoralement.

immortal, *adj.* and *n.* immortel *m.*

immortality, *n.* immortalité *f.*

immortalize, *vb.* immortaliser.

immovable, *adj.* fixe, immuable, inébranlable.

immune, *adj.* immunisé.

immunity, *n.* exemption *f.,* immunité *f.*

immunize, *vb.* immuniser.

immutable, *adj.* immuable, inaltérable.

impact, *n.* choc *m.,* impact *m.*

impair, *vb.* affaiblir, altérer, compromettre.

impale, *vb.* empaler.

impart, *vb.* donner, communiquer, transmettre.

impartial, *adj.* impartial.

impasse, *n.* impasse *f.*

impassioned, *adj.* passionné.

impassive, *adj.* impassible.

impatience, *n.* impatience *f.*

impatient, *adj.* impatient.

impeach, *vb.* attaquer, accuser, récuser.

impede, *vb.* entraver, empêcher.

impediment, *n.* entrave *f.,* obstacle *m.,* empêchement *m.*

impel, *vb.* pousser, forcer.

impending, *adj.* imminent.

impenetrable, *adj.* impénétrable.

impenitent, *adj.* impénitent.

imperative, 1. *n.* (*gramm.*) impératif *m.* **2.** *adj.* (*gramm.*) impératif; urgent, impérieux.

imperceptible, *adj.* imperceptible.

imperfect, *adj.* and *n.* imparfait *m.*

imperfection, *n.* imperfection *f.*

imperial, *adj.* impérial.

imperialism, *n.* impérialisme *m.*

imperil, *vb.* mettre en péril, exposer au danger.

imperious, *adj.* impérieux, arrogant.

impersonal, *adj.* impersonnel.

impersonate, *vb.* personnifier, représenter.

impersonation, *n.* personnification *f.,* incarnation *f.*

impersonator, *n.* personnificateur *m.*

impertinence, *n.* impertinence *f.*

impervious, *adj.* impénétrable, imperméable.

impetuous, *adj.* impétueux.

impetus, *n.* élan *m.,* vitesse acquise *f.*

impinge, *vb.* se heurter à, empiéter sur.

implacable, *adj.* implacable.

implant, *vb.* inculquer, implanter.

implement, *n.* outil *m.*

implicate, *vb.* impliquer, entremêler.

implication, *n.* implication *f.*

implicit, *adj.* implicite.

implied, *adj.* implicite, tacite.

implore, *vb.* implorer.

imply, *vb.* impliquer.

impolite, *adj.* impoli.

imponderable, *adj.* impondérable.

import, 1. *n.* article (*m.*) d'importation, importation *f.* **2.** *vb.* importer.

importance, *n.* importance *f.*

important, *adj.* important.

importation, *n.* importation *f.*

importune, *vb.* importuner.

impose (on), *vb.* imposer (à).

imposition, *n.* imposition *f.*

impossibility, *n.* impossibilité *f.*

impossible, *adj.* impossible.

impotence, *n.* impuissance *f.*

impotent, *adj.* impuissant.

impound, *vb.* confisquer.

impoverish, *vb.* appauvrir.

impractical, *adj.* pas pratique.

impregnable, *adj.* imprenable, inexpugnable.
impregnate, *vb.* imprégner, féconder.
impresario, *n.* imprésario *m.*
impress, *vb.* (imprint) imprimer; (affect) faire une impression à.
impression, *n.* impression *f.*
impressive, *adj.* impressionnant.
imprison, *vb.* emprisonner.
imprisonment, *n.* emprisonnement *m.*
improbable, *adj.* improbable.
impromptu, *adv., adj.* et *n.* impromptu *m.*
improper, *adj.* (inaccurate) impropre; (unbecoming) malséant.
improve, *vb.* améliorer, *tr.*
improvement, *n.* amélioration *f.*
improvise, *vb.* improviser.
impudent, *adj.* insolent, effronté, impertinent.
impugn, *vb.* attaquer, contester, impugner.
impulse, *n.* impulsion *f.*
impulsion, *n.* impulsion *f.*
impulsive, *adj.* impulsif.
impunity, *n.* impunité *f.*
impure, *adj.* impur.
impurity, *n.* impureté *f.*
impute, *vb.* imputer.
in, *prep.* en; (with art. or adj.) dans; (town) à.
inability, *n.* incapacité *f.*
inaccurate, *adj.* inexact.
inadequate, *adj.* insuffisant.
inadvertent, *adj.* inattentif, négligent, involontaire.
inalienable, *adj.* inaliénable.
inane, *adj.* inepte, niais, bête.
inappropriate, *adj.* mal à propos.
inaugural, *adj.* inaugural.
inaugurate, *vb.* inaugurer.
inauguration, *n.* inauguration *f.*
inborn, *adj.* inné.
inbred, *adj.* inné.
Inca, *n.* Inca *m.*
incandescence, *n.* incandescence *f.*
incandescent, *adj.* incandescent.
incantation, *n.* incantation *f.*, conjuration *f.*
incapable, *adj.* incapable.
incapacitate, *vb.* rendre incapable, priver de capacité légale.

incarcerate, *vb.* incarcérer, emprisonner.
incarnate, 1. *vb.* incarner. **2.** *adj.* incarné, fait chair.
incarnation, *n.* incarnation *f.*
incendiary, 1. *n.* incendiaire *m.* **2.** *adj.* incendiaire, séditieux.
incense, *n.* encens *m.*
incentive, *n.* stimulant *m.*, aiguillon *m.*
inception, *n.* commencement *m.*, début *m.*
incessant, *adj.* incessant, continuel.
incest, *n.* inceste *m.*
inch, *n.* pouce *m.*
incidence, *n.* incidence *f.*
incident, *n.* incident *m.*
incidental, *adj.* fortuit.
incidentally, *adv.* incidemment, en passant.
incinerator, *n.* incinérateur *m.*
incipient, *adj.* naissant, qui commence.
incision, *n.* incision *f.*, entaille *f.*
incisive, *adj.* incisif, tranchant.
incisor, *n.* incisive *f.*
incite, *vb.* inciter, instiguer.
inclination, *n.* inclinaison *f.*, penchant *m.*
incline, *vb.* incliner.
inclose, *see* enclose.
include, *vb.* comprendre.
inclusive, *adj.* inclusif.
incognito, *adj. and adv.* incognito.
income, *n.* revenu *m.*
incomparable, *adj.* incomparable.
incompetent, *adj.* incompétent.
inconsiderate, *adj.* peu prévenant.
inconvenience, 1. *n.* inconvénient *m.* **2.** *vb.* incommoder.
inconvenient, *adj.* incommode.
incorporate, *vb.* incorporer.
incorrigible, *adj.* incorrigible.
increase, 1. *n.* augmentation *f.* **2.** *vb.* augmenter.
incredible, *adj.* incroyable.
incredulity, *n.* incrédulité *f.*
incredulous, *adj.* incrédule.
increment, *n.* augmentation *f.*, accroissement *m.*
incriminate, *vb.* incriminer.
incrimination, *n.* incrimination *f.*
incrust, *vb.* incruster.
incubator, *n.* incubateur *m.*

inculcate, vb. inculquer.
incumbency, n. période (f.) d'exercice, charge f.
incumbent, 1. n. titulaire m., bénéficiaire m. **2.** adj. couché, posé, appuyé.
incur, vb. encourir.
incurable, adj. incurable.
indebted, adj. endetté.
indecent, adj. indécent.
indecisive, adj. indécis.
indeed, adv. en effet.
indefatigable, adj. infatigable, inlassable.
indefinite, adj. indéfini.
indefinitely, adv. indéfiniment.
indelible, adj. indélébile, ineffaçable.
indemnify, vb. garantir, indemniser, dédommager.
indemnity, n. garantie f., indemnité f., dédommagement m.
indent, vb. denteler, découper, entailler.
indentation, n. découpage m., renfoncement m., endentement m.
independence, n. indépendance f.
independent, adj. indépendant.
in-depth, adj. profond.
index, n. index m.
India, n. Inde f.
Indian, 1. n. Indien m. **2.** adj. indien.
indicate, vb. indiquer.
indication, n. indication f.
indicative, adj. and n. indicatif m.
indicator, n. indicateur m.
indict, vb. accuser, inculper.
indictment, n. accusation f., inculpation f., réquisitoire m.
indifference, n. indifférence f.
indifferent, adj. indifférent.
indigenous, adj. indigène.
indigent, adj. indigent, pauvre.
indigestion, n. dyspepsie f., indigestion f.
indignant, adj. indigné.
indignation, n. indignation f.
indignity, n. indignité f., affront m.
indirect, adj. indirect.
indiscreet, adj. indiscret.
indiscretion, n. imprudence f.
indiscriminate, adj. aveugle, qui ne fait pas de distinction.
indispensable, adj. indispensable.

indisposed, adj. (unwilling) peu enclin, peu disposé; (ill) indisposé, souffrant.
individual, 1. n. individu m. **2.** adj. individuel.
individuality, n. individualité f.
individually, adv. individuellement.
indivisible, adj. indivisible.
indoctrinate, vb. endoctriner, instruire.
indolent, adj. indolent, paresseux.
Indonesia, n. Indonésie f.
indoor, adj. d'intérieur.
indoors, adv. à la maison.
indorse, vb. endosser, appuyer, sanctionner.
induce, vb. (persuade) persuader; (produce) produire.
induct, vb. installer, conduire.
induction, n. induction f.; installation f.
inductive, adj. inductif.
indulge, vb. contenter, favoriser.
indulgence, n. indulgence f.
indulgent, adj. indulgent.
industrial, adj. industriel.
industrialist, n. industriel m.
industrious, adj. travailleur.
industry, n. industrie f.; (diligence) assiduité f.
inebriated, adj. sou.
ineligible, adj. inéligible.
inept, adj. inepte, mal à propos.
inert, adj. inerte, apathique.
inertia, n. inertie f.
inevitable, adj. inévitable.
inexplicable, adj. inexplicable.
infallible, adj. infaillible.
infamous, adj. infâme.
infamy, n. infamie f.
infancy, n. (première) enfance f.
infant, n. enfant m.f.
infantile, adj. enfantin, infantile.
infantryman, n. soldat (m.) d'infanterie, fantassin m.
infatuated, adj. infatué, entiché.
infect, vb. infecter.
infection, n. infection f.
infectious, adj. infectieux, infect, contagieux.
infer, vb. déduire.
inference, n. inférence f.
inferior, adj. and n. inférieur m.

inferiority complex, n. complexe (m.) d'infériorité.

infernal, adj. infernal.

inferno, n. enfer m.

infest, vb. infester.

infidel, n. infidèle m., incroyant m.

infidelity, n. infidélité f.

infighting, n. querelles (f.pl.) internes.

infiltrate, vb. infiltrer.

infinite, adj. and n. infini m.

infinitesimal, adj. infinitésimal.

infinitive, n. infinitif m.

infinity, n. infinité f.

infirm, adj. infirme, faible, maladif.

infirmary, n. infirmerie f.

infirmity, n. infirmité f.

inflame, vb. enflammer, tr.

inflammable, adj. inflammable.

inflammation, n. inflammation f.

inflammatory, adj. incendiaire, inflammatoire.

inflate, vb. gonfler.

inflation, n. (currency) inflation f.

inflection, n. inflection f.

inflict, vb. (penalty) infliger.

infliction, n. infliction f., châtiment m.

influence, n. influence f.

influential, adj. influent.

influenza, n. grippe f., influenza f.

inform, vb. (tell) informer.

informal, adj. (without formality) sans cérémonie.

informant, n. informateur m.

information, n. renseignements m.pl.

informative, adj. instructif.

informer, n. indicateur m.

infringe, vb. enfreindre, violer.

infuriate, vb. rendre furieux.

ingenious, adj. ingénieux.

ingenuity, n. ingéniosité f.

ingrained, adj. enraciné.

ingredient, n. ingrédient n.

inhabit, vb. habiter.

inhabitant, n. habitant m.

inhale, vb. inhaler, aspirer, humer.

inherent, adj. inhérent.

inherit, vb. hériter.

inheritance, n. héritage m.

inhibit, vb. empêcher; (psychology) inhiber.

inhibition, n. inhibition f., défense expresse f., prohibition f.

inhuman, adj. inhumain.

inimical, adj. ennemi, hostile, défavorable.

inimitable, adj. inimitable.

iniquity, n. iniquité f.

initial, 1. n. initiale f. 2. adj. initial. 3. vb. parafer.

initialize, vb. initialiser.

initiate, vb. (begin) commencer; (admit) initier.

initiation, n. commencement m., début m., initiation f.

initiative, n. initiative f.

inject, vb. injecter.

injection, n. injection f.

injunction, n. injonction f., ordre m.

injure, vb. (harm) nuire à; (wound) blesser; (damage) abîmer.

injurious, adj. (harmful) nuisible; (offensive) injurieux.

injury, n. (person) préjudice m.; (body) blessure f.; (thing) dommage m.

injustice, n. injustice f.

ink, n. encre f.

inland, adj. and n. intérieur m.

inlet, n. entrée f., admission f., débouché m.

inmate, n. habitant m., hôte m., pensionnaire m.

inn, n. auberge f.

innate, adj. inné.

inner, adj. intérieur.

inning, n. tour (m.) de batte.

innocence, n. innocence f.

innocent, adj. innocent.

innocuous, adj. inoffensif.

innovation, n. innovation f.

innuendo, n. insinuation f., allusion malveillante f.

innumerable, adj. innombrable.

inoculate, vb. inoculer.

inoculation, n. inoculation f., vaccination préventive f.

inoffensive, adj. inoffensif.

input, n. entrée (f.) (de données).

inquest, n. enquête f.

inquire (about), vb. se renseigner (sur).

inquiry, n. (investigation) recherche f.; (question) demande f.; (official) enquête f.

inquisition, *n.* Inquisition *f.*; enquête *f.*, recherche *f.*

inquisitive, *adj.* curieux, questionneur, indiscret.

inroad, *n.* incursion *f.*, invasion *f.*, empiètement *m.*

insane, *adj.* fou *m.*, folle *f.*

insanity, *n.* folie *f.*, insanité *f.*, démence *f.*

inscribe, *vb.* inscrire, graver.

inscription, *n.* inscription *f.*

insect, *n.* insecte *m.*

insecticide, *n.* insecticide *m.*

insecure, *adj.* peu sûr.

insensitive, *adj.* insensible.

inseparable, *adj.* inséparable.

insert, *vb.* insérer.

insertion, *n.* insertion *f.*

inside, 1. *n.* dedans *m.* **2.** *adj.* intérieur. **3.** *prep.* à l'intérieur de. **4.** *adv.* (en) dedans.

insidious, *adj.* insidieux.

insight, *n.* perspicacité *f.*, pénétration *f.*

insignia, *n.* insignes *m.pl.*

insignificance, *n.* insignifiance *f.*

insignificant, *adj.* insignifiant.

insinuate, *vb.* insinuer.

insinuation, *n.* insinuation *f.*

insipid, *adj.* insipide, fade.

insist, *vb.* insister.

insistence, *n.* insistance *f.*

insistent, *adj.* qui insiste, importun.

insolence, *n.* insolence *f.*

insolent, *adj.* insolent.

insomnia, *n.* insomnie *f.*

inspect, *vb.* examiner, inspecter.

inspection, *n.* inspection *f.*

inspector, *n.* inspecteur *m.*

inspiration, *n.* inspiration *f.*

inspire, *vb.* inspirer.

install, *vb.* installer.

installation, *n.* installation *f.*, montage *m.*

installment, *n.* acompte *m.*, versement partiel *m.*, paiement à compte *m.*

instance, *n.* exemple *m.*

instant, *n.* instant *m.*

instantaneous, *adj.* instantané.

instantly, *adv.* à l'instant.

instead, *adv.* au lieu de cela.

instead of, *prep.* au lieu de.

instigate, *vb.* instiguer.

instill, *vb.* instiller, faire pénétrer, inculquer.

instinct, *n.* instinct *m.*

instinctive, *adj.* instinctif.

institute, *vb.* instituer.

institution, *n.* institution *f.*

instruct, *vb.* instruire.

instruction, *n.* instruction *f.*

instructive, *adj.* instructif.

instructor, *n.* (*mil.*) instructeur *m.*; (university) chargé (*m.*) de cours.

instrument, *n.* instrument *m.*

instrumental, *adj.* instrumental, contributif (à).

insufferable, *adj.* insupportable, intolérable.

insufficient, *adj.* insuffisant.

insular, *adj.* insulaire.

insulate, *vb.* isoler.

insulation, *n.* isolement *m.*, isolation *f.*

insulator, *n.* isolant *m.*, isolateur *m.*

insulin, *n.* insuline *f.*

insult, 1. *vb.* insulter. **2.** *n.* insulte *f.*

insuperable, *adj.* insurmontable.

insurance, *n.* assurance *f.*

insure, *vb.* assurer.

insurgent, *adj. and n.* insurgé *m.*

insurrection, *n.* insurrection *f.*, soulèvement *m.*

intact, *adj.* intact.

intake, *n.* admission(s) *f.pl.*; (technical) prise *f.*

intangible, *adj.* intangible, impalpable.

integral, *adj.* intégrant.

integrate, *vb.* intégrer, compléter, rendre entier.

integrity, *n.* intégrité *f.*

intellect, *n.* (mind) esprit *m.*; (faculty) intellect *m.*

intellectual, *adj. and n.* intellectuel *m.*

intelligence, *n.* intelligence *f.*; (information) renseignements *m.pl.*

intelligent, *adj.* intelligent.

intelligentsia, *n.* l'intelligence *f.*

intelligible, *adj.* intelligible.

intend, *vb.* avoir l'intention de; (destine for) destiner à.

intense, *adj.* intense.

intensify, *vb.* intensifier.

intensity, *n.* intensité *f.*

intensive, adj. intensif.

intent, adj. (i. on) (absorbed in) absorbé dans; (determined to) déterminé à.

intention, n. intention f.

intentional, adj. intentionnel, voulu, fait exprès.

inter, vb. enterrer.

interact, vb. communiquer, avoir une action réciproque.

intercede, vb. intervenir, intercéder.

intercept, vb. intercepter, capter.

interchange, n. échange m.

intercom, n. interphone m.

intercourse, n. commerce m., relations f.pl., rapports m.pl.

interdict, vb. interdire, prohiber.

interest, 1. n. intérêt m. 2. vb. intéresser.

interesting, adj. intéressant.

interface, n. entreface f.

interfere, vb. (person) intervenir (dans); (i. with) (hinder) gêner.

interference, n. (person) intervention f.

interim, adv. entre temps, en attendant.

interior, adj. and n. intérieur m.

interject, vb. lancer, émettre.

interjection, n. interjection f.

interloper, n. intrus m.

interlude, n. intermède m., interlude m.

intermarry, vb. se marier.

intermediary, n. intermédiaire m.f.

intermediate, adj. and n. intermédiaire m.f.

interment, n. enterrement m.

intermission, n. interruption f., relâche f.; (theater) entr'acte m.

intermittent, adj. intermittent.

intern, 1. n. interne m. 2. vb. interner.

internal, adj. interne.

Internal Revenue Service, n. fisc m.

international, adj. international.

internationalism, n. internationalisme m.

interne, n. interne m.

interplay, n. effect (m.) réciproque, interaction f.

interpolate, vb. interpoler.

interpose, vb. interposer, tr.

interpret, vb. interpréter.

interpretation, n. interprétation f.

interpreter, n. interprète m.f.

interrogate, vb. interroger, questionner.

interrogation, n. interrogation f.

interrogative, 1. adj. interrogateur. 2. n. interrogatif m.

interrupt, vb. interrompre.

interruption, n. interruption f.

intersect, vb. entrecouper, intersecter, entrecroiser.

intersection, n. intersection f.

intersperse, vb. entremêler, parsemer, intercaler.

intertwine, vb. (s') entrelacer.

interval, n. intervalle m.

intervene, vb. intervenir.

intervention, n. intervention f.

interview, n. entrevue f.; (press) interview m.f.

intestine, n. intestin m.

intimacy, n. intimité f.

intimate, adj. intime.

intimidate, vb. intimider.

intimidation, n. intimidation f.

into, prep. en; (with art. or adj.) dans.

intonation, n. intonation f.

intone, vb. entonner, psalmodier.

intoxicate, vb. enivrer.

intoxication, n. intoxication f., ivresse f.

intractable, adj. très difficile.

intransigent, adj. intransigeant.

intravenous, adj. intraveineux.

intrepid, adj. intrépide, brave, courageux.

intricacy, n. complexité f., nature compliquée f.

intricate, adj. compliqué.

intrigue, n. intrigue f.

intrinsic, adj. intrinsèque.

introduce, vb. (bring in) introduire; (present) présenter.

introduction, n. introduction f.; (presenting) présentation f.

introductory, adj. introductoire, d'introduction.

introspection, n. introspection f., recueillement m.

introvert, n. introverti m.

intrude on, vb. importuner.

intruder, n. intrus m.

intuition, n. intuition f.

intuitive, *adj.* intuitif.

inundate, *vb.* inonder.

invade, *vb.* envahir.

invader, *n.* envahisseur *m.,* transgresseur *m.*

invalid, *adj. and n.* infirme *m.f.*

invaluable, *adj.* inestimable.

invariable, *adj.* invariable.

invasion, *n.* invasion *f.*

invective, *n.* invective *f.*

inveigle, *vb.* attirer, séduire, leurrer.

invent, *vb.* inventer.

invention, *n.* invention *f.*

inventive, *adj.* inventif, trouveur.

inventor, *n.* inventeur *m.*

inventory, *n.* inventaire *m.*

inverse, *adj.* inverse.

invertebrate, 1. *n.* invertébré *m.* **2.** *adj.* invertébré.

invest, *vb.* investir; (money) placer.

investigate, *vb.* faire des recherches (sur).

investigation, *n.* investigation *f.*

investment, *n.* placement *m.*

inveterate, *adj.* invétéré, enraciné.

invidious, *adj.* odieux, haïssable, ingrat.

invigorate, *vb.* fortifier, vivifier.

invincible, *adj.* invincible.

invisible, *adj.* invisible.

invitation, *n.* invitation *f.*

invite, *vb.* inviter.

invocation, *n.* invocation *f.*

invoice, *n.* facture *f.*

invoke, *vb.* invoquer.

involuntary, *adj.* involontaire.

involve, *vb.* (implicate) impliquer; (entail) entraîner.

invulnerable, *adj.* invulnérable.

inward, *adj.* intérieur.

iodine, *n.* iode *m.*

Iran, *n.* Iran *m.*

Iraq, *n.* Irak *m.,* Iraq *m.*

irate, *adj.* en colère, courroucé, furieux.

Ireland, *n.* Irlande *f.*

iridium, *n.* iridium *m.*

iris, *n.* iris *m.*

Irish, *adj.* irlandais.

Irishman, *n.* Irlandais *m.*

irk, *vb.* ennuyer.

iron, *n.* fer *m.*

ironworks, *n.* fonderie de fonte *f.,* usine métallurgique *f.*

irony, *n.* ironie *f.*

irrational, *adj.* irrationnel, déraisonnable, absurde.

irrefutable, *adj.* irréfutable, irrécusable.

irregular, *adj.* irrégulier.

irregularity, *n.* irrégularité *f.*

irrelevant, *adj.* non pertinent, hors de propos.

irresistible, *adj.* irrésistible.

irresponsible, *adj.* irresponsable.

irreverent, *adj.* irrévérent, irrévérencieux.

irrevocable, *adj.* irrévocable.

irrigate, *vb.* irriguer, arroser.

irrigation, *n.* irrigation *f.*

irritability, *n.* irritabilité *f.*

irritable, *adj.* irritable, irascible.

irritant, *n.* irritant *m.*

irritate, *vb.* irriter.

irritation, *n.* irritation *f.*

Islam, *n.* Islam *m.*

Islamic, *adj.* islamique.

island, *n.* île *f.*

isolate, *vb.* isoler.

isolation, *n.* isolement *m.*

isolationist, *n.* isolationniste *m.*

isosceles, *adj.* isoscèle.

Israel, *n.* Israël *m.*

Israeli 1. *n.* Israëlien *m.* **2.** *adj.* israëlien.

issuance, *n.* délivrance *f.*

issue, 1. *n.* (way out, end) issue *f.;* (result) résultat *m.;* (question) question *f.;* (publication) numéro *m.;* (money, bonds) émission *f.* **2.** *vb.* (come out) sortir; (publish) publier; (money) émettre.

isthmus, *n.* isthme *m.*

it, *pron.* (subject) il *m.;* elle *f.;* (object) le *m.,* la *f.;* (of it) en; (in it, to it) y.

Italian, 1. *n.* (person) Italien *m.;* (language) italien *m.* **2.** *adj.* italien.

italics, *n.* italique *m.*

Italy, *n.* Italie *f.*

itch, 1. *n.* démangeaison *f.* **2.** *vb.* démanger.

item, *n.* (article) article *m.;* (detail) détail *m.*

itemize, *vb.* détailler.

itinerant, *adj.* ambulant.
itinerary, *n.* itinéraire *m.*
its, 1. *adj.* son *m.,* sa *f.,* ses *pl.* **2.** *pron.* le sien *m.,* la sienne *f.*

itself, *pron.* lui-même *m.,* elle-même *f.;* (reflexive) se.
ivory, *n.* ivoire *m.*
ivy, *n.* lierre *m.*

J

jab, *n.* coup *m.,* coup sec *m.* **2.** *vb.* piquer, donner un coup sec.
jackal, *n.* chacal *m.*
jackass, *n.* âne *m.,* idiot *m.*
jacket, *n.* (man) veston *m.;* (woman) jaquette *f.*
jackknife, *n.* couteau (*m.*) de poche.
jack-of-all-trades, *n.* maître Jacques *m.,* factotum *m.,* homme (*m.*) à tous les métiers.
jade, *n.* (horse) rosse *f.,* haridelle *f.;* (woman) drôlesse *f.,* coureuse *f.;* (mineral) jade *m.*
jaded, *adj.* surmené, éreinté, blasé, fatigué.
jagged, *adj.* déchiqueté, entaillé, dentelé.
jaguar, *n.* jaguar *m.*
jail, *n.* prison *f.*
jailer, *n.* gardien *m.,* geôlier *m.*
jam, 1. *n.* foule *f.,* presse *f.;* (traffic) embouteillage *m.;* (food) confiture *f.* **2.** *vb.* serrer, presser.
Jamaica, *n.* Jamaïque *f.*
jamb, *n.* jambage *m.,* montant *m.,* chambranle *m.*
jangle, 1. *n.* cliquetis *m.* **2.** *vb.* cliqueter.
janitor, *n.* concierge *m.*
January, *n.* janvier *m.*
Japan, *n.* Japon *m.*
Japanese, 1. *n.* (person) Japonais *m.;* (language) japonais *m.* **2.** *adj.* japonais.
jar, 1. *n.* (container) pot *m.;* (sound) son (*m.*) discordant; (shock) secousse *f.* **2.** *vb.* secouer, heurter.
jargon, *n.* jargon *m.*
jasmine, *n.* jasmin *m.*
jaundice, *n.* jaunisse *f.*
jaunt, *n.* petite excursion *f.,* balade *f.*
javelin, *n.* javelot *m.,* javeline *f.*

jaw, *n.* mâchoire *f.*
jay, *n.* geai *m.*
jaywalk, *vb.* se promener d'une façon distraite ou imprudente.
jazz, *n.* jazz *m.*
jealous, *adj.* jaloux.
jealousy, *n.* jalousie *f.*
jeans, *n.* jeans *m.pl.*
jeer, 1. *n.* raillerie *f.;* moquerie *f.,* huée *f.* **2.** *vb.* se moquer de, huer.
jelly, *n.* gelée *f.*
jellyfish, *n.* méduse *f.*
jeopardize, *vb.* exposer au danger, mettre en danger, hasarder.
jeopardy, *n.* danger *m.,* péril *m.*
jerk, *n.* saccade *f.;* (person) pauvre type *m.*
jerkin, *n.* justaucorps *m.,* pourpoint *m.*
jerky, *adj.* saccadé, coupé.
jersey, *n.* jersey *m.,* tricot (*m.*) de laine.
Jerusalem, *n.* Jérusalem *f.*
jest, 1. plaisanterie *f.,* raillerie *f.,* badinage *m.* **2.** *vb.* plaisanter, railler, badiner.
jester, *n.* railleur *m.,* farceur *m.,* bouffon *m.*
Jesuit, *n.* jésuite *m.*
Jesus, *n.* Jésus *m.*
jet, *n.* (mineral) jais *m.;* (water, gas) jet *m.;* (**j. plane**) avion (*m.*) à réaction.
jet lag, *n.* (réaction au) décalage (*m.*) horaire.
jetsam, *n.* épaves *f.pl.*
jettison, *vb.* se délester.
jetty, *n.* jetée *f.,* môle *m.*
Jew, *n.* Juif *m.,* Juive *f.*
jewel, *n.* bijou *m.*
jeweler, *n.* bijoutier *m.,* jouaillier *m.*
jewelry, *n.* bijouterie *f.*
Jewish, *adj.* juif *m.,* juive *f.*
jib, *n.* foc *m.*

jibe, vb. être en accord, s'accorder.

jiffy, n. instant m., clin d'œil m.

jig, 1. n. gigue f.; calibre m., gabarit m. **2.** vb. danser la gigue, sautiller.

jilt, vb. délaisser, plaquer, planter.

jingle, 1. n. tintement m., cliquetis m. **2.** vb. tinter, cliqueter.

jinx, n. porte-malheur m.

jittery, adj. très nerveux.

job, n. (work) travail m.; (employment) emploi m.

jobber, n. intermédiaire m., marchandeur m., sous-traitant m.

jockey, n. jockey m.

jocular, adj. facétieux, jovial, rieur.

jocund, adj. enjoué.

jodhpurs, n. pantalon (m.) d'équitation.

jog, 1. n. coup m., secousse f., cahot m. **2.** vb. pousser, secouer, cahoter; faire du jogging.

jogging, n. jogging m.

joggle, 1. n. petite secousse f. **2.** vb. secouer légèrement.

join, vb. (things) joindre; (group, etc.) se joindre à.

joiner, n. menuisier m.

joint, 1. n. joint m.; (anatomy) articulation f. **2.** adj. (in common) commun; (in partnership) co-.

jointly, adv. ensemble, conjointement.

joist, n. solive f., poutre f.

joke, 1. n. plaisanterie f. **2.** vb. plaisanter.

joker, n. farceur m., blagueur m.; joker m.

jolly, adj. joyeux.

jolt, 1. n. cahot m., choc m., secousse f. **2.** vb. cahoter, secouer, ballotter.

jonquil, n. jonquille f.

Jordan, n. Jordanie f.

jostle, vb. coudoyer tr.

jot, vb. **(j. down)** noter.

jounce, 1. n. cahot m., secousse f. **2.** vb. cahoter.

journal, n. journal m.

journalism, n. journalisme m.

journalist, n. journaliste m.f.

journey, 1. n. voyage m. **2.** vb. voyager.

journeyman, n. compagnon m.

jovial, adj. jovial, gai.

jowl, n. mâchoire f.

joy, n. joie f.

joyful, adj. joyeux.

joyous, adj. joyeux.

joystick, n. manette f.

jubilant, adj. réjoui, jubilant, exultant.

jubilee, n. jubilé m.

Judaism, n. judaïsme m.

judge, 1. n. juge m. **2.** vb. juger.

judgment, n. jugement m.

judicial, adj. judiciaire.

judiciary, adj. judiciaire.

judicious, adj. judicieux, sensé.

jug, n. cruche f.

juggle, vb. jongler.

jugular, adj. jugulaire.

juice, n. jus m.

juicy, adj. juteux.

July, n. juillet m.

jumble, 1. n. brouillamini m., fouillis m., fatras m. **2.** vb. brouiller, mêler confusément.

jump, n. saut m. **2.** vb. sauter.

jumper cables, n. câbles (m.pl.) de démarrage.

jumpy, adj. nerveux.

junction, n. jonction f.; (rail) embranchement m.

juncture, n. jointure f., jonction f., conjoncture f.

June, n. juin m.

jungle, n. jungle f., brousse f.

junior, adj. and n. (age) cadet m.; (rank) subalterne m.

juniper, n. genévrier m., genièvre m.

junk, n. (waste) rebut m.

junket, n. jonchée f.; festin m.; partie de plaisir f.

jurisdiction, n. juridiction f.

jurisprudence, n. jurisprudence f.

jurist, n. juriste m., légiste m.

juror, n. juré m., membre du jury m.

jury, n. jury m.

just, 1. adj. juste. **2.** adv. (exactly) juste; (barely) à peine; **(have j.)** venir de.

justice, n. justice f.

justifiable, adj. justifiable, justifié.

justification, n. justification f.

justify, vb. justifier.
jut, vb. être en saillie.

jute, n. jute m.
juvenile. adj. juvénile.

K

kale, n. chou m.
kaleidoscope, n. kaléidoscope m.
kangaroo, n. kangourou m.
karakul, n. karakul m., caracul m.
karat, n. carat m.
karate, n. karaté m.
keel, n. quille f.
keen, adj. (edge) aiguisé; (pain, point) aigu; (look, mind) pénétrant; (k. on) enthousiaste de.
keep, vb. tenir; (reserve, protect, retain) garder; (remain) rester; (continue) continuer à.
keeper, n. gardien m.
keepsake, n. souvenir m.
keg, n. caque f., barillet m., tonnelet m.
kennel, n. chenil m.
Kenya, n. Kenya m.
kerchief, n. fichu m., mouchoir m.
kernel, n. (grain) grain m.; (nut) amande f.; (fig.) noyau m.
kerosene, n. pétrole m.
ketchup, n. sauce (f.) piquante à base de tomates.
kettle, n. bouilloire f.
kettledrum, n. timbale f.
key, n. clef, clé f.; (piano, typewriter) touche f.
keyboard, n. clavier m.
keyhole, n. entrée (f.) de clef.
khaki, n. kaki m.
kick, 1. n. coup (m.) de pied; (gun) recul m. **2.** vb. donner un coup de pied à.
kid, n. (animal, skin) chevreau m.; (child) gosse m.f.
kidnap, vb. enlever de vive force.
kidnapper, n. auteur (m.) de l'enlèvement, ravisseur m.
kidney, n. rein m.; (food) rognon m.
kidney bean, n. haricot nain m.
kill, vb. tuer.
killer, n. tueur m., meurtrier m.
killing, n. meurtre m.
kiln, n. four (céramique) m., séchoir m.
kilobyte, n. kilo-octet m.

kilocycle, n. kilocycle m.
kilogram, n. kilogramme m.
kilohertz, n. kilohertz m.
kilowatt, n. kilowatt m.
kilt, n. kilt m.
kimono, n. kimono m.
kin, n. (relation) parent m.
kind, 1. n. genre m. **2.** adj. aimable.
kindergarten, n. jardin (m.) d'enfants, école maternelle f.
kindle, vb. allumer, tr.
kindling, n. allumage m., bois d'allumage m.
kindly, adv. avec bonté.
kindness, n. bonté f.
kindred, 1. n. parenté f., affinité f. **2.** adj. analogue.
kinetic, adj. cinétique.
king, n. roi m.
kingdom, n. royaume m.
kink, 1. n. nœud m., tortillement m. **2.** vb. se nouer.
kinky, adj. excentrique.
kiosk, n. kiosque m.
kipper, n. kipper m., hareng (m.) légèrement salé et fumé.
kiss, 1. n. baiser m. **2.** vb. embrasser.
kitchen, n. cuisine f.
kite, n. cerf-volant m.
kitten, n. petit chat m.
kitty, n. (money) cagnotte f.
kleptomania, n. kleptomanie f.
kleptomaniac, n. kleptomane m.
knack, n. tour de main m., talent m., truc m.
knapsack, n. havresac m.
knead, vb. pétrir, malaxer.
knee, n. genou m.
kneecap, n. genouillère f.
kneel, vb. s'agenouiller.
knell, n. glas m.
knickers, n. pantalon m.; (underwear) culotte f.
knife, n. couteau m.
knight, n. chevalier m.
knit, vb. (with needles) tricoter.
knob, n. bouton m.
knock, 1. n. coup m. **2.** vb. frapper.

knot, *n.* nœud *m.*

knotty, *adj.* plein de nœuds.

know, *vb.* savoir; (be acquainted with) connaître.

knowledge, *n.* connaissance *f.*; (learning) savoir *m.*

knuckle, *n.* articulation *(f.)* du doigt, jointure *(f.)* du doigt.

Kodak, *n.* kodak *m.*

Koran, *n.* Coran *m.*

Korea, *n.* Corée *f.*

Kosher, *adj.* kascher.

L

lab, *n.* labo *m.*

label, *n.* étiquette *f.*

labor, 1. *n.* travail *m.*; (workers) ouvriers *m.pl.* **2.** *vb.* peiner.

laboratory, *n.* laboratoire *m.*

laborer, *n.* travailleur *m.*

laborious, *adj.* laborieux.

labor union, *n.* syndicat *m.*

laburnum, *n.* cytise *m.*

labyrinth, *n.* labyrinthe *m.*

lace, *n.* dentelle *f.*; (string) lacet *m.*

lacerate, *vb.* lacérer, déchirer.

laceration, *n.* lacération *f.*

lack, 1. *n.* manque *m.* **2.** *vb.* manquer de.

lackadaisical, *adj.* affecté.

laconic, *adj.* laconique.

lacquer, *n.* vernis-laque *m.*

lactic, *adj.* lactique.

lactose, *n.* lactose *f.*

lacy, *adj.* de dentelle.

ladder, *n.* échelle *f.*

ladle, *n.* cuiller *(f.)* à pot.

lady, *n.* dame *f.*

ladybug, *n.* coccinelle *f.*

lag behind, *vb.* rester en arrière.

lagoon, *n.* lagune *f.*

laid-back, *adj.* décontracté.

lair, *n.* tanière *f.*, repaire *m.*

laissez faire, *n.* laisser-faire *m.*

laity, *n.* les laïques *m.pl.*

lake, *n.* lac *m.*

lamb, *n.* agneau *m.*

lame, *adj.* boiteux.

lament, *vb.* se lamenter (sur); (mourn) pleurer.

lamentable, *adj.* lamentable, déplorable.

lamentation, *n.* lamentation *f.*

laminate, *vb.* laminer, écacher.

lamp, *n.* lampe *f.*

lampoon, 1. *n.* pasquinade *f.*, satire *f.* **2.** *vb.* lancer des satires.

lance, *n.* lance *f.*

land, 1. *n.* terre *f.* **2.** *vb.* (boat) débarquer; (plane) atterrir.

landholder, *n.* propriétaire foncier *m.*

landing, *n.* débarquement *m.*, mise à terre *f.*

landlord, *n.* propriétaire *m.f.*

landmark, *n.* borne *f.*

landscape, *n.* paysage *m.*

landslide, *n.* éboulement *m.*

landward, *adv.* vers la terre.

lane, *n.* (country) sentier *m.*; (town) ruelle *f.*; (highway) voie *f.*

language, *n.* langue *f.*; (form of expression) langage *m.*

languid, *adj.* languissant.

languish, *vb.* languir.

languor, *n.* langueur *f.*

lanky, *adj.* grand et maigre.

lanolin, *n.* lanoline *f.*

lantern, *n.* lanterne *f.*

lap, *n.* (of body) genoux *m.pl.*; (of track) tour *(m.)* (de piste).

lapel, *n.* revers *m.*

lapin, *n.* lapin *m.*

lapse, 1. *n.* (of time) laps *m.*; (error) faute *f.* **2.** *vb.* passer.

laptop computer, *n.* portable *m.*

larceny, *n.* larcin *m.*, vol *m.*

lard, *n.* saindoux *m.*

large, *adj.* grand.

largely, *adv.* en grande partie.

largo, *n.* largo *m.*

lariat, *n.* lasso *m.*

lark, *n.* alouette *f.*

larkspur, *n.* pied d'alouette *m.*, delphinium *m.*

larva, *n.* larve *f.*

laryngitis, *n.* laryngite *f.*

larynx, *n.* larynx *m.*

lascivious, *adj.* lascif.

laser, *n.* laser *m.*

lash, 1. *n.* (whip) lanière *f.*; (blow)

coup (m.) de fouet. 2. vb. fouetter.

lass, n. jeune fille f.

lassitude, n. lassitude f.

lasso, n. lasso m.

last, 1. adj. dernier; (at l.) enfin. **2.** vb. durer.

lasting. adj. durable.

latch, n. loquet m.

late, adj. and adv. (on in day, etc.) tard; (after due time) en retard; (dead) feu; (recent) dernier.

latecomer, n. retardataire m.

lately, adv. dernièrement.

latent, adj. latent, caché.

lateral, adj. latéral.

lath, n. latte f.

lathe, n. tour m.

lather, n. (soap) mousse f.; (horse) écume f.

Latin, 1. n. (person) Latin m.; (language) latin m. **2.** adj. latin.

Latin America, n. Amérique (f.) latine.

latitude, n. latitude f.

latrine, n. latrine f.

latter, adj. and pron. dernier.

lattice, n. treillis m.

laud, vb. louer.

laudable, adj. louable.

laudanum, n. laudanum m.

laudatory, adj. élogieux.

laugh, n. rire m.

laugh (at), vb. rire (de).

laughable, adj. risible.

laughter, n. rire m.

launch, 1. n. (boat) chaloupe f. **2.** vb. lancer, tr.

launder, vb. blanchir.

launderette, n. buanderie f., laverie (f.) (automatique).

laundry, n. (works) blanchisserie f.; (washing) lessive f.

laundryman, n. blanchisseur m.

laureate, adj. and n. lauréat m.f.

laurel, n. laurier m.

lava, n. lave f.

lavaliere, n. lavallière f.

lavatory, n. lavabo m.; cabinet (m.) de toilette.

lavender, n. lavande f.

lavish, 1. adj. (person) prodigue; (thing) somptueux. **2.** vb. prodiguer.

law, n. loi f.; (jurisprudence) droit m.

law court, n. tribunal m.

lawful, adj. légal.

lawless, adj. sans loi.

lawn, n. pelouse f.

lawsuit, n. procès m.

lawyer, n. (counselor) avocat m.; (attorney) avoué m.; (jurist) jurisconsulte m.

lax, adj. lâche, mou, relâché.

laxative, n. laxatif m.

laxity, n. relâchement m.

lay, 1. vb. poser; (l. off) licencier. **2.** adj. laïque.

layer, n. couche f.

layman, n. laïque m.

lazy, adj. paresseux.

lead, 1. n. plomb m.; (pencil) mine f. **2.** vb. mener, conduire.

leaden, adj. de plomb.

leader, n. chef m.

leading, adj. principal.

lead pencil, n. crayon (m.) à la mine de plomb.

leaf, n. feuille f.

leaflet, n. feuillet m.

leafy, adj. feuillu.

league, n. (compact) ligue f.; (measure) lieue f.

League of Nations, n. La Société (f.) des Nations.

leak, 1. n. (liquid) fuite f.; (boat) voie (f.) d'eau. **2.** vb. fuir; faire eau.

leakage, n. fuite d'eau f.

leaky, adj. qui coule, qui fait eau.

lean, 1. adj. maigre. **2.** vb. intr. (l. against) s'appuyer sur; (stoop) se pencher. **3.** vb., tr., appuyer.

leap, vb. sauter.

leap year, n. année bissextile f.

learn, vb. apprendre.

learned, adj. savant, docte.

learning, n. science f., instruction f., érudition f.

lease, n. bail m.

leash, n. laisse f., attache f.

least, 1. n. moins m. **2.** adj. (le) moindre. **3.** adv. (le) moins.

leather, n. cuir m.

leathery, adj. coriace.

leave, 1. n. permission f. **2.** vb. laisser; (go away from) quitter.

leaven, 1. *n.* levain *m.* 2. *vb.* faire lever, modifier.

Lebanon, *n.* Liban *m.*

lecherous, *adj.* lascif, libertin.

lecture, *n.* conférence *f.*

lecturer, *n.* conférencier *m.*

ledge, *n.* bord *m.*; (of rocks) chaîne *f.*

ledger, *n.* grand livre *m.*

lee, *n.* côté (*m.*) sous le vent.

leech, *n.* sangsue *f.*

leek, *n.* poireau *m.*

leer, 1. *n.* œillade *f.*, regard de côté *m.* 2. *vb.* lorgner.

leeward, *adj. and adv.* sous le vent.

left, *adj. and adv.* gauche *f.*; (on, to the l.) à gauche.

leftist, *n.* gaucher *m.*; (politics) gauchiste *m.*

left wing, *n.* l'aile gauche *f.*; (politics) la gauche.

leg, *n.* (man, horse) jambe *f.*; (most animals) patte *f.*

legacy, *n.* legs *m.*

legal, *adj.* légal.

legalize, *vb.* rendre légal.

legation, *n.* légation *f.*

legend, *n.* légende *f.*

legendary, *adj.* légendaire.

legible, *adj.* lisible.

legion, *n.* légion *f.*

legislate, *vb.* faire les lois.

legislation, *n.* législation *f.*

legislator, *n.* législateur *m.*

legislature, *n.* législature *f.*

legitimate, *adj.* légitime.

legume, *n.* légume *m.*

leisure, *n.* loisir *m.*

leisurely, *adv.* à loisir.

lemon, *n.* citron *m.*

lemonade, *n.* citron (*m.*) pressé.

lend, *vb.* prêter.

length, *n.* (dimension) longueur *f.*; (time) durée *f.*

lengthen, *vb.* allonger, *tr.*

lengthwise, *adv.* en long.

lengthy, *adj.* assez long.

lenient, *adj.* indulgent.

lens, *n.* lentille *f.*; (camera) objectif *m.*

Lent, *n.* carême *m.*

Lenten, *adj.* de carême.

lentil, *n.* lentille *f.*

lento, *adv.* lento.

leopard, *n.* léopard *m.*

leotard, *n.* maillot (*m.*) (de danseur, etc.).

leper, *n.* lépreux *m.*

leprosy, *n.* lèpre *f.*

lesbian, 1. *adj.* lesbien 2. *n.* lesbienne *f.*; tribade *f.*

lesion, *n.* lésion *f.*

less, 1. *adj.* (smaller) moindre; (not so much) moins de. 2. *adv.* (l. than) moins (de).

lessen, *vb.* diminuer.

lesser, *adj.* moindre.

lesson, *n.* leçon *f.*

lest, *conj.* de peur que . . . (ne).

let, *vb.* laisser; (lease) louer.

letdown, *n.* déception *f.*

lethal, *adj.* mortel.

lethargic, *adj.* léthargique.

lethargy, *n.* léthargie *f.*

letter, *n.* lettre *f.*

letterhead, *n.* en-tête de lettre *m.*

lettuce, *n.* laitue *f.*

leukemia, *n.* leucémie *f.*

levee, *n.* lever *m.*

level, 1. *adj.* (flat) égal; (l. with) au niveau de. 2. *n.* niveau *m.*

lever, *n.* levier *m.*

levity, *n.* légèreté *f.*

levy, 1. *n.* levée *f.* 2. *vb.* lever.

lewd, *adj.* impudique.

lexicon, *n.* lexique *m.*

liability, *n.* responsabilité *f.*

liable, *adj.* (responsible for) responsable de; (subject to) sujet à.

liar, *n.* menteur *m.*

libation, *n.* libation *f.*

libel, *n.* diffamation *f.*

libelous, *adj.* diffamatoire.

liberal, *adj.* libéral; (generous) généreux.

liberalism, *n.* libéralisme *m.*

liberality, *n.* libéralité *f.*

liberate, *vb.* libérer.

liberation, *n.* libération *f.*

libertine, 1. *n.* libre-penseur *m.* 2. *adj.* libertin.

liberty, *n.* liberté *f.*

libidinous, *adj.* libidineux.

libido, *n.* libido *m.*

librarian, *n.* bibliothécaire *m.f.*

library, *n.* bibliothèque *f.*

libretto, *n.* livret *m.*

Libya, *n.* Libye *f.*

license, *n.* permis *m.*; (tradesmen)

patente *f.*; (abuse of freedom) licence *f.*

licentious, *adj.* licencieux.

lick, *vb.* lécher.

licorice, *n.* réglisse *f.*

lid, *n.* couvercle *m.*

lie, 1. *n.* mensonge *m.* **2.** *vb.* (fib) mentir; (recline) être couché; (l. down) se coucher; (be situated) se trouver.

lien, *n.* privilège *m.*

lieutenant, *n.* lieutenant *m.*

life, *n.* vie *f.*

lifeboat, *n.* bateau *(m.)* de sauvetage.

life buoy, *n.* bouée *(f.)* de sauvetage.

lifeguard, *n.* maître-nageur *m.*

life insurance, *n.* assurance-vie *f.*

lifeless, *adj.* sans vie.

life preserver, *n.* appareil *(m.)* de sauvetage.

life sentence, *n.* condamnation *(f.)* à perpétuité.

life style, *n.* manière de vivre *f.*

life-support system, *n.* respirateur *(m.)* artificiel.

lifetime, *n.* vie *f.*, vivant *m.*

lift, *vb.* lever.

ligament, *n.* ligament *m.*

ligature, *n.* ligature *f.*

light, 1. *n.* lumière *f.* **2.** *adj.* (not heavy) léger; (not dark) clair. **3.** *vb.* allumer, *tr.*

lighten, *vb.* (relieve) alléger, *tr.*; (brighten) éclairer, *tr.*

lighter, *n.* (cigarette) briquet *m.*

lighthouse, *n.* phare *m.*

lighting, *n.* éclairage *m.*

lightly, *adv.* légèrement.

lightness, *n.* légèreté *f.*

lightning, *n.* (flash of) éclair *m.*

lightweight, 1. *adj.* léger. **2.** *n.* (boxing) poids *(m.)* léger.

lignite, *n.* lignite *m.*

likable, *adj.* agréable.

like, 1. *adj.* pareil. **2.** *vb.* aimer; plaire à. **3.** *prep.* comme.

likelihood, *n.* probabilité *f.*

likely, *adj.* probable.

liken, *vb.* comparer.

likeness, *n.* ressemblance *f.*

likewise, *adv.* de même.

lilac, *n.* lilas *m.*

lilt, 1. *n.* forte cadence *f.* **2.** *vb.* chanter gaiement.

lily, *n.* lis *m.*; (l. of the valley) muguet *m.*

limb, *n.* membre *m.*; (tree) grosse branche *f.*

limber, 1. *adj.* souple, flexible. **2.** *vb.* assouplir.

limbo, *n.* limbes *m.pl.*

lime, *n.* (mineral) chaux *f.*; (tree) tilleul *m.*; (fruit) lime *f.*, citron *(m.)* vert.

limelight, *n.* lumière oxhydrique *f.*

limestone, *n.* pierre à chaux *f.*, calcaire *m.*

limewater, *n.* eau de chaux *f.*

limit, 1. *n.* limite *f.* **2.** *vb.* limiter.

limitation, *n.* limitation *f.*

limitless, *adj.* sans limite, sans bornes.

limousine, *n.* limousine *f.*

limp, 1. *adj.* flasque. **2.** *vb.* boiter.

limpid, *adj.* limpide.

linden, *n.* tilleul *m.*

line, *n.* ligne *f.*

lineage, *n.* lignée *f.*, race *f.*

lineal, *adj.* linéaire.

linen, *n.* (cloth) toile *f.*; (sheets, etc.) linge *m.*

linger, *n.* s'attarder.

lingerie, *n.* lingerie *f.*

linguist, *n.* linguiste *m.f.*

linguistic, *adj.* linguistique.

linguistics, *n.* linguistique *f.*

liniment, *n.* liniment *m.*

lining, *n.* (clothes) doublure *f.*

link, 1. *n.* (chain) chaînon *m.*; (fig.) lien *m.* **2.** *vb.* (re)lier.

linoleum, *n.* linoléum *m.*

linseed, *n.* graine *(f.)* de lin.

lint, *n.* charpie *f.*

lion, *n.* lion *m.*

lip, *n.* lèvre *f.*

lipstick, *n.* rouge *(m.)* à lèvres.

liquefy, *vb.* liquéfier.

liqueur, *n.* liqueur *f.*

liquid, *adj. and n.* liquide *m.*

liquidate, *vb.* liquider.

liquidation, *n.* liquidation *f.*, acquittement *m.*

liquor, *n.* boisson *(f.)* alcoolique.

lisp, *vb.* zézayer.

list, 1. *n.* liste *f.* **2.** *vb.* enregistrer.

listen (to), *vb.* écouter.

listless, *adj.* inattentif.

litany, n. litanie f.

literacy, n. degré (m.) d'aptitude à lire et à écrire.

literal, adj. littéral.

literary, adj. littéraire.

literate, adj. lettré.

literature, n. littérature f.

lithe, adj. flexible, pliant.

lithograph, vb. lithographier.

lithography, n. lithographie f.

litigant, n. plaideur m.

litigation, n. litige m.

litmus, n. tournesol m.

litter, n. (vehicle, animals' bedding) litière f.; (disorder) fouillis m.; (animals' young) portée f.

little, 1. n. and adv. peu m. **2.** adj. (small) petit; (not much) peu (de).

liturgical, adj. liturgique.

liturgy, n. liturgie f.

live, vb. vivre.

livelihood, n. vie f., subsistance f., gagne-pain m.

lively, adj. vif m., vive f.

liven, vb. animer, activer.

liver, n. foie m.

livery, n. livrée f.

livestock, n. bétail m.

livid, adj. livide, blême.

lizard, n. lézard m.

llama, n. lama m.

lo, interj. voilà.

load, 1. n. (cargo) charge f.; (burden) fardeau m. **2.** vb. charger.

loaf, 1. n. pain m. **2.** vb. flâner.

loafer, n. fainéant m.

loam, n. terre grasse f.

loan, 1. n. (thing) prêt m.; (borrowing) emprunt m. **2.** vb. prêter.

loath, adj. fâché, peiné.

loathe, vb. détester.

loathing, n. dégoût m.

loathsome, adj. dégoûtant.

lobby, 1. n. (hall) vestibule m.; (politics) groupe (m.) de pression. **2.** vb. faire pression sur.

lobe, n. lobe m.

lobster, n. homard m.

local, adj. local.

locale, n. localité f., scène f.

locality, n. localité f.

localize, vb. localiser.

locate, vb. localiser.

location, n. placement m.

lock, 1. n. (door) serrure f.; (hair) mèche f. **2.** vb. fermer à clef.

locker, n. armoire f.; (baggage) consigne automatique f.

locket, n. médaillon m.

lockjaw, n. tétanos m.

locksmith, n. serrurier m.

locomotion, n. locomotion f.

locomotive, n. locomotive f.

locust, n. sauterelle f.

locution, n. locution f.

lode, n. filon m.

lodge, vb. loger.

lodger, n. locataire m.

lodging, n. logement m.

loft, n. grenier m.

lofty, adj. élevé; (proud) hautain.

log, n. (wood) bûche f.; (boat) loch m.

logarithm, n. logarithme m.

loge, n. loge f.

logic, n. logique f.

logical, adj. logique.

logo, n. emblème m.

loins, n. reins m.pl.

loiter, vb. flâner.

lollipop, n. sucre d'orge m., sucette f.

London, n. Londres m.

lone, lonely, lonesome, adj. solitaire.

loneliness, n. solitude f.

long, 1. adj. long m., longue f. **2.** adv. longtemps.

longevity, n. longévité f.

long for, vb. désirer ardemment.

longing, n. désir ardent m.

longitude, n. longitude f.

longitudinal, adj. longitudinal.

look, 1. n. regard m.; aspect m. **2.** vb. (l. at) regarder; (l. for) chercher; (l. after) soigner; (seem) paraître.

looking glass, n. miroir m.

loom, 1. n. métier m. **2.** vb. se dessiner.

loop, n. boucle f.

loophole, n. meurtrière f., échappatoire f.

loose, adj. (not tight) lâche; (detached) détaché; (morals) relâché.

loosen, vb. desserrer.

loot, 1. n. butin m. **2.** vb. piller.

lop, vb. élaguer, ébrancher.

loquacious, adj. loquace.

lord, n. seigneur m.; (title) lord m.

lordship, n. seigneurie f.

lorgnette, n. lorgnette f.

lose, vb. perdre.

loss, n. perte f.

lot, n. (fortune) sort m.; (land) terrain m.; (much) beaucoup.

lotion, n. lotion f.

lottery, n. loterie f.

lotus, n. lotus m., lotos m.

loud, adj. fort; (noisy) bruyant. 2. adv. haut.

loudspeaker, n. haut-parleur m.

lounge, 1. n. sofa m.; hall m. 2. vb. flâner.

louse, n. pou m.

lout, n. rustre m.

louver, n. auvent m.

lovable, adj. aimable.

love, 1. n. amour m. 2. vb. aimer.

love affair, n. liaison (f.) amoureuse.

lovely, adj. beau m., belle f.

lover, n. amoureux m.

low, adj. bas m., basse f.

lowboy, n. commode basse f.

lowbrow, adj. peu intellectuel.

lower, vb. baisser.

lowly, adj. humble.

loyal, adj. loyal.

loyalist, n. loyaliste m.f.

loyalty, n. loyauté f.

lozenge, n. pastille f.

lubricant, n. lubrifiant m.

lubricate, vb. lubrifier.

lucid, adj. lucide.

luck, n. chance f.

lucky, adj. (person) heureux.

lucrative, adj. lucratif.

ludicrous, adj. risible.

lug, vb. traîner, tirer.

luggage, n. bagages m.pl.

lukewarm, adj. tiède.

lull, n. moment (m.) de calme.

lullaby, n. berceuse f.

lumbago, n. lumbago m.

lumber, n. bois (m.) de charpente.

luminous, adj. lumineux.

lump, 1. n. (gros) morceau m. 2. vb. (l. together) mettre en tas.

lumpy, adj. grumeleux.

lunacy, n. folie f.

lunar, adj. lunaire.

lunatic, n. aliéné m.

lunch, 1. n. déjeuner m. 2. vb. déjeuner.

luncheon, n. déjeuner m.

lung, n. poumon m.

lunge, 1. n. botte f. 2. vb. se fendre.

lurch, 1. n. embardée f. 2. vb. faire une embardée.

lure, vb. (animal) leurrer; (attract) attirer.

lurid, adj. blafard, sombre.

lurk, vb. se cacher, rôder.

luscious, adj. délicieux.

lush, adj. luxuriant.

lust, n. luxure f.

luster, n. lustre m.

lustful, adj. lascif, sensuel.

lustrous, adj. brillant, lustré.

lusty, adj. vigoureux.

lute, n. luth m.

Lutheran, n. Luthérien m.

Luxemburg, n. Luxembourg m.

luxuriant, adj. exubérant.

luxurious, adj. (thing) luxueux.

luxury, n. luxe m.

lying, n. mensonge m.

lymph, n. lymphe f.

lynch, vb. lyncher.

lyre, n. lyre f.

lyric, adj. lyrique.

lyricism, n. lyrisme m.

lyrics, n. (of song) paroles f.pl.

M

macaroni, n. macaroni m.

machine, n. machine f.

machine gun, n. mitrailleuse f.

machinery, n. machines f.pl.; (fig.) mécanisme m.

machinist, n. machiniste m.

machismo, n. phallocratie f.

macho, 1. adj. phallocrate, macho. 2. n. homme phallocrate.

mackerel, n. maquereau m.

mackinaw, n. mackinaw m.

macrobiotic, adj. macrobiotique.

mad, adj. fou m., folle f.

madness, n. folie f.

Madagascar, n. Madagascar m.

madam, n. madame f.

madcap, n. and adj. écervelé.

madden, vb. exaspérer.

made, *adj.* fait, fabriqué.

mafia, *n.* mafia *f.*

magazine, *n.* revue *f.*

maggot, *n.* ver *m.*

magic, **1.** *n.* magie *f.* **2.** *adj.* magique.

magician, *n.* magicien *m.*

magistrate, *n.* magistrat *m.*

magnanimous, *adj.* magnanime.

magnate, *n.* magnat *m.*

magnesium, *n.* magnésium *m.*

magnet, *n.* aimant *m.*

magnetic, *adj.* magnétique.

magnificence, *n.* magnificence *f.*

magnificent, *adj.* magnifique.

magnify, *vb.* grossir.

magnitude, *n.* grandeur *f.*

mahogany, *n.* acajou *m.*

maid, *n.* (servant) bonne *f.*; (old m.) vieille fille *f.*

maiden, *adj.* de jeune fille.

mail, **1.** *n.* courrier *m.* **2.** *vb.* envoyer par la poste.

mailbox, *n.* boîte (*f.*) aux lettres.

mail carrier, mailman, *n.* facteur *m.*

maim, *vb.* estropier, mutiler.

main, *adj.* principal.

mainframe, *n.* unité centrale (d'un informateur) *f.*

mainland, *n.* terre (*f.*) ferme.

mainly, *adv.* surtout.

mainspring, *n.* grand ressort *m.*; mobile essentiel *m.*

maintain, *vb.* maintenir; (support) soutenir.

maintenance, *n.* entretien *m.*

maize, *n.* maïs *m.*

majestic, *adj.* majestueux.

majesty, *n.* majesté *f.*

major, **1.** *n.* (*mil.*) commandant *m.*; (school) sujet (*m.*) principal. **2.** *adj.* majeur.

majority, *n.* majorité *f.*

major scale, mode, or key, *n.* ton majeur *m.*, mode majeur *m.*

make, **1.** *n.* fabrication *f.* **2.** *vb.* faire.

make-believe, **1.** *n.* trompe l'œil *m.* **2.** *vb.* feindre.

maker, *n.* fabricant *m.*

makeshift, **1.** *n.* expédient *m.* **2.** *adj.* provisoire.

make-up, *n.* (face) maquillage *m.*

maladjusted, *adj.* mal adapté, mal ajusté.

maladjustment, *n.* mauvaise adaptation *f.*

malady, *n.* maladie *f.*

malaria, *n.* malaria *f.*

male, *adj.* and *n.* mâle *m.*

malevolent, *adj.* malveillant.

malice, *n.* méchanceté *f.*

malicious, *adj.* méchant.

malign, *vb.* calomnier.

malignant, *adj.* malin *m.*, maligne *f.*

mall, *n.* centre (*m.*) commercial.

malleable, *adj.* malléable.

malnutrition, *n.* mauvaise hygiène (*f.*) alimentaire.

malpractice, *n.* faute (*f.*) professionnelle.

malt, *n.* malt *m.*

Malta, *n.* Malte *f.*

mammal, *n.* mammifère *m.*

man, *n.* homme *m.*

manage, **1.** *vb. tr.* (administer) gérer; (conduct) diriger; (person, animal) dompter. **2.** *vb. intr.* se tirer d'affaire; (m. to) réussir à.

management, *n.* direction *f.*, gestion *f.*

manager, *n.* directeur *m.*; (household) ménager *m.*; gérant *m.*

mandate, *n.* (politics) mandat *m.*

mandatory, *adj.* obligatoire.

mandolin, *n.* mandoline *f.*

mane, *n.* crinière *f.*

maneuver, *n.* manœuvre *f.*

manganese, *n.* manganèse *m.*

manger, *n.* mangeoire *f.*

mangle, *vb.* mutiler.

manhood, *n.* virilité *f.*

mania, *n.* (craze) manie *f.*; (madness) folie *f.*

maniac, *adj.* and *n.* fou *m.*, folle *f.*

manic-depressive, *n.* and *adj.* maniaco-dépressif *m.*

manicure, *n.* (person) manucure *m.f.*; (care of hands) soin (*m.*) des mains.

manifest, **1.** *adj.* manifeste. **2.** *vb.* manifester.

manifesto, *n.* manifeste *m.*

manifold, *adj.* (varied) divers; (numerous) nombreux.

manipulate, *vb.* manipuler.

mankind, *n.* genre (*m.*) humain.

manly, *adj.* viril.

man-made, *adj.* artificiel.

manner, *n.* manière *f.*; (customs) mœurs *f.pl.*

mannerism, *n.* maniérisme *m.,* affectation *f.*

manor, *n.* manoir *m.*

manpower, *n.* main-d'œuvre *f.*

mansion, *n.* (country) château *m.;* (town) hôtel *m.*

manslaughter, *n.* homicide involontaire *m.*

mantel, *n.* (framework) manteau *m.;* (shelf) tablette *f.*

mantle, *n.* manteau *m.*

manual, *adj. and n.* manuel *m.*

manufacture, 1. *n.* manufacture *f.;* (product) produit *(m.)* manufacturé. **2.** *vb.* fabriquer.

manufacturer, *n.* fabricant *m.*

manure, *n.* fumier *m.*

manuscript, *adj. and n.* manuscrit *m.*

many, 1. *adj.* beaucoup de, un grand nombre de; **(too m.)** trop de; **(so m.)** tant de; **(how m.)** combien de. **2.** *pron.* beaucoup.

map, *n.* carte *(f.)* géographique.

maple, *n.* érable *m.*

mar, *vb.* gâter.

marble, *n.* marbre *m.*

march, 1. *n.* marche *f.* **2.** *vb.* marcher.

March, *n.* mars *m.*

mare, *n.* jument *f.*

margarine, *n.* margarine *f.*

margin, *n.* marge *f.*

marijuana, *n.* marijuana *f.;* marie-jeanne *f.*

marinate, *vb.* faire mariner.

marine, 1. *n.* (ships) marine *f.;* (soldier) fusilier *(m.)* marin. **2.** *adj.* marin; (insurance) maritime.

mariner, *n.* marin *m.*

marionette, *n.* marionnette *f.*

marital, *adj.* conjugal.

maritime, *adj.* maritime.

marjoram, *n.* marjolaine *f.*

mark, 1. *n.* marque *f.;* (target) but *m.;* (school) point *m.* **2.** *vb.* marquer.

market, 1. *n.* marché *m.* **2.** *vb.* commercialiser.

marketing, *n.* marketing *m.*

market place, *n.* place *(f.)* du marché.

market research, *n.* étude *(f.)* de marché.

marmalade, *n.* confiture *f.*

maroon. 1. *adj. n.* rouge *(m.)* foncé. **2.** *vb.* abandonner (dans une île déserte).

marquee, *n.* (tente) marquise *f.*

marquis, *n.* marquis *m.*

marriage, *n.* mariage *m.*

married, *adj.* marié.

marrow, *n.* moelle *f.*

marry, *vb.* épouser; se marier (avec).

marsh, *n.* marais *m.*

marshal, *n.* maréchal *m.*

marshmallow, *n.* guimauve (plant) *f.*

martial, *adj.* martial.

martinet, *n.* officier *(m.)* strict sur la discipline.

martyr, *n.* martyr *m.*

martyrdom, *n.* martyre *m.*

marvel, 1. *n.* merveille *f.* **2.** *vb.* **(m. at)** s'étonner de.

marvelous, *adj.* merveilleux.

Marxist, *n. and adj.* marxiste *m.f.*

mascara, *n.* mascara *m.*

mascot, *n.* mascotte *f.*

masculine, *adj.* masculin.

mash, *n.* (food) purée *f.*

mask, 1. *n.* masque *m.* **2.** *vb.* masquer.

masochist, *n.* masochiste *m.f.*

mason, *n.* maçon *m.*

masquerade, *n.* mascarade *f.,* bal masqué *m.*

mass, *n.* masse *f.*

Mass, *n.* messe *f.*

massacre, 1. *n.* massacre *m.* **2.** *vb.* massacrer.

massage, *n.* massage *m.*

masseur, *n.* masseur *m.*

massive, *adj.* massif.

mass media, *n.* mass-media *m.pl.*

mass meeting, *n.* réunion *f.*

mass production, *n.* fabrication *(f.)* en série.

mast, *n.* mât *m.*

master, 1. *n.* maître *m.* **2.** *vb.* maîtriser.

masterpiece, *n.* chef-d'œuvre *m.*

mastery, *n.* maîtrise *f.*

masticate, *vb.* mâcher.

mat, n. (door) paillasson m.

match, 1. n. (for fire) allumette f.; (equal) égal m.; (marriage) mariage m.; (person to marry) parti m.; (sport) partie f. 2. vb. assortir, tr.

match box, n. boîte (f.) d'allumettes.

mate, 1. n. (fellow-worker) camarade m.f.; (of pair) compagnon m.; compagne f.; (boat) officier m. 2. vb. s'accoupler.

material, 1. n. matière f.; (cloth) étoffe f. 2. adj. matériel.

materialism, n. matérialisme m.

materialize, vb. matérialiser, tr.; se réaliser, intr.

maternal, adj. maternel.

maternity, n. maternité f.

math, n. maths f.pl.

mathematical, adj. mathématique.

mathematics, n. mathématiques f.pl.

matinee, n. matinée f.

mating, n. accouplement m.

mating season, n. saison (f.) des amours.

matriarch, n. femme (f.) qui porte les chausses.

matrimony, n. mariage m.

matrix, n. matrice f.

matron, n. (institution) intendante f.

matter, 1. n. (substance) matière f.; (subject) sujet m.; (question, business) affaire f.; (what is the m.?) qu'est-ce qu'il y a? 2. vb. importer.

mattress, n. matelas m.

mature, 1. adj. mûr. 2. vb. mûrir.

maturity, n. maturité f.; (comm.) échéance f.

maudlin, adj. larmoyant.

mausoleum, n. mausolée m.

maxim, n. maxime f.

maximum, n. maximum m.

may, vb. pouvoir.

May, n. mai m.

maybe, adv. peut-être.

mayhem, n. mutilation f.

mayonnaise, n. mayonnaise f.

mayor, n. maire m.

maze, n. labyrinthe m.

me, pron. (unstressed direct and in-direct) me; (alone, stressed, with prep.) moi.

meadow, n. (small) pré m.; (large) prairie f.

meager, adj. maigre.

meal, n. (repast) repas m.; (grain) farine f.

mean, 1. n. (math.) moyenne f.; (m.s. financial) moyens m.pl.; (m.s. way to do) moyen m. 2. adj. humble; (stingy) avare; (contemptible) méprisable. 3. vb. (signify) vouloir dire; (purpose) se proposer (de); (destine) destiner (à).

meaning, n. sens m.

meaningful, adj. significatif.

meanness, n. méchanceté f.

meantime, meanwhile, adv. sur ces entrefaites.

measles, n. rougeole f.

measure, 1. n. mesure f. 2. vb. mesurer.

measurement, n. mesurage m.

meat, n. viande f.

mechanic, n. mécanicien m.; (auto) garagiste m.

mechanical, 1. adj. mécanique. 2. (fig.) machinal.

mechanism, n. mécanisme m.

mechanize, vb. mécaniser.

medal, n. médaille f.

meddle, vb. se mêler (de).

media, n. media m.pl.

median, n. médian.

mediate, vb. agir en médiateur.

medical, adj. médical.

medicate, vb. médicamenter.

medication, n. médicament m.

medicine, n. médecine f.

medieval, adj. médiéval.

mediocre, adj. médiocre.

mediocrity, n. médiocrité f.

meditate, vb. méditer.

meditation, n. méditation f.

Mediterranean, 1. adj. méditerranéen. 2. n. (M. Sea) Méditerranée f.

medium, 1. n. milieu m.; (agent) intermédiaire m.; (psychic person) médium m. 2. adj. moyen.

medley, n. mélange m.

meek, adj. doux m., douce f.

meekness, n. douceur f.

meet, vb. rencontrer, tr.; (become

acquainted with) faire la connaissance de; (expenses) faire face à.

meeting, *n.* réunion *f.*

megabyte, *n.* méga-octet *m.*

megahertz, *n.* mégahertz *m.*

megaphone, *n.* mégaphone *m.*

melancholic, *adj.* mélancolique.

melancholy, *n.* mélancolie *f.*

mellow, *adj.* moelleux.

melodious, *adj.* mélodieux.

melodrama, *n.* mélodrame *m.*

melody, *n.* mélodie *f.*

melon, *n.* melon *m.*

melt, *vb.* fondre.

meltdown, *n.* fusion *f.*

member, *n.* membre *m.*

membership, *n.* adhésion *f.*

membrane, *n.* membrane *f.*

memento, *n.* mémento *m.*

memo, *n.* note *f.*

memoir, *n.* mémoire *m.*

memorable, *adj.* mémorable.

memorandum, *n.* mémorandum *m.*

memorial, 1. *n.* souvenir *m.,* monument *m.* 2. *adj.* commémoratif.

memorize, *vb.* apprendre par cœur.

memory, *n.* mémoire *f.*

menace, 1. *n.* menace *f.* 2. *vb.* menacer.

menagerie, *n.* ménagerie *f.*

mend, *vb.* (clothes) raccommoder; (correct) corriger.

mendacious, *adj.* menteur.

mendicant, *n. and adj.* mendiant *m.*

menial, *adj.* servile.

meningitis, *n.* méningite *f.*

menstruation, *n.* menstruation *f.*

menswear, *n.* habillements masculins *m.pl.*

mental, *adj.* mental.

mentality, *n.* mentalité *f.*

menthol, *n.* menthol *m.*

mention, 1. *n.* mention *f.* 2. *vb.* mentionner; **(don't m. it)** il n'y a pas de quoi.

menu, *n.* menu *m.*

mercantile, *adj.* mercantile.

mercenary, *adj. and n.* mercenaire *m.*

merchandise, *n.* marchandise(s) *f.(pl.).*

merchant, 1. *n.* négociant *m.* 2. *adj.* marchand.

merchant marine, *n.* marine marchande *f.*

merciful, *adj.* miséricordieux.

merciless, *adj.* impitoyable.

mercury, *n.* mercure *m.*

mercy, *n.* miséricorde *f.;* **(at the m. of)** à la merci de.

mere, *adj.* simple.

merely, *adv.* simplement.

merge, *vb.* fusionner.

merger, *n.* fusion *f.*

merit, 1. *n.* mérite *m.* 2. *vb.* mériter.

meritorious, *adj.* (person) méritant; (deed) méritoire.

mermaid, *n.* sirène *f.*

merriment, *n.* gaieté *f.*

merry, *adj.* gai.

merry-go-round, *n.* carrousel *m.*

mesh, *n.* maille *f.*

mesmerize, *vb.* magnétiser.

mess, 1. *n.* (muddle) fouillis *m.;* gâchis *m.;* (mil.) popote *f.* 2. *vb.* gâcher.

message, *n.* message *m.*

messenger, *n.* messager *m.,* coursier *m.*

messy, *adj.* (dirty) malpropre.

metabolism, *n.* métabolisme *m.*

metal, *n.* métal *m.*

metallic, *adj.* métallique.

metamorphosis, *n.* métamorphose *f.*

metaphor, *n.* métaphore *f.*

metaphysics, *n.* métaphysique *f.*

meteor, *n.* météore *m.*

meteorology, *n.* météorologie *f.*

meter, 1. *n.* (measure) mètre *m.;* (device) compteur *m.*

method, *n.* méthode *f.*

meticulous, *adj.* méticuleux.

metric, *adj.* métrique.

metropolis, *n.* métropole *f.*

metropolitan, *adj.* métropolitain.

mettle, *n.* ardeur *f.*

Mexican, 1. *n.* Mexicain *m.* 2. *adj.* mexicain.

Mexico, *n.* Mexique *m.*

mezzanine, *n.* mezzanine *f.*

microbe, *n.* microbe *m.*

microchip, *n.* microplaquette *f.,* puce *f.*

microcomputer, *n.* micro-ordinateur *m.*

microcosm, n. microcosme m.
microfiche, n. microfiche f.
microfilm, n. microfilm m.
microform, n. microforme f.
microphone, n. microphone m.
microscope, n. microscope m.
microscopic, adj. microscopique.
microwave, n. micro-onde f.; **(m. oven)** four (m.) à micro-ondes.
mid, adj. mi-.
middle, 1. n. milieu m. **2.** adj. du milieu.
middle-aged, adj. d'un certain âge.
Middle Ages, n. moyen âge m.
middle class, n. classe moyenne f., bourgeoisie f.
Middle East, n. Moyen Orient m.
midget, n. nain m.
midnight, n. minuit m.
midriff, n. diaphragme m.
midwife, n. sage-femme f.
mien, n. mine f.; air m.
might, n. puissance f.
mighty, adj. puissant.
migraine, n. migraine f.
migrate, vb. émigrer.
migration, n. migration f.
mike, n. (colloquial) micro m.
mild, adj. doux m., douce f.
mildew, n. rouille f.
mile, n. mille m.
mileage, n. kilométrage m.
milestone, n. borne routière f.
militarism, n. militarisme m.
military, adj. militaire.
militia, n. milice f.
milk, n. lait m.
milkman, n. laitier m.
milky, adj. laiteux.
mill, 1. n. (grinding) moulin m.; (spinning) filature f.; (factory) usine f. **2.** vb. (grind) moudre; (crowd) fourmiller.
millennium, n. millénaire m.
miller, n. meunier m.
millimeter, n. millimètre m.
milliner, n. modiste f.
millinery, n. modes f.pl.
million, n. million m.
millionaire, adj. and n. millionnaire m.f.
mimic, 1. n. mime m. **2.** adj. mimique. **3.** vb. imiter.
mince, vb. (chop) hacher.
mind, 1. n. esprit m.; (opinion) avis

m.; (desire) envie f. **2.** vb. (heed) faire attention à; (listen to) écouter; (apply oneself to) s'occuper de; (take care) prendre garde; (look after) garder; **(never m.)** n'importe.
mindful, adj. attentif.
mine, 1. n. mine f. **2.** pron. le mien m., la mienne f., les miens m.pl., les miennes f.pl.
mine field, n. champ (m.) de mines.
miner, n. mineur m.
mineral, adj. and n. minéral m.
mine sweeper, n. dragueur (m.) de mines.
mingle, vb. mêler, tr.
miniature, n. miniature f.
miniaturize, vb. miniaturiser.
minimize, vb. réduire au minimum.
minimum, n. minimum m.
minimum wage, n. salaire minimum m.
mining, n. exploitation minière f., pose de mines f.
minister, n. ministre m.
ministry, n. ministère m.
mink, n. vison m.
minnow, n. vairon m.
minor, adj. and n. mineur m.
minority, n. minorité f.
minstrel, n. ménestrel m.
mint, n. (plant) menthe f.; (place) Hôtel (m.) de la Monnaie.
minus, prep. moins.
minute, 1. n. minute f.; (of meeting) procès-verbal m. **2.** adj. (very small) minuscule; (detailed) minutieux.
miracle, n. miracle m.
miraculous, adj. miraculeux.
mirage, n. mirage m.
mire, n. boue f., bourbier m.
mirror, n. miroir m.
mirth, n. gaieté f.
misadventure, n. mésaventure f., contretemps m.
misappropriate, vb. détourner, dépréder.
misbehave, vb. se conduire mal.
miscellaneous, adj. divers.
mischief, n. (harm) mal m.; (mischievousness) malice f.

mischievous, *adj.* espiègle; (wicked) méchant.

misconstrue, *vb.* mal interpréter, tourner en mal.

misdemeanor, *n.* délit *m.*

miser, *n.* avare *m.f.*

miserable, *adj.* (unhappy) malheureux; (wretched) misérable.

miserly, *adj.* avare.

misery, *n.* (affliction) souffrance(s) *f.(pl.);* (poverty) misère *f.*

misfit, *n.* vêtement manqué *m.;* inadapté *m.*, inapte *m.*

misfortune, *n.* malheur *m.*

misgiving, *n.* doute *m.*

mishap, *n.* mésaventure *f.*

mislead, *vb.* tromper, égarer.

misplace, *vb.* mal placer.

misprint, *n.* faute *(f.)* d'impression.

mispronounce, *vb.* mal prononcer, estropier.

miss, *vb.* manquer; (**I m. you**) vous me manquez.

miss, *n.* mademoiselle *f.*

missile, *n.* projectile *m.*

missing, *adj.* (thing) qui manque; (person) disparu.

mission, *n.* mission *f.*

missionary, *adj. and n.* missionnaire *m.f.*

misspell, *vb.* mal orthographier.

mist, *n.* brume *f.*

mistake, 1. *n.* erreur *f.* 2. *vb.* (misunderstand) comprendre mal; (make a mistake) se tromper (de).

mister, *n.* monsieur *m.*

mistletoe, *n.* gui *m.*

mistreat, *vb.* maltraiter.

mistress, *n.* maîtresse *f.*

mistrust, 1. *n.* méfiance *f.* 2. *vb.* se méfier de.

misty, *adj.* brumeux.

misunderstand, *vb.* mal comprendre.

misuse, *vb.* (misapply) faire mauvais usage (de); (maltreat) maltraiter.

mite, *n.* denier *m.*, obole *f.*

mitigate, *vb.* atténuer.

mitten, *n.* moufle *f.*

mix, *vb.* mêler, *tr.*

mixture, *n.* mélange *m.*

mix-up, *n.* embrouillement *m.*

moan, 1. *n.* gémissement *m.* 2. *vb.* gémir.

moat, *n.* fossé *m.*

mob, 1. *n.* foule *f.;* (pejorative) populace *f.* 2. *vb.* assaillir.

mobile, *adj.* mobile.

mobile phone, *n.* téléphone *(m.)* portatif.

mobilization, *n.* mobilisation *f.*

mobilize, *vb.* mobiliser.

mock, *vb.* (**m. at**) se moquer de; (imitate) singer.

mockery, *n.* moquerie *f.*

mod, *adj.* à la mode.

mode, *n.* mode *f.*

model, *n.* modèle *m.*

modem, *n.* modem *m.*

moderate, 1. *adj.* modéré. 2. *vb.* modérer.

moderation, *n.* modération *f.*

modern, *adj.* moderne.

modernize, *vb.* moderniser.

modest, *adj.* modeste.

modesty, *n.* modestie *f.*

modify, *vb.* modifier.

modish, *adj.* à la mode.

modulate, *vb.* moduler.

module, *n.* module *m.*

moist, *adj.* moite.

moisten, *vb.* humecter.

moisture, *n.* humidité *f.*

molar, *n. and adj.* molaire *f.*

molasses, *n.* mélasse *f.*

mold, 1. *n.* (casting) moule *m.;* (mildew) moisissure *f.* 2. *vb.* (shape) mouler; (get moldy) moisir.

moldy, *adj.* moisi.

mole, *n.* (animal) taupe *f.;* (spot) grain *(m.)* de beauté.

molecule, *n.* molécule *f.*

molest, *vb.* molester.

mollify, *vb.* adoucir, apaiser.

molten, *adj.* fondu, coulé.

moment, *n.* moment *m.*

momentary, *adj.* momentané.

momentous, *adj.* important.

mommy, *n.* maman *f.*

Monaco, *n.* Monaco *f.*

monarch, *n.* monarque *m.*

monarchy, *n.* monarchie *f.*

monastery, *n.* monastère *m.*

Monday, *n.* lundi *m.*

monetary, *adj.* monétaire.

money, n. argent m.; (comm.) monnaie f.
money order, n. mandat m.
mongrel, n. métis m.
monitor, n. moniteur m.
monk, n. moine m.
monkey, n. singe m.
monologue, n. monologue m.
monoplane, n. monoplan m.
monopolize, vb. monopoliser.
monopoly, n. monopole m.
monosyllable, n. monosyllabe m.
monotone, n. monotone m.
monotonous, adj. monotone.
monotony, n. monotonie f.
monsoon, n. mousson f.
monster, n. monstre m.
monstrosity, n. monstruosité f.
monstrous, adj. monstrueux.
month, n. mois m.
monthly, adj. mensuel.
monument, n. monument m.
monumental, adj. monumental.
mood, n. humeur f.; (gramm.) mode m.
moody, adj. de mauvaise humeur.
moon, n. lune f.
moonlight, 1. n. clair (m.) de lune. 2. vb. travailler au noir.
moor, n. lande f.
mooring, n. amarrage m.
moot, adj. discutable.
mop, n. balai (m.) à laver.
mope, vb. bouder.
moped, n. cyclomoteur m.
moral, 1. n. morale f.; (m.s) moralité f. 2. adj. moral.
morale, n. moral m.
moralist, n. moraliste m.f.
morality, n. moralité f.; (ethics) morale f.
morally, adv. moralement.
morbid, adj. morbide.
more, 1. pron. en . . . davantage. 2. adj. and adv. plus; (m. than) plus de; (no m.) ne . . . plus.
moreover, adv. de plus.
mores, n. mœurs f.pl.
morgue, n. morgue f.
morning, n. matin m.; (length of m.) matinée f.; (good m.) bonjour.
Morocco, n. Maroc m.
moron, n. idiot m.
morose, adj. morose.
morphine, n. morphine f.

Morse code, n. l'alphabet Morse m.
morsel, n. morceau m.
mortal, adj. and n. mortel m.
mortality, n. mortalité f.
mortar, n. mortier m.
mortgage, 1. n. hypothèque f. 2. vb. hypothéquer.
mortician, n. entrepreneur (m.) de pompes funèbres.
mortify, vb. mortifier.
mortuary, adj. mortuaire.
mosaic, 1. n. mosaïque f. 2. adj. en mosaïque.
Moscow, n. Moscou m.
Moslem, adj. and n. musulman m.
mosque, n. mosquée f.
mosquito, n. moustique m.
moss, n. mousse f.
most, 1. n. le plus. 2. adj. le plus (de); la plupart. 3. adv. (with adj. and vb.) le plus; (intensive) très.
mostly, adv. pour la plupart; (time) la plupart du temps.
moth, n. papillon (m.) de nuit; (clothes) mite f.
mother, n. mère f.
mother-in-law, n. belle-mère f.
mother-of-pearl, n. nacre f.
mother tongue, n. langue (f.) maternelle.
motif, n. motif m.
motion, n. mouvement m.; (gesture) signe m.; (proposal) motion f.
motionless, adj. immobile.
motion-picture, n. film m.
motivate, vb. motiver.
motive, n. motif m.
motley, 1. adj. bigarré. 2. n. livrée de bouffon m.
motor, n. moteur m.
motorboat, n. canot (m.) automobile.
motorcycle, n. motocyclette f.
motorist, n. automobiliste m.
motto, n. devise f.
mound, n. tertre m.
mount, 1. n. (hill) mont m.; (horse, structure) monture f. 2. vb. monter.
mountain, n. montagne f.
mountain bike, n. vélo (m.) tout terrain, VTT m.

mountaineer, n. montagnard m., alpiniste m.

mountainous, adj. montagneux.

mountebank, n. saltimbanque m., charlatan m.

mourn, vb. pleurer.

mournful, adj. triste.

mourning, n. deuil m.

mouse, n. souris f.

mouth, n. bouche f.

mouthful, n. bouchée f.

mouthpiece, n. embouchure f., embout m.

movable, adj. mobile.

move, vb. mouvoir, tr.; remuer; (stir) bouger; (affect with emotion) émouvoir; (change residence) déménager; (propose) proposer.

movement, n. mouvement m.

movie, n. film m.

movie camera, n. caméra f.

moving, 1. n. déménagement m. 2. adj. touchant.

mow, vb. faucher; (lawn) tondre.

Mr., n. M. m. (abbr. for Monsieur).

Mrs., n. Mme. f. (abbr. for Madame).

much, adj., pron. and adv. beaucoup (de); (**too m.**) trop (de); (**so m.**) tant (de); (**how m.**) combien (de).

mucilage, n. mucilage m.

muck, n. fumier m.

mucous, adj. muqueux.

mud, n. boue f.

muddy, adj. boueux.

muff, n. manchon m.

muffin, n. petit pain m.

muffle, vb. emmitoufler.

mug, 1. n. gobelet m., pot m., chope f. 2. vb. attaquer.

muggy, adj. lourd, moite.

mulatto, n. mulâtre m.

mule, n. mulet m.

mullah, n. mollah m.

multicolored, adj. multicolore.

multifarious, adj. divers.

multinational, adj. multinational.

multiple, adj. multiple.

multiplication, n. multiplication f.

multiplicity, n. multiplicité f.

multiply, vb. multiplier, tr.

multitude, n. multitude f.

mumble, vb. marmonner.

mummy, n. (embalmed) momie f.; maman f.

mumps, n. oreillons m.pl.

munch, vb. mâcher.

mundane, adj. banal.

municipal, adj. municipal.

munificent, adj. munificent.

munition, n. munition(s) f.(pl.).

mural, n. (painting) peinture (f.) murale.

murder, n. meurtre m.

murderer, n. meurtrier m.

murmur, 1. n. murmure m. 2. vb. murmurer.

muscle, n. muscle m.

muscular, adj. musculaire; (strong) musculeux.

muse, 1. n. muse f. 2. vb. méditer.

museum, n. musée m.

mushroom, n. champignon m.

music, n. musique f.

musical, adj. musical; (person) musicien.

musical comedy, n. comédie musicale f.

musician, n. musicien m.

Muslim, adj. and n. musulman m.

muslin, n. mousseline f.

mussel, n. moule f.

must, vb. devoir; falloir (used impersonally, il faut que).

mustache, n. moustache f.

mustard, n. moutarde f.

muster, vb. rassembler, tr.

musty, adj. moisi, suranné.

mutation, n. mutation f.

mute, adj. muet.

mutilate, vb. mutiler.

mutiny, n. mutinerie f.

mutter, vb. grommeler.

mutton, n. mouton m.

mutual, adj. mutuel.

muzzle, n. muselière f.

my, adj. mon m., ma f., mes pl.

myopia, n. myopie f.

myriad, n. myriade f.

myself, pron. moi-même; (reflexive) me.

mysterious, adj. mystérieux.

mystery, n. mystère m.

mystic, adj. mystique.

mystify, vb. mystifier.
myth, n. mythe m.

mythical, adj. mythique.
mythology, n. mythologie f.

N

nab, vb. attraper, saisir.
nag, vb. gronder.
nail, 1. n. (person, animal) ongle m.; (metal) clou m.; (**n. polish**) vernis (m.) à ongles. **2.** vb. clouer.
naïve, adj. naïf m., naïve f.
naked, adj. nu.
name, 1. n. nom m. **2.** vb. nommer.
namely, adv. à savoir.
namesake, n. homonyme m.
nanny, n. nounou f.
nap, n. petit somme m.
nape, n. nuque f.
napkin, n. serviette f.
narcissus, n. narcisse m.
narcotic, adj. and n. narcotique m.
narrate, vb. raconter.
narrative, n. récit m.
narrow, adj. étroit.
narrow-minded, adj. à l'esprit étroit.
nasal, adj. nasal.
nasty, adj. méchant.
natal, adj. natal.
nation, n. nation f.
national, adj. national.
nationalism, n. nationalisme m.
nationality, n. nationalité f.
nationalization, n. nationalisation f.
nationalize, vb. nationaliser.
nationwide, 1. adj. à l'échelle du pays entier. **2.** adv. à travers tout le pays.
native, 1. n. autochtone m.f.; (non-European) indigène m.f. **2.** adj. natif; (place) natal; (language) maternel.
nativity, n. naissance f.
NATO, n. OTAN f.
natural, adj. naturel.
naturalist, n. naturaliste m.f.
naturalize, vb. naturaliser.
naturalness, n. naturel m.
nature, n. nature f.
naughty, adj. méchant.
nausea, n. nausée f.
nauseous, adj. nauséeux.
nautical, adj. marin.

naval, adj. naval.
nave, n. nef f.
navigable, adj. navigable.
navigate, vb. naviguer.
navigation, n. navigation f.
navigator, n. navigateur m.
navy, n. marine f.
navy yard, n. arsenal maritime m.
Nazi, n. Nazi m.
near, 1. adj. proche. **2.** adv. près. **3.** prep. près de.
nearly, adv. de près; (almost) presque.
near-sighted, adj. myope.
neat, adj. soigné, net.
neatness, n. propreté f.
nebula, n. nébuleuse f.
nebulous, adj. nébuleux.
necessary, adj. nécessaire.
necessity, n. nécessité f.
neck, 1. n. cou m. **2.** vb. se peloter.
necklace, n. collier m.
necktie, n. cravate f.
nectar, n. nectar m.
need, 1. n. besoin m. **2.** vb. avoir besoin de.
needful, adj. nécessaire.
needle, n. aiguille f.
needle point, n. pointe d'aiguille f.
needless, adj. inutile.
needy, adj. nécessiteux.
nefarious, adj. infâme.
negative, adj. négatif.
neglect, 1. n. négligence f. **2.** vb. négliger (de).
negligee, n. négligée f.
negligent, adj. négligent.
negligible, adj. négligeable.
negotiate, vb. négocier.
negotiation, n. négociation f.
Negro, adj. and n. nègre m.
neighbor, n. voisin m.; (fellow man) prochain m.
neighborhood, n. voisinage m.
neighborly, adj. amical.
neither, 1. adj. and pron. ni l'un ni l'autre. **2.** adv. non plus. **3.** conj. (**n. . . . nor**) ni . . . ni.
neon, n. néon m.

neophyte, n. néophyte m.
nephew, n. neveu m.
nepotism, n. népotisme m.
nerve, n. nerf m.
nerve-racking, adj. angoissant.
nervous, adj. nerveux.
nervous system, n. système nerveux m.
nest, n. nid m.
nestle, vb. se nicher.
net, 1. n. filet m. **2.** adj. net m., nette f.
Netherlands, the, n. les Pays-Bas m.pl., Hollande f.
network, n. réseau m.
neuralgia, n. névralgie f.
neurology, n. neurologie f.
neurotic, adj. and n. névrosé m.
neutral, adj. and n. neutre m.
neutron, n. neutron m.
neutron bomb, n. bombe (f.) à neutrons.
never, adv. jamais.
nevertheless, adv. néanmoins.
new, adj. nouveau m., nouvelle f.; (not used) neuf m., neuve f.
newborn, adj. nouveau né.
newlyweds, n. jeunes mariés m.pl.
news, n. (piece of news) nouvelle f.
newsboy, n. vendeur (m.) de journaux.
newscast, n. journal parlé m., informations f.pl.
newscaster, n. présentateur m.
newspaper, n. journal m.
newsreel, n. film (m.) d'actualité.
newsstand, n. kiosque (m.) à journaux.
New Testament, n. le Nouveau Testament m.
new year, n. nouvel an m.
New Zealand, n. Nouvelle-Zélande f.
next, 1. adj. prochain. **2.** adv. ensuite. **3.** prep. auprès de.
nibble, vb. grignoter.
nice, n. (person) gentil; (thing) joli.
niche, n. niche f., (fig.) place f., situation f.
nick, n. entaille f.
nickel, n. nickel m.
nickname, n. surnom m.
nicotine, n. nicotine f.
niece, n. nièce f.

Nigeria, n. Nigéria m.f.
niggardly, adj. chiche.
night, n. nuit f.; (evening) soir m.
nightclub, n. boîte (f.) de nuit, établissement (m.) de nuit.
nightgown, n. chemise (f.) de nuit.
nightingale, n. rossignol m.
nightly, adv. tous les soirs; toutes les nuits.
nightmare, n. cauchemar m.
night-school, n. cours (m.) du soir.
nimble, adj. agile.
nine, adj. and n. neuf m.
nineteen, adj. and n. dix-neuf m.
ninety, adj. and n. quatre-vingt-dix m.
ninth, adj. and n. neuvième m.f.
nip, 1. n. pincement m., pincade f. **2.** vb. pincer.
nipple, n. mamelon m.
nitrogen, n. nitrogène m.
no, 1. adj. pas de. **2.** interj., adv. non.
nobility, n. noblesse f.
noble, adj. noble.
nobleman, n. gentilhomme m.
nobly, adv. noblement.
nobody, pron. personne.
nocturnal, adj. nocturne.
nod, 1. n. signe (m.) de la tête. **2.** vb. incliner la tête.
node, n. nœud m.
no-frills, adj. simple.
noise, n. bruit m.
noiseless, adj. silencieux.
noisome, adj. puant, fétide.
noisy, adj. bruyant.
nomad, n. nomade m.f.
nominal, adj. nominal.
nominate, vb. (appoint) nommer; (propose) désigner.
nomination, n. (appointment) nomination f.; (proposal) désignation f.
nominee, n. personne nommée f., candidat choisi m.
nonaligned, adj. (in politics) non-aligné.
nonchalant, adj. nonchalant.
noncombatant, adj. and n. non-combattant m.
noncommissioned, adj. sans brevet.

noncommittal, *adj.* qui n'engage à rien.

nondescript, *adj.* indéfinissable.

none, *pron.* aucun.

nonentity, *n.* nullité *f.*

nonplussed, *adj.* perplexe.

non-proliferation, *n.* non-prolifération *f.*

nonresident, *n.* and *adj.* non-résident *m.*

nonsense, *n.* absurdité *f.*

non-smoker, *n.* non-fumeur *m.*

nonstop, *adj.* sans arrêt.

noodles, *n.* nouilles *f.pl.*

nook, *n.* coin *m.,* recoin *m.*

noon, *n.* midi *m.*

noose, *n.* nœud coulant *m.*

nor, *conj.* ni; (and not) et ne . . . pas.

norm, *n.* norme *f.*

normal, *adj.* normal.

normally, *adv.* normalement.

Normandy, *n.* Normandie *f.*

north, *n.* nord *m.*

North America, *n.* Amérique *(f.)* du Nord.

northeast, *n.* nord-est *m.*

northern, *adj.* du nord.

North Pole, *n.* pôle nord *m.*

northwest, *n.* nord-ouest *m.*

Norway, *n.* Norvège *f.*

Norwegian, 1. *n.* (person) Norvégien *m.;* (language) norvégien *m.* **2.** *adj.* norvégien.

nose, *n.* nez *m.*

nosebleed, *n.* saignement *(m.)* du nez.

nose dive, *n.* vol piqué *m.*

nostalgia, *n.* nostalgie *f.*

nostril, *n.* narine *f.;* (animals) naseau *m.*

nostrum, *n.* panacée *f.,* remède *(m.)* de charlatan.

nosy, *adj.* curieux.

not, *adv.* (ne) pas.

notable, *adj.* and *n.* notable *m.*

notary, *n.* notaire *m.*

notation, *n.* notation *f.*

note, 1. *n.* note *f.;* (letter, finance) billet *m.;* (distinction) marque *f.* **2.** *vb.* noter.

notebook, *n.* (small) carnet *m.;* (large) cahier *m.*

noted, *adj.* célèbre.

notepaper, *n.* papier *(m.)* à notes.

noteworthy, *adj.* remarquable, mémorable.

nothing, *pron.* rien.

notice, 1. *n.* (announcement) avis *m.;* (attention) attention *f.;* (forewarning) préavis *m.* **2.** *vb.* remarquer.

noticeable, *adj.* remarquable; apparent.

notification, *n.* notification *f.*

notify, *vb.* avertir.

notion, *n.* idée *f.*

notoriety, *n.* notoriété *f.*

notorious, *adj.* notoire.

notwithstanding, 1. *adv.* tout de même. **2.** *prep.* malgré.

noun, *n.* substantif *m.*

nourish, *vb.* nourrir.

nourishment, *n.* nourriture *f.*

novel, 1. *n.* roman *m.* **2.** *adj.* nouveau, original.

novelist, *n.* romancier *m.*

novelty, *n.* nouveauté *f.*

November, *n.* novembre *m.*

novice, *n.* novice *m.f.*

now, *adv.* maintenant; **(n. and then)** de temps en temps.

nowadays, *adv.* de nos jours.

nowhere, *adv.* nulle part.

nozzle, *n.* ajutage *m.,* jet *m.*

nuance, *n.* nuance *f.*

nuclear, *adj.* nucléaire.

nuclear physics, *n.* physique nucléaire *f.*

nuclear warhead, *n.* cône *(m.)* de charge nucléaire.

nuclear waste, *n.* déchets nucléaires *m.pl.*

nucleus, *n.* noyau *m.*

nude, *adj.* and *n.* nu *m.*

nugget, *n.* pépite *f.*

nuisance, *n.* (thing) ennui *m.;* (person) peste *f.*

nuke, 1. *n.* arme nucléaire *f.* **2.** *vb.* détruire avec des armes nucléaires.

nullify, *vb.* annuler, nullifier.

numb, 1. *adj.* engourdi. **2.** *vb.* engourdir.

number, 1. *n.* nombre *m.;* (in a series, street, etc.) numéro *m.* **2.** *vb.* compter, numéroter.

numeral, *n.* chiffre *m.*

numerical, *adj.* numérique.

numerous, *adj.* nombreux.

nun, n. religieuse f., nonne f.
nuncio, n. nonce m.
nuptial, adj. nuptial.
nurse, 1. n. (hospital) infirmière f.; (wet-n.) nourrice f. **2.** vb. soigner; (suckle) allaiter.
nursery, n. (children) chambre (f.) des enfants; (plants) pépinière f.
nurture, 1. n. nourriture f. **2.** vb. nourrir, entretenir.

nut, 1. n. noix f.; (metal) écrou m. **2.** adj. (n.s) (colloquial) dingue.
nutcracker, n. casse-noix m.
nutmeg, n. muscade f.
nutrition, n. nutrition f.
nutritious, adj. nutritif.
nutshell, n. coquille (f.) de noix; (in a n.) en deux mots.
nylon, n. nylon m.
nymph, n. nymphe f.

O

oak, n. chêne m.
oar, n. rame f.
oasis, n. oasis f.
oath, n. serment m.; (curse) juron m.
oatmeal, n. farine (f.) d'avoine.
oats, n. avoine f.
obdurate, adj. obstiné, têtu.
obedience, n. obéissance f.
obedient, adj. obéissant.
obeisance, n. salut m.
obelisk, n. obélisque m.
obese, adj. obèse.
obey, vb. obéir à.
obituary, n. nécrologe m.
object, 1. n. objet m. **2.** vb. objecter.
objection, n. objection f.
objectionable, adj. répréhensible.
objective, adj. and n. objectif m.
obligation, n. obligation f.
obligatory, adj. obligatoire.
oblige, vb. obliger.
oblivion, n. oubli m.
obnoxious, adj. odieux.
oboe, n. hautbois m.
obscene, adj. obscène.
obscure, adj. obscur.
obsequious, adj. obséquieux.
observance, n. observance f.
observation, n. observation f.
observe, vb. observer.
observer, n. observateur m.
obsess, vb. obséder.
obsession, n. obsession f.
obsolescence, n. vieillissement m.
obsolete, adj. désuet.
obstacle, n. obstacle m.
obstetrician, n. médecin-accoucheur m.
obstinate, adj. obstiné.

obstreperous, adj. tapageur.
obstruct, vb. obstruer.
obstruction, n. obstruction f.
obtain, vb. obtenir.
obtrude, vb. mettre en avant.
obtuse, adj. obtus.
obviate, vb. prévenir, éviter.
obvious, adj. évident.
occasion, n. occasion f.
occasional, adj. (not regular) de temps en temps.
occult, adj. occulte.
occupant, n. occupant m.
occupation, n. occupation f.; (vocation) métier m.
occupy, vb. occuper.
occur, vb. (happen) avoir lieu; (come to the mind) se présenter à l'esprit.
occurrence, n. occurrence f.
ocean, n. océan m.
o'clock, see **clock.**
octagon, n. octogone m.
octave, n. octave f.
October, n. octobre m.
octopus, n. poulpe m.
ocular, adj. oculaire.
oculist, n. oculiste m.f.
odd, adj. (not even) impair; (unmatched) dépareillé; (strange) bizarre.
oddity, n. singularité f.
odds, n. inégalité f., (betting) cote f.
odious, adj. odieux.
odor, n. odeur f.
of, prep. de.
off, 1. adv. (away) à . . . de distance; (cancelled) rompu. **2.** prep. de.

offend, vb. offenser; **(o. against the law)** enfreindre la loi.

offender, n. offenseur m.; (law) délinquant m.

offense, n. offense f.; (transgression) délit m.

offensive, 1. n. offensive f. **2.** adj. (mil., etc.) offensif; (word, etc.) offensant.

offer, 1. n. offre f. **2.** vb. offrir.

offering, n. offre f., offrande f.

offhand, 1. adj. spontané. **2.** adv. sans préparation.

office, n. (service) office m.; (function) fonctions f.pl.; (room) bureau m.

officer, n. (mil.) officier m.; (public) fonctionnaire m.

official, n. officiel m.

officiate, vb. officier.

officious, adj. officieux.

off-line, adj. and adv. (computer) (en mode) autonome.

off-peak, adj. aux heures creuses.

offshore, 1. adv. vers le large. **2.** adj. du côté de la terre.

offspring, n. descendant m.

often, adv. souvent.

oil, n. huile f.

oilcloth, n. toile cirée f.

oily, adj. huileux.

ointment, n. onguent m.

okay, interj. très bien, d'accord.

old, adj. vieux (vieil) m., vieille f.; **(how o. are you?)** quel âge avez-vous?

old-fashioned, adj. démodé.

Old Testament, n. l'Ancien Testament m.

olfactory, adj. olfactif.

oligarchy, n. oligarchie f.

olive, n. (tree) olivier m.; (fruit) olive f.

ombudsman, n. (in France) médiateur m.; (in Quebec) protecteur (m.) du citoyen.

omelet, n. omelette f.

omen, n. présage m.

ominous, adj. de mauvais augure.

omission, n. omission f.

omit, vb. omettre.

omnibus, n. omnibus m.

omnipotent, adj. omnipotent, tout-puissant.

on, prep. sur.

once, adv. une fois; (formerly) autrefois; **(at o., without delay)** tout de suite; **(at o., at the same time)** à la fois.

one, 1. adj. un; (only) seul. **2.** n. un. **3.** pron. un; (indefinite subject) on, (indefinite object) vous; **(the o.)** celui; **(this o.)** celui-ci; **(that o.)** celui-là; **(which o.)** lequel.

oneself, pron. soi-même; (reflexive) se.

one-sided, adj. unilatéral.

one-way, adj. (street, traffic) à sens unique; non connecté.

onion, n. oignon m.

onionskin, n. pelure (f.) d'oignon, (paper) papier pelure m.

on-line, adj. and adv. en ligne; connecté.

only, 1. adj. seul. **2.** adv. seulement.

onslaught, n. assaut m.

onward, adj. and adv. en avant.

opal, n. opale f.

opaque, adj. opaque.

OPEC, n. OPEP f.

open, 1. adj. ouvert; **(o.-minded)** à l'esprit ouvert. **2.** vb. ouvrir.

opening, n. ouverture f.

opera, n. opéra m.

opera glasses, n. jumelles f.pl.

operate, vb. opérer; (put into operation) actionner.

operatic, adj. d'opéra.

operation, n. opération f.; (functioning) fonctionnement m.

operator, n. opérateur m.; (switchboard) standardiste m.f.

operetta, n. opérette f.

opinion, n. opinion f.

opponent, n. adversaire m.f.

opportunism, n. opportunisme m.

opportunity, n. occasion f.

oppose, vb. (put in opposition) opposer; (resist) s'opposer à.

opposite, 1. adj. opposé. **2.** adv. vis-à-vis. **3.** prep. en face de.

opposition, n. opposition f.

oppress, vb. opprimer.

oppression, n. oppression f.

oppressive, adj. oppressif; (heat, etc.) accablant.

opt, vb. **(o. for)** opter pour; **(o. out of)** refuser de participer à.

optic, adj. optique.

optician, n. opticien m.

optimism, n. optimisme m.

optimistic, adj. optimiste.

option, n. option f.

optional, adj. facultatif.

optometry, n. optométrie f.

opulent, adj. opulent, riche.

or, conj. ou; (with negative) ni.

oracle, n. oracle m.

oral, adj. oral.

orange, n. orange f.

orangeade, n. orangeade f.

oration, n. discours m.

orator, n. orateur m.

oratory, n. art (m.) oratoire.

orbit, n. orbite f.

orchard, n. verger m.

orchestra, n. orchestre m.

orchid, n. orchidée f.

ordain, vb. ordonner.

ordeal, n. épreuve f.

order, 1. n. ordre m.; (comm.) commande f. **2.** vb. ordonner; (comm.) commander.

orderly, adj. ordonné.

ordinance, n. ordonnance f.

ordinary, adj. and n. ordinaire m.

ordination, n. ordination f.

ore, n. minerai m.

organ, n. (music) orgue m.; (body) organe m.

organdy, n. organdi m.

organic, adj. organique.

organism, n. organisme m.

organist, n. organiste m.f.

organization, n. organisation f.; (group) organisme m.

organize, vb. organiser.

orgasm, n. orgasme m.

orgy, n. orgie f.

orient, vb. orienter.

Orient, n. Orient m.

Oriental, 1. n. Oriental m. **2.** adj. oriental.

orientation, n. orientation f.

orifice, n. orifice m.

origin, n. origine f.

original, adj. (new, unique) original; (from the origin) originel.

originality, n. originalité f.

originate from, vb. provenir de.

ornament, n. ornement m.

ornamental, adj. ornemental.

ornate, adj. orné.

ornithology, n. ornithologie f.

orphan, n. orphelin m.

orphanage, n. orphelinat m.

orthodox, adj. orthodoxe.

orthopedics, n. orthopédie f.

osmosis, n. osmose f.

ostensible, adj. prétendu.

ostentation, n. ostentation f.

ostentatious, adj. plein d'ostentation, ostentatoire.

osteopath, n. ostéopathe m.f.

ostracize, vb. ostraciser.

ostrich, n. autruche f.

other, adj. and pron. autre.

otherwise, adv. autrement.

ought, vb. devoir.

ounce, n. once f.

our, adj. notre sg., nos pl.

ours, pron. le nôtre.

ourself, pron. nous-même; (reflexive) nous.

oust, vb. évincer.

ouster, n. éviction f.

out, adv. dehors.

outbreak, n. (beginning) commencement m.; (insurrection) révolte f., éruption f.

outburst, n. éruption f.

outcast, n. paria m.

outcome, n. résultat m.

outdated, adj. suranné.

outdoors, adv. dehors.

outer, adj. extérieur.

outfit, n. équipement m.; (clothes) tenue f.

outgrow, vb. devenir trop grand pour.

outgrowth, n. conséquence f.

outing, n. promenade f.

outlandish, adj. bizarre.

outlaw, 1. vb. proscrire. **2.** n. hors-la-loi m.

outlet, n. issue f.; prise (f.) de courant.

outline, 1. n. contour m.; (general idea) aperçu m. **2.** vb. (drawing) tracer; (plan) exposer à grands traits.

out of, prep. hors de; (because of) par; (without) sans.

out-of-date, adj. suranné.

output, n. rendement m.

outrage, n. outrage m.

outrageous, adj. outrageant.

outrank, vb. occuper un rang supérieur.

outright, adv. complètement.

outrun, vb. dépasser.

outset, n. début m.

outside, 1. adv. dehors. **2.** prep. en dehors de.

outsider, n. étranger m.

outskirts, n. limites f.pl.

outstanding, adj. exceptionnel; non réglé.

outward, adj. extérieur.

oval, adj. and n. ovale m.

ovary, n. ovaire m.

ovation, n. ovation f.

oven, n. four m.

over, 1. prep. (on) sur; (above) au-dessus de; (beyond) au delà de; (more than) plus de. **2.** adv. (all o.) partout; (more) davantage; (finished) fini; (with adj.) trop.

overbearing, adj. arrogant.

overcast, adj. (weather) couvert.

overcoat, n. pardessus m.

overcome, vb. vaincre; (be o. by) succomber à.

overdose, n. dose (f.) excessive, overdose f.

overdue, adj. arriéré, échu.

overflow, vb. déborder.

overhaul, vb. examiner en détail, remettre au point.

overhead, 1. adj. (comm.) général. **2.** adv. en haut.

overkill, n. exagération rhétorique f.

overlook, vb. (look onto) avoir vue sur; (neglect) négliger.

overnight, adv. pendant la nuit.

overpower, vb. (subdue) subjuguer; (crush) accabler.

overrule, vb. décider contre.

overrun, vb. envahir.

overseas, adv. outre-mer, à l'étranger.

oversee, vb. surveiller.

oversight, n. inadvertance f.

overstuffed, adj. rembourré.

overt, adj. manifeste.

overtake, vb. rattraper; (accident, etc.) arriver à.

overthrow, vb. renverser.

overtime, n. heures (f.pl.) supplémentaires.

overture, n. ouverture f.

overturn, vb. renverser, tr.

overview, n. vue d'ensemble f.

overweight, n. excédent m.

overwhelm, vb. accabler (de).

overwork, vb. surmener, tr.

owe, vb. devoir.

owing, 1. prep. à cause de, en raison de. **2.** adj. dû.

owl, n. hibou m.

own, 1. adj. propre. **2.** vb. posséder; (admit) avouer; (acknowledge) reconnaître.

owner, n. propriétaire m.f.

ox, n. bœuf m.

oxygen, n. oxygène m.

oxygen mask, n. masque (m.) d'oxygène.

oyster, n. huître f.

ozone, n. ozone m.; (o. hole) trou (m.) d'ozone; (o. layer) couche (f.) d'ozone.

P

pace, 1. n. (step) pas m.; (gait) allure f. **2.** vb. arpenter.

pacemaker, n. stimulateur (m.) cardiaque.

pacific, adj. pacifique.

Pacific Ocean, n. océan Pacifique m.

pacifism, n. pacifisme m.

pacify, vb. pacifier.

pack, 1. n. paquet m.; (animals) meute f.; (persons) bande f. **2.** vb. emballer; (crowd) entasser.

package, n. paquet m.

packet, n. paquet m.

packing, n. emballage m.

pact, n. pacte m., contrat m.

pad, 1. n. (stuffing) bourrelet m.; (cotton, ink) tampon m.; (paper) bloc m. **2.** vb. (clothes) ouater; (stuff) bourrer.

padding, n. remplissage m., rembourrage m.

paddle, n. pagaie f.

paddock, n. enclos m.

padlock, n. cadenas m.

pagan, adj. and n. païen m.

page, *n.* (book) page *f.;* (attendant) page *m.*

pageant, *n.* spectacle *m.*

pager, *n.* récepteur *(m.)* d'appels.

pagoda, *n.* pagode *f.*

pail, *n.* seau *m.*

pain, 1. *n.* douleur *f.;* (trouble) peine *f.* 2. *vb.* (hurt) faire mal (à); (distress) faire de la peine (à).

painful, *adj.* douloureux.

painstaking, *adj.* soigneux.

paint, 1. *n.* peinture *f.* 2. *vb.* peindre.

painter, *n.* peintre *m.*

painting, *n.* peinture *f.*

pair, *n.* paire *f.*

pajamas, *n.* pyjama *m.*

Pakistan, *n.* Pakistan *m.*

pal, *n.* copain *m.*

palace, *n.* palais *m.*

palatable, *adj.* d'un goût agréable, agréable au palais.

palate, *n.* palais *m.*

palatial, *adj.* qui ressemble à un palais, magnifique.

pale, *adj.* pâle.

paleness, *n.* pâleur *f.*

Palestine, *n.* Palestine *f.*

palette, *n.* palette *f.*

pall, 1. *n.* drap funéraire *m.* 2. *vb.* s'affadir.

pallbearer, *n.* porteur (d'un cordon du poêle) *m.*

pallid, *adj.* pâle, blême.

palm, *n.* (tree) palmier *m.;* (branch) palme *f.;* (hand) paume *f.*

palpable, *adj.* manifeste.

palpitate, *vb.* palpiter.

paltry, *adj.* mesquin.

pamper, *vb.* choyer.

pamphlet, *n.* brochure *f.*

pan, *n.* (cooking) casserole *f.*

panacea, *n.* panacée *f.*

Pan-American, *adj.* panaméricain.

pancake, *n.* crêpe *f.*

pancreas, *n.* pancréas *m.*

pandemonium, *n.* tumulte *m.,* chaos *m.*

pander to, *vb.* flatter bassement.

pane, *n.* (window) vitre *f.*

panel, *n.* panneau *m.*

pang, *n.* angoisse *f.*

panic, *n.* panique *f.*

panorama, *n.* panorama *m.*

pant, *vb.* haleter.

pantomime, *n.* pantomime *m.*

pantry, *n.* office *f.*

pants, *n.* pantalon *m.*

panty hose, *n.* collant *m.*

papal, *adj.* papal.

paper, *n.* papier *m.*

paperback, *n.* livre *(m.)* de poche.

par, *n.* pair *m.,* égalité *f.*

parable, *n.* parabole *f.*

parachute, *n.* parachute *m.*

parade, *n.* parade *f.*

paradise, *n.* paradis *m.*

paradox, *n.* paradoxe *m.*

paraffin, *n.* paraffine *f.*

paragon, *n.* modèle *m.*

paragraph, *n.* alinéa *m.,* paragraphe *m.*

parakeet, *n.* perruche *f.*

parallel, 1. *n.* (line) parallèle *f.;* (geography, comparison) parallèle *m.* 2. *adj.* parallèle.

paralyze, *vb.* paralyser.

paramedic, *n.* assistant médical *m.*

parameter, *n.* paramètre *m.*

paramount, *adj.* souverain.

paranoia, *n.* paranoïa *f.*

paranoid, *adj.* paranoïaque.

paraphrase, *vb.* paraphraser.

parasite, *n.* parasite *m.*

parcel, *n.* paquet *m.;* (p. post) colis postal *m.*

parch, *vb.* dessécher, *tr.*

parchment, *n.* parchemin *m.*

pardon, 1. *n.* pardon *m.* 2. *vb.* pardonner.

pare, *vb.* (fruit) peler.

parent, *n.* père *m.;* mère *f.;* (parents) parents *m.pl.*

parentage, *n.* naissance *f.*

parenthesis, *n.* parenthèse *f.*

parish, *n.* paroisse *f.*

Parisian, 1. *n.* Parisien *m.* 2. *adj.* parisien.

parity, *n.* parité *f.,* égalité *f.*

park, 1. *n.* parc *m.* 2. *vb.* stationner.

parking lot, *n.* parking *m.*

parking meter, *n.* parcmètre *m.*

parley, *n.* conférence *f.,* pourparler *m.*

parliament, *n.* parlement *m.*

parliamentary, *adj.* parlementaire.

parlor, *n.* petit salon *m.*

parochial, *adj.* paroissial; (limited in outlook) de clocher.

parody, n. parodie f.

parole, 1. n. parole f. **2.** vb. libérer conditionnellement.

paroxysm, n. paroxysme m.

parrot, n. perroquet m.

parsley, n. persil m.

parsimonious, adj. parcimonieux.

parson, n. pasteur m.

part, 1. n. (of a whole) partie f.; (share) part f. **2.** vb. (divide) diviser; (share) partager; (of people) se séparer.

partake of, vb. participer à.

partial, adj. partiel; (favoring) partial.

participant, adj. and n. participant m.

participate, vb. participer.

participation, n. participation f.

participle, n. participe m.

particle, n. particule f.

particular, 1. n. détail m. **2.** adj. particulier; (person) exigeant.

parting, n. séparation f.; (hair) raie f.

partisan, n. partisan m.

partition, n. partage m.; (wall) cloison f.

partly, adv. en partie.

partner, n. associé m.

part of speech, n. partie (f.) du discours.

partridge, n. perdrix f.

part-time, adj. and adv. à temps partiel.

party, n. (faction) parti m.; (social) réception f.; (group of people) groupe m.; (law) partie f.

pass, 1. n. (mountain) col m.; (permission) laissez-passer m. **2.** vb. passer.

passable, adj. traversable, passable, assez bon.

passage, n. passage m.

passenger, n. (land) voyageur m.; (sea, air) passager m.

passer-by, n. passant m.

passion, n. passion f.

passionate, adj. passionné.

passive, adj. and n. passif m.

Passover, n. Pâque f.

passport, n. passeport m.

password, n. mot (m.) de passe.

past, 1. adj. and n. passé m. **2.** prep. (beyond) au delà de; (more than)

plus de; **(half p. four)** quatre heures et demie.

paste, 1. n. pâte f.; (glue) colle f. **2.** vb. coller.

pasteurize, vb. pasteuriser.

pastime, n. passe-temps m.

pastor, n. pasteur m.

pastry, n. pâtisserie f.

pasture, n. pâturage m.

pasty, adj. empâté, pâteux.

pat, vb. taper.

patch, 1. n. pièce f. **2.** vb. rapiécer.

patchwork, n. patchwork m.

patent, n. brevet (m.) d'invention.

patent leather, n. cuir (m.) verni.

paternal, adj. paternel.

paternity, n. paternité f.

path, n. sentier m.

pathetic, adj. pathétique.

pathology, n. pathologie f.

pathos, n. pathétique m.

patience, n. patience f.

patient, 1. n. malade m.f. **2.** adj. patient.

patio, n. patio m.

patriarch, n. patriarche m.

patriot, n. patriote m.f.

patriotic, adj. patriotique.

patriotism, n. patriotisme m.

patrol, n. patrouille f.

patrolman, n. agent (de police) m.; patrouilleur m.

patron, n. protecteur m.; (comm.) client m.

patronize, vb. subventionner; traiter avec condescendance.

pattern, n. modèle m.; (design) dessin m.; schéma m.

pauper, n. indigent m., pauvre m.; mendiant m.

pause, n. pause f.

pave, vb. paver.

pavement, n. pavé m.; (sidewalk) trottoir m.

pavestone, n. pavé m.

pavilion, n. pavillon m.

paw, n. patte f.

pawn, 1. n. pion m. **2.** vb. mettre en gage, engager.

pay, 1. n. salaire m. **2.** vb. payer.

payment, n. paiement m.

pay phone, n. cabine (f.) téléphonique.

pea, n. pois m.

peace, n. paix f.

peaceable, peaceful, adj. paisible.

peach, n. pêche f.

peacock, n. paon m.

peak, n. sommet m.

peal, 1. n. retentissement m. **2.** vb. sonner, retentir.

peanut, n. arachide f.

pear, n. poire f.

pearl, n. perle f.

peasant, n. paysan m.

pebble, n. caillou m.

peck, vb. becqueter.

peculiar, adj. particulier; (unusual) singulier.

pecuniary, adj. pécuniaire.

pedagogue, n. pédagogue m.

pedagogy, n. pédagogie f.

pedal, n. pédale f.

pedant, n. pédant m.

peddle, vb. colporter.

peddler, n. colporteur m., camelot m.

pedestal, n. piédestal m.

pedestrian, n. piéton m.

pediatrician, n. pédiatre m.

pedigree, n. généalogie f.

pee, vb. (colloquial) faire pipi.

peek, 1. n. coup d'œil furtif m. **2.** vb. regarder à la dérobée.

peel, 1. n. pelure f. **2.** vb. peler.

peep, vb. regarder furtivement.

peer, 1. n. pair m. **2.** vb. scruter.

peevish, adj. irritable.

peg, n. cheville f.

pejorative, adj. péjoratif.

pelican, n. pélican m.

pelt, 1. n. peau f., fourrure f. **2.** vb. lancer, jeter.

pelvis, n. bassin m.

pen, n. plume f.; (ballpoint) stylo (m.) à bille.

penalty, n. peine f.

penance, n. pénitence f.

penchant, n. penchant m.

pencil, n. crayon m.

pendant, n. pendentif m.

pending, prep. pendant.

penetrate, vb. pénétrer.

penetration, n. pénétration f.

penicillin, n. pénicilline f.

peninsula, n. péninsule f.

penis, n. pénis m.

penitent, 1. adj. pénitent, contrit. **2.** n. pénitent m.

penknife, n. canif m.

penniless, adj. sans le sou.

penny, n. sou m.

pension, n. pension f.

pensive, adj. pensif.

Pentecost, n. Pentecôte f.

pent-up, adj. refoulé.

penury, n. pénurie f.

people, 1. n. gens m.f.pl.; (of a country) peuple m. **2.** vb. peupler.

pep, n. énergie f.

pepper, n. poivre m.

per, prep. par; **(p. hour)** par heure; **(p. year)** par an.

perambulator, n. voiture (f.) d'enfant.

perceive, vb. apercevoir, tr.

percent, pour cent.

percentage, n. pourcentage m.

perceptible, adj. perceptible.

perception, n. perception f.

perch, 1. n. (for birds) perchoir m.; (fish) perche f. **2.** vb. se percher.

perdition, n. perte f.

peremptory, adj. péremptoire.

perennial, adj. perpétuel; (plant) vivace.

perfect, adj. parfait.

perfection, n. perfection f.

perforation, n. perforation f.

perform, vb. accomplir; (theater) jouer.

performance, n. (task) accomplissement m.; (theater) représentation f.

perfume, n. parfum m.

perfunctory, adj. fait pour la forme, superficiel.

perhaps, adv. peut-être.

peril, n. péril m.

perilous, adj. périlleux.

perimeter, n. périmètre m.

period, n. période f.; (full stop) point m.

periodic, adj. périodique.

periodical, n. périodique m.

peripheral, adj. périphérique.

periphery, n. périphérie f.

perish, vb. périr.

perishable, adj. périssable.

perjury, n. parjure m.

permanent, adj. permanent.

permeate, vb. filtrer.

permissible, adj. admissible.

permission, n. permission f.

permit, 1. n. permis m. **2.** vb. permettre.

pernicious, adj. pernicieux.

peroxide, n. eau (f.) oxygénée.

perpendicular, adj. perpendiculaire, vertical.

perpetrate, vb. perpétrer.

perpetual, adj. perpétuel.

perplex, vb. mettre dans la perplexité.

perplexity, n. perplexité f., embarras m.

persecute, vb. persécuter.

persecution, n. persécution f.

perseverance, n. persévérance f.

persevere, vb. persévérer.

Persian, adj. persan; **(P. Gulf)** golfe (m.) persique.

persist, vb. persister.

persistent, adj. persistant.

person, n. personne f.

personage, n. personnage m.

personal, adj. personnel.

personal computer, n. ordinateur (m.) personnel.

personality, n. personnalité f.

personally, adv. personnellement.

personnel, n. personnel m.

perspective, n. perspective f.

perspiration, n. transpiration f.

perspire, vb. transpirer.

persuade, vb. persuader.

persuasive, adj. persuasif.

pertain, vb. appartenir.

pertinent, adj. pertinent.

perturb, vb. troubler.

Peru, n. Pérou m.

peruse, vb. lire attentivement.

pervade, vb. pénétrer.

perverse, adj. entêté (dans l'erreur).

perversion, n. perversion f.

pessimism, n. pessimisme m.

pester, vb. importuner.

pestilence, n. pestilence f.

pet, n. (animal) animal (m.) familier.

petal, n. pétale m.

petition, n. pétition f.

petrified, adj. mort de peur.

petroleum, n. pétrole m.

petticoat, n. jupon m.

petty, adj. insignifiant.

petulant, adj. boudeur.

pew, n. banc (m.) (d'église).

phantom, n. fantôme m.

pharmacist, n. pharmacien m.

pharmacy, n. pharmacie f.

phase, n. phase f.

phenomenal, adj. phénoménal.

phenomenon, n. phénomène m.

philanthropy, n. philanthropie f.

Philippines, n. Philippines f.pl.

philosopher, n. philosophe m.

philosophical, adj. philosophique.

philosophy, n. philosophie f.

phobia, n. phobie f.

phone, 1. n. téléphone m. **2.** vb. téléphoner.

phone booth, n. cabine (f.) téléphonique.

phonetics, n. phonétique f.

phonograph, n. phonographe m.

photocopier, n. photocopieur m.

photocopy, 1. n. photocopie f. **2.** vb. photocopier.

photograph, photography, n. photographie f.

photographer, n. photographe m.

phrase, n. expression f.; (gramm.) bout (m.) de phrase.

physical, adj. physique.

physical therapy, n. kinésithérapie f.

physician, n. médecin m.

physics, n. physique f.

physiology, n. physiologie f.

pianist, n. pianiste m.f.

piano, n. piano m.

pick, 1. vb. (choose) choisir; (gather) cueillir. **2.** n. pioche f.

pickles, n. conserves (f.pl.) au vinaigre.

picnic, n. pique-nique m.

picture, n. tableau m.; (motion picture) film m.

picturesque, adj. pittoresque.

pie, n. tarte f.

piece, n. morceau m.

pier, n. jetée f.; quai m.

pierce, vb. percer.

piety, n. piété f.

pig, n. cochon m.

pigeon, n. pigeon m.

pigeonhole, n. (for papers, etc.) case f.

pigment, n. pigment m.

pigtail, n. natte f.

pile, 1. n. (construction) pieu m.; (heap) tas m. **2.** vb. entasser.

pilgrim, n. pèlerin m.
pilgrimage, n. pèlerinage m.
pill, n. pilule f.
pillage, 1. n. pillage m. **2.** vb. piller.
pillar, n. pilier m.
pillow, n. oreiller m.
pillowcase, n. taie (f.) d'oreiller.
pilot, n. pilote m.
pimp, n. maquereau m., souteneur m.
pimple, n. bouton m.
pin, 1. n. épingle f. **2.** vb. épingler.
pinball, n. flipper m.
pinch, vb. pincer.
pine, 1. n. pin m. **2.** vb. languir.
pineapple, n. ananas m.
pink, adj. and n. rose m.
pinnacle, n. pinacle m.
pint, n. pinte f.
pioneer, n. pionnier m.
pious, adj. pieux.
pipe, n. tuyau m.; (smoking) pipe f.
pipeline, n. pipeline m.
piper, n. (bagpipe) joueur (m.) de cornemuse.
piquant, adj. piquant.
pirate, n. pirate m.
pistol, n. pistolet m.
piston, n. piston m.
pit, n. fosse f.
pitch, 1. n. (substance) poix f.; (throw) jet m.; (height) hauteur f.; (music) ton m. **2.** vb. (throw) lancer.
pitcher, n. (vessel) cruche f.; (baseball) lanceur m.
pitfall, n. trappe f.
pitiful, adj. pitoyable.
pitiless, adj. impitoyable.
pity, 1. n. pitié f.; (what a p.!) quel dommage! **2.** vb. plaindre.
pivot, n. pivot m., axe m.
pizza, n. pizza f.
placate, vb. calmer.
place, 1. n. endroit m.; (locality) lieu m.; (position occupied) place f. **2.** vb. mettre.
placid, adj. placide.
plagiarize, vb. plagier.
plague, n. (disease) peste f.; (fig.) fléau m.
plaid, n. (blanket) plaid m.; (textile) tartan m.
plain, 1. n. plaine f. **2.** adj. (clear)

clair; (simple) simple; (of person) quelconque.
plaintiff, n. demandeur m., plaignant m.
plan, 1. n. plan m. **2.** vb. prévoir, projeter.
plane, n. (surface) plan m.; (tool) rabot m.; (tree) platane m.; (airplane) avion m.
planet, n. planète f.
plank, n. planche f.
planning, n. planification f.; (family p.) planning (m.) familial.
plant, 1. n. plante f. **2.** vb. planter.
plantation, n. plantation f.
planter, n. planteur m.
plasma, n. plasma m.
plaster, n. plâtre m.
plastic, adj. plastique.
plate, n. plaque f.; (for eating) assiette f.
plateau, n. plateau m.
platform, n. plate-forme f.; (railroad) quai m.
platinum, n. platine f.
platonic, adj. platonique.
platoon, n. (military) section f.
platter, n. plat m.
plausible, adj. plausible.
play, 1. n. jeu m.; (drama) pièce (f.) de théâtre. **2.** vb. jouer; (game) jouer à; (instrument) jouer de.
player, n. jouer m.; (theater) acteur m.
playful, adj. enjoué.
playground, n. (children) terrain (m.) de jeu.
playmate, n. camarade (m.f.) de jeu.
playwright, n. dramaturge m.
plea, n. défense f.; (excuse) excuse f.
plead, vb. plaider; (allege) alléguer.
pleasant, adj. agréable.
please, vb. plaire à; (satisfy) contenter; (if you p.) s'il vous plaît.
pleasure, n. plaisir m.
pleat, n. pli m.
pledge, n. gage m.; (promise) engagement m.
plentiful, adj. abondant.
plenty, n. abondance f.
pliable, adj. pliable.
pliers, n. pinces f.pl.

plight, n. état m.

plot, 1. n. (literature) intrigue f.; (conspiracy) complot m. **2.** vb. comploter.

plow, 1. n. charrue f. **2.** vb. labourer.

pluck, n. courage m.

plug, n. tampon m.; (electric) prise (f.) de courant.

plum, n. prune f.

plumber, n. plombier m.

plume, n. panache m.

plump, adj. grassouillet.

plunder, vb. piller.

plunge, 1. n. plongeon m. **2.** vb. plonger.

pluperfect, n. plus-que-parfait m.

plural, adj. and n. pluriel m.

plus, n. plus m.

pneumonia, n. pneumonie f.

poach, vb. (of eggs) pocher.

poacher, n. braconnier m.

pocket, n. poche f.

pocketbook, n. sac (m.) à main.

podiatrist, n. podologue m.f.

poem, n. poésie f.; (long) poème f.

poet, n. poète m.

poetic, adj. poétique.

poetry, n. poésie f.

poignant, adj. poignant.

point, 1. n. point m.; (sharp end) pointe f. **2.** vb. (gun, etc.) pointer; (indicate) désigner.

pointed, adj. pointu; (ironical) mordant.

poise, n. équilibre m.

poison, 1. n. poison m. **2.** vb. empoisonner.

poisonous, adj. empoisonné; (plant) vénéneux; (animal) venimeux.

Poland, n. Pologne f.

polar, adj. polaire.

polar bear, n. ours (m.) blanc.

Pole, n. Polonais m.

pole, n. (geography) pôle m.; (wood) perche f.

polemic, n. polémique f.

police, n. police f.

policeman, n. agent (m.) de police.

policy, n. politique f.; (insurance) police f.

polio, n. polio f.

Polish, adj. and n. polonais m.

polish, vb. polir; (shoes) cirer.

polite, adj. poli.

politic, political, adj. politique.

politician, n. politicien m.

politics, n. politique f.

poll, n. (voting) scrutin m.; (opinion) sondage m.

pollen, n. pollen m.

pollute, vb. polluer.

polygamy, n. polygamie f.

pomegranate, n. grenade f.

pomp, n. pompe f.

pompous, adj. pompeux.

pond, n. étang m.

ponder, vb. réfléchir.

ponderous, adj. pesant.

pony, n. poney m.

poodle, n. caniche m.

pool, n. mare f.; (swimming) piscine f.

poor, adj. pauvre.

pop, n. petit bruit (m.) sec.

pope, n. pape m.

popular, adj. populaire.

popularity, n. popularité f.

population, n. population f.

porcelain, n. porcelaine f.

porch, n. véranda f.

porcupine, n. porc-épic m.

pore, n. pore m. **2.** vb. (p. over) s'absorber dans.

pork, n. porc m.

pornography, n. pornographie f.

porous, adj. poreux.

porpoise, n. marsouin m.

port, n. (harbor) port m.; (naut.) bâbord m.; (wine) porto m.

portable, adj. portatif.

portal, n. portail m.

portfolio, n. portefeuille m.

portion, n. portion f.

portrait, n. portrait m.

portray, vb. (paint) peindre; (describe) dépeindre.

Portugal, n. Portugal m.

Portuguese, 1. n. (person) Portugais m.; (language) portugais m. **2.** adj. portugais.

pose, 1. n. pose f. **2.** vb. poser.

position, n. position f.

positive, 1. n. positif m. **2.** adj. positif.

possess, vb. posséder.

possession, n. possession f.

possibility, n. possibilité f.

possible, *adj.* possible.
possibly, *adv.* il est possible que . . .; (perhaps) peut-être.
post, 1. *n.* (mail) poste *f.;* (wood) poteau *m.;* (place) poste *m.* **2.** *vb.* (mail) mettre à la poste; (placard) afficher.
postage, *n.* affranchissement *m.*
postal, *adj.* postal.
post card, *n.* carte (*f.*) postale.
poster, *n.* affiche *f.*
posterior, *adj.* postérieur.
posterity, *n.* postérité *f.*
post office, *n.* bureau (*m.*) de poste.
postman, *n.* facteur *m.*
postmark, *n.* cachet (*m.*) de la poste.
postpone, *vb.* remettre.
postscript, *n.* post-scriptum *m.*
posture, *n.* posture *f.*
postwar, *adj.* d'après-guerre.
pot, *n.* pot *m.;* (saucepan) marmite *f.;* (marijuana) herbe *f.,* kif *m.*
potato, *n.* pomme (*f.*) de terre; (French-fried p.s) frites *f.pl.*
potent, *adj.* puissant.
potential, *adj. and n.* potentiel *m.*
pottery, *n.* poterie *f.*
pouch, *n.* sac *m.*
poultry, *n.* volaille *f.*
pound, *n.* livre *f.*
pour, *vb.* verser; (rain) tomber à verse.
pout, *vb.* bouder.
poverty, *n.* pauvreté *f.*
powder, *n.* poudre *f.*
power, *n.* pouvoir *m.;* (nation, mathematics) puissance *f.*
powerful, *adj.* puissant.
powerless, *adj.* impuissant.
practical, *adj.* pratique.
practically, *adv.* pratiquement.
practice, 1. *n.* (exercise) exercice *m.;* (habit) habitude *f.;* (not theory) pratique *f.* **2.** *vb.* pratiquer; (piano, etc.) s'exercer (à).
practiced, *adj.* expérimenté.
pragmatic, *adj.* pragmatique.
prairie, *n.* savane *f.*
praise, 1. *n.* éloge *m.* **2.** *vb.* louer.
prank, *n.* fredaine *f.*
pray, *vb.* prier.
prayer, *n.* prière *f.*
preach, *vb.* prêcher.

preacher, *n.* prédicateur *m.*
precarious, *adj.* précaire.
precaution, *n.* précaution *f.*
precede, *vb.* précéder.
precedent, *n.* précédent *f.*
precept, *n.* précepte *m.*
precinct, *n.* circonscription *f.*
precious, *adj.* précieux.
precipice, *n.* précipice *m.*
precipitate, *vb.* précipiter.
precise, *adj.* précis.
precision, *n.* précision *f.*
preclude, *vb.* empêcher.
precocious, *adj.* précoce.
precondition, *n.* condition (*f.*) requise.
predecessor, *n.* prédécesseur *m.*
predestination, *n.* prédestination *f.*
predicament, *n.* situation (*f.*) difficile.
predict, *vb.* prédire.
predispose, *vb.* prédisposer.
predominant, *adj.* prédominant.
preempt, *vb.* (acquire) acquérir d'avance; (forestall) prévenir.
prefabricate, *vb.* préfabriquer.
preface, *n.* préface *f.*
prefer, *vb.* préférer.
preferable, *adj.* préférable.
preference, *n.* préférence *f.*
prefix, *n.* préfixe *m.*
pregnant, *adj.* enceinte.
prejudice, *n.* préjugé *m.*
preliminary, *adj.* préliminaire.
prelude, *n.* prélude *m.*
premarital, *adj.* avant le mariage.
premature, *adj.* prématuré.
premeditate, *vb.* préméditer.
premier, *n.* premier ministre *m.*
première, *n.* première *f.*
premise, *n.* (place) lieux *m.pl.;* (logic) prémisse *f.*
premium, *n.* prix *m.*
preoccupation, *n.* préoccupation *f.*
preparation, *n.* préparation *f.;* préparatifs *m.pl*
preparatory, *adj.* préparatoire.
prepare, *vb.* préparer, *tr.*
preponderant, *adj.* prépondérant.
preposition, *n.* préposition *f.*
preposterous, *adj.* absurde.
prerequisite, *n.* nécessité (*f.*) préalable.

prerogative, *n.* prérogative *f.*

prescribe, *vb.* prescrire.

prescription, *n.* prescription *f.;* (medical) ordonnance *f.*

presence, *n.* présence *f.*

present, 1. *adj.* présent. **2.** *n.* présent *m.;* (gift) cadeau *m.* **3.** *vb.* présenter.

presentable, *adj.* présentable.

presentation, *n.* présentation *f.*

presently, *adv.* tout à l'heure.

preservative, *n.* préservateur *m.,* conservateur *m.*

preserve, 1. *n.* (jam) confiture *f.* **2.** *vb.* (protect) préserver; (keep) conserver.

preside, *vb.* présider.

president, *n.* président *m.*

press, 1. *n.* presse *f.* **2.** *vb.* presser; (iron) repasser.

press conference, *n.* conférence (*f.*) de presse.

pressure, *n.* pression *f.*

prestige, *n.* prestige *m.*

presume, *vb.* présumer.

presumptuous, *adj.* présomptueux.

pretend, *vb.* (claim, aspire) prétendre; (feign) simuler.

pretense, *n.* faux semblant *m.*

pretentious, *adj.* prétentieux.

pretext, *n.* prétexte *m.*

pretty, *adj.* joli.

prevail, *vb.* prévaloir; **(p. upon)** décider.

prevalent, *adj.* répandu.

prevent, *vb.* (impede) empêcher; (forestall) prévenir.

prevention, *n.* empêchement *m.*

preventive, *adj.* préventif.

preview, *n.* avant-première *f.*

previous, *adj.* antérieur.

prewar, *adj.* d'avant-guerre.

prey, *n.* proie *f.*

price, *n.* prix *m.*

priceless, *adj.* inestimable.

prick, 1. *n.* piqûre *f.* **2.** *vb.* piquer.

pride, *n.* orgueil *m.*

priest, *n.* prêtre *m.*

prim, *adj.* guindé.

primarily, *adv.* principalement.

primary, *adj.* premier; (school, geology) primaire.

prime, 1. *n.* comble *m.* **2.** *adj.* premier, de première qualité. **3.** *vb.* amorcer.

primitive, *adj.* primitif.

prince, *n.* prince *m.*

princess, *n.* princesse *f.*

principal, *adj.* principal.

principle, *n.* principe *m.*

print, 1. *n.* (mark) empreinte *f.;* (book) impression *f.;* (photo) épreuve *f.* **2.** *vb.* imprimer.

printout, *n.* feuille (*f.*) imprimée produite par un ordinateur.

prior, 1. *adj.* antérieur. **2.** *adv.* **(p. to doing)** avant de faire.

priority, *n.* priorité *f.*

prism, *n.* prisme *m.*

prison, *n.* prison *f.*

prisoner, *n.* prisonnier *m.*

privacy, *n.* intimité *f.,* solitude *f.,* vie (*f.*) privée.

private, *adj.* particulier; (not public) privé.

privation, *n.* privation *f.*

privilege, *n.* privilège *m.*

prize, *n.* prix *m.*

probability, *n.* probabilité *f.*

probable, *adj.* probable.

probation, *n.* **(on p.)** en liberté (*f.*) surveillée.

probe, *vb.* sonder.

problem, *n.* problème *m.*

procedure, *n.* procédé *m.*

proceed, *vb.* procéder; (advance) avancer.

process, *n.* (method) procédé *m.,* processus *m.;* (progress) développement *m.*

procession, *n.* cortège *m.;* (religious) procession *f.*

proclaim, *vb.* proclamer.

proclamation, *n.* proclamation *f.*

procrastinate, *vb.* différer.

procure, *vb.* procurer.

prodigal, *adj. and n.* prodigue *f.*

prodigy, *n.* prodige *m.*

produce, *vb.* produire.

product, *n.* produit *m.*

production, *n.* production *f.*

production line, *n.* chaîne (*f.*) (de fabrication).

productive, *adj.* productif.

profane, *adj.* profane.

profess, *vb.* professer.

profession, *n.* profession *f.*

professional, *adj.* professionnel.

professor, *n.* professeur *m.*

proficient, *adj.* capable.

profile, *n.* profil *m.*

profit, 1. *n.* profit *m.* **2.** *vb.* profiter.

profitable, *adj.* profitable.

profound, *adj.* profond.

profuse, *adj.* (of thing) profus; (of person) prodigue.

program, 1. *n.* programme *m.* **2.** *vb.* programmer.

programming, *n.* programmation *f.*

progress, *n.* progrès *m.;* (motion forward) marche *f.*

progressive, *adj.* progressif.

prohibit, *vb.* défendre.

prohibition, *n.* défense *f.*

prohibitive, *adj.* prohibitif.

project, 1. *n.* projet *m.* **2.** *vb.* projeter; (jut out) faire saillie.

projection, *n.* projection *f.;* (jutting out) saillie *f.*

projector, *n.* projecteur *m.*

proletariat, *n.* prolétariat *m.*

proliferation, *n.* prolifération *f.*

prologue, *n.* prologue *m.*

prolong, *vb.* prolonger.

prominent, *adj.* saillant.

promiscuous, *adj.* (indiscriminate) sans distinction.

promise, 1. *n.* promesse *f.* **2.** *vb.* promettre.

promote, *vb.* (raise) promouvoir; (encourage) encourager.

promotion, *n.* promotion *f.*

prompt, 1. *adj.* prompt. **2.** *n.* (computer) message *(m.)* (de guidage). **3.** *vb.* provoquer, (theater) souffler.

pronoun, *n.* pronom *m.*

pronounce, *vb.* prononcer.

pronunciation, *n.* prononciation *f.*

proof, *n.* (evidence) preuve *f.;* (test) épreuve *f.*

prop, *n.* appui *m.*

propaganda, *n.* propagande *f.*

propagate, *vb.* propager, *tr.*

propel, *vb.* propulser.

propeller, *n.* hélice *f.*

proper, *adj.* propre; (respectable, fitting) convenable.

property, *n.* propriété *f.*

prophecy, *n.* prophétie *f.*

prophesy, *vb.* prophétiser.

prophet, *n.* prophète *m.*

prophetic, *adj.* prophétique.

proportion, *n.* proportion *f.*

proportionate, *adj.* proportionné.

proposal, *n.* proposition *f.;* demande *(f.)* en mariage.

propose, *vb.* proposer, *tr.*

proposition, *n.* (proposal, grammar) proposition *f.;* (undertaking) affaire *f.*

proprietor, *n.* propriétaire *m.f.*

prosaic, *adj.* prosaïque.

proscribe, *vb.* proscrire.

prose, *n.* prose *f.*

prosecute, *vb.* poursuivre.

prosecution, *n.* poursuites *(f.pl.)* judiciaires.

prosecuting attorney, *n.* procureur *m.*

prospect, *n.* perspective *f.*

prospective, *adj.* en perspective.

prosper, *vb.* prospérer.

prosperity, *n.* prospérité *f.*

prosperous, *adj.* prospère.

prostate, *n.* prostate *f.*

prostitute, 1. *n.* prostituée *f.* **2.** *vb.* prostituer.

prostrate, *adj.* prosterné.

protagonist, *n.* protagoniste *m.*

protect, *vb.* protéger.

protection, *n.* protection *f.*

protective, *adj.* protecteur.

protector, *n.* protecteur *m.*

protégé, *n.* protégé *m.*

protein, *n.* protéine *f.*

protest, 1. *n.* protestation *f.;* *(comm.)* protêt *m.* **2.** *vb.* protester.

Protestant, 1. *n.* Protestant *m.* **2.** *adj.* protestant.

protocol, *n.* protocole *m.*

protrude, *vb.* saillir.

proud, *adj.* fier.

prove, *vb.* prouver; (test) éprouver.

proverb, *n.* proverbe *m.*

provide (with) *vb.* pourvoir (de), *tr.*

providence, *n.* (foresight) prévoyance *f.;* (divine) providence *f.*

province, *n.* province *f.*

provincial, *adj. and n.* provincial *m.*

provision, *n.* (stock) provision *f.*

provocation, *n.* provocation *f.*

provoke, *vb.* provoquer; (irritate) irriter.

prowess, n. prouesse f.
prowl, vb. rôder.
proximity, n. proximité f.
prude, n. prude f.
prudence, n. prudence f.
prudent, adj. prudent.
prune, n. pruneau m.
Prussia, n. Prusse f.
Prussian, 1. n. Prussien m. **2.** adj. prussien.
pry, vb. fureter.
psalm, n. psaume m.
psychedelic, adj. psychédélique.
psychiatry, n. psychiatrie f.
psychoanalysis, n. psychanalyse f.
psychological, adj. psychologique.
psychology, n. psychologie f.
psychothérapie, n. psychothérapie f.
ptomaine, n. ptomaïne f.
public, 1. n. public m. **2.** adj. public m., publique f.
publication, n. publication f.
publicity, n. publicité f.
public transport, n. transports (m.pl.) en commun.
publish, vb. publier.
publisher, n. éditeur m.
pudding, n. pouding m.
puddle, n. flaque f.
puff, n. (smoke etc.) bouffée f.
pugnacious, adj. batailleur, combattif.
pull, vb. tirer.
pulley, n. poulie f.
pulp, n. pulpe f.
pulpit, n. chaire f.
pulsar, n. pulsar m.
pulsate, vb. battre.
pulse, n. pouls m.
pump, 1. n. pompe f. **2.** vb. pomper.

pumpkin, n. potiron m.; citrouille f.
pun, n. calembour m.
punch, 1. n. (tool) poinçon m.; (blow) coup (m.) de poing; (beverage) punch (m.) **2.** vb. (pierce) percer; (pummel) gourmer.
punctual, adj. ponctuel.
punctuate, vb. ponctuer.
puncture, n. piqûre f.
punish, vb. punir.
punishment, n. punition f.
pupil, n. (school) élève m.f.; (eye) pupille f.
puppet, n. marionnette f.
puppy, n. petit chien m.
purchase, 1. n. achat m. **2.** vb. acheter.
pure, adj. pur.
puree, n. purée f.
purge, vb. purger.
purify, vb. purifier.
puritan, n. puritain m.
purity, n. pureté f.
purple, adj. violet.
purpose, n. but m.; **(to the p.)** à propos.
purposely, adv. exprès.
purse, n. bourse f.
pursue, vb. poursuivre.
pursuit, n. poursuite f.; (occupation) occupation f.; **(p. plane)** avion (m.) de chasse.
push, 1. n. poussée f. **2.** vb. pousser.
pussy(cat), n. minet m.
put, vb. mettre.
puzzle, 1. n. problème m. **2.** vb. embarrasser.
pyramid, n. pyramide f.
Pyrenees, n. Pyrénées f.pl.
python, n. python m.

Q

quadrangle, n. cour f.
quadraphonic, adj. quadriphonique.
quail, n. caille f.
quaint, adj. (strange) étrange.
quake, vb. trembler.
qualification, n. (reservation) ré-

serve f.; (aptitude) compétence f.; (description) qualification f.
qualify, vb. qualifier; (modify) modifier.
quality, n. qualité f.
qualm, n. scrupule m.
quandary, n. dilemme m.
quantity, n. quantité f.

quarantine, *n.* quarantaine *f.*

quarrel, 1. *n.* querelle *f.* **2.** *vb.* se quereller.

quarry, *n.* carrière *f.*

quart, *n.* (approximately) litre *m.*

quarter, *n.* quart *m.;* (district, moon, beef) quartier *m.*

quarterly, *adj.* trimestriel.

quartet, *n.* quatuor *m.*

quartz, *n.* quartz *m.*

quasar, *n.* quasar *m.*

quaver, *vb.* chevroter.

queen, *n.* reine *f.*

queer, *adj.* bizarre.

quell, *vb.* réprimer.

quench, *vb.* éteindre.

querulous, *adj.* récriminateur.

query, *n.* question *f.*

quest, *n.* recherche *f.*

question, 1. *n.* question *f.* **2.** *vb.* interroger; (raise questions) mettre en doute.

questionable, *adj.* douteux.

question mark, *n.* point *(m.)* d'interrogation.

questionnaire, *n.* questionnaire *m.*

quibble, *vb.* ergoter.

quick, 1. *adj.* rapide; (lively) vif. **2.** *adv.* vite.

quicken, *vb.* accélérer.

quiet, 1. *n.* tranquillité *f.* **2.** *adj.* tranquille.

quilt, *n.* courtepointe *f.*

quinine, *n.* quinine *f.*

quip, *n.* mot *(m.)* piquant.

quit, *vb.* quitter.

quite, *adv.* tout à fait.

quiver, *vb.* trembloter.

quiz, 1. *n.* petit examen *m.* **2.** *vb.* examiner.

quorum, *n.* quorum *m.*

quota, *n.* (share) quote-part *f.;* (immigration, etc.) contingent *m.*

quotation, *n.* citation *f.;* *(comm.)* cote *f.*

quote, *vb.* citer.

quotient, *n.* quotient *m.*

R

rabbi, *n.* rabbin *m.*

rabbit, *n.* lapin *m.*

rabble, *n.* tourbe *f.*

rabid, *adj.* enragé.

rabies, *n.* rage *f.*

race, 1. *n.* (people) race *f.;* (contest) course *f.* **2.** *vb.* lutter à la course (avec).

race-track, *n.* piste *f.*

racial, *adj.* racial.

racism, *n.* racisme *m.*

rack, *n.* râtelier *m.;* (torture) chevalet *(m.)* de torture.

racket, *n.* (tennis) raquette *f.;* (noise) tintamarre *m.*

radar, *n.* radar *m.*

radiance, *n.* éclat *m.*

radiant, *adj.* radieux.

radiate, *vb.* irradier.

radiation, *n.* rayonnement *m.*

radiator, *n.* radiateur *m.*

radical, *adj. and n.* radical *m.*

radio, *n.* télégraphie *(f.)* sans fil *(commonly* T.S.F.), radio *f.*

radioactive, *adj.* radio-actif.

radish, *n.* radis *m.*

radium, *n.* radium *m.*

radius, *n.* rayon *m.*

raft, *n.* radeau *m.*

rafter, *n.* chevron *m.*

rag, *n.* chiffon *m.*

rage, *n.* rage *f.*

ragged, *adj.* en haillons.

ragweed, *n.* ambrosie *f.*

raid, *n.* (police) descente *f.;* *(mil.)* raid *m.* **2.** *vb.* faire un raid sur.

rail, *n.* (bar) barre *f.;* (railroad) rail *m.*

railroad, *n.* chemin *(m.)* de fer.

railway station, *n.* gare *f.*

rain, 1. *n.* pluie *f.* **2.** *vb.* pleuvoir.

rainbow, *n.* arc-en-ciel *m.*

raincoat, *n.* imperméable *m.*

rainfall, *n.* chute *(f.)* de pluie.

rain forest, *n.* forêt *(f.)* tropicale humide.

rainy, *adj.* pluvieux.

raise, vb. (bring up, erect, promote) élever; (lift) lever; (plants) cultiver.

raisin, n. raisin (m.) sec.

rake, 1. n. râteau m. **2.** vb. râteler.

rally, n. (mil.) ralliement m.; (meeting) rassemblement m.

ram, n. bélier m.

ramble, vb. rôder; (speech) divaguer.

ramp, n. rampe f.

rampart, n. rempart m.

rancid, adj. rance.

random, n. hasard m.

range, 1. n. (scope) étendue f.; (mountains) chaîne f.; (distance) portée f.; (stove) fourneau m. **2.** vb. s'étendre.

rank, 1. n. rang m. **2.** vb. ranger, tr.

ransack, vb. (search) fouiller; (pillage) saccager.

ransom, n. rançon f.

rant, vb. fulminer.

rap, 1. n. coup m.; (r. music) rap m. or f. **2.** vb. frapper.

rape, n. viol m.

rapid, adj. rapide; rapid m.

rapture, n. ravissement m.

rare, adj. rare; (meat) saignant.

rascal, n. coquin m.

rash, 1. n. éruption f. **2.** adj. téméraire.

raspberry, n. framboise f.

rat, n. rat m.

rate, 1. n. taux m.; (speed) vitesse f.; (at any r.) en tout cas; (first-r.) de premier ordre. **2.** vb. estimer.

rather, adv. plutôt.

ratify, vb. ratifier.

rating, n. classement m.; (TV r.s) Audimat m.

ration, n. ration f.

rational, adj. raisonnable; (mathematics, philosophy) rationnel.

rat race, n. foire (f.) empoigne.

rattle, n. (toy) hochet m.; (noise) fracas m.

raucous, adj. rauque.

rave, vb. délirer; (r. about) s'extasier sur.

raven, n. corbeau m.

ravenous, adj. vorace.

raw, adj. cru.

ray, n. rayon m.

rayon, n. rayonne f.

razor, n. rasoir m.

reach, 1. n. portée f. **2.** vb. atteindre; (extend) étendre, tr.; (arrive) arriver à.

react, vb. réagir.

reaction, n. réaction f.

reactionary, adj. réactionnaire.

read, vb. lire.

reader, n. (person) lecteur m.; (book) livre (m.) de lecture.

readily, adv. promptement.

ready, adj. prêt.

real, adj. réel.

realist, n. réaliste m.f.

reality, n. réalité f.

realization, n. réalisation f.

realize, vb. (notice) s'apercevoir de; (make real) réaliser, tr.

really, adv. vraiment.

realm, n. royaume m.

Realtor, n. agent (m.) immobilier.

reap, vb. moissonner.

rear, 1. n. (hind part) queue f.; (mil.) arrière-garde f. **2.** adj. situé à l'arrière. **3.** vb. élever.

rear-view mirror, n. rétroviseur m.

reason, 1. n. raison f. **2.** vb. raisonner.

reasonable, adj. raisonnable.

reassure, vb. rassurer.

rebate, n. rabais m.

rebel, 1. adj. and n. rebelle m.f. **2.** vb. se rebeller.

rebellion, n. rébellion f.

rebellious, adj. rebelle.

rebirth, n. renaissance f.

rebound, n. rebond m.

rebuff, vb. repousser.

rebuke, 1. n. réprimande f. **2.** vb. réprimander.

rebuttal, n. réfutation f.

recall, vb. (call back) rappeler; (remember) se rappeler.

recap, vb. récapituler.

recede, vb. s'éloigner.

receipt, n. (for payment) quittance f.

receive, vb. recevoir.

receiver, n. (phone) récepteur m.

recent, adj. récent.

receptacle, n. réceptacle m.; récipient m.

reception, n. réception f.; (welcoming) accueil m.

receptive, adj. réceptif.

recess, n. recoin m.; (parliament) vacances f.pl.; (school) récréation f.

recession, n. récession f.

recipe, n. recette f.

reciprocal, adj. réciproque.

reciprocate, vb. payer de retour.

recite, vb. réciter.

reckless, adj. téméraire.

reckon, vb. compter.

reclaim, v. (person) corriger; (land) défricher.

recline, vb. reposer, tr.

recognition, n. reconnaissance f.

recognize, vb. reconnaître.

recoil, vb. reculer.

recollect, vb. se rappeler.

recommend, vb. recommander.

recommendation, n. recommandation f.

recompense, n. récompense f.

reconcile, vb. réconcilier.

record, 1. n. (register) registre m.; (mention) mention f.; (known facts of person) antécédents m.pl.; (sports) record m.; (phonograph) disque m. 2. vb. enregistrer.

record player, n. tourne-disques m.

recount, vb. raconter.

recoup, vb. récupérer.

recover, vb. recouvrer; (from illness) se rétablir.

recovery, n. recouvrement m.; (health) rétablissement m.

recreation, n. récréation f.

recruit, 1. n. recrue f. 2. vb. recruter.

rectangle, n. rectangle m.

rectify, vb. rectifier.

recuperate, vb. se rétablir, intr.

recur, vb. revenir.

recycle, vb. recycler.

recycling, n. recyclage m.

red, adj. and n. rouge m.

red tape, n. paperasse f.

redeem, vb. racheter.

redemption, n. rachat m.; (theology) rédemption f.

redo, vb. refaire.

redress, 1. n. justice f.; réparation f. 2. vb. redresser, réparer; faire justice à.

reduce, vb. réduire.

reduction, n. réduction f.; (on price) remise f.

redundant, adj. superflu.

reed, n. roseau m.; (music) anche f.

reef, n. récif m.

reel, n. bobine f.

refer, vb. référer.

referee, n. arbitre m.

reference, n. référence f.

referendum, n. référendum m.

refill, vb. remplir (à nouveau).

refine, vb. raffiner.

refinement, n. raffinement m.

reflect, vb. réfléchir.

reflection, n. réflexion f.

reflex, adj. and n. réflexe m.

reform, 1. n. réforme f. 2. vb. réformer, tr.

reformation, n. réforme f.

refractory, adj. réfractaire.

refrain from, vb. se retenir de.

refresh, vb. rafraîchir.

refreshment, n. rafraîchissement m.

refrigerator, n. frigidaire m.

refuge, n. refuge m.

refugee, n. réfugié m.

refund, 1. n. remboursement m. 2. vb. rembourser.

refurbish, vb. remettre à neuf.

refusal, n. refus m.

refuse, 1. n. rebut m. 2. vb. refuser.

refute, vb. réfuter.

regain, vb. regagner.

regal, adj. royal.

regard, 1. n. égard m.; (r.s, compliments) amitiés f.pl. 2. vb. regarder.

regardless of, adj. sans tenir compte de.

regent, adj. and n. régent m.

regime, n. régime m.

regiment, n. régiment m.

region, n. région f.

register, 1. n. registre m. 2. vb. enregistrer; (letter) recommander.

registration, n. enregistrement m.

regret, 1. n. regret m. 2. vb. regretter.

regroup, vb. (se) regrouper.

regular, adj. régulier.

regularity, n. régularité f.

regulate, vb. régler.

regulation, n. règlement m.

regulator, n. régulateur m.

rehabilitate, *vb.* réhabiliter.

rehearse, *vb.* répéter.

reign, 1. *n.* règne *m.* 2. *vb.* régner.

reimburse, *vb.* rembourser.

rein, *n.* rêne *f.*

reindeer, *n.* renne *m.*

reinforce, *vb.* renforcer.

reinforcement, *n.* renfort *m.*

reinstate, *vb.* rétablir, réintégrer.

reject, *vb.* rejeter.

rejoice, *vb.* réjouir, *tr.*

rejoin, *vb.* (join again) rejoindre; (reply) répliquer.

relapse, 1. *n.* rechute *f.* 2. *vb.* rechuter.

relate, *vb.* raconter; (have reference to) se rapporter (à); (r. to) entrer en rapport avec.

relation, *n.* relation *f.;* (relative) parent *m.*

relationship, *n.* rapport *m.,* relations *f.pl.*

relative, 1. *n.* parent *m.* 2. *adj.* relatif.

relax, *vb.* relâcher.

relay, 1. *n.* relais *m.* 2. *vb.* relayer.

release, 1. *n.* délivrance *f.* 2. *vb.* libérer.

relent, *vb.* se laisser attendrir.

relevant, *adj.* pertinent.

reliability, *n.* sûreté *f.*

reliable, *adj.* digne de confiance.

reliant, *adj.* confiant.

relic, *n.* relique *f.*

relief, *n.* (ease) soulagement *m.;* (help) secours *m.;* (projection) relief *m.*

relieve, *vb.* (ease) soulager; (help) secourir.

religion, *n.* religion *f.*

religious, *adj.* religieux.

relinquish, *vb.* abandonner.

relish, 1. *n.* goût *m.* 2. *vb.* goûter.

relocate, *vb.* s'installer ailleurs.

reluctant, *adj.* peu disposé (à).

rely upon, *vb.* compter sur.

remain, *vb.* rester.

remainder, *n.* reste *m.*

remark, 1. *n.* remarque *f.* 2. *vb.* remarquer.

remarkable, *adj.* remarquable.

remedy, 1. *n.* remède *m.* 2. *vb.* remédier à.

remember, *vb.* se souvenir de.

remembrance, *n.* souvenir *m.*

remind of, *vb.* rappeler à (person recalling).

reminisce, *vb.* raconter ses souvenirs.

remiss, *adj.* negligent.

remission, *n.* rémission *f.*

remit, *vb.* remettre.

remnant, *n.* reste *m.,* vestige *m.,* (of cloth) coupon *m.*

remorse, *n.* remords *m.*

remote, *adj.* éloigné; (vague) vague.

removable, *adj.* transportable.

removal, *n.* enlèvement *m.*

remove, *vb.* enlever.

rend, *vb.* déchirer.

render, *vb.* rendre.

rendezvous, *n.* rendez-vous *m.*

renew, *vb.* renouveler.

renewal, *n.* renouvellement *m.*

renounce, *vb.* (give up) renoncer à; (repudiate) répudier.

renovate, *vb.* renouveler.

renown, *n.* renommée *f.*

rent, 1. *n.* loyer *m.* 2. *vb.* louer.

repair, 1. *n.* réparation *f.* 2. *vb.* réparer.

repay, *vb.* (give back) rendre; (refund) rembourser.

repeat, *vb.* répéter.

repel, *vb.* repousser.

repent, *vb.* se repentir (de).

repentance, *n.* repentir *m.*

repertoire, repertory, *n.* répertoire *m.*

repetition, *n.* répétition *f.*

replace, *vb.* (place again) replacer; (take place of) remplacer.

replay, *n.* répétition *f.*

replenish, *vb.* réapprovisionner.

reply, 1. *n.* réponse *f.* 2. *vb.* répondre.

report, 1. *n.* rapport *m.;* (rumor) bruit *m.* 2. *vb.* rapporter; (inform against) dénoncer.

report card, *n.* bulletin (*m.*) scolaire.

repose, *n.* repos *m.*

represent, *vb.* représenter.

representation, *n.* représentation *f.*

representative, 1. *n.* représentant *m.;* (politics) député *m.* 2. *adj.* représentatif.

repress, *vb.* réprimer.

reprimand, n. réprimande f.

reprisals, n. représailles f.pl.

reproach, 1. n. reproche m. **2.** vb. faire des reproches à.

reproduce, vb. reproduire, tr.

reproduction, n. reproduction f.

reproof, n. réprimande f.

reprove, vb. réprimander.

reptile, n. reptile m.

republic, n. république f.

republican, adj. and n. républicain m.

repudiate, vb. répudier.

repugnant, adj. répugnant.

repulse, vb. repousser.

repulsive, adj. répulsif.

reputation, n. réputation f.

repute, 1. n. renom m. **2.** vb. réputer.

request, 1. n. requête f. **2.** vb. demander.

require, vb. exiger.

requirement, n. exigence f.

requisite, adj. nécessaire.

requisition, n. réquisition f.

rescind, vb. annuler.

rescue, 1. n. délivrance f. **2.** vb. délivrer.

research, n. recherche f.

resemble, vb. ressembler à.

resent, vb. être froissé de.

reservation, n. réserve f.

reserve, 1. n. réserve f. **2.** vb. réserver.

reservoir, n. réservoir m.

reside, vb. résider.

residence, n. résidence f.

resident, 1. n. habitant m. **2.** adj. résidant.

resign, vb. résigner; (from post) se démettre (de), démissionner.

resignation, n. résignation f.; (from post) démission f.

resist, vb. résister à.

resistance, n. résistance f.

resolute, adj. résolu.

resolution, n. résolution f.

resolve, vb. résoudre.

resonant, adj. résonnant.

resort, 1. n. (resource) ressource f.; (recourse) recours m.; (place) lieu (m.) de séjour. **2.** vb. avoir recours.

resound, vb. résonner.

resource, n. ressource f.

respect, 1. n. respect m.; (reference) rapport m. **2.** vb. respecter.

respectable, adj. respectable.

respectful, adj. respectueux.

respective, adj. respectif.

respiration, n. respiration f.

respite, n. répit m.

respond, vb. répondre.

response, n. réponse f.

responsibility, n. responsabilité f.

responsible, adj. responsable.

rest, 1. n. (repose) repos m.; (remainder) reste m.; **(the r.,** the others) les autres m.f.pl. **2.** vb. se reposer.

restaurant, n. restaurant m.

restful, adj. qui repose.

restive, adj. agité.

restless, adj. (anxious) inquiet.

restoration, n. restauration f.

restore, vb. remettre; (repair) restaurer.

restrain, vb. contenir.

restraint, n. contrainte f.

restrict, vb. restreindre.

result, 1. n. résultat m. **2.** vb. résulter.

resume, vb. reprendre.

résumé, n. résumé m.

resurrect, vb. ressusciter.

retail, n. détail m.

retain, vb. retenir.

retaliate, vb. user de représailles.

retard, vb. retarder.

retarded, adj. arriéré.

reticent, adj. réservé.

retina, n. rétine f.

retire, vb. se retirer.

retort, n. riposte f.

retract, vb. (se) rétracter.

retreat, 1. n. retraite f. **2.** vb. se retirer.

retribution, n. châtiment m.

retrieve, vb. recouvrer.

retrospect, n. renvoi m., **(in r.)** coup d'œil (m.) rétrospectif.

return, 1. n. retour m.; (returns, comm.) recettes f.pl. **2.** vb. (give back) rendre; (go back) retourner; (come back) revenir.

reunion, n. réunion f.

reunite, vb. réunir.

reveal, vb. révéler.

revel, vb. s'ébattre.

revelation, n. révélation f.

revelry, n. bacchanale f.

revenge, 1. n. vengeance f. **2.** vb. (**r. oneself**) se venger.

revenue, n. revenu m.

reverberate, vb. réverbérer, réfléchir, répercuter.

revere, vb. révérer.

reverence, n. révérence f.

reverend, adj. révérend.

reverent, adj. respectueux.

reverie, n. rêverie f.

reverse, 1. n. (opposite) contraire m.; (defeat, medal) revers m.; (gear) marche (f.) arrière. **2.** vb. renverser.

revert, vb. revenir.

review, n. revue f.

revise, vb. réviser.

revision, n. révision f.

revival, n. renaissance f.; (religious) réveil m., renouveau m.

revive, vb. revivre, intr.; faire vivre, tr.

revoke, vb. révoquer.

revolt, 1. n. révolte f. **2.** vb. se révolter.

revolution, n. révolution f.

revolutionary, adj. révolutionnaire.

revolve, vb. tourner, intr.

revolver, n. revolver m.

reward, 1. n. récompense f. **2.** vb. récompenser.

rewind, vb. rembobiner.

rheumatism, n. rhumatisme m.

Rhine, n. Rhin m.

Rhone, n. Rhône m.

rhinoceros, n. rhinocéros m.

rhubarb, n. rhubarbe f.

rhyme, 1. n. rime f. **2.** vb. rimer.

rhythm, n. rythme m.

rhythmical, adj. rythmique.

rib, n. côte f.

ribbon, n. ruban m.

rice, n. riz m.

rich, adj. riche.

rid, vb. débarrasser.

riddle, n. énigme f.

ride, 1. n. promenade f. **2.** vb. (horse) aller à cheval; (vehicle) aller en voiture.

rider, n. (on horse) cavalier m.

ridge, n. crête f.

ridicule, 1. n. ridicule m. **2.** vb. se moquer de.

ridiculous, adj. ridicule.

rifle, n. fusil m.

rift, n. désaccord m.

rig, 1. n. (vessel) gréement m.; (outfit) tenue f. **2.** vb. gréer.

right, 1. n. droit m.; (not left) droite f. **2.** adj. (straight, not left) droit; (correct, proper) juste; (be r., of person) avoir raison; (all r.) c'est bien. **3.** adv. (straight) droit; (not left) à droite; (justly) bien.

righteous, adj. vertueux.

righteousness, n. justice f.

right of way, n. droit de passage m.; (automobiles) priorité (f.) de passage.

right wing, n. la droite.

rigid, adj. rigide.

rigor, n. rigueur f.

rigorous, adj. rigoureux.

rim, n. bord m.; (wheel) jante f.

ring, 1. n. anneau m.; (ornament) bague f.; (circle) cercle m.; (arena) arène f.; (sound) son m.; (phone) coup (m.) de téléphone. **2.** vb. sonner.

rinse, vb. rincer.

riot, n. émeute f.

rip, 1. n. fente f. **2.** vb. fendre, tr.

ripe, adj. mûr.

ripen, vb. mûrir.

ripoff, n. vol m. **2.** vb. voler.

ripple, 1. n. (on water) ride f. **2.** vb. rider, tr.

rise, 1. n. (ground) montée f.; (increase) augmentation f.; (rank) avancement m. **2.** vb. se lever.

risk, 1. n. risque m. **2.** vb. risquer.

rite, n. rite m.

ritual, adj. rituel.

rival, 1. adj. and n. rival m. **2.** vb. rivaliser avec.

rivalry, n. rivalité f.

river, n. fleuve m.

river bank, n. rive f., berge f.

rivet, n. rivet m.

Riviera, n. Côte (f.) d'Azur.

road, n. route f.

roam, vb. errer (par).

roar, vb. (person) hurler; (lion) rugir; (bull, sea) mugir; (thunder, cannon) gronder; (laughter) éclater de.

roast, 1. n. rôti m. **2.** vb. rôtir.

rob, vb. voler.

robber, n. voleur m.

robbery, n. vol m.

robe, n. robe f.

robin, n. rouge-gorge m.

robot, n. automate m., robot m.

robust, adj. robuste.

rock, 1. n. rocher m. **2.** vb. balancer; (child) bercer. **3.** adj. (music) rock.

rocket, n. fusée f.

rocking chair, n. fauteuil (m.) à bascule.

rocky, adj. rocheux.

rod, n. verge f.

rodent, adj. and n. rongeur m.

roe, n. (animal) chevreuil m.; (of fish) œufs (m.pl.) de poisson.

rogue, n. coquin m.

roguish, adj. coquin.

role, n. rôle m.

roll, 1. n. rouleau m.; (bread) petit pain m.; (list) liste f.; (r.-call) appel m.; (boat) roulis m. **2.** vb. rouler.

roller, n. rouleau m.

roller skate, n. patin (m.) à roulette.

Roman, 1. n. Romain m. **2.** adj. romain.

romance, n. roman (m.) de chevalerie.

Romania, n. Roumanie f.

Romanian, 1. n. (person) Roumain m.; (language) roumain m. **2.** adj. roumain.

romantic, adj. romanesque; (poetry, music) romantique.

romp, 1. n. tapage m. **2.** vb. batifoler.

roof, n. toit m.

room, n. (space) place f.; (private use) chambre f.; (public use) salle f.

roommate, n. camarade (m.f.) de chambre.

rooster, n. coq m.

root, 1. n. racine f.; (source) source f. **2.** vb. enraciner, tr.

rope, n. corde f.

rosary, n. rosaire m.

rose, n. rose f.

rosemary, n. romarin m.

rosin, n. colophane f.

rosy, adj. de rose.

rot, 1. n. pourriture f. **2.** vb. pourrir.

rotary, adj. rotatoire.

rotate, vb. tourner.

rotation, n. rotation f.

rotten, adj. pourri.

rouge, n. rouge m.

rough, adj. rude; (sea weather) gros m., grosse f.

round, 1. adj. rond. **2.** n. rond m.; (circuit) tournée f.

round trip, n. voyage (m.) aller et retour.

rouse, vb. (wake) réveiller; (stir up) secouer.

rout, n. (mil.) déroute f.

route, n. route f.

routine, n. routine f.

rove, vb. errer (par).

rover, n. rôdeur m.

row, 1. n. rang m.; dispute f. **2.** vb. ramer.

rowboat, n. barque f.

rowdy, adj. tapageur.

rowing, n. aviron m.

royal, adj. royal.

royalty, n. royauté f.; (of author) droits (m.pl.) d'auteur.

rub, vb. frotter.

rubber, n. caoutchouc m.

rubbish, n. rebuts m.pl.; (nonsense) bêtises f.pl.

ruby, n. rubis m.

rudder, n. gouvernail m.

ruddy, adj. rouge.

rude, adj. (rough) rude; (impolite) impoli.

rudiment, n. rudiment m.

rue, vb. regretter.

ruffian, n. bandit m.

ruffle, n. (frill) fraise f.

rug, n. tapis m.

rugged, adj. (rough) rude; (uneven) raboteux.

ruin, 1. n. ruine f. **2.** vb. ruiner.

ruinous, adj. ruineux.

rule, 1. n. règle f.; (authority) autorité f. **2.** vb. gouverner; (decide) décider.

ruler, n. souverain m.; (for lines) règle f.

rum, n. rhum m.

rumba, n. rumba f.

rumble, vb. gronder.
rumor, n. rumeur f.
run, vb. intr. courir; (of engine) marcher; (of colors) déteindre; (of liquids) couler; (**r. away**) s'enfuir.
run-down, adj. épuisé.
rung, n. échelon m.
runner, n. (person) coureur m.; (table) chemin (m.) de table.
running, n. course f., gestion f., direction f.
rupture, n. rupture f.
rural, adj. rural.
rush, 1. n. (haste) hâte f.; (onrush) ruée f.; (air, water) coup m.;

(plant) jonc m. **2.** vb. se précipiter, intr.
Russia, n. Russie f.
Russian, 1. n. (person) Russe m.f.; (language) russe m. **2.** adj. russe.
rust, 1. n. rouille f. **2.** vb. rouiller, tr.
rustic, adj. rustique.
rustling, n. (leaves) bruissement m.; (skirt) frou-frou m.
rusty, adj. rouillé.
rut, n. ornière f.
ruthless, adj. impitoyable.
rye, n. seigle m.; (whiskey) whisky m.

S

Sabbath, n. sabbat m.
saber, n. sabre m.
sable, n. zibeline f.
sabotage, 1. n. sabotage m. **2.** vb. saboter.
saboteur, n. saboteur m.
saccharin, n. saccharine f.
sachet, n. sachet m.
sack, 1. n. sac m. **2.** vb. saccager.
sacrament, n. sacrement m.
sacred, adj. sacré.
sacrifice, 1. n. sacrifice m. **2.** vb. sacrifier.
sacrilege, n. sacrilège m.
sad, adj. triste.
sadden, vb. attrister, tr.
saddle, n. selle f.
sadism, n. sadisme m.
sadistic, adj. sadique.
sadness, n. tristesse f.
safe, 1. n. coffre-fort m. **2.** adj. sûr; (**s. and sound**) sain et sauf; (**s. from**) à l'abri de.
safeguard, vb. sauvegarder.
safe sex, n. rapports (m.pl.) sexuels sans risques.
safety, n. sûreté f., sécurité f.
safety pin, n. épingle (f.) anglaise.
sag, vb. s'affaisser.
sage, n. (person) sage m.; (plant) sauge f.
sail, 1. n. voile f. **2.** vb. naviguer; (depart) partir.
sailboat, n. canot (m.) à voiles.
sailor, n. marin m.
saint, adj. and n. saint m.

sake, n. (**for the s. of**) pour l'amour de.
salad, n. salade f.
salami, n. salami m.
salary, n. appointements m.pl.
sale, n. vente f.
salesman, n. vendeur m.
sales tax, n. impôt (m.) sur les ventes.
saliva, n. salive f.
salmon, n. saumon m.
salt, 1. n. sel m. **2.** vb. saler.
salute, 1. n. salut m. **2.** vb. saluer.
salvage, n. sauvetage m.
salvation, n. salut m.
salve, n. onguent m.
same, 1. adj. and pron. même. **2.** adv. de même.
sample, n. échantillon m.
sanatorium, n. sanatorium m.
sanctify, vb. sanctifier.
sanction, n. sanction f.
sanctity, n. sainteté f.
sanctuary, n. sanctuaire m.
sand, n. sable m.
sandal, n. sandale f.
sandwich, n. sandwich m.
sandy, adj. sablonneux.
sane, adj. sain d'esprit.
sanitary, adj. sanitaire.
sanitary napkin, n. serviette (f.) hygiénique.
sanitation, n. hygiène f.
sanity, n. santé (f.) d'esprit.
Santa Claus, n. Père Noël m.
sap, n. sève f.

sapphire, n. saphir m.

sarcasm, n. sarcasme m.

sardine, n. sardine f.

Sardinia, n. Sardaigne f.

sash, n. ceinture f.

satellite, n. satellite m.

satellite dish, n. antenne (f.) parabolique.

satellite television, n. télévision (f.) par cable.

satin, n. satin m.

satire, n. satire f.

satisfaction, n. satisfaction f.

satisfactory, adj. satisfaisant.

satisfy, vb. satisfaire.

saturate, vb. saturer.

Saturday, n. samedi m.

sauce, n. sauce f.

saucer, n. soucoupe f.

saucy, adj. impertinent.

Saudi Arabia, n. Arabie (f.) Saoudite.

sausage, n. saucisse f.

savage, adj. and n. sauvage m.f.

save, vb. sauver; (put aside) mettre de côté.; (economize) épargner.

saving, n. épargne f.

savings bank, n. caisse (f.) d'épargne.

savior, n. sauveur m.

savor, n. saveur f.

savory, adj. savoureux.

saw, 1. n. scie f. 2. vb. scier.

say, vb. dire.

scab, n. croûte f., gale f.

scaffold, n. échafaud m.

scald, vb. échauder.

scale, 1. n. (fish) écaille f.; (balance) balance f.; (series, graded system, map) échelle f.; (music) gamme f. 2. vb. escalader.

scallop, n. coquille (f.) Saint-Jacques; (sewing) feston m.

scalp, 1. n. cuir (m.) chevelu m. 2. vb. scalper.

scan, 1. vb. (examine) scruter; (verse) scander. 2. n. échographie f.

scandal, n. scandale m.

scandalous, adj. scandaleux.

Scandinavia, n. Scandinavie f.

Scandinavian, 1. n. Scandinave m.f. 2. adj. scandinave.

scant(y), adj. limité, faible.

scar, n. cicatrice f.

scarce, adj. rare.

scare, vb. effrayer.

scarf, n. écharpe f.

scarlet, adj. and n. écarlate f.; (s. fever) scarlatine f.

scary, adj. effrayant.

scathing, adj. cinglant.

scatter, vb. éparpiller.

scavenger, n. boueur m.

scenario, n. scénario m.

scene, n. scène f.

scenery, n. (theater) décors m.pl.; (landscape) paysage m.

scent, 1. n. parfum m., odeur f. 2. vb. flairer, sentir.

schedule, n. horaire m.

scheme, n. plan m.

schizophrenic, adj. and n. schizophrène m.f.

scholar, n. savant m.

scholarship, n. (school) bourse f.

school, n. école f.

sciatica, n. sciatique f.

science, n. science f.

science fiction, n. science-fiction f.

scientist, n. scientifique m.f.

scissors, n. ciseaux m.pl.

scoff at, vb. se moquer de.

scold, vb. gronder.

scoop out, vb. évider.

scope, n. (extent) portée f.; (outlet) carrière f.

scorch, vb. roussir.

score, n. (games) points m.pl.; (twenty) vingtaine f.; (music) partition f.

scorn, 1. n. mépris m. 2. vb. mépriser.

scornful, adj. dédaigneux.

Scotch, Scottish, adj. écossais.

Scotchman, Scotsman, n. Écossais m.

Scotch tape, n. ruban adhésif m.

Scotland, n. Écosse f.

scour, vb. nettoyer.

scourge, n. fléau m.

scout, n. éclaireur m.; (boy s.) boy-scout m.

scowl, vb. se renfrogner.

scramble, vb. avancer péniblement.

scrap, 1. n. petit morceau m. 2. vb. mettre au rebut.

scrape, scratch, 1. n. égratignure f. 2. vb. gratter.

scream, 1. *n.* cri *m.* **2.** *vb.* crier.

screen, *n.* écran *m.;* **(folding s.)** paravent *m.*

screen play, *n.* scénario *m.*

screw, 1. *n.* vis *f.* **2.** *vb.* visser, *tr.*

screwdriver, *n.* tournevis *m.*

scribble, *vb.* griffonner.

script, *n.* écriture *f.,* scénario *m.*

scroll, *n.* rouleau *m.*

scrub, *vb.* frotter.

scruple, *n.* scrupule *m.*

scrupulous, *adj.* scrupuleux.

scrutinize, *vb.* scruter.

scuba-diving, *n.* plongée *(f.)* soumarine.

sculptor, *n.* sculpteur *m.*

sculpture, *n.* sculpture *f.*

scythe, *n.* faux *f.*

sea, *n.* mer *f.*

seabed, *n.* lit *(m.)* de la mer.

seacoast, *n.* littoral *m.*

seagull, *n.* mouette *f.*

seal, 1. *n.* (animal) phoque *m.;* (stamp) sceau *m.* **2.** *vb.* sceller.

seam, *n.* couture *f.*

seaport, *n.* port *(m.)* de mer.

search, 1. *n.* recherche *f.* **2.** *vb.* chercher.

seasickness, *n.* mal *(m.)* de mer.

season, 1. *n.* saison *f.* **2.** *vb.* assaisonner.

seat, 1. *n.* siège *m.* **2.** *vb.* asseoir.

seat-belt, *n.* ceinture *(f.)* de sécurité.

seclude, *vb.* isoler.

second, 1. *adj.* sûr. **2.** *vb.* **(make s.)** mettre en sûreté; (make fast) fixer; (obtain) obtenir.

secondary, *adj.* secondaire.

secret, *adj. and n.* secret *m.*

secretary, *n.* secrétaire *m.f.*

sect, *n.* secte *f.*

section, *n.* section *f.*

sectional, *adj.* régional.

secular, *adj.* (church) séculier; (education) laïque; (time) séculaire.

secure, 1. *adj.* sûr. **2.** *vb.* **(make s.)** mettre en sûreté; (make fast) fixer; (obtain) obtenir.

security, *n.* sûreté *f.;* (comm.; law) caution *f.;* (finance, *pl.*) valeurs *f.pl.*

sedative, *adj. and n.* sédatif *m.*

sediment, *n.* sédiment *m.*

seduce, *vb.* séduire.

see, *vb.* voir.

seed, *n.* semence *f.;* (vegetables, etc.) graine *f.*

seek, *vb.* chercher.

seem, *vb.* sembler.

seep, *vb.* suinter.

segment, *n.* segment *m.*

segregate, *vb.* séparer.

seize, *vb.* saisir.

seizure, *n.* crise *f.,* attaque *f.*

seldom, *adv.* rarement.

select, *vb.* choisir.

selection, *n.* sélection *f.*

self, *n.* moi *m.,* personne *f.*

self-centered, *adj.* égocentrique.

selfish, *adj.* égoïste.

selfishness, *n.* égoïsme *m.*

self-righteous, *adj.* suffisant.

self-service, *adj. and n.* libre-service *m.*

sell, *vb.* vendre, *tr.*

semantics, *n.* sémantique *f.*

semester, *n.* semestre *m.*

semicircle, *n.* demi-cercle *m.*

semicolon, *n.* point-virgule *m.*

seminary, *n.* séminaire *m.*

Semite, *n.* Sémite *m.f.*

senate, *n.* sénat *m.*

senator, *n.* sénateur *m.*

send, *vb.* envoyer; **(s. back)** renvoyer.

senile, *adj.* sénile.

senior, *adj. and n.* (age) aîné *m.;* (rank) supérieur *m.*

senior citizen, *n.* personne *(f.)* du troisième âge.

seniority, *n.* ancienneté *f.*

sensation, *n.* sensation *f.*

sensational, *adj.* sensationnel.

sense, *n.* sens *m.*

sensible, *adj.* (wise) sensé; (appreciable) sensible.

sensitive, *adj.* sensible.

sensual, *adj.* sensuel.

sensuous, *adj.* sensuel.

sentence, *n.* (gramm.) phrase *f.;* (law) sentence *f.*

sentiment, *n.* sentiment *m.*

sentimental, *adj.* sentimental.

separate, 1. *adj.* séparé. **2.** *vb.* séparer, *tr.*

separation, *n.* séparation *f.*

September, *n.* septembre *m.*

sequence, *n.* suite *f.*

serene, *adj.* serein.

serenade, *n.* sérénade *f.*

serene, *adj.* serein.

sergeant, *n.* sergent *m.*

serial, *n.* roman-feuilleton *m.*

series, *n.* série *f.*

serious, *adj.* sérieux.

sermon, *n.* sermon *m.*

serpent, *n.* serpent *m.*

serum, *n.* sérum *m.*

servant, *n.* (domestic) domestique *m.f.*; (public) employé *m.*

serve, *vb.* servir.

service, *n.* service *m.*; (church) office *m.*

service station, *n.* station-service *f.*

servitude, *n.* servitude *f.*

session, *n.* session *f.*

set, 1. *n.* ensemble *m.* **2.** *adj.* fixe; (decided) résolu. **3.** *vb. tr.* (put) mettre; (regulate) régler; (jewels) monter; (fix) fixer. **4.** *vb. intr.* (sun, etc.) se coucher; **(s. about)** se mettre à.

settle, *vb.* (establish) établir, *tr.*; (fix) fixer; (decide) décider; (arrange) arranger; (pay) payer; **(s. down to,** *intr.*) se mettre à.

settlement, *n.* (colony) colonie *f.*; (accounts) règlement *m.*

settler, *n.* colon *m.*

seven, *adj. and n.* sept *m.*

seventeen, *adj. and n.* dix-sept *m.*

seventh, *adj. and n.* septième *m.f.*

seventy, *adj. and n.* soixante-dix *m.*

sever, *vb.* séparer, couper.

several, *adj. and pron.* plusieurs.

severe, *adj.* sévère.

severity, *n.* sévérité *f.*

sew, *vb.* coudre.

sewer, *n.* égout *m.*

sex, *n.* sexe *m.*

sexism, *n.* sexisme *m.*

sexist, *adj.* sexiste.

sexual, *adj.* sexuel.

shabby, *adj.* (clothes) usé; (person) mesquin.

shack, *n.* cabane *f.*

shade, 1. *n.* ombre *f.*; (colors) nuance *f.*; (window) store *m.* **2.** *vb.* ombrager.

shadow, *n.* ombre *f.*

shady, *adj.* ombragé; (not honest) louche.

shaft, *n.* (mine) puits *m.*

shaggy, *adj.* poilu, hirsute.

shake, *vb. tr.* secouer; trembler; **(s. hands)** serrer la main à.

shallow, *adj.* peu profond.

shame, *n.* honte *f.*

shameful, *adj.* honteux.

shampoo, *n.* shampooing *m.*

shape, 1. *n.* forme *f.* **2.** *vb.* former.

share, 1. *n.* part *f.*; (finance) action *f.* **2.** *vb.* partager.

shareholder, *n.* actionnaire *m.*

shark, *n.* requin *m.*

sharp, *adj.* (cutting) tranchant; (clever) fin; (piercing) perçant; (music) dièse.

sharpen, *vb.* aiguiser.

shatter, *vb.* briser.

shave, *vb.* raser, *tr.*

shaving brush, *n.* blaireau *m.*

shaving cream, *n.* crème (*f.*) à raser.

shawl, *n.* châle *m.*

she, *pron.* elle.

sheaf, *n.* (grain) gerbe *f.*

shear, *vb.* tondre.

shears, *n.* cisailles *f.pl.*

sheath, *n.* étui *m.*

shed, 1. *n.* hangar *m.* **2.** *vb.* verser.

sheen, *n.* lustre *m.*

sheep, *n.* mouton *m.*

sheet, *n.* (bed) drap *m.*; (paper, metal) feuille *f.*

shelf, *n.* rayon *m.*

shell, *n.* coquille *f.*; (of building) carcasse *f.*; (explosive) obus *m.*

shellac, *n.* laque *f.*

shellfish, *n.* coquillages *m.pl.*

shelter, 1. *n.* abri *m.* **2.** *vb.* abriter.

shepherd, *n.* berger *m.*

sherbet, *n.* sorbet *m.*

sherry, *n.* xérès *m.*

shield, *n.* bouclier *m.*

shift, 1. *n.* (change) changement *m.*; (workers) équipe *f.*; (expedient) expédient *m.*; (shirt) chemise *f.* **2.** *vb.* changer; **(s. gears)** changer de vitesse.

shin, *n.* tibia *m.*

shine, *vb.* briller, *intr.*; (shoes) cirer.

shiny, *adj.* luisant.

ship, *n.* navire *m.*; vaisseau *m.*

shipment, *n.* envoi *m.*

shirk, *vb.* esquiver.

shirt, *n.* chemise *f.*

shiver, 1. *n.* frisson *m.* 2. *vb.* frissonner.

shock, 1. *n.* choc *m.* 2. *vb.* choquer.

shock absorber, *n.* amortisseur *m.*

shoe, *n.* soulier *m.,* chaussure *f.*

shoelace, *n.* lacet *m.*

shoemaker, *n.* cordonnier *m.*

shoot, *vb.* tirer; (person) fusiller; (hit) atteindre; (rush) se précipiter.

shop, 1. *n.* boutique *f.;* (factory) atelier *m.* 2. *vb.* faire des emplettes.

shopping, *n.* achats *m.pl.*

shop window, *n.* vitrine *f.*

shore, *n.* rivage *m.*

short, *adj.* court.

shortage, *n.* manque *m.,* insuffisance *f.*

short-circuit, *n.* court-circuit *m.*

shorten, *vb.* raccourcir.

shorthand, *n.* sténographie *f.*

short story, *n.* nouvelle *f.*

shot, *n.* coup *m.*

should, *vb.* devoir (in conditional).

shoulder, *n.* épaule *f.*

shoulder blade, *n.* omoplate *f.*

shout, 1. *n.* cri *m.* 2. *vb.* crier.

shove, *vb.* pousser.

shovel, *n.* pelle *f.*

show, 1. *n.* (exhibition) exposition *f.;* (spectacle, performance) spectacle *m.;* (semblance) semblant *m.;* (display) parade *f.* 2. *vb.* montrer, *tr.*

shower, *n.* (rain) averse *f.;* (washing) douche *f.*

shrapnel, *n.* éclats *(m.pl.)* d'obus.

shrewd, *adj.* sagace.

shriek, 1. *n.* cri *(m.)* perçant. 2. *vb.* hurler.

shrill, *adj.* aigu.

shrimp, *n.* crevette *f.*

shrine, *n.* châsse *f.*

shrink, *vb.* rétrécir, *tr.*

shroud, *n.* linceul *m.*

shrub, *n.* arbrisseau *m.*

shudder, 1. *n.* frisson *m.* 2. *vb.* frissonner.

shun, *vb.* fuir.

shut, *vb.* fermer.

shuttle, 1. *n.* navette *f.* 2. *vb.* faire la navette.

shutter, *n.* volet *m.*

shy, *adj.* timide.

sick, *adj.* malade.

sickness, *n.* maladie *f.*

side, *n.* côté *m.*

sidewalk, *n.* trottoir *m.*

siege, *n.* siège *m.*

sieve, *n.* tamis *m.*

sift, *vb.* cribler.

sigh, 1. *n.* soupir *m.* 2. *vb.* soupirer.

sight, *n.* vue *f.;* (spectacle) spectacle *m.*

sightseeing, *n.* tourisme *m.*

sign, 1. *n.* signe *m.;* (placard) enseigne *f.* 2. *vb.* signer.

signal, *n.* signal *m.*

signature, *n.* signature *f.*

significance, *n.* (meaning) signification *f.;* (importance) importance *f.*

significant, *adj.* significatif.

signify, *vb.* signifier.

sign language, *n.* langage *(m.)* des sourds-muets.

silence, *n.* silence *m.*

silent, *adj.* silencieux.

silicon, *n.* silicium *m.;* **(s. chip)** microplaquette *f.*

silk, *n.* soie *f.*

silken, *adj.* de soie.

silly, *adj.* sot *m.,* sotte *f.*

silver, 1. *n.* argent *m.* 2. *adj.* d'argent.

silverware, *n.* argenterie *f.*

similar, *adj.* semblable.

simple, *adj.* simple.

simplicity, *n.* simplicité *f.*

simplify, *vb.* simplifier.

simply, *adv.* simplement.

simultaneous, *adj.* simultané.

sin, 1. *n.* péché *m.* 2. *vb.* pécher.

since, 1. *adv., prep.* depuis. 2. *conj.* (time) depuis que; (cause) puisque.

sincere, *adj.* sincère.

sincerity, *n.* sincérité *f.*

sinful, *adj.* (person) pécheur *m.,* pécheresse *f.;* (act) coupable.

sing, *vb.* chanter.

singer, *n.* chanteur *m.*

single, *adj.* (only one) seul; (particular) particulier; (not married) célibataire.

singular, *adj. and n.* singulier *m.*

sinister, *adj.* sinistre.

sink, 1. *n.* (kitchen) évier *m.,* (bathroom) lavabo *m.* 2. *vb.* enfoncer.

tr.; (vessel) couler à fond; (diminish, weaken) baisser.

sinner, n. pécheur m.; pécheresse f.

sinus, n. sinus m.

sip, vb. siroter.

sir, n. monsieur m.; (title) Sir m.

sirloin, n. aloyau m.

sister, n. sœur f.

sister-in-law, n. belle-sœur f.

sit, vb. (s. down) s'asseoir; (be seated) être assis.

sitcom, n. comédie (f.) de situation.

site, n. emplacement m.

sit-in, n. occupation (f.) de (locaux).

situate, vb. situer.

situation, n. situation f.

six, adj. and n. six m.

sixteen, adj. and n. seize m.

sixteenth, adj. and n. seizième m.f.

sixth, adj. and n. sixième m.f.

sixty, adj. and n. soixante m.

size, n. grandeur f.; (person) taille f.; (shoes, gloves) pointure f.; (book, packaged merchandise) format m.

skate, 1. n. patin m. **2.** vb. patiner.

skateboard, n. planche (f.) à roulettes.

skeleton, n. squelette m.

skeptic, n. sceptique m.f.

skeptical, adj. sceptique.

sketch, 1. n. croquis m. **2.** vb. esquisser.

ski, 1. n. ski m. **2.** vb. faire du ski.

skill, n. adresse f.

skillful, adj. adroit.

skim, vb. (milk) écrémer; (book) feuilleter; (surface) effleurer.

skin, 1. n. peau f. **2.** vb. écorcher.

skinny, adj. maigre.

skip, vb. sauter.

skirt, n. jupe f.

skull, n. crâne m.

sky, n. ciel m.

skyscraper, n. gratte-ciel m.

slab, n. dalle f.

slack, adj. lâche.

slacken, vb. (slow up) ralentir; (loosen) relâcher.

slacks, n. pantalon m.

slander, 1. n. calomnie f. **2.** vb. calomnier.

slang, n. argot m.

slant, 1. n. (slope) pente f.; (bias) biais m. **2.** vb. incliner.

slap, 1. n. claque f. **2.** vb. gifler.

slash, n. taillade f.

slate, n. ardoise f.

slaughter, 1. n. (people) massacre m.; (animals) abattage m. **2.** vb. massacrer; abattre.

slaughterhouse, n. abattoir m.

slave, n. esclave m.f.

slavery, n. esclavage m.

slay, vb. tuer.

sled, n. traîneau m.

sleep, 1. n. sommeil m.; (go to s.) s'endormir. **2.** vb. dormir.

sleeping bag, n. sac de couchage m.

sleeping pill, n. somnifère m.

sleepy, adj. somnolent; (be s.) avoir sommeil.

sleet, 1. n. grésil m. **2.** vb. grésiller.

sleeve, n. manche f.

sleigh, n. traîneau m.

slender, adj. mince; svelte.

slice, n. tranche f.

slide, 1. n. (sliding) glissade f.; (microscope) lamelle f.; (lantern) plaque (f.) de projection. **2.** vb. glisser.

slight, adj. léger; mince.

slim, adj. mince.

sling, 1. n. fronde f.; (medical) écharpe f. **2.** vb. (throw) lancer; (hang) suspendre.

slip, 1. n. (sliding) glissade f.; (tongue, pen) lapsus m.; (mistake) faux pas m.; (paper) fiche f.; (garment) sous-jupe f. **2.** vb. glisser; (err) faire une faute.

slipper, n. pantoufle f.

slippery, adj. glissant.

slit, 1. n. fente f. **2.** vb. fendre.

slogan, n. mot (m.) d'ordre; (politics) cri (m.) de guerre.

slope, 1. n. pente f. **2.** vb. incliner.

sloppy, adj. mal soigné.

slot, n. fente f.

slow, adj. lent; (clock) en retard.

slowness, n. lenteur f.

sluggish, adj. paresseux.

slum, n. quartier (m.) pauvre.

slumber, vb. sommeiller.

sly, adj. (crafty) rusé; (secretive) sournois.

smack, 1. *n.* (a bit) soupçon *m.*; (noise) claquement *m.* 2. *vb.* gifler.

small, *adj.* petit.

smallpox, *n.* petite vérole *f.*

smart, 1. *adj.* (clever) habile; (stylish) élégant. 2. *vb.* cuire.

smash, 1. *vb.* briser, *tr.* 2. *n.* coup *m.*; (*fig.*) collision *f.*

smear, 1. *n.* tache *f.* 2. *vb.* salir.

smell, 1. *n.* odeur *f.* 2. *vb.* sentir.

smelt, 1. *n.* éperlan *m.* 2. *vb.* fondre.

smile, 1. *n.* sourire *m.*

smite, *vb.* frapper.

smog, *n.* brouillard (*m.*) mélangé de fumée.

smoke, 1. *n.* fumée *f.* 2. *vb.* fumer.

smolder, *vb.* couver.

smooth, 1. *adj.* lisse. *vb.* lisser.

smother, *vb.* étouffer.

smug, *adj.* suffisant.

smuggle, *vb.* faire passer en contrebande.

snack, *n.* casse-croute *m.*

snag, *n.* obstacle (*m.*) caché.

snail, *n.* escargot *m.*

snake, *n.* serpent *m.*

snap, 1. *n.* (bite) coup (*m.*) de dents; (sound) coup (*m.*) sec. 2. *vb.tr.* (with teeth) happer; (sound) faire claquer.

snapshot, *n.* instantané *m.*

snare, *n.* piège *m.*

snarl, *vb.* grogner.

snatch, *vb.* saisir.

sneak, *vb.* se glisser furtivement.

sneakers, *n.* tennis *m.pl.*, basket *m.pl.*

sneer, *vb.* ricaner.

sneeze, 1. *n.* éternuement *m.* 2. *vb.* éternuer.

sniff, *vb.* renifler.

snob, *n.* snob *m.*

snore, *vb.* ronfler.

snorkel, *n.* tuba *m.*

snow, 1. *n.* neige *f.* 2. *vb.* neiger.

snug, *adj.* confortable.

snuggle, *vb.* se pelotonner.

so, *adv.* si; tellement; (thus) ainsi; (**s. that**) de sorte que.

soak, *vb.* tremper.

soap, *n.* savon *m.*

soar, *vb.* prendre son essor.

sob, 1. *n.* sanglot *m.* 2. *vb.* sangloter.

sober, *adj.* (sedate) sérieux; (not drunk) qui n'est pas ivre.

soccer, *n.* football *m.*

sociable, *adj.* sociable.

social, *adj.* social.

socialism, *n.* socialisme *m.*

socialist, *adj.* and *n.* socialiste *m.f.*

social worker, *n.* assistant (*m.f.*) social.

society, *n.* société *f.*

sociology, *n.* sociologie *f.*

sock, *n.* chaussette *f.*

socket, *n.* douille *f.*

sod, *n.* motte *f.*

soda, *n.* soude *f.*; (**s. water**) eau (*f.*) de Seltz.

sofa, *n.* canapé *m.*

soft, *adj.* doux *m.*, douce *f.*; (yielding) mou *m.*, molle *f.*

soften, *vb.* amollir, *tr.*

software, *n.* logiciel *m.*

soil, 1. *n.* terroir *m.* 2. *vb.* souiller.

sojourn, 1. *n.* séjour *m.* 2. *vb.* séjourner.

solace, *n.* consolation *f.*

solar, *adj.* solaire.

soldier, *n.* soldat *m.*

sole, *n.* (shoe) semelle *f.*; (fish) sole *f.*

solemn, *adj.* solennel.

solemnity, *n.* solennité *f.*

solicit, *vb.* solliciter.

solicitous, *adj.* empressé.

solid, *adj.* and *n.* solide *m.*

solidity, *n.* solidité *f.*

solidarity, *n.* solidarité *f.*

solitary, *adj.* solitaire.

solitude, *n.* solitude *f.*

solo, *n.* solo *m.*

solution, *n.* solution *f.*

solve, *vb.* résoudre.

solvent, *adj.* (*comm.*) solvable.

somber, *adj.* sombre.

some, 1. *adj.* quelque; (partitive) de. 2. *pron.* certains; (with verb) en.

somebody, someone, *pron.* quelqu'un.

something, *pron.* quelque chose *m.*

sometime, *adv.* (past) autrefois; (future) quelque jour.

sometimes, *adv.* quelquefois.

somewhat, *adv.* quelque peu.

somewhere, *adv.* quelque part.

son, *n.* fils *m.*

song, n. chanson f.; chant m.

son-in-law, n. gendre m.

soon, adv. bientôt, tôt.

soot, n. suie f.

soothe, vb. calmer.

sophisticated, adj. blasé.

soprano, n. soprano m.

sordid, adj. sordide.

sore, adj. (aching) douloureux; (have a s. throat, etc.) avoir mal à....

sorrow, n. tristesse f., douleur f., chagrin m.

sorrowful, adj. (person) affligé.

sorry, 1. adj. désolé, triste; (be s.) regretter. 2. interj. pardon!

sort, 1. n. sorte f. 2. vb. trier.

soul, n. âme f.

sound, 1. n. son m. 2. adj. (healthy) sain, solide. 3. vb. sonner.

soundproof, adj. insonorisé.

soup, n. potage m., soupe, f.

sour, adj. aigre.

source, n. source f.

south, n. sud m.

South America, n. Amérique (f.) du Sud.

southeast, n. sud-est m.

southern, adj. du sud.

South Pole, n. pôle sud m.

southwest, n. sud-ouest m.

souvenir, n. souvenir m.

Soviet, adj. soviétique; (S. Union) Union (f.) soviétique.

sow, vb. semer.

spa, n. station (f.) thermale.

space, n. espace m.

space shuttle, n. navette spatiale f.

spacious, adj. spacieux.

spade, n. bêche f.; (cards) pique m.

Spain, n. Espagne f.

span, n. (hand) empan m.; (bridge) travée f.

Spaniard, n. Espagnol m.

Spanish, adj. and n. espagnol m.

spank, vb. fesser.

spanking, n. fessée f.

spare, 1. adj. (in reserve) de réserve. 2. vb. épargner.

spark, n. étincelle f.

sparkle, vb. étinceler.

sparrow, n. moineau m.

spasm, n. spasme m.

speak, vb. parler.

speaker, n. (public) orateur m.

spec, n. (on s.) à tout hasard.

special, adj. spécial.

specialist, n. spécialiste m.f.

specially, adv. spécialement.

specialty, n. spécialité f.

species, n. espèce f.

specific, adj. spécifique.

specify, vb. spécifier.

specimen, n. spécimen m.

spectacle, n. spectacle m.

spectacular, adj. spectaculaire.

spectator, n. spectateur m.

speculate, vb. spéculer.

speculation, n. spéculation f.

speech, n. (address) discours m.; (utterance) parole f.

speed, n. vitesse f.

speedometer, n. compteur (m.) (de vitesse).

speedy, adj. rapide.

spell, 1. n. (incantation) charme m.; (period) période f. 2. vb. épeler.

spelling, n. orthographe f.

spend, vb. (money) dépenser; (time) passer.

sphere, n. sphère f.

spice, n. épice f.

spider, n. araignée f.

spike, n. pointe f.

spill, vb. répandre, tr.

spin, vb. (thread) filer; (twirl) tourner.

spinach, n. épinards m.pl.

spine, n. épine f.; (backbone) épine (f.) dorsale.

spiral, 1. n. spirale f. 2. adj. spiral.

spirit, n. esprit m.

spiritual, adj. spirituel.

spiritualism, n. spiritisme m.; spiritualisme m.

spit, 1. n. (saliva) crachat m.; (for roast) broche f. 2. vb. cracher.

spite, n. dépit m.; (in s. of) malgré.

spiteful, adj. méchant.

splash, vb. éclabousser.

splendid, adj. splendide.

splendor, n. splendeur f.

splinter, n. éclat m.

split, vb. fendre.

spoil, 1. n. butin m. 2. vb. gâter.

sponge, n. éponge f.

sponsor, n. (law) garant m.

spontaneity, n. spontanéité f.

spontaneous, adj. spontané.

spool, n. bobine f.

spoon, n. cuiller f.

spoonful, n. cuillerée f.

sporadic, adj. sporadique.

sport, n. sport m.; (fun) jeu m.

spot, 1. n. (stain) tache f.; (place) endroit m. **2.** vb. tacher; (recognize) reconnaître.

spotless, adj. immaculé.

spouse, n. époux m., épouse f.

spout, 1. n. (teapot, etc.) bec m. **2.** vb. jaillir.

sprain, n. entorse f.

sprawl, vb. s'étaler.

spray, n. (sea) embrun m.

spread, 1. n. étendue f. **2.** vb. étendre, tr.

spreadsheet, n. tableur m.

spree, (go on a s.) faire la noce.

sprightly, adj. éveillé.

spring, 1. n. (season) printemps m.; (source) source f.; (leap) saut m.; (device) ressort m. **2.** vb. (leap) sauter; (water) jaillir.

sprinkle, vb. asperger.

spry, adj. alerte.

spur, 1. n. éperon m. **2.** vb. éperonner.

spurious, adj. faux m., fausse f.

spurn, vb. repousser.

spurt, 1. n. jet m. **2.** vb. jaillir.

spy, 1. n. espion m. **2.** espionner, apercevoir.

squad, n. escouade f.

squadron, n. escadron m.

squalid, adj. misérable.

squall, n. rafale f.

squander, vb. gaspiller.

square, 1. n. (geom.) carré m.; (in town) place f. **2.** adj. carré.

squash, 1. n. (vegetable) courge f.; (game) squash m. **2.** vb. écraser.

squat, vb. s'accroupir.

squeak, 1. vb. crier, grincer. **2.** n. grincement m.

squeeze, vb. serrer; (lemon) presser.

squid, n. calamar m.

squirrel, n. écureuil m.

squirt, vb. seringuer.

stab, vb. poignarder.

stability, n. stabilité f.

stabilize, vb. stabiliser.

stable, 1. n. écurie f. **2.** adj. stable.

stack, n. (hay) meule f.; (pile) pile f.; (chimney) souche f.

staff, n. (stick) bâton m.; (mil.) état-major m.; (personnel) personnel m.

stage, n. (theater) scène f.; (in development) période f.; (stopping-place) étape f.

stagflation, n. stagflation f.

stagger, vb. (totter) chanceler.

stagnant, adj. stagnant.

stain, 1. n. tache f. **2.** vb. (spot) tacher; (color) teinter.

staircase, stairway, n. escalier m.

stairs, n. escalier m.

stake, 1. n. (post) pieu m.; (at s.) en jeu. **2.** vb. (gaming) mettre au jeu.

stale, adj. (bread) rassis; (food) pas frais.

stalk, 1. n. tige f. **2.** vb. traquer.

stall, 1. n. (stable, church) stalle f. **2.** vb. temporiser.

stamina, n. vigueur f.

stammer, vb. bégayer.

stamp, 1. n. timbre(-poste) m. **2.** vb. (letter) timbrer; (with foot) frapper du pied.

stampede, n. sauve-qui-peut n.; débandade f.

stand, 1. n. (position) position f.; (resistance) résistance f.; (stall) étalage m.; (vehicles) station f. **2.** vb. tr. (put) poser; (endure) supporter. **3.** vb. intr. (upright) se tenir debout; (be situated, be located) se trouver; (stop) s'arrêter.

standard, n. (flag) étendard m.; (measure, etc.) étalon m.; (living, etc.) niveau m.

stanza, n. strophe f.

staple, 1. n. agrafe f. **2.** vb. agrafer.

stapler, n. agrafeuse f.

star, n. étoile f.; (movie) vedette f.

starch, n. amidon m.

stare, vb. regarder fixement.

stark, adj. pur, austère.

start, 1. n. (beginning) commencement m.; (surprise, etc.) tressaillement m. **2.** vb. commencer, tressaillir.

startle, vb. effrayer.

starvation, n. faim f.

starve, vb. intr. mourir de faim.

state, 1. n. état m. **2.** vb. déclarer.

statement, n. déclaration f.

statesman, n. homme (m.) d'état.

static, adj. statique.

station, n. (railroad) gare f.; (bus, subway) station f.

stationary, adj. stationnaire.

stationery, n. papeterie f.

statistics, n. statistique f.

statue, n. statue f.

stature, n. stature f.

statute, n. statut m.

stay, vb. rester.

steady, adj. ferme; (constant) soutenu.

steak, n. bifteck m.

steal, vb. voler.

steam, n. vapeur f.

steamboat, n. bateau (m.) à vapeur.

steamship, n. vapeur m.

steel, n. acier m.

steep, adj. raide.

steeple, n. clocher m.

steer, 1. n. jeune bœuf m. 2. vb. gouverner.

stem, n. (plant) tige f.

stenographer, n. sténographe m.f.

stenography, n. sténographie f.

step, 1. n. pas m.; (of staircase) marche f. 2. vb. faire un pas.

stereo, n. stéréo f.; chaîne (f.) stéréo.

stepbrother, n. demi-frère m.

stepdaughter, n. belle-fille f.

stepfather, n. beau-père m.

stepmother, n. belle-mère f.

stepsister, n. belle-soeur f.

stereophonic, adj. stéréophonique.

stereotype, n. stéréotype m.

sterile, adj. stérile.

stern, adj. sévère.

stethoscope, n. stéthoscope m.

stew, n. ragoût m.

steward, n. (airline) steward m.

stewardess, n. (airline) hôtesse (f.) de l'air.

stick, 1. n. bâton m. 2. vb. (paste) coller, tr.; (remain) rester.

sticker, n. autocollant m.

sticky, adj. gluant.

stiff, adj. raide.

stiffness, n. raideur f.

stifle, vb. étouffer.

still, 1. adj. tranquille. 2. adv. encore. 3. conj. cependant.

stillness, n. tranquillité f.

stimulant, n. stimulant m.

stimulate, vb. stimuler.

stimulus, n. stimulant m.

sting, 1. n. piqûre f. 2. vb. (prick) piquer; (smart) cuire.

stingy, adj. mesquin.

stink, 1. vb. puer. 2. n. puanteur f.

stir, 1. vb. remuer (person, intr.) bouger. 2. n. mouvement m.

stitch, 1. n. (sewing) point m.; (knitting) maille f. 2. vb. coudre.

stock, n. (goods on hand) marchandise f.pl.; (finance) valeurs f.pl., action f.

stockbroker, n. agent de change m.

stock exchange, n. Bourse f.

stocking, n. bas m.

stole, n. étole f.

stomach, n. estomac m.; (s. ache) mal (m.) à l'estomac.

stone, n. pierre f.

stool, n. escabeau m.

stoop, vb. se pencher.

stop, 1. n. arrêt m. 2. vb. arrêter, tr.; (prevent) empêcher (de); (cease) cesser.

storage, n. emmagasinage m.

store, 1. n. (shop) magasin m.; (supply) provision f. 2. vb. emmagasiner.

storm, 1. n. orage m. 2. vb. prendre d'assaut.

stormy, adj. orageux.

story, n. histoire f.; (floor) étage m.

stout, adj. gros m., grosse f.

stove, n. fourneau m.

straight, adj. and adv. droit.

straighten, vb. redresser.

strain, 1. n. effort m. 2. vb. (stretch) tendre; (filter) passer.

strait, n. (geography) détroit m.

strand, n. (beach) plage f.; (hair) mèche f.; (thread) fil m.

strange, adj. étrange; (foreign) étranger.

stranger, n. étranger m.

strangle, vb. étrangler.

strap, n. courroie f.

strategic, adj. stratégique.

strategy, n. stratégie f.

straw, n. paille f.

strawberry, n. fraise f.

stray, adj. égaré.

streak, 1. n. raie f. **2.** vb. rayer.

stream, n. courant m.; (small river) ruisseau m.

streamline, vb. caréner, simplifier, moderniser.

street, n. rue f.

strength, n. force f.

strengthen, vb. fortifier.

strenuous, adj. énergique.

streptococcus, n. streptocoque m.

stress, 1. n. force f.; tension f.; (gramm.) accent m. **2.** vb. accentuer.

stretch, vb. étendre, tr.

stretcher, n. brancard m.

strict, adj. strict.

stride, n. enjambée f.

strife, n. lutte f.

strike, 1. n. grève f. **2.** vb. frapper; (match, tr.) allumer; (clock) sonner; (workers) se mettre en grève.

string, n. ficelle f.; (music) corde f.

string bean, n. haricot vert m.

strip, 1. n. bande f. **2.** vb. dépouiller.

stripe, n. bande f.; (mil.) galon m.

strive, vb. s'efforcer (de).

stroke, 1. n. coup m., caresse f. **2.** vb. caresser.

stroll, n. tour m.

stroller, n. poussette f.

strong, adj. fort.

structure, n. structure f.

struggle, 1. n. lutte f. **2.** vb. lutter.

stub, n. souche f.

stubborn, adj. opiniâtre, obstiné, têtu.

student, n. étudiant m.

studio, n. atelier m.

studious, adj. studieux.

study, 1. n. étude f.; (room) cabinet (m.) de travail. **2.** vb. étudier.

stuff, 1. n. (materials) matériaux m.pl.; (textile) étoffe f. **2.** vb. bourrer; (cooking) farcir.

stuffing, n. bourre f.; (cooking) farce f.

stumble, vb. trébucher.

stump, n. (tree) souche f.

stun, vb. étourdir.

stunt, n. tour (m.) de force.

stupid, adj. stupide.

stupidity, n. stupidité f.

sturdy, adj. vigoureux.

stutter, vb. bégayer.

style, n. style m.

stylish, adj. élégant.

subconscious, adj. subconscient.

subdue, vb. subjuguer.

subject, 1. n. sujet m. **2.** adj. (people, country) assujetti; (liable) sujet. **3.** vb. assujettir.

sublet, vb. sous-louer.

sublimate, vb. sublimer.

sublime, adj. sublime.

submarine, n. sous-marin m.

submerge, vb. submerger.

submission, n. soumission f.

submit, vb. soumettre, tr.

subnormal, adj. sous-normal.

subordinate, adj. and n. subordonné a.

subpoena, n. citation f.

subscribe, vb. (consent, support) souscrire; (to paper, etc.) s'abonner.

subscription, n. souscription f.; (to paper, etc.) abonnement m.

subsequent, adj. subséquent, ultérieur.

subsidy, n. subvention f.

substance, n. substance f.

substantial, adj. substantiel; (well-to-do) aisé.

substitute, 1. n. remplaçant m., remplacement m. **2.** vb. substituer.

substitution, n. substitution f.

subterfuge, n. subterfuge m., faux-fuyant m.

subterranean, adj. souterrain.

subtitle, n. sous-titre m.

subtle, adj. subtil.

subtract, vb. soustraire.

suburb, n. faubourg m., banlieue f.

subversive, adj. subversif.

subway, n. métro(politain) m.

succeed, vb. (come after) succéder à; (be successful) réussir (à).

success, n. succès m.

successful, adj. heureux.

succession, n. succession f.

successive, adj. successif.

successor, n. successeur f.

succumb, vb. succomber.

such, adj. tel; (intensive, **s. a** + adj.) un . . . aussi + adj.

suck, vb. sucer.

suction, n. succion f.

sudden, *adj.* soudain.

sue, *vb.* poursuivre.

suffer, *vb.* souffrir.

suffice, *vb.* suffire.

sufficient, *adj.* suffisant.

suffocate, *vb.* suffoquer.

sugar, *n.* sucre *m.*

suggest, *vb.* suggérer.

suggestion, *n.* suggestion *f.*

suicide, 1. *n.* suicide *m.* 2. *vb.* **(commit s.)** se suicider, *intr.*

suit, 1. *n.* (law) procès *m.;* (clothes) (man's) complet *m.,* (woman's) tailleur *m.;* (cards) couleur *f.* 2. *vb.* convenir (à).

suitable, *adj.* convenable.

suitcase, *n.* valise *f.*

sulk, *vb.* bouder.

sulphur, *n.* soufre *m.*

sum, *n.* somme *f.*

summary, 1. *n.* résumé *m.,* abrégé *m.* 2. *adj.* sommaire, immédiat.

summer, *n.* été *m.*

summit, *n.* sommet *m.*

summon, *vb.* (convoke) convoquer; (bid to come) appeler.

sun, *n.* soleil *m.*

sunburn, *n.* hâle *m.,* coup *(m.)* de soleil.

Sunday, *n.* dimanche *m.*

sunglasses, *n.* lunettes *(f.pl.)* de soleil.

sunny, *adj.* ensoleillé.

sunshine, *n.* soleil *m.*

suntan, *n.* bronzage *m.*

superb, *adj.* superbe.

superficial, *adj.* superficiel.

superfluous, *adj.* superflu.

superimpose, *vb.* superposer.

superintendent, *n.* surveillant *m.*

superior, *adj. and n.* supérieur *m.*

superiority, *n.* supériorité *f.*

superlative, *n.* superlatif *m.*

supermarket, *n.* supermarché *m.*

supernatural, *adj. and n.* surnaturel *m.*

superpower, *n.* superpuissance *f.*

supersede, *vb.* remplacer.

superstar, *n.* superstar *m.*

superstition, *n.* superstition *f.*

superstitious, *adj.* superstitieux.

superstore, *n.* hypermarché *m.*

supervise, *vb.* surveiller.

supper, *n.* souper *m.*

supplement, *n.* supplément *m.*

supply, 1. *n.* approvisionnement *m.;* provision *f.* 2. *vb.* fournir (de).

support, 1. *n.* appui *m.,* soutien *m.* 2. *vb.* soutenir; (bear) supporter; (back up) appuyer.

suppose, *vb.* supposer.

suppress, *vb.* supprimer.

suppression, *n.* suppression *f.*

supreme, *adj.* suprême.

surcharge, *n.* prix *(m.)* supplémentaire; (tax) surtaxe *f.*

sure, *adj.* sûr.

surf, *n.* ressac *m.*

surface, *n.* surface *f.*

surfboard, *n.* planche *(f.)* de surf.

surfing, *n.* surf *m.*

surge, *n.* houle *f.*

surgeon, *n.* chirurgien *m.*

surgery, *n.* chirurgie *f.*

surpass, *vb.* surpasser.

surplus, *n.* surplus *m.*

surprise, 1. *n.* surprise *f.* 2. *vb.* surprendre.

surrender, *vb.* rendre, *tr.*

surround, *vb.* entourer.

survey, 1. *vb.* contempler; (investigate) examiner. 2. *n.* enquête *f.*

survival, *n.* survivance *f.,* survie *f.*

survive, *vb.* survivre.

susceptible, *adj.* susceptible (de).

suspect, 1. *vb.* soupçonner. 2. *adj. and n.* suspect *m.*

suspend, *vb.* suspendre.

suspense, *n.* incertitude *f.;* **(in s.)** en suspens; (film, book) suspense *m.*

suspension, *n.* suspension *f.*

suspicion, *n.* soupçon *m.*

suspicious, *adj.* soupçonneux; (questionable) suspect.

sustain, *vb.* soutenir.

swallow, 1. *n.* (bird) hirondelle *f.* 2. *vb.* avaler.

swamp, *n.* marais *m.*

swan, *n.* cygne *m.*

swap, *vb.* échanger.

swarm, *n.* essaim *m.*

sway, 1. *n.* (rule) domination *f.;* (motion) oscillation *f.* 2. *vb.* (rule) gouverner; (motion) se balancer.

swear, *vb.* jurer.

sweat, 1. *n.* sueur *f.* 2. *vb.* suer.

sweater, *n.* pull-over *m.*

Swede, *n.* Suédois *m.*

Sweden, *n.* Suède *f.*

Swedish, adj. and n. suédois m.

sweep, 1. n. (bend) courbe f.; (movement) mouvement (m.) circulaire. **2.** vb. balayer.

sweepstakes, n. poule f.

sweet, adj. doux m., douce f.; sucré.

sweetheart, n. chéri m., chérie f.

sweetness, n. douceur f.

swell, vb. gonfler, tr.; enfler, tr.

swift, adj. rapide.

swim, vb. nager.

swimsuit, n. maillot de bain m.

swindle, vb. escroquer.

swine, n. cochon m.

swing, vb. balancer, tr.

Swiss, 1. n. Suisse m. **2.** adj. suisse, helvétique.

switch, n. (elect.) interrupteur m.

switchboard, n. standard m.

Switzerland, n. Suisse f.

sword, n. épée f.

syllable, n. syllabe f.

symbol, n. symbole m.

symbolic, adj. symbolique.

symmetry, n. symétrie f.

sympathetic, adj. compatissant.

sympathy, n. compassion f.

symphony, n. symphonie f.

symptom, n. symptôme m.

synagogue, n. synagogue f.

synchronize, vb. synchroniser, tr.

syndicate, n. syndicat m.

syndrome, n. syndrome m.

synonym, n. synonyme m.

synthetic, adj. synthétique.

syphilis, n. syphilis f.

Syria, n. Syrie f.

syringe, n. seringue f.

syrup, n. sirop m.

system, n. système m.

systems analyst, n. analyste-programmeur m.

systematic, adj. systématique.

T

tabernacle, n. tabernacle m.

table, n. table f.

tablecloth, n. nappe f.

tablespoon, n. cuiller (f.) à soupe.

tablet, n. tablette f.

tabloid, n. (t. press) la presse (f.) populaire.

tack, 1. n. (nail) broquette f. **2.** vb. clouer.

tackle, 1. n. matériel m. **2.** vb. s'attaquer à.

tact, n. tact m.

tag, n. étiquette f.

tail, n. queue f.

tailor, n. tailleur m.

take, vb. prendre; (lead) conduire; (carry) porter; (t. off) (plane) décoller.

tale, n. conte m.

talent, n. talent m.

talk, 1. n. conversation f. **2.** vb. parler.

talkative, adj. bavard.

tall, adj. grand.

tame, adj. (animal) apprivoisé.

tamper, vb. toucher à.

tampon, n. tampon hygiénique m.

tan, 1. n. (leather) tan m.; (skin) hâle m.; (color) tanné m. **2.** vb. tanner.

tangible, adj. tangible.

tangle, n. embrouillement m.

tank, n. réservoir m.; (mil.) char (m.) d'assaut.

tap, 1. n. (water) robinet m.; (knock) petit coup m. **2.** vb. frapper légèrement.

tape, n. ruban m.

tape recorder, n. magnétophone m.

tapestry, n. tapisserie f.

tar, n. goudron m.

target, n. cible f.

tariff, n. tarif m.

tarnish, vb. ternir, tr.

tarragon, n. estragon m.

tart, 1. n. tarte f. **2.** adj. âpre.

task, n. tâche f.

taste, 1. n. goût m. **2.** vb. goûter.

tasty, adj. savoureux.

taut, adj. raide.

tavern, n. taverne f.

tax, 1. n. impôt m. **2.** vb. imposer.

taxi, n. taxi m.

taxi driver, n. chauffeur (m.) de taxi.

taxpayer, n. contribuable m.

tea, n. thé m.

teach, vb. enseigner; (to do) apprendre à.

teacher, n. instituteur m.; (school) professeur m.

team, n. (animals) attelage m.; (people) équipe f.

teapot, n. théière f.

tear, 1. n. larme f.; (rip) déchirure f. **2.** vb. déchirer.

tease, vb. taquiner.

teaspoon, n. cuiller (f.) à thé.

technical, adj. technique.

technician, n. technicien m.

technique, n. technique f.

technological, adj. technologique.

tedious, adj. ennuyeux.

teenager, n. adolescent m.

telegram, n. télégramme m.

telegraph, n. télégraphe m.

telephone, 1. n. téléphone m. **2.** vb. téléphoner.

telephone booth, n. cabine (f.) téléphonique.

telephone directory, n. annuaire m. (du téléphone).

telescope, n. télescope m.

televise, vb. téléviser.

television, n. télévision f.

tell, vb. dire; (story, etc.) raconter.

teller, n. (bank) caissier m., guichetier m.

temper, n. (humor) humeur f.; (lose one's t.) s'emporter; (anger) colère f.; (metals) trempe f.

temperament, n. tempérament m.

temperamental, adj. instable.

temperance, n. tempérance f.

temperate, adj. (habit) sobre; (climate) tempéré.

temperature, n. température f.

tempest, n. tempête f.

template, n. patron m.

temple, n. temple m.; (forehead) tempe f.

temporary, adj. temporaire, provisoire.

tempt, vb. tenter.

temptation, n. tentation f.

ten, adj. and n. dix m.

tenant, n. locataire m.f.

tend, vb. tendre, intr.; (care for) soigner.

tendency, n. tendance f.

tender, adj. tendre.

tenderness, n. tendresse f.

tendon, n. tendon m.

tenement, n. taudis m.

tennis, n. tennis m.

tenor, n. (music) ténor m.

tense, adj. tendu.

tension, n. tension f.

tent, n. tente f.

tentative, adj. tentatif, expérimental.

tenth, adj. and n. dixième m.f.

term, n. terme m.; (school) trimestre m.; (conditions) conditions f.pl.; (political) mandat m.

terminal, 1. n. (electricity) borne f.; (computer) terminal m.; (airport) aérogare f. **2.** adj. incurable, terminal.

terrace, n. terrasse f.

terrible, adj. terrible.

terrific, adj. fantastique.

terrify, vb. terrifier.

territory, n. territoire m.

terror, n. terreur f.

test, 1. n. épreuve f. **2.** vb. mettre à l'épreuve.

testament, n. testament m.

testify, vb. témoigner (de); (declare) affirmer.

testimony, n. témoignage m.

text, n. texte m.

textile, adj. textile.

texture, n. texture f.

Thai, 1. n. Thaïlandais m. **2.** adj. thaïlandais.

than, conj. que; (with numerals) de.

thank, vb. remercier; (t. you) merci.

thankful, adj. reconnaissant.

that sg., **those** pl., **1.** adj. ce, cet m., cette f., ces pl.; (opposed to *this*) ce . . . -là, etc. **2.** *demonstrative pron.* celui-là m., celle-là f., ceux-là m.pl., celles-là f.pl.; (object not named) cela, abbr. ça; (**what is t.?**) qu'est-ce que c'est que ça? **3.** *relative pron.* qui (subject); que (object). **4.** *conj.* que; (purpose) pour que.

the, art. le m., la f., les pl.

theater, n. théâtre m.

theft, n. vol m.

their, adj. leur sg., leurs pl.

theirs, pron. le leur m., la leur f., les leurs pl.

them, *pron.* eux *m.,* elles *f.;* (unstressed, with verb) les (direct), leur (indirect).

theme, *n.* thème *m.*

themselves, *pron.* eux-mêmes *m.,* elles-mêmes *f.;* (reflexive) se.

then, *adv.* alors; (after that) ensuite.

thence, *adv.* (place) de là; (reason) pour cette raison.

theology, *n.* théologie *f.*

theoretical, *adj.* théorique.

theory, *n.* théorie *f.*

therapy, *n.* thérapie *f.*

there, *adv.* là; (with verb) y.

therefore, *adv.* donc.

thermometer, *n.* thermomètre *m.*

thermonuclear, *adj.* thermonucléaire.

thermostat, *n.* thermostat *m.*

these, *see* **this.**

they, *pron.* ils *m.,* elles *f.*

thick, *adj.* épais.

thicken, *vb.* épaissir, *tr.*

thickness, *n.* épaisseur *f.*

thief, *n.* voleur *m.*

thigh, *n.* cuisse *f.*

thimble, *n.* dé *m.*

thin, *adj.* mince.

thing, *n.* chose *f.*

think (of), *vb.* penser (à).

thinker, *n.* penseur *m.*

third, 1. *n.* tiers *m.* **2.** *adj.* troisième.

Third World, *n.* Tiers Monde *m.*

thirst, *n.* soif *f.*

thirsty, *adj.* **(be t.)** avoir soif.

thirteen, *adj. and n.* treize *m.*

thirty, *adj. and n.* trente *m.*

this, *sg.* **these** *pl.,* **1.** *adj.* ce, cet *m.,* cette *f.,* ces *pl.;* (opposed to *that*) ce . . . -ci, *etc.* **2.** *demonstrative pron.* celui-ci *m.,* celle-ci *f.,* ceux-ci *m.pl.,* celles-ci *f.pl.;* (object not named) ceci.

thorough, *adj.* complet.

those, *see* **that.**

though, *conj.* quoique.

thought, *n.* pensée *f.*

thoughtful, *adj.* pensif.

thoughtless, *adj.* étourdi.

thousand, *adj. and n.* mille *m.*

thread, *n.* fil *m.*

threat, *n.* menace *f.*

threaten, *vb.* menacer.

three, *adj. and n.* trois *m.*

thrift, *n.* économie *f.*

thrill, 1. *n.* tressaillement *m.* **2.** *vb.* tressaillir, *intr.;* faire frémir, *tr.*

thriller, *n.* livre *(m.)* /film *(m.)* à suspense.

thrive, *vb.* prospérer.

throat, *n.* gorge *f.*

throne, *n.* trône *m.*

through, *prep. and adv.* à travers; **(be t.)** avoir fini.

throughout, *adv.* partout.

throw, *vb.* jeter.

thrust, *n.* pousser.

thumb, *n.* pouce *m.*

thumbtack, *n.* punaise *f.*

thunder, 1. *n.* tonnerre *m.* **2.** *vb.* tonner.

Thursday, *n.* jeudi *m.*

thus, *adv.* ainsi.

thwart, *vb.* contrarier.

thyme, *n.* thym *m.*

thyroid, *n.* thyroïde *f.*

ticket, *n.* billet *m.*

tickle, *vb.* chatouiller.

ticklish, *adj.* chatouilleux.

tide, *n.* marée *f.*

tidy, *adj.* ordonné, en ordre.

tie, 1. *n.* lien *m.;* **(neck-t.)** cravate *f.* **2.** *vb.* attacher; (bind) lier; (knot) nouer.

tier, *n.* gradin *m.*

tiger, *n.* tigre *m.*

tight, *adj.* serré; (drunk) gris.

tighten, *vb.* serrer.

tile, *n.* (roof) tuile *f.*

till, 1. *prep.* jusqu'a. **2.** *conj.* jusqu'à ce que.

tilt, *vb.* pencher.

timber, *n.* (building) bois *(m.)* de construction.

time, 1. *n.* temps *m.;* (occasion) fois *f.;* (clock) heure *f.;* **(what t. is it?)** quelle heure est-il?; **(have a good t.)** s'amuser bien. **2.** *vb.* (race) chronométrer; (program) minuter.

timeless, *adj.* éternel.

timetable, *n.* horaire *m.*

timid, *adj.* timide.

timidity, *n.* timidité *f.*

tin, *n.* étain *m.*

tin foil, *n.* papier *(m.)* d'aluminium.

tint, *n.* teinte *f.*

tiny, adj. tout petit.

tip, 1. n. (money) pourboire m.; (end) bout m. **2.** vb. (money) donner un pourboire à; **(t. over)** renverser.

tire, 1. n. (car, etc.) pneu m. **2.** vb. fatiguer.

tired, adj. fatigué.

tissue, n. tissu m.; mouchoir m.

title, n. titre m.

to, prep. à; **(in order t.)** pour.

toast, n. pain (m.) grillé.

tobacco, n. tabac m.

today, adv. aujourd'hui.

toe, n. orteil m.

together, adv. ensemble.

toil, vb. travailler dur.

toilet, n. toilettes f.pl.; **(t. paper)** papier (m.) hygiénique.

token, n. témoignage m.; (coin) jeton m.

tolerance, n. tolérance f.

tolerant, adj. tolérant.

tolerate, vb. tolérer.

toll, n. péage m.

tomato, n. tomate f.

tomb, n. tombeau m.

tomorrow, adv. demain.

ton, n. tonne f.

tone, n. ton m.

tongue, n. langue f.

tonic, adj. and n. tonique f.

tonight, adv. cette nuit; (evening) ce soir.

tonsil, n. amygdale f.

tonsillitis, n. amygdalite f.

too, adv. trop; (also) aussi.

tool, n. outil m.

tooth, n. dent f.

toothache, n. mal (m.) de dents.

toothbrush, n. brosse (f.) à dents.

toothpaste, n. dentifrice m.

top, n. (mountain, etc.) sommet m.; (table) dessus m.

topcoat, n. pardessus m.

topic, n. sujet m.

torch, n. torche f.

torment, 1. n. tourment m. **2.** vb. tourmenter.

tornado, n. tornade f.

torrent, n. torrent m.

torture, 1. n. torture f. **2.** vb. torturer.

toss, vb. (throw) jeter; s'agiter.

total, adj. and n. total m.

totalitarian, adj. totalitaire.

touch, 1. n. (touching) attouchement m.; (sense) toucher m.; (small amount) pointe f.; (contact) contact m. **2.** vb. toucher.

touching, adj. touchant.

tough, adj. dur.

tour, 1. n. tour m. **2.** vb. visiter.

tourist, n. touriste m.f.

tournament, n. tournoi m.

tow, vb. remorquer.

toward, prep. (place, time) vers; (feelings, etc.) envers.

towel, n. serviette f.

tower, n. tour f.

town, n. ville f.

toy, n. jouet m.

trace, n. trace f.

track, n. piste f.; (railroad) voie f.

tract, n. (space) étendue f.

tractor, n. tracteur m.

trade, 1. n. commerce m.; (job) métier m. **2.** vb. commercer, échanger.

trader, n. commerçant m.

trade union, n. syndicat m.

tradition, n. tradition f.

traditional, adj. traditionnel.

traffic, n. circulation f.

tragedy, n. tragédie f.

tragic, adj. tragique.

trail, n. trace f.

train, 1. n. train m.; (dress) traîne f.; (retinue) suite f. **2.** vb. (sports) entraîner, tr.; (mil.) exercer, tr.

trait, n. trait m.

traitor, n. traître m.

tramp, n. (steps) bruit (m.) de pas; (person) chemineau m.

tranquil, adj. tranquille.

tranquillity, n. tranquillité f.

transaction, n. opération f.

transcript, n. transcription f.

transfer, 1. n. transport m.; (ticket) billet (m.) de correspondance. **2.** vb. transférer, tr.

transform, vb. transformer.

transfusion, n. transfusion f.

transistor, n. transistor m.

transition, n. transition f.

translate, vb. traduire.

translation, n. traduction f.

transmit, vb. transmettre.

transparent, adj. transparent.

transplant, 1. vb. transplanter. **2.** n. transplantation f.

transport, transportation, 1. n. transport m. **2.** vb. transporter.

transsexual, adj. transsexuel.

transvestite, adj. travesti.

trap, 1. n. piège m. **2.** vb. prendre au piège.

trash, n. (rubbish) rebut m.

trauma, n. traumatisme m.

travel, 1. n. voyage m. **2.** vb. voyager.

traveler, n. voyageur m.

traveler's check, n. chèque (m.) de voyage.

tray, n. plateau m.

treacherous, adj. traître.

tread, vb. marcher.

treason, n. trahison f.

treasure, 1. n. trésor m. **2.** vb. tenir beaucoup à.

treasurer, n. trésorier m.

treasury, n. trésor m.

treat, vb. traiter.

treatment, n. traitement m.

treaty, n. traité m.

tree, n. arbre m.

trek, n. voyage (m.) difficile.

tremble, vb. trembler.

tremendous, adj. terrible.

trench, n. tranchée f.

trend, n. tendance f., mode f.

trespass, vb. empiéter.

triage, n. présélection f.

trial, n. (law) procès m.; (test) épreuve f.

triangle, n. triangle m.

tribe, n. tribu f.

tribulation, n. tribulation f.

tributary, 1. n. (river) affluent m. **2.** adj. tributaire.

tribute, n. tribut m.

trick, 1. n. ruse f. **2.** vb. duper.

trickle, vb. dégouliner.

tricky, adj. astucieux.

trifle, n. bagatelle f.

trigger, 1. n. détente f. **2.** vb. déclencher.

trim, 1. adj. soigné, svelte. **2.** vb. (put in order) arranger; (adorn) garnir; (cut) tailler.

Trinity, n. Trinité f.

trinket, n. breloque f.

trip, 1. n. voyage m. **2.** vb. trébucher.

triple, adj. and n. triple m.

trite, adj. rebattu.

triumph, n. triomphe m.

triumphant, adj. triomphant.

trivial, adj. trivial.

trolley-car, n. tramway m.

troop, n. troupe f.

trophy, n. trophée m.

tropic, n. tropique m.

trot, 1. n. trot m. **2.** vb. intr. trotter.

trouble, 1. n. (misfortune) malheur m.; (difficulty) difficulté f.; (inconvenience, med.) dérangement m. **2.** vb. (worry) inquiéter, tr.; (inconvenience) déranger; (afflict) affliger.

troublesome, adj. gênant.

trough, n. auge f.

trousers, n. pantalon m.

trousseau, n. trousseau m.

trout, n. truite f.

truce, n. trêve f.

truck, n. camion m.

true, adj. vrai.

truly, adv. vraiment.

trumpet, n. trompette f.

trunk, n. (clothes) malle f.; (body, tree) tronc m.

trust, 1. n. confiance f.; (business) trust m. **2.** vb. se confier à; (entrust) confier.

trustworthy, adj. digne de confiance.

truth, n. vérité f.

truthful, adj. sincère.

try, vb. essayer; (law) mettre en jugement.

tryst, n. rendez-vous m.

T-shirt, n. maillot m., tee-shirt m.

tub, n. baignoire f.

tube, n. tube m.

tuberculosis, n. tuberculose f.

tuck, 1. n. (fold) pli m. **2.** vb. ranger, rentrer.

Tuesday, n. mardi m.

tug, 1. n. (boat) remorqueur m. **2.** vb. (pull) tirer; (boat) remorquer.

tuition, n. (frais de l')enseignement m.

tulip, n. tulipe f.

tumble, vb. (fall) tomber.

tummy, n. ventre m.

tumor, n. tumeur f.

tumult, n. tumulte m.

tuna, n. thon m.

tune, 1. *n.* air *m.*; (concord, harmony) accord *m.* **2.** *vb.* accorder.

Tunisia, *n.* Tunisie *f.*

tunnel, *n.* tunnel *m.*

turban, *n.* turban *m.*

turf, *n.* gazon *m.*

Turk, *n.* Turc *m.*, Turque *f.*

turkey, *n.* dindon *m.*

Turkey, *n.* Turquie *f.*

Turkish, 1. *n.* (language) turc *m.* **2.** *adj.* turc *m.*, turque *f.*

turmoil, *n.* tumulte *m.*

turn, 1. *n.* tour *m.*; (road) détour *m.* **2.** *vb.* tourner, virer.

turning point, *n.* tournant *m.*

turnip, *n.* navet *m.*

turnover, *n.* (money) chiffre *(m.)* d'affaires.

turnpike, *n.* autoroute *(f.)* à péage.

turret, *n.* tourelle *f.*

turtle, *n.* tortue *f.*

tutor, 1. *n.* précepteur *m.* **2.** *vb.* donner des leçons particulières à.

TV, *n.* télé *f.*

twelfth, *adj.* and *n.* douzième *m.f.*

twelve, *adj.* and *n.* douze *m.*

twentieth, *adj.* and *n.* vingtième *m.f.*

twenty, *adj.* and *n.* vingt *m.*

twice, *adv.* deux fois.

twig, *n.* brindille *f.*

twilight, *n.* crépuscule *m.*

twin, *adj.* and *n.* jumeau *m.*, jumelle *f.*

twine, *n.* ficelle *f.*

twinkle, *vb.* scintiller.

twirl, *vb.* (faire) tournoyer.

twist, *vb.* tordre.

two, *adj.* and *n.* deux *m.*

tycoon, *n.* magnat *m.*

type, 1. *n.* type *m.*; (printing) caractère *m.* **2.** *vb.* taper à la machine.

typewriter, *n.* machine *(f.)* à écrire.

typhoid fever, *n.* fièvre *(f.)* typhoïde.

typical, *adj.* typique.

typist, *n.* dactylo(graphe) *m.f.*

tyranny, *n.* tyrannie *f.*

tyrant, *n.* tyran *m.*

U

ubiquitous, *adj.* omniprésent.

udder, *n.* mamelle *f.*

Uganda, *n.* Ouganda *m.*

ugliness, *n.* laideur *f.*

ugly, *adj.* laid.

ulcer, *n.* ulcère *m.*

ulterior, *adj.* ultérieur.

ultimate, *adj.* dernier.

ultrasound, *n.* ultrason *m.*

umbrella, *n.* parapluie *m.*

umpire, *n.* arbitre *m.f.*

unable, *adj.* incapable; (u. to) dans l'impossibilité de.

unanimous, *adj.* unanime.

uncalled for, *adj.* déplacé.

uncanny, *adj.* bizarre.

uncertain, *adj.* incertain.

uncle, *n.* oncle *m.*

unconscious, 1. *n.* inconscient *m.* **2.** *adj.* (aware) inconscient; (faint) sans connaissance; (u. of) sans conscience de.

uncouth, *adj.* grossier.

uncover, *vb.* découvrir.

under, 1. *prep.* sous. **2.** *adv.* au-dessous.

underdeveloped, *adj.* sous-développé.

underestimate, *vb.* sous-estimer.

undergo, *vb.* subir.

underground, *adj.* souterrain, clandestin.

underline, *vb.* souligner.

underneath, *adv.* en-dessous.

underpants, *n.pl.* caleçon *m.*, slip *m.*

underprivileged, *adj.* défavorisé.

undershirt, *n.* gilet *(m.)* de dessous.

understand, *vb.* comprendre.

understatement, *n.* litote *f.*

undertake, *vb.* entreprendre.

undertaker, *n.* entrepreneur *(m.)* de pompes funèbres.

underwear, *n.,* sous-vêtements *m.pl.*

underworld, *n.* (crime) milieu *m.*, pègre *f.*

undo, *vb.* défaire.

undress, vb. déshabiller, tr.
uneasy, adj. gêné.
uneven, adj. inégal.
unexpected, adj. inattendu.
unfair, adj. injuste.
unfit, adj. peu propre (à).
unfold, vb. déplier.
unforgettable, adj. inoubliable.
unfortunate, adj. malheureux.
unhappy, adj. malheureux.
uniform, adj. and n. uniforme n.
unify, vb. unifier.
union, n. union f.
unique, adj. unique.
unisex, adj. unisexuel.
unison, n. (in u.) à l'unisson.
unit, n. unité f.
unite, vb. unir, tr.
United Kingdom, n. Royaume (m.) Uni.
United Nations, n. Nations (f.pl.) Unies.
United States, n. États-Unis m.pl.
unity, n. unité f.
universal, adj. universel.
universe, n. univers m.
university, n. université f.
unless, conj. à moins que . . . ne.
unlike, adj. dissemblable.
unload, vb. décharger.
unlock, vb. ouvrir.
untie, vb. dénouer.
until, conj. jusqu'à ce que.
unusual, adj. insolite.
up, prep. vers le haut de.

upbringing, n. éducation f.
update, vb. mettre à jour.
uphold, vb. soutenir.
upholster, vb. tapisser.
upon, prep. sur.
upper, adj. supérieur.
upright, adj. droit.
uprising, n. soulèvement m.
uproar, n. vacarme m.
upset, vb. renverser.
upstairs, adv. en haut.
uptight, adj. tendu, crispé.
upward, 1. adj. dirigé en haut. 2. adv. en montant.
uranium, n. uranium m.
urban, adj. urbain.
urge, vb. (beg) prier.
urgency, n. urgence f.
urgent, adj. urgent.
us, pron. nous.
use, 1. n. usage m. 2. vb. employer, se servir de.
useful, adj. utile.
useless, adj. inutile.
usher, n. huissier m.
usual, adj. usuel.
utensil, n. ustensile m.
uterus, n. utérus m.
utilize, vb. utiliser, se servir de.
utmost, 1. n. le plus; (all one can) tout son possible. 2. adj. (greatest) le plus grand.
utter, 1. adj. absolu. 2. vb. prononcer; (cry) pousser.
utterance, n. émission f.

V

vacancy, n. vide m., vacance f.
vacant, adj. vide.
vacate, vb. quitter, évacuer.
vacation, n. vacances f.pl.
vaccinate, vb. vacciner.
vaccine, n. vaccin m.
vacuum, n. vide m.; (v. cleaner) aspirateur m.
vagina, n. vagin m.
vagrant, adj. vagabond.
vague, adj. vague.
vain, adj. vain.
valiant, adj. vaillant.
valid, adj. valide.
valise, n. valise f.

valley, n. vallée f.
valor, n. valeur f.
valuable, adj. de valeur.
value, 1. n. valeur f. 2. vb. évaluer.
value-added tax, n. taxe à la valeur ajoutée f.
valve, n. soupape f.
van, n. camionnette f.
vandal, n. vandale m.f.
vanguard, n. avant-garde f.
vanilla, n. vanille f.
vanish, vb. s'évanouir.
vanity, n. vanité f.
vanquish, vb. vaincre.
vapor, n. vapeur f.

variable, *adj.* variable.

variation, *n.* variation *f.*

varied, *adj.* varié.

variety, *n.* variété *f.*

various, *adj.* divers.

varnish, *n.* vernis *m.*

vary, *vb.* varier.

vase, *n.* vase *m.*

vasectomy, *n.* vasectomie *f.*

vassal, *n.* vassal *m.*

vast, *adj.* vaste.

vat, *n.* cuve *f.*

vault, *n.* voûte *f.*

veal, *n.* veau *m.*

vegetable, *n.* légume *m.*

vegetarian, *n.* végétarien *m.*

vehement, *adj.* véhément.

vehicle, *n.* véhicule *m.*

veil, *n.* voile *m.*

vein, *n.* veine *f.*

velocity, *n.* vitesse *f.*

velvet, *n.* velours *m.*

vending machine, *n.* distributeur (*m.*) automatique

venereal, *adj.* vénérien.

vengeance, *n.* vengeance *f.*

vent, *n.* ouverture *f.*

ventilate, *vb.* ventiler.

venture, 1. *n.* aventure *f.* 2. *vb.* hasarder, *tr.*

verb, *n.* verbe *m.*

verbose, *adj.* verbeux.

verdict, *n.* verdict *m.*

verge, *n.* bord *m.*

verify, *vb.* vérifier.

vermouth, *n.* vermouth *m.*

versatile, *adj.* versatile.

verse, *n.* vers *m.pl.*; (line of poetry) vers *m.*

version, *n.* version *f.*

vertical, *adj.* vertical.

vertigo vertige *m.*

very, *adv.* très.

vessel, *n.* vaisseau *m.*

vest, *n.* gilet *m.*

veteran, *n.* vétéran *m.*

veterinarian, *n.* vétérinaire *m.f.*

veto, *n.* véto *m.*

vex, *vb.* vexer.

viaduct, *n.* viaduc *m.*

vibrate, *vb.* vibrer.

vibration, *n.* vibration *f.*

vice, *n.* vice *m.*

vicinity, *n.* voisinage *m.*

vicious, *adj.* méchant.

victim, *n.* victime *f.*

victor, *n.* vainqueur *m.*

victorious, *adj.* victorieux.

victory, *n.* victoire *f.*

videocassette recorder, *n.* magnétoscope *m.*

videodisc, *n.* vidéodisque *m.*

videotape, *n.* bande vidéo *f.*

Vietnam, *n.* Viêt-nam *m.*

view, *n.* vue *f.*

vigil, *n.* veille *f.*

vigilant, *adj.* vigilant.

vigor, *n.* vigueur *f.*

vile, *adj.* vil, abominable.

village, *n.* village *m.*

villain, *n.* scélérat *m.*

vindicate, *vb.* défendre.

vindictive, *adj.* vindicatif.

vine, *n.* vigne *f.*

vinegar, *n.* vinaigre *m.*

vineyard, *n.* vigne *f.*, vignoble *m.*

vintage, *n.* (grapes gathered) vendange *f.*; (year of wine) année *f.*, millésime, *m.*

viola, *n.* alto *m.*

violate, *vb.* violer.

violation, *n.* violation *f.*

violence, *n.* violence *f.*

violent, *adj.* violent.

violet, 1. *n.* violette *f.* 2. *adj.* violet.

violin, *n.* violon *m.*

virgin, *n.* vierge *f.*

virile, *adj.* viril.

virtual, *adj.* vrai.

virtual reality, *n.* réalité (*f.*) virtuelle.

virtue, *n.* vertu *f.*

virtuous, *adj.* vertueux.

virus, *n.* virus *m.*

visa, *n.* visa *m.*

visible, *adj.* visible.

vision, *n.* vision *f.*

visit, 1. *n.* visite *f.* 2. *vb.* visiter.

visitor, *n.* visiteur *m.*

visual, *adj.* visuel.

vital, *adj.* vital.

vitality, *n.* vitalité *f.*

vitamin, *n.* vitamine *f.*

vivacious, *adj.* vif *m.*, vive *f.*

vivid, *adj.* vif *m.*, vive *f.*

vocabulary, *n.* vocabulaire *m.*

vocal, *adj.* vocal.

vocation, *n.* vocation *f.*

vodka, *n.* vodka *f.*

vogue, *n.* vogue *f.*

voice, *n.* voix *f.*

void, *adj.* (law) nul.

volcano, *n.* volcan *m.*

volley, *n.* (gun fire) salve *f.* **volleyball,** *n.* volley(-ball) *m.*

volt, *n.* volt *m.*

voltage, *n.* tension *f.,* voltage *m.*

volume, *n.* volume *m.*

voluntary, *adj.* volontaire.

volunteer, 1. *n.* volontaire *m.* **2.** *vb.* s'engager.

vomit, *vb.* vomir.

vote, 1. *n.* vote *m.* **2.** *vb.* voter.

voter, *n.* votant *m.*

vouch for, *vb.* répondre de.

vow, *n.* vœu *m.*

vowel, *n.* voyelle *f.*

voyage, *n.* voyage *m.*

vulgar, *adj.* vulgaire.

vulnerable, *adj.* vulnérable.

vulture, *n.* vautour *m.*

W

wade, *vb.* traverser à gué.

wafer, *n.* gaufrette *f.*

waffle, *n.* gaufre (américaine) *f.*

wag, *vb.* agiter.

wage, *vb.* (war) faire la guerre.

wages, *n.* salaire *m.*

wagon, *n.* chariot *m.*

wail, *vb.* gémir.

waist, *n.* taille *f.*

wait (for), *vb.* attendre.

waiter, *n.* garçon *m.,* serveur *m.*

waitress, *n.* serveuse *f.*

wake (up), *vb.* réveiller, *tr.;* s'éveiller, *intr.*

Wales, *n.* pays (*m.*) de Galles.

walk, 1. *n.* promenade *f.* **2.** *vb.* marcher; **(take a w.)** se promener.

Walkman, *n.* baladeur *m.,* walkman *m.*

wall, *n.* mur *m.*

wallcovering, *n.* tenture *f.*

wallet, *n.* portefeuille *m.*

wallpaper, *n.* papier peint *m.;* papier à tapisser *m.*

walnut, *n.* noix *f.*

walrus, *n.* morse *m.*

waltz, *n.* valse *f.*

wander, *vb.* errer.

want, 1. *n.* besoin *m.* **2.** *vb.* vouloir.

war, *n.* guerre *f.*

ward, *n.* (hospital) salle *f.;* (charge) pupille *m.f.*

ware, *n.* marchandises *f.pl.*

warehouse, *n.* entrepôt *m.*

warhead, *n.* ogive *f.*

warlike, *adj.* guerrier.

warm, 1. *adj.* chaud; **(be w.)** avoir chaud. **2.** *vb.* chauffer.

warmth, *n.* chaleur *f.*

warn, *vb.* avertir.

warning, *n.* avertissement *m.*

warp, *vb.* détourner.

warrant, 1. *n.* mandat *m.* **2.** *vb.* garantir.

warranty, *n.* garantie *f.*

warrior, *n.* guerrier *m.*

warship, *n.* navire (*m.*) de guerre.

wash, *vb.* laver, *tr.*

washing machine, *n.* laveuse mécanique *f.*

washroom, *n.* salle (*f.*) de bain.

wasp, *n.* guêpe *f.*

waste, 1. *n.* (money) gaspillage *m.;* (time) perte *f.;* (rubbish) déchets *m.pl.* **2.** *vb.* gaspiller, perdre.

wastepaper basket, *n.* corbeille (*f.*) à papier.

watch, 1. *n.* (timepiece) montre *f.;* (guard) garde *f.* **2.** *vb.* veiller.

watchful, *adj.* vigilant.

watchmaker, *n.* horloger *m.*

watchman, *n.* gardien *m.*

water, *n.* eau *f.*

waterbed, *n.* aqualit *m.*

water color, *n.* aquarelle *f.*

watercress, *n.* cresson *m.*

waterfall, *n.* chute (*f.*) d'eau.

waterproof, *adj.* imperméable.

wave, 1. *n.* (sea) vague *f.;* (sound) onde *f.;* **(permanent w.)** ondulation (*f.*) permanente. **2.** *vb.* agiter; (hair) onduler; saluer.

waver, *vb.* vaciller.

wax, *n.* cire *f.*

way, *n.* (road) chemin *m.;* (distance) distance *f.;* (direction) côté *m.;* (manner) manière *f.*

we, *pron.* nous.
weak, *adj.* faible.
weaken, *vb.* affaiblir.
weakness, *n.* faiblesse *f.*
wealth, *n.* richesse *f.*
wealthy, *adj.* riche.
weapon, *n.* arme *f.*
wear, *vb.* porter; (w. down) user; (w. out) épuiser.
weary, *adj.* las.
weasel, *n.* belette *f.*
weather, *n.* temps *m.*
weave, *vb.* tisser.
weaver, *n.* tisserand *m.*
web, *n.* (fabric) tissu *m.*; (spider) toile *f.*
wedding, *n.* noces *f.pl.*
wedge, *n.* coin *m.*
Wednesday, *n.* mercredi *m.*
weed, *n.* mauvaise herbe *f.*
week, *n.* semaine *f.*
weekday, *n.* jour (*m.*) de semaine.
weekend, *n.* week-end *m.*, fin de semaine *f.*
weekly, *adj.* hebdomadaire.
weep, *vb.* pleurer.
weigh, *vb.* peser.
weight, *n.* poids *m.*
weird, *adj.* mystérieux.
welcome, *adj.* bienvenu.
welfare, *n.* bien-être *m.*
welfare work, *n.* travail (*m.*) social.
well, 1. *n.* (water) puits *m.* **2.** *adv.* bien.
well-known, *adj.* bien connu.
well-meaning, *adj.* bien intentionné.
well-off, *adj.* aisé.
Welsh, *adj.* gallois.
west, *n.* ouest *m.*
western, *adj.* de l'ouest.
westward, *adv.* vers l'ouest.
wet, 1. *adj.* mouillé; (weather) pluvieux. **2.** *vb.* mouiller.
whale, *n.* baleine *f.*
wharf, *n.* quai *m.*
what, 1. *adj.* quel. **2.** *pron.* (*relative, that which*) ce qui (subject), ce que (object); *interr.* qu'est-ce qui; quoi. **3.** *interj.* quoi!
whatever, 1. *adj.* quelque . . . qui (subject), . . . que (object). **2.** *pron.*

quoi qui (subject), . . . que (object).
wheat, *n.* blé *m.*
wheel, *n.* roue *f.*
wheel chair, *n.* fauteuil (*m.*) roulant.
when, *conj.* quand.
whenever, *conj.* toutes les fois que.
where, *conj.* où.
wherever, *conj.* partout où.
whether, *conj.* soit que; (if) si.
which, 1. *adj.* quel. **2.** *pron.* (*relative*) qui; lequel; *interr.* lequel.
whichever, *pron.* n'importe lequel.
while, *conj.* pendant que; (whereas) tandis que.
whim, *n.* caprice *m.*, lubie *f.*
whip, *n.* fouet *m.*
whirl, *vb.* faire tourner, *tr.*; tourner sur soi, *intr.*
whirlpool, *n.* tourbillon *m.*
whirlwind, *n.* tornade *f.*
whisker, *n.* (man) favori *m.*; (animals) moustache *f.*
whiskey, *n.* whiskey *m.*
whisper, *vb.* chuchoter.
whistle, 1. *n.* sifflet *m.* **2.** *vb.* siffler.
white, *adj.* blanc *m.*, blanche *f.*
who, *pron.* qui.
whoever, *pron.* qui que.
whole, *adj.* entier.
wholesale, *adj. and adv.* en gros.
wholesome, *adj.* sain.
wholly, *adv.* entièrement.
whom, *pron.* (relative) que; lequel; *interr.* qui.
whooping cough, *n.* coqueluche *f.*
whose, *pron.* (relative) dont; *interr.* de qui.
why, *adv.* pourquoi.
wicked, *adj.* méchant.
wickedness, *n.* méchanceté *f.*
wide, *adj.* large.
widen, *vb.* élargir, *tr.*
widespread, *adj.* répandu.
widow, *n.* veuve *f.*
widower, *n.* veuf *m.*
width, *n.* largeur *f.*
wield, *vb.* manier.
wife, *n.* femme *f.*
wig, *n.* perruque *f.*
wild, *adj.* sauvage.
wilderness, *n.* désert *m.*

wildlife, *n.* faune *f.*

will, 1. *n.* volonté *f.*; **(last w.)** testament *m.* 2. *vb.* vouloir; (bequeath) léguer.

willful, *adj.* obstiné.

willing, *adj.* bien disposé.

willpower, *n.* volonté *f.*

wilt, *vb.* flétrir.

win, *vb.* gagner.

wind, *n.* vent *m.*

window, *n.* fenêtre *f.*

windshield, *n.* pare-brise *m.*

windsurfing, *n.* planche *(f.)* à voile.

windy, *adj.* venteux.

wine, *n.* vin *m.*

wing, *n.* aile *f.*

wink, 1. *n.* clin *(m.)* d'œil. 2. *vb.* clignoter.

winner, *n.* gagnant *m.*

winter, *n.* hiver *m.*

wipe, *vb.* essuyer.

wire, *n.* fil *(m.)* de fer.

wireless, *n.* télégraphie *(f.)* sans fil *(abbr.* T.S.F.).

wisdom, *n.* sagesse *f.*

wise, *adj.* sage.

wish, 1. *n.* désir, souhait *m.* 2. *vb.* désirer, souhaiter.

wit, *n.* esprit *m.*

witch, *n.* sorcière *f.*

with, *prep.* avec.

withdraw, *vb.* retirer, *tr.*

wither, *vb.* flétrir.

withhold, *vb.* refuser.

within, *adv.* dedans.

without, *prep.* sans.

witness, *n.* témoin *m.*

witty, *adj.* spirituel.

wizard, *n.* sorcier *m.*

woe, *n.* malheur *m.*

wolf, *n.* loup *m.*

woman, *n.* femme *f.*

womb, *n.* matrice *f.*

wonder, *vb.* (ask oneself) se demander; (be surprised) être étonné.

wonderful, *adj.* merveilleux.

woo, *vb.* faire la cour à.

wood, *n.* bois *m.*

wooden, *adj.* de bois.

wool, *n.* laine *f.*

woolen, *adj.* de laine.

word, *n.* mot *m.*

word processing, *n.* traitement *(m.)* de texte.

word processor, *n.* machine *(f.)* de traitement de texte.

work, 1. *n.* travail *m.* 2. *vb.* travailler.

workaholic, *n.* bourreau *(m.)* de travail.

worker, *n.* travailleur *m.*

working class, *n.* classe *(f.)* ouvrière.

workman, *n.* ouvrier *m.*

world, *n.* monde *m.*

worldly, *adj.* mondain.

worldwide, *adj.* mondial.

worm, *n.* ver *m.*

worn, *adj.* usé.

worry, 1. *n.* souci *m.* 2. *vb.* tracasser, préoccuper, *tr.*

worse, 1. *adj.* pire. 2. *adv.* pis.

worship, 1. *n.* culte *m.* 2. *vb.* adorer.

worst, 1. *adj.* (le) pire. 2. *adv.* (le) pis.

worth, *n.* valeur *f.*; **(be w. while to)** valoir la peine de.

worthless, *adj.* indigne; (without value) sans valeur.

worthy, *adj.* digne.

would, *vb.* vouloir.

wound, 1. *n.* blessure *f.* 2. *vb.* blesser.

wrap, *vb.* envelopper, emballer.

wrapping, *n.* couverture *f.*, emballage *m.*

wrath, *n.* courroux *m.*

wreath, *n.* couronne *f.*

wreck, *n.* (ship) naufrage *m.*; (remains) débris *m.pl.*

wrench, *vb.* tordre.

wrestle, *vb.* lutter.

wretched, *adj.* misérable.

wring, *vb.* tordre.

wrinkle, 1. *n.* ride *f.* 2. *vb.* rider *tr.*

wrist, *n.* poignet *m.*

wristwatch, *n.* montre-bracelet *f.*

write, *vb.* écrire.

writer, *n.* écrivain *m.*

writhe, *vb.* se tordre.

writing, *n.* écriture *f.*

wrong, 1. *n.* tort *m.* 2. *adj.* faux *m.*, fausse *f.*; **(be w.)** avoir tort.

X, Y, Z

xerox, *vb.* photocopier.
x-rays, *n.* rayons X *m.pl.*
xylophone, *n.* xylophone *m.*
yacht, *n.* yacht *m.*
yam, *n.* igname *f.*
yard, *n.* (house, etc.) cour *f.*; (lumber, etc.) chantier *m.*; (measure) yard *m.*
yarn, *n.* fil *m.*
yawn, 1. *n.* bâillement *m.* **2.** *vb.* bâiller.
year, *n.* an *m.*; (duration) année *f.*
yearly, *adj.* annuel.
yearn for, *vb.* soupirer après.
yeast, *n.* levure *f.*
yell, *vb.* hurler.
yellow, *adj. and n.* jaune *m.*
yes, *adv.* oui; (after negative question) si.
yesterday, *adv.* hier.
yet, 1. *adv.* encore. **2.** *conj.* néanmoins.
Yiddish, *n.* yiddish *m.*
yield, *vb.* (resign, submit) céder; (produce) produire.
yoga, *n.* yoga *m.*
yogurt, *n.* yaourt *m.*
yoke, *n.* joug *m.*
yolk, *n.* jaune *m.*
you, *pron.* vous; (familiar, *sg.*) tu (subject), toi (object), te (object, unstressed, with verb).
young, *adj.* jeune.
your, *adj.* votre *sg.*, vos *pl.*; (familiar form) ton *m.sg.*, ta *f.sg.*, tes *pl.*
yours, *pron.* le vôtre; *m.*, la vôtre *f.*, les vôtres *pl.*, (familiar form) le tien *m.*, la tienne *f.*, les tiens *m.pl.*, les tiennes *f.pl.*
yourself, *pron.* vous-même; (familiar form) toi-même; (reflexive) vous, te.
youth, *n.* jeunesse *f.*
youthful, *adj.* (young) jeune; (of youth) de jeunesse.
Yugoslavia, *n.* Yougoslavie *f.*
yuppie, *n.* yuppie *m.*
zap, *vb.* (kill) descendre; (computer) effacer; (TV) zapper.
zeal, *n.* zèle *m.*
zealous, *adj.* zélé.
zebra, *n.* zèbre *m.*
zenith, *n.* zénith *m.*
zero, *n.* zéro *m.*
zest, *n.* entrain *m.*; (taste) saveur *f.*
zip code, *n.* code postal *m.*
zipper, *n.* fermeture *f.* éclair.
zone, *n.* zone *f.*
zoo, *n.* jardin *(m.)* zoologique.
zoology, *n.* zoologie *f.*
zoom, 1. *vb.* passer en trombe. **2.** *n.* zoom *m.*
zucchini, *n.* courgette *f.*

Numerals

Cardinal

1 un, une	21 vingt et un	75 soixante-quinze
2 deux	22 vingt-deux	76 soixante-seize
3 trois	23 vingt-trois	77 soixante-dix-sept
4 quatre	24 vingt-quatre	78 soixante-dix-huit
5 cinq	25 vingt-cinq	79 soixante-dix-neuf
6 six	26 vingt-six	80 quatre-vingts
7 sept	27 vingt-sept	81 quatre-vingt-un
8 huit	28 vingt-huit	82 quatre-vingt-deux
9 neuf	29 vingt-neuf	90 quatre-vingt-dix
10 dix	30 trente	91 quatre-vingt-onze
11 onze	31 trente et un	92 quatre-vingt-douze
12 douze	32 trente-deux	100 cent
13 treize	40 quarante	101 cent un
14 quatorze	50 cinquante	102 cent deux
15 quinze	60 soixante	200 deux cents
16 seize	70 soixante-dix	300 trois cents
17 dix-sept	71 soixante et onze	301 trois cent un
18 dix-huit	72 soixante-douze	1,000 mille
19 dix-neuf	73 soixante-treize	5,000 cinq mille
20 vingt	74 soixante-quatorze	1,000,000 un million

Ordinal

1st premier, première	19th dix-neuvième
2nd deuxième, second	20th vingtième
3rd troisième	21st vingt-et-unième
4th quatrième	22nd vingt-deuxième
5th cinquième	30th trentième
6th sixième	40th quarantième
7th septième	50th cinquantième
8th huitième	60th soixantième
9th neuvième	70th soixante-dixième
10th dixième	80th quatre-vingtième
11th onzième	90th quatre-vingt-dixième
12th douzième	100th centième
13th treizième	101st cent-unième
14th quatorzième	102nd cent-deuxième
15th quinzième	103rd cent-troisième
16th seizième	300th trois-centième
17th dix-septième	1,000th millième
18th dix-huitième	1,000,000th millionième

Days of the Week

Sunday	dimanche
Monday	lundi
Tuesday	mardi
Wednesday	mercredi
Thursday	jeudi
Friday	vendredi
Saturday	samedi

Months

January	janvier
February	février
March	mars
April	avril
May	mai
June	juin
July	juillet
August	août
September	septembre
October	octobre
November	novembre
December	décembre

Weights and Measures

The French use the *Metric System* of weights and measures, a decimal system in which multiples are shown by the prefixes **déci-** (one-tenth); **centi-** (one hundredth); **milli-** (one thousandth); **hecto-** (hundred); and **kilo-** (thousand).

1 centimètre	=	.3937 inch
1 mètre	=	39.37 inches
1 kilomètre	=	.621 mile
1 centigramme	=	.1543 grain
1 gramme	=	15.432 grains
100 grammes	=	3.527 ounces
1 kilogramme	=	2.2046 pounds
1 tonne	=	2.204 pounds
1 centilitre	=	.338 ounce
1 litre	=	1.0567 quart (liquid); .908 quart (dry)
1 kilolitre	=	264.18 gallons

Useful Words and Phrases

Good day.	Bonjour.
Good afternoon.	Bonjour.
Good evening.	Bonsoir.
Good night.	Bonne nuit.
Good-bye.	Au revoir.
How are you?	Comment allez-vous?
Fine, thank you.	Très bien, merci.
Glad to meet you.	Enchanté de faire votre connaissance.
Thank you very much.	Merci beaucoup.
You're welcome.	Pas de quoi.
Please.	S'il vous plaît.
Good luck.	Bonne chance.
To your health.	A votre santé.
I am lost.	Je me suis égaré(e).
Please help me.	Aidez-moi, s'il vous plaît.
Do you understand?	Comprenez-vous?
I don't understand.	Je ne comprends pas.
Speak slowly, please.	Parlez lentement, s'il vous plaît.
Please repeat.	Répétez, s'il vous plaît.
I don't speak French.	Je ne parle pas français.
Do you speak English?	Parlez-vous anglais?
Does anyone here speak English?	Y a-t-il quelqu'un qui parle anglais?
How do you say . . . in French?	Comment dit-on . . . en français?
What do you call this?	Comment appelle-t-on ceci?
What is your name?	Comment vous appelez-vous?
My name is . . .	Je m'appelle . . .
I am an American.	Je suis américain.
May I introduce . . .	Permettez-moi de vous présenter . . .
How is the weather?	Quel temps fait-il?
What time is it?	Quelle heure est-il?
What is it?	Qu'est-ce que c'est?
I would like . . .	Je voudrais . . .
Please give me . . .	S'il vous plaît, donnez-moi . . .
Please bring me . . .	S'il vous plaît, apportez-moi . . .
How much does this cost?	Combien est ceci?
It is too expensive.	C'est trop cher.

May I see something cheaper?	Pourrais-je voir quelque chose à meilleur marché?
May I see something better?	Pourrais-je voir quelque chose de meilleur?
It is not exactly what I want.	Ce n'est pas exactement ce que je cherche.
I want to buy . . .	Je voudrais acheter . . .
Do you accept traveler's checks?	Acceptez-vous les chèques de voyage?
I want to eat.	Je voudrais manger.
Can you recommend a restaurant?	Pouvez-vous recommander un restaurant?
I am hungry.	J'ai faim.
I am thirsty.	J'ai soif.
May I see the menu?	Pourrais-je voir le menu?
Check, please.	L'addition, s'il vous plaît.
Is service included in the bill?	Le service est-il compris?
Where can I get a taxi?	Où pourrais-je trouver un taxi?
What is the fare to . . .	Quel est le tarif jusqu'à . . . ?
Please take me to this address.	Veuillez me conduire à cette adresse.
I have a reservation.	J'ai une réservation.
Where is the nearest drugstore?	Où est la pharmacie la plus proche?
Is there a hotel here?	Y a-t-il un hôtel ici?
Where is . . . ?	Où est . . . ?
Where is the men's (women's) room?	Où est la toilette pour messieurs (dames)?
What is the way to . . . ?	Quelle est la route de . . . ?
Take me to . . .	Conduisez-moi à . . .
I need . . .	J'ai besoin de . . .
I am ill.	Je suis malade.
Please call a doctor.	Appelez un docteur, s'il vous plaît.
Is there any mail for me?	Y a-t-il du courrier pour moi?
Please call the police.	Appelez la police, s'il vous plaît.
I want to send a telegram.	Je voudrais envoyer un télégramme.
Where can I change money?	Où puis-je changer de l'argent?
Where is the nearest bank?	Où est la banque la plus proche?
Will you accept checks?	Acceptez-vous des chèques?
What is the postage?	Quel est l'affranchissement?
Where can I mail this letter?	Où est-ce que je peux mettre cette lettre à la poste?

Please help me with my baggage	S'il vous plaît, aidez-moi avec mes bagages.
Right away.	Tout de suite.
Help!	Au secours!
Who is it?	Qui est-ce que c'est?
Come in.	Entrez.
Stop.	Arrêtez.
Hurry.	Dépêchez-vous.
Go on.	Continuez.
Right.	A droite.
Left.	A gauche.
Straight ahead.	Tout droit.
Hello! *(on telephone)*	Allô!
As soon as possible.	Aussitôt que possible.
Pardon me.	Pardon *or* Pardonnez-moi *or* Je m'excuse.
Look out!	Attention! *or* Faites attention!
Just a minute!	Un instant!

Signs

Caution	Attention	**Go Slow**	Ralentir
Danger	Danger	**No smoking**	Défense de fumer
Exit	Sortie	**No admittance**	Défense d'entrer
Entrance	Entrée	**Women**	Dames
Stop	Halte, Arrêtez	**Men**	Hommes
Closed	Fermé	**Lavatory**	Lavabos, toilettes
Open	Ouvert		

FOOD AND MENU TERMS

LES ENTRÉES *f.pl.* — APPETIZERS

artichaut *m.*	artichoke
assiette *f.* de charcuterie	cold cuts
assiette *f.* de crudités	raw vegetables
céleri *m.* rémoulade *f.*	shredded celery root in mayonnaise sauce
champignons *m.pl.* à la grecque	mushrooms in oil, lemon juice and herbs
coeur *m.* de palmier	hearts of palm
coquilles *f.pl.* St. Jacques	bay scallops in cream sauce
escargots *m.pl.*	snails (usually in garlic butter)
moules *f.pl.* (rémoulade)	mussels (in mayonnaise)
pâté *m.* de foie	liver pâté
pâté de campagne	pork pâté
pâté impérial	spring roll
salade *f.* verte	green salad
salade niçoise	salad usually including tuna, tomatoes, green beans, anchovies and olives
sardines *f.pl.* à l'huile	sardines in oil
saucisse *f.*	small fresh sausage
saucisson *m.*	large sausage, like salami
saucisson à l'ail	garlic sausage
saumon *m.* fumé	smoked salmon
terrine *f.*	cold pâté baked in earthenware casserole
thon *m.* mayonnaise	tuna salad with mayonnaise

POTAGES *m.pl.* AND SOUPES *f.pl.* — SOUPS

bisque *f.*	shellfish soup
bouillabaisse *f.*	Provençal fish soup
bouillon *m.*	clear broth
consommé *m.* (de volaille)	clear (chicken) soup
petite marmite *f.*	meat and vegetable broth cooked in earthenware casserole
pistou *m.*	rich vegetable, bean and pasta soup flavored with basil, garlic and olive oil
potage *m.* aux légumes	vegetable soup
potage crème Saint-Germain	cream of pea soup
soupe *f.* à l'oignon	onion soup
vichyssoise *f.*	cold, creamy leek and potato soup

LES PLATS *m.pl*	MAIN COURSES
Viandes *f.pl.*	Meats
agneau *m.*	lamb
carré *m.* d'agneau	rack of lamb
côte *f.* d'agneau	lamb chop
gigot *m.* d'agneau	leg of lamb
bifteck *m.*	steak
blanquette *f.*	traditional stew of veal, chicken, lamb or seafood in cream sauce
boeuf *m.* bourguignon	stew of beef chunks and vegetables in Burgundy wine sauce
boudin *m.*	meat sausage
boudin blanc	white sausage of veal, chicken or pork
boudin noir	pork blood sausage
brochette *f.*	cubes of meat or fish and vegetables cooked on skewer
chateaubriand *m.*	thick beef fillet, traditionally served with sautéed potatoes and sauce
côtelette *f.*	thin chop or cutlet
entrecôte *m.* or *f.*	beef rib steak
escalope *f.*	thin slice of meat or fish
filet mignon *m.*	filet mignon
jambon *m.*	ham
jarret *m.* (de veau, de porc, de boeuf)	knuckles (veal, pork, beef)
lapin *m.*	rabbit
pavé *m.*	thick slice of boned beef or calf's liver
porc *m.*	pork
carré de porc	pork loin
steak *m.* frites	steak with French fries
steak *m.* tartare	raw chopped steak
tournedos *m.*	center part of beef fillet
tripes *f.pl.* à la mode de Caen	beef entrails, carrots, leeks, and onions, cooked in water, cider and Calvados
veau *m.*	veal
côte de veau	veal chop

Volailles *f.pl.*	**Poultry**
caille *f.*	quail
canard *m.*	duck
canard à la presse	roast duck with sauce of natural juices, red wine and cognac
canard sauvage	wild duck, usually mallard
caneton *m.*	young male duck
coq *m.* (au vin)	mature male chicken (cooked in wine sauce)
coq jaune	chicken cooked in the local wine with butter, cream and tarragon
coq *m.* de bruyère	wood grouse
coquelet *m.* (sauté)	sautéed baby rooster
foie *f.*	liver
fricassé *m.*	stewed or sautéed mixture of fish or meat
perdrix *f.*	partridge
poulet *m.* rôti	roast chicken
poulet à la Kiev	chicken Kiev
poulet impérial	Vietnamese chicken
poulet basquaise	chicken Basque-style with tomatoes and sweet peppers
poulet fermier	free-range chicken
Fruits *m.pl.* **de Mer and Poissons** *m.pl.*	**Fish**
bar *m.*	bass
colin *m.*	hake
coquillage *m.*	shellfish
crevettes *f.pl.*	shrimp
escargots *m.pl.*	snails
grenouilles *f.pl.*	frogs' legs
homard *m.*	lobster
huîtres *f.pl.*	oysters
langouste *f.*	crayfish
langoustines *f.pl.*	prawns
moules *f.pl.*	mussels
saumon *m.*	salmon
sôle *f.*	sole
thon *m.*	tuna
truite *f.*	trout
turbot *m.*	turbot
Légumes *m.pl.*	**Vegetables**
asperges *f.pl.*	asparagus
avocat *m.*	avocado
brocoli *m.*	broccoli

carotte *f.*	carrot
champignons *m.pl.*	mushrooms
chou-fleur *m.*	cauliflower
choux *m.*	cabbage
concombre *m.*	cucumber
courgette *f.*	zucchini
endive *f.*	chicory, endive
fenouil *m.*	fennel
flageolet *m.*	small kidney-shaped bean
haricots *m.pl.*	beans
haricots rouges	kidney beans
haricots verts	string beans
laitue *f.*	lettuce
maïs *m.*	corn
navet *m.*	turnip
petits pois *m.pl.*	green peas
poireaux *m.pl.*	leeks
poivron (doux) *m.*	(sweet bell) pepper

OEUFS *m.pl.* — EGGS

oeuf *m.* **à la coque**	soft-boiled egg
oeuf brouillé	scrambled egg
oeuf dur	hard-boiled egg
oeuf poché	poached egg
oeuf sur le plat	fried egg

DESSERTS *m.pl.* — DESSERTS

crème *f.* **caramel**	caramel custard
flan *m.*	custard
gâteau *m.*	cake
glace *f.*	ice cream
marron *m.* **glacé**	glazed chestnut
mousse *f.* **au chocolat**	chocolate mousse
oeufs *m.pl.* **à la neige**	poached meringues in custard sauce
pêche *f.* **melba**	poached peach with vanilla ice cream and raspberry sauce
petit-four *m.*	tiny cake
poire *f.* **belle Hélène**	pear with ice cream, cookie and hot chocolate sauce
profiteroles *f.pl.*	ice cream–filled cream puffs topped with hot chocolate sauce
sorbet *m.*	sorbet
tarte *f.* **aux fruits**	fruit pie

FRUITS *m.pl.*	FRUITS
abricot *m.*	apricot
banane *f.*	banana
cantaloup *m.*	cantaloupe
cerise *f.*	cherry
citron *m.*	lemon
figue *f.*	fig
fraise *f.*	strawberry
framboise *f.*	raspberry
melon *m.*	melon
myrtille *f.*	bilberry
pamplemousse *f.*	grapefruit
pêche *f.*	peach
pomme *f.*	apple
pruneau *m.*	prune

BOISSONS *f.pl.*	DRINKS, BEVERAGES
sans alcool	(nonalcoholic)
café *m.*	coffee
eau *f.* minérale	mineral water
jus *m.*	juice
jus d'orange	orange juice
jus de tomate	tomato juice
jus de raisin	grape juice
lait *m.*	milk
thé *m.*	tea
avec alcool	(alcoholic)
champagne *m.*	champagne
cognac *m.*	cognac
vin *m.*	wine
vin rouge	red wine
vin blanc	white wine
vin rosé	rosé wine